48.00

هاراب

المعجم المدرسي
انجليزي ـ عربي

HARRAP'S
ENGLISH-ARABIC
BASIC LEARNER'S
DICTIONARY

P. H. Collin

Edited by Nagi Abboud

قاموس مختصر
انجليزي عربي
للمبتدىء في
درس الانجليزية

خطوط الغلاف : حسَن المسعود

HARRAP

First published in Great Britain 1986
by HARRAP BOOKS Ltd
Chealsea House, 26 Market Square,
Bromley, Kent BR1 1NA
© Harrap Books Limited 1986
Distribution Al Mouhit

All rights reserved. No part of this publication
may be reproduced in any form or by any means
without the prior permission of Harrap Books Ltd

ISBN 0-245-53933-6

Dépôt légal: Octobre 1986

Reprinted 1987, 1988, 1991
Printed in France by Maury-Eurolivres S.A.
45300 Manchecourt

Typeset by Computype Limited, England

Pronunciation

The following signs are used to show the pronunciation of words in the dictionary.

Words are also marked with a sign (') to show where the strong beat should be placed, but you must remember that this is only a guide, and that the pronunciation of a word can change depending on the position of the word in a sentence.

æ	back	ə	afraid	ð	then	r	round
ɑː	farm	əʊ	boat	dʒ	just	s	some
ɒ	top	əʊə	lower	f	fog	ʃ	short
aɪ	pipe	ɜː	word	g	go	t	too
aʊ	how	iː	heap	h	hand	tʃ	chop
aɪə	fire	ɪ	hit	j	yes	θ	thing
aʊə	flower	ɪə	hear	k	catch	v	voice
ɔː	bought	uː	school	l	last	w	was
ɔɪ	toy	ʊ	book	m	mix	z	zoo
e	fed	ʌ	but	n	nut	ʒ	treasure
eə	hair	b	back	ŋ	sing		
eɪ	take	d	dog	p	penny		

Alphabet

These are the letters of the English alphabet, showing how they are pronounced.

Aa	eɪ	**Hh**	eɪtʃ	**Oo**	əʊ	**Vv**	viː
Bb	biː	**Ii**	aɪ	**Pp**	piː	**Ww**	ˈdʌblju:
Cc	siː	**Jj**	dʒeɪ	**Qq**	kjuː	**Xx**	eks
Dd	diː	**Kk**	keɪ	**Rr**	ɑː	**Yy**	waɪ
Ee	iː	**Ll**	el	**Ss**	es	**Zz**	zed
Ff	ef	**Mm**	em	**Tt**	tiː		
Gg	dʒiː	**Nn**	en	**Uu**	juː		

Aa

a, an [eɪ, æn or ə, ən] *article*

أ) أداة تنكير بمعنى « واحد » أو « ما »

(*a*) not a special one; **I want a glass of water; a big car; he has a good job; an empty house; a useful knife.**

ب) أي ـ كل ـ في كل ـ لكل ... (هذا البرتقال سعره ٥٠ قرشاً لكل كيلو واحد .)

(*b*) for each/in each; **these oranges cost 50p a kilo; the car was doing 30 kilometres an hour.**

Note: **an** *is used in front of words beginning with* **a, e, i, o, u** *and with* **h** *if the* **h** *is not pronounced* (**an apple; an hour**); **a** *is used in front of all the other letters and also* **u** *where* **u** *is pronounced* **ju** (**a university**)

able [ˈeɪbl] *adjective*

قادر ـ باستطاعة (أحد أن)

he wasn't able to breathe = he could not breathe; **will you be able to come to the party?** = can you come to the party? **he wasn't able to find the house.**

Note: **able** *is used with* **to** *and a verb*

ability [əˈbɪlɪti] *noun*

قدرة ـ استطاعة

being able to do something; **I'll do it to the best of my ability** = as well as possible.

about [əˈbaʊt] *adverb & preposition*

أ) بخصوص

(*a*) concerning; **tell me about your holiday; what do you want to speak to me about? he is worried about his health.**

ب) تقريباً

(*b*) more or less; **the room is about three metres square; the next train leaves at about four o'clock; she's about twenty years old; the town is about ten kilometres from here.**

ت) في عدة أماكن

(*c*) in several places; **he left his papers lying about on the floor.**

ث) على وشك

(*d*) **to be about to do something** = to be going to do something; **I was just about to go out when you phoned.**

above [əˈbʌv] *adverb & preposition*

فوق

higher than; **the plane flew above the clouds; the temperature was above 40°.**

abroad [əˈbrɔd] *adverb*

خارج البلاد ـ في الخارج ـ في بلاد أخرى

in another country; to another country; **he lives abroad; they are going abroad on holiday.**

absence [ˈæbsəns] *noun*

غياب ـ عدم وجود

not being here/there; **in the absence of Mr Smith** = when Mr Smith is not here/there.

absent [ˈæbsənt] *adjective*

غائب ـ غير موجود

not here/not there; **three children are absent because they are ill.**

absolutely [ˈæbsəlutli] *adverb*

على الاطلاق

really/completely; **you're absolutely right; the weather was absolutely awful.**

one 1

accent

accent ['æksənt] *noun*

لهجة ـ طريقة معينة باللفظ

way of pronouncing words; **he speaks English with an Irish accent; she has a southern accent.**

accept [ək'sept] *verb*

أ) يقبل ـ يرضى بـ

a) to take (something which someone is giving you); **will you accept this little present?**

ب) يوافق على شيء ما

(b) to agree (to do something); **I invited her to the party and she accepted.**

accepts—accepting—accepted— has accepted

accident ['æksɪdənt] *noun*

أ) صدفة : (رأيتها بالصدفة في المحطة ..)

(a) something which happens by chance; **I met her by accident at the bus stop.**

ب) حادث مؤسف

(b) unpleasant thing which happens; **she had an accident and had to go to hospital; three people were killed in the accident on the motorway.**

accidentally [æksɪ'dentəlɪ] *adverb*

أ) بالصدفة ـ صدفةً

(a) by chance; **I found the missing watch accidentally.**

ب) جرّاء حادث ـ بحادث

(b) in an accident; **he was killed accidentally.**

accompany [ə'kʌmpnɪ] *verb*

أ) يرافق ـ يلازم

(a) to go with; **he accompanied his wife to hospital; roast beef accompanied by boiled potatoes.**

ب) يرافق المغني أو العازف بآلة موسيقية ما أو بالغناء

(b) to play the piano, etc., while someone else is singing; **he was accompanying the singer on the piano; she accompanied herself on the piano.**

accompanies—accompanying— accompanied—has accompanied

act

according to [ə'kɔːdɪŋ tʊ] *adverb*

وفقاً لـ ، بحَسَب

as someone says or writes; **according to the newspaper, today is a public holiday; according to the TV, it will be fine tomorrow.**

account [ə'kaʊnt] *noun*

أ) حساب (يوضع في البنك)

(a) amount of money kept in a bank; **how much money do you have in your account? he put £10 into his bank account.**

ب) بسبب

(b) **on account of** = because of; **the trains are late on account of the fog.**

ache [eɪk] *noun*

ألم ، وجع

pain; (*used with other words to show where you have a pain: see* **headache, toothache**)

across [ə'krɒs] *adverb & preposition*

أ) عَبْرَ ، من جانب إلى آخر .

(a) from one side to the other; **he swam across the river; don't run across the road; the river is 50 metres across.**

ب) في الجانب الآخر ـ إلى الجانب الآخر .

(b) on the other side; **he lives across the street; their house is across the street from ours** = it is just opposite our house.

act [ækt] *verb*

أ) يلعب دوراً (في تمثيلية) ـ يمثل

(a) to take part in a play/film, etc.; **she's acted on TV many times; he acted the part of Hamlet in the film.**

ب) يفعل ـ يتصرَّفُ بطريقة ما

(b) to do something; **he had to act quickly to save his sister.**

acts—acting—acted—has acted

action ['ækʃn] *noun*

فعْل ـ تصرُّف ـ نشاط

thing which has been done; **he regretted his action** = he was sorry for what he had done.

2   *two*

actual　　　　　　　　　　　　　　　　　　　　　　　　　　**admire**

active ['æktɪv] *adjective*

نشيط ـ عملي ـ رشيق ـ فَعّال

lively/doing something; **although he is over eighty, he is still very active.**

actor ['æktə] *noun*

ممثل (في المسرح أو في السينما)

man who acts in a play.

actress ['æktrəs] *noun*

ممثلة (في المسرح أو السينما)

woman who acts in a play.
plural **actresses**

act upon, *verb*

يعمل بموجب ـ يتصرف بحسب شيء ما

to do something as the result of something which has been said; **he acted upon your suggestion.**

actual ['æktjʊəl] *adjective*

حقيقي ـ واقعي

real; **what are the actual figures for the number of children in school?**
actually, *adverb*

حقاً ـ بالحقيقة ـ بالفعل ـ بالواقع

really; **is he actually going to sell his shop?**

ad [æd] *see* **advertisement**

اعلان

add [æd] *verb*

أ) يجمع

(*a*) to put numbers together; **if you add ten and fifteen you get twenty-five.**

ب) يضيف ـ يزيد

(*b*) to put more of something; **if your coffee isn't sweet enough, add some more sugar; she added a few words at the end of the letter.**
adds—adding—added—has added

addition [ə'dɪʃn] *noun*

جَمْع (الأرقام)

putting numbers together; **she is good at addition, but not at multiplication.**
add up, *verb*

يجمع

to put several numbers together; **if you add up all these figures, the answer should be a thousand.**
Note: **add the numbers up** *or* **add up the numbers,** *but only* **add them up**
add up to, *verb*

يبلغ مجموعه : (ان الأموال التي نفقناها تبلغ أكثر من ١٠٠ جنيه)

to make a total; **the sums of money we have spent add up to over £100.**

address [ə'dres] **1.** *noun*

١ ـ عنوان

number of a house, name of a street and town where someone lives or where an office is; **what is the address of the new bookshop? write all their addresses on a piece of paper; her address is: 15 High Street, Bradford, Yorkshire.**
plural **addresses**
2. *verb*

٢ ـ يُدَوِّن العنوان على رسالة . يرسل (رسالة) إلى ، أو باسم شخص ما

to write the details of name, where someone is/where a house is, on an envelope; **the letter is addressed to your father.**
addresses—addressing—addressed—has addressed

adjective ['ɒdʒɪktɪv] *noun*

صفة ـ نعت

word used to describe what a noun is like; **in the phrase 'a big green door', 'big' and 'green' are both adjectives.**

admire [əd'maɪə] *verb*

يكون معجباً بـ ـ يُعجب بـ

to look at something with pleasure; to be impressed by something; **he was admiring my new car.**
admires—admiring—admired—has admired
admiration [ɒdmə'reɪʃn] *noun*

إعجاب

feeling of pleasure in something; **I have a great admiration for his work.**

three　　　　　　　　　　　　　　　　　　　　　　　　　　**3**

admit

admit [əd'mɪt] *verb*

أ) يصلح لـ ـ يكون صالحاً لـ ـ يسمح (بدخول شخصاً ما)

(a) to allow (someone) to go in; **this ticket admits one person; children are admitted free.**

ب) يعترف (بفعل أو بقول أو بشعور أو بتصرف ما)

(b) to say that something is true; **he admitted he was the person who broke the window/he admitted to having broken the window.**

admits—admitting—admitted—has admitted

adult ['ɒdʌlt, ə'dʌlt] *noun & adjective*

بالغ (شخص بلغ سن الرشد).

grown-up (person/animal); **the price for adults is £1; an adult elephant.**

advantage [əd'vɒːntɪdʒ] *noun*

أ) افضلية ـ ميزة.

(a) something useful which will help you to be successful; **it will be an advantage if you can speak Italian.**

ب) يستفيد من ـ ينتهز فرصة

(b) **to take advantage of** = to use something to help yourself; **we took advantage of the fine weather and went on a picnic.**

adventure [əd'ventʃə] *noun*

مغامرة ـ مجازفة

new and exciting thing which happens; **he told us of his adventures while he was crossing the desert.**

adverb ['ɒdvɜːb] *noun*

حال ـ ظرف (تستعمل adverb في القواعد والصرف فقط).

word which is used to describe a verb or an adjective; **in the sentence 'he drives quickly', the word 'quickly' is an adverb.**

advert ['ɒdvɜːt] *see* **advertisement**

اعلان

advise

advertise ['ɒdvətaɪz] *verb*

يعلن عن (في الصحف أو التلفيزيون ...)

to show that something is for sale/that you want something; **he advertised his car in the newspaper; the company is advertising for new secretaries; jobs are advertised in the local paper.**

advertises—advertising—advertised—has advertised

advertisement [ɒd'vɜːtɪzmənt], **advert** ['ɒdvɜːt], **ad** [ɒd] *noun*

إعلان

notice which shows that something is for sale/that you want something; **if you want to sell the carpet, put an ad in the paper; I sold the carpet through an advert in the paper; she answered an advertisement in the paper and got a better job.**

ملاحظة : تستعمل كلمة ad وكلمة advert في الكلام وقليلاً ما تستعمل في الكتابة

Note: **advert** *and* **ad** *are used in ordinary speaking, but not usually in writing*

advice [əd'vaɪs] *noun*

نصيحة

suggestion about what should be done; **he went to the teacher for advice on how to do his homework; she would not listen to my advice; my advice to you is that you should take a long holiday; the doctor's advice was to stay in bed; he took the doctor's advice and went to bed.**

no plural: **some advice; a piece of advice**

advise [əd'vaɪz] *verb*

ينصح

to suggest what should be done; **the doctor advised him to stay in bed; she advised me to sell my car; I would advise you to drive slowly.**

advises—advising—advised—has advised

advise against, *verb*

4   four

aeroplane

ينصح بعدم ...

to suggest that something should not be done; **I wanted to learn to fly, but she advised against it; the doctor advised against going to bed late.**

aeroplane ['eərə:pleɪn] *noun* (*American*: **airplane**)

طائرة

machine which flies in the air; **the passengers got into the aeroplane.**

afford [ə'fɔ:d] *verb*

يستطيع الانفاق على ـ يكون بقدرته ان ينفق أمواله على شيء ما أو على شراء شيء ما .

to have enough money to pay for something; **I can't afford a new pair of shoes; how can you afford two holidays a year?**
affords—affording—afforded—has afforded

afraid [ə'freɪd] *adjective*

ا) يخاف من ـ يخشى .

(*a*) **to be afraid (of)** = to be frightened (by); **I am afraid of snakes; she's afraid of the dark; he's afraid to climb on to the roof.**

ب) آسف من القول ان ...

(*b*) **to be afraid** = to be sorry to say; **I'm afraid we have no seats left; I'm afraid she's ill; have you got a watch?—no, I'm afraid not.**

Note: **afraid** *cannot be used in front of a noun:* **she's afraid** *but a* **frightened** *girl*

after ['ɑ:ftə] **1.** *preposition*

١ ـ أ) بعدَ ـ ما بعد ـ عقب .

(*a*) **following/next; if today is Monday, the day after tomorrow is Wednesday; he arrived after me; I must go to bed—it's after midnight; they came in one after the other.**

ب) يبحث عن ـ يفتش على ـ يكون مستاء من .

(*b*) **to be after** = to be looking for/to be angry with; **the police are after him; if**

five

again

you eat all the cake, your mother will be after you; what's he after? = what does he want?
2. *conjunction*

٢ ـ بعد ان ـ (في الفترة التي تلي) بعدما

following a time; **after the rain came the grass started to grow; after the driver got in, the bus set off; phone me after you get home.**

ملاحظة : تستعمل **after** مع عدة أفعال **look after, take after**

Note: **after** *is used with many verbs:* **look after; take after,** *etc.*

after all, *adverb*

ا) في النهاية ، بالرغم من كل شيء

(*a*) in the end/in spite of everything; **he changed his mind and decided to go to the party after all.**

ب) في أي حال

(*b*) in any case; **I think I shall stay at home—after all, I have no work to do at the office and it's a fine day.**

afternoon [ɑ:ftə'nu:n] *noun*

بعد الظهر

part of the day between the morning and the evening; **I always have a little sleep in the afternoon; she doesn't work on Tuesday afternoons; we met at 3 o'clock in the afternoon; I will try to catch the afternoon train; can you come to see me this afternoon or tomorrow afternoon?**

afterwards ['ɑ:ftəwədz] *adverb*

بعدئذ

later/next; **we'll go shopping first, and visit the museums afterwards; he was very well before lunch, but felt ill afterwards.**

again [ə'geɪn *or* ə'gen] *adverb*

مرة أخرى ـ مرة ثانية

another time/once more; **he sang the song again; you must come to see us again.**

مجدداً ـ مرة أخرى .

once again = another time; **once again, the car refused to start.**

5

against

مرة أخرى بعد عدة مرات
yet again = once more after many times; **he is back in hospital yet again.**

against [əˈgenst] *preposition*

أ) ملامس لـ ـ متكىء على ـ على ـ بـ
(a) touching; **the ladder is leaning against the wall; he hit his head against a low branch.**

ب) مخالف للقانون .
(b) **against the rules/against the law** = not as the rules say/as the law says; **it's against the law to open the shop on a Sunday; you can't hold the football in your hands—it's against the rules; have you anything against my going out this evening?** = do you agree that I can go out? **she was against the idea of going to the cinema.**

ث) ضد ـ مقابل .
(c) opposite; **our school is playing against the girls' school at football; it's hard cycling against the wind.**

age [eɪdʒ] *noun*

أ) عمر ـ سن
(a) number of years which you have lived; **what's your age on your next birthday? he was sixty years of age; she looks younger than her age; old age** = period when you are old.

ب) منذ مدة طويلة
(b) **for ages** = for a very long time; **I've been waiting here for ages.**

aged, *adjective*

أ) بالغ من العمر
(a) [eɪdʒd] with a certain age; **a boy aged twelve; he died last year, aged 64.**

ب) عجوز ـ مسن
(b) [ˈeɪdʒɪd] very old; **an aged man.**

agent [ˈeɪdʒnt] *noun*

وكيل
person who acts for you, usually in another country; **he is the agent for Japanese cars; Mr Smith is our agent in Australia.**

air

ago [əˈgəʊ] *verb*

منذ ، في الماضي
in the past; **I saw him five minutes ago; she left home two years ago; it all happened a long time ago.**

agree [əˈgriː] *verb*

يتفق (في الرأي مع) يوافق على
to say that you think the same way as someone; to say yes; **I agree with you that we need a new car; we asked her to come with us and she agreed.**
agrees—agreeing—agreed—has agreed

agreement, *noun*

اتفاقية ـ اتفاق ـ معاهدة ـ مص
action of agreeing; **he nodded to show his agreement; they are in agreement with our plan** = they agree with it.

ahead [əˈhed] *adverb*

في المتقدمة ـ متقدم على ـ في الطليعة ـ إلى الأمام
in front; **our team was losing, but now we are ahead; ahead of us was a big old house; he has a lot of work ahead of him; we walked on ahead of the others; run on ahead and keep some seats for us.**

aim [eɪm] *verb*

أ) يصوّب
(a) to point at; **he aimed his gun at the policeman.**

ب) يسعى إلى (تحقيق شيء ما)
(b) to intend to do something; **we aim to save enough money to go on holiday.**
aims—aiming—aimed—has aimed

air [eə] *noun*

هواء ـ جوّ
mixture of gases which you can't see, but which you breathe; **the air felt cold; he kicked the ball up into the air.**

بواسطة الطائرة ـ جواً ـ بالبريد الجوي .

6

six

alcohol

by air = in an aircraft; **we are travelling to France by air; I must send this letter by air.**

aircraft, noun

طائرة ـ سفينة هواء

machine which flies in the air; **the pilot got into the aircraft.**

Note: plural is **aircraft: one aircraft, six aircraft**

air force, noun

سلاح الطيران .

all the aircraft used in war, with the people who fly them; **he's joining the air force.**

air hostess, noun

مضيفة الطائرة

woman who looks after the passengers in an aircraft.

plural: **air hostesses**

airplane, noun

طائرة

American = **aircraft**

airport, noun

مطار

place where aircraft land and take off; **we are due to leave London Airport at five o'clock; you can take a bus to the airport.**

alcohol ['ælkəhɒl] noun

كحول

liquid which makes you drunk if you drink too much of it.

alcoholic [ælkə'hɒlɪk] adjective

كحولي ـ يحتوي على كحول

containing alcohol; **an alcoholic drink.**

alike [ə'laɪk] adjective

متشابه ـ متماثل على قدم المساواة .

looking almost the same; **the two brothers are very alike.**

Note: **alike** is only used after a verb

alive [ə'laɪv] adjective

على قيد الحياة ـ حيّ ـ

seven

all

living/not dead; **the fish is still alive, even though it was caught an hour ago; my grandfather was alive when the first aeroplanes flew.**

Note: **alive** cannot be used in front of a noun: **the fish is alive** but **a live fish**

all [ɔ:l] 1. adjective & pronoun

١ ـ جميع ـ كل ـ بالاجماع

every; everything/everyone; **all the tomatoes are red; are all the children here? we all like chocolate; let's sing the song all together** = everyone at the same time.

٢ ـ تماماً ـ على الاطلاق

2. adverb

completely; **the ground was all white after the snow fell; I forgot all about her birthday.**

فجأةً

all at once = suddenly; **all at once the telephone rang.**

لا ، ابداً ـ بالتأكيد لا .

not at all = certainly not; **do you mind waiting for ten minutes?—not at all!**

بمفردك ـ بدون مساعدة أحد

all by yourself = alone; **he was all by himself; I'm all by myself; she did it all by herself.**

أ) في كل الأماكن : (كان السكر مرشوشاً على كل مساحة الكعكة) (دلقت الماء على كل الطاولة)

all over = (a) everywhere; **there was sugar all over the cake; she poured water all over the table.**

ب) كل شيء انتهى (كان كل شيء قد انتهى لما عدنا إلى البيت)

(b) finished; **when it was all over we went home.**

all right, adjective

أ) حسناً ـ بخير .

(a) fine/well; **I was sick yesterday, but I'm all right now.**

7

allow

ب) حسناً سأفعل

(b) will you answer the telephone for me?—**all right** = yes, I will.
all the same, *adverb*

بالرغم من كل ذلك .

in spite of this; **I don't like parties, but I shall come to yours all the same.**

allow [ə'lau] *verb*

يسمح بـ

to say that someone can do something; **you are not allowed to walk on the grass; he allowed me to see his stamp collection; are we allowed to sit down?**
allows—allowing—allowed—has allowed

almost ['ɔ:lməust] *adverb*

تقريباً

nearly; not quite; **he is almost as tall as I am; hurry up, it's almost time for the train to leave.**

alone [ə'ləun] *adjective*

منفرد بنفسه ـ متوحد

with no one else; **she was all alone in the house; I want to talk to you alone** = just the two of us together.

along [ə'lɒŋ] 1. *preposition*

١ ـ على طول (الطريق أو النهر...)

by the side of; **there are trees along both sides of the road; he was walking along the bank of the river.**
2. *adverb*

٢ ـ يصاحب ـ يأتي بصحبة شخص ما

to go along/to come along = to go/to come; **come along with us; he went along to the police station to report the accident.**

aloud [ə'laud] *adverb*

بصوت عالٍ

in a voice which can be heard; **he was reading the newspaper aloud; I was just thinking aloud** = just saying what I was thinking.

alphabet ['ælfəbet] *noun*

الابجدية

the 26 letters which are used to write words; **A is the first letter of the alphabet.**
alphabetical ['ælfəbetɪkl] *adjective*

ابجدي ـ مرتب حسب أحرف الأبجدية

like in the alphabet; **the telephone book has all the names in alphabetical order** = arranged by letters as they come in the alphabet.

already [ɔ:l'redɪ] *adverb*

الآن ـ سابقاً ـ في ذلك الحين ـ قبل الآن .

by this time; **it is already past ten o'clock; has he finished work already?** = so quickly; **I've seen that film already** = I have seen it before.

also ['ɔ:lsəu] *adverb*

ايضاً

as well/at the same time; **he sings and can also play the piano; she came to dinner, and her son also came.**

although [ɔ:l'ðəu] *conjunction*

بالرغم عن ، مع أنَّ

in spite of the fact that; **although it was snowing, it was not very cold; although he is eighty, he still goes running every morning;** *see also* **though.**

altogether [ɔ:ltə'geðə] *adverb*

١) الكل معاً ـ في المجموع .

(a) putting everything together; **the shirt is £10 and the tie is £5, that makes £15 altogether.**

ب) كلياً ـ تماماً .

(b) completely; **he forgot about it altogether.**

8   **eight**

always

always [ˈɔːlweɪz] *adverb*

دائماً .

every time/all the time; **he is always later; it always rains when we want to go for a walk; in tropical countries it is always hot; she's always in a hurry.**

am [æm] *see* **be**

ملاحظة : انظر إلى كلمة be .

a.m. [ˈeɪˈem] *adverb*

قبل الظهر .

in the morning; **I have to get up at 6 a.m. every day; she's going to catch the 10 a.m. train to Edinburgh.**

ملاحظة : ان لفظة a.m. تستعمل للاشارة إلى الوقت الصحيح وكلمة o'clock في هذه الحال تحذف

Note: **a.m.** *is usually used to show the exact hour and the word* **o'clock** *is left out*

ambulance [ˈæmbjʊləns] *noun*

سيارة اسعاف

van for taking sick people to hospital; **the injured man was taken away in an ambulance.**

America [əˈmerɪkə] *noun*

أ) اميركا أو أمريكا (القارة)

(*a*) large area of land (North America and South America) between the Atlantic and Pacific Oceans.

ب) الولايات المتحدة الأميركية .

(*b*) (*also* **the United States**) large country on the other side of the Atlantic Ocean from Europe; **we're going to America on holiday; they live in America.**

ملاحظة : للمزيد من الدقة ، من المستحسن استعمال the United States أو the US للاشارة إلى هذا البلد المعين .

Note: if you want to be clear it is better to refer to the country as **the United States** *or* **the US**

amuse

American, 1. *adjective*

١ ـ اميركي ، من صنع اميركا

referring to the United States; **the American President; she drives an American car.**

2. *noun*

٢ ـ اميركي الجنسية

person who lives in the United States; **Americans make very good ice cream.**

among [əˈmʌŋ] *preposition*

أ) في وسط ـ بين

(*a*) in the middle of; **the birds built their nests among the leaves; among the people at the party was a man who reads the news on TV.**

ب) ما بين

(*b*) between; **the cake was divided among the children.**

amount [əˈmaʊnt] **1.** *noun*

١ ـ كمّية

quantity; **she drinks a large amount of tea; he gave away his money in large amounts.**

2. *verb*

٢ ـ يبلغ (السعر ، المجموع)

to add up (to); **the bill amounted to £100.**

amounts—amounting— amounted—has amounted

amuse [əˈmjuːz] *verb*

يسلّي ـ يرفّه

to make someone happy; **they amused themselves playing football; the teacher amused the children by showing them a film.**

amuses—amusing—amused—has amused

amusement, *noun*

الترفيه ـ التسلية

being happy; **he poured a bucket of water over his head to the great amusement of the children.**

an

amusing, *adjective*

مسلي ـ مُرَفِّه .

which makes you happy; **the film was very amusing; I didn't find the book very amusing.**

an [æn *or* ən] *see* **a**

ملاحظة : انظر إلى كلمة a

and [ænd *or* ənd] *conjunction*

و (حرف العطف)

which shows two things are connected in some way; **my mother and father; he likes apples and pears; he was running and singing at the same time; come and sit down.**

ملاحظة : تستعمل and في الأرقام بعد المئة : (سبعمئة واثنين ...)

Note: **and** *is used to say numbers after 100:* **seven hundred and two (702)**

and so on, *adverb*

وهلّم جرّاً .

in the same way; **he talked about gardens, flowers, and so on** = and other similar things.

anger [ˈæŋgə] *noun*

غضب

being annoyed; **he showed his anger by banging on the table.**

angry [ˈæŋgrɪ] *adjective*

غاضب ـ ساخط

annoyed; **he's angry with his children because they broke a window; she gets angry if the trains are late; everyone is angry about the price of petrol.**

angry—angrier—angriest

angrily, *adverb*

بغضب

in an angry way.

animal [ˈænɪməl] *noun*

حيوان

living and moving thing; **dogs and cats are animals, and man is also an animal; we went to see the animals in the zoo.**

ankle [ˈæŋkl] *noun*

كاحل (جزء من الرجل)

joint where your foot is connected to your leg; **he twisted his ankle** = he hurt it by bending it in an odd direction.

annoy [əˈnɔɪ] *verb*

يزعج ، يضايق

to make (someone) angry; **it annoys me to have to go out in the rain.**

annoys—annoying—annoyed—has annoyed

annoyed, *adjective*

منزعج ، متضايق

angry; **he's annoyed because we all forgot his birthday; she's annoyed with the dog because it ate her chocolates.**

annoying, *adjective*

مزعج

which makes you angry; **it's annoying to have to wait for a bus.**

another [əˈnʌðə] *adjective & pronoun*

١) آخر ـ إضافي .

(*a*) one more; **would you like another cup of tea?**

ب) آخر ، مختلف

(*b*) a different (one); **she fell down and made her dress dirty, so she had to change into another one;** *see also* **each other, one another.**

answer [ˈɑːnsə] **1.** *noun*

١ ـ جواب ـ اجابة .

reply/words spoken or written when someone has spoken to you or asked you a question; **I phoned the office, but there was no answer; have you had an answer to your letter yet?**
2. *verb*

٢ ـ يجاوب ـ يرد على

anxious

to reply/to speak or write words after someone has spoken to you or asked you a question; **he hasn't answered my letter; when he asked them if they had enjoyed the book, they all answered 'no';** to answer the phone = to speak into it when it rings.

answers—answering— answered—has answered

answer back, verb

يجاوب بعنف أو بوقاحة .

to answer in a rude way; **if you answer back like that the teacher will be angry with you.**

anxious ['æŋʃəs] adjective

ا) قَلِق - مهموم

(a) worried; **my sister is still ill—I am anxious about her.**

ب) مُتلهف إلى ، منتظر بفارغ الصبر

(b) eager; **she was anxious to get home; I was anxious to see him.**

any ['enɪ] 1. adjective & pronoun

١ - ا) أيّ من - اية من

(a) it doesn't matter which; **take any one you like; come any day next week.**

ب) بعض - قليل من .

(b) some; **have you any salt? is there any cake left? would you like any more coffee?**

ت) لا شيء

(c) not . . . any = none; **there aren't any cakes left; give me your money—I haven't got any.**
2. adverb

٢ - لا أكثر .

not . . . any + comparative = not even a little; **I can't sing any louder; the car won't go any faster.**

anybody ['enɪbɒdɪ], anyone ['enɪwʌn] pronoun

ا) أيا كان

apart

(a) it doesn't matter who; **anybody can learn to ride a bicycle; anybody can do it, can't they?**

ب) شخص ما

(b) some person; **can anybody lend me ten pounds? I didn't meet anybody** = I met no one.

anyhow ['enɪhaʊ] adverb

في أي حال

in any case; in spite of it all; **it was raining, but I didn't want to go out anyhow.**

anyone ['enɪwʌn] see anybody

أياً كان

anything ['enɪθɪŋ] pronoun

ا) أي شيء

(a) it doesn't matter what; **you can take anything you want; our dog will eat anything.**

ب) شيء ما

(b) something; **did anything happen during the night? has anything made you ill? do you want anything more to drink? he didn't eat anything** = he ate nothing.

anyway ['enɪweɪ] adverb

في اية حال

in any case; in spite of it all; **it was raining but I didn't want to go out anyway; the doctor told me to stay in bed, but I'm still going to the party anyway.**

anywhere ['enɪweə] adverb

ا) في أي مكان

(a) it doesn't matter where; **put the book down anywhere.**

ب) في مكان ما

(b) somewhere; **is there anywhere where I can put this box? I haven't seen it anywhere.**

apart [ə'pɑːt] adverb

منفصل - متفرق - عن بعضهم البعض - عن بعضها البعض .

eleven

11

apartment

separate; **the two towns are very far apart; the watch came apart in my hands** = it came to pieces; **they live apart now** = they don't live together any more.

باستثناء ـ ما عدا

apart from = except; **they all wore black hats, apart from me.**

apartment [ə'pɑ:tmənt] *noun*

شقة (في مبنى).

American = **flat**

appear [ə'pɪə] *verb*

أ) يظهر

(*a*) to start being seen; **a ship suddenly appeared in the distance; a man appeared at the door.**

ب) يبدو ، يتراءى

(*b*) to seem; **he appears to be ill; it appears to be raining.**

appears—appearing—appeared—has appeared

appearance [ə'pɪərəns] *noun*

مظهر ، ظهور

how a person or thing looks; **you could tell from her appearance that she had been climbing trees; he put in an appearance at the meeting** = he came for a short time.

apple ['æpl] *noun*

تفاحة

common hard round sweet fruit, growing on a tree; **apple pie; don't eat that green apple—it isn't ripe yet.**

apple tree, *noun*

شجرة تفاح

tree which apples grow on.

apply [ə'plaɪ] *verb*

أ) يقدم طلب ـ (لوظيفة ما)

(*a*) to ask for a job; **she applied for a job as a teacher; he applied to join the police force.**

approach

ب) ينطبق على

(*b*) to refer to; **this applies to all of you; the rule applies to visitors only.**

applies—applying—applied—has applied

application [æplɪ'keɪʃn] *noun*

تقديم طلب (عمل أو وظيفة)

asking for a job (usually in writing); **if you are applying for the job, you must fill in an application form.**

appoint [ə'pɔɪnt] *verb*

يعيّن

to give someone a job; **he was appointed headmaster.**

appoints—appointing—appointed—has appointed

appointment, *noun*

أ) تعيين (شخص لرتبة أو وظيفة)

(*a*) giving someone a job; **on his appointment as headmaster** = when he was appointed headmaster.

ب) موعد (المقابلة)

(*b*) arrangement to see someone at a particular time; **I have an appointment with the doctor/to see the doctor on Tuesday; can I make an appointment to see Dr Jones? I'm very busy—I've got appointments all day.**

appreciate [ə'pri:ʃieɪt] *verb*

يُقَدّر

to notice how good something is; **he always appreciates good food.**

appreciates—appreciating—appreciated—has appreciated

approach [ə'prəʊtʃ] *verb*

يقترب من

to go/to come nearer; **as policeman approached, all the children ran away; the time is approaching when we will have to decide what to do.**

approaches—approaching—approached—has approached

12 *twelve*

approve

approve [ə'pruːv] *verb*

يؤيّد ـ يرضى ان ـ يكون راضياً على ـ يكون موافقاً على ـ يوافق على

to approve of something = to think that something is good; **I don't approve of noisy children; the police don't approve of fast cars; he approves of staying in bed.**

approves—approving—approved—has approved

April ['eɪprəl] *noun*

شهر نيسان (ابريل)

fourth month of the year; **his birthday is in April; she died on April 20th; we went on holiday last April; today is April 5th.** *Note:* **April 5th:** *say* 'the fifth of April' *or* 'April the fifth'

apron ['eɪprən] *noun*

مريلة ، مريول

cloth or plastic cover which you wear in front of your clothes to stop them getting dirty; **put on an apron if you are going to do the washing up.**

are [ɑː] *see* **be**

ملاحظة : انظر إلى كلمة be

area ['eərɪə] *noun*

أ) مساحة

(*a*) measurement of the space occupied by something; **to measure the area of a room you must multiply the length by the width; the area of the garden is 250 square metres.**

ب) منطقة ـ حي سكني

(*b*) district; **the houses in this area are very expensive; the police are searching the area round the school.**

aren't [ɑːnt] *see* **be**

ملاحظة : انظر إلى كلمة be

argue ['ɑːgjuː] *verb*

يناقش ـ يجادل

to discuss something without agreeing/ to quarrel; **she argued with the waiter about the bill.**

argues—arguing—argued—has argued

argument ['ɑːgjʊmənt] *noun*

جدال ـ نقاش ـ نزاع

discussing something without agreeing; **they got into an argument about money.**

arithmetic [ə'rɪθmətɪk] *noun*

علم الحساب

calculating with numbers.

arm [ɑːm] *noun*

أ) ذراع (الانسان)

(*a*) part of the body which goes from your hand to your shoulder; **his arm hurt after he fell down; she broke her arm skiing; lift your arms up above your head.**

ب) ذراع (الكرسي)

(*b*) part of a chair which you can rest your arms on; **he sat on the arm of my chair.**

ت) سلاح ـ أسلحة

(*c*) **arms** = weapons.

armchair, *noun*

كرسي ذو ذراعين

chair with arms.

armed, *adjective*

مسلح

(person) who carries weapons; **the soldiers were armed with knives; are the policemen all armed? the armed forces** = the army, navy and air force.

army ['ɑːmɪ] *noun*

جيش

all the soldiers of a country; **the British army; he left school and joined the army.**

plural **armies**

thirteen 13

around

around [əˈraʊnd] *preposition*

أ) يحيط بـ ـ حول

(a) surrounding; **the water was all around the house.**

ب) تقريباً ، حوالي

(b) about; **the car costs around £4,000.**

arrange [əˈreɪndʒ] *verb*

أ) يرتب

(a) to put in order; **she arranged the books in rows; the books are arranged in alphabetical order.**

ب) ينظم ـ ينسّق

(b) to organize; **we arranged to meet at 6 o'clock.**

arranges—arranging—arranged—has arranged

arrangement, *noun*

ترتيب ـ تنظيم

way in which something is put in order, way in which something is organized; **all the arrangements have been made for the wedding.**

arrest [əˈrest] *verb*

يلقي القبض على

to catch someone and keep him (usually at a police station) because the police believe he has done something wrong; **the policeman arrested the burglar; he was arrested as he was climbing out of the window.**

arrests—arresting—arrested—has arrested

arrive [əˈraɪv] *verb*

يصل

to reach a place; **the plane arrives in London at 4 o'clock; we arrived at the cinema after the film had started; she arrived home tired out.**

arrives—arriving—arrived—has arrived

Note: you **arrive in a town,** *but* **arrive at a place**

arrival, *noun*

as

أ) وصول ـ قدوم .

(a) reaching a place; **the time of arrival is 4 o'clock.**

ب) شخص قادم

(b) person who has arrived; **he's a new arrival.**

ت) قسم من المطار خاص بالقادمين

(c) **arrivals** = part of an airport dealing with passengers who are arriving.

art [ɑːt] *noun*

فن

painting/drawing, etc.

art gallery, *noun*

معرض للرسوم واللوحات الفنية

building where paintings are put on show.

article [ˈɑːtɪkl] *noun*

أ) صنف ـ قطعة .

(a) thing/object; **article of clothing** = piece of clothing.

ب) أداة (مثل أداة التعريف)

(b) part of speech/word showing a noun (*such as* **a** *house,* **the** *tree*).

ت) مقالة (في الصحف أو المجلّات)

(c) piece of writing in a newspaper; **did you read the article about/on Germany in yesterday's paper?**

artificial [ɑːtɪˈfɪʃl] *adjective*

إصطناعي

which is made by man/which is not the real thing; **artificial wood; he has an artificial leg.**

artist [ˈɑːtɪst] *noun*

فنان

person who paints/draws, etc.

as [æz *or* əz] *conjunction*

أ) بما ان ـ لأن ـ طالما

(a) because; **as you can't drive you must go by bus.**

ب) في حين ـ بينما

(b) at the same time; **as he was opening the door, the telephone rang.**

14 fourteen

ash

ت) كما ـ مثلما ـ بنفس الطريقة

(c) in a certain way; **leave it as it is; you must do as the policeman tells you.**

فيما يتعلق

as for = concerning; **as for you—you must stay here.**

ابتداء من

as from = from a time; **as from tomorrow** = starting from tomorrow.

كما لو أن

as if = in the same way as; **he walks very slowly, as if he had hurt his leg; she looks as if she's going to cry; it looks as if it's going to rain.**

بنفس القدر ـ بنفس الكمية

as ... as = like; **he is as tall as me; as green as grass.**

كما لو أن

as though = as if

أيضاً

as well = also/too; **he ate his piece of cake and mine as well; we visited the castle and the old church as well.**

كذلك أيضاً ـ بالاضافة إلى

as well as = together with; **he has a house in the country as well as a house in town; as well as teaching English, he also teaches football.**

ash [æʃ] noun

رماد

grey dust left when something has burnt; **he dropped cigarette ash on to the carpet.**

no plural: ashes means pieces of ash

ashamed [əˈʃeɪmd] adjective

مخجول ـ شاعر بالخجل

sorry because you have done something wrong; **he was ashamed of what he had done; don't be ashamed of making mistakes; she was ashamed of her old clothes; I'm ashamed of you!**

ask [ɑːsk] verb

أ)يسأل ـ يطلب

fifteen

astonish

(a) to put a question; **ask someone to teach you how to swim; he asked the policeman the way to the post office; she went to the railway station to ask about cheap tickets to London.**

ب) يدعو إلى

(b) to invite; **we asked them in for a cup of tea; don't ask her out—she always wants expensive meals.**

asks—asking—asked—has asked

ask for, verb

يطلب

to say that you want something; **he asked for more money; someone knocked at the door and asked for my father; he asked for his pencil back** = said that he wanted to have the pencil which he had lent.

asleep [əˈsliːp] adjective

نائم

sleeping; **he was asleep and didn't hear the telephone ring; she fell asleep in front of the TV** = she began to sleep.

ملاحظة : لا تستعمل asleep أمام الاسم ، بل تستعمل بعد الفعل .

Note: **asleep** *cannot be used in front of a noun:* **the cat is asleep** *but* **a sleeping cat**

assistant [əˈsɪstənt] noun

مساعد ـ معاون ـ نائب

person who helps; **my assistant will come to meet you; shop assistant** = person who works in a shop.

astonish [əˈstɒnɪʃ] verb

يدهش

to surprise; **I was astonished to see that she had got married.**

astonishes—astonishing—astonished—has astonished

astonishing, adjective

مدهش ـ مذهل

15

at

which surprises; **it's astonishing how many people speak English well;** an **astonishing number of the students passed their exams.**

astonishment, noun

دهشة .

great surprise; **to his astonishment, she suddenly started to sing.**

at [æt *or* ət] *preposition*

أ) عند (تستعمل لتحديد الوقت أو الزمان)

(*a*) (*showing time*) **at ten o'clock; at night; at the weekend.**

ب) عند (تستعمل لتحديد المكان)

(*b*) (*showing place*) **meet me at the corner of the street; at the top of the mountain; she's not at home; he's at work.**

ت) تستعمل لتعيين السرعة(بسرعة ٥٠ كيلومتر بالساعة)

(*c*) (*showing speed*) **the train was travelling at 50 kilometres an hour.**
Note: **at** *is often used after verbs:* **look at; point at,** *etc.*

ate [et] *see* **eat**

ملاحظة : انظر إلى كلمة eat

attach [ə'tætʃ] *verb*

يربط ـ يعلّق

to fix/to fasten; **the seat belt is attached to the floor of the car; the boat was attached with a chain.**
attaches—attaching—attached—has attached

attack [ə'tæk] **1.** *noun*

١ - أ) هجوم

(*a*) starting to fight; **they made an attack on the castle.**

ب) نوبة مرضية

(*b*) sudden illness; **he had an attack of fever.**
2. *verb*

٢ - يهجم على ـ يهاجم

attract

to start to fight; **three big men attacked him and stole his money; the old lady was attacked by robbers.**
attacks—attacking—attacked—has attacked

attempt [ə'tempt] **1.** *noun*

١ ـ محاولة

try; **he made an attempt to break the record for the high jump.**
2. *verb*

٢ ـ يحاول

to try; **she attempted to climb the mountain.**
attempts—attempting—attempted—has attempted

attend [ə'tend] *verb*

يحضر (اجتماعاً أو جلسةً)

to be present at; **will you attend the meeting tomorrow?**
attends—attending—attended—has attended

attend to, *verb*

يهتم بـ

to deal with; **the doctor is attending to his patients.**

attention [ə'tenʃn] *noun*

انتباه

careful thinking; **the boy in the back row was not paying attention to what the teacher was saying; attention please!**

attract [ə'trækt] *verb*

يجذب ـ يلفت (الانتباه)

to make something come to you; **bees are attracted by flowers; to attract attention** = to make people notice what you are doing.
attracts—attracting—attracted—has attracted

attractive [ə'træktɪv] *adjective*

جذاب ـ فاتن ـ ساحر

16   *sixteen*

August · awkward

pleasant to look at; **an attractive town**; **she's a very attractive girl**.

August [ˈɔːɡəst] *noun*

آب ـ أغسطس

eighth month of the year; **my birthday is in August**; **today is August 15th**; **I start my new job next August**.
Note: **August 15th:** *say* 'the fifteenth of August' *or* 'August the fifteenth'

aunt [ɑːnt] *noun*

عمة ـ خالة ـ زوجة العم أو الخال

sister of your mother or father; wife of your uncle; **here is Aunt Mary**.

automatic [ɔːtəˈmætɪk] *adjective*

آلي ـ أوتوماتيكي

which works by itself, with no one making it work; **an automatic door** = door which opens as you come to it.

آلياً ـ بشكل آلي أو اوتوماتيكي

automatically [ɔːtəˈmætɪklɪ] *adverb*
working by itself; **the door opens automatically**; **when smoke comes into the room it automatically makes a bell ring**.

autumn [ˈɔːtəm] *noun (American:* **fall**)

خريف

season of the year between summer and winter; **in cold countries, the leaves turn brown and fall off the trees in autumn**; **we go on holiday in the autumn**; **the building will be finished next autumn**; **I started work last autumn**.

average [ˈævrɪdʒ] **1.** *noun*

١ ـ معدل ـ متوسط

middle figure out of two or more; **we scored 10, 12 and 17, so our average is 13**; **to work out an average you must add all the figures together and then divide by the number of figures which you have added**.
2. *adjective*

٢ ـ معتدل ـ متوسط ، مقبول ـ غير بارز

ordinary/not very good; **he gets average marks in school**; **she is just an average worker**.

avoid [əˈvɔɪd] *verb*

يتجنب ـ يتفادى

to try not to do something; to try not to hit something; **I want to avoid going out in the rain**; **the car managed to avoid the lamppost**.
avoids—avoiding—avoided—has avoided

awake [əˈweɪk] **1.** *verb*

١ ـ أ) يوقظ .

(*a*) to wake someone up; **he was awoken by the sound of thunder**.

ب) يستيقظ

(*b*) to wake up; **he awoke when he heard the sound of thunder**.
awakes—awaking—awoke—has awoken

2. *adjective*

٢ ـ مستيقظ ـ

not asleep; **he was still awake at 2 o'clock**; **the baby is wide awake** = very awake.
Note: **awake** *cannot be used in front of a noun*

away [əˈweɪ] *adverb*

بعيداً عن ـ جانباً

not here; far; **they went away on holiday**; **the nearest town is six kilometres away**; **go away! put that knife away**.

awful [ˈɔːfʊl] *adjective*

شنيع ـ كريه .

very bad; **what an awful smell! he has an awful cold**.

awkward [ˈɔːkwəd] *adjective*

حَرِج ـ مرتبك ـ صعب المنال

difficult to reach/to find/to deal with; **that cupboard is in a very awkward**

seventeen

awoke | back

place; he was in a very awkward situation.

awoke [ə'wəuk]., **awoken** [ə'wəukn]
see **awake**

ملاحظة : انظر إلى كلمة awake

axe [æks] *noun*

فأس

tool with a sharp metal head for chopping wood; he chopped the tree down with an axe.

Bb

baby ['beɪbɪ] *noun*

طفل ـ طفلة .

(a) very young child; **babies start to walk when they are about 12 months old; I've known Mary since she was a baby; Mrs Smith had her baby last week** = she gave birth to the baby last week.

ب) حديث السن .

(b) small animal; **baby elephant**.
plural **babies**
Note: if you do not know the sex of a baby you can refer to it as **it**: **the baby was sucking its thumb**

back [bæk] **1.** *noun*

١ ـ أ) ظَهْر (جزء من الجسم ما بين العنق والخصر)

(a) part of the body from your neck downwards to your waist, which is not in front; **he lay down on his back and looked at the sky; she carried her bag on her back; he hurt his back lifting up the sack; he stood with his back to the wall.**

ب) خَلْف ـ

(b) other side to the front; **he wrote his name on the back of the photograph; she wrote the address on the back of the envelope; he sat in the back of the car and went to sleep; his bedroom is in the back of the house; he put his trousers on back to front** = the wrong way round.
2. *adjective*

٢ ـ خَلْفي

on the opposite side to the front; he knocked at the back door; the back tyre of my bicycle is flat.
3. *adverb*

٣ ـ أ) إلى الخلف ـ إلى الوراء .

(a) towards the back; **he stepped back; she leant back against the wall.**

ب) (تستعمل **back** مع بعض الأفعال للتعبير عن العودة إلى حالة سابقة وليس لها ترجمة حرفية بالعربية مثلاً : رد الأموال **to pay back** عاد إلى **to get back** (to

(b) (*showing how things were before*) **can you pay me back the £10 which you owe me? he went back into the house; she gave me back my book; he only got back home at 10 o'clock.**
4. *verb*

٤ ـ يتراجع ـ يعود (بشيء ما) إلى الوراء

to go backwards; **he backed his car into the garage; she backed away from him** = she went away from him backwards.
backs—backing—backed—has backed

ملاحظة : تستعمل كلمة **back** غالباً بعد الفعل

Note: **back** *is often used after verbs:* **to give back; to go back; to pay back,** *etc.*

background ['bækgraund] *noun*

خلفية

part (of a picture) which is in the distance; **the picture shows a house with a**

bacon

background of dark trees; her blue dress stands out against the white background; can you see the two ships in the background?

back up, verb

يدعم ـ يساعد

to help someone; **nobody would back her up in her argument with the boss.**

backwards, adverb

إلى الوراء

from the front towards the back; **he stepped backwards into the lake;** 'tab' is 'bat' spelt backwards; **backwards and forwards** = from one side to the other several times; **the policeman walked backwards and forwards in front of the shop.**

bacon ['beɪkn] noun

لحم خنزير مملّح

salty meat from a pig; **we had bacon and eggs for breakfast; can I have some more bacon please? he's already eaten three pieces of bacon and two eggs.**
no plural: **some bacon; a slice of bacon/a piece of bacon**

bad [bæd] adjective

أ) سيّء ـ ضار

(*a*) not good; of poor quality; **too much butter is bad for you; this apple's going bad; she's good at maths but bad at English.**

ب) رديء ـ مزعج

(*b*) unpleasant; **she's got a bad cold; he had a bad accident in his car.**
bad—worse—worst

لا بأس به

not bad = quite good; **this cake isn't bad; what did you think of the film?—not bad!**

badly, adverb

بشكل سيىء ـ بشكل ملحّ ـ بحاجة ماسة

in a bad way; **he did badly in his English exam; your hair badly needs cutting** = it is very long.
badly—worse—worst

bad-tempered, adjective

حاد المزاج

he's always bad-tempered = he is always annoyed.

bag [bæg] noun

كيس ـ حقيبة

something made of paper/cloth, etc., in which you can carry things; **a bag of potatoes; he put the apples in a paper bag; she carried her clothes in an old bag; string bag** = bag made of string like a net; **shopping bag** = bag for carrying shopping in; **sleeping bag** = comfortable warm bag for sleeping in.

baggage ['bægɪdʒ] noun

حقائب السفر

cases/bags, etc., which you take with you when you travel containing your clothes; **put all the baggage into the back of the car; we have too much baggage—we will have to pay extra.**
no plural: **some baggage; a lot of baggage**

bake [beɪk] verb

يَخْبُز

to cook in an oven; **she baked a cake; do you like baked potatoes?**
bakes—baking—baked—has baked

baker, noun

خَبّاز

person who makes bread and cakes; **the baker's** = shop where you can buy bread and cakes; **he bought a loaf of bread at the baker's; the baker's is next door to the butcher's.**

nineteen 19

balance

balance ['bæləns] 1. *noun*

١ ـ توازن

not falling; **he stood on the top of the fence and kept his balance** = did not fall off.
2. *verb*

٢ ـ يحفظ توازنه

to stand on something narrow without falling; **he was balancing on top of the fence; how long can you balance on one foot?**

balances—balancing—balanced—has balanced

ball [bɔːl] *noun*

كرة

round thing for throwing/kicking/for playing games; **tennis ball; he kicked the ball into the goal; I threw the ball and he caught it.**

ball point pen, ball pen, *noun*

قلم حبر ناشف

pen which writes using a small ball covered with ink.

balloon [bə'luːn] *noun*

بالون ـ مُنطاد

large round thing which you blow up with air or gas; **they blew up balloons for the party.**

banana [bə'nɑːnə] *noun*

موز

long yellow fruit which grows in hot countries; **he was peeling a banana; the children like to eat bananas; banana split** = dessert made of bananas, cream, ice cream and nuts.

band [bænd] *noun*

أ) شريط

(*a*) thin piece of material for tying things together; **the papers were held together with a rubber band.**

ب) فرقة موسيقية

bank

(*b*) group of people, esp. people who play music together; **the soldiers marched after the band; the band played music; a dance band.**

bandage ['bændɪdʒ] 1. *noun*

١ ـ ضمادة للجروح

piece of cloth which you wrap round a wound; **he head was covered in bandages; put a bandage round your knee.**
2. *verb*

٢ ـ ضمّد ، أو لف بالضمادة

to wrap a piece of cloth round a wound; **she bandaged his leg; his arm is bandaged up.**

bandages—bandaging—bandaged—has bandaged

bang [bæŋ] 1. *noun*

١ ـ دويّ انفجار ـ صوت مفاجىء وقوي

sudden loud noise like that made by a gun; **the gun went bang; there was a bang and the chimney fell down.**
2. *verb*

٢ ـ يطرق (الباب) بقوة ـ يخبط بقوة (على الطاولة)

to make a loud noise; **can't you stop the door banging? he banged on the table with his hand.**

bangs—banging—banged—has banged

bank [bæŋk] 1. *noun*

١ ـ أ) شاطىء نهر (أو بحيرة)

(*a*) land along the two sides of a river or at the edge of a lake; **he sat on the bank of the river, trying to catch fish.**

ب) مصرف ـ بنك .

(*b*) place where you can leave your money safely; **how much money do you have in the bank? he put all his money in the bank; she took all her money out of the bank to buy a car.**
2. *verb*

٢ ـ يودع أموال

20   *twenty*

bank holiday

to put money away in a bank; **have you banked the money yet?**
banks—banking—banked—has banked

bank account, *noun*

حساب مصرفي

arrangement which you make with a bank to keep your money safely; **I put all my savings in my bank account; he opened/closed a bank account** = he started/stopped keeping money in a bank.

bank holiday, *noun*

يوم عطلة - عطلة رسمية

day when most people are on holiday and the banks are closed; **Christmas Day is a bank holiday.**

bank on, *verb*

يعتمد على - يتّكل على

to be sure that something will happen; **don't bank on getting any money from your father; you can bank on the weather being bad for the school sports day.**

bar [baː] *noun*

أ) قطعة - لوح (من الشكولاتة، من الصابون)

(*a*) piece of something hard; **a bar of soap; a bar of chocolate.**

ب) قضيب (من الخشب أو المعدن)

(*b*) long piece of wood or metal; **he escaped from the prison by sawing through the bars** = pieces of metal in front of the windows.

ت) مكان لشرب الخمرة

(*c*) room where you can buy alcohol; **a bar in a hotel.**

ث) مقهى صغير (لتناول مأكولات أو مشروبات معينة)

(*d*) small shop where you can buy special things; **sandwich bar** = small restaurant which mainly sells sandwiches;

coffee bar = small restaurant which sells coffee, cakes and sandwiches.

bare [beə] *adjective*

أ) عار

(*a*) not covered by clothes; **the children had bare feet; her dress left her arms bare.**

ب) عارٍ من الورق (يقال عن الشجر)

(*b*) with no leaves; **in winter the branches of the trees are bare.**

barely, *adverb*

بالكاد - بالجهد

almost not/hardly; **we have barely enough money to pay the bill** = we have only just enough money; **he barely had time to sit down before the telephone rang.**

bargain ['baːɡɪn] *noun*

صفقة - صفقة رابحة

something which you buy at a lower price than normal; **£50 return to New York is a bargain; you should buy that fur coat—it's a bargain.**

bark [baːk] **1.** *noun*

١ - أ) قشرة جذع الشجرة

(*a*) hard outside of a tree trunk.

ب) نباح

(*b*) noise made by a dog.
2. *verb*

٢ - ينبح

(*of a dog*) to make a noise; **the dog barked at the postman; I can hear a dog barking.**
barks—barking—barked—has barked

base [beɪs] *noun*

قاعدة

bottom part/part which something stands on; **a glass with a heavy base.**

baseball, *noun*

twenty-one 21

basin

لعبة البيزبول (لعبة اميركية تستعمل كرة صغيرة ويتخاصم فيها فريقين)

American game played between two teams using a hard ball; **do you want to watch the baseball game on TV? he's playing in the school baseball team.**

basic ['beɪsɪk] *adjective*

أساسي

very simple/which everything else comes from; **you should know basic maths if you want to work in a shop; a basic dictionary** = dictionary which contains the most common words.

basin ['beɪsn] *noun*

مغسلة - حوض للاغتسال

large bowl; **wash basin** = bowl in a kitchen or bathroom, where you can wash your hands, etc.

basket ['bɑːskɪt] *noun*

سلّة -

container made of thin pieces of wood, etc.; **throw those papers into the waste paper basket; if you're going shopping, don't forget your shopping basket.**

bath [bɑːθ] **1.** *noun*

١ - أ) حوض الاستحمام - مغطس

(a) large container for water, in which you can wash your whole body; **is the bath clean? there's a shower and a bath in the bathroom.**

ب) الاستحمام

(b) washing your whole body; **after you've been playing football you need a hot bath; my father has a cold bath every morning.**

ت) حمّام بالماء (الساخنة أو الباردة)

(c) the water in a bath; **I like to lie in a hot bath.**

ث) حمّام السباحة - مسابح عامة

(d) **swimming baths** = large building with a swimming pool.

be

Note: **one bath** [bɑːθ] *but* **two baths** [bɑːðz]

2. *verb*

٢ - يستحم

to wash all over; **he's bathing the baby. baths** [bɑːθs]—**bathing** ['bɑːθɪŋ]— **bathed** [bɑːθt]—**has bathed**

bathroom, *noun*

غرفة الحمّام

room in a house, with a bath, washbasin and usually lavatory; **where's the bathroom? can I use your bathroom, please? the bathroom scales must be wrong— I'm heavier than I was yesterday.**

bathe [beɪð] *verb*

أ) يسبح

(a) to swim; **we were bathing in the sea before breakfast.**

ب) يغسل - يحمّم

(b) to wash (a wound); **he bathed his knee with boiled water. bathes—bathing** ['beɪðɪŋ]— **bathed** [beɪðd]—**has bathed**

battery ['bætəri] *noun*

بطارية

something which stores electric power and is used to make something work; **the torch needs a new battery; you ought to change the batteries in the radio.** *plural* **batteries**

battle ['bætl] *noun*

معركة - كفاح

fight between armies; **the French navy was defeated in the battle of Trafalgar.**

be [biː] **1.** *verb*

١ - أ) (للدلالة على حالة ما) : يكون - (من فعل كان)

ملاحظة : ان فعل to be لا يستعمل في العربية إلا في المستقبل (سيكون) أو في الماضي (كان) - اما في الحاضر فتستعمل

Bathroom

حمام

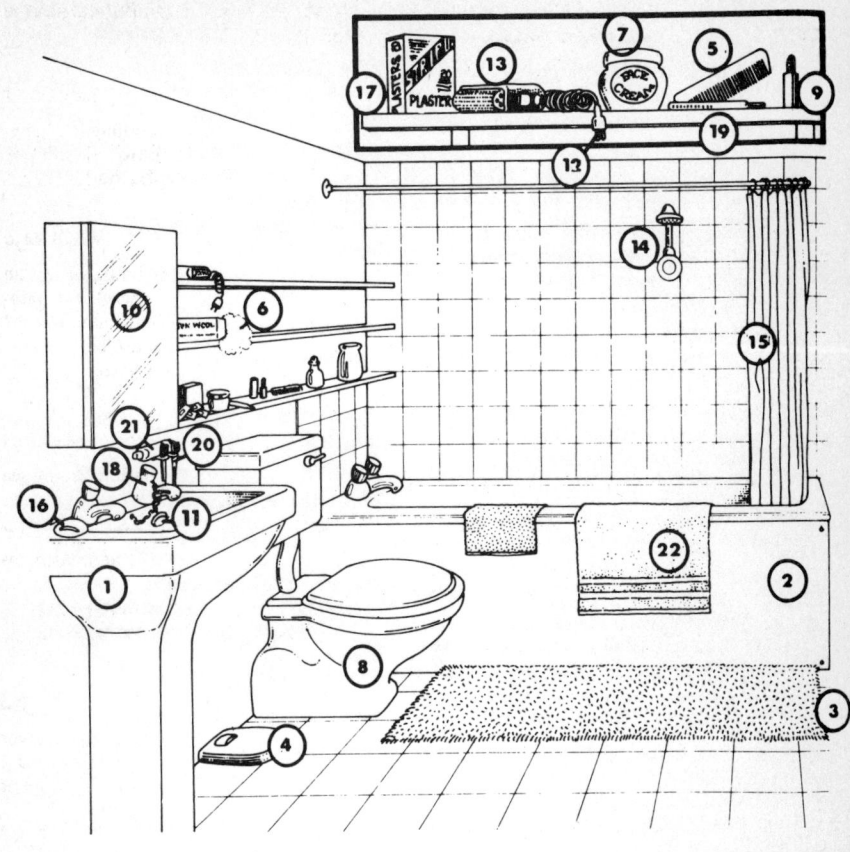

1. basin	١ ـ مغسلة	12. plug (on razor)	١٢ ـ مأخذ الكهرباء في آلة الحلاقة
2. bath	٢ ـ مغطس	13. razor	١٣ ـ آلة حلاقة
3. bathmat	٣ ـ بساط الحمام	14. shower	١٤ ـ مضخة ماء
4. bathroom scales	٤ ـ ميزان	15. shower curtain	١٥ ـ ستائر الحمام
5. comb	٥ ـ مشط	16. soap	١٦ ـ صابون
6. cotton wool	٦ ـ قطن	17. sticking plaster	١٧ ـ لاصقة
7. face cream	٧ ـ كريم (مستحضر تجميلي للوجه)	18. tap	١٨ ـ حنفية
8. lavatory	٨ ـ مرحاض	19. thermometer	١٩ ـ ميزان الحرارة
9. lipstick	٩ ـ أحمر الشفاة	20. toothbrush	٢٠ ـ فرشاة أسنان
10. mirror	١٠ ـ مرآة	21. toothpaste	٢١ ـ معجون أسنان
11. plug (in washbasin)	١١ ـ سدادة المغسلة	22. towel	٢٢ ـ منشفة

twenty-three

beach

كلمة هو أو هي بدلاً من فعل كان ، وفي معظم الأحوال تحذف تماماً : نقول مثلاً : السماء زرقاء أو السماء هي زرقاء

(a) (showing a state) the sky is blue; he is taller than his father; tomatoes are red; it's cold today; are you hungry?

ب) (للدلالة على العمر أو السن) في ... من عمره . مثلاً : هو في السادسة عشر من عمره

(b) (showing age/time) he's sixteen; she's only two years old; it's nearly six o'clock; it's time to go to bed; it will soon be summer.

ت) (للدلالة على السعر) يبلغ سعره ـ سعره هو ... مثلاً : سعر الطماطم ٣٠ درهماً .

(c) (showing price) tomatoes are 30p a pound; sandwiches are 25p each.

ث) (للدلالة على المهنة) مثلاً : امه هي استاذة

(d) (showing occupation) his mother is a teacher; she wants to be a doctor.

ج) (للدلالة على الطول أو القامة) مثلا : يبلغ ١٧٠ سنتم في القامة

(e) (showing size, height, etc.) he's six foot tall; the table is more than two metres long; the post office is very close to our house.

ح) (للدلالة على وجود شيء ما) مثلاً : هناك جمهور ينتظر الحافلة

(f) (showing that something exists) there's a crowd of people waiting for the bus; there are only two chocolates left in the box.

خ) ذهب (في الماضي فقط) مثلاً : هل سبق وذهبت إلى ألمانيا

(g) (in the perfect = go) have you ever been to Germany? she has been to see the film three times.

2. *making a part of a verb*

٢ ـ أ) (لوضع الفعل في صيغة الحاضر المستمر) مثلاً : وهو يقرأ

(a) (making the present continuous) don't talk to him when he's reading; I'm waiting for the bus; they are hoping to go on holiday next week.

ب) (لوضع الفعل في صيغة الماضي المستمر) مثلاً : كان يغني ـ كانوا يسيرون .

(b) (making the past continuous) she was singing in the bath; they were walking in the street when it started to rain.

ت) (لوضع الفعل في صيغة المستقبل المستمر) سيكون مسافراً

(c) (making the future continuous) he will be flying to Paris tomorrow morning.

ث) لصيغة الفعل المجهول

(d) (showing the passive) she was knocked down by a bus; the children were told to go home.

ـ في الحاضر

Present: I am, you are, he is, we are, they are

ـ في صيغة مختصرة

Short forms: I'm, you're, he's, we're, they're

ـ في النفي

Negative: I'm not; you're not or you aren't; he's not or he isn't; we're not or we aren't; they're not or they aren't

ـ في المستقبل

Future: I will be/I shall be

ـ في الماضي المتواصل

Past: I was, you were, he was, we were, they were

ـ في الماضي وبصيغة النفي

Negative: I wasn't, you weren't, he wasn't, we weren't, they weren't

ـ في الماضي

Perfect: I have been, you have been, he/she/it has been, they have been

beach [biːtʃ] *noun*

شاطىء البحر

sandy part by the edge of the sea; we sat on the beach and ate our sandwiches; let's go to the beach this afternoon; some

bean

of the beaches are covered with oil. *plural* **beaches**

bean [biːn] *noun*

لوبياء - فاصولياء

vegetable which produces seeds which you can eat; **green beans; baked beans.**

bear [beə] *noun*

دُب

large wild animal covered with fur; **bears like honey; polar bear** = big white bear which lives in the snow near the North Pole.

beard [ˈbɪəd] *noun*

لحية - شعر الذقن

hair growing on a man's chin; **Father Christmas has a long white beard.**

beat [biːt] **1.** *noun*

١ - إيقاع

regular sound; **the beat of a drum; keep in time with the beat of the music.**
2. *verb*

٢ - أ) يضرب

(*a*) to hit; **he used to beat his wife with a stick.**

ب) ينتصر على - يفوز على - يغلب

(*b*) to win against someone; **our team beat the Germans 3-0; he was easily beaten in the long jump.**

ت) يخفق

(*c*) to make a regular sound; **his heart was beating fast.**
beats—beating—beat—has beaten

beat up, *verb*

يضرب على نحو متكرر

to hit someone hard many times; **the old lady was beaten up by the burglars.**
Note: **they beat the old man up** *or* **they beat up the old man,** *but only* **they beat him up**

twenty-five

bed

beautiful [ˈbjuːtɪfəl] *adjective*

جميل - ظريف

very nice (to look at); **the beautiful colours of the autumn leaves; what beautiful weather! a beautiful Christmas cake.**

became [bɪˈkeɪm] *see* **become**
أصبح (انظر إلى كلمة become)

because [bɪˈkɒz] *conjunction*

لأن

for this reason; **I was late because I missed the bus; he's wet because it's raining; she's fat because she eats too much.**

بسبب

because of = on account of; due to; **the trains are late because of the fog; we don't use the car because of the price of petrol.**

become [bɪˈkʌm] *verb*

يصبح - يتحول إلى

to change into something different; **he wants to become a dentist; the sky became dark and the wind became stronger; they became friends; she's become rather deaf.**
becomes—becoming—became—has become

bed [bed] *noun*

سرير

piece of furniture for sleeping on; **lie down on the bed if you're tired; she always goes to bed at 9 o'clock; he was sitting in bed drinking a cup of coffee; come on, get out of bed—it's time for breakfast; she's in bed with a cold; have you made your bed?** = have you made it tidy after having slept in it?
bed and breakfast, *noun*

النزول في فندق وطعام الفطور فقط

staying the night (in a hotel, etc.) and

Bedroom

غرفة النوم

1. bed	١ ـ سرير	10. photograph	١٠ ـ صورة
2. blanket	٢ ـ بطانية	11. pillow	١١ ـ وسادة
3. chest of drawers	٣ ـ خزانة بدوارج	12. plant	١٢ ـ شتلة ـ غرسة
4. curtain	٤ ـ ستار	13. pyjamas	١٣ ـ ثياب النوم (منامة)
5. door	٥ ـ باب	14. sheet	١٤ ـ شرشف
6. drawer	٦ ـ درج	15. slippers	١٥ ـ خف
7. lamp	٧ ـ مصباح كهربائي	16. wardrobe	١٦ ـ خزانة الملابس
8. mattress	٨ ـ فراش	17. window	١٧ ـ نافذة
9. mirror	٩ ـ مرآة		

twenty-six

bee

having breakfast, but no other meals; **I only want to have bed and breakfast.**

bedclothes, *plural noun*

شراشف وأغطية السرير

sheets and blankets which cover a bed; **he woke up when all his bedclothes fell off.**

bedroom, *noun*

غرفة نوم

room where you sleep; **my bedroom is on the ground floor; shut your bedroom door if you want to be quiet.**

bedtime, *noun*

وقت النوم

time when you usually go to bed; **9 o'clock is my bedtime; go to bed—it's past your bedtime.**

bee [bi:] *noun*

نحلة

small insect which makes honey; **bees were going from flower to flower.**

beehive, *noun*

خلية النحل ـ قفير

box where bees are kept.

beef [bi:f] *noun*

لحم بقر

meat from a cow; **roast beef and boiled potatoes; would you like another slice of beef?**

ملاحظة : لا تستعمل beef إلا في المفرد
no plural: **some beef; a piece of beef/ a slice of beef**

been [bi:n] *see* **be.**

انظر إلى كلمة be

beer ['bɪə] *noun*

بيرة

type of alcohol; **can I have a glass of**

begin

beer? three beers please = three glasses of beer.

ملاحظة : في الجمع تعني كؤوس من البيرة
plural only used to mean **glasses of beer**

before [bɪ'fɔ:] **1.** *adverb*

١ ـ قبل ذلك ـ من قبل

earlier; **why didn't you tell me before? I didn't see him on Tuesday, I saw him the day before.**
2. *preposition*

٢ ـ قبل

earlier than; **he got here before me; make sure you arrive before 10.30; G comes before L in the alphabet.**
3. *conjunction*

٣ ـ قبل ان

earlier than; **before you sit down, can you pass me the salt? think carefully before you answer my question; before coming in, wipe your shoes on the mat.**

beg [beg] *verb*

يستعطي ـ يستجدي ـ يلتمس ـ يطلب الحسنة من

to ask (especially to ask for money); **I beg your pardon** = excuse me.
begs—begging—begged—has begged

beggar, *noun*

متوسل ـ شحاذ

person who asks for money or food.

began [bɪ'gæn] *see* **begin**
ملاحظة : انظر إلى كلمة begin

begin [bɪ'gɪn] *verb*

يبدأ

to start; **it began to rain; she began to cry; he's beginning to understand; they all began talking at once.**
begins—beginning—began—has begun

twenty-seven 27

beginner

beginner, *noun*

مُبتدىء ـ قليل الخبرة

person who is beginning; **he can't play well, he's only a beginner.**

beginning, *noun*

ابتداء ـ بداية ـ مطلع ـ مستهل

first part; **the beginning of the story is rather dull; hurry up if you want to see the beginning of the film.**

behave [bɪ'heɪv] *verb*

يسلك ـ يتصرف بأدب ـ يتصرف بطريقة معينة

to do things (usually well); **the children behaved (themselves) very well when they stayed with their granny; after she was ill she began to behave very strangely; if you don't behave, you'll have to stay in your bedroom** = if you are naughty.

behaves—behaving—behaved— has behaved

behaviour, *noun* (*American;* **behavior**)

سلوك ـ طريقة التصرّف ـ تصرّف

way of doing things; **his behaviour was very strange; the police said that the behaviour of the young people at the football match was very bad.**

behind [bɪ'haɪnd] **1.** *preposition*

١ ـ خلف ـ وراء (شيء ما)

at the back of; **they hid behind the curtain; my pen has fallen behind the sofa; he was second, only three metres behind the winner.**

2. *adverb*

٢ ـ إلى الوراء ـ في المؤخرة ـ إلى الخلف

at the back; **he was second, only three metres behind; she's left her ticket behind** = she has forgotten to take her ticket with her; **he stayed behind to watch TV** = stayed at home when the others went out.

3. *noun*

below

٣ ـ مؤخر (جزء من الجسم الذي يجلس عليه)

part of the body which you sit on; **he kicked my behind.**

being [biːɪŋ] *see* **human**

كائن ـ كينونة ـ (انظر إلى كلمة human)

believe [bɪ'liːv] *verb*

يعتقد ـ يؤمن ـ يصدق

to be sure that something is true, although you can't prove it; **people used to believe that the earth was flat; I believe I have seen him before; never believe what he tells you; do you believe in flying saucers?**

believes—believing—believed— has believed

bell [bel] *noun*

جرس ـ ناقوس

metal object, shaped like a cup, which rings if you hit it or when you shake it; electric machine which rings if you push a button; **he rang the door bell; you ought to have a bell on your bicycle; they rang the church bells at the wedding.**

belong [bɪ'lɒŋ] *verb*

أ) يخصّ

(*a*) to be the property of someone; **this hat belongs to my sister; who does this house belong to? the old watch used to belong to my mother.**

ب) ينتمي إلى ـ ينتسب إلى

(*b*) to be a member of; **I belong to a youth club.**

belongs—belonging—belonged— has belonged

below [bɪ'ləʊ] **1.** *adverb*

١ ـ إلى الأسفل

lower down; **he looked down from the hill at the town below.**

2. *preposition*

28 twenty-eight

belt

٢ ـ تحت

lower down than something else; **the temperature was below 60°; can you see below the surface of the water?**

belt [belt] *noun*

حزام

long piece of leather, etc., which goes round your waist to keep your trousers up or to attach a coat; **you will have to tighten your belt; seat belt** = belt in a car/in a plane which holds you safely in your seat.

bend [bend] **1.** *noun*

١ ـ تعويج ـ منعطف (في طريق) عكفة

curved shape; **the road is full of bends; he drove too fast round the bend; the pipe under the washbasin has two bends in it.**
2. *verb*

٢ ـ أ ـ يلوي

(*a*) to make something curved; to be curved; **he bent the pipe into the shape of an S; the road bends and then goes straight.**

ب ـ ينحني

(*b*) to lean towards the ground; **he bent down to tie up his shoe; she was bending over the table.**
bends—bending—bent—has bent

beneath [bɪˈniːθ] **1.** *adverb*

١ ـ إلى أدنى ـ إلى الأسفل

below; **he looked down from the roof at the people walking beneath.**
2. *preposition*

٢ ـ تحت ـ دون

under; **the ball was stuck beneath the sofa; the ground was soft beneath his feet.**

bent [bent] *adjective*

معكوف ـ ملوي ـ منحني

curved; **a bent pipe;** *see also* **bend**

twenty-nine

best

beside [bɪˈsaɪd] *preposition*

إلى جانب ـ بجانب

at the side of (something); next to; **he sat down beside me; his house is just beside the post office; put the teapot beside the milk jug.**

besides 1. *preposition*

١ ـ عدا عن ـ علاوة على

other than; **he has two other cars besides the red one; besides the football team, our town has a cricket team and a swimming club.**
2. *adverb*

٢ ـ بالاضافة إلى

(*a*) as well as; **besides managing the shop, he also teaches in the evening.**

٣ ـ في اية حال ـ وفوق كل ذلك

(*b*) in any case; **I don't want to go for a picnic—besides, the car won't start.**

best [best] **1.** *adjective*

١ ـ الأفضل ـ الأحسن

very good—better than anything else; **this is the best book I've read this year; what is the best way of cleaning a carpet? he put on his best suit to go to the wedding; she's the best swimmer in the team.**
2. *noun*

٢ ـ قدر المستطاع ـ أفضل ما يستطيع ـ أقصى الجهد

thing which is better than anything else; **you must do your best** = do as well as you can; **he did his best—but he still didn't win.**
3. *adverb*

٣ ـ بأفضل طريقة ـ على أحسن وجه

in the best way; **which of the sisters plays the piano best? the engine works best when it's warm; oranges grow best in hot countries.**
best *is the superlative of* **good** *and* **well**

29

better

better ['betə] 1. *adjective*

١ - أ) أفضل - أحسن

(*a*) very good (compared to something else); **the weather became better; this book is better than the one I was reading last week; he's better at maths than at history; vegetables are better for you than meat** = make you healthier.

ب) أحسن صحياً

(*b*) healthy again; **I had a cold last week, but now I'm better; I hope you're better soon.**

2. *adverb*

٢ - أ) بطريقة أفضل

(*a*) very well (compared to something else; **she plays the piano better than her sister; these scissors cut cloth better than those ones.**

ب) بحالة أحسن - في تحسن

(*b*) not as ill; **he had a cold but now he's getting better.**

من المستحسن ان

had better = it would be a good thing if; **you had better hurry up, if you want to catch the train; she'd better go to bed if she's got a cold; hadn't you better answer the phone?**

better is the comparative of good and well

between [bɪ'twiːn] *preposition*

بين

in the space separating two things; **there's a wall between his office and mine; the plane flies between London and Edinburgh; I'm busy between 10 o'clock and 2.30; can you come to see me between now and next Monday? she can't tell the difference between butter and margarine.**

في ما بين

in between = in the middle; **he had a meeting at 12.00 and another at 2 p.m. but managed to play a game of tennis in between.**

30

bill

beyond [bɪ'jɒnd] *preposition*

إلى ما وراء - إلى ما بعد

further than; **I can see your house, but I can't see anything beyond it because of the fog; to find the post office, you have to go about 100 metres beyond the traffic lights.**

bicycle ['baɪsɪkl] *noun*

درّاجة

vehicle with two wheels, which is ridden by one person who makes it go forward by pushing pedals; **he went to school by bicycle; she's going to do the shopping on her bicycle; he can drive but he can't ride a bicycle** = he doesn't know how to ride one.

*Note: often called a **bike***

big [bɪg] *adjective*

كبير - ضخم

of a large size; **I don't want a little piece of cake— I want a big one; his father has the biggest car in our street; I'm not afraid of him—I'm bigger than he is.**

big—bigger—biggest

bike [baɪk] *noun*

درّاجة

(*short way of saying*) bicycle; **he came to school by bike; she fell off her bike; she's going to the shops on her bike.**

bill [bɪl] *noun*

أ) فاتورة بالحساب

(*a*) piece of paper showing the amount of money you have to pay (in a restaurant, etc.); **she invited me to have a meal, and then asked me to pay the bill; I must pay the telephone bill.**

ب) منقار

(*b*) hard part outside a bird's mouth; **the hen was pulling at the grass with its bill.**

ت) (بالاميركية) ورقة عملة

(*c*) *American* = **note**; **a 5 dollar bill.**

thirty

bind

bind [baɪnd] *verb*

يربط ـ يحزم

to tie; to fasten; **the burglars bound his hands and feet with string.**
binds—binding—bound [baʊnd]—has bound

bird [bɜːd] *noun*

عصفور

animal with wings and feathers; **the little birds were learning to fly; most birds can fly well, but some can't; the birds were singing in the trees; in the winter we put a bird table in the garden, and put food on it for the birds.**

birth [bɜːθ] *noun*

ولادة ـ مولد

being born; **date of birth** = date when you were born.
birthday, *noun*

عيد ميلاد ـ تاريخ الولادة

date on which you were born; **my birthday is on June 15th; her birthday is next week; he's just had his birthday** = it was only a few days ago; **he'll be 21 next birthday** = on his next birthday he will be 21 years old; **what do you want for your birthday?** = what presents do you want?; **he got a calculator for his birthday; birthday party** = party held for a birthday; **birthday card** = card sent to someone to wish him good luck on his birthday; **birthday cake** = cake made specially for a birthday.

عيد سعيد (تعبير للمعايدة بذكرى عيد ميلاد شخص ما)

Happy Birthday = greeting to someone on a birthday.

biscuit ['bɪskɪt] *noun (American:* **cookie**)

بسكوت

small hard cake, usually sweet; **I like chocolate biscuits best; cheese and biscuits** = cheese with dry hard cakes which are not sweet.

black

bit [bɪt] *noun*

أ) قطعة صغيرة

(*a*) small piece; **he tied up the parcel with a bit of string; can I have another bit of cake, please? he's taking my watch to bits** = putting it in pieces to see what is wrong with it.

ب) قليلاً ـ بعض الشيء ـ كمية قليلة من ـ فترة قصيرة

(*b*) **a bit** = a little; **the photograph is a bit too dark; let him sleep a bit longer; have you got a piece of wood a little bit bigger than this one? wait a bit, I'm not ready yet.**

ت) انظر إلى كلمة bite

(*c*) *see* **bite**

قطعةً قطعةً ـ شيئاً فشيئاً ـ على مراحل

bit by bit = not all at the same time/ little by little; **he painted the house bit by bit.**

bite [baɪt] *verb*

يعضّ ـ يلدغ ـ يلسع

to cut with your teeth; **the dog bit the postman; he bit a piece out of the apple; she was bitten by an insect.**
bites—biting—bit—has bitten

bitter ['bɪtə] *adjective*

مُرّ

not sweet; **lemons are bitter, but oranges are sweet.**
bitter—more bitter—bitterest

black [blæk] *adjective & noun*

أسود

of the darkest colour, the opposite to white; **he was wearing a black hat; we have a black and white TV** = one which does not show pictures in colour; **why did you paint your front door black?**

blackbird

black coffee = coffee with no milk in it.
black—blacker—blackest

blackbird, *noun*

شحرور (عصفور صغير)

common bird which lives in gardens; the male is black with a yellow bill.

blackboard, *noun*

سبّورة ـ لوح أسود (للكتابة بالطبشورة)

large board on the wall of a classroom which you can write on with chalk.

blade [bleɪd] *noun*

شفرة

flat piece of metal; **this knife has a very sharp blade; the boat's propeller has three blades; my penknife has six blades.**

blame [bleɪm] 1. *noun*

١ ـ لوم ـ ملامة ـ توبيخ

saying that someone has done something wrong; **his sister broke the window, but he got the blame.**
2. *verb*

٢ ـ يلوم ـ يُوَبِّخ

to say that someone has done something wrong; **his father blamed him for breaking the window; don't blame me if the car won't start** = don't say it is my fault; **I don't blame you for asking for more money** = I think you are doing the right thing when you ask for more money.
blames—blaming—blamed—has blamed

blank [blæŋk] *adjective*

أبيض ـ بدون أي كتابة عليه ـ على بياض (شيك) ـ مفرغ

(paper) with nothing written on it; **a blank cheque; write your name in the blank space.**

blanket [ˈblæŋkɪt] *noun*

بطانية ـ حرام

thick woollen cover which you put over yourself to keep you warm in bed; **he woke up when his blankets fell off.**

bled [bled] *see* **bleed**

ملاحظة : انظر إلى كلمة bleed

bleed [bliːd] *verb*

ينزف دماً ـ يدمي

to lose blood; **his knee is bleeding; my nose began to bleed; when she cut her finger it bled.**
bleeds—bleeding—bled—has bled

blew [bluː] *see* **blow**

ملاحظة : انظر إلى كلمة blow

blind [blaɪnd] *adjective*

أعمى ـ ضرير ـ مكفوف

not able to see; **a blind man with a white stick; after her illness she became blind.**

block [blɒk] 1. *noun*

١ ـ أ) كتلة (حجرية أو خشبية)

(*a*) large piece; **they used blocks of stone to make the wall; a block of wood fell on his foot.**

ب) صف من المباني أو محلات متلاصقة

(*b*) group of houses forming a square with streets on all sides; **go for a walk round the blocks; a block of flats** = large building containing several flats.
2. *verb*

٢ ـ يسدّ ـ يوقف ـ يحبط .

to stop something moving; **the pipe was blocked by a dead bird; the accident blocked the road for several hours.**
blocks—blocking—blocked—has blocked

blood [blʌd] *noun*

دم ـ دماء

red liquid in your body; **the police followed the spots of blood to find the wounded man; blood was pouring from the cut in his hand.**

blouse

blouse [blauz] *noun*

بلوزة ـ قميص نسائي

shirt (worn by a woman); **she wore a skirt and a blouse.**

blow [bləu] *verb*

يهبُّ (الهواء) ـ ينفخ ـ يعصف ـ يتمخّط (الأنف)

to make air move; **the wind blew hard all day; blow on your soup to make it cool; because she has a cold, she keeps blowing her nose** = she blows through her nose into a handkerchief to get rid of liquid in her nose.

blows—blowing—blew [blu:]**—has blown**

blow away, *verb*

يبعد بالنفخ ـ يبتعد بفعل قوة الهواء

to (make something) go away by blowing; **the wind blew away the smoke; his hat blew away.**

blow down, *verb*

يسقط بالنفخ ـ يسقط بفعل قوة الهواء

to (make something) fall down by blowing; **the trees were blown down by the wind; the fence has blown down.**

blow off, *verb*

يطيح بالنفخ

to (make something) go away by blowing; **the wind blew off her hat; all the leaves were blown off the trees.**

blow out, *verb*

يطفىء بالنفخ

to (make something) go out by blowing; **you must blow out the candles on your birthday cake; the lamp has blown out; all the papers blew out of the window.**

blow up, *verb*

أ) ينفخ (بالون)

(*a*) to make something get bigger by blowing into it; **to blow up a balloon; your front tyre needs blowing up.**

boat

ب) يفجّر

(*b*) to destroy something with a bomb; **the soldiers blew up the bridge.**

Note: **the wind blew the smoke away** *or* **blew away the smoke; they blew the bridge up** *or* **they blew up the bridge,** *etc., but only* **the wind blew it away, they blew it up,** *etc.*

blue [blu:] *adjective & noun*

أزرق

of a colour like the colour of the sky in the daytime; **the car is light blue; they live in the house with the dark blue door; she was dressed all in blue; have you a cloth of a darker blue than this?**

blue—bluer—bluest

blunt [blʌnt] *adjective*

كليل ـ غير حاد

not sharp/which does not cut well; **don't try to cut your meat with a blunt knife; these scissors are blunt—they need sharpening.**

blunt—blunter—bluntest

board [bɔ:d] *noun*

لوح خشبي

large flat piece of wood, etc.; **write this sentence on the board** = on the blackboard.

boast [bəust] *verb*

يتباهى ـ يتفاخر بـ ـ يفتخر بـ ـ يعتزّ بـ

to talk very proudly of something (especially something which you have done); **he was boasting that he had scored three goals; she's always boasting about her new car.**

boasts—boasting—boasted—has boasted

boat [bəut] *noun*

سفينة ـ زورق ـ مركب

ship; **a sailing boat** = boat which goes with sails; **a fishing boat** = boat used to

thirty-three 33

body

catch fish at sea; **we took the boat across to France; when is the next boat to New York? they went to Australia by boat.**

body [bɒdɪ] *noun*

أ) جسد ـ جسم ـ بدن

(a) main part of an animal/of a person (not including the head and arms and legs).

ب) جثة

(b) all of an animal/of a person; **the dead man's body was found several days later.**
plural **bodies**

boil [bɔɪl] *verb*

أ) يغلي (الماء)

(a) to heat water (or another liquid) until it changes into a gas; (*of water, etc.*) to change into a gas because it is very hot; **the soup's boiling; can you boil some water for me to make the tea? the kettle's boiling** = the water in the kettle is boiling.

ب) يسلق (في الماء المغلي)

(b) to cook (vegetables/eggs, etc.) in boiling water; **I had a boiled egg for breakfast; I don't like the smell of boiling cabbage; hard-boiled egg** = egg which has been boiled so long that it is hard.
boils—boiling—boiled—has boiled

boil over, *verb*

يفور اثناء الغليان

to rise up when boiling in a pan and pour over the side; **the milk boiled over and made a mess on the stove.**

bomb [bɒm] **1.** *noun*

١ ـ قنبلة ـ قذيفة

large shell which is dropped from an aircraft or placed on the ground in order to blow up buildings; **bombs were falling on the town; the enemy dropped bombs on the bridges; his house was destroyed by a bomb.**
2. *verb*

٢ ـ يقذف بالقنابل ـ يقصف

to drop a bomb on something from an aircraft; **the enemy tried to bomb the railway lines; they bombed the hospital.**
bombs—bombing—bombed—has bombed

bone [bəʊn] *noun*

عظيم ـ عظمة ـ حسكة (السمكة)

one of the solid pieces which make the skeleton of an animal's body; **he fell over and broke a bone in his ankle; don't try to eat the fish bones.**

book [bʊk] **1.** *noun*

١ ـ أ) كتاب

(a) printed pages attached together with a cover; **I'm reading a book on gardening; he wrote a book about elephants.**

ب) دفتر ـ مجموعة من الأوراق ـ دفتر شيكات ـ مجموعة طوابع ـ رزمة (من الكبريت)

(b) pages attached together; **exercise book** = notebook which you can write exercises in; **cheque book** = cheques attached together in a cover; **a book of stamps** = several stamps in a little paper cover; **a book of matches** = cardboard matches attached together in a paper cover.
2. *verb*

٢ ـ يحجز (مكاناً أو مقعد أو طاولة أو غرفة)

to reserve a place/a seat/a table in a restaurant/a room in a hotel; **have you booked a table for the party? I want to book a room for Friday night; I'm sorry the concert is sold out—all the seats have been booked.**
books—booking—booked—has booked

bookcase, *noun*

خزانة كتب

Body

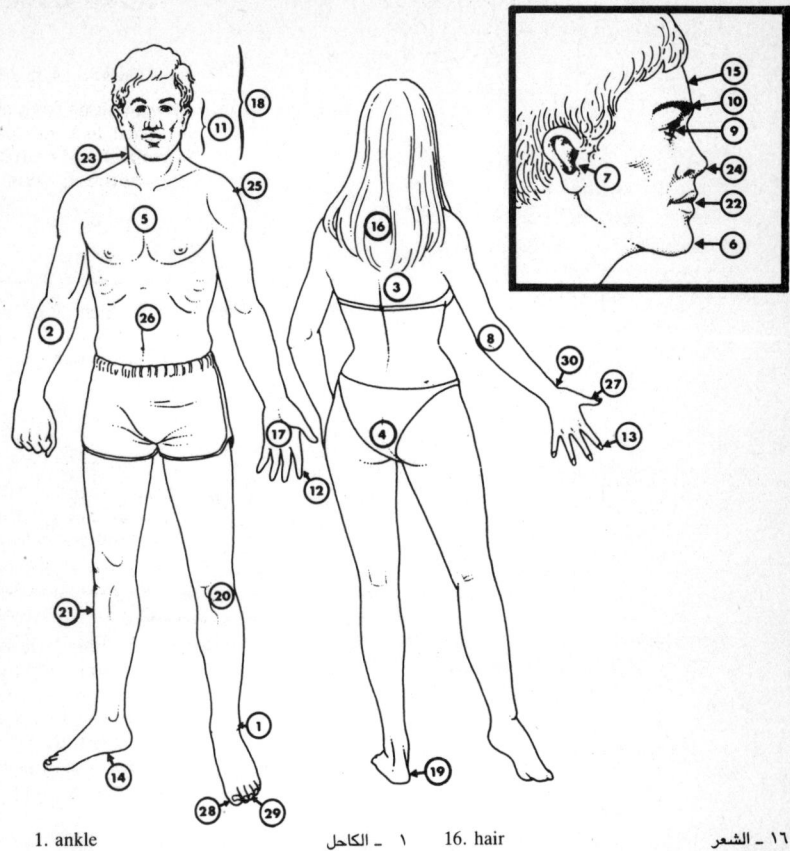

الجسم

1. ankle	١ ـ الكاحل	16. hair	١٦ ـ الشعر
2. arm	٢ ـ الذراع	17. hand	١٧ ـ اليد
3. back	٣ ـ الظهر	18. head	١٨ ـ الرأس
4. behind	٤ ـ القعر	19. heel	١٩ ـ العقب
5. chest	٥ ـ الصدر	20. knee	٢٠ ـ الركبة
6. chin	٦ ـ الذقن	21. leg	٢١ ـ الساق
7. ear	٧ ـ الاذن	22. mouth	٢٢ ـ الفم
8. elbow	٨ ـ الكوع	23. neck	٢٣ ـ الرقبة
9. eye	٩ ـ العين	24. nose	٢٤ ـ الانف
10. eyebrow	١٠ ـ الحاجب	25. shoulder	٢٥ ـ الكتف
11. face	١١ ـ الوجه	26. stomach	٢٦ ـ المعدة ـ البطن
12. finger	١٢ ـ الاصبع	27. thumb	٢٧ ـ إبهام اليد
13. fingernail	١٣ ـ ظفر الاصبع	28. toe	٢٨ ـ إصبع القدم
14. foot	١٤ ـ القدم	29. toenail	٢٩ ـ ظفر إصبع القدم
15. forehead	١٥ ـ الجبين	30. wrist	٣٠ ـ المعصم

thirty-five

boot

cupboard with shelves for keeping books.

book in(to), *verb*

٢ ـ يحجز (غرفةً) في (مكان ما)

to reserve a room in a hotel; **I've booked into the Castle Hotel.**

booking office, *noun*

شباك التذاكر ـ غرفة حجز التذاكر

small office in a cinema/theatre, etc., where you can buy tickets.

bookshelf, *noun*

رَفّ كتب

shelf for keeping books.
plural **bookshelves**

bookshop, *noun*

مكتبة

shop which sells books.

book up, *verb*

يحجز جميع التذاكر ـ يحجز مكاناً بأكمله

to reserve (everything); **the hotel is booked up** = all the rooms are booked.

boot [buːt] *noun*

جزمة ـ حذاء عالي الساق

strong shoe which goes above your ankle; **she was wearing long black boots; the children wore boots in the rain; football boots** = boots to wear when playing football; **ski boots** = boots to wear when skiing.

border [ˈbɔːdə] *noun*

حدّ ـ حدود (بين بلدين)

line separating two countries; **the border between France and Spain goes along the tops of mountains; border guards** = soldiers guarding the border.

bored [bɔːd] *adjective*

ضَجِر

not interested; **I get bored sitting in the office all day; she's bored—ask her to go to the cinema.**

both

boring, *adjective*

مُضْجِر

which makes you lose interest/not interesting; **he went to sleep watching a boring film on TV; she thinks cricket is so boring.**

born [bɔːn] *verb*

يُولَدُ ـ مولود

to be born = to begin to live; **he was born in Germany; she was born in 1962.**
Note: **born** *is usually only used with* **was** *or* **were**

borrow [ˈbɒrəʊ] *verb*

يستعير ـ يقترض

to take something for a short time with the permission of the owner; **can I borrow your car to go to the shops? he borrowed £10 from me, and never paid it back; she borrowed three books from the library.**

**borrows—borrowing—
borrowed—has borrowed**
Note: compare **lend**

boss [bɒs] *noun*

مدير (في شركة) ـ رئيس (في عصابة)

person in charge; **do you like the new boss? I have to ask the boss if I can have a holiday.**
plural **bosses**

both [bəʊθ] *adjective & pronoun & conjunction*

كلا ـ كلتا ـ معاً ـ على حد سواء

two people/two things together; **both my socks have holes in them; you can't eat both of the cakes; both the children were ill; hold the handle in both hands; we both like honey; they both fell down on the ice; both the teacher and his wife were ill; he ate both his cake and my cake.**

bother

bother [ˈbɒðə] 1. *noun*

١ ـ إنزعاج ـ قلق ـ مصدر قلق

thing which is annoying or worrying; **he had a lot of bother mending the car.**
2. *verb*

٢ ـ يزعج نفسه

to take trouble to do something; to worry about something; **she didn't bother to send us a bill; don't bother about cleaning the room.**
bothers—bothering—bothered—has bothered

bottle [ˈbɒtl] *noun*

زجاجة ـ قنّينة

glass container for liquids; **wine bottle; milk bottle; he drinks a bottle of milk a day; open another bottle of orange juice; you can buy beer in bottles or in cans; he was drinking beer out of the bottle.**

bottom [ˈbɒtəm] *noun*

أ) قعر ـ قاع ـ أسفل

(*a*) lowest part; **there was some jam left in the bottom of the jar; the ship sank to the bottom of the sea; turn right at the bottom of the hill; he's at the bottom of his class** = he gets the worst marks.

ب) نهاية ـ آخر

(*b*) far end; **the apple tree is at the bottom of the garden.**

ت) عجيزة ـ مؤخرة الشخص

(*c*) part of the body on which you sit; *see also* **behind**.

bought [bɔːt] *see* **buy**

ملاحظة : انظر إلى كلمة buy

bound [baʊnd] *see* **bind**

ملاحظة : انظر إلى كلمة bind

bowl [bəʊl] *noun*

وعاء مجوف

wide container with higher sides than a plate; **a bowl of soup; soup bowl** = bowl specially made for soup; **washing up bowl** = plastic bowl for washing dirty dishes in.

box [bɒks] *noun*

علبة ـ صندوق

container; **a box of biscuits/of matches; put the cakes into a box; she ate boxes of chocolates.**
plural **boxes**

boy [bɔɪ] *noun*

صبي ـ ولد ـ فتى

male child; **they have three children—two boys and a girl; the boys were playing in the field; paper boy** = boy who delivers newspapers to your house.
plural **boys**

brain [breɪn] *noun*

دماغ ـ مخ ـ مقدرة عقلية ـ ذكاء

part of the inside of your head which you think with; **use your brain** = think hard; **he's got brains** = he's clever.

brake [breɪk] 1. *noun*

١ ـ فرملة ـ فرامل

thing which stops a car/a bicycle, etc.; **he put on the brakes; he drove the car with the brake on; you should use your brakes when you go down the hill.**
2. *verb*

٢ ـ يُفَرْمِل

to stop a car/a bicycle by putting on the brakes; **the motorcyclist braked as he turned the corner.**
brakes—braking—braked—has braked

branch [brɑːntʃ] *noun*

أ) غصن (شجرة)

(*a*) part of a tree, growing out of the main trunk; **the children were swinging in the branches of the trees; they jumped from branch to branch.**

brave

(b) فرع (شركة أو مؤسسة)

(b) office of a bank/of a shop; **the local branch of the Midland Bank; the bank has branches in all large towns; branch manager** = manager in charge of a branch.
plural **branches**

brave [breɪv] *adjective*

شجاع - جريء

not afraid of danger; **he's a brave man—he saved the little boy from the burning house.**
brave—braver—bravest

bravely, *adverb*

بشجاعة

in a brave way; **he bravely jumped into the water to save the little girl.**

bread [bred] *noun*

خبز

food made from flour and water cooked in an oven; **go to the baker's and buy a loaf of bread; cut three slices of bread; the children were eating bread and butter** = slices of bread covered with butter; **brown bread** = bread made from brown flour.
no plural: **some bread; a loaf of bread; a slice of bread/a piece of bread**

break [breɪk] **1.** *noun*

١ - أ) تَوَقُّف

(a) space; interruption; **he spoke for two hours without a break** = without stopping; **the sun came through a break in the clouds.**

ب) استراحة قصيرة

(b) short rest; **there is a ten minute break in the middle of the morning; the children drink milk during break; coffee break/tea break** = short rest in the middle of work, when you drink coffee or tea; **we'll have a coffee break now.**
2. *verb*

break

٢ - يكسر

to make something go to pieces; to go to pieces; **he dropped the cup on the floor and broke it; it fell on the floor and broke; I can't use the lift because it's broken; she fell off the wall and broke her leg.**
breaks—breaking—broke—has broken

break down, *verb*

يتعطّل - يصيبه خلل .

to stop working; **the car broke down and we had to push it.**

breakfast ['brekfəst] *noun*

الفطور - طعام الصباح

first meal of the day; **I had a boiled egg for breakfast; she didn't have any breakfast because she was in a hurry; we have breakfast at 7.30 every day.**

break in(to), *verb*

يقتحم (منزلاً أو مكاناً بغاية السرقة)

to get into a house without permission; **burglars broke in during the night; he was caught breaking into the bookshop.**

break off, *verb*

أ) يكسر - ينزع

(a) to make something come apart by breaking; **he broke the handle off a cup; the branch was broken off the tree.**

يتوقف فجأة

(b) to stop suddenly; **he broke off in the middle of his story; they broke off the discussion.**

break up, *verb*

أ) يتحطم - يتفتت

(a) to come to pieces; **the ship was breaking up on the rocks.**

ب) يتوقف - يقطع (استمرارية شيء ما)

(b) to stop being together; **the meeting broke up at 3 p.m.; school breaks up next week** = the school holidays start next week.

breath

breath [breθ] *noun*

نَفَس - تَنَفُّس

air which goes into and out of your body when you breathe; **he ran so fast he was out of breath; stop for a moment to get your breath back; she took a deep breath and dived into the water.**

breathe [bri:ð] *verb*

يتنفس

to take air in and out of your body through your nose or mouth; **can fish breathe under water? he breathed in the smoke from the fire, and it made him cough.**
breathes—breathing—breathed—has breathed

brick [brɪk] *noun*

طوب فخاري

block of earth, baked in an oven, and used to build houses; **a brick house; the wall is built of bricks; he threw a brick through the window.**

bridge [brɪdʒ] *noun*

جسر - كوبري

thing built across a road/a river, etc., so that traffic can cross from one side to the other; **the road crosses the river by a very long bridge; the river goes under the bridge; a railway bridge** = bridge which carries a railway.

bright [braɪt] *adjective*

١) ساطع - مشرق

(*a*) which shines; which has a very strong colour; **bright sunshine; they have painted their house bright orange.**

ب) ذكي - لامع

(*b*) intelligent; **he's a bright little boy; both their children are very bright.**
bright—brighter—brightest

brightly, *adverb*

على نحو ساطع

in a bright way; **brightly coloured flags.**

thirty-nine

Britain

bring [brɪŋ] *verb*

يجلب - يحمل

to carry something to this place; to come with something or someone to this place; **bring me the money; he brought his father with him; he's bringing his friends along to the party.**
brings—bringing—brought [brɔːt]—has brought

bring back, *verb*

يجيء بـ - يُعيد - يأتي بـ

to carry something back; **bring back my book—I want it; he brought back some presents from his visit to France.**

bring down, *verb*

يُنزل - يأتي به إلى أسفل

to carry something down to here; **can you bring down my coat from the bedroom?**

bring in, *verb*

يجلب إلى الداخل

to carry something or somebody in here; to come with something or somebody in here; **he brought his boots in with him; don't bring your friends in—I've washed the floor.**

bring up, *verb*

يُربي

to look after and educate a child; **he was brought up by his uncle; I was brought up in Scotland.**
Note: **he brought some presents back** *or* **he brought back some presents; she brought the dog in** *or* **she brought in the dog,** *etc.; but only* **he brought them back, she brought it in,** *etc.*

Britain [ˈbrɪtn] *noun*

بريطانيا (جزء من المملكة المتحدة)

part of the United Kingdom, a country consisting of Scotland, Wales and England; **he's come back to live in Britain; most people in Britain speak English; is this car made in Britain?**

39

broke

ملاحظة : عادةً يطلق عليها اسم بريطانيا العظمى

Note: usually called **Great Britain**

British 1. *adjective*

١ ـ بريطاني

referring to Britain; **the British people; the British car industry.**
2. *plural noun*

٢ ـ البريطانيون

the British = the people who live in or come from Britain; **the British make good beer; the Germans fought the British in the Second World War.**

broke, broken [brəʊk, brəʊkn] *see* **break**

ملاحظة : انظر إلى كلمة **break**

brother [ˈbrʌðə] *noun*

أخ ـ شقيق

male who has the same mother and father as another child; **he's my brother; that girl has three brothers; her brother's a doctor.**

brought [brɔːt] *see* **bring**

ملاحظة : انظر إلى كلمة **bring**

brown [braʊn] *adjective & noun*

بُنّي (اللون البُني) ـ أسمر

of a colour like the colour of earth or wood; **he has brown hair and blue eyes; in autumn the leaves turn brown and fall off the trees; you're very brown—you must have been sitting in the sun for a long time; I like brown bread better than white; she was wearing dark brown shoes.**

brown—browner—brownest

brush [brʌʃ] **1.** *noun*

١ ـ فرشاة

thing with a handle and stiff hairs or wire which you use for cleaning dust off the floor/for cleaning your teeth with toothpaste/for putting paint on a wall, etc.; **you must have a stiff brush to get all the mud off your shoes; if you paint with a thin brush you will make fine lines; he was painting white lines on the road with a large brush.**
plural **brushes**
2. *verb*

٢ ـ يفرك بالفرشاة

to clean with a brush; **have you brushed your shoes? don't forget to brush your teeth after meals.**
brushes—brushing—brushed—has brushed

brush off, *verb*

ينظف بالفرشاة

to clean something off with a brush; **he brushed the mud off his trousers.**

brush up, *verb*

يُحسِّن ـ يستعيد براعته في ...

to make better/to improve; **you must brush up your German if you are going to work in Germany.**

bucket [ˈbʌkɪt] *noun*

دلو

large round container with a handle on top, used for carrying liquids; **she got a bucket of water from the river; they threw buckets of water on the fire; the children built castles on the sand with their buckets.**

build [bɪld] *verb*

يَبني ـ يُشيد

to make something by putting pieces together/by putting bricks/stones, etc., on top of each other; **the house was built in 1900; we are building a new church; the government is going to build a motorway across this field; he built the model plane out of pieces of wood.**
builds—building—built [bɪlt]**—has built**

builder, *noun*

bulb

البناء ـ الباني

person who makes houses/offices, etc.

building, *noun*

مبنى ـ عمارة

thing which has been built (such as a house/a railway station/a factory, etc.); **the bomb destroyed several buildings; his office is on the top floor of the building; they will have to knock several buildings down to build the new motorway.**

bulb [bʌlb] *noun*

أ) مصباح كهربائي .

(*a*) glass ball which produces electric light; **we must get a new bulb for the light in the kitchen; I can't use the torch—it hasn't got a bulb.**

ب) بصلة الزرع

(*b*) thick round part of a plant, which you put in the soil and which grows into a flower.

bump [bʌmp] **1.** *noun*

١ ـ أ) إرتطام خفيف

(*a*) slight knock against something; **the plane landed with a bump.**

ب) وَرَم ـ انتفاخ

(*b*) slightly raised part; **he has a bump on the back of his head; the car went slowly over the bumps in the road.**
2. *verb*

٢ ـ يصدم ـ يرتطم .

to knock slightly; **the car bumped into a tree; I bumped into her at the bus stop** = I met her by chance.
bumps—bumping—bumped—has bumped

bunch [bʌntʃ] *noun*

باقة ـ ربطة (من الزهور ...)
حزمة (من العنب ، موز)

group of flowers tied together; group of grapes/of bananas; **the children picked bunches of flowers; when you go shopping can you buy a bunch of grapes?**
plural **bunches**

burst

burglar [ˈbɜːglə] *noun*

لص

person who breaks into a house to steal things; **burglars broke into the house and stole our silver; he woke up to find a burglar in his bedroom.**

buries [ˈberɪz], **buried** [ˈberɪd] *see* **bury**

ملاحظة : انظر إلى كلمة bury

burn [bɜːn] *verb*

يحرق ـ يحترق

to destroy by fire; to be on fire; **call the firemen—the school is burning! all our papers were burnt in the fire; she burnt her hand on the hot frying pan; look, you've burnt the sausages** = cooked them too much, so that they are black.
burns—burning—burnt/burned—has burnt/burned

burn down, *verb*

يحرق بالكامل

to burn completely; **he was playing with matches and burnt the house down; the school burnt down before the firemen arrived.**

burst [bɜːst] *verb*

ينفجر ـ يفجر ـ ينفجر (عاطفياً ، بالبكاء ...)

to break; **he blew up the balloon until it burst; she burst all the balloons with a pin; don't eat so much or you'll burst; he burst into tears** = he suddenly started to cry; **she burst out laughing** = she suddenly started to laugh.
burst—bursting—burst—has burst

forty-one

bury

bury [ˈberɪ] *verb*

يدفن ـ يخفي ـ يطمر

to put something into the ground; to cover; **the dog has buried a bone in the garden; the path was buried under the snow; he died on Monday and was buried on Friday.**
buries—burying—buried—has buried

bus [bʌs] *noun*

حافلة ـ باص

motor vehicle for carrying many passengers; **why do you go by bus?—it's cheaper than the train; she takes the bus every morning to go to work; he missed the last bus and had to walk home; London buses are red; a school bus takes the children to school; the number 6 bus goes to Oxford Street.**
plural **buses**

bus stop, *noun*

موقف الحافلة

place where you can get on or off a bus; **there was a long queue of people waiting at the bus stop.**

bush [bʊʃ] *noun*

شجيرة

plant which is smaller than a tree; **a rose bush.**
plural **bushes**

bushy, *adjective*

ملتف الاغصان ـ كثيف ـ كث

(*of hair*) growing close together; **he has bushy eyebrows.**

business [ˈbɪznɪs] *noun*

مهنة ـ عمل ـ تجارة ـ عمل تجاري ...

work of buying or selling things; company which buys or sells things; **he runs a secondhand car business; she's in business selling dresses; they do business with several European countries.**
plural **businesses**

butter

businessman, *noun*

رجل الأعمال

man who buys or sells things; man who runs a business.
plural **businessmen**

busy [ˈbɪzɪ] *adjective*

مشغول ـ ناشط الحركة

occupied with doing something; **he was busy washing the car; the shop is very busy today** = there are a lot of customers; **she's busy with her exams; I was too busy to buy you a present.**
busy—busier—busiest

but [bʌt] *conjunction suggesting the opposite*

إلاّ أن ـ لولا ان ـ لكن ـ غير أن ـ سوى ـ إلاّ

he is very tall, but his sister is quite short; I would like to come, but I am not free that evening; but you said you would give me £10!

butcher [ˈbʊtʃə] *noun*

جزّار ـ تاجر اللحوم

man who sells meat; **the butcher's** = shop where you can buy meat; **go to the butcher's and buy some sausages; the butcher's is closed on Mondays; the butcher is on holiday.**

butter [ˈbʌtə] *noun*

زُبَدَة

solid yellow stuff made from cream; **he was spreading butter on a piece of bread; fry the onions in butter.**
no plural: **some butter; a piece of butter**

butterfly, *noun*

فراشة

insect with large brightly coloured wings.
plural **butterflies**

button

button ['bʌtn] **1.** *noun*

١ - (أ) زِرّ

(*a*) small round object attached to clothes which you use to fasten one part of the clothing to another; **his coat has buttons down the front; do up the buttons on your coat; can you sew this button on?**

ب) زِر كهربائي

(*b*) small round object which you push to ring a bell, etc.; **push the button to open the doors of the lift; push the top button if you want a cup of coffee.**
2. *verb*

٢ - يزرر - يتزرر

to attach with buttons; **he buttoned up his coat, because it was cold.**
buttons—buttoning—buttoned—has buttoned
Note: **button your coat up** *or* **button up your coat,** *but only* **button it up**

buy [baɪ] *verb*

يشتري

to get something by paying money; **I bought a book on my way home; he was bought a new car; she's buying a house; what have you bought her for Christmas? he bought his wife a fur coat; I've bought myself a new watch; he wants to buy a car for his sister.**
buys—buying—bought [bɔːt]**—has bought**

buyer, *noun*

الشاري

person who buys.

by [baɪ] **1.** *preposition*

١ - (أ) بالقرب من - بجوار

(*a*) near; **the house by the traffic lights; sit down here by the fire.**

ب) عند (الساعة الخامسة)

bye(-bye)

(*b*) before; **try to get home by teatime; you must finish your homework by Friday.**

ت) بواسطة - جرّاء - بسبب

(*c*) (*showing means or method*) **send the letter by air; he goes to school by bus; she made the cake by mixing eggs and flour; he caught a cold by standing in the rain.**

ث) من تأليف - من صنع - من تصميم - من تلحين - بواسطة - بـ -

(*d*) (*showing the person or thing that did something*) **a play by Shakespeare; now here is some music by the school band; the postman was bitten by the dog; I was knocked down by a bus.**

ج) بنفسه - بمفرده - بنفسك - بمفردك

(*e*) (**all**) **by yourself** = alone; **she's all by herself all day; he built his house by himself; you can find the house by yourself.**

ح) بـ (تدل على كمية أو مبلغ)

(*f*) (*showing amount*) **fares have been increased by 10%; they beat us by 10 goals to 2.**
2. *adverb*

٢ - بجانب - بجوار

past; **he drove by without stopping.**

على العموم

by and large = generally/mostly; **by and large, fat people are happier than thin ones.**

على فكرة . وبالمناسبة

by the way used to introduce something which does not seem very important; **by the way, did you see the TV programme on cars yesterday?**

bye (-bye) [baɪ('baɪ)] *interjection*

وداعاً - مع السلامة

used when you are leaving someone; **bye!—see you on Thursday!**

forty-three 43

Cc

cabbage ['kæbɪdʒ] *noun*

كُرُنْب ـ ملفوف (نوع من الخضروات)

green vegetable of which you eat the leaves; **we had a salad of raw cabbage and tomatoes; the kitchen smells of boiled cabbage; he has a row of cabbages in the garden.**
Note: as food, cabbage does not have a plural: some cabbage; a spoonful of cabbage; as plants you can count two cabbages, etc.

cage [keɪdʒ] *noun*

قفص

box made of thick metal bars or wire, which you keep wild animals or birds in; **the little yellow bird was singing in its cage; the white mouse ran across the cage.**

cake [keɪk] *noun*

كعكة ـ (كاتو)

food made by baking flour, sugar, eggs, dried fruit, etc., in an oven; **he had a birthday cake with six candles on it; a Christmas cake; would you like some more cake? have a slice of chocolate cake.**
Note: as food cake does not have a plural: some cake; a piece of cake; when it means a particular piece of food it can have a plural: she baked ten cakes; there are no cakes left in the shop

calculate ['kælkjʊleɪt] *verb*

يحسب (رياضياً)

to find the answer to a sum; **he tried to calculate how much he had spent on petrol; can you calculate the distance from London to Amsterdam in kilometres? I calculate that I have spent two hours on the phone to America.**
calculates—calculating—calculated—has calculated

calculator, *noun*

آلة حاسبة

machine for calculating; **I added up the bill on my pocket calculator.**

calendar ['kælɪndə] *noun*

تقويم ـ روزنامة

piece of paper showing the days and months of a year; **he pinned the calendar on to the wall by his desk; tear off the next page on the calendar—today is November 1st.**

calf [kɑːf] *noun*

عجل

baby cow; **a cow and her calf.**
plural **calves** [kɑːvz]

call [kɔːl] **1.** *noun*

١ ـ مكالمة هاتفية

speaking by telephone; **I want to make a (phone) call to Canada; there were three calls for you while you were out.**
2. *verb*

٢ ـ ا) ينادي ـ يصيح ـ يصرخ

(*a*) to shout to tell someone to come; **call the children—it's time for tea; call me at 7 o'clock** = wake me at 7; **call a taxi** = shout to a taxi to come.

ب) يسمّي ـ يعطي إسماً ـ يطلق اسماً على ...

(*b*) to give someone or something a name; **his son is called Peter; his name is James, but everyone calls him Jim; we**

44   *forty-four*

calm

call our cat Natasha; what do you call this machine for spreading glue?

ت) يكلم هاتفياً

(c) to telephone; if he comes, tell him I'll call him when I'm in the office; Mr Smith is out—shall I ask him to call you back? = to phone you.

ث) يقوم بزيارة ـ يأتي إلى ـ يذهب إلى

(d) to visit; the police called at the house, but there was no one there; can you call at the baker's to get a loaf of bread? he called on me at 10 o'clock.

calls—calling—called—has called

callbox, noun

حجيرة الهاتف ـ غرفة التلفون العمومي

tall square box with windows, with a public telephone inside; I'm phoning from the callbox outside the post office.

plural **callboxes**

call off, verb

يلغي

to decide not to do something which was planned; he's called off his visit to the USA.

call up, verb

يستدعي ـ يدعو إلى الالتحاق (بالجيش)

to tell people to join the armed forces; thousands of men were called up at the beginning of the war.

calm [kɑ:m] *adjective*

هادىء

quiet; not rough; not excited; the sea is very calm; a calm evening; stay calm—don't lose your temper.

calm—calmer—calmest

calmly, *adverb*

بهدوء . بطريقة هادئة

in a calm way; he calmly walked into the burning house.

calves [kɑ:vz] *see* **calf**

ملاحظة : انظر إلى كلمة calf

forty-five

can

came [keɪm] *see* **come**

ملاحظة : انظر إلى كلمة come

camera ['kæmərə] *noun*

آلة تصوير

machine for taking photographs; he took a picture of the church with his new camera; have you got a film in your camera? cine-camera = camera for taking films.

camp [kæmp] *verb*

مُخَيَّم

to go on holiday in a tent; we go camping every summer; a camping holiday; we camped by the side of the lake.

camps—camping—camped—has camped

camping ground, *noun*

أرض معدّة للتخييم

area specially arranged for people to camp.

camping site/camp site, *noun*

مكان يصلح لنصب المخيم

place where you can camp.

can [kæn] **1.** *noun*

١ ـ علبة معدنية

round metal container for keeping food or drink; he opened a can of beer.

2. *verb used with other verbs*

٢ ـ أ) يستطيع

(a) to mean be able; he can swim, but he can't ride a bicycle; you can't run as fast as I can; can you remember what the policeman said?

ب) يُسمح لِـ ـ يُمكن ان

(b) to mean be allowed; he says we can go in; the policeman says we can't park here.

ت) (للطلب بلطف وأدب) هل من الممكن ان

(c) (*in asking politely*) can we come in? can you shut the door, please?

I can, you can, he can, we can, they can

45

canal

Negative: **cannot,** *usually* **can't**
Past: **could, could not,** *usually* **couldn't**
Note: **can** *and* **could** *do not have to* **to** *and are only used with other verbs*

canal [kə'næl] *noun*

قناة

river made by men for ships to pass along; **the Suez Canal.**

candle ['kændl] *noun*

شمعة

stick of white or coloured stuff which will burn and give a light; **there were six candles on her birthday cake; the electricity has gone off—can you light a candle?**

candy ['kændɪ] *noun*

سكر نبات ـ حبّة من الكراميـل ـ حبّة سكرية

American = **sweet**

canned [kænd] *adjective*

مُعَلّب

in a can; **canned fruit.**

cannot ['kænɒt *see* **can**

ملاحظة : انظر إلى كلمة can

can't [kɑːnt] *see* **can**

ملاحظة : انظر إلى كلمة can

cap [kæp] *noun*

١) قبعة

(*a*) flat hat with a hard piece sticking out over your face; **he was wearing an old black cap; an officer's cap.**

ب) غطاء (لزجاجة أو قلم)

(*b*) top which covers something; **screw the cap back on the bottle; a silver pen with a black cap.**

capital ['kæpɪtl] *noun*

١) عاصمة

(*a*) main town in a country, where the government is; **Rome is the capital of Italy; what is the capital of the United States?**

ب) حرف استهلالي
حرف كبير

(*b*) large form of a letter of the alphabet; **Rome begins with a capital R; write your name in capitals.**

ت) رأس مال

(*c*) money which you can use to start a business, or put in a bank to make interest.

no plural for (c)

captain ['kæptɪn] *noun*

ربّان ـ قبطان

officer in charge of a ship/of an aircraft; **go to see the captain; Captain Smith.**

car [kɑː] *noun*

سيارة

small motor vehicle for carrying people; **he's bought a new car; her car was stolen last night.**

car park, *noun*

موقف للسيارات

special place where you can leave a car while you are not using it; **park your car in one of the car parks in the centre of the town.**

caravan ['kærəvæn] *noun*

قافلة

van on wheels which you can live in, and which you pull behind a car; **we went on holiday with our caravan to Scotland.**

card [kɑːd] *noun*

١) بطاقة (للمعايدة ـ للتمنيات)

(*a*) piece of stiff paper with a picture on it which you can send with a message; **he sent me a card from Italy; how much does it cost to send a card to Canada? birthday card** = card which you send to someone to wish them a happy birth-

care

day; **Christmas card** = card which you send to someone at Christmas; *see also* **postcard**

ب) ورقة لعب - ورقة كوتشينة

(b) piece of stiff paper with a picture or pattern on it, used to play various games; **a pack of cards; they were playing cards; do you want a game of cards?**

cardboard, *noun*

كرتون - ورق مقوّي

thick piece of card; **we put our books into cardboard boxes.**
no plural: **some cardboard; a piece of cardboard**

care [ˈkeə] **1.** *noun*

١ - أ) انتباه - عناية - اهتمام - حرص - رعاية

(a) attention; **take care when you cross the road** = watch out; **he took care to lock the door; take care not to be late.**

ب) بواسطة

(b) (*on a letter*) **Mr Brown, care of Mrs Green** = Mr Brown, at the address of Mrs Green.
2. *verb*

٢ - يهتم - يعتني - يبالي

to worry; to mind; **he doesn't care if his car is dirty; he couldn't care less** = he doesn't worry at all.

cares—caring—cared—has cared

care for, *verb*

أ) يرغب - يريد

(a) to like; **would you care for another piece of cake? I don't care for this music very much.**

ب) يعتني

(b) to look after; **nurses were caring for the injured people.**

careful, *adjective*

حذر - منتبه - يَقظ

taking care; **he was careful not to make any noise; be careful, that glass is valu-**

forty-seven

carrot

able! she is very careful about what she eats.

carefully, *adverb*

بانتباه - بحرص - بحذر

with great care; **carry the eggs carefully! drive carefully!**

careless, *adjective*

لا مبالٍ

without care; **he was careless and made mistakes in his homework; she made several careless mistakes.**

cargo [ˈkɑːgəʊ] *noun*

الشحن (البحري أو الجوي)

goods which are carried (on a ship or aircraft); **cargo ship** = ship which does not carry any passengers.
plural **cargoes**

carpet [ˈkɑːpɪt] *noun*

سجادة - بساط

thick wool material for covering the floor, stairs, etc.; **he spilt his coffee on the carpet; we have bought a new carpet for the dining room.**

carriage [ˈkærɪdʒ] *noun*

حافلة (قطار) - عربة قطار

wagon on a train for passengers; **they got into a 'no smoking' carriage.**

carried [ˈkærɪd], **carries** [ˈkærɪz] *see* **carry**

ملاحظة : انظر إلى كلمة carry

carrot [ˈkærət] *noun*

جزرة

long orange root vegetable; **boiled carrots; carrot salad; can you go to the greengrocer's and buy two kilos of carrots?**

47

carry

carry ['kærɪ] *verb* يحمل ـ ينقل

to lift something and move it to another place; **they had to carry the piano up the stairs; the bus was carrying sixty passengers; the box was too heavy to carry. carries—carrying—carried—has carried**

carry on, *verb* يواصل

to continue/to go on doing something; **when the teacher came into the room, the children carried on talking.**

carry out, *verb* ينفذ (خطّة) ـ يقوم بتنفيذ (عمل ما)

to do (something which has been planned); **they carried out a search for the missing children.**
Note: **we carried the plan out** *or* **we carried out the plan,** *but only* **we carried it out.**

case [keɪs] *noun* حقيبة

suitcase/box with a handle, for carrying your clothes, etc., in; **he was packing his case; I lost my cases at the airport; put the gun in its case.**

in any case = whatever may happen/and yet; **he's late but in any case it doesn't matter.** في أي حال

in case = because something might happen; **take your coat in case it is cold; I always carry an umbrella in case it rains.** في حال

in that case = if that happens. في هذا الحال

cash [kæʃ] *noun* نقد ـ أوراق مالية تُدفع نقداً

money either in notes or coins; **he paid for the car in cash; can I pay by cheque** as I haven't very much cash on me?
no plural: **some cash; a lot of cash**

catch

cassette [kə'set] *noun* كاسيت ـ شريط تسجيلي

plastic box with a tape on which music or words can be recorded; **a cassette recorder; he played a cassette of Spanish music.**

castle ['kɒːsl] *noun* قصر

large building with strong walls which soldiers can defend; **Windsor Castle; the soldiers shut the castle gate.**

cat [kæt] *noun* قطّ ـ هرّ ـ قطة ـ هرّة

furry pet with a long tail; **the cat sat in front of the fire; what a beautiful cat! she gave the cat some fish to eat.**

catch [kætʃ] *verb*

١) يمسك بـ ـ
(a) to hold something which someone has thrown/which is flying in the air; **see if you can catch the ball; she caught the ball in her left hand.**

ب) يقبض على ـ يصطاد
(b) to stop and hold (an animal); **we caught three fish; he sat by the river all day but didn't catch anything; our cat is good at catching mice.**

ت) يلحق بـ
(c) to get on (a bus/a train, etc.) before it goes; **you will have to run if you want to catch the 9 o'clock bus; he caught the last plane to Paris.**

ث) يُصاب (بمرض ما)
(d) to get a disease; **he caught a cold from standing in the rain; she caught mumps.**

ج) يفاجىء ـ يعثر على
(e) to find someone doing something wrong; **she caught him stealing apples;**

48   *forty-eight*

caught

the police caught the burglar as he was climbing out of the window.

ح) يدرك - يفهم

(f) to hear; **I didn't quite catch what you said.**

catches—catching—caught [kɔ:t] **—has caught**

catch up, verb

يلحق بـ -

to join someone who is moving in front of you; **if you run you will catch the others up/catch up with the others; he walked so slowly that we soon caught him up/soon caught up with him.**

caught [kɔ:t] see **catch**

انظر إلى كلمة **catch**

cause [kɔ:z] **1.** noun

١ - سبب

reason why something happens; **what was the cause of the accident?**
2. verb

٢ - يسبّب - يتسبّب

to make something happen; **the accident was caused by thick fog.**

causes—causing—caused—has caused

ceiling ['si:lɪŋ] noun

سقف

top part which covers a room; **each room has four walls, a floor and a ceiling; flies can walk on the ceiling; he painted the bathroom ceiling.**

cellar ['selə] noun

قبو

rooms in a house which are underground; **we keep our washing machine in the cellar.**

cement [sɪ'ment] noun

أ) إسمنت

(a) powder which you mix with sand and water to make concrete; **he bought a bag of cement.**

ب) مادة لاصقة قوية

(b) strong glue used for making models. *no plural*

cent [sent] noun

«سِنْت» (جزء من مئة من دولار)

small coin used in the USA and in many other countries, which is one hundredth of a dollar; **this book only costs twenty-five cents (25c).**
cent *is usually written* **c** *with numbers:* **25c**

centimetre ['sentɪmi:tə] noun (*American:* **centimeter**)

سنتمتر (جزء مئوي من متر)

measurement of how long something is; one hundredth part of a metre; **the table is sixty centimetres (60 cm) wide.**
centimetre *is usually written* **cm** *with figures*

centre ['sentə] noun (*American:* **center**)

أ) وسط - قلب

(a) middle; **a tree was growing in the centre of the field; the centre of the town is very old; this chocolate has coffee cream in the centre.**

ب) مركز

(b) large building; **sports centre** = place where several different sports can be played; **shopping centre** = group of several shops together in one place.

central, adjective

مركزي

of the centre; **central heating** = heating which heats the whole house from one heater.

century ['sentʃərɪ] noun

قرن (مئة سنة)

hundred years; **the nineteenth (19th) century** = the period from 1800 to 1899;

cereal

a 19th century church.
plural **centuries**

cereal ['sɪərɪəl] *noun*

أ) النبات الحبي - حبوب

(a) plant whose seeds are used for food, especially to make flour; **the farmer grows cereals; a cereal crop.**

ب) طعام مؤلف من الحبوب كالذرة والقمح ..

(b) food made of seeds of corn, etc., which you eat at breakfast; **he ate a bowl of cereal; you put milk and sugar on your cereal.**

ceremony ['serɪmənɪ] *noun*

حفلة رسمية - احتفال

official event; **the prize-giving ceremony will be held in the school hall.**
plural **ceremonies**

certain ['sɜːtn] *adjective*

أ) متأكد - أكيد - واثق

(a) sure; **the police are certain he is the thief; this horse is certain to win the race; he locked the door to make certain that no one could steal his money.**

ب) شخص

(b) (person/thing) which you don't know or which you are not sure of; **a certain Mr Smith called while you were out; certain plants can make you ill if you eat them.**

ت) بعض

(c) a certain amount = some; **the storm did a certain amount of damage; painting the house will take a certain amount of time.**

certainly, *adverb*

بالتأكيد - من غير ريب

of course; **will you come to the party?—certainly I'll come; please tell him to write to me—certainly, sir.**

chance

chain [tʃeɪn] **1.** *noun*

١ ـ سلسلة

number of metal rings attached together to make a long line; **he wore a gold cross on a chain round his neck; that dog should be kept on a chain** = should be attached with a chain.
2. *verb*

٢ ـ يقيّد ـ يربط بسلسلة

to attach with a chain; **the dog was chained to the gate.**
chains—chaining—chained—has chained

chair [tʃeə] *noun*

كرسي

piece of furniture which you sit on; **someone has been sitting in my chair; pull up a chair and have some supper; this chair is very hard and not very comfortable.**

chairman, *noun*

رئيس الجلسة

person who is in charge of a meeting; **Mr Smith was the chairman at the meeting.**

chalk [tʃɔːk] *noun*

طباشير ـ طبشورة ـ مادة الكلس

soft white rock; a piece of material for writing on a blackboard; **the hills are made of chalk; there are chalk hills along the south coast; he wrote on the blackboard with coloured chalk.**

chance [tʃɑːns] *noun*

أ) امكانية

(a) possibility; **has he any chance of winning?—yes, I think he has a good chance of winning; is there any chance of getting a cup of tea? there is no chance of the weather turning cold.**

ب) مناسبة . فرصة

(b) opportunity; **I've been waiting for the chance to speak to the manager; he**

change

never had the chance to visit the United States.

ت) صدفة

(c) luck; **it was quite by chance that we were travelling on the same bus.**
Note: **chance of —ing** = possibility, but **chance to** = opportunity

change [tʃeɪndʒ] **1.** *noun*

١ - أ) تغيير - تبديل

(a) being different; **we usually go on holiday in August, but this year we're going in July for a change; a cup of tea is a nice change after several cups of coffee; I think it's a change for the better** = I think it has improved things.

ب) قطع نقد صغيرة

(b) **small change** = money in coins; **I have only got a £5 note, I've no small change at all; have you got change for a £1 note?**

ت) ما يرد من فائض القيمة المدفوعة

(c) money which you get back when you have given more than the correct price; **the book is £3.50, so you get £1.50 change from £5; you've given me too much change.**
no plural for (b) and (c)

2. *verb*

٢ - أ) يتغيَّر - يغيِّر - يبدِّل

(a) to make something different; to become different; **London has changed a lot in the last few years; he's changed so much since I saw him last, that I didn't recognize him; I've changed my mind** = I've decided to do something different.

ب) يغيّر ملابسه

(b) to put on different clothes; **he changed into his old clothes before mending the car; go into my bedroom if you want to change your dress.**

ت) يستبدل -

(c) to give something in place of something else; **you ought to change your car tyres; can you change a £5 note?** = can

charge

you give me small change for it? **to get to London you will have to change at Birmingham** = to get on to another train or bus.

changes—changing—changed— has changed

character ['kærəktə] *noun*

أ) طبع - شخصية

(a) part of you which makes you different from other people; all your personal qualities; **she has a strong character; he's a weak character.**

ب) دور (في مسرحية)

(b) person in a play/book; **at the end of the play all the main characters are dead.**

charge [tʃɑːdʒ] **1.** *noun*

١ - أ) ثمن - رسم

(a) money which you have to pay to do something; **there is no charge for service; we will send the parcel free of charge** = without asking you to pay.

ب) تهمة

(b) statement by the police which says someone has done something wrong; **he was kept in prison on a charge of trying to kill the Prime Minister.**

ت) مسؤول عن - مُتولٍّ أمر العناية بـ

(c) **in charge of** = giving orders to/being the head of; **he is in charge of the department; who's in charge here? he took charge of the class while the teacher was out of the room.**

2. *verb*

٢ - أ) يُسعِّر - يطلب ثمناً مقابل ...

(a) to make someone pay; **they charged me £1 for two glasses of orange juice; how much do you charge for cleaning the car?**

ب) يَتهم

(b) (*of the police*) to say that someone has done something wrong; **he was charged with stealing the silver.**

fifty-one 51

chase

charges—charging—charged— has charged

chase [tʃeɪs] *verb*

يطارد

to run after someone to try to catch him; the policeman chased the burglar; he was chased by two dogs.
chases—chasing—chased—has chased

cheap [tʃiːp] *adjective*

رخيص

not costing a lot of money; **the coat is much cheaper than that one**; choose the cheapest sort of meat; I bought these books cheap in the market; how much is a cheap return ticket to London?
cheap—cheaper—cheapest

cheat [tʃiːt] *verb*

يغش - يخدع

to trick someone so that he loses; to break rules; **don't play cards with Paul—he cheats**; the teacher caught him cheating in the exams; the shopkeeper tried to cheat me out of 50p by giving me the wrong change.
cheats—cheating—cheated—has cheated

check [tʃek] **1.** *noun*

١ - (١) تفحص - فحص - تدقيق

(*a*) making sure/test to be sure; **the car has to go to the garage for a check**; the police made a check on everyone who was in the building.
(*b*) American = **cheque**

2. *verb*

٢ - يتأكد من - يتفحص - يتفقد - يدقق بـ

to make sure; to test; **don't forget to check if the doors are all locked**; he checked the times of trains with the booking office; I asked the garage to check the brakes.

52

cheer up

checks—checking—checked— has checked

check in(to), *verb*

يصل إلى فندق ويسجل اسمه

to arrive and register at a hotel; **they checked in at 10 p.m.**; he's checked into room 15.

check out, *verb*

يدفع حساب الفندق ويغادره

to leave a hotel; **they checked out in the morning**; I'm checking out of room 15.

check up, *verb*

يتأكد من

to make sure; **can you check up if the doors are locked?** he checked up on the times of trains to London.

check-up, *noun*

فحص طبي - فحص للتأكد من سلامة الجسم أو السيارة أو آلة ما

test; **I must go to the dentist for a check-up** = to see if there is something wrong with my teeth.

cheek [tʃiːk] *verb*

خَدّ - وجنة

fat parts of your face on each side of your nose; **a little girl with red cheeks**.

cheer up [ˈtʃɪərʌp] *verb*

يُبهج - يُشجّع - يشعر بالابتهاج

to become happier; to make someone happier; **this funny film will soon cheer you up**; she cheered up after we had been to see her.
cheers—cheering—cheered—has cheered

cheerful [ˈtʃɪəfʊl] *adjective*

مبتهج - مرح

happy; **he's always cheerful, even when things go wrong**; you must try to keep cheerful; they sang a cheerful song as they worked.

fifty-two

cheese

cheerfully, *adverb*

بمرح ـ بابتهاج

in a happy way; **the children played cheerfully in the garden.**

cheese [tʃiːz] *noun*

جبنة

solid food made from milk; **a piece of cheese; at the end of the meal; we'll have biscuits and cheese; can I have a pound of cheese, please? cream cheese** = soft cheese; **blue cheese** = cheese with blue bits in it.

plural **cheeses** *is only used to mean different sorts of cheese or several large round blocks of cheese. Usually no plural:* **some cheese; a piece of cheese**

chemist [ˈkemɪst] *noun*

الصيدلي

person who makes medicines and sells them; **the chemist's** = shop where you can buy medicine, soap, toothpaste, etc.; **go to the chemist's to get some cough medicine; the chemist's is next door to the post office.**

cheque [tʃek] *noun* (*American:* **check**)

شيك (مصرفي)

note asking a bank to pay money from your account to someone else's account; **I wrote a cheque for £10; can I pay by cheque?** *see also* **traveller's cheque**

cheque book, *noun*

دفتر الشيكات

book made of several cheques attached together.

chess [tʃes] *noun*

الشطرنج ـ لعبة الشطرنج

game for two people, played on a board with black and white squares; **would you like a game of chess? she plays chess very well; he's no good at chess.**

no plural

chest [tʃest] *noun*

أ) صندوق

(*a*) large box; **he kept his money in a large chest.**

ب) صَدْر (الانسان)

(*b*) top part of your body where your heart and lungs are; **he hit me in the chest; she has a cold on the chest** = she coughs badly.

chest of drawers, *noun*

خزانة ذات أدراج

piece of furniture made of several drawers one on top of the other.

chew [tʃuː] *verb*

يَمْضَغ

to crush with your teeth; **he was chewing a piece of meat; you should chew your food slowly.**

chews—chewing—chewed—has chewed

chewing gum, *noun*

مضيغة ـ « علكة »

sweet stuff which you can chew for a long time but do not swallow.

chicken [ˈtʃɪkɪn] *noun*

أ) فَروج

(*a*) young hen; **the chickens were running all round the farm.**

ب) لحم الدجاج

(*b*) meat from a hen or cock; **we had roast chicken for dinner; would you like another slice of chicken? can I have a chcken sandwich?**

no plural for (b): **some chicken; a slice of chicken/a piece of chicken**

chief [tʃiːf] **1.** *adjective*

١ ـ رئيسي ـ أول ـ أعلى ـ أكبر

most important; **he's the chief engineer;**

fifty-three 53

child

what is the chief cause of traffic accidents?
2. *noun*

٢ ـ الرئيس

person in charge, especially the leader of a group of people.

chiefly, *adverb*

خاصةً ـ خصوصاً

in an important way/mainly.

child [tʃaɪld] *noun*

طفل ـ طفلة

young boy or girl; **when I was a child TV didn't exist; here is a photograph of him as a child; all the children were playing in the field; when do the children come out of school? how many children have they got?** = how many sons or daughters?

plural **children** ['tʃɪldrən]

childhood, *noun*

الطفولة

time when you were a child; **he had a happy childhood in the country; she spent her childhood in Canada.**

chimney ['tʃɪmnɪ] *noun*

مُسْتَوْقَد ـ مَدْخَنَة

tall tube for taking away the smoke from a fire; **the smoke poured out of the chimney; all the smoke went up the chimney.**

plural **chimneys**

chin [tʃɪn] *noun*

ذَقْن

bottom part of your face, beneath your mouth; **she hit him on the chin; he rested his chin on his hand while he was thinking.**

china ['tʃaɪnə] *noun*

الصيني (خزف نفيس) ـ آنية من الصيني
(فنجان أو صحن أو كأس ...)

hard white material for making cups/

chocolate

plates, etc.; **a china teacup; put all the china away in the cupboard** = put all the cups/saucers/plates, etc.

no plural: **some china; a piece of china** = a cup/a saucer, etc.

chip [tʃɪp] 1. *noun*

١ ـ أ) رقاقة (من الخشب أو الحجر)

(a) little piece of wood/stone, etc.; **chips of stone flew in all directions.**

ب) رقاقة من البطاطس مقلية

(b) long thin piece of potato, fried in deep oil; **fish and chips; can I have some more chips?**
2. *verb*

٢ ـ يقطع أو يشظي على شكل رقاقات

to take off in little pieces; **he chipped the old paint off the door.**

chips—chipping—chipped—has chipped

chipped, *adjective*

مُقَطَّع بشكل رقاقات

with a little piece broken off;
a chipped cup; this plate is chipped.

chocolate ['tʃɒklət] *noun*

أ) شوكولا

(a) sweet food made from seeds of tropical tree; **can I have a piece of chocolate? his mother made a chocolate cake; a bar of chocolate costs 20p; plain chocolate** = dark brown chocolate; **milk chocolate** = light brown sweet chocolate.

ب) قطعة أو حبة شوكولا

(b) a single sweet made from chocolate; **a box of chocolates; John ate six chocolates, and then felt ill.**

ت) شراب مصنوع من الشوكولا المسحوق

(c) drink made from chocolate powder; **I always have a cup of hot chocolate before I go to bed.**

ث) لون الشوكولا

(d) brown colour, like chocolate; **we**

54 fifty-four

choice

have a chocolate-coloured carpet in the sitting room.
no plural for (a), (c) or (d)

choice [tʃɔɪs] *noun*

إختيار - خَبَار
مجموعة يمكن الاختيار منها

choosing/something which you choose; **the shop has a wonderful choice of shoes** = very many types of shoes for you to choose from; **I don't like her choice of music; have you made your choice yet?**

choose [tʃuːz] *verb*

يختار - ينتقي - يقرّر

to decide to take something/to buy something/ to do something; **have you chosen what you want to eat? in the end, they chose to go to Germany on holiday; there are too many tours to choose from—I can't decide which one to choose; don't take too long choosing a book to read on holiday.**
chooses—choosing—chose [tʃəʊz]—has chosen [tʃəʊzn]

chop [tʃɒp] **1.** *noun*

١ ـ قطعة ـ شرحة (من اللحم)

piece of meat on a curved bone from a pig or sheep; **we had lamp chops and potatoes; a pork chop.**
2. *verb*

٢ ـ يقطع بفأس أو بسكين

to cut something into pieces with an axe/a knife; **he's in the garden chopping up wood for the fire; chop the onions into little pieces; they chopped down the tree** = made it fall down by cutting it with an axe.
chops—chopping—chopped—has chopped

Christian ['krɪstʃən] *noun & adjective*

مسيحي - نصراني

(person) who believes in Jesus Christ;

cigarette

اسم التنصير : الاسم الذي يسبق اسم العائلة

Christian name = a person's first name; **I know his name is Smith, but what's his Christian name?**

Christmas ['krɪstməs] *noun*

عيد الميلاد (٢٥ ديسمبر)

Christian holiday on December 25th, the birthday of Jesus Christ; **Christmas Day** = December 25th; **Christmas tree** = tree which is brought into the house at Christmas; **Christmas cake/pudding** = special cake/pudding eaten on Christmas Day; **what did you get for Christmas?** = what presents did you get? **have you opened your Christmas presents yet? Christmas card** = special card sent to friends at Christmas; **Father Christmas** = man in a long red coat, with a long white beard, who is supposed to bring presents to children on Christmas Day.

church [tʃɜːtʃ] *noun*

كنيسة

building where Christians pray to God; **we go to church on Sundays; this is St Mary's Church.**
plural **churches**

cigar [sɪˈgɑː] *noun*

سيجار

thick brown roll of tobacco which you can light and smoke; **he was smoking a long cigar.**

cigarette [sɪgəˈret] *noun*

سيجارة

chopped tobacco rolled up in paper which you can light and smoke; **how many cigarettes does he smoke a day? she went into the shop to buy a packet of cigarettes.**

fifty-five 55

cine-camera

cine-camera ['sɪnɪkæmərə] *noun*

آلة تصوير أفلام متحركة

camera for taking films; **he took a film of the race with his cine-camera.**

cinema ['sɪnəmə] *noun*

سينما

building where you can watch films; **we went to the cinema on Saturday night; what's on at the cinema this week?** = which film is being shown?

circle ['sɜːkl] *noun*

مستديرة

round shape; ring; **draw a circle in the middle of the piece of paper; the children sat in a circle.**

city ['sɪtɪ] *noun*

مدينة

large town; **which is the largest city in the United States? traffic is a big problem in large cities.**
plural **cities**

citizen, *noun*

مدني ـ أحد سكان المدن

person who lives in a town or country; **a citizen of London; a British citizen.**

claim [kleɪm] *verb*

أ) يطالب بـ

(*a*) to ask for something as a right; **he claimed the prize.**

ب) يعلن حق المطالبة بـ

(*b*) to say that you own something; **we found a watch in the street, but no one has come to claim it.**

ت) يدّعي

(*c*) to say something is true (but without being able to prove it); **he claimed he was a relative of mine; she claims that the police attacked her.**
claims—claiming—claimed—has claimed

clean

clap [klæp] *verb*

يصفّق

to hit your hands together several times to show that you are pleased; **when the play finished everyone started clapping; they all clapped the headmaster when he said the school would have a day's holiday.**
claps—clapping—clapped—has clapped

class [klɑːs] *noun*

أ) صف (في مدرسة) ـ درس

(*a*) group of people (usually children) who study together; **the French class; there are thirty children in Simon's class; we go to evening classes to learn German** = lessons in German given in the evening.

ب) طبقة اجتماعية

(*b*) people of the same group in society; **working class** = people who mainly work with their hands; **middle class** = people who have studied for their jobs, such as doctors/teachers, etc.

ت) نوعية (ممتازة ـ متوسطة ...)

(*c*) level at which something is judged; **first class** = very good; **second class** = not very good.

ث) درجة (في الطائرة : أولى ـ سياحية ...)

(*d*) type of seats or service in a plane/on a train; **he always travels first class; first class passengers; the tourist class fare is much less than the first class.**
plural **classes**

classroom, *noun*

حجرة الدراسة ـ غرفة التدريس

room in a school where children are taught; **when the teacher came into the classroom all the children stood up.**

clean [kliːn] **1.** *adjective*

١ ـ نظيف

not dirty; **have you got a clean handkerchief? these plates aren't clean; you**

clear

won't get any food if your hands aren't clean.

clean—cleaner—cleanest

2. *verb*

٢ - يُنظِّف

to make clean, by taking away dirt; **have you cleaned your teeth today? don't forget to clean your shoes; she was cleaning the bathroom when the telephone rang.**

cleans—cleaning—cleaned—has cleaned

cleaner's, *noun*

منظّف (محل لتنظيف الثياب) - مصبغة

shop where clothes are cleaned; **I'm taking my suit to the cleaner's.**

clean out, *verb*

ينظّف إلى أقصى حد

to make very clean; **you must clean out your room; she was cleaning out the kitchen cupboards.**

clean up, *verb*

ينظّف تماماً

to make everything tidy (after a party, etc.).

clear ['klɪə] 1. *adjective*

١ - أ) سالك - صافٍ

(*a*) with nothing in the way; **the road is clear now; have you got a clear view of the TV picture? a clear blue sky.**

ب) واضح - مفهوم

(*b*) easily understood; **he made it clear that he wanted us to leave; the words on the medicine bottle are not very clear.**

ت) شفّاف - نقي

(*c*) which is not covered and which you can easily see through; **clear glass.**

clear—clearer—clearest

2. *verb*

٢ - يزيل العقبات - ينظّف - يرفع (الأطباق عن المائدة)

to take something away which is blocking; **they cleared the streets of snow/they** cleared the snow from the streets; he's clearing a blocked pipe in the kitchen; to clear the table = to take away knives/forks/plates, etc., after a meal.

clears—clearing—cleared—has cleared

clear away, *verb*

يزيل تماماً

to remove something completely; **can you help to clear away the snow from the path?**

clearly, *adverb*

بالطبع - بكل تأكيد - بوضوح

plainly/obviously; **he clearly did not like her dress.**

clear off, *verb*

ينصرف

to go away; **clear off! I don't want you here.**

clear out, *verb*

أ) ينصرف

(*a*) to go away; **clear out! I don't want you here.**

ب) يفرّغ تماماً

(*b*) to empty completely; **can you clear out the cupboards in your bedroom?**

clear up, *verb*

أ) ينظّف تماماً

(*a*) to clean completely; **we had to clear up the mess after the party.**

ب) يحل مشكلة - يوضح

(*b*) to solve a problem; **the police finally cleared up the mystery.**

ت) يتحسن (الطقس)

(*c*) to get better; **I hope the weather clears up because tomorrow is our sports day.**

Note: **clear that mess up** or **clear up that mess**, but only **clear it up**

clever ['klevə] *adjective*

بارع - ذكي - ماهر - موهوب

intelligent/able to learn quickly; **she's**

climb

very clever at business; he's clever with his hands = he's good at making things with his hands; she's the cleverest person in the family.
clever—cleverer—cleverest

climb [klaɪm] *verb*

يتسلق

to go up; he climbed up a tree; the children climbed over the wall; she climbed through the window and down the wall by a rope; the car climbed the steep hill with some difficulty; when you have climbed Everest, there is nothing higher to climb; he goes climbing every weekend = he climbs mountains.
climbs—climbing—climbed—has climbed

clock [klɒk] *noun*

ساعة كبيرة

machine which shows the time; **the school clock is always right; your clock is five minutes slow; the clock has stopped—it needs winding up;** *see also* **o'clock.**

close¹ [kləʊs] *adjective & adverb*

قريب ـ على مقربة من ـ بالقرب من

very near/just next to something; **our house is close to the post office; keep close by me if you don't want to get lost; go further away—you're too close.**
close—closer—closest

close² [kləʊz] *verb*

يُغلق ـ يقفل

to shut; **please close the window; would you mind closing the door? the shops are closed in Sundays; he closed his book and turned on the TV.**
closes—closing—closed—has closed

close down, *verb*

ينقطع عن العمل ـ يتوقف عن الانتاج

to stop a business; **the shop closed down last week; they're going to close down the factory.**

cloth [klɒθ] *noun*

قطعة من القماش

piece of material made of cotton, etc.; **wipe the floor with a wet cloth; face cloth** = cloth for washing your face; **dish cloth** = cloth for washing dishes.

clothes [kləʊðz] *plural noun*

ثياب

things which you wear to cover your body and keep you warm; **he hasn't any clothes on; the policeman took off his clothes and jumped into the river; you ought to put some clean clothes on; they haven't had any new clothes for years.**

clothing, *noun*

انظر إلى كلمة cloth

clothes.
no plural: **some clothing; a piece of clothing**

cloud [klaʊd] *noun*

سحابة ـ غيمة

light white or grey mass floating in the air; **I think it is going to rain—look at those clouds; the aircraft flew above the clouds; clouds of smoke poured out of the house.**

cloudy, *adjective*

ملبد بالغيوم ـ غائم

where the sky is covered with clouds; **a dull cloudy day; the weather turned cloudy; when it's cloudy, it isn't easy to take good photographs.**
cloudy—cloudier—cloudiest

club [klʌb] *noun*

١) نادٍ

(*a*) group of people who have the same interest or form a team; place where these people meet; **youth club; I'm joining a swimming club; our town has one**

fifty-eight

Clothes

الثياب

1. belt	١ - حزام	16. pocket	١٦ - جيب
2. boot	٢ - جزمة	17. pullover	١٧ - كنزة صوفية
3. button	٣ - زر	18. purse	١٨ - الجزدان
4. cap	٤ - قبعة	19. raincoat	١٩ - معطف واقٍ للمطر
5. collar	٥ - قبّة - ياقة	20. sandal	٢٠ - خُفّ
6. dress	٦ - فستان	21. shirt	٢١ - قميص
7. glove	٧ - قفاز	22. shoe	٢٢ - حذاء
8. handbag	٨ - حقيبة يد	23. shorts	٢٣ - بنطلون قصير (شورت)
9. handkerchief	٩ - منديل	24. skirt	٢٤ - تنورة
10. hat	١٠ - قبعة	25. sleeve	٢٥ - كُمّ
11. heel	١١ - عقب (الحذاء)	26. sock	٢٦ - جورب
12. helmet	١٢ - خوذة	27. suit	٢٧ - بذّة - طقم
13. jacket	١٣ - سترة	28. tie	٢٨ - رباط العنق
14. jeans	١٤ - بنطلون « الجينس »	29. trousers	٢٩ - بنطلون - سروال ضيّق
15. overalls	١٥ - وزرة	30. zip	٣٠ - سحابة

fifty-nine

59

cm

of the best football clubs in the country; the sports club is near the police station.

ب) الاسباتي (في ورق اللعب)

(b) one of the suits in a game of cards, shaped like a black leaf; **the ten of clubs.**

ت) عصا غليظ

(c) large stick

cm *see* **centimetre**
ملاحظة : انظر إلى كلمة centimetre

Co. *see* **company**
ملاحظة : انظر إلى كلمة company

coach [kəʊtʃ] **1.** *noun*

١ - أ) حافلة

(a) large comfortable bus for travelling long distances; **we took the coach to Scotland; when does the coach leave for London? we all went on a coach tour to France; I get sick on long coach journeys.**

ب) مركبة قطار

(b) wagon for passengers on a train; **a train with eight coaches.**

ث) مدرّب - مدرّس

(c) person who trains people to play a sport; **tennis coach; he's a football coach.**

plural **coaches**

2. *verb*

٢ - يـدرّب - يعمل كمـدرّب أو كمدرس خصوصي

to train people to play a sport; **he's coaching the England tennis team.**
coaches—coaching—coached—has coached

coal [kəʊl] *noun*

فحم

black mineral which you can burn to make heat; **put some more coal on the fire; the electric power station burns coal.**

no plural: **some coal; a bag of coal; a lump of coal**

coffee

coast [kəʊst] *noun*

ساحل

part of the land by the sea; **after ten days, they saw the coast of Africa in the distance; the south coast is the warmest part of the country.**

coat [kəʊt] *noun*

أ) معطف - سُرّة

(a) thing which you wear on top of other clothes to keep yourself warm; **you'll need to put on a coat—it's just started to snow; she was wearing a fur coat.**

ب) طبقة (من الدهان)

(b) **a coat of paint** = paint covering something; **we gave the door two coats of paint** = we painted the door twice.

cock [kɒk] *noun*

ذكر الطائر - ديك

male bird (especially a male chicken).

cocoa [ˈkəʊkəʊ] *noun*

كاكاو

chocolate powder used to make a drink; drink made from this powder; **I always have a cup of cocoa in the evening; put a spoonful of cocoa into each cup.**

coffee [ˈkɒfɪ] *noun*

أ) قهوة

(a) drink made from a powder from the seeds of a tropical plant; **would you like a cup of coffee? this coffee is too bitter; black coffee/white coffee** = coffee without milk/with milk in it.

ب) فنجان من القهوة

(b) cup of coffee; **three coffees and two teas, please.**

ت) لون القهوة - بني غامق

(c) orange-brown colour, like coffee; **we have a coffee-coloured carpet in the sitting room.**

no plural except when it means **a cup of coffee**

coin

coffee cup, *noun* فنجان قهوة
special small cup for coffee.

coffee pot, *noun* ركوة القهوة
special pot for making coffee in.

coffee table, *noun* طاولة القهوة
low table for putting cups/glasses, etc. on.

coin [kɔin] *noun*
قطعة معدنية ـ نقد معدني ـ عملة معدنية
piece of metal money; **he gave me my change in 10p and 5p coins; this telephone box takes 10p coins; I've dropped a coin inside the piano.**

cold [kəuld] **1.** *adjective*
١ ـ بارد ـ مشعر بالبرد ـ مقرور ـ قارس
not warm; not hot; **you'll have to wash in cold water; the weather is colder than last week; they say it will be even colder tomorrow; it's so cold—I think it's going to snow; if you're cold, come and sit by the fire; my hands are cold, but my toes are warm; start eating, or your soup will get cold.**
cold—colder—coldest
2. *noun*
٢ ـ زكام ـ رشح
illness, when you sneeze and cough; **he caught a cold by standing in the rain; she's got a cold, so she can't go out; mother's in bed with a cold; don't come near me—I've got a cold.**

collar ['kɒlə] *noun*
١) قبّة ـ ياقة
(*a*) part of a coat/shirt, etc., which goes round your neck; **my shirt collar's too tight; she turned up her coat collar because of the wind.**
ب) طوق
(*b*) piece of leather which goes round an animal's neck; **our dog has his name written on his collar.**

colour

collect [kə'lekt] *verb*
أ) يجيء بـ ـ
(*a*) to fetch something or someone; **my wife collects the children from school at 4 o'clock; can you collect my suit from the cleaner's?**
ب) يُجَمِّع (الطوابع ...)
(*b*) to bring together various things; **he collects stamps.**
ت) يُجبي (الأموال ، الضرائب)
(*c*) to ask people to give money; **I'm collecting for the old people's home.**
collects—collecting—collected—has collected

collection [kə'lekʃn] *noun*
تشكيلة ـ مجموعة
group of things which have been brought together; **he showed me his collection of gold coins; have you seen his stamp collection?**

college ['kɒlidʒ] *noun*
كلّية ـ مبنى الكلّية
place where people study after they have left secondary school; **I'm going to college to study engineering.**

colour ['kʌlə] *noun* (American: **color**) لون
red/blue/yellow, etc., which allows you to tell the difference between two things which are exactly the same in shape and size; **what colour is your hat?—it's a pale blue colour; I don't like the colour of her dress; all the pictures in the book are in colour; his socks are the same colour as his shirt; colour TV/colour film** = TV/film in all colours, and not just black and white.

colour-blind, *adjective*
مصاب بالعمى اللوني ـ شخص
لا يستطيع التفريق بين لونين
not able to tell the difference between certain colours; **he's colour-blind.**

coloured, *adjective*

sixty-one 61

come

in colour; **a coloured postcard; a book with coloured pictures.**

comb [kəʊm] 1. *noun*

ملوّن

١ - مشط

thing with many long teeth for making your hair tidy.

2. *verb*

٢ - يمشط (الشعر)

to make your hair tidy, using a comb; **she was combing her hair; have you combed your hair?**
combs—combing—combed—has combed

come [kʌm] *verb*

يجيء

(*a*) to move towards here; **come and see me again soon; he came to see me yesterday; they came to school by car; hide behind the door, there's a policeman coming; come up to my room for a cup of coffee; the teacher told him to come in.**

ب) يأتي

(*b*) to happen; **what comes after B in the alphabet? T comes before U; what comes next in the programme?**
comes—coming—came [keɪm]—has come

come across, *verb*

يجد بالصدفة

to find by chance; **I came across this book in a little shop.**

come along, *verb*

يرافق - يأتي مع - ملاحظة: في صيغة الأمر تعني: هيّا، إسرع

to go with someone; **come along with us = walk with us; come along, or you'll miss the bus! = hurry up.**

come apart, *verb*
to break into pieces; **the watch came apart in my hands.**

come back, *verb*

command

يعود

to return; **he left the house to go to work, but came back for his newspaper; come back here, I want to talk to you.**

come of, *verb*

ينتج عن

to be a result of; **nothing came of his plan.**

come off, *verb*

أ) يسقط - يسقط عن

(*a*) to fall off; to stop being attached; **the button has come off my shirt; the handle came off in my hand.**

ب) يزول

(*b*) to disappear; **the ink won't come off the tablecloth.**

come on, *verb*

أ) إسرع - هيّا

(*a*) to hurry; **come on, or we'll be late.**

ب) يحصل - يأتي

(*b*) to arrive; **there's a storm coming on; I think I have a cold coming on.**

come out, *verb*

أ) يزول

(*a*) to disappear; **the ink marks won't come out.**

ب) يصدر

(*b*) to appear for sale; **the magazine comes out on Fridays.**

come to, *verb*

يَبْلُغُ

to add up to; **the bill comes to more than £10.**

comfortable [ˈkʌmftəbl] *adjective*

مريح

soft; (chair) which is soft to sit on; **what a comfortable bed! the seats in the cinema aren't very comfortable; make yourself comfortable = choose a soft chair, etc.**

command [kəˈmɑːnd] *noun*

أ) أمر - إصدار الأوامر

(*a*) order; **the soldiers were given the command to stop fighting.**

committee

ب) قيادة - إمرة

(b) in command = in charge of (soldiers); who is in command here?

committee [kə'mɪtɪ] noun

لجنة

official group of people who decide/organize; the tennis club committee organizes the matches; he's on the committee of the youth club; would you like to join the committee? there's a committee meeting at 10 o'clock.

common ['kɒmən] adjective

أ) عادي

(a) ordinary/happening very frequently; accidents are quite common on this part of the motorway; that's a common mistake.

ب) مشترك - عمومي - عام

(b) in common = belonging to more than one person; we have two things in common—we are all English and we all have red hair.

common—commoner—commonest

common sense, noun

الفطرة السليمة - الحكم على الأشياء بصورة سليمة

good sense; it's common sense to lock your car at night.

companion [kəm'pænjən] noun

رفيق

person who travels or lives with someone.

company ['kʌmpnɪ] noun

أ) شركة (تجارية)

(a) business firm; the company is doing well; John Smith and Company.

ب) رفقة - عشرة

(b) being together with other people; will you keep me company? = will you stay with me so that I am not lonely?

complain

plural **companies** but no plural for (b)
Note: **Company** is written **Co.** in names of companies: **John Smith & Co.**

compare [kəm'peə] verb

يقارن - يشبّه

to look at two things to see how they are different; try on the two pairs of shoes to compare them; you can't compare tinned fruit to/with fresh fruit; compared with/to his father, he is not very tall.

compares—comparing—compared—has compared

comparative [kəm'pærətɪv] noun

صيغة التفضيل

form of an adjective or adverb which compares; 'Fatter' is the comparative of 'fat'; 'faster' is the comparative of 'fast'.

comparison, noun

مقارنة

way of comparing; you can't make a comparison between the two men.

competition [kɒmpə'tɪʃn] noun

منافسة - مباراة

test where several people try to win a prize; a crossword competition; she entered a competition to win a holiday in Spain.

complain [kəm'pleɪn] verb

يشكو

to say that something is not good; she complained about the food; he is complaining of pains in his legs; we will complain to the police about the noise from the restaurant.

complains—complaining—complained—has complained

complaint, noun

شكوى

saying that something is wrong; the manager wouldn't listen to the complaints from the customers.

sixty-three

complete

complete [kəm'pliːt] **1.** *adjective*

١) كامل

whole/with all parts; **I have a complete set of the new stamps; he has read the complete works of Shakespeare.**
2. *verb*

٢) يُكْمِل ـ يُنهي

to finish; **he completed the whole job in two days.**

completes—completing—
completed—has completed

completely, *adverb*

بالكامل ـ تماماً

totally/all; **the house was completely destroyed; I completely forgot about her birthday.**

concern [kən'sɜːn] **1.** *noun*

١ ـ أ) مؤسسة (تجارية أو صناعية)

(*a*) business; **a large industrial concern.**

ب) قلق ـ اهتمام

(*b*) being worried about something; **concern for poor people; his health is giving cause for concern.**
2. *verb*

يهم ـ يتعلق بـ ـ هو من شأن

to deal with; to be connected with; **it doesn't concern you** = it hasn't anything to do with you; **as far as food is concerned** = referring to food; **as far as I'm concerned** = as for me.

concerns—concerning—
concerned—has concerned

concerned, *adjective*

قلق

worried; **I really am concerned about your health.**

concerning, *preposition*

في ما يتعلق بـ ـ في ما يختص بـ .

about; **I want to talk to you concerning your son's behaviour.**

concert ['kɒnsət] *noun*

حفلة موسيقية

pieces of music played in public; **we went to a Beethoven concert last night.**

confuse

concrete ['kɒŋkriːt] *noun*

إسمنت

hard material like stone, made by mixing cement, sand and water together; **a concrete pavement; they made a path out of concrete.**
no plural

condition [kən'dɪʃn] *noun*

١) حالة

(*a*) state; **the old car is in very good condition; he is ill, and his condition is getting worse; living conditions are very bad.**

ب) شرط

(*b*) term/something which has to be agreed before something else is done; **I will come on condition that you pay me** = only if you pay me; **I don't agree with some of the conditions in the contract.**

conduct ['kɒndʌkt] **1.** *noun*

١ ـ طريقة التصرف ـ سلوك ـ تصرّف

way of behaving; **the teacher sent him out of the classroom because his conduct was so bad; she got a prize for good conduct.**
2. [kən'dʌkt] *verb*

٢ ـ يقود (جوقة موسيقية)

to be in charge of an orchestra.

conducts—conducting—
conducted—has conducted

conductor [kən'dʌktə] *noun*

١) قائد (الجوقة الموسيقية)

(*a*) man who is in charge of an orchestra.

ب) قاطع التذاكر

(*b*) man who takes the money from the passengers in a bus.

confuse [kən'fjuːz] *verb*

يُربك ـ يشوش

to make someone think wrongly; to make things difficult for someone to understand; **if you all ask questions at**

congratulate

the same time, you will only confuse the teacher; there was a confusing noise of voices.
confuses—confusing—confused—has confused

congratulate [kəŋ'grætjʊleɪt] *verb*

يهنىء

to give someone good wishes/to praise someone for having done something; **we want to congratulate you on winning the prize.**
congratulates—congratulating—congratulated—has congratulated

congratulations [kəŋgrætjʊ'leɪʃnz] *plural noun*

تهنئة - تهاني

good wishes to someone on having done something: **congratulations on your success!/on your 21st birthday!**

conjunction [kən'dʒʌŋkʃn]

حرف عطف أو جر أو نفي

word (like **and** or **but**) which joins two parts of a sentence.

connect [kə'nekt] *verb*

يَصِل (أشياء ببعضها البعض) - يوصّل

to join; **the cooker is connected to the gas pipe; have you connected the electric wires to the mains?**
connects—connecting—connected—has connected

connection [kə'nekʃn] *noun*

وصلة - علاقة

something which joins; **what is the connection between the dead man and the murderer? is there any connection between the bombs and the election?**

بخصوص - بشأن

in connection with = concerning/referring to; **I want to speak to you in connection with your letter.**

contain

conscience ['kɒnʃəns] *noun*

ضمير - وجدان

feeling which tells you if you have done something wrong; **he has a guilty conscience** = he knows he has done something wrong.

conscious ['kɒnʃəs] *adjective*

واعٍ - مُتيقّظ

knowing what is happening around you; **he became conscious of two red eyes looking at him in the dark; it was two days after the accident before she became conscious.**

consider [kən'sɪdə] *verb*

ينظر (في أمر) - يفكر (في أمر)

to think about something; **he is considering going on holiday to Spain; have you considered complaining to the manager?**
considers—considering—considered—has considered

considerable, *adjective*

كثير - باهظ

quite large; **he lost a considerable amount of money; she has put a considerable amount of effort into her shop.**

considerably, *adverb*

بمقدار كبير

quite a lot; **he's considerably thinner than he was last year.**

consist of [kən'sɪstɒv] *verb*

يتضمن على - يتألف من

to be made of; **our English class consists of twenty girls and two boys; he had a snack consisting of an apple and a glass of milk.**
consists—consisting—consisted—has consisted

contain [kən'teɪn] *verb*

يحتوي على

to hold; **this bottle contains two litres of milk; he had a box containing a knife, a piece of thread and some buttons.**

contents

contains—containing—contained—has contained

container, *noun*

وعاء ـ حاوية

thing (such as a box/a bottle) which holds something; **have you a container for this soft cheese? the container cracked, and all the contents spilled out into the road.**

contents ['kɒntents] *plural noun*

أ) محتويات

(*a*) things which are held in a container; **he turned the box upside down and the contents fell out on to the floor; the police were inspecting the contents of her suitcases.**

ب) محتويات الرسالة أو الكتاب

(*b*) what is written in a book/letter, etc.; **she wouldn't tell me the contents of the letter.**

continue [kən'tɪnjuː] *verb*

يستمرّ ـ يتابع

to go on doing something/to do something which you were doing before; **the talks continued for three days; the snow continued to fall for 24 hours; they continued their conversation; they continued eating as if nothing had happened.**

continues—continuing—continued—has continued

continual, *adjective*

مستمر

which goes on all the time without stopping; which happens again and again; **there were continual interruptions.**

continuous, *adjective*

مستمر ـ بدون توقف

put together without breaks or stops; **a continuous performance in a cinema** = where there are no intervals between the films.

cook

control [kən'trəʊl] **1.** *noun*

١ ـ سيطرة

power/keeping in order; **he has no control over his children; the fireman brought the fire under control** = stopped it from spreading; **the fire got out of control** = spread quickly.
2. *verb*

٢ ـ يسيطر ـ يَضْبُط

to keep in order; **the police were controlling the traffic; we can't control the sales of foreign cars; the government controls the price of bread.**

controls—controlling—controlled—has controlled

control tower, *noun*

برج المراقبة

tall building at an airport where the radio station is.

convenient [kən'viːnjənt] *adjective*

مناسب ـ ملائم

suitable; handy; **the house is convenient for the shops** = is near to the shops, so it is easy to do the shopping; **let's find a convenient spot for a picnic; when is the most convenient time for us to meet?**

conversation [kɒnvə'seɪʃn] *noun*

مكالمة ـ حديث ـ محادثة

talking; **they had a long conversation about their holidays; he suddenly changed the subject of the conversation.**

cook [kʊk] **1.** *noun*

١ ـ طاهي

person who gets food ready; **she's a very good cook** = she makes very good food.
2. *verb*

٢ ـ أ) يطهو ـ يطبخ

(*a*) to get food ready; **you should learn how to cook—it's quite easy; I'm cooking breakfast; how do you cook cabbage?**

cool

(b) (of food) to be got ready; **supper is cooking in the oven; how long does this meat take to cook? the chicken isn't cooked enough; a cooked breakfast** = breakfast of eggs, bacon, etc.

cooks—cooking—cooked—has cooked

cooker, *noun*

ب) يستوي

فرن منزلي ـ طبّاخة (على الغاز أو الكهرباء ...)

stove for cooking; **we have a fridge and a gas cooker in the kitchen.**

cookie, *noun*

بسكوت ـ كعك صغير

American = **biscuit**

cool [ku:l] **1.** *adjective*

١ ـ بارد ـ مرطّب

not very warm/quite cold; **the weather has suddenly become cooler; keep this bottle in a cool place; what I want is a long, cool drink.**

cool—cooler—coolest

2. *verb*

٢ ـ يبرد ـ يميل إلى البرودة

to become cool; **wait until your soup has cooled; put the milk in the fridge to cool.**

cools—cooling—cooled—has cooled

cool down, *verb*

تنخفض حرارته ـ يبرد

to become cool; **has your soup cooled down enough? we sat in the shade of a tree to cool down.**

cool off, *verb*

يخفف عنه الحر

(of people) to become cool; **we cooled off by going for a swim.**

copy ['kɒpɪ] **1.** *noun*

١ ـ أ) نسخة

(a) thing which is made to look like something else; **this isn't a real picture by Picasso, it's only a copy; to type a letter and make two copies.**

corner

ب) عدد (من كتاب ـ من مجلة)

(b) a book/a newspaper; **have you got a copy of Shakespeare's plays? I've lost my copy of 'The Times'.**

plural **copies**

2. *verb*

٢ ـ ينسخ ـ يقلّد

to make something which looks like something else; to imitate; **she copied the letter; he copies his father's way of walking.**

copies—copying—copied—has copied

cork [kɔ:k] *noun*

أ) فلّين

(a) very light material from the bark of a tree; **the floor was covered with cork.**

ب) سدادة من الفلّين

(b) round piece of this material, used to close a wine bottle; **he pulled the cork out of the bottle; the cork won't go back into the bottle.**

corkscrew, *noun*

فتاحة زجاجات

tool with a pointed screw and a handle, used to pull corks out of bottles.

corn [kɔ:n] *noun*

أ) ذُرة

(a) cereal crop; **the farmer grows corn.**

ب) ذرة ذات حب كبير

(b) **sweet corn** = type of cereal crop with big seeds.

no plural

cornflakes, *plural noun*

ذرة محمصة تأكل عادة في الصباح

breakfast cereal made from corn.

corner ['kɔ:nə] *noun*

زاوية

place where two walls, sides or streets join; **the shop is on the corner of the street; put the chair in the far corner of the room; the police car went round the corner at top speed; she was waiting at**

correct

the street corner; he turned the corner = went round the corner.

correct [kə'rekt] 1. *adjective*

١ - صحيح

right; **what is the correct time? you have to give correct answers to all the questions if you want to win a prize; your answer isn't correct—try again.**
2. *verb*

٢ - يصحح

to show the mistakes in something; to put faults right; **the teacher is correcting our homework; you must try to correct your spelling; the car keeps turning to the left—can you correct this fault?**

corrects—correcting—corrected—has corrected

correction [kə'rekʃn] *noun*

تصحيح

showing the mistake in something; making something correct.

correctly, *adverb*

بطريقة صحيحة - بشكل صحيح

in a correct way; **he answered all the questions correctly and won the prize.**

corridor ['kɒridɔː] *noun*

ممر - دهليز

long, narrow passage inside a building: **his room is at the end of the corridor; she ran down the corridor.**

cost [kɒst] 1. *noun*

١ - كلفة - سعر

amount which you have to pay for something; **what is the cost of a cinema ticket? the cost of living** = amount which you pay for food, heating, etc.
2. *verb*

٢ - تبلغ قيمته - يُكلّف

to have a price; **apples cost 50p a kilo; petrol seems to cost more all the time; this table cost me £50; what does it cost?** = how much is it?

costs—costing—cost—has cost

could

cotton ['kɒtn] *noun*

قطن

thread from a tropical plant; cloth made from this thread; **a cotton shirt; I'm trying to thread the cotton through this needle.**

cotton wool, *noun*

قطن طبي أو جراحي

soft white stuff used to put on wounds, etc.

cough [kɒf] 1. *noun*

١ - سعال - كحّة

noise made when you send air out of your lungs suddenly because your throat hurts; **he gave a little cough to attract the waiter's attention; I have got a bad cough** = my throat hurts, which makes me cough frequently.
2. *verb*

٢ - يسعل - يكحّ

to send air out of your lungs suddenly because your throat hurts; **the smoke made me cough; he has a cold and keeps on coughing and sneezing.**

coughs—coughing—coughed—has coughed

could [kʊd] *verb used with other verbs*

ملاحظة : فعل يستعمل مع أفعال أخرى

أ) قدِر - استطاع - كان قادراً على

(*a*) *to mean* was able/were able/would be able; **he fell down and couldn't get up; you could still catch the train if you ran fast.**

ب) سُمح لـ - كان مسموحاً ان

(*b*) *to mean* was allowed/were allowed; **the policeman said we could cross the road.**

ت) (يستعمل للطلب بلطف)

(*c*) (*in asking politely*) **could you pass me the sugar, please? could you shut the door?**
Negative: **could not,** *usually* **couldn't**

Note: **could** *is the past of* **can**; **could** *does not have* **to** *and is only used with other verbs*

council

council ['kaʊnsl] *noun*

مجلس ـ مجلس بلدي

group of people elected to run something; **town council** = elected committee which runs a town; **he lives in a council house** = in a house which belongs to the town and which is let for a small rent.

count [kaʊnt] *verb*

أ) يعدّ (الأرقام)

(a) to say numbers in order; **the little girl can count up to ten; count to three, and then start running.**

ب) يجمع (الأرقام أو الكميات)

(b) to add up to a total; **can you count how many books we have? he counted up the figures on the bill.**

ت) يحسب ـ يشمل ـ يأخذ بعين الاعتبار

(c) to include; **there were thirty people, if you count the children; we have four television sets, not counting the one which doesn't work.**
counts—counting—counted—has counted

count on, *verb*

يعتمد على ـ يتكل على

to expect; **can I count on you to help? don't count on having fine weather for your wedding.**

country ['kʌntrɪ] *noun*

أ) بلد ـ دولة ـ قطر

(a) area of land which is separate and which governs itself; **the countries of Western Europe; the countries in the United Nations.**

ب) الريف ـ الأرياف ـ (خارج المدن)

(b) area which is not the town; **he has a house in the country/a country house.**
plural **countries,** *but no plural for (b)*

countryside, *noun*

الريف

large area away from towns; **the English countryside.**
no plural

cover

couple [kʌpl] *noun*

زوج ، اثنان

two things/two people; **it will only take a couple of minutes; there are a couple of questions I want to ask; he ate a couple of sandwiches; the book only costs a couple of pounds** = about £2; **a married couple** = two people who are married.

course [kɔːs] *noun*

أ) مدى (وقت)

(a) passing of time; **in the course of the last few years** = during the last few years.

ب) دورة دراسية ـ برنامج دراسي ـ مجموعة فصول أو دروس .

(b) series of lessons; **I'm taking a course in mathematics; she's taking a painting course.**

ت) طبق

(c) dish of food for part of a meal; **the first course is soup, and then you can have roast chicken.**

طبعاً ـ بالتأكيد

of course = naturally; **he is rich, so of course he has a big car; are you coming with us?—of course! do you want to lose all your money?—of course not!**

cousin ['kʌzn] *noun*

ابن أو ابنة عم أو عمة ـ ابن أو ابنة خال أو خالة

son or daughter of your uncle or aunt; **he went to stay with his cousin; I've had a letter from Cousin Charles.**

cover ['kʌvə] **1.** *noun*

١ ـ أ) غطاء ـ غلاف

(a) thing put over something to keep it clean, etc.; **keep a cover over your typewriter when you are not using it; book with a hard cover** = book with stiff cardboard back and front.

ب) يحتمي بـ

(b) **to take cover** = to hide/to shelter; **when people began to shoot, the policeman took cover behind a wall.**
2. *verb*

sixty-nine

Countryside

الريف

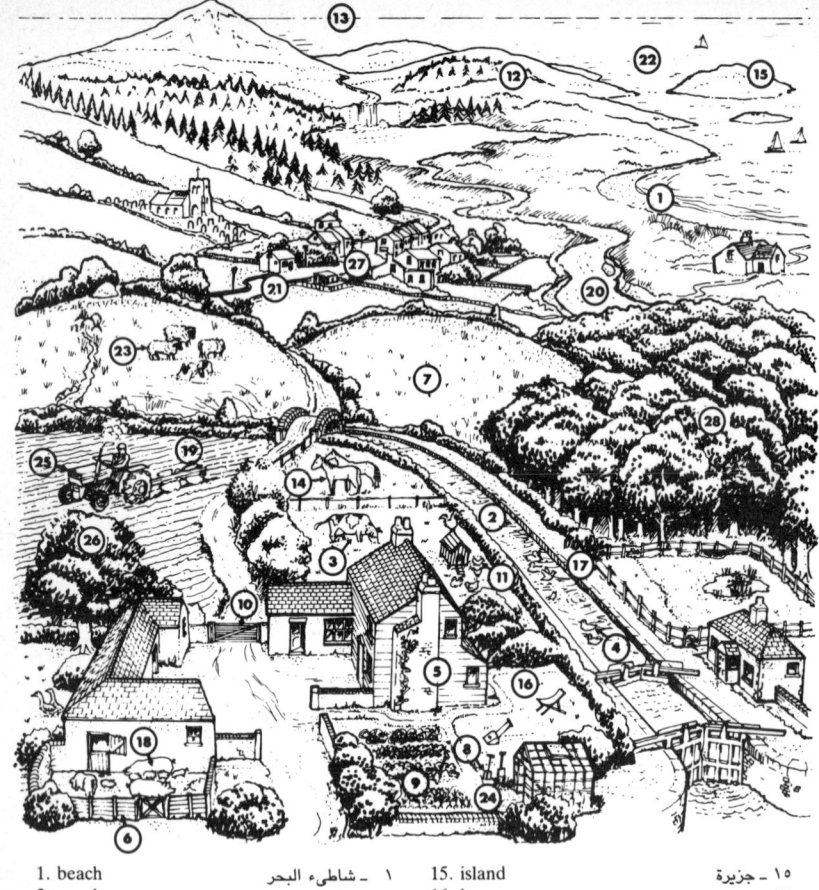

1. beach	١ ـ شاطىء البحر	15. island	١٥ ـ جزيرة
2. canal	٢ ـ قناة	16. lawn	١٦ ـ مرج
3. cow	٣ ـ بقرة	17. path	١٧ ـ سبيل ـ درب
4. duck	٤ ـ بطة	18. pig	١٨ ـ خنزير
5. farmhouse	٥ ـ بيت المزرعة	19. plough	١٩ ـ محراث
6. fence	٦ ـ سياج	20. river	٢٠ ـ نهر
7. field	٧ ـ حقل	21. road	٢١ ـ طريق
8. fork	٨ ـ شوكة	22. sea	٢٢ ـ بحر
9. garden	٩ ـ حديقة	23. sheep	٢٣ ـ غنم
10. gate	١٠ ـ بوابة	24. spade	٢٤ ـ رفش
11. hen	١١ ـ دجاجة	25. tractor	٢٥ ـ جرارة
12. hill	١٢ ـ تل	26. tree	٢٦ ـ شجرة
13. horizon	١٣ ـ الافق	27. village	٢٧ ـ قرية
14. horse	١٤ ـ فرس ـ حصان	28. wood	٢٨ ـ غابة

cow

to put something over something to keep it clean, etc.; **you should cover the floor with newspapers before you start painting the ceiling; she covered her face with her hands.**
covers—covering—covered—has covered

cover up, verb

يغطي بالكامل

to cover completely; = **he covered up the mark on the wall with white paint.**

cow [kaʊ] noun

أ) بقرة

(a) large female animal, kept to produce milk and used for meat; **a field of cows; the farmer was milking a cow.**

ب) أنثى بعض الحيوانات
ملاحظة: لحم البقر يسمى beef

(b) female of some animals; **a cow elephant.**
Note: the meet from a cow is beef

cowboy, noun

راعي البقر

man who looked after cows in the west of the USA, now usually a character in films.

crack [kræk] 1. noun

١ ـ شق ـ صدع

thin break; **there's a crack in this glass; we looked through a crack in the fence** = through a long thin hole.
2. verb

٢ ـ أ) يتشقّق ـ يتصدّع

(a) to make a thin break in something; to split; **the stone cracked the window; she cracked a bone in her leg; he dropped the cup and it cracked.**

ب) يقول نكتة

(b) **to crack a joke** = to tell a joke.
cracks—cracking—cracked—has cracked

crane [kreɪn] noun

رافعة

tall machine for lifting heavy objects;

creep

they lifted the parts of the factory roof with a crane.

crash [kræʃ] 1. noun

١ ـ أ) حادث ارتطام أو تحطم

(a) accident where cars/planes, etc. are damaged; **he was killed in a car crash; none of the passengers was hurt in the crash; crash helmet** = hard hat worn by motorcyclists, etc.

ب) دوي التحطم أو الارتطام

(b) loud noise; **the chair fell over with a crash; there was a crash, and the plates lay on the floor in pieces.**
plural **crashes**
2. verb

٢ ـ أ) يصطدم ـ يرتطم ـ يتحطم

(a) (of vehicles) to hit something and be damaged; **the car crashed into the wall; the plane crashed** = it hit the ground.

ب) يحدث دوياً نتيجة التحطم

(b) to make a loud noise; **the tree came crashing down; the pile of plates crashed on to the floor.**
crashes—crashing—crashed—has crashed
3. adjective

٣ ـ بسرعة ـ سريع (دورة دراسية)

rapid; **he took a crash course in German** = a course to learn German very quickly.

cream [kri:m] noun

أ) قشطة ـ كريمة

(a) rich part of milk full of fat which rises to the top; **I like fruit and cream; single cream** = thin liquid cream; **double cream** = thick stiff cream.

ب) مستحضر تجميلي (كريمة تستعمل لنعومة البشرة)

(b) soft paste; **face cream** = paste for putting on your face to make the skin soft.

creep [kri:p] verb

يسير بدون ضجة ـ يزحف ـ يتسلل

to walk very quietly, usually bent low down; **he crept into the bank; she crept**

seventy-one 71

crew

downstairs in the dark; he crept up behind the policeman and hit him with a stick.

creeps—creeping—crept [krept]—has crept

crew [kru:] *noun*

طاقم (سفينة أو طائرة)

group of people who work on a boat/aircraft, etc.; **the plane had twenty passengers and a crew of six; when the ship began to sink, the crew jumped into the water.**

cricket ['krɪkɪt] *noun*

لعبة الكريكت

game played between two teams of eleven players using a hard ball; **I haven't played cricket this year; our school has a cricket match this afternoon; we beat the Australians at cricket last year.**

cried [kraɪd], **cries** [kraɪz] *see* **cry**

ملاحظة : انظر إلى كلمة cry

crime [kraɪm] *noun*

جريمة

action which is against the law; **it is a crime to steal someone's money; the police are trying to reduce crime in London** = reduce the number of crimes.

criminal ['krɪmɪnl] *noun*

مجرم

person who has done a crime; **the policeman arrested a group of criminals.**

crisp [krɪsp] **1.** *adjective*

١ ـ محمص

dry; making a cracking noise when broken; **the snow is crisp; the biscuits aren't crisp—they must have got wet.**

crisp—crisper—crispest

2. *noun*

٢ ـ قطعة من البطاطة المقلية والصلبة

thin slice of potato, fried until it is hard;

cross

a bag of crisps; do you like crisps which taste of bacon, or just with salt?

crop [krɒp] *noun*

غلّة ـ محصول زراعي

vegetables/plants, etc., grown for food; **we have a good crop of tomatoes this year; the apple crop will be small; root crops** = vegetables like carrots, where you eat the root and not the leaves.

cross [krɒs] **1.** *adjective*

١ ـ مغتاظ ـ غاضب

angry/annoyed; **mother's cross with you for drawing on the dining room wall; don't be cross—he didn't do it on purpose.**

2. *noun*

٢ ـ صليب

shape made of an upright line with another going across it, used as a sign of the Christian church; **there is a cross on the top of the church; the Red Cross** = international organization which provides medical help.

plural **crosses**

3. *verb*

٣ ـ يَعبُر ـ يقطع (الطريق) يجلس مربع الساقين

to go across; **don't cross the road without looking to see if there is any traffic coming; he crossed the river in a small boat; the road crosses the railway line about 2 km from here; she sat down and crossed her legs** = put one leg over the other.

crosses—crossing—crossed—has crossed

crossing, *noun*

أ) عبور

(*a*) action of going across; **how long is the crossing from England to France? we had a rough crossing** = the sea was rough.

ب) مَعبر

(*b*) place where you go across; **you must cross the street at the zebra crossing;**

crowd

cars have to take care at the railway crossing.

cross off, cross out, *verb*

يحذف

to put a line through something which has been written, to show that it should not be there; **he was ill, so we crossed his name off the list; I can't read her letter—she's crossed out so many words.**

crossroads, *noun*

مفترق الطرق

place where two roads cross.

crossword, *noun*

الكلمات المتقاطعة

puzzle where small squares have to be filled with letters to spell words; **I can't do today's crossword in the paper; he's mad about crosswords; I finished the crossword in 25 minutes.**

crowd [kraʊd] **1.** *noun*

١ ـ حشد ـ جمهور ـ عدد كبير من الناس

large number of people; **there were crowds of people trying to do their Christmas shopping; a crowd of tourists rushed into the museum.**

2. *verb*

٢ ـ يحشد ـ يزدحم

to come together in a crowd; **people crowded in to the shops to do their Christmas shopping; the train was crowded = was full of people.**

crowds—crowding—crowded—has crowded

cruel [kruːl] *adjective*

قاسٍ ـ عديم الشفقة

which likes to cause pain; **it is cruel to hit your dog with a stick.**

crush [krʌʃ] *verb*

يسحق

to squash; **he sat on my hat and crushed it flat.**

crushes—crushing—crushed—has crushed

cupboard

cry [kraɪ] **1.** *noun*

١ ـ صيحة ـ بكاء

shout; **no one heard his cries for help.**
plural **cries**

2. *verb*

٢ ـ يبكي ـ يصيح

to have tears coming out of your eyes; **she cried when her mother took away her toys; onions make me cry; why is the baby crying? she cries every time she sees this film.**

cries—crying—cried—has cried

cup [kʌp] *noun*

ا) فنجان

(a) small bowl with a handle for drinking tea or coffee, etc., **tea cup** = large cup for drinking tea; **coffee cup** = little cup for drinking coffee; **he was drinking milk out of a cup.**

ب) احتواء الفنجان (من السائل)

(b) drink contained in a cup; **would you like a cup of tea? she drank two cups of coffee.**

ت) كأس (جائزة الفوز بمباراة رياضية) ـ الكأس النهائي

(c) silver jar given as a prize for winning a sports competition; **he has won three cups at sailing; cup final** = last game in a football competition, where the winner is given the cup.

cupful [ˈkʌpfʊl] *noun*

كمية (من السائل) بقدر احتواء فنجان

quantity which a cup can hold; **add two cupfuls of sugar.**

cupboard [ˈkʌbəd] *noun*

دولاب أو خزانة لها رفوف

piece of furniture with shelves and doors; **put the flour in the cupboard; the plates are on the top shelf in the kitchen cupboard; the cupboard doors are painted white.**

seventy-three 73

cure

cure ['kjuə] **1.** *noun*

١ ـ علاج

way of making an illness better; **there is no cure for an ordinary cold.**
2. *verb*

٢ ـ يشفي ـ يعالج

to make better; **he was completely cured; can you cure bad eyesight? this disease can't be cured.**
cures—curing—cured—has cured

curious ['kjuəriəs] *adjective*

١) فضولي ـ محب للاستطلاع

(*a*) wanting to know; **I am curious to know if they are married; she is curious to find out who sent the flowers.**

غريب الأطوار ـ عجيب

(*b*) strange; **what a curious house! he has the curious habit of pulling the end of his nose.**

curl [kɜ:l] **1.** *noun*

١ ـ جعدة شعر

piece of hair which twists into a small ring.
2. *verb*

٢ ـ يتجعّد

to twist into small rings; **her hair curls; the smoke curled up from the fire.**
curls—curling—curled—has curled

curl up, *verb*

ينطوي على نفسه بشكل كرة

to roll up into a ball; **the cat was curled up in front of the fire; the little girl was curled up in the armchair.**

curly, *adjective*

جَعْدُ أو معَقوص

twisting into small rings; **she has long, curly hair.**
curly—curlier—curliest

current ['kʌrənt] **1.** *noun*

١ ـ تيار (كهرباء أو مياه)

water/electricity which flows; **the current in the river is strong; the boat was carried away by the current; the electric current is too weak to make the machine work.**
2. *adjective*

٢ ـ جاري (ما يجري في الوقت الحاضر)

referring to the present time; **current affairs** = things which are happening at the present time; **current account** = account in a bank from which you can take money when you want.

currently, *adverb*

في الوقت الحاضر

at the present time.

curtain ['kɜ:tən] *noun*

١) ستار

(*a*) long piece of cloth hanging in front of a window, etc.; **can you open the curtains? draw the curtains—it is getting cold** = close the curtains.

ب) ستار المسرح

(*b*) long piece of cloth hanging in front of the stage in a theatre; **the curtain goes up at 8.30** = the play begins at 8.30.

curve [kɜ:v] **1.** *noun*

١ ـ منعطف

line which bends round; road which bends round; **be careful when you drive round this curve; the car takes the curves very well** = is easy to drive round curves; **the cloth has a pattern of curves and straight lines.**
2. *verb*

٢ ـ يُقَوَّس ـ ينعطف

to make a round shape; to bend round; **the road curves round the hill.**
curves—curving—curved—has curved

curved, *adjective*

مقوَّس ـ منحنٍ

with a shape which is not straight or flat; **a curved line; a curved front window in a car.**

cushion

cushion ['kʊʃn] *noun*

وسادة

bag filled with feathers or soft material, used for sitting on; **the sofa has three cushions; the chair with a red cushion.**

customer ['kʌstəmə] *noun*

زبون ‐ عميل

person who buys things in a shop; person who is eating in a restaurant; **will you serve this customer, please? we had no customers, so we shut the shop early.**

customs ['kʌstəmz] *plural noun*

جمارك ‐ جمرك

government department which charges tax on goods coming into a country; **when you come into the country, you have to pass through customs; the customs officer asked me to open my suitcase; customs duty** = tax which you have to pay to take goods into a country.

cut [kʌt] **1.** *noun*

١ ‐ جرح

place where something has been cut; **I had a bad cut on my leg; put a bandage on your cut.**
2. *verb*

٢ ‐ أ) يَقصّ ‐ يقطع بمقص أو سكين

(*a*) to make an opening, using a knife/scissors, etc.; to remove a piece of something, using a knife/scissors, etc.; **he cut the meat with his knife; she cut her finger on the broken glass; when are you going to get your hair cut? cut the cake into six pieces; he cut himself shaving.**

ب) يقلّل ‐ يُخَفِّض

(*b*) to reduce the number of something; **accidents have been cut by 10%.**
cuts—cutting—cut—has cut

cut down, *verb*

أ) يقطع من الجذع

(*a*) to make a tree fall down by using an axe/a saw, etc.; **he cut the tree down/he cut down the tree.**

ب) يخفِّض

(*b*) to reduce; **he's trying to cut down the number of cigarettes he smokes; the police hope that speed limits will cut down the number of accidents.**

cut off, *verb*

أ) يَقْتَطِع

(*a*) to take away part of something by using a knife, etc.; **he cut off a piece of cake; she cut off a little piece of string.**

ب) يَعْزِل

(*b*) to keep someone separate; **she was cut off from her friends by a crowd of schoolchildren; the tide came in and cut off the children on some rocks.**

cut out, *verb*

أ) يقطع قسماً ‐ يقتطع

(*a*) to remove a small piece from a large piece; **she cut out the photograph from the newspaper; he cut the photograph out with a pair of scissors.**

ب) يكف عن

(*b*) to stop; **he's trying to cut out smoking; she's decided to cut out sweets.**

cut up, *verb*

يقطع قطعاً صغيرة

to make into small pieces; **cut the meat up into little pieces.**
Note: **he cut the tree down** *or* **he cut down the tree; she cut out the picture** *or* **she cut the picture out,** *etc.,* but only **he cut it down, she cut it out,** *etc.*

cycle [saɪkl] **1.** *noun*

١ ‐ درَّاجة

bicycle/vehicle with two wheels, which is ridden by one person who makes it go forward by pushing pedals; **he fell off his cycle; let's go for a cycle ride.**
2. *verb*

٢ ‐ يستعمل الدراجة للذهاب أو الإياب أو التنقل

dad

to go by bicycle; **he cycles to school every day**; **he was cycling down the hill.**

cycles—cycling—cycled—has cycled

Dd

dad [dæd], **daddy** ['dædɪ] *noun*

أب ـ بابا ـ والد

child's name for father; **come over here, Dad, and look at my book**; **my dad has bought a new car.**
*Note: spelt **Dad** or **Daddy** when used to speak to your father, but **dad** and **daddy** when used to talk about a father*

daily ['deɪlɪ] **1.** *adjective*

١ ـ يومي

happening or appearing every day; **a daily newspaper**; **you should do daily exercises to keep fit.**
2. *adverb*

٢ ـ يومياً

every day; **take the medicine twice daily.**

damage ['dæmɪdʒ] **1.** *noun*

١ ـ ضرر ـ ملاحظة : لا تستعمل هذه الكلمة بالجمع

harm done to things; **the storm caused a lot of damage**; **flood damage** = damage caused by a flood.
no plural
2. *verb*

٢ ـ يضرّ ـ يُلحق بأضرار

to harm something; **the car was badly damaged in the accident**; **if it rains hard it'll damage the crops.**
damages—damaging— damaged—has damaged

76

dare

cyclist, *noun*

راكب الدرّاجة

person who rides a bicycle; **hundreds of cyclists crossed the bridge.**

dance [dɑːns] **1.** *noun*

١ ـ رقصة ـ رقص

way of moving in time to music; **dance band** = group of people who play music for people to dance.
2. *verb*

٢ ـ يرقص

to move in time to music; **he was dancing with my sister**; **the crowds were dancing in the streets**; **I'm having dancing lessons.**
dances—dancing—danced—has danced

danger ['deɪndʒə] *noun*

خَطَر

possibility of harm or death; **in dry weather there's a danger of forest fires**; **he's in danger of losing his job** = he may easily lose his job; **she's out of danger** = not likely to die.

dangerous, *adjective*

مُخْطِر ـ خَطِر

which can cause harm or death; **don't touch the electric wires—they're dangerous**; **it's dangerous to walk on railway lines.**

dare ['deə] *verb*

١) يجرؤ ـ يتجرّأ

(*a*) to be brave enough to do something dangerous or rude; **I would never dare**

seventy-six

dark

(to) jump from that wall; he doesn't dare/he dare not go out of the house; how dare you tell me what to do! I dare say he's ill = perhaps he is ill.

ب) يتحدّى

(b) to say that someone is not brave enough to do something; **I dared him to steal some sweets from the shop.**
dares—daring—dared—has dared
Note: he doesn't dare = he dare not

dark [dɒːk] **1.** *adjective*

١ ـ أ) مُظلم

(a) with very little light; **during the storm the sky turned quite dark; switch the lights on—it's getting too dark to read; in the winter it gets dark early; the sky got darker and darker as night came on.**

ب) غامق (اللون)

(b) not a light colour; **his shirt is dark green.**

ت) اسمر ـ أسود أو بُنّي الشعر

(c) with black or brown hair; **he's dark, but his sister is fair; he has dark hair.**
dark—darker—darkest
2. *noun*

٢ ـ ظلام ـ ظلمة

lack of light; **she is afraid of the dark; cats can see in the dark; we're completely in the dark** = we don't understand.

darkness, *noun*

٢ ـ ظلام ـ ظلمة

being dark; **the house was in complete darkness** = there were no electric lights on in the house.

date [deɪt] *noun*

أ) تاريخ (اليوم أو الشهر أو السنة)

(a) number of a day or year, name of a month (when something happened); **what's the date today? what are the dates of the Second World War? do you remember the date of your last letter?**

seventy-seven

day

ب) موعد ـ وقت اللقاء المتفق عليه

(b) time agreed for a meeting, usually between a boy and girl; **let's make it a date, shall we? I asked her out for a date.**

حديث ـ عصري

up to date = very modern/using very recent information; **the new telephone book is completely up to date; keep me up to date on what has been happening** = tell me all the latest information about what has been happening.

قديم ـ غير متناسب مع العصر الحديث

out of date = not modern; **this old book is quite out of date** = the information in it is not recent.

daughter [ˈdɔːtə] *noun*

إبنة

girl child of a parent; **they have two sons and one daughter; have you met my daughter, Mary?**

day [deɪ] *noun*

أ) يوم

(a) period of 24 hours; **there are 365 days in the year; July has 31 days; Christmas Day is December 25th; what day is it today?** = is it Monday, Tuesday, etc.? **I saw him the day before yesterday; we will meet the day after tomorrow; he phones me every other day** = once every two days; **I saw him only the other day** = I saw him very recently.

ب) نهار

(b) period from morning until night, when it is light; **he works all day in the office, and then goes to German classes in the evening; it will take me two days to finish this work.**

كل يوم ـ باليوم الواحد

a day = every day; **he eats a loaf of bread a day.**

77

dead

طوال النهار

all day = the whole day; **he's been working hard all day.**

daylight, *noun*

ضوء النهار

light during the day; **the robbers attacked the bank in full daylight.**

daytime, *noun*

فترة النهار ـ وقت النهار

period of light between morning and night; **he works at night, and sleeps during the daytime.**

dead [ded] *adjective*

أ) ميّت

(*a*) not alive; **my grandparents are both dead; dead fish were floating in the lake; the wind blew piles of dead leaves into the road**

ب) كامل ـ تام

(*b*) complete; **dead silence; the car came to a dead stop.**

deadly, *adjective*

مميت

likely to kill; **these plants are deadly poisonous.**
deadly—deadlier—deadliest

deaf [def] *adjective*

أطرش

not able to hear; **you have to shout when you speak to Mr Jones because he's deaf.**
deaf—deafer—deafest

deal [di:l] 1. *noun*

١ ـ أ) صفقة ـ اتفاق (بيع أو شراء)

(*a*) business agreement; **we did a deal with a German company to buy steel.**

ب) مقدار كبير ـ مبلغ وفير ـ كمية ضخمة ..

(*b*) **a good deal of/a great deal of** = a lot; **he made a great deal of money; we wasted a good deal of time.**

78

debt

2. *verb*

٢ ـ أ) يوزع (أوراق اللعب)

(*a*) to hand out cards in a game; **he dealt me three cards.**

ب) يرتب (الأمور) ـ يتعامل مع (أشخاص)

(*b*) **to deal with** = to organize things; to have to do with; **don't worry about the passports—I will deal with them; the government is trying to deal with the problem of crime; I don't like dealing with difficult people.**

ت) يعمل بـ ـ يتاجر بـ

(*c*) **to deal in** = to do business in; **he deals in old cars**
deals—dealing—dealt [delt]—has dealt

dear [dɪə] *adjective*

أ) عزيز ـ حميم

(*a*) well liked; **a very dear friend; I met dear old Mrs Jones.**

ب) عزيزي (تستعمل في مقدمة الرسالة قبل اسم المُرسَل إليه)

(*b*) (*at the beginning of a letter*) **Dear Mr Smith; Dear John; Dear Sir.**

ت) غالٍ ـ مكلف كثيراً

(*c*) which costs a lot of money; **oranges are dearer than apples; he always orders the dearest food in the restaurant.**

ث) آه . يا إلهي ـ يا للهول

(*d*) **oh dear!** = what a nuisance!/how annoying!
dear—dearer—dearest

death [deθ] *noun*

موت ـ مصرع

dying; end of life; **his sudden death shocked his friends; he met his death in a car crash** = he died in a crash.

debt [det] *noun*

دَيْن

money which is owed to someone; **he**

seventy-eight

December

got into debt = he started to owe money; **he is in debt** = he owes money; **he is out of debt** = he doesn't owe money any more.

December [dɪ'sembə] *noun*

شهر ديسمبر ـ كانون الأول

twelfth and last month of the year; her birthday is in December; she was born on December 20th; we went on holiday last December; today is December 6th. *Note:* **December 6th**: *say* 'the sixth of December' *or* 'December the sixth'

decide [dɪ'saɪd] *verb*

يقرّر

to make up your mind to do something; have you decided where to go for your holiday? they decided to stay at home; he decided not to go away.
decides—deciding—decided—has decided

decision [dɪ'sɪʒn] *noun*

قرار

making up your mind to do something; they have been talking for hours, but still haven't reached a decision.

deck [dek] *noun*

ظهر السفينة

flat floor in a ship/on a bus; the restaurant is on the third deck; there are seats on the top deck.

declare [dɪ'kleə] *verb*

صرّح ب ـ أعلن عن

to tell a customs man that you have goods which you may have to pay tax on; anything to declare? I want to declare three bottles of wine.
declares—declaring—declared—has declared

deep [diːp] *adjective*

أ) عميق

(a) which goes a long way down; be careful—the water is very deep here; this is the deepest mine in Europe; the water is only two metres deep.

ب) غامق (اللون)

(b) dark; the carpet is a deep chocolate colour.
deep—deeper—deepest

degree

defeat [dɪ'fiːt] **1.** *noun*

١ ـ هزيمة

loss of a battle/of a vote; the government had to resign after its defeat in the election; the defeat of the French army at Agincourt.
2. *verb*

٢ ـ يهزم

to beat someone in a battle/a vote; the government was defeated; Napoleon defeated the German army.
defeats—defeating—defeated—has defeated

defend [dɪ'fend] *verb*

يدافع عن

to protect someone/something from an attack; the town was defended by a large army.
defends—defending—defended—has defended

defence, *noun* (*American:* **defense**) protection against an attack; defence of a country against an enemy.

degree [dɪ'griː] *noun*

أ) درجة

(a) (*in science*) part of a series of measurements; a circle has 360° (*say* 'three hundred and sixty degrees'); the temperature is only 20° (*say* 'twenty degrees').

ب) شهادة جامعية

(b) he has a degree in English = he studied English at university and passed his exams.
Note: with figures **degree** *is written* °

seventy-nine 79

delay

delay [dɪ'leɪ] **1.** *noun*

١ ـ تأخير

time when something/someone is late; **the meeting started after twenty minutes' delay/after a delay of twenty minutes; I am sorry for the delay in answering your letter.**
2. *verb*

٢ ـ يتأخر

to make something/someone late; **the train was delayed by snow; the fog has delayed all planes**
delays—delaying—delayed—has delayed

delight [dɪ'laɪt] **1.** *noun*

١ ـ إستمتاع ـ ابتهاج ـ سرور

enjoyment; pleasure; **he takes delight in being rude to people** = he enjoys it; **our cat's greatest delight is sleeping in front of the fire.**
2. *verb*

٢ ـ يتمتع ـ يستمتع

to delight in = to enjoy; **he delights in being rude to his friends.**
delights—delighting—delighted—has delighted

delighted, *adjective*

مسرور

very pleased; **I'd be delighted to come to your party; she was delighted with her present.**

delightful, *adjective*

مُمتع ـ مُسِر

very pleasant; **what delightful weather! they gave a delightful party.**

deliver [dɪ'lɪvə] *verb*

يُسلِّم ـ يُوصِل

to bring something to someone; **the postman delivers the mail to our house; can you deliver this parcel for me? the shop will deliver the new table tomorrow.**
delivers—delivering—delivered—has delivered

depend on

demand [dɪ'mɒːnd] **1.** *noun*

١ ـ يَطْلُب

asking for something; **this book is in great demand** = everyone is asking for it.
2. *verb*

٢ ـ يطلب بإلحاح

to ask for something and expect to get it; **she demanded to see the manager; he is demanding his money back.**
demands—demanding—demanded—has demanded

dentist ['dentɪst] *noun*

طبيب الأسنان

person who looks after your teeth; **I must go to the dentist—I've got toothache; she had to wait for an hour at the dentist's; I hate going to see the dentist.**

department [dɪ'pɑːtmənt] *noun*

قسم (في مؤسسة أو متجر) دائرة حكومية ـ وزارة

part of a large organization/of a large shop; **if you want cheese, you must go to the food department; he is manager of the sales department; Department of Education** = part of the government which deals with education.

departure [dɪ'pɑːtʃə] *noun*

رحلة ـ (في المطار) : قسم المغادرة

going away; **departures** = part of an airport dealing with passengers who are leaving.

depend on [dɪ'pend'ɒn] *verb*

أ) يعتمد على

(*a*) to be sure that something will happen/that someone will do something; **he depends on his wife to look after the house; we're depending on you to pay for the food.**

ب) يتوقَّف على

(*b*) to happen because of something; **whether or not we go on a picnic depends**

depth

on the weather; depending on her exam results she will go to university or start work in an office.
depends—depending—depended—has depended

depth [depθ] *noun*

عمق

measurement of how deep something is; **what is the depth of the pool? the river is at least 6 metres in depth.**
no plural

describe [dɪ'skraɪb] *verb*

يَصِف

to say or write what something/someone is like; **can you describe the man who stole the money? she described how her car suddenly hit a tree; the police asked her to describe what happened.**
describes—describing—described—has described

description [dɪ'skrɪpʃn] *noun*

وَصْف

saying or writing what something/someone is like; **her description of the accident.**

desert ['dezət] *noun*

صحراء

place which is very dry and covered with sand; **the Sahara desert; he lived for three years on a desert island.**

deserted [dɪ'zɜːtɪd] *adjective*

مهجور ـ خالٍ من السكان

with no people; **the town is quite deserted on Sunday afternoons; they camped in a deserted spot in the mountains.**

deserve [dɪ'zɜːv] *verb*

يستحق

he deserves a prize = he ought to have a prize because what he has done is very good; **she deserves to be punished** = she ought to be punished.
deserves—deserving—deserved—has deserved

develop

desk [desk] *noun*

مكتب (الطاولة التي تستعمل للكتابة)

table for writing (sometimes with drawers); **put the papers away in your desk; he was sitting at his desk when the telephone rang.**

dessert [dɪ'zɜːt] *noun*

حلويات (بعد الطعام)

sweet food which you eat at the end of a meal; **what's for dessert? we'll have ice cream for dessert.**

destroy [dɪ'strɔɪ] *verb*

يُدمِّر ـ يُتلف

to ruin completely; **the house was destroyed by fire; she destroyed all his letters.**
destroys—destroying—destroyed—has destroyed

detail ['diːteɪl] *noun*

تفاصيل

small part of a description; **he went into a lot of detail when describing the accident; she told us how to get to her house, but left out the most important detail—the name of the street.**

develop [dɪ'veləp] *verb*

أ) يطوِّر ـ يتطور
(*a*) to grow or make grow; to use for a better purpose; **the town is going to develop the land near the railway station; tourism is a rapidly developing industry.**
ب) يُحَسِّن ـ يتحسَّن
(*b*) to start to get; **she developed a cold; he developed a liking for chocolate.**
ت) بدأ يميل أو يتطور نحو ...
(*c*) to make a film ready to print photographs from it.

eighty-one   **81**

diamond

develops—developing—developed—has developed

development, noun

تطور ـ تطوير

thing which develops; being developed.

diamond ['daɪəmənd] noun

أ) ألماس

(a) very valuable stone.

ب) الديناري (في ورق اللعب)

(b) one of the red suits in a game of cards; **the ten of diamonds.**

dictionary ['dɪkʃənrɪ] noun

قاموس ـ معجم

book which lists words in alphabetical order and gives their meanings or translates them into another language; **a French dictionary; if you don't understand the word, look it up in a dictionary.**

plural **dictionaries**

did [dɪd], **didn't** [dɪdnt] *see* **do**

ملاحظة : انظر إلى كلمة do

die [daɪ] verb

أ) يموت ـ يفارق الحياة

(a) to stop living; **his father died last year; she died in a car crash; if you take a fish out of water it will die.**

ب) متلهف على ـ بحاجة ماسة إلى

(b) **dying for** = very keen to have; **I'm dying for a cup of tea** = I would like a cup of tea very much.

dies—dying—died—has died

die away, verb

يخفّ (صوت) يتضاءل ـ يتلاشى ـ يختفي

to get fainter; **the sound of the car died away.**

die down, verb

يخف حدةً ـ يتضاءل ـ يتلاشى

to get less; **the fire began to die down.**

dinner

difference ['dɪfrəns] noun

فرق ـ فارق

way in which two things are not the same; **can you tell the difference between butter and margarine? you can use water or oil—it doesn't make any difference** – the result is the same.

different, adjective

مختلف

not the same; **living in the country is different from living in the town; I went to six different shops, but couldn't find what I wanted; he looks different—I think he has had his hair cut.**

difficult ['dɪfɪkəlt] adjective

صعب

hard to do; not easy; **the examination was very difficult—half the students failed; it is difficult to find somewhere to park on Saturday mornings.**

difficulty, noun

صعوبة

problem/thing which is not easy; **the difficulty is how to start the car; she has difficulty in getting up in the morning.**

plural **difficulties**

dig [dɪg] verb

يَحْفُر

to make a hole in the ground; **he was digging in his garden; the prisoner dug a hole under the prison wall; we dug up an old coin** = found it while digging.

digs—digging—dug—has dug

dining room ['daɪnɪŋ rʊm] noun

غرفة الطعام

room in a house where you usually eat; **we were sitting the dining room having supper; come into the dining room—dinner is ready; he was doing his homework on the dining room table.**

dinner ['dɪnə] noun

طعام الغذاء (أو العشاء)

main meal (either eaten at 1 o'clock or

82   eighty-two

direct

in the evening); **we were having dinner in the dining room when the telephone rang; we always have dinner at 7.30; would you like to come to dinner next week? eat up your dinner; hurry up, it's almost time for dinner; what's for dinner?**

*Note: if you call the midday meal **dinner**, then you call the evening meal **supper**; if you call the evening meal **dinner**, then you call the midday meal **lunch**.*

dinnertime, *noun*

وقت العشاء

time when you usually have dinner; **it's almost dinnertime; 7 o'clock is my dinnertime.**

direct [daɪ'rekt *or* dɪ'rekt] **1.** *adjective & adverb*

١ ‏- مباشر - بدون توقف - مباشرةً

straight; **the plane flies direct to Paris; a direct flight to Paris** = flight with no stops or where you do not have to change planes.
2. *verb*

٢ - يوجّه - يشير الطريق

to tell someone where to go; **the policeman was directing the traffic; can you direct me to the Post Office?** = can you tell me how to get to the Post Office?
directs—directing—directed—has directed

direction [daɪ'rekʃn *or* dɪ'rekʃn] *noun*

أ) اتجاه - وجهة

(*a*) way in which you are going; **turn round—you are going in the wrong direction; the station is in the other direction; leaves were blowing in all directions** = everywhere.

ب) توجيهات - إرشادات

(*b*) **directions** = telling how to do something; **the policeman gave us directions for getting to the station; I can't use this, as there are no directions how to switch it on.**

eighty-three

discover

dirt [dɜːt] *noun*

وَسَخ - وحل - غبار

material which is not clean, like mud, dust, earth, etc.; **don't sit in the dirt—you'll get your clothes dirty.**

dirty, *adjective*

وَسِخ - قَذِر

not clean; **if you lie on the ground you will get your clothes dirty; we must wash all these dirty plates; you can't have any dinner if your hands are dirty.**
dirty—dirtier—dirtiest

disappear [dɪsə'pɪə] *verb*

يختفي - يغيب عن الأنظار

not to be seen any more; **the thieves disappeared when they heard the police coming; the sun disappeared behind the clouds.**
disappears—disappearing—disappeared—has disappeared

disappointed [dɪsə'pɔɪntɪd] *adjective*

خائب الأمل

sad, because something has not happened which you hoped would happen or because it is not what you expected it to be; **she is very disappointed because she did not get the job; they were disappointed with the hotel.**

disappointment, *noun*

خيبة أمل

being disappointed; **to her great disappointment she didn't get the job.**

discover [dɪ'skʌvə] *verb*

يكتشف

to find something, especially something new; **who discovered America? scientists are trying to discover a cure for this disease; he discovered a hole in the floor under his bed.**
discovers—discovering—discovered—has discovered

83

discuss

discuss [dɪ'skʌs] *verb*

يناقش ـ يبحث ـ يتحدث عن

to talk about a problem/a subject; **they started discussing politics; we were discussing how to get to Scotland; they discussed the best way of getting to Scotland.**
discusses—discussing—discussed—has discussed

discussion [dɪ'skʌʃn] *noun*

مناقشة ـ حديث

general talk about a problem; **the discussion went on for hours, but no decision was taken.**

disease [dɪ'ziːz] *noun*

مَرَض

serious illness (of people/animals/plants, etc.); **he caught a disease in the tropics; she is suffering from a very serious disease.**

dish [dɪʃ] *noun*

أ) صحن

(*a*) large plate for serving food; **a vegetable dish.**

ب) الأواني (الصحون والطناجر .. الخ)

(*b*) **dishes** = plates/cups, etc.; **can I wash all these dirty dishes?**

ت) طبق من الأكل ـ طبخة

(*c*) (plate of) food; **you ought to have a meat dish to start with.**
plural **dishes**

dishcloth, *noun*

فوطة (لغسل الأواني)

cloth for washing dishes.

dishwasher, *noun*

آلة غسيل الأواني

machine for washing dishes; **put all the dirty plates in the dishwasher.**

distance ['dɪstəns] *noun*

مسافة

space between one thing and another; **what is the distance between the police station and the post office? can you see that white house in the distance?** = far away; **long distance race** = very long race.

divide

district ['dɪstrɪkt] *noun*

محافظة جغرافية ـ اقليم ـ منطقة

area; **he lives in a country district; district nurse** = nurse who travels around visiting sick people at home.

disturb [dɪ'stɜːb] *verb*

يزعج ـ يضايق

to worry someone/to stop someone working by talking, etc.; **don't disturb him when he's working; sorry to disturb you, but could you lend me your pen?**
disturbs—disturbing—disturbed—has disturbed

dive [daɪv] *verb*

يغوص

to go down head first; **he dived into the water; she dived off the rocks into the sea.**
dives—diving—dived—has dived

divide [dɪ'vaɪd] *verb*

أ) يقسّم ـ يجزّىء

(*a*) to cut into parts; **he divided the cake up between the children** = he gave them each a piece.

ب) يقسم (الأعداد)

(*b*) to see how many of one number there are in another; **can you divide 27 by 9? 27 divided by 9 gives 3.**
divides—dividing—divided—has divided

division [dɪ'vɪʒn] *noun*

تقسيم ـ عملية القسمة (في الحساب)

cutting into parts; seeing how many of one number there are in another; **I am good at multiplication but not at division.**

84   *eighty-four*

do

do [duː] *verb*

أ) ملاحظة : تستعمل كلمة do مع الفعل للاستفهام ؛ هل الأمر يهمك ؟ هل ضحك ؟

(a) (*used with other verbs to make questions*) **does it matter? did he laugh? do your parents live in England? do you smoke? did she go with them?**

ب) ملاحظة : تستعمل كلمة do مع الفعل للنفي : لا يهمني الأمر . لم يضحك

(b) (*used with other verbs to make the negative*) **it doesn't matter; he didn't laugh; my parents don't live in England; I don't smoke; she didn't go with them.**

ت) تستعمل أيضاً للتأكيد : من فضلك اجلس ـ هو يحب البوظة بالتأكيد ...

(c) (*used to make a verb stronger*) **please do sit down; he does like ice cream!**

ث) تستعمل بدل الفعل مع so و neither : أنا لا أدخن ـ وأنا أيضاً

(d) (*used instead of another verb with* **so** *and* **neither**) **I don't smoke—neither do I; he likes chocolate—so does she** = she likes chocolate too.

ج) تستعمل في الجوابات القصيرة على الأسئلة : هل يهمك الأمر ؟ نعم يهمني

(e) (*used in short answers instead of another verb*) **does it matter?—yes, it does; do you live here?—yes, I do; did he laugh?—no, he didn't; do your parents live in England?—yes, they do.**

ح) تستعمل بدل الفعل في آخر الجملة للسؤال : انت تعيش هنا ، أليس كذلك

(f) (*used instead of another verb at the end of a question or statement*) **you live here, don't you? it doesn't look very nice, does it? it rains a lot, doesn't it!**

خ) تستعمل بدل الفعل : لا آكل بقدر ما هي تأكل

(g) (*used instead of another verb*) **I don't eat as much as she does; she arrived before we did; he speaks English better than I do.**

د) تستعمل في صيغة الأمر للنهي : لا تلعب في الطريق

(h) (*telling someone not to do something*) **don't play in the road! don't put that chair there! don't go away!**

ذ) تستعمل مع كلمات في آخرها ing :

(i) (*with nouns ending in* **-ing**) **she's doing the washing up; he always does the cooking.**

ر) تستعمل في بعض التعابير : كيف حالك ـ هو ناجح في عمله ـ هذا يكفي ـ هذا غير كافٍ أبداً ـ تجري السيارة بسرعة ١٠٠ ميلاً بالساعة

(j) (*used in certain expressions*) **how do you do? he's doing very well in his new job; he's a difficult person to do business with; that will do** = that's enough; **that won't do at all** = that's not satisfactory; **the car was doing 100 miles an hour** = was travelling at 100 miles an hour; **what do you do for a living?** = what is your job?

ز) تستعمل مع بعض الكلمات : اذهب وفرش أسنانك ـ يجب أن اسرح شعري ـ هو يغسل الصحون

(k) (*with things*) **go and do your teeth** = brush your teeth; **I must do my hair** = arrange my hair; **he's doing the dishes** = he's washing them; **have you done your homework? what have you been doing?** *see also* **make do with.**

I do/you do/he, she, it does [dʌz]/ **they do**
doing—did [dɪd]**—has done** [dʌn]
Negative: **do not**, *usually* **don't** [dəʊnt]; **does not**, *usually* **doesn't** [dʌznt]; **did not**, *usually* **didn't** [dɪdnt]

do away with, *verb*

يتخلص من ـ يحذف ـ يلغي

to get rid of something; **the government did away with tax on food.**

do up, *verb*

يزرّر

to fasten; **do up your buttons; can you do up the zip at the back of my dress?**
Note: **do your buttons up** *or* **do up your buttons** *but only* **do them up**

do with, *verb*

eighty-five 85

dock

أ) يخص ـ له علاقة بـ

(a) to concern; **it is nothing to do with me; it is something to do with my new book.**

ب) يفعل

(b) **what have you done with my hat?** = where did you put my hat?

do without, verb

يمكنه الاستغناء عن : هل يمكنك الاستغناء عن السيارة

to be able to manage without something; **can you do without a car? we had to do without tea; plants can't do without water.**

dock [dɒk] **1.** noun

١ ـ رصيف المرفأ ـ حوض

place near a town where ships tie up to load and unload; **dry dock** = dock which can be emptied of water for ships to be repaired; **the ship is in dock.**
2. verb

٢ ـ يرسي السفينة في الحوض

to come into dock; **we will be docking in twenty minutes.**
docks—docking—docked—has docked

doctor [ˈdɒktə] noun

طبيب

person who examines people when they are ill to find out what is wrong with them; **I have an appointment with Dr Jones; if you have a pain in your chest, you ought to see a doctor; he has gone to the doctor's.**
doctor is shortened to Dr with names

does [dʌz], **doesn't** [dʌznt] see **do**
ملاحظة : انظر إلى كلمة do

dog [dɒg] noun

كَلْب

animal kept as a pet, which barks, and waves its tail when it is pleased; **our dog bit the postman; I must take the dog out for a walk.**

dollar [ˈdɒlə] noun

دولار (العملة المستعملة في اميركا و في عدة دول أخرى)

money used in the USA and in many other countries; **this book costs four dollars ($4)**
dollar is written **$** with numbers: **$20, $525,** etc.
Note: with the word **bill, dollar** is singular: **five dollars,** but **a five dollar bill**

donkey [ˈdɒŋkɪ] noun

حمار

grey farm animal, like a small horse, but with long ears; **I haven't seen him for donkey's years** = for a very long time.

don't [dəʊnt] see **do**
ملاحظة : انظر إلى كلمة do

door [dɔː] noun

باب

piece of wood/metal, etc., which closes an entrance; **our house has a blue door; shut the oven door; he opened the door with his key; the back door leads out into the garden, and the front door on to the street; someone is knocking at the door; they live two doors away** = two houses away; see also **next door.**

dot [dɒt] noun

نُقْطَة

round spot; **her dress is blue with white dots.**

double [dʌbl] **1.** adjective

١ ـ أ) عدد مزدوج

(a) with two similar parts; **double figures** = numbers from 10 to 99.

doubt

ب) ضِعْف ـ مزدوج

(b) twice as big/twice as much/twice as many; **I am double your age** = I am twice as old as you; **double bed** = bed for two people.

2. *verb*

٢ ـ يضاعف

to multiply by two; **think of a number, and then double it.**

doubles—doubling—doubled— has doubled

doubt [daʊt] *verb*

يشك بـ

not to be sure of something; **I doubt if he will come** = I don't think he will come.

doubts—doubting—doubted— has doubted

doubtful, *adjective*

مرتاب ـ غير متأكد

not certain; **I am doubtful if he will ever come.**

down [daʊn] 1. *preposition*

١ ـ أ) إلى أسفل

(a) towards the bottom; **he went down the stairs; she fell down the ladder; they ran down the hill.**

ب) في الأسفل

(b) at the bottom; **he is not down here; it was cool down below.**

ت) هناك في الأسفل

(c) away from where the person is speaking; **I'm just going down the road to buy something.**

2. *adverb*

٢ ـ أ) (بمعنى نحو الأسفل)

(a) towards the bottom; **put your case down on the floor; he sat down on the sofa; she lay down on the carpet.**

ب) (بمعنى على الورق)

(b) on paper; **did you write down the phone number? I'll just take down your address.**

eighty-seven

drag

ت) (بمعنى نحو الجنوب)

(c) towards the south; **I'm going down to London tomorrow (from Edinburgh).**

3. *adjective*

٣ ـ منخفض

at the bottom; **the sun is down.**

Note: **down** *is often used with verbs:* **to go down; to break down; to fall down,** *etc.*

downhill, *adverb*

نزولاً إلى أسفل الجبل

towards the bottom of a hill; **the road went downhill for three kilometres.**

downstairs, *adverb & noun*

الطابق الأسفل ـ الدور الأسفل

(on or to) the ground floor of a house; **he lives downstairs; the downstairs of the house is larger than the upstairs; the dining room is downstairs; come downstairs at once! did you leave your watch downstairs?**

downwards, *adverb*

نحو الأسفل

towards the bottom; **he put the card face downwards on the table.**

dozen [dʌzn] *noun*

أ) درزنة ـ (اثني عشر)

(a) twelve; **two dozen eggs** = 24 eggs; **a dozen bottles of beer.**

ب) كثيراً ـ مراراً

(b) **dozens** = lots; **I've been there dozens of times.**

Note: after numbers **dozen** *does not take an* **-s**: *two dozen, ten dozen, etc.*

drag [dræg] *verb*

يَجُرّ

to pull something heavy along; **he dragged the sack into the corner; he was dragging a table behind him.**

drags—dragging—dragged—has dragged

87

drain

drain [dreɪn] **1.** *noun*

١ ـ أنبوب ـ مجرور ـ مصرف مياه

pipe for carrying dirty water from a house; **there is an awful smell—the drains must be blocked.**
2. *verb*

٢ ـ يصرّف المياه

to remove liquid which is not needed; **the water will slowly drain away; the land needs draining.**

drains—draining—drained—has drained

drainpipe, *noun*

أنبوب ـ مجرور

pipe on the outside of a house which takes water down to the drains; **he got into the house by climbing up a drainpipe.**

drank [dræŋk] *see* **drink**

ملاحظة: انظر إلى كلمة **drink**

draw [drɔː] **1.** *noun*

١ ـ تعادل

result of a game where there is no winner; **the game ended in a draw, 2-2.**
2. *verb*

٢ ـ أ) يرسم

(*a*) to make a picture with a pen or pencil; **he drew a picture of the church; what is he doing?—he is drawing the church.**

ب) يسحب

(*b*) to pull; **can you draw the curtains—it is getting dark.**

ت) انتهى بالتعادل . (مباراة)

(*c*) not to have a winner in a game; **the teams drew 1-1.**

draws—drawing—draw—has drawn

drawer, *noun*

دُرج ـ جارور

part of a desk or cupboard like an open box which slides in or out; **my desk has three drawers; chest of drawers** = piece of furniture with several drawers for clothes.

drawing, *noun*

رسمة ـ صورة مرسومة

picture done with a pen or pencil; **here is a drawing of the church; drawing pin** = pin with a large flat head, used for pinning papers; **drawing room** = living room.

draw up, *verb*

أ) يتوقف على حافة (الطريق)

(*a*) to come close and stop; **the car drew up to the side of the road.**

ب) يصمّم ـ يَعدُ (خطة) ـ يُجَهّز (لائحة)

(*b*) to prepare and write down; **he drew up a plan to build three new schools; we've drawn up a list of people to invite to the party.**

dream [driːm] **1.** *noun*

١ ـ حلم

events which you think you see happening while you are asleep; **I had a bad dream about spiders.**
2. *verb*

٢ ـ يحلم

to think you see something happening while you are asleep; **I dreamt I was swimming; I wouldn't dream of wearing green shoes** = I would never even think of it.

dreams—dreaming—dreamed/ dreamt [dremt]**—has dreamed/ dreamt**

dress [dres] **1.** *noun*

١ ـ أ) ثوب نسائي ـ فستان

(*a*) piece of woman's/girl's clothing, covering the body from the neck down to the knees or below; **she was wearing a green dress.**

ب) ملابس خاصة

(*b*) special clothes; **he was wearing even-**

drew

ing dress = black suit, with a black or white tie.
plural **dresses** *for (a); no plural for (b)*

2. *verb*

٢ - يرتدي (الثياب)

to put on clothes; **he (got) dressed, and then had breakfast; she was dressed in white.**

dresses—dressing—dressed—has dressed

drew [dru:] *see* **draw**

ملاحظة : انظر إلى كلمة **draw**

dried [draɪd], **drier** ['draɪə], **dries** [draɪz], **driest** ['draɪəst] *see* **dry**

ملاحظة : انظر إلى كلمة **dry**

drink [drɪŋk] **1.** *noun*

١ - أ) مشروب - شراب

(*a*) liquid which you swallow; **have a drink of water; I always have a hot drink before I go to bed; would you like a drink?** = are you thirsty? **soft drinks** = drinks (like orange juice) with no alcohol.

ب) مشروب (يحتوي على كحول)

(*b*) alcoholic drink; **would you like a drink? I'll order drinks.**

2. *verb*

٢ - أ) يشرب

(*a*) to swallow liquid; **he drank two cups of coffee; someone has drunk my beer! what would you like to drink?**

ب) يتعاطى الكحول

(*b*) to drink alcoholic drinks; **he never drinks/he doesn't drink.**

drinks—drinking—drank—has drunk

drink up, *verb*

يشرب بالكامل

to drink all of something; **drink up your milk.**

Note: **drink your milk up** *or* **drink up your milk** *but only* **drink it up**

drop

drip [drɪp] *verb*

يُنَقِّط

to fall in drops; **the water dripped off the table on to the floor; your coat is dripping wet** = so wet that drops fall off it; **the tap is dripping** = drops of water are falling from it.

drips—dripping—dripped—has dripped

drive [draɪv] **1.** *noun*

١ - رحلة بالسيارة - جولة بالسيارة - نُزهة

car journey; **let's go for a drive; I don't like long drives.**

2. *verb*

٢ - يقود (سيارة أو شاحنة ...) يوصل (أحداً بواسطة السيارة)

(*a*) to make a car/lorry, etc., travel in a certain direction; **I can swim, but I can't drive; he's taking driving lessons; he was driving a tractor; can I drive you to the station?** = can I take you to the station in my car? **in Great Britain, cars drive on the left hand side of the road.**

ب) يجعل (أحداً) يشعر بـ

(*b*) to make; **the noise is driving her mad.**

drives—driving—drove [drəʊv]**—has driven**

driver, *noun*

سائق

person who drives a car/a bus, etc.; **he's a bus driver; the driver of the car was injured in the accident.**

driving test, *noun*

امتحان المرور - امتحان لقيادة السيارات

test to see if you can drive a car; **he's just passed his driving test; she is taking her driving test tomorrow.**

drop [drɒp] **1.** *noun*

١ - أ) قطرة (مياه أو سائل)

(*a*) small quantity of liquid which falls; **a drop of water fell on my head; drops of rain splashed into the river; would you like a drop of wine?**

eighty-nine

drove

ب) سقوط ـ هاوية
(b) distance which you might fall; **there is a drop of four metres from the window to the ground.**
2. *verb*

٢ ـ يقع ـ يُسقط ـ يتساقط
to fall; to let something fall; **he dropped the cup and broke it; the prices are dropping.**
drops—dropping—dropped—has dropped

drop in, *verb*

يزور
to visit; **he dropped in to have a cup of tea; drop in for coffee if you're passing.**

drop off, *verb*

يغرق في النوم
to begin to sleep; **she dropped off in front of the TV.**

drove [drəʊv] *see* **drive**
ملاحظة: انظر إلى كلمة **drive**

drown [draʊn] *verb*

يغرق
to die or to be killed by being unable to breathe under water; **he fell into the sea and (was) drowned; the drowning man shouted for help; six people drowned when the boat sank.**
drowns—drowning—drowned—has drowned

drug [drʌg] *noun*

أ) دواء
(a) medicine; **the doctors are trying to cure him with a new drug.**

ب) مُخَدِّر
(b) something which it becomes a habit to take; **he takes drugs.**

drum [drʌm] *noun*

طَبْل
large round musical instrument covered with a tight skin, and which you play by hitting it with a stick; **he plays the drums in a band.**

drunk [drʌŋk] *adjective*

سَكْران
ill because of drinking too much alcohol; *see also* **drink**.

dry [draɪ] 1. *adjective*

١ ـ جاف
not wet; **don't sit on that chair—the paint isn't dry yet; it hasn't rained for weeks so the earth is very dry.**
dry—drier—driest
2. *verb*

٢ ـ يَجُفّ ـ يُجفِّف ـ ينشف
to stop being wet; to wipe something until it is dry; **the washing is drying in the sun; can you dry the dishes for me?**
dries—drying—dried—has dried

dry out, *verb*

يصبح جافاً تماماً ـ يجفف بالكامل
to dry completely; **hang up your coat until it dries out; I must dry out my wet shoes.**
Note: **dry your coat out** or **dry out your coat** but only **dry it out**

duck [dʌk] 1. *noun*

١ ـ طير البط ـ لحم البط
farm bird, also a wild bird, which lives near water and can swim; meat from this bird used as food; **we're going to feed the ducks; we're having roast duck for dinner.**
Note: as a food **duck** *does not have a plural:* **some duck; a slice of duck**
2. *verb*

٢ ـ يحني رأسه بسرعة
to lower your head quickly to avoid hitting or being hit by something; **he ducked as the stone went past his head; tall people have to duck as they go through that door.**
ducks—ducking—ducked—has ducked

due

due [dju:] 1. *adjective*

١ - أ) متوقع - منتظر
(*a*) expected; **the train is due to arrive at 10.00.**

ب) المطلوب دفعها - مستحق دفعها
(*b*) which ought to be paid; **the rent is due next week.**

ت) من جرّاء - بسبب
(*c*) **due to** = caused by; **the cracks in the wall are due to the traffic; the plane is late due to fog.**

2. *adverb*

٢ - في اتجاه
straight (in a direction); **the boat sailed due west.**

dug [dʌg] *see* **dig**

ملاحظة : انظر إلى كلمة **dig**

dull [dʌl] *adjective*

أ) مُضْجر - مُمل
(*a*) not exciting; **he went to sleep watching a rather dull film on TV; life here is very dull—nothing ever happens.**

ب) مظلم - باهت
(*b*) not bright; **dull weather; the car is painted dull grey.**

dull—duller—dullest

dumb [dʌm] *adjective*

أخرس
not able to speak.

during ['djuəriŋ] *preposition*

أثناء - خلال
for the time something lasts/while something lasts; **he went to sleep during the TV film; during the war we never had any butter.**

dying

dust [dʌst] 1. *noun*

١ - غبار
dirt like powder; **the table is covered with dust; wipe the dust off your shoes.**

2. *verb*

٢ - يمسح الغبار عن
to wipe dust off something; **have you dusted the dining room table?**

dusts—dusting—dusted—has dusted

dustbin, *noun*

سَلَّة النفايات - سلة القمامة
metal or plastic container for rubbish.

dustman, *noun*

موظف يعمل بتجميع النفايات في البيوت
man employed by the town to remove rubbish from houses.

plural **dustmen**

dusty, *adjective*

مُغَبَّر - مليء بالغبار
covered with dust; **the top of the car is dusty; we walked for miles along a dusty road.**

dusty—dustier—dustiest

duty ['dju:ti] *noun*

أ) رسم جمركي
(*a*) tax which has to be paid; **you have to pay duty if you want to bring cigarettes into the country.**

ب) واجب
(*b*) something which has to be done (especially in a certain job); **what are your duties as manager of the sales department?**

plural **duties**

dying ['daiiŋ] *see* **die**.

ملاحظة : انظر إلى كلمة **die**

ninety-one 91

Ee

each [iːtʃ] 1. *adjective referring to single things or people separately*

١ - كلَّ

every; **each house has a number; he was holding a knife in each hand; each one of us has a bicycle.**
2. *pronoun*

٢ - أ) كل (للأشخاص) كل واحد

(a) every person; **they have two cars each/each of them has two cars; she gave them each a cake/she gave them a cake each.**

ب) كل (للأشياء)

(b) every thing; **each of the houses has three bedrooms/the houses have three bedrooms each.**

بعضهم بعضاً

each other = both of two people/of two things; **they were talking to each other; we always send each other Christmas cards; the cups fit into each other.**

eager [ˈiːɡə] *adjective*

مُتَلَهِّف

wanting to do something/keen; **he is eager to get into the top team; she was eager to start work as soon as possible.**

ear [ɪə] *noun*

أ) أذن

(a) part of the head which is used for hearing; **donkeys have long ears; have you washed your neck and ears? he's up to his ears in work** = he has a lot of work to do.

ب) موهبة موسيقية

(b) sense of music; **he has a good ear for music; she can play the piano by ear** = without reading printed notes.

earache [ˈɪəreɪk] *noun*

ألم الأذن

pain in your ear.

early [ˈɜːli] 1. *adverb*

١ - أ) باكراً ، قبل الأوان

(a) before the proper time; **the train arrived five minutes early; we must get up early tomorrow as we have a lot of work to do; can you come earlier next time?**

ب) باكراً ، في أوائل

(b) at the beginning of a period of time; **we went out early in the afternoon; early in the year.**
2. *adjective*

٢ - مبكّر - قبل الموسمي - في مطلع (الشهر أو السنة)

which happens at the beginning of a period of time; **early vegetables; I caught an early train; these flowers open in early summer; we hope to meet you at an early date; early closing day** = day when shops close for the afternoon.

early—earlier—earliest

earn [ɜːn] *verb*

يحصّل (من المال) - يكسب (من المال)

to get money by working; **he earns £50 a week; how much does a taxi driver earn?**

earns—earning—earned—has earned

earnings, *plural noun*

مكسب - محصول (من المال)

money which you earn; **he gave all his earnings to his wife.**

earth [ɜːθ] *noun*

أ) الأرض (الكرة الأرضية)

(a) the star on which we live; **the earth**

92   *ninety-two*

easier

goes round the sun; the space station came back to earth.

ب) التربة
(b) soil; sow your seeds in fine earth.

ملاحظة: تستعمل on earth لتدعيم السؤال وتقوية المعنى
on earth (phrase used to make questions stronger) = why on earth did you do that? who on earth is going to read this book? how on earth did he find all that money?

easier ['i:zɪə], **easiest** ['i:zɪəst], **easily** ['i:zɪlɪ] see **easy**
ملاحظة: انظر إلى كلمة easy

east [i:st] **1.** noun

١ - الشرق
direction of where the sun rises; the sun rises in the east and sets in the west; the town is to the east of the mountains; the Far East/the Middle East/the Near East = countries to the east of India/to the east of Egypt and west of Pakistan/to the east of the Mediterranean.
2. adjective

٢ - الشرقي (مكان أو منطقة أو حدود)
referring to the east; the East End of London; the east coast.
3. adverb

٣ - شرقاً . نحو الشرق
towards the east; the ship is sailing east; go due east for ten kilometres.

eastern, adjective

شرقي - شرقية
of the east; Poland is in eastern Europe; the capital is in the eastern part of the country.

Easter ['i:stə] noun

عيد الفصح (عند المسيحيين)
Christian holiday in the spring, the time of Christ's death and return to life; Easter egg = chocolate egg eaten at Easter; we have two days off at Easter; are you going away for the Easter holidays? we often have a picnic on Easter Monday; we went to Germany last Easter.

easy ['i:zɪ] adjective

سهل - متيسّر
not difficult; the exam is too easy—everyone passed; it's easy to understand why he passed the exam; the house is within easy reach of the station = is quite close to the station.
easy—easier—easiest

easily, adverb

بسهولة
without difficulty; I could do the exam easily; she is easily the tallest in the class = quite a lot taller than all the others.

eat [i:t] verb

يأكل
to chew and swallow food; can I have something to eat? I haven't eaten anything since breakfast; he ate all the cakes; who has eaten my chocolates?
eats—eating—ate [et]—**has eaten** ['i:tn]

eat away, verb

يتآكل
to destroy bit by bit; the rocks have been eaten away by the sea.

eat up, verb

يأكل بالكامل
to finish eating/eat everything; eat up your meat!
Note: eat up your meat or eat your meat up, but only eat it up

edge

edge [edʒ] noun

أ) حافة - طرف
(a) side of a flat object; don't put your cup so close to the edge of the table; he lay down on the flat roof of the building and looked over the edge; she stood the coin on its edge; the knife has a very sharp edge.

ب) شفير - حدود - طرف
(b) line separating two quite different things; he stood at the edge of the water; the house is built on the edge of the town.

ninety-three

educate

educate ['edju:keɪt] *verb*

يتثقف ـ يتلقّى التربية

to teach someone; **he was educated in Scotland** = he went to school in Scotland.

educates—educating—educated—has educated

education [edju:'keɪʃn] *noun*

تربية ـ ثقافة

teaching; **adult education** = teaching of adults; **further education** = teaching of people who have left school; **higher education** = teaching people at university.

effect [ɪ'fekt] *noun*

تأثير ـ جدوى

result; **he poured water on the fire but it had no effect; this rule comes into effect on January 1st** = starts working.

effective, *adjective*

فعّال ـ مؤثر

which has the right effect; **his way of making the children keep quiet is very effective.**

effort ['efət] *noun*

جهد

using your mind or the muscles of your body; **he made an effort and painted the whole house; it took a lot of effort to carry the food to the top of the mountain; if he made an effort he would pass his exams.**

e.g. ['i:'dʒi:]

مثلاً

for example; **some fruit, e.g. lemons, are very sour.**

egg [eg] *noun*

أ) بيضة

(*a*) round object with a hard shell, produced by a female bird, which contains a baby bird; **the birds have laid three eggs in their nest.**

eight

ب) بيض ـ بيض

(*b*) egg of a hen, used as food; **I had a boiled egg for breakfast; can I have bacon and eggs? this cake is made with three eggs.**

eight [eɪt] number 8

ثمانية (العدد ٨)

she ate eight sandwiches; he's eight (years old); come to see us at eight (o'clock).

eighteen, number 18

ثمانية عشر (العدد ١٨)

there are eighteen children in the class; she's eighteen (years old); the train leaves at eighteen fifteen (18.15).

eighteenth, 18th, *adjective & noun*

الثامن عشر ـ الثامنة عشر

the eighteenth of May/May the eighteenth (May 18th); the eighteenth name on the list; it's her eighteenth birthday tomorrow.

eighth, 8th, *adjective & noun*

الثامن ـ الثامنة

the eighth of May/May the eighth (May 8th); an eighth of the time; Henry the Eighth (Henry VIII); her eighth birthday is next Tuesday.

Note: with dates **eighth** *is usually written* **8th: May 8th, 1979; October 8th, 1880;** *with names of kings and queens* **eighth** *is usually written* **VIII: King Henry VIII**

eightieth, 80th, *adjective & noun*

الثمانين

an eightieth of the money; tomorrow is grandfather's eightieth birthday.

eighty, number 80

ثمانين (العدد ٨٠)

you need more than eighty bricks to build a wall; he's eighty (years old); she's in her eighties = she is between 80 and 89 years old.

Note: **eighty-one** (81), **eighty-two** (82) *but* **eighty-first** (81st), **eighty-second** (82nd), *etc.*

either ['aɪðə] **1.** *adjective & pronoun*

١ - أ) أي واحد

(*a*) one or the other; **I don't believe either of them; you can use either car—it doesn't matter which.**

ب) كلّ من

(*b*) each of two; **they sat on either side of him** = one on each side.

2. *adverb*

٢ - إما ... (أو)

(*showing choice*) **either you come to see us or we'll go to see you; he's either ill or he doesn't want to come.**

3. *conjunction*

٣ - ولا ... أيضاً . وليس ... أيضاً

(*with a negative, making a statement stronger*) **he isn't French, and he isn't English either; you don't want to go, and I don't want to either; it wasn't on the TV news, and it wasn't on the radio either.**

elbow ['elbəʊ] *noun*

مرفق (الذراع)

place where your arm bends in the middle; **don't put your elbows on the table; he pushed me with his elbow.**

elect [ɪ'lekt] *verb*

ينتخب

to choose by voting; **he was elected Prime Minister.**

elects—electing—elected—has elected

election [ɪ'lekʃn] *noun*

انتخاب

act of choosing by voting; **general election** = election where the voters choose the members of a parliament; **he was elected a member of parliament in the last general election.**

electricity [ɪlek'trɪsəti] *noun*

كهرباء

current used to make light/heat/power; **the motor is run by electricity; the house is in the country and doesn't have any electricity.**

no plural

electric [ɪ'lektrɪk] *adjective*

كهربائي - يعمل على الكهرباء

worked by electricity; used for carrying electricity; **electric light; an electric saw; don't touch that electric wire.**

electrical, *adjective*

كهربائي

referring to electricity; **he is studying electrical engineering; they are mending an electrical fault.**

electrician [elek'trɪʃn] *noun*

أخصائي بالكهرباء

person who repairs electric wires/puts in electric machines, etc.

elephant ['elɪfənt] *noun*

فيل

very large animal, living in Africa or India, with large ears, and a long trunk; **you can go for a ride on an elephant.**

elevator ['elɪveɪtə] *noun*

مصعد

American = **lift**

eleven [ɪ'levn] number 11

أحدَ عشر (العدد ١١)

you can't eat eleven ice creams all by yourself! he's eleven (years old); come and see me at eleven (o'clock).

eleventh, 11th, *adjective & noun*

الحادي عشر

the eleventh of May/May the eleventh (May 11th); he came eleventh in the race; it's his eleventh birthday tomorrow.

else [els] **1.** *adjective*

١ - آخر (شخص أو شيء أو مكان)

(*after pronouns*) other; **anyone else** = any other person; **anything else** = any other thing; **somebody else** = some other person; **is there anyone else who**

employ

hasn't got a ticket? did you see anyone else? is there anything else you would like to eat? I couldn't go to the concert, so someone else took my ticket; who else was there? there was nowhere else to put it; can we go somewhere else?

2. *adverb*

٢ ـ أو بالاحرى ـ وإلاّ

or else = or if not; come in or else stay outside; you must have a ticket, or else you won't be able to get in.

elsewhere, *adverb*

في مكان آخر

somewhere else; if you can't find it here, I should look elsewhere.

employ [ɪm'plɔɪ] *verb*

أ) يوظّف ـ يعيّن (موظف أو عامل)

(*a*) to pay someone for regular work; the factory employs a staff of two hundred; she is employed as a secretary.

ب) يستخدم ـ يستعمل ـ يستهلك

(*b*) to use; don't employ too much force.

employs—employing—employed—has employed

employee [emplɔɪ'i:] *noun*

مُوظَّف

person who is paid for doing work; the firm has two hundred employees.

employer [ɪm'plɔɪə] *noun*

رب العمل

person who gives work to people and pays them for it.

employment, *noun*

عمل ـ وظيفة

regular paid work.

empty ['emtɪ] 1. *adjective*

١ ـ فارغ

with nothing inside; the bottle is empty; find an empty bottle and fill it with water; the fridge is empty—we must buy some more food.

empty—emptier—emptiest

2. *verb*

engine

٢ ـ يفرَغ ـ يُفرغ

to take everything out; he emptied the water out of the bottle; she emptied the box on to the table.

empties—emptying—emptied—has emptied

end [end] 1. *noun*

١ ـ نهاية ـ آخر

last part of something; tie the ends of the piece of string together; go to the end of the road and turn left; we missed the end of the TV film, because we had to go to dinner; wait until the end of the month.

في النهاية ـ أخيراً

in the end = finally/at last; in the end the police let him go home.

بدون توقف

on end = with no breaks; he worked for hours on end.

2. *verb*

٢ ـ ينتهي

to finish; to come to an end; the film ends with the wedding of the boy and girl; the game should end about 4 o'clock; the game ended in a draw.

ends—ending—ended—has ended

end up, *verb*

ينتهي (به) الأمر : وانتهى بنا الأمر في بيت صديقتي ...

to finish; we all ended up at my girl friend's house; he ended up getting arrested by the police.

enemy ['enəmɪ] *noun*

عدوّ ـ خصم

person who you fight in a war; person who you don't like; the enemy aircraft dropped bombs on our town.

plural **enemies**

engine ['endʒɪn] *noun*

مُحرِّك (السيارة أو القطار)

machine which drives something; my car has a small engine and can't go very fast; the train is driven by an electric engine.

96   ninety-six

England — enter

engineer [endʒɪ'nɪə] *noun*

مهندس ميكانيكي

person who looks after engines or other machinery; **he works as a telephone engineer.**

engineering, *noun*

الهندسة الميكانيكية

study of machinery.
no plural

England ['ɪŋglənd] *noun*

إنجلترا

country which is the largest part of Great Britain; **they have come to live in England; why do you want to go to England for your holiday? England is north of France.**

English ['ɪŋglɪʃ] **1.** *adjective*

١ ـ إنجليزي

referring to England; **do you like English cheese? English weather can be very good; is she English or American?**
2. *noun*

٢ ـ أ) الانجليز (الشعب الانجليزي)

(*a*) **the English** = people who live in or come from England; **the English like playing cricket.**

ب) الانجليزية (اللغة الانجليزية)

(*b*) language spoken in Britain, the USA, Australia and many other countries; **he speaks English very well; what is the English for 'pommes frites'?**

Englishman,   Englishwoman *noun*

انجليزي (شخص)

man or woman from England.
plural **Englishmen, Englishwomen**

إنجليزية (إمرأة)

enjoy [ɪn'dʒɔɪ] *verb*

يهوى ـ يتمتع ـ يمرح

to take pleasure in something; **I enjoy going to the cinema; did you enjoy the film on TV last night? we didn't enjoy the game at all; to enjoy yourself** = to have a good time; **the children are making a lot of noise—they must be enjoying themselves; did she enjoy herself at the party?**
enjoys—enjoying—enjoyed—has enjoyed

enjoyable, *adjective*

ممتع

which people enjoy; **we had an enjoyable day by the sea.**

enjoyment, *noun*

متعة ـ مرح

pleasure

enough [ɪ'nʌf] **1.** *adjective*

١ ـ كافٍ

as much as is needed; **have you got enough money to pay the bill? there isn't enough light to take a photograph.**
2. *pronoun*

٢ ـ ما يكفي

as much of something as is needed; **have you had enough to eat?**
3. *adverb*

٣ ـ بما يكفي ـ بصورة كافية ـ بمقدار كافٍ

as much as is needed; **you are not walking quickly enough; your hands aren't clean enough; this knife isn't sharp enough; he doesn't work hard enough.**

enquire [ɪŋ'kwaɪə], **enquiry** [ɪŋ'kwaɪərɪ] *see* **inquire, inquiry**

ملاحظة : انظر إلى كلمة inquire

enter ['entə] *verb*

يدخل

to go in; **he entered the room; the burglars entered the house through a bedroom window.**
enters—entering—entered—has entered

entrance, *noun*

مدخل ـ دخول

way in; going in; **this is the main entrance** = the main door; **entrance—10p** = it costs 10p to go in.

ninety-seven 97

envelope

envelope ['envələup] *noun*

مُغَلَّف

flat paper cover which you put a letter into before sending it; **don't forget to lick the envelope and put a stamp on it.**

equal ['iːkwəl] **1.** *adjective*

١ - مساوٍ

exactly the same in quantity/size, etc., as something else; **weigh three equal amounts of sugar; the two bits of string are not equal in length.**
2. *verb*

٢ - أ) يُساوي

(a) to be exactly the same in quantity; **two and four equals six (2 + 4 = 6); ten take away two equals eight (10 − 2 = 8).**

ب) ينافس - يضاهي - يساوي

(b) to be as good/clever/fast, etc., as someone else; **he equalled the world record; there's no one to equal him at tennis.**

equals—equalling—equalled— has equalled
Note: **equals** *is written* **=** *when used in sums:* **6 + 4 = 10**

equipment [ɪ'kwɪpmənt] *noun*

معدات - تجهيزات

things which you need to do something; **office equipment; he brought his camping equipment with him; the soldiers carried their equipment on their backs.**
no plural: **some equipment; a piece of equipment**

escape [ɪ'skeɪp] **1.** *verb*

١ - فرَّ - هرب - نجا

to get away; **he escaped from prison by climbing over a wall.**
escapes—escaped—escaping— has escaped
2. *noun*

٢ - فرار - هَرَبْ . نجاة

getting away from prison/from a dangerous situation; **we had a narrow escape when the train hit our car** = we were almost killed.

98

even

especially [ɪ'speʃlɪ] *adverb*

خاصةً - خصوصاً - خصيصاً

specially/in particular; **he's especially fond of chocolates; you mustn't go out without a coat, especially when it's raining.**

etc. [et'setərə]

إلخ ... (إلى آخره)

and so on; **vegetables, such as carrots, potatoes, etc.**

Europe ['juərəp] *noun*

أوروبا

group of countries to the west of Asia and north of Africa; **Germany and Holland are countries in Europe; many tourists come to Europe for their holidays.**

European [juərə'piːən] *adjective*

أوروبّي

of Europe; **the European countries; he collects European stamps.**

even ['iːvn] **1.** *adjective*

١ - أ) مزدوج (يقال عن الأرقام التي تقسّم على ٢)

(a) **even numbers** = numbers which can be divided by 2; **on the left side of the street, all the houses have even numbers.**

ب) متعادل

(b) with equal scores; **at the end of the competition, the two teams were even.**
2. *adverb*

٢ - حتى (تدل على الدهشة) : حتى أبرع الطلاب يستطيع ان يرتكب أغلاط فادحة

(showing surprise or making an expression stronger) **even the cleverest students can make silly mistakes; even the biggest apples were rotten** = not only the small ones, but also the large ones; **he even tried to swim across the lake** = he did many strange things, and in particular tried to swim across the lake; **that film was bad, but this one is even worse.**

حتى ولو

even if = it doesn't matter if; **he never wears a coat, even if it's snowing.**

ninety-eight

evening

ومع ذلك ـ ولكن رغم ذلك

even so = in spite of what has happened; but still; **it poured with rain, but even so we had our picnic.**

رغم ان ـ بالرغم ان

even though = although; **he didn't wear a coat, even though it was snowing.**

evening ['i:vnɪŋ] *noun*

مساء

late part of the day, when it is getting dark; **this evening** = today in the evening; **I'll meet you this evening after work; I saw him yesterday evening; the accident took place at 9 o'clock in the evening; we arrived in New York in the morning, having left London the evening before; on Sunday evening we stayed in to watch television; we always watch television on Sunday evenings.**

event [ɪ'vent] *noun*

أ) حدث

(*a*) thing which happens; **strange events took place in the church at night.**

ب) مباريات رياضية

(*b*) sports competition; **field events** = jumping and throwing competitions; **track events** = running races.

ever ['evə] *adverb*

أ) ابداً

(*a*) at any time; **nothing ever happens; did you ever meet Mr Smith? have you ever been to the USA? I hardly ever see her** = almost never; **he sang better than ever.**

ب) دائماً ـ ومنذ ذلك الحين ـ إلى الأبد

(*b*) always; **ever since** = from that time on; **for ever** = always; **it has gone for ever** = it has disappeared and will never come back; *see also* **however, whatever, whenever, wherever, whoever.**

every ['evrɪ] *adjective*

كلّ (كل يوم ـ كل مساء ...)

each; **every day; every evening; we have**

exam

a party every Christmas; every time we go on a picnic it rains; I bought six apples and every one of them was rotten; every other day = on one day, not on the next, but on the day after that (e.g. on Monday, Wednesday, Friday, etc.); **every two hours** = with a period of 2 hours in between; **have your car checked every 5,000 miles** = when it has travelled 5,000, 10,000, etc. miles.

everybody, everyone, *pronoun*

كل الناس ـ كل واحد

all people; **everybody/everyone is going to the party; I sent Christmas cards to everybody/everyone at work; everybody/everyone has to show their tickets; everybody is here, aren't they?**
Note: **everybody** *and* **everyone** *are followed by* **they/their/themselves,** *etc. but the verb stays singular, except when followed by a question:* **is everyone enjoying themselves?** *but* **not everyone works here do they?**

everything, *pronoun*

كل شيء

all things; **have you brought everything with you? everything was dark in the house; the burglars stole everything that was valuable.**

everywhere, *adverb*

في كل مكان ـ في كل الأنحاء

in all places; **there were papers everywhere; I have looked everywhere for the key and I can't find it; everywhere was white after the snow had fallen.**

exact [ɪg'zækt] *adjective*

صحيح

very correct; **this is an exact copy; what is the exact time?**

exactly, *adverb*

على نحو دقيق ـ تماماً

very correctly; **the time is exactly 16.24; he looks exactly like his brother** = completely.

exam [ɪg'zæm] *see* **examination**

ملاحظة : انظر إلى كلمة examination

ninety-nine 99

examine

examine [ɪgˈzæemɪn] *verb*

يمتحن ـ يتفحّص ـ يفحص

to look at something/someone carefully to see if everything is correct; to see if someone knows something; **the doctor examined the sick man's heart; the boxes were examined by the customs men.**

examines—examing—examined—has examined

examination [ɪgzæmɪˈneɪʃn], **exam** [ɪgˈzæm] *noun*

امتحان ـ فحص

looking at something to see if everything is correct or at someone to see if he knows something; **there is a written examination in French; he passed his English exam; she was sad when she failed her music exams.**

Note: exam is used mainly in speaking

example [ɪgˈzɑmpl] *noun*

مَثَل ـ مِثَال

something chosen to show something; **this is a good example of German poetry; for example** = to name one thing out of many; **he is keen on keeping fit—for example, he goes running every morning; to set an example** = to show people how to behave, by doing things yourself; **he sets everyone a good example by getting up early; she sets a bad example to everyone else in the office.**

excellent [ˈekələnt] *adjective*

ممتاز

very good; **we had an excellent meal.**

except [ɪkˈsept] *preposition & conjunction*

ما عدا ـ سوى ـ باستثناء

other than; not including; **you can eat anything except fish; he doesn't do anything except sit and watch television; the party was very good, except that there wasn't enough to eat.**

excited [ɪkˈsaɪtɪd] *adjective*

مبتهج ـ مسرور

very lively and happy because you hope something will happen; **the children were excited at the thought of going on holiday; don't get too excited—you may not win the prize.**

excitement, *noun*

إبتهاج ـ حماس

being excited; **what's all the excitement about? the children are in a state of excitement before Christmas.**

exciting, *adjective*

مثير

which makes you excited; **an exciting film; the news is really exciting.**

excuse 1. *noun* [ɪkˈskjuːs]

١ ـ سبب غير مقنع ـ ذريعة ـ مُبَرِّر

reason for doing something wrong or not expected; **his excuse for not coming was that he had a cold.**

2. *verb* [ɪkˈskjuːz]

٢ ـ يَعْذُر ـ يأسف لـ ـ يقدم اعتذاره لـ ...
ملاحظة : تأتي عبارة excuse me بمعنى أنا آسف أو عدم المؤاخذة ...

to pardon/forgive someone for a small mistake; **excuse me** = I am sorry; **excuse me, can you tell me how to get to the post office? excuse me for being so late; excuse me for interrupting.**

excuses—excusing—excused—has excused

exercise [ˈeksəsaɪz] *noun*

أ) تمرين (رياضي أو جسماني)

(*a*) use of your muscles as a way of keeping fit; **regular exercise is good for your heart; you ought to do five minutes' exercises every morning; he doesn't get/take enough exercise—that's why he's too fat.**

ب) تمرين (علمي أو ثقافي أو لغوي...)

(*b*) written work done as practice; **have you done all your maths exercises?**

exercise book, noun

دفتر التمارين

notebook in which you write exercises or homework.

exhibition [eksɪ'bɪʃn] noun

معرض

show/putting things for people to look at; **an exhibition of modern art; we went to a furniture exhibition.**

exist [ɪg'zɪst] verb

يعيش ‐ له وجود ‐ يتواجد

to live/to be; **can fish exist out of water? don't be silly—such a thing doesn't exist.**

exists—existing—existed—has existed

exit ['egzɪt] noun

مَخْرَج

way out (of a building, etc.); **use the exit at the back of the room; passengers must go in by the front door—the back door is the exit; turn off the motorway at exit 12.**

expect [ɪk'spekt] verb

يتوقع ‐ ينتظر من (أحد) ان ...

to think/to hope that something is going to happen or is true; **I expect it will rain; I expect she is tired after a day at the office; he expects his wife to do all the work for him; do you think it's going to snow?—yes, I expect so.**

expects—expecting—expected—has expected

expensive [ɪk'spensɪv] adjective

غالي الثمن ‐ قيِّم ‐ باهظ

dear/which costs a lot of money; **he was wearing an expensive watch; I'll buy two watches—they're not very expensive; this hotel is more expensive than I expected.**

experiment [ɪk'sperɪmənt] noun

تجربة (علمية)

scientific test; **he did some experiments to show that water boils at a temperature of 100°.**

explain [ɪk'spleɪn] verb

يشرح ‐ يفسِّر

to give reasons for something; to make something clear; **can you explain why it is colder in winter than in summer? she tried to explain what had happened, but the policeman didn't listen; he explained that the car hadn't stopped at the red light.**

explains—explaining—explained—has explained

explanation [eksplə'neɪʃn] noun

شرح ‐ تفسير

reason for something; **the police asked him for an explanation of his strange behaviour; there is no explanation for this sudden cold weather.**

expression [ɪk'spreʃn] noun

أ) تعبير

(a) word or group of words; **'for donkey's years' is an expression meaning 'for a long time'.**

ب) تعبير الوجه ‐ ملامح

(b) look on your face which shows what you think; **she had a sad expression; his expression showed that he was annoyed.**

extra ['ekstrə] adjective & adverb

إضافي

more than usual; **the first class ticket will cost you an extra £10/will cost you £10 extra; you should find some extra strong string/some extra thick paper.**

extremely [ɪk'stri:mlɪ] adverb

في منتهى ‐ للغاية ‐ إلى أقصى حد

very much; **he is extremely small; this watch is extremely expensive.**

eye [aɪ] noun

عَيْن

part of your head which you see with;

face

she has blue eyes; **shut your eyes while we all hide; I've got something in my eye; to keep an eye on something** = to watch something carefully/to look after something, so that it doesn't get harmed or stolen; **can you keep an eye on the house while we are on holiday?**

eyebrow, *noun*

حاجب (العين)

small line of hair above your eye; **he raised his eyebrows** = he looked surprised.

eyelid, *noun*

جفن (العين)

piece of skin which covers the eye.

eyesight, *noun*

نَظَر ـ قوة البصر

being able to see; **he has got very good eyesight.**
no plural

Ff

face [feɪs] **1.** *noun*

١ ـ أ) وجه (الانسان)

(*a*) front part of your head, where your eyes, nose and mouth are; **don't forget to wash your face and hands; he tried to keep a straight face** = he tried not to laugh; **he was making funny faces and the children laughed.**

ب) واجهة (الأشياء)

(*b*) front part of something; **a clock face; to put the picture face downwards on the table.**
2. *verb*

٢ ـ يواجه

to have your face towards; **please face the camera; the house faces east.**

faces—facing—faced—has faced

facecloth, *noun*

قطعة قماش لغسل الوجه

small square of cloth for washing your face and body.

face up to, *verb*

يواجه (مصاعب أو مخاطر)

to agree that an unpleasant situation exists and try to deal with it; **he faced up to the fact that he wasn't fit enough for the race; you must try to face up to the problem.**

fact [fækt] *noun*

واقع ـ حقيقة

something which is real and true; **it is a fact that he did well in his exams; tell me all the facts so that I can decide what to do.**

في الواقع ـ بطبيعة الحال

in fact = actually/really; **he said he was going to the office when in fact he went to the cinema.**

factory [ˈfæktrɪ] *noun*

معمل ـ مصنع

building where things are made; **a shoe factory; he works in a car factory; he runs a factory which makes furniture.**
plural **factories**

fail [feɪl] *verb*

يفشل ـ يخفق

not to be successful in doing something/ not to succeed/not to do something which you are trying to do; **the car failed to stop at the red light; she has failed her**

faint

exams again; he failed his driving test three times.
fails—failing—failed—has failed

failure ['feɪljə] *noun*

فشل

not a success; **he tried to make a machine to change gas into oil, but it was a failure.**

faint [feɪnt] 1. *verb*

١ - يغيب عن الوعي - يُغشى عليه

to fall down and not know what is happening/to stop being conscious; **she fainted when she saw the blood; it was so hot standing in the sun that he fainted.**
faints—fainting—fainted—has fainted

2. *adjective*

٢ - ضئيل - ضعيف - خفيف

not very clear/difficult to see or hear; **we could hear a faint noise behind the door; there's a faint smell of paint.**
faint—fainter—faintest

fair [feə] *adjective*

أ) فاتح اللون - أشقر (الشعر)

(*a*) light coloured (hair); **she's got fair hair; he's dark, but his sister is fair.**

ب) متوسط (النجاح)

(*b*) not very good; **her work was only fair.**

ت) عادل

(*c*) right/correct; **it isn't fair to eat all the cake yourself; that's not fair—you must let everyone play with the ball; the teacher was very fair when she marked our exams.**

ث) مقبول (طقس)

(*d*) bright (weather); **the TV says it will be fair tomorrow.**
fair—fairer—fairest

fairly, *adverb*

تماماً - بكل معنى الكلمة

quite; **I'm fairly certain I have met him before; he has been working here a fairly short time.**

family

Note the order of words **he's a fairly good student** *but* **he's quite a good student**

fall [fɔːl] 1. *noun*

١ - أ) سقوط - هبوط

(*a*) dropping (of something); **there has been a heavy fall of snow; falls** = waterfall.

ب) سقطة

(*b*) losing balance; **she had a fall and hurt her back.**

ت) فصل الخريف (في اميركا)

(*c*) *American* = **autumn**
2. *verb*

٢ - يسقط - يهوي

to drop down; **he fell down the stairs; she fell off the wall; did he fall into the water or did someone push him? don't put the bottle on the cushion—it will fall over.**
falls—falling—fell—has fallen

fall asleep, *verb*

يغرق في النوم - يتغلب عليه النوم

to go to sleep; **he fell asleep in front of the TV.**

fall off, *verb*

ينخفض - يهبط

to get smaller; **the number of tourists has fallen off this summer.**

fall through, *verb*

يفشل - يخفق

not to take place as planned; **the trip to London fell through.**

family ['fæmlɪ] *noun*

عائلة - أسرة

group of people who are related to each other, especially mother, father and children; **John is the youngest in our family; the Jones family have gone on holiday to Spain; they have a very big family—two sons and three daughters.**
plural **families,** *but* **family** *can be used as a plural*

one hundred and three 103

famous

famous ['feɪməs] *adjective*

مشهور ـ شهير

well known; **he's a famous singer; that restaurant is famous for its cakes.**

far [fɑː] *adverb & adjective*

بعيد (أ

(*a*) a long way away; **the post office is not far from here; how far is it from London to Edinburgh?**

ب) بكثير (أرخص ـ أفضل ـ أحسن) :
ركوب الحافلة أرخص بكثير من ركوب سيارة الأجرة ؛ ان الطعام في هذا المطعم ألذ بكثير من طعام البيت

(*b*) much; **it is far cheaper to go by bus than to take a taxi; the food in this restaurant is far nicer than at home.**

بدون أي نسبة ـ بالتأكيد

by far = very much; **it is by far the cheapest way to travel; this car uses by far the least amount of petrol.**

حتى الآن

so far = up till now; **so far the weather has been beautiful; have you enjoyed the holiday so far?**

far—farther/further— farthest/furthest

fare [feə] *noun*

أجرة ـ سعر الرحلة ـ تسعيرة

money which you pay for a journey; **bus fares have increased again; what is the fare from London to Edinburgh? return fare** = price for a journey to a place and back again; **the return fare is twice the ordinary fare.**

farm [fɑːm] *noun*

مزرعة

land used for growing crops and keeping animals; **he's going to work on the farm during the holidays; we spent six weeks on a farm; you can buy eggs and vegetables at the farm.**

104

fat

farmer, *noun*

مزارع

man who looks after or owns a farm.

farmhouse, *noun*

مزرعة ـ مبنى المزرعة

house where the farmer and his family live.

farmyard, *noun*

باحة المزرعة

place round a farmhouse where tractors are kept/where cows are milked, etc.

fast [fɑːst] *adjective & adverb*

أ) سريع ـ بسرعة ـ سبّاقة (ساعة)

(*a*) quick; quickly; **this is a fast train to London—it doesn't stop anywhere; if you walk fast you can catch up with the children in front; my watch is fast** = is showing a time which is later than the correct time; **my watch is five minutes fast** = is showing a time five minutes later than the correct time (e.g. 7.15 instead of 7.10).

ب) غارق في النوم

(*b*) **fast asleep** = sleeping so that it is difficult to wake up.

fast—faster—fastest

fasten ['fɑːsn] *verb*

يربط بحزم ـ يُثَبّت

to fix tightly; **fasten your seat belt when you drive a car; the dress is fastened with a zip down the back.**

fastens—fastening—fastened— has fastened

fasten up, *verb*

يحكّم التثبيت أو الربط

to attach completely; **you should fasten up your coat.**

Note: **you fasten your coat up** or **you fasten up your coat,** but only **you fasten it up**

fat [fæt] **1.** *adjective*

١ ـ سمين ـ بدين

big and round; **you ought to eat less— you're getting too fat; that fat man has a**

one hundred and four

father

very thin wife; he's the fattest boy in the class.
fat—fatter—fattest

2. *noun*

٢ ـ دُهْنَة ـ شحم

part of meat which is white; solid white material used for cooking; **if you don't like the fat, cut it off; fry the eggs in some fat.**

father [ˈfɑːðə] *noun*

أب ـ والد

man who has a son or daughter; **ask your father if you can borrow his car; Jane is coming to tea with her father and mother.**

faucet [ˈfɔːsət] *noun*

ملاحظة: انظر إلى كلمة **tap**

American = **tap**

fault [fɒlt] *noun*

خطأ ـ غلطة ـ غلط ـ خلل

making a mistake/being to blame for something going wrong; not being correct; **whose fault is it that we haven't any food? it's all your fault—if you hadn't stayed in bed all morning we would be at the seaside by now; the engineer is trying to mend an electrical fault.**

favourite [ˈfeɪvrɪt] *adjective & noun*
(*American*: **favorite**)

مُفَضَّل ـ الـمُـفَـضَّل

(thing/person) which you like best; **what is your favourite ice cream? which film star is your favourite? this is my favourite TV programme.**

feather [ˈfeðə] *noun*

ريش ـ ريشة

soft thing which grows on a bird's body; **a duck with green feathers on its head.**

February [ˈfebruəri] *noun*

فبراير ـ شباط (ثاني شهر في السنة)

second month of the year; **his birthday is in February; she died on February 6th; we are moving to a new house next February; today is February 7th.**
Note: **February 7th**: *say* 'the seventh of February' *or* 'February the seventh'

fed [fed] *see* **feed**

ملاحظة: انظر إلى كلمة **feed**

fed up [ˈfedʌp] *adjective*

حَكَمه الملل: لقد مَلِيت من الاستماع إلى تلك الأحاديث

sad/unhappy because you have had enough of something; **I'm fed up with listening to all this talk; she's fed up with school.**

feed [fiːd] *verb*

يُطْعِم ـ يُؤَكِّل

to give food (to someone/an animal); **it's time to feed the cows; how can you feed the family when you haven't any money? cows feed on grass.**
feeds—feeding—fed [fed]**—has fed**

feel [fiːl] *verb*

أ) يشعر ـ يَحُسّ

(*a*) to touch (usually with your fingers); **feel how soft the cushion is; when the lights went out we had to feel our way to the door.**

ب) يبدو (عند اللمس)

(*b*) to give a sensation when touched; **the knife felt cold; the floor feels hard.**

ت) يشعر

(*c*) to have a sensation; **I felt the table move; did you feel the lift go down suddenly? I feel cold/warm/happy/hungry, etc.; when she saw the film she felt sad; are you feeling better?**

ث) يعتقد

(*d*) to believe/to think; to have an opinion; **he feels it would be wrong to leave the children alone in the house; the police felt that the accident was the fault of the driver of the car.**
feels—feeling—felt [felt]**—has felt**

feet / fifteen

feeling, *noun*

شعور ـ إحساس

sensation/something which you feel; **I had a feeling that someone was watching me.**

feel like, *verb*

ينتاب (أحداً) شعورٌ : انتابني شعور بأن
أسبح .. يريد ـ يشتهي

I felt like going for a swim = I suddenly wanted to go for a swim; **do you feel like a cup of tea?** = would you like a cup of tea?

feet [fi:t] *see* **foot**

ملاحظة : انظر إلى كلمة foot

fell [fel] *see* **fall**

ملاحظة : انظر إلى كلمة fall

felt [felt] *see* **feel**

ملاحظة : انظر إلى كلمة feel

female ['fi:meɪl] *adjective & noun*

أنثى

(animal/plant) of the same sex as a woman or girl; **a female cat.**

fence [fens] *noun*

سياج

wooden or wire wall used to keep people or animals inside or out of a place; **you need a strong wire fence round the chickens; the sheep pushed through the hole in the fence; he was leaning on the garden fence.**

ferry ['ferɪ] *noun*

معدّية (مركب للمسافات القصيرة)

boat which carried goods or people across water; **we will take the ferry to France; a car ferry** = boat which carries cars and lorries.

plural **ferries**

fetch [fetʃ] *verb*

يَجْلُب ـ يأتي بـ

to go and bring something/someone; **it's time to fetch the children from school; I'll come and fetch you from the office** = pick you up in my car; **can you fetch another bag of sugar from the grocer's?**
fetches—fetching—fetched—has fetched

fever ['fi:və] *noun*

حُمَّى

sickness when the temperature of your body is very high; **you must stay in bed until the fever has gone.**

few [fju:] *adjective & noun*

أ) قليل (من الأصدقاء)

(*a*) not many; **he has few friends; we go to fewer parties than last year.**

ب) بعض (الصور) (الدقائق) ـ بضعة

(*b*) **a few** = some; **take a few photographs and we will choose which one is best; I'll be ready in a few minutes.**
few—fewer—fewest

field [fi:ld] *noun*

أ) حقل

(*a*) piece of ground on a farm, surrounded by a fence; **the cows are all in the field; a field of grass.**

ب) ميدان الملعب

(*b*) piece of ground for playing a game; **the crowd is going to the football field.**

fifteen [fɪf'ti:n] *number* 15

خمســة عشر ـ خمس عشرة (العــدد ١٥)
الخامس عشر

there are fifteen players in a rugby football team; he's fifteen (years old); come and see me in fifteen minutes time; the train leaves at eighteen fifteen (18.15).

fifteenth, 15th, *adjective & noun*
the fifteenth of May/May the fifteenth (May 15th); that's the fifteenth phone call I've had this morning; it's his fifteenth birthday next week.

fight

fifth [fɪfθ] **5th,** *adjective & noun*

الخامس

the fifth of June/June the fifth (June 5th); Henry the Fifth (Henry V); a fifth = 20%; he spends a fifth of his time writing letters; it's her fifth birthday tomorrow.

خُمس (بالغ ٢٠٪ من مبلغ أو كمية أو عدد ...)

Note: with dates **fifth** *is usually written* **5th:** *June 5th, 1935; December 5th, 1981; with names of kings and queens* **fifth** *is usually written* **V: King Henry V**

fifty [fɪftɪ] *number* 50

خمسون (العدد ٥٠)

I've made fifty pots of marmalade; he's fifty (years old); she's in her fifties = she is between 50 and 59 years old.
Note: **fifty-one** (51), **fifty-two** (52), *but* **fifty-first** (51st), **fifty-second** (52nd), *etc.*

fiftieth, 50th, *adjective & noun*

الخمسون ـ جزء من خمسين (يبلغ ٢٪)

a fiftieth = 2%; she came fiftieth in the race; it's his fiftieth birthday on Monday.

fight [faɪt] *verb*

يتقاتل ـ يكافح ـ يقاتل ـ يقاوم ـ يخوض (معركة) ـ يلاكم

to try to beat someone using force; **the boys are fighting in the street; the police are fighting to reduce traffic accidents; doctors are fighting against disease; the two dogs were fighting over a bone.**
fights—fighting—fought [fɔːt]—**has fought**

figure ['fɪgə] *noun*

رَقْم ـ عدد

written number; **write two hundred and twenty three in figures; double figures** = between 10 and 99; **his salary is in five figures** = he earns more than £10,000.

film

fill [fɪl] *verb*

أ) يملأ ـ يصبّ

(a) to make something full; **he filled the box with books; she was filling the bottle with water.**

ب) يحشو (الأسنان) بحشوة معدنية ..

(b) **to fill a tooth** = to put metal into a hole in a tooth to stop it going bad.
fills—filling—filled—has filled

fill in, *verb*

يزوّد بمعلومات معينة ـ يملأ الفراغ بمعلومات

to write in the blank spaces; **fill in your name and address; fill in the missing words.**

filling, *noun*

حشوة

metal put into a hole in your tooth by a dentist; **I had to have two fillings when I went to the dentist's.**

filling station, *noun*

محطة ملء ـ محطة للتزويد بالوقود ـ محطة بنزين

petrol station/place where you can buy petrol; **stop at the next filling station to ask the way.**

fill up, *verb*

أ) يملأ بالكامل ـ يملأ تماماً

(a) to make something completely full; **fill her up** = please fill the car with petrol; **he filled up the bottle and screwed on the top.**

ب) يملأ الفراغ بالمعلومات المطلوبة

(b) to write in all the blank spaces in a form; **fill up the form as soon as possible.**
Note: **fill the glass up** *or* **fill up the glass** *but only* **fill it up**

film [fɪlm] *noun*

أ) فيلم سنمائي

(a) moving pictures shown at a cinema, taken with a cine camera; **have you seen this Charlie Chaplin film? we watched the film on TV.**

ب) فيلم للتصوير ـ فيلم للكاميرة

(b) roll of material which you put into a

one hundred and seven   **107**

finally

camera which is used for taking photographs or moving pictures; **I must buy a film before I go on holiday; do you want a colour film or a black and white one?**

finally ['faɪnəlɪ] *adverb*

أخيراً ـ في النهاية

in the end; **the car wouldn't start, there were no buses, so finally we had to walk; we waited for half an hour, and he finally arrived at 8.30.**

find [faɪnd] *verb*

١) يكتشف ـ يُلاقي ـ يَلْقي

(a) to discover something (either by chance or by looking for it) which was hidden or lost; to discover something which was not known before; **I found a 50p coin in the street; did she find the book she was looking for? scientists have found that cold water helps a headache; doctors are still trying to find a cure for colds.**

ب) يَعْتَقِد أن

(b) to feel/to have an opinion; **I found this film very interesting; he finds his work too easy.**

finds—finding—found [faʊnd]— **has found**

find out, *verb*

يكتشف ـ يستطلع

to discover (a fact); **the police are trying to find out why she went to Edinburgh; I'm going to the library to find out about how to look after tropical fish.**

find time, *verb*

يُوجد بعض الوقت (لغرض معين)

to make enough time to do something; **in spite of all his work, he found time to phone his wife.**

fine [faɪn] 1. *adjective*

١ ـ أ) جميل (الطقس) ـ مُشمس

(a) good (weather); **we'll go for a picnic if it is fine tomorrow; let's hope it stays fine for the cricket match.**

finish

ب) بصحة جيدة ـ حَسَن

(b) well/good; **I was ill yesterday, but I'm feeling fine today; how are things?— fine!**

ت) رفيع ـ رقيق ـ ناعم

(c) very thin/very small; **sharpen your pencil to a very fine point; I can't read this book—the print is too fine.**

fine—finer—finest

2. *noun*

٢ ـ غرامة

money which you have to pay for doing something wrong; **I had to pay a £10 fine for parking on the yellow lines.**

3. *verb*

٣ ـ يُغَرِّم

to make someone pay money for having done something wrong; **he was fined £10 for parking on yellow lines.**

fines—fining—fined—has fined

finger ['fɪŋgə] *noun*

إصبع

one of the five parts at the end of your hand, but usually not including your thumb; part of a glove into which a finger goes; **she wears a ring on her little finger; he touched the switch with his finger; to keep your fingers crossed** = to hope that something will happen as you want it to happen.

fingernail, *noun*

ظفر (الاصبع)

thin hard part covering the end of a finger; **she painted her fingernails red.**

fingerprint, *noun*

بصمة (الاصبع)

mark left by a finger when you touch something; **the police found fingerprints near the broken window.**

finish ['fɪnɪʃ] *verb*

يُنْهي ـ ينتهي من ـ يُكْمِل ـ يأتي على

to do something completely; to come to an end; **I've finished my homework; tell me when you've finished reading the book; we can't watch TV until we've**

fire

finished the washing up; the film finished at 10.30.
finishes—finishing—finished—has finished

finish off, *verb*

ينهي تماماً

to do something completely; **have you finished off your work?**

finish up, *verb*

أ) ينتهي (به) الأمر في ..

(*a*) to be in the end; **we got lost and finished up in south London.**

ب) يأتي على

(*b*) to eat something completely; **you must finish up your potatoes** = eat them all.

Note: **he finished his work off** *or* **he finished off his work, finish up your meat** *or* **finish your meat up,** *etc, but only* **finish it off, finish it up,** *etc.*

finish with, *verb*

ينتهي من استعمال (أو فعل شيء ما) : هل انتهيت من قراءة الصحيفة ؟

to finish using something; **have you finished with the newspaper? can I borrow the tin opener when you've finished with it?**

fire ['faɪə] **1.** *noun*

١ ـ نار

something which is burning/which heats; **we sat in front of a gas fire; we made a big fire in the garden to burn the dead leaves.**

يشتعل ـ تنتقل النار (إليه)

to catch fire = to start to burn because of something else which is burning; **the house caught fire; take that carpet away—it might catch fire.**

يُضرم النار في

to set fire to = to make something start burning; **his cigarette set fire to the chair.**

مشتعل

on fire = burning; **phone the fire station—the house is on fire.**
2. *verb*

first

٢ ـ يطلق النار

to shoot a gun; **the police fired at the car; we could hear the guns firing in the distance.**
fires—firing—fired—has fired

fireman, *noun*

الاطفائي

man who tries to put out fires; **the firemen were fighting the fire in the town centre.**
plural **firemen**

fireplace, *noun*

مُسْتَوْقَد ـ مُصطَلَى

place in a room where you can light a fire with coal or wood to heat the room.

firm [fɜːm] **1.** *noun*

١ ـ شركة

business company; **he works for a firm of engineers; it is the biggest engineering firm in the country.**

2. *adjective*

٢ ـ قوي ـ راسخ ـ صلب ـ ثابت

solid/strong; **make sure that chair is firm before you sit on it.**
firm—firmer—firmest

firmly, *adverb*

بحزم ـ بعزم ـ بشدة

in a strong way; **she told them firmly to keep quiet.**

first [fɜːst] **1. 1st** *adjective & noun*

١ ـ أوّل ـ الأول

referring to one; **my birthday is on the first of August/August the first (August 1st); King Charles the First (Charles I); it's the baby's first birthday on Tuesday; the post office is the first building on the left.**
Note: with dates **first** *is usually written* **1st: August 1st, 1980: December 1st, 1669;** *with names of kings and queens* **first** *is usually written* **I: King Charles I**

2. *adverb*

one hundred and nine 109

fish

٢ - أ) في الطليعة - أولاً

(a) at the beginning/before doing anything else; **he came first in the race; do your homework first, and then we can go out.**

ب) لأول مرّة

(b) for the first time; **when did you first go to Germany?**

في البداية

at first = at the beginning; **he didn't like his job at first but later got used to it; at first I didn't want to go to the party, but then I changed my mind.**

first class, noun & adverb
الدرجة الأولى - من الدرجة الأولى - في الدرجة الأولى

most expensive seats in a train or plane; most expensive and fastest way of sending a letter; **a first class ticket to Edinburgh; he always travels first class; send that letter first class—I want it to arrive quickly; first class is always very comfortable.**

fish [fɪʃ] noun

سمك - سمكة

animal which lives in water and which you can usually eat; **look at all those fish in the lake; I caught six little fish; we're having fish and chips for dinner.**
plural is usually **fish: some fish; three fish**

fishing, noun

صيد السمك

sport where you try to catch fish; **he goes fishing every weekend.**

fit [fɪt] **1.** adjective

١ - سليم - مهيّأ - مُعَدّ

in good condition for something; **he isn't fit enough to work** = he is still too ill to work; **you'll have to get fit before the football match.**
fit—fitter—fittest

2. verb

٢ - أ) يلائم مقاييس الجسم

(a) to be the right size/shape; **he's grown so tall that his trousers don't fit him any more; these shoes don't fit me—they're too tight.**

ب) يزوّد بـ - يُعدُّ - يطابق

(b) to put in place; **I want to fit a new bath in the bathroom; the sitting room has a fitted carpet** = has a carpet which is made to cover all the floor.
fits—fitting—fitted—has fitted

fit in, verb

يتطابق مع - يستوعب

to arrange something so that it goes into the space allowed for it; **I don't think I can fit in any holidays this year as I have too much work; how can you fit everything into that little box?**

five [faɪv] number 5

خمس - خمسة (العدد ٥)

she drank five cups of coffee; he's five (years old); come for tea at five (o'clock).

fix [fɪks] verb

أ) ثبّت - ربط

(a) to fasten/to attach; **he fixed the cupboard to the wall; she fixed a notice to the post with string.**

ب) يُصلح (خللاً)

(b) to mend; **can you fix the car engine for me?**

ت) يحدد (موعداً)

(c) to arrange; **the meeting has been fixed for next week.**
fixes—fixing—fixed—has fixed

fix up, verb

يتخذ الترتيبات أو الاستعدادات

to arrange; **we've fixed up for a car to meet us at the airport; can you fix me up with a room for two nights?**

flag

flag [flæg] noun

أ) عَلَم - راية

(a) piece of cloth with a pattern on it which is attached to a pole, to show a country/a club, etc.; **each ship carries the flag of its country; a ship flying the**

flame

British flag; for the party, we hung flags across the street.

(ب) بطاقة تبرعات (للجمعيات الخيرية)

(b) small paper sign sold to get money for sick people, etc.; he was selling flags for the Red Cross.

flame [fleɪm] *noun*

شُعلة

bright light coming from something which is burning; **the flame of a candle; the house was in flames** = was burning; **the car burst into flames** = suddenly started to burn.

flash [flæʃ] **1.** *noun*

١ ـ لَمْع ـ بَرْق ـ موجز للأخبار

sudden light; **a flash of lightning;** if you want to take a photograph in the dark, you should use a flash; **a news flash** = short piece of important news.
plural **flashes**
2. *verb*

٢ ـ أ) يلْمَع

(a) to shine (a light) very quickly; **the light flashed twice; a police car has a blue flashing light; he flashed his torch in my eyes.**

ب) ينطلق بسرعة البرق

(b) to go very quickly; **the car flashed past the traffic lights.**
flashes—flashing—flashed—has flashed

flat [flæt] **1.** *adjective & adverb*

١ ـ منبسط ـ مستو ـ مُسَطَّح ممَهَّد ـ مُفَرَّغ من الهواء (يقال عَنْ عجلة السيارة)

level; **a flat road; spread the paper out flat on the table; the soldiers lay flat on the ground; a flat tyre** = tyre which has lost all the air in it.

ينفذ كل طاقته في ـ يعمل بجهد

flat out = at full speed/working very hard; **he worked flat out to finish his work on time.**

2. *noun (American:* **apartment)**

٢ ـ شقة (في مبنى) ـ دور ـ طابق

flood

separate group of rooms for one family, usually in a building with several similar groups of rooms; **they live in a block of flats; their flat is on the top floor; he has a flat in London and a house in the country.**

flew [fluː] *see* **fly**

ملاحظة : انظر إلى كلمة fly

flies [flaɪz] *see* **fly**

ملاحظة : انظر إلى كلمة fly

flight [flaɪt] *noun*

أ) رحلة بالطائرة

(a) journey through the air; **the flight to New York leaves in 15 minutes; there are six flights a day to Glasgow; when does the New York flight leave? how long is the flight from London to Madrid? the flight lasts about 3 hours.**

ب) مجموعة متواصلة من درجات سلّم

(b) **flight of stairs** = set of stairs which go up straight; **turn left at the top of the first flight of stairs.**

float [fləʊt] *verb*

يَعُوم ـ يطفو

to lie on top of a liquid/not to sink; **leaves were floating on the lake; he put his model boat into the water and it floated.**
floats—floating—floated—has floated

flood [flʌd] **1.** *noun*

١ ـ فيضان ـ طوفان

large amount of water over land which is usually dry; **after the rainstorm there were floods in the valley.**
2. *verb*

٢ ـ يغمر بالمياه

to cover with a large amount of water; **the fields were flooded; the washing machine flooded the kitchen floor.**
floods—flooding—flooded—has flooded

one hundred and eleven 111

floor

floor [flɔː] *noun*

أ) أرض (الحجرة)

(a) part of a room on which you walk; put that box down on the floor; she lay on the floor and looked up at the ceiling.

ب) دور ـ طابق (في بناية)

(b) all the rooms on one level in a building; **the shop is on the ground floor** = the floor which is level with the street; **his office is on the second floor**; he walked up the stairs to the top floor.

flour ['flaʊə] *noun*

طحين ـ دقيق (قمح مطحون)

seeds of cereal crushed to powder, used for making bread and cakes, etc.; **brown flour** = flour where most of the seed is left in; **white flour** = flour where only the centre of the seed has been crushed.

no plural

flow [fləʊ] *verb*

يجري (يقال عن سائل) : كانت المياه تجري في الأنابيب

to go past like a liquid; the water flowed down the pipe; the traffic was flowing around the square; the river flows into the sea.

flows—flowing—flowed—has flowed

flower ['flaʊə] **1.** *noun*

١ ـ زهرة

part of a plant which usually has a bright colour, which attracts bees, and which then forms fruit; she picked a bunch of flowers; **the apple trees are in flower** = they are covered with flowers.

2. *verb*

٢ ـ يُزْهِر

to produce flowers; the apple trees flowered early this year; this plant only flowers once every ten years.

flowers—flowering—flowered—has flowered

fold

flown [fləʊn] *see* **fly**

ملاحظة : انظر إلى كلمة fly

flu [fluː] *noun*

الانفلونزا (مرض)

common illness like a bad cold, but with a fever; he's in bed with flu; she caught flu and had to stay at home; there is a lot of flu about in the winter.

fly [flaɪ] **1.** *noun*

١ ـ ذبابة

small insect with two wings, often living in houses; try to kill that fly; flies can walk on the ceiling.

plural **flies**

2. *verb*

٢ ـ أ) يقود طائرة ـ يطير ـ يسافر بالطائرة

(a) to move through the air; to make (a plane) move through the air; he is flying his own plane; the birds flew away; I'm flying to Hong Kong next week; to go from London to Italy you have to fly over France; he has flown across the Atlantic twice.

ب) يرفع راية (يقال عن سفينة)

(b) to put up (a flag); the ship was flying a British flag.

flies—flying—flew—has flown

fog [fɒg] *noun*

ضباب

thick cloud near the ground which it is difficult to see through; the planes couldn't take off because of fog; the fog is so thick that you must drive slowly.

foggy, *adjective*

مُضبّب ـ كثيف الضباب

covered in a fog; foggy weather; he walked around the foggy streets; don't drive fast when it's foggy.

foggy—foggier—foggiest

fold [fəʊld] *verb*

يَطْوي ـ يَثْني

to bend something so that part of it is on top of the rest; he folded the letter and

112　　　　　　　　　　　　　　　　*one hundred and twelve*

follow

put it in an envelope; he folded the letter and put it in an envelope; he folded up the newspaper; **to fold your arms** = to rest one arm on the other across your chest.
folds—folding—folded—has folded

follow ['fɒləʊ] *verb*

أ) يَتْبَع ـ يمشي وراء ـ يلاحق

(a) to come after or behind; **follow me and I will show you the way; C follows B in the alphabet; the police followed the man across the town; look at the following pages.**

ب) يلي

(b) to be the result of something; **if he wrote the letter, it follows that he must have known the news.**
follows—following—followed—has followed

fond of ['fɒnd 'ɒv] *adjective*

مُولع بـ ـ مُغْرَم بـ

having a liking for; **I'm fond of food; she's fond of dancing** = she likes dancing; **he's very fond of cheese; I'm not very fond of loud music.**
fond—fonder—fondest

food [fu:d] *noun*

طعام ـ غذاء ـ قوت ـ مأكولات

things which you eat; **this restaurant is famous for its food; do you like Chinese food? we went on a picnic but forgot to bring the food; this food tastes funny.**
food *is usually used in the singular*

foot [fʊt] *noun*

أ) قَدَم ـ سيراً على الأقدام

(a) end part of your leg on which you stand; **he has got big feet; you trod on my foot; on foot** = walking; **we went to the shops on foot; don't wait for the bus—it's quicker to go on foot; he put his foot in it** = he said something by mistake which annoyed someone.

one hundred and thirteen

foot

ب) سفح ـ أسفل ـ قعر ـ أدنى

(b) bottom part/end; **he sat at the foot of the stairs; the house is at the foot of the hill; the page number is at the foot of the page.**

ت) قدم (قياس للمسافة أو الطول يقارب ٣٠ سنتمتر)

(c) measurement of how long something is (= 30 centimetres); **the table is three feet/three foot wide; he is almost six foot tall; she is five foot six inches tall (5″ 6′;** *say* **'she's five foot six').**
plural **feet**
Note: often with numbers **foot** *has no plural:* **six foot tall; three foot wide**
Note: with numbers **foot** *is often written* ′: **a 6′ ladder; he is 5′ 6″ (five foot six);** *see also* **inch**

football, *noun*

أ) كرة القدم (نفسها)

(a) ball used for kicking; **he was kicking a football about in the garden; throw me that football.**

ب) لعبة كرة القدم ـ القدم

(b) game played by two teams with a ball which can be kicked; **rugby football** = type of football played with an egg-shaped ball which is thrown as well as kicked; **a football match; they were playing football in the field; come and have a game of football; do you always watch the football matches/games on TV?**

football field, football ground, *noun*

ملعب (لكرة القدم)

place where football is played.

footpath, *noun*

ممرّ المشاة ـ رصيف

path for people to walk on, but not to ride on.

footstep, *noun*

ضجة خطوات

sound made by a foot touching the ground; **we heard quiet footsteps outside the room.**

113

for

for [fɔː] *preposition*

١) لِغَرَضْ

(a) (*showing how something is used*) **this box is for old papers; what's that key for? what did she say that for?** = why did she say that?

ب) بمناسبة

(b) (*showing why something is given*) **what did your parents give you for Christmas? what shall we buy John for his birthday?**

ت) لـ - إلى

(c) (*showing person who gets something*) **the postman has brought a parcel for you; this present is for your mother.**

ث) لِمُدّة

(d) (*showing how long something happens*) **he has gone to the United States for a week; I have been waiting for hours.**

ج) نحو - باتجاه

(e) (*showing direction*) **is this the train for London?**

اما بالنسبة لـ

as for = as far as something is concerned; **as for me, I'm going to bed.**

إلى الأبد - دائماً

for ever = always; **I will love you for ever.**

مثلاً

for example/for instance = to show one thing among many; **large animals, for example elephants, are expensive to feed.**
Note: **for example** *is often written* **e.g.**

دائماً

for good = for always; **he left the house for good.**

forbid [fəˈbɪd] *verb*

يَمْنع - يُحظِّر

to tell someone not to do something; **smoking is forbidden in the cinema; the committee has forbidden any discussion of the plan; the rules of football forbid you to touch the ball.**

114

forget

forbids—forbidding—forbade [fəˈbæd]**—has forbidden**

force [fɔːs] 1. *noun*

١ - أ) قوة

(a) strength; **the tree was blown down by the force of the wind.**

ب) قوة منظمة ـ مجموعة من

(b) group of people in uniform; **the police force** = all the police; **the armed forces** = the army, navy, and air force.
2. *verb*

٢ - يُجْبِر - يُرْغم

to make someone do something; **they forced him to lie on the floor; she was forced to do whatever they wanted.**
forces—forcing—forced—has forced

forehead [ˈfɒrɪd] *noun*

جبين - جبهة

part of your face above your eyes.

foreign [ˈfɒrɪn] *adjective*

أجنبي - غريب (عادة أو لغة)

not belonging to your own country; **he speaks several foreign languages.**

foreigner, *noun*

أجنبي (شخص)

person who comes from another country.

forest [ˈfɒrɪst] *noun*

غابة

large area covered with trees; **many wild animals live in the forests of South America.**

forgave [fəˈgeɪv] *see* **forgive**

ملاحظة: انظر إلى كلمة forgive

forget [fəˈget] *verb*

يَنْسى

not to remember; **he forgot to put on his trousers; he's forgotten how to play cricket; I forgot all about my appoint-**

one hundred and fourteen

forgive

ment with the dentist; don't forget to lock the door.
forgets—forgetting—forgot [fəˈgɒt]—forgotten [fəˈgɒtn]

forgive [fəˈgɪv] *verb*

يَغْفِر - يصفح - يعفو عن - يسامِح - يتسامح مع

to stop being angry with someone who has done something bad; **she forgave him when he said he was sorry; please forgive me for being so late.**
forgives—forgiving—forgave [fəˈgeɪv]—has forgiven

forgot [fəˈgɒt], **forgotten** [fəˈgɒtn], *see* **forget**

ملاحظة : انظر إلى كلمة forget

fork [fɔːk] *noun*

شوكة (للطعام) - مِذراة

tool with a handle at one end and several sharp points at the other, used for picking things up especially when eating; **you can't eat soup with a knife and fork; use your fork to eat your meat—don't use your fingers; each person had a knife, fork and spoon; garden fork** = very large fork used for digging.

form [fɔːm] *noun*

أ) شكل - هيئة

(*a*) shape; **she has a ring in the form of a letter A.**

ب) استمارة - ورقة طلب

(*b*) paper with blank spaces which you have to write in; **you have to fill in a form when you want to pay your tax.**

ت) حالة

(*c*) state/condition; **our team was in good form and won easily; he's in good form today** = he is very amusing/is doing things well; **off form** = not very well/slightly ill.

ث) صف (مستوى معيَّن في التعليم في المدارس)

(*d*) class (in school); **he's in the top form; the little children are in the first

forward

form; sixth form** = class of children who are about 18 years old.

former [ˈfɔːmə] *adjective*

سالف . سابق

at an earlier time; **he's a former army officer** = he used to be an officer in the past.

formerly, *adverb*

سابقًا

at an earlier time; **this house was formerly a railway station; she was formerly the headmistress of the local school.**

fortnight [ˈfɔːtnaɪt] *noun*

أسبوعان - (١٤ يومًا)

two weeks; **we are going away for a fortnight to France; I'll see you in a fortnight's time; we met a fortnight ago.**

fortunate [ˈfɔːtʃənət] *adjective*

سعيد الحظ - محظوظ

lucky; **how fortunate that you happened to be there!**
fortunately, *adverb*

لحسن الحظ

luckily.

forty [ˈfɔːtɪ] *number* 40

أربعون (العدد ٤٠)

he's forty (years old); she has forty pairs of shoes; he's in his forties = he is between 40 and 49 years old.
Note: **forty-one** (41), **forty-two** (42), *but* **forty-first** (41st), **forty-second** (42nd), *etc.*

fortieth, 40th, *adjective & noun*

الأربعون

she came fortieth in the race; it's my fortieth birthday tomorrow.

forward [ˈfɔːwəd] 1. *adverb* (*also* **forwards**)

١ - نحوَ - باتجاه

towards the front; **he ran forward to shake my hand; the police asked the**

115

fought

crowd to move forward; see also **backwards**.
2. *noun*

٢ ـ اللاعب الأمامي (في لعبة الكرة)

player in football and other games who plays in the front row.

fought [fɔ:t] *see* **fight**

ملاحظة : انظر إلى كلمة **fight**

found [faʊnd] *see* **find**

ملاحظة : انظر إلى كلمة **find**

four [fɔ:] number 4

أربع ـ أربعة (العدد ٤)

she's four (years old); come and see me at four (o'clock); a square has four corners.

fourteen, number 14

أربع عشرة ـ أربعة عشر

I have fourteen books to read for my exam; she's fourteen (years old).

fourteenth, 14th, *adjective & noun*

الرابع عشر ـ الرابعة عشر

she came fourteenth in her race; the fourteenth of July/July the fourteenth (July 14th); it was his forteenth birthday yesterday.

fourth, 4th, *adjective & noun*

الرابع ـ الرابعة ـ رُبع (أي ٢٥٪)

they live in the fourth house from the corner; the fourth of August/August the fourth (August 4th); Charles the Fourth (Charles IV); it's her fourth birthday tomorrow; a fourth = 25%.
Note: instead of 'a fourth' or 'a fourth part' you usually say 'a quarter'.
Note: with dates **fourth** *is usually written* **4th**: *June 4th, 1979; August 4th, 1981; with names of kings and queens* **fourth** *is usually written* **IV**: **King Charles IV**

frame [freɪm] *noun*

هيكل

main part of a building/ship/bicycle,

freeze

etc., which holds it together; **the bicycle has a very light frame; I've broken the frame of my glasses; picture frame** =

هيكل خشبي يحيط بصورة أو بلوحة

wooden edge round a picture.

free [fri:] *adjective*

أ) غير مشغول ـ شاغر

(*a*) not busy/not occupied; **are you free tonight? there is a table free in the corner of the restaurant.**

ب) مَجَّاني

(*b*) not costing any money; **if you cut off the top of the cereals box you can get a free book; I didn't pay anything for my ticket—I got it free! children are admitted free, but adults have to pay £1.**

ت) حرّ

(*c*) able to do what you want/not forced to do anything; **he's free to do what he wants; it's a free country.**
free—freer—freest

freeze [fri:z] *verb*

أ) يَتَجمَّد (بفعل البرد) ـ يشعر ببرد شديد

(*a*) to be so cold that water turns to ice; **it is freezing outside; they say it will freeze tomorrow; I'm freezing** = I'm very cold.

ب) يُثَلَّج ـ يصبح جليداً

(*b*) to make something very cold; to become very cold; **I'll cook some frozen peas to eat with the fish; we freeze a lot of vegetables from our garden; the river has frozen over** = is covered with ice.
freezes—freezing—froze [frəʊz]—**has frozen** ['frəʊzn]

freezer, *noun*

ثلاجة

powerful refrigerator which keeps food frozen.

freeze up, *verb*

يصبح جليداً بالكامل

to freeze completely; **all the pipes in the house froze up.**

116　　　　　　　　　　　　　　　　　　　　　*one hundred and sixteen*

frequent

frequent ['fri:kwənt] *adjective*

متكرر ـ مألوف

which happens or comes often; **there are frequent trains to London; she is a frequent visitor.**

frequently, *adverb*

كثيراً ـ تكراراً

happening often; **it frequently rains in the west of the country.**

fresh [freʃ] *adjective*

١) نظيف ـ غير مستعمل

(*a*) not used/not dirty; **I'll get some fresh towels; fresh air** = open air; **they came out of the mine into the fresh air.**

ب) طازج

(*b*) recently made; **fresh bread.**

ت) طازج وطبيعي (غير مُعلّب أو مثلّج)

(*c*) not tinned or frozen; **fresh fish; fresh fruit salad; fresh vegetables are expensive in winter.**

fresh—fresher—freshest

Friday ['fraɪdɪ] *noun*

الجمعة (يوم الجمعة)

day between Thursday and Saturday, the fifth day of the week; **he came to see me last Friday; we always go to the cinema on Fridays; I'll see you next Friday; today is Friday, June 20th.**

fridge [frɪdʒ] *noun*

ثلاجة ـ برّاد (لحفظ الأطعمة باردة وطازجة)

refrigerator/machine in the kitchen for keeping food cold; **put the butter in the fridge; there's no milk left in the fridge; shut the fridge door.**

fried [fraɪd] *see* **fry**

ملاحظة : انظر إلى كلمة fry

friend [frend] *noun*

صديق

person whom you know well and like; **Henry is my best friend; she's going on holiday with some friends from college;**

to make friends with someone = to get to know and like someone; **these are the people we made friends with on holiday.**

friendly, *adjective*

ودود ـ محب ـ صديق

kind/helpful; **don't be afraid of the dog—he's very friendly; we're on friendly terms with the people who live next door** = we are friends.

friendly—friendlier—friendliest

fries [fraɪz] *see* **fry**

ملاحظة : انظر إلى كلمة fry

frighten [fraɪtn] *verb*

يُرعب ـ يرتعب

to make someone afraid; **the noise frightened me; a frightening film about insects which eat people.**

frightens—frightening—frightened—has frightened

frightened, *adjective*

مرتعب

afraid; **I'm frightened of spiders; don't leave me alone—I'm frightened of the dark.**

frog [frɒg] *noun*

ضِفْدَع

small animal with no tail, which lives in water or on land and can jump; **a little green frog jumped into the river.**

from [frɒm] *preposition*

أ) من (٢ من أصل ٣)

(*a*) out of; **take two from three, and you have one left; he comes from America.**

ب) من (من مكان إلى آخر)

(*b*) (*showing where something starts or started*) **the bee moved from flower to flower; I'll be at home from 9 o'clock in the morning; she works from Monday to Friday; it is 2 km from here to the post office; here's a letter from Peter.**

ت) عن

(*c*) (*showing difference*) **I can't tell**

front

butter from margarine; your job is very different from mine.

(د) بسبب

(d) (showing cause) he died from his disease; she suffers from colds.

front [frʌnt] noun

واجهة (مبنى) ـ جبهة (عسكرية) ـ صفحة أمامية (من كتاب)

part of something which faces forwards; the front of the house faces south; there is a picture of the Tower of London on the front of the book; he spilt soup down the front of his shirt; there was a photograph of him on the front page of the newspaper.

مواجه لـ ـ بمقابل

in front of = on the front side of something; he was standing in front of the bus when it suddenly started; there are two people in front of me in the queue; park your car in front of the house.

frost [frɒst] noun

جليد (سائل مجمّد)

freezing weather when the temperature is below the freezing point of water; there was a frost last night.

froze [frəʊz], **frozen** ['frəʊzn] see **freeze**

ملاحظة: انظر إلى كلمة **freeze**

fruit [fruːt] noun

ثَمَرة

part of a plant which contains the seeds, and which is often eaten; can you buy me some fruit at the market? his garden is full of fruit trees; we ought to eat all the fruit quickly or it will go bad; **fruit salad** = pieces of fruit chopped up and mixed together.

no plural: **some fruit/a lot of fruit**

fry [fraɪ] verb

يَقْلي (بالزيت أو السمن)

to cook in hot oil or fat; fried eggs; do you want your eggs fried or boiled? he was frying onions in the kitchen.

fries [fraɪz]—**frying—fried** [fraɪd]—**has fried**

frying pan, noun

مِقْلاة

wide pan with low sides and a long handle, used for frying.

fun

full [fʊl] adjective

أ) ملىء ـ مقتظ ـ حاشد ـ حافل

(a) with as much inside as possible; **is the bottle full? the bag is full of apples; the bus was so full we couldn't get on; I'm full up** = I have eaten so much that I can't eat any more.

ب) كامل

(b) complete; you must write down the full details of your job; he got **full marks** = 100%; children over 12 must pay **full fare** = the same fare as an adult; **full moon** = when the moon is round.

نقطة : (علامة توقف كامل للجملة)

full stop = dot (.) at the end of a written sentence.

full—fuller—fullest

fun [fʌn] noun

تسلية ـ مرح ـ هزل ـ مزاح

amusement; **we had some fun on the beach** = we enjoyed ourselves; **to make fun of someone** = to laugh at someone; **for fun** = as a joke; she poured water down his neck for fun.

funny, adjective

أ) مُضْحك

(a) which makes you laugh; we saw a funny programme on TV; she wore a funny hat; let me tell you a funny story about my brother.

ب) غريب ـ غير طبيعي

(b) strange/odd; he was behaving in a funny way; there's a funny smell in the kitchen.

funny—funnier—funniest

fur

fur [fɜː] *noun*

فرو

thick hair on an animal; **our cat has soft white fur; the lady was wearing a fur coat.**

furry, *adjective*

فروي - مفري

covered with fur; **a little furry animal.**

furnish [ˈfɜːnɪʃ] *verb*

يُجهّز بالأثاث - يزوّد بالمفروشات

to put chairs/tables/beds, etc., into a room or house; **they have a small furnished flat** = a flat with all the furniture provided.

furnishes—furnishing— furnished—has furnished

furniture [ˈfɜːnɪtʃə] *noun*

مفروشات - أثاث

tables / chairs / beds / cupboards, etc.; **someone has stolen all our furniture; you should move the furniture out of the room before you paint the ceiling.**

no plural: **some furniture; a lot of furniture; a piece of furniture**

garage

further [ˈfɜːðə] *adverb & adjective*

أ) إلى مسافة أبعد

(a) at a greater distance away; **can you move further back? they went further away; the post office is further away than the police station; Edinburgh is further from London than Paris.**

ب) مزيد من - إضافي

(b) more; **we want further information; can you give me further details of when the accident took place?**

furthest, *adverb & adjective*

الأبعد مسافةً

at the greatest distance; **he lives furthest from the office; the furthest distance I have travelled by train is 800 km.**

future [ˈfjuːtʃə] *noun*

أ) مستقبل

(a) time which has not yet happened; **in the future, I will try to eat less; I'll be more careful in future** = next time this happens.

ب) فعل المضارع

(b) (*also* **future tense**) part of a verb which shows that something will happen; **'he will go' and 'he is going to go' are forms of the future of 'to go'.**

Gg

gallon [ˈgælən] *noun*

غالون : (مقياس للسوائل)

measurement of liquids which equals eight pints or 4.5 litres; **the car does thirty miles to the gallon** = each gallon of petrol is enough to drive thirty miles; **the bucket can hold two gallons.**

game [geɪm] *noun*

أ) لعبة - مباراة

(a) sport which you play, and which you can win because of your skill, strength or luck; **would you like a game of tennis? he's not very good at games; our side have won all their games this year.**

ب) جزء من المباراة

(b) single round which is part of a tennis match; **he's winning by six games to three.**

garage [ˈgærɪdʒ] *noun*

أ) مَرْآب للسيارات

(a) small building where you can keep a car; **put the car into the garage; he drove**

one hundred and nineteen 119

garden

the car out of the garage; don't forget to lock the garage door.

(ب) مَرْأب (لاصلاح السيارات)

(b) business where petrol is sold and cars, etc., are repaired; **where's the nearest garage?—my car has broken down; I can't drive you to the station—my car is in the garage.**

garden ['gɑ:dn] *noun*

أ) حديقة ـ بستان

(a) (*American:* **yard**) ground used for growing vegetables, flowers, etc., usually near a house; **he grows tomatoes in his back garden; your mother's sitting in the garden.**

ب) حديقة عامة

(b) **public gardens** = place belonging to a town where there are flowers and grass and where people can go to walk around and enjoy themselves.

garden centre, *noun*

مشتل ـ مكان لبيع الشتل وحبوب الزهر والأشجار

place which sells plants/seeds, etc., and equipment for gardening.

gardener, *noun*

البستاني ـ الجنائني

person who looks after a garden.

gardening, *noun*

الاعتناء بالبستان

looking after a garden; **he likes gardening; she does some gardening every Saturday.**

gas [gæs] *noun*

أ) غاز

(a) something which, like air, has no shape and cannot usually be seen; often produced from coal or found underground, and used to cook or heat; **a gas cooker; we heat our house by gas; there is a gas fire in the dining room.**

(ب) (بالاميركية) ـ وقود ـ بنزين

(b) *American* = **petrol**
plural **gases** *is only used to mean different types of gas*

general

gate [geɪt] *noun*

أ) بوابة خارجية ـ مدخل

(a) outside door which is in an open wall or fence; **if you leave the gate open, the sheep will get out of the field; shut the gate; there is a white gate in the garden wall.**

ب) بوابة (تقود إلى الطائرة)

(b) door which leads to an aircraft at an airport; **go to gate 25 for flight AB193.**

gather ['gæðə] *verb*

أ) يَجْمَع ـ يَتَجَمَّع

(a) to bring together/to collect; **she was gathering peas; the speaker gathered up his papers; the children gathered round the Christmas tree.**

ب) يعتقد ـ يستنتج

(b) to understand; **I gather you're leaving for Africa tomorrow; did you gather who will be speaking at the ceremony? gathers—gathering—gathered—has gathered**

gave [geɪv] *see* **give**

ملاحظة : انظر إلى كلمة give

general ['dʒenrəl] **1.** *adjective*

١ ـ عام ـ يخصّ الجميع

not particular; which concerns everything or everybody; **there was a general feeling of excitement; a general election** = election where all the voters in a country can vote; **in general** = normally; **in general, the winters are wet and cold.**
2. *noun*

٢ ـ لواء (جنرال) : قائد برتبة لواء

important officer in the army; **General Robinson.**

generally, *adverb*

عموماً ـ في العموم ـ عادة

normally; **we generally spend our holidays in Holland.**

generous

generous ['dʒenrəs] *adjective*

كريم - سخي

willing to give money, etc.; **she is very generous with her money; that's very generous of you; the firm will give a very generous sum** = will give a lot of money.

gentle ['dʒentl] *adjective*

لطيف - دَمِث

soft; kind; **the doctor has gentle hands; you must be gentle when you are holding a little baby.**

gentle—gentler—gentlest

gentleman, *noun*

أ) سيد (طريقة مهذبة للتعبير عن رجل ما)

(*a*) (*polite way of referring to men*) **well, gentlemen, you may sit down.**

ب) نبيل الأخلاق ومهذب

(*b*) polite man; **he's a real gentleman.**

geography ['dʒɒgrəfɪ] *noun*

جغرافية - علم الجغرافية

study of the earth/weather/countries, etc.; **geography is my best subject; he got top marks in geography; I've lost my geography book.**

no plural

get [get] *verb*

أ) ينال - يحصل على - يملك

(*a*) to have/receive; **I got a letter this morning; she will get £10 for cutting the grass; he gets more money than I do.**

ب) يصل إلى

(*b*) to arrive; **we got home late; when will you get to London?**

ت) يصبح - يصير في حالة ما

(*c*) to become; **he's getting old; she got fat from eating too much; the light got brighter and brighter; this towel's getting dirty.**

ث) يجعل - يجبر على

(*d*) to make something happen; to pay someone to do something; to persuade someone to do something; **I must get my shoes mended; can you get the garage to fill up my car? I'll try and get him to bring his car.**

ج) يَجب على ... يجب ان ... يتعَيَّن على

(*e*) to have got to = must; **you have got to come** = you must come; **he left early because he had got to drive a long way; has she got to work all night?**

يُمنى بـ - يُصاب بـ

(*f*) to catch (a disease); **I think I'm getting a cold; she's got flu.**

ملاحظة : تستعمل مع الأفعال الماضية أو الصفات ولا تترجم حرفياً بالعربية

(*g*) used with adjectives or past of verbs to mean to do; **I got my work finished in time; she's getting the dinner ready.**

gets—getting—got [gɒt]—has got

get across, *verb*

أ) يَعْبُر - يَجعله يعبر

(*a*) to go across; **they got across the river by boat.**

ب) يجعله مفهوماً - يُوَضِّح

(*b*) to make someone understand; **we managed to get the message across, although no one understood English; I'm trying to get across to him that he has to work harder.**

get along, *verb*

ينجح في تدبير شيء ما - ينسجم مع

to manage/to work; **we seem to get along quite well without any electricity.**

get around, *verb*

يَتَنَقل

to move about; **since she had the accident she gets around on two sticks; the news soon got around that he was married.**

get away, *verb*

يفرّ - يهرب

to escape; **the burglars got away in a stolen car.**

get back, *verb*

أ) يعود - يرجع

(*a*) to return; **we got back home very late; when did you get back from holiday?**

get

ب) يسترد

(b) to get something again which you had before; **he got his book back; I want to get my coat back.**

get down, verb

أ) ينزل

(a) to go down; **she got down off the ladder.**

ب) يجلب إلى الأرض أو إلى أسفل

(b) to bring down; **can you get that box down for me?**

get down to, verb

يبدأ بالتركيز على

to start working hard; **he will have to get down to work if he wants to pass his exams.**

get dressed, verb

يرتدي ثيابه

to put your clothes on; **he got dressed quickly because he didn't want to be late for work; she was getting dressed when the phone rang.**

get in, verb

يَدْخل

to go inside (a car, etc.); **hurry up and get in—the train is waiting to leave; she got in and sat down; the burglars got in through the kitchen window.**

get into, verb

يدخل

to go inside (a car, etc.); **he got into the car and sat down; I was getting into bed when the phone rang; the burglars got into the house through the kitchen window.**

Note: **get into** *is followed by a noun*

get off, verb

يترجّل (عن دراجة أو حافلة)

to come down from; **he got off his bicycle; you must get off the bus at the next stop.**

get on, verb

أ) يدخل إلى - يصعد إلى - يركب

(a) to go into (a bus, etc.); **we got on the bus at the post office; she got on her bike and rode away.**

ب) يتقدم في السن - يصبح عجوزاً

(b) to become old; **he's getting on and is quite deaf.**

get on with, verb

أ) ينسجم مع - يتفق بلا طباع مع

(a) to be friendly with someone; **he gets on very well with everyone; I didn't get on with the boss.**

ب) يتابع

(b) to continue to do some work; **I must get on with my homework.**

get out, verb

أ) يستخرج

(a) to take out; **get your books out of the box; he was getting his car out of the garage.**

ب) يخرج

(b) to go outside; **she was getting out of her car; the lorry stopped and the driver got out; the burglars got out through the front door.**

get over, verb

يتغلب على (مرض أو صعوبة أو مشكلة)

to become better after an illness or shock; **he got over his cold; she never got over her mother's death.**

get through, verb

أ) يمرّ من خلال

(a) to go through; **the sheep got through the hole in the hedge.**

ب) يجتاز (امتحان) بنجاح

(b) to be successful; **she got through all her exams.**

get up, verb

ينهض

to stand up; to get out of bed; **he got up from his chair and walked out of the room; what time did you get up? I was getting up when the phone rang.**

girl [gɜ:l] *noun*

فتاة

female child; **she's only a little girl; they have three children—two boys and a**

give

girl; he met a girl at the bus stop; my sister goes to the girls' school.

give [gɪv] *verb*

يعطي - يَمنح - يهب

to pass something to someone (e.g. as a present); **I gave him a watch for his birthday; give me another apple; she gave him a kiss; you ought to give that book to the teacher.**
gives — giving — gave [geɪv] **— has given**

give back, *verb*

يُعيد

to hand something back to someone; **give me back my watch/give me my watch back; he gave back everything he had stolen.**

give in, *verb*

يستسلم

to agree with something even if you did not like it before; **we asked him every day if we could go to the cinema, and in the end he gave in** = he said we could go.

give out, *verb*

يَنْفَذ

to come to an end; **the battery has given out so I can't use my radio.**

give up, *verb*

يَكُفُّ عن

to stop doing something; **he's given up smoking; I give up!** = I will never guess the answer, please tell me.

glad [glæd] *adjective*

مسرور - مبتهج

pleased; **I'm glad to see you; we're glad you came; she was glad to sit down.**

glass [glɒːs] *noun*

أ) زجاج

(*a*) material which you can see through, used to make windows; **the doors are made of glass; a glass roof; the car has black glass windows.**
no plural: **some glass; a piece of glass**

go

ب) كأس

(*b*) thing to drink out of, usually made of glass; **put the glasses on the table; he broke a glass as he was washing up; give him some more milk, his glass is empty.**

ت) ملء كأس أو إناء

(*c*) contents of a glass; **he drinks a glass of milk every evening; two glasses of wine.**
plural **glasses** *for (b) and (c)*

glasses, *plural noun*

نظارتان

pieces of glass which you wear in front of your eyes to help you see better; **she was wearing dark glasses; he has glasses with gold frames; can you see my glasses anywhere?**

glove [glʌv] *noun*

قفاز

piece of clothing which you wear on your hand; **the doctor was wearing rubber gloves; I've bought a new pair of gloves; put your gloves on if you are going to play in the snow.**

glue [gluː] **1.** *noun*

١ - غراء

material which sticks things together; **you can mend the broken cup with glue; he put some glue on the teacher's chair.**
no plural: **some glue; a tube of glue**
2. *verb*

٢ - يُغَرِّي

to stick things together with glue; **he glued the handle on to the cup; she's glued the pieces together.**
glues — glueing — glued — has glued

go [gəʊ] *verb*

أ) يذهب - يرحـل - يسافـر - يجتاز - يمضي - يتسلق - ينزل

(*a*) to move from one place to another; **he has gone to New York; she went from London to Berlin; they all went across the street; he went down the stairs; the**

one hundred and twenty-three   **123**

goal

car went up the hill; do you go to school by bus? she has gone shopping; we all went for a walk.

ب) يجري - يدور - يعمل بالطريقة الملائمة
(b) to work; my watch won't go; the car is going smoothly; I'm trying to get my motorbike to go.

ت) يذهب
(c) to leave; it's time for us to go.

ث) ينطبق - يكون موضعه في أو على
(d) to fit; this box won't go into the back of the car; this book goes on the top shelf.

ج) يصبح
(e) to become; she went pale; he went bright red; the old lady is going deaf.
goes—going—went [went]**—has gone** [gɔn]

to be going to, verb

يوشك ان - يعزم ان
to be just about to do something; to intend to do something; that tree is going to fall down; are you going to sing? it's going to be fine tomorrow; I am going to read my newspaper.

go away, verb

ينصرف - يبتعد
to leave; they went away and we never saw them again.

go back, verb

يعود إلى
to return; he went back home; let's all go back to the bus stop.

go on, verb

أ) يثابر - يواصل
(a) to continue; go on, don't stop; he went on singing; go on with your work.

ب) يجري - يحدث
(b) to happen; what has been going on here?

go without, verb

يبقى من غير (الحصول على)
not to have something which you usually have; he got up late and had to go without breakfast; we haven't enough money so we'll have to go without a holiday this year.

good

goal [gəʊl] noun

أ) مرمى
(in games) (a) two posts between which you have to kick the ball to score a point.

ب) هدف
(b) point scored by kicking the ball between the posts; he scored a goal; our team scored six goals.

goalkeeper, noun

حارس المرمى
player in football who stands in front of the goal to stop the ball going in.

God [gɒd] noun

الله
person who made the world and to whom people pray.

gold [gəʊld] noun

ذهب
valuable yellow-coloured metal; a gold chain; she has a gold ring on her left hand; that ring isn't made of gold; gold is worth more than silver.
no plural: **some gold; a piece of gold**
golden, adjective

ذهبي - مذهب
coloured like gold; her golden hair; golden wedding = day when you have been married for fifty years.

goldfish, noun

السمك الذهبي
small orange fish which is kept as a pet; he has two goldfish in a glass bowl.
no plural: **one goldfish; three goldfish**

good [gʊd] adjective

أ) جيد - حسن - لذيذ
(a) not bad; we had a good meal; did you have a good time at the party?

ب) شاطر - بارع
(b) clever; he's good at making things out of wood; she's good with her hands.

124 **one hundred and twenty-four**

got

ت) مطيع - مهذب

(c) well behaved; **be a good girl! and I'll give you a sweet.**

ث) وافر - كثير

(d) **a good deal of/a good many** = a lot of; **he made a good deal of money; a good many people know her.**

بصورة نهائية - نهائياً - دائماً

for good = for ever; **he left the town for good.**

لا منفعة منه . معطوب

no good = useless/which doesn't work; **this radio's no good.**

good—better ['betə]**—best** [best]

goodbye, *noun & interjection used when leaving someone*

وداعاً - استودعكم الله

say goodbye to Aunt Anne; Goodbye! we'll see you again next week.

good-looking, *adjective*

وسيم - جميل الملامح - جذاب

attractive/pleasant to look at; **she's a good-looking girl; he's very good-looking.**

good morning/good afternoon/ good evening, *interjections used when meeting or leaving someone in the morning/afternoon/evening*

صباح الخير - بعد الظهر سعيد - مساء الخير

good morning, Mrs Smith; I must say good afternoon to Aunt Jane.

goodnight, *interjection used when leaving someone late in the evening*

تصبحون على خير

goodnight! sleep well!

goods, *plural noun*

البضائع

things, especially things for sale; **the goods will be on sale tomorrow; the shop sells goods from various countries.**

got [gɒt] *see* **get**

ملاحظة : انظر إلى كلمة get

govern ['gʌvn] *verb*

يَحْكم (دولة أو بلد)

to rule (a country); **the country is gov-**

grand

erned by a group of army officers. governs—governing— governed—has governed

government ['gʌvnmənt] *noun*

حكومة

group of people who rule a country; **the Prime Minister is head of the government; a military government; government employees are asking for more money.**

gradually ['grædʒuəlɪ] *adverb*

تدريجياً

little by little; **he gradually got better after his operation; the snow gradually melted.**

gram [græm] *noun*

غرام (أو جرام) (لقياس الوزن) : ١٠٠٠ غرام تساوي كيلوغرام واحد

measure of weight; **a thousand grams make one kilogram; I want 500 g.** (*say* **five hundred grams**) **of butter.**

Note: when used with numbers **gram** *is usually written* **g**

grand [grænd] *adjective*

أ) كبير

(a) looking large and important; **a grand entrance; grand piano** = large horizontal piano.

ب) رائع - ممتاز

(b) very good; **that's a grand idea; it's a grand day for a picnic.**

grand—grander—grandest

grandchild, *noun*

حفيد - حفيدة

child of a son or daughter; **old Mr and Mrs Smith have one son and three grandchildren.**

plural **grandchildren**

granddaughter, *noun*

حفيدة

daughter of a son or daughter; **old Mr and Mrs Smith have only girls in their family—they have a daughter and three granddaughters.**

grape

grandfather, *noun* جَدّ ـ سَلَفْ

father of a mother or father; **both my father's father and my mother's father are still alive, so I have two grandfathers; grandfather clock** = tall clock which stands on the floor.

Note: often called **grandad** *or* **grandpa**

grandmother, *noun* جدّة ـ سَلَفَة

mother of a mother or father; **both my grandmothers are still alive.**

Note: often called **granny** *or* **grandma**

grandparents, *plural noun*
الجدّين (الجد والجدة)

parents of a mother or father; **my wife's grandparents are staying with us.**

grandson, *noun*

حفيد (ذكر)

son of a son or daughter; **old Mr and Mrs Smith have three grandsons.**

grape [greɪp] *noun* عِنَب

fruit of a climbing plant, which can be eaten or used for making wine; **have another grape; what a beautiful bunch of grapes!**

grapefruit [ˈgreɪpfruːt] *noun* ليمون الجنة

large round yellow fruit, of the same family as oranges and lemons; **we had grapefruit for breakfast; a jar of grapefruit marmalade.**
no plural: **one grapefruit, two grapefruit**

grass [grɑːs] *noun* عشب

low green plant, which is eaten by cows and sheep in fields, or used in gardens to make lawns; **the grass is getting too long;**

great

keep off the grass! we'll sit on the grass and have our picnic.
no plural

grateful [ˈgreɪtful] *adjective*
شاكر ـ مُقِرٌّ بالجميل

showing thanks; **she was grateful for all the help she received.**

grave [greɪv] *noun*

قَبْر

place where a dead person is buried; **his grave is covered with flowers.**

gray [greɪ] *adjective*
ملاحظة: انظر إلى كلمة grey
American = **grey**

grease [griːs] **1.** *noun*
١ ـ شحم (لتشحيم المحرك أو السيارة ...)
thick oil used to put on machines to make them work smoothly; **have you put any grease on your back wheel?**
2. *verb*

٢ ـ يُشحّم

to put grease on a machine; **he was greasing the engine.**
greases—greasing—greased—has greased

greasy, *adjective*
مُزَيَّت ـ مُدْهِن ـ دُهْنِي
covered with grease; **don't wipe your greasy hands on your shirt.**
greasy—greasier—greasiest

great [greɪt] *adjective*
أ) كبير ـ كثير
(*a*) large; **he was carrying a great pile of books; she's eating a great big sandwich; a great deal of** = a lot of; **there's a great deal of work to do.**

ب) عظيم ـ شهير
(*b*) important/famous; **London is a great city; Picasso was a great artist.**
great—greater—greatest

Great Britain, *noun*

greedy

country formed of England, Scotland and Wales; **he came to live in Great Britain ten years ago.**

greatly, *adverb*

كثيراً ـ جداً

very much; **we greatly enjoyed the party.**

greedy [ˈgriːdɪ] *adjective*

شَرِه ـ طمّاع

always wanting to eat a lot of food; **don't be greedy—leave some for the others.**

greedy—greedier—greediest

green [griːn] *adjective & noun*

أخضر

of a colour like the colour of leaves; **her coat is bright green; I have painted the door dark green; he was dressed all in green; have you any paint of a lighter green than this? you can go ahead—the traffic lights are green.**

green—greener—greenest

greengrocer, *noun*

بقّال ـ بيّاع الخضار

person who sells fruit and vegetables; **the greengrocer's** = shop where you can buy fruit and vegetables; **can you go to the greengrocer's and buy some potatoes? I buy all my fruit at the greengrocer's in the High Street.**

greet [griːt] *verb*

يُرحِّب بـ ـ

to welcome someone whom you are meeting; **he greeted his mother as she got off the bus.**

greets—greeting—greeted—has greeted

greetings, *plural noun*

ترحيب ـ تحيّة ـ تمنيّات طيبة

good wishes; **to send someone birthday greetings.**

ground

بريطانيا العظمى

grew [gruː] *see* **grow**

ملاحظة: انظر إلى كلمة grow

grey [greɪ] *adjective & noun (American:* gray)

رمادي (اللون)

of a colour like a mixture of black and white; **his hair is quite grey; a grey-haired man; she was dressed all in grey; the clouds are grey—I think it is going to rain; he was wearing dark grey trousers.**

grey—greyer—greyest

grocer [ˈgrəʊsə] *noun*

بقّال ـ سمّان

person who sells sugar/butter/tins of food, etc.; **the grocer's** = shop where you can buy sugar/butter/tins of food, etc.; **can you go to the grocer's and get me a tin of beans? we buy our tea at the grocer's in the High Street.**

groceries, *plural noun*

البقالة (ما يبيعه البقّال)

things which you buy at a grocer's; **my bag is full of groceries.**

ground [graʊnd] *noun*

أ) أرض

(*a*) soil/earth; **you must dig the ground in the winter.**

ب) سطح الأرض

(*b*) surface of the earth; **the house was burnt to the ground; it has been so dry that the ground is hard; let's sit on the ground to have our picnic; he lay down on the ground and went to sleep.**

ت) أرض مخصصة لغرض معين

(*c*) place where you play a game; **football ground/cricket ground.**

ground floor, *noun*

الدور الأرضي (من مبنى)

floor (in a shop, block of flats, etc.) which is level with the street; **the clothes department is on the ground floor; he lives in a ground floor flat.**

Note: Americans call the **ground floor** *the* **first floor**

one hundred and twenty-seven 127

group

grounds, *plural noun*

أ) الأرض المحيطة لمبنى والتابعة له
(a) land around a big house; **they had a party in the grounds of the castle.**

ب) أساس ـ دوافع
(b) reasons; **what grounds have you got for saying that he should have more money?**

group [gru:p] *noun*

أ) مجموعة ـ جماعة
(a) several people/animals/things which are all close together; **a group of policemen waited at the corner of the street; let's meet at that group of trees over there.**

ب) مجموعة (من نفس الجنس أو متشابهة)
(b) way of putting similar things together; **blood group** = type of blood; **age group** = all people of a certain age.

ت) جوقة ـ فرقة موسيقية
(c) small number of people who play music together.

grow [grəʊ] *verb*

أ) يَنْمو ـ يكبر ـ ينبت
(a) to become larger (as a plant); **these trees grow very tall; cabbages grow well in our garden.**

ب) يُنْبِتُ ـ يَزرع
(b) to make plants grow; **we are growing cabbages; farmers grow grass to feed their cows.**

ت) يكبُر (يزداد طولاً أو حجماً أو عدداً)
(c) to become taller/bigger; **your son has grown since I last saw him; the population is growing very fast.**

ث) يتحول تدريجياً ـ يصبح تدريجياً
(d) to become; **it's growing colder at nights now; he grew richer all the time.**

grows—growing—grew [gru:]—**has grown**

grown-up, *noun*

البالغ ـ الراشد ـ بالغ ـ راشد
adult; **there are three grown-ups and ten children.**

guess

grow up, *verb*

يصبح بالغاً ـ يبلغ سن الرشد
to become an adult; **what do you want to do when you grow up/when you've grown up?**

growth, *noun*

نموّ ـ ازدياد ـ نشوء
increase in size; **the growth of the population since 1960.**

guard [gɑ:d] **1.** *noun*

أ) حارس ـ حرس
(a) person who protects someone or something; **armed guards were at the door of the bank.**

ب) وضع دفاعي ـ تَيَقُّظ ـ عُثِر عليه مباغتةً أو عندما لم يكن متيقظاً
(b) protection against attack; **he is on guard** = is watching out in case someone might attack; **to be caught off guard** = to be caught by surprise.

ت) كمساري قطار
(c) person in charge of a train who tells the driver when to start.

2. *verb*

٢ ـ يحرس ـ يحمي
to protect; to take care of; **the soldiers were guarding the castle.**

guards—guarding—guarded—has guarded

guess [ges] **1.** *verb*

١ ـ أ) يَخْزُر
(a) to try to imagine or think of something; **guess who is coming to see us; can you guess what we are having for dinner? he guessed right** = he got the right answer.

ب) يَظُن
(b) to think; to suppose; **I guess it's my turn to do the washing up.**

guesses—guessing—guessed—has guessed

2. *noun*

٢ ـ تَخْمين ـ حَزْر ـ ظَنّ
opinion which you reach without having

128   **one hundred and twenty-eight**

guest

any information; **do you know who is coming to see us?—I'll give you three guesses; I don't know if the answer is right—I only made a guess.**
plural **guesses**

guest [gest] *noun*

ضَيْف ـ نَزيل

person who comes to see someone and has a meal or stays the night; visitor; **all the guests in the hotel had to leave because of the fire.**

guide [gaɪd] 1. *noun*

١ ـ المرشد ـ الدليل

person/book which shows you how to do something/where to go; **I'll act as your guide to London; read this guide to doing repairs in the house.**
2. *verb*

٢ ـ يرشد ـ يدلُّ ـ يُهْدي

to show someone round a town/building/museum, etc.; **he guided his visitors round the town; guided tour** = tour where the tourists are led by a guide.
guides—guiding—guided—has guided

guide book, *noun*

دليل (كتاب يجمع معلومات وعناوين وأرقام هاتف ...)

book which tells you where to go; **a guide book to London.**

guide dog, *noun*

كلب مُدَرَّب لهداية العُمْيان

dog which shows a blind person where to go.

habit

guilty ['gɪltɪ] *adjective*

مُذْنِب

having something wrong; **the judge decided he was guilty of murder.**
guilty—guiltier—guiltiest

guitar [gɪ'taː] *noun*

قيثارة (آلة موسيقية)

musical instrument with several strings, which you play by pulling the strings with your fingers; **he likes to play the guitar; Spanish guitar music.**

gum [gʌm] *noun*

أ) مَضيغَةْ ـ عِلْكة

(*a*) sweet stuff which you chew but do not swallow.

ب) صَمْغ

(*b*) type of glue.

gun [gʌn] *noun*

مُسَدَّس ـ بندقيّة

weapon which you shoot with; **the policeman pulled out his gun; she took his gun and shot him dead.**

gym [dʒɪm] *noun*

حالة مخصصة للألعاب الرياضية

large hall where you can do exercises, play games, etc.; **we are going to watch a tennis game in the school gym.**

Hh

habit ['hæbɪt] *noun*

عادة

regular way of doing things; **he got into the habit of swimming every day before breakfast; she's got out of the habit of taking any exercise; from force of habit**

had

= because you do it regularly; **I wake up at 6 o'clock from force of habit.**

had [hæd] *see* **have**

انظر إلى كلمة have

hair [heə] *noun*

أ) شعرة

(*a*) long thread growing on your head/on the body of an animal; **the dog has left hairs all over the armchair; there's a hair in my soup; you're beginning to get some grey hairs.**

plural **hairs**

ب) شعر

(*b*) mass of hairs growing on your head; **she's got long black hair; you ought to wash your hair; his hair is too long; he is going to have his hair cut.**

no plural

haircut, *noun*

قص الشعر ـ حلاقة

cutting of hair on your head; **you need a haircut.**

hairdresser, *noun*

المُزَيِّن ـ الحَلَّاق

person who cuts/washes, etc., your hair; **you must go to the hairdresser's before the party; I met her at the hairdresser's.**

hairy, *adjective*

مكسوّ بالشعر

covered with hair; **a hairy dog; he's got hairy arms.**

hairy—hairier—hairiest

half [hɒːf] **1.** *noun*

١ ـ نصف ـ شَطْر

one of two equal parts; **he cut the apple in half; half the apple fell on the floor; our team scored a goal in the first half** = in the first part of the football match; **half of six is three.**

plural **halves** [hɑːvz]

2. *adjective*

٢ ـ نصف ـ بمقدار النصف

divided into two parts; **half an apple;**

130

ham

two and a half hours; I only want half a cup of coffee.

3. *adverb*

٣ ـ نصفيّاً . جزئياً

not completely; **the work is only half finished; this book is half as big/half as thick as that one** = it is only 50% of the size; **but this book is half as big again** = it is 150% of the size of that one.

نصف الساعة : (تعالَ إلى بيتي في السادسة والنصف)

half past = 30 minutes after an hour; **come and see me at half past six (6.30).**

half term, *noun*

عطلة نصف السنة

short holiday in the middle of a school term; **we went away for a few days at half term.**

hall [hɔːl] *noun*

أ) حجرة الجلوس ـ الصالون

(*a*) small room when you go into a house, where you can leave your coat, etc.; **don't stand in the hall, come into the dining room; I've left my umbrella in the hall.**

ب) صالة

(*b*) large room for meetings; **we all eat in the school hall; concert hall** = large building where the town council meets and where the town is governed.

hallo [həˈləʊ] *interjection showing a greeting (American:* **hi***)*

مَرْحباً ـ السلام عليكم

hallo, John, I'm glad to see you; he called hallo from the other side of the street.

also spelt **hello, hullo**

ham [hæm] *noun*

لحم مملّح (اجمالاً من فخذ الخنزير)

salt meat from the leg of a pig, usually eaten cold; **he had a ham salad; can I have two ham sandwiches, please? would you like another slice of ham?**

no plural: **some ham; a slice of ham**

one hundred and thirty

hammer

hammer ['hæmə] *noun*

مطرقة

heavy metal tool for knocking nails into wood, etc.; **he hit his thumb with the hammer.**

hand [hænd] **1.** *noun*

١ - أ) يَد

(*a*) part of the body at the end of each arm, which you use for holding things; **he had a cup in each hand; to shake hands** = to greet someone by holding their right hand; **he shook hands with me; can you lend a hand?** = can you help? **give me a hand with the washing up** = help me; **the car has changed hands** = it has a new owner; **they walked along hand in hand** = holding each other by the hand.

ب) عقرب (الساعة)

(*b*) one of the two pieces on a clock which turn round and point to the figures; **the hour hand/the minute hand.**

باليدين (لا بالآلات أو الأدوات)

by hand = using your hands and tools, but not large machines; **he made the table by hand.**

2. *verb*

٢ - يناول - يُسلِّم باليد

to pass; **can you hand me that book? he handed me all his money.**

hands—handing—handed—has handed

handbag, *noun*

حقيبة يد

small bag which women carry to hold their money/pens/handkerchiefs, etc.

handful, *noun*

حفنة - قبضة

amount you can hold in your hand; **he gave me a handful of pound notes; only a handful of people came** = very few.

handkerchief ['hæŋkətʃiːf] *noun*

منديل - مَحرمة - وشاح

piece of cloth or paper for wiping your nose; **he blew his nose into his handker-**

handwriting

chief; have you got a handkerchief, my glasses are dirty?

handmade, *adjective*

صنع يدوي

made by hand without using a machine; **a handmade table; a box of handmade chocolates.**

handle ['hændl] **1.** *noun*

مَقبَض - مَسكَة

part of an object which you hold in your hand to pick it up/to open it, etc.; **he turned the door handle; she broke the handle off the cup; the handle of my suitcase is broken.**

2. *verb*

٢ - أ) يلمس بيدة - يَمسّ

(*a*) to touch with your hands; **don't handle the fruit, please;**

ب) يعالج (موضوعاً أو مشكلة) يقوم بالمهمة جيداً

(*b*) to manage; **do you think she can handle all the work in the department? handles—handling—handled—has handled**

handlebars, *plural noun*

مقوَد الدراجة

bar on the front of a bicycle or motor-cycle which steers the front wheel; **hold on to the handlebars.**

handsome ['hænsəm] *adjective*

وسيم - جذاب

good-looking/very pleasant to look at; **a handsome young man.**

ملاحظة : تستعمل هذه الكلمة للرجال ولا للنساء أو الأطفال

Note: usually used of men, but not women or children

handwriting ['hændraɪtɪŋ] *noun*

كتابة - خط

writing done by hand; **his handwriting is very difficult to read;** *see also* **writing.**

handy

handy ['hændɪ] *adjective*

قريب - في متناول اليد - سهل الاستعمال - مفيد

useful; in convenient place; **a handy hammer; keep the salt handy when you are cooking; the shops are handy; these scissors will come in handy** = will be useful.

handy—handier—handiest

hang [hæŋ] *verb*

يُعَلِّق - يدلّي

to attach (something) above the ground (to a nail or to a hook, etc.); to be attached above the ground (to a nail, a hook, etc.); **hang your coat on the hook; I like that picture hanging over the fireplace; she hung the photograph over her bed; he's hanging the lights on the Christmas tree.**

hangs—hanging—hung ['hʌŋ]—**has hung**

hang on, *verb*

ينتظر لفترة وجيزة

to wait; **hang on a moment please.**

happen ['hæpn] *verb*

أ) يَحْدث - يَحْصُل - يصادف
يقع بالصدفة

(a) to take place; **the accident happened at the corner of the street; how did it happen? something has happened to make the train late; she's late—something must have happened; what's happened to his brother?** = what is his brother doing now?

ب) يحصل بالصدفة - يتواجد بالصدفة

(b) to be (by chance); **I happened to be there when the fire started; the house happened to be empty; we happened to meet him at the pub; do you happen to have a map of London?**

happens—happening—happened—has happened

happy ['hæpɪ] *adjective*

مسرور - سعيد

very pleased; **I'm happy to say we're going to have a holiday; we're so happy to hear that you are better; she's not very happy in her job; are you happy with the plans for the new school? Happy Birthday/Happy Christmas/Happy New Year** = greetings said to someone on their birthday/at Christmas/at the New Year; **many Happy Returns of the Day** = greetings said to someone on their birthday.

happy—happier—happiest

happily, *adverb*

بمرح - بسرور - بسعادة

in a happy way; **the children played happily for hours.**

harbour ['hɑːbə] *noun* (*American:* harbor)

ميناء - مرفأ

place where ships tie up; **the sailing boats are all in the harbour; the ships tried to reach the harbour in the storm.**

hard [hɑːd] **1.** *adjective*

١ - أ) صَلْب - قاس

(a) not soft; **this bed is too hard; the cake is so hard I can't bite it.**

ب) صَعْب - عويص - ثقيل السمع

(b) difficult; **today's crossword is too hard—I can't finish it; if the exam is too hard, nobody will pass; he's hard of hearing** = he is rather deaf.

ت) (شتاء) قاس - بارد

(c) **a hard winter** = very cold winter.

hard—harder—hardest

2. *adverb*

٢ - بقوة ، بشدة - بكثرة - بغزارة - باجتهاد

with a lot of effort; **hit the nail hard with the hammer; it's snowing hard; if we all work hard, we'll earn a lot of money.**

hardly, *adverb*

بالكاد - قليلاً ما - نادراً ما

almost not; **I hardly know her; it hardly ever rains in the desert** = almost never; **hardly anyone came to the meeting** = almost no one.

harm

hard up, *adjective*

في عوز شديد ـ محروم حرمانا شديداً

with very little money; **I'm rather hard up at the moment so I can't lend you any money.**

harm [hɑ:m] 1. *noun*

أذى ـ ضرر

damage (esp. to a person); **walking to work every day won't do you any harm; I hope my guitar won't come to any harm if I leave it on the chair; there's no harm in phoning him** = it might possibly be useful to phone him.
2. *verb*

يُؤذي ـ يَضُرّ ـ يسيء إلى

to damage/to hurt; **the dog won't harm you; walking to work every day won't harm you.**
harms—harming—harmed—has harmed

harmful, *adjective*

مؤذٍ ـ مُضِرّ

which causes damage; **bright light can be harmful to your eyes.**

harmless, *adjective*

غير مؤذٍ ـ غير مُضِرّ

which causes no damage; **the dog is old—he's quite harmless.**

hat [hæt] *noun*

قُبَّعة

piece of clothing which you wear on your head; **take your hat off when you go into a church; she put on her new hat; keep it under your hat!** = keep it secret.

hate [heɪt] *verb*

كُرهَ ـ بُغَضَ

not to like at all; **I hate cold eggs; she hates getting up in the morning.**
hates—hating—hated—has hated

have [hæv] *verb*

أ) يملك ـ يحوز ـ يحتوي على

(*a*) (*also* **to have got**) to possess; **he has (got) a lot of money; she has (got) a new green car; have you got enough to eat? to you have enough to eat? he has (got) very big muscles.**

ب) يتناول (الطعام) ـ يقوم بـ

(*b*) to take/to eat, etc.; **have you had any breakfast? I have sugar in my coffee; I'm going to have a bath; we had a long walk.**

ت) يطلب من شخص عملاً ما

(*c*) to get someone to do something and pay them for it; **he is having his house painted; you ought to have your hair cut.**

ث) يستعمل هذا الفعل لصيغة الماضي : (أكلَ طعامه ـ هل انتهيت من العمل ؟)

(*d*) (*used to form the past of verbs*) **he has eaten his breakfast; have you finished your work? she hadn't seen him for two days; if they had asked me I would have said yes.**

Present: **I/you have; he/she/it has; we/you/they have**
having—had—has had

Negative: **I haven't,** *etc.;* **he hasn't,** *etc.*

Note the short forms (only used to form the past of verbs and with got): **I've; you've; he's; she's; it's; we've; they've**

have got, *verb*

أ) يملك (بمعنى لديه أو لديك أو لديهم) مثلاً : لديه كثير من المال .

(*a*) to possess; **he's got a lot of money; she has got a new green car; have you got enough to eat? he's got very big muscles.**

ب) يَجِبُ ان ـ يَضطرّ إلى ـ عليك أو عليه ـ أو عليهم ـ الخ) . مثلاً : عليك ان تفعل ما يقوله الطبيب

(*b*) (*used to mean must*) **you've got to do what the doctor says; have they got to get up early tomorrow? have you got to go so soon?**

have (got) to do with, *verb*

يعني : (هذا لا يعنيك بتاتاً)

to concern; **that's got nothing to do with you.**

he

يجب ـ من المفروض ان ...

have to, *verb used with other verbs to mean* must; **you have to do what the policeman says; in England you have to drive on the left; I had to walk to work because I missed the bus; do you have to go so soon?**

he [hiː] *pronoun referring to a man or boy, and some male animals*

هو (ضمير مذكر، للأشخاص وبعض الحيوانات فقط)

he's my father; he and I went there together; I'm angry with John—he's eaten all the chocolates; don't be frightened of the dog—he won't hurt you.
Note: when it is the object, he becomes him: he hit the ball/the ball hit him; when it follows the verb be, he usually becomes him: who's that?—it's him, the man who stole my bike!

head [hed] **1.** *noun*

١ ـ أ) رأس

(*a*) top part of the body, which contains the eyes/nose/mouth/brain, etc.; **can you stand on your head? he hit his head on the low branch; she rolled head over heels down the hill** = rolled over and over like a ball; **he shook his head** = he moved his head from side to side to mean 'no'; **she tried to do the sum in her head** = using her brain, and not writing it down.

ب) أول ـ مقدم (الصف) ـ طليعة (اللائحة)

(*b*) first place/top part; **he stood at the head of the queue; whose name is at the head of the list?**

ت) رئيس ـ مدير (مدرسة أو مؤسسة)

(*c*) most important person; **he's the head of the sales department; head waiter; head teacher.**

ث) وجه القطعة النقدية

(*d*) top side of a coin, usually with a picture of the head of a king on it; **let's**

health

play heads or tails = let's throw a coin in the air to see which side comes down on top; **heads you win** = if the coin falls with the top side up, then you will win.
2. *verb*

٢ ـ أ) يَضَع في رأس اللائحة ـ يكون في الطليعة

(*a*) to be the first/to lead; **his name heads the list.**

ب) يتّجه . يتوجه نحوَ

(*b*) to go towards; **they are heading north; he headed for the manager's office.**
heads—heading—headed—has headed

headache ['hedeɪk] *noun*

صداع

pain in your head; **I must lie down—I have a headache; she can't come with us because she's got a headache.**

headlights, *plural noun*

المصابيح الأمامية

main white lights on the front of a car.

headline, *noun*

عناوين الصحف ـ رأسية الصحيفة

words in capital letters on the front page of a newspaper; **did you see the headlines about the Prime Minister? the newspaper headline says TAXES TO BE RAISED.**

headmaster, *noun*

مدير المدرسة

man who is in charge of a school.

headmistress, *noun*

مديرة المدرسة

woman who is in charge of a school.
plural **headmistresses**

health [helθ] *noun*

عافية ـ صحّة ـ سلامة

being well/not being ill; **he's in good health; your health/good health!** = greetings said to someone when you drink with them; **health service** = organisation in a country which is in charge of doctors/hospitals, etc.

134 *one hundred and thirty-four*

heap

healthy, *adjective*

صحّي ـ نافع للصحّة ـ مُعافى

likely to make you well; being a farmer is a healthy job; this town is the healthiest place in England.
healthy—healthier—healthiest

heap [hi:p] **1.** *noun*

١ ـ كومة ـ ركام

large pile; he brushed the dead leaves into heaps; he threw the papers on to the heap in the middle of the table.

2. *verb*

٢ ـ يُكَوِّم ـ يُكدِّس

to put into a heap; he heaped his plate with potatoes; the snow is heaped up by the wall of the house.
heaps—heaping—heaped—has heaped

hear ['hɪə] *verb*

أ) يسمع

(a) to catch sounds with your ears; can you hear footsteps? I can't hear what you're saying because of the noise of the aircraft; I heard her shut the front door; we heard him singing in the bath.

ب) يعلم ـ يتلقّى معلومات ان ـ يعلم عن طريق السمع

(b) to get information; I hear you're going to Denmark on holiday; have you heard that the Prime Minister has died? where did you hear that?—I heard it on the news.
hears—hearing—heard [hɜ:d]—has heard

heart [hɑ:t] *noun*

أ) قلب

(a) part of the body which beats regularly as it pumps blood round the body; the doctor listened to his heart; he has heart trouble.

ب) وسط (الغابة أو المدينة)

(b) centre/middle; he lives in the heart of the forest; she has a house in the heart of the city.

one hundred and thirty-five

heat

ث) ملاحظة : تأخذ كلمـة learnt عدة معاني حسب التعابير المستعملة : مثلاً : يحفظ عن ظهر القلب ـ يتأثر كثيراً ـ يفقد اهتمامه بالشيء ـ يحزن

(c) he learnt the whole book by heart = so that he could repeat it from memory; don't take it to heart = don't be too sad about it; his heart isn't in it = he has lost interest in it; my heart sank when I heard the news = I suddenly became sad.

ث) الكوبة (ورقة لعب تحمل صورة قلب)

(d) one of the suits in a game of cards, shaped like a red heart; the six of hearts.

heart attack, *noun*

نوبة قلب

bad illness when your heart stops working for a short time.

hearty, *adjective*

وافر

strong/big; she ate a hearty breakfast.

heat [hi:t] **1.** *noun*

أ) حَرارة ـ حَرّ

(a) being hot; the heat of the sun made the road melt.

ب) شوط (من مباراة)

(b) one part of a sports competition; there are three heats before the main competition; dead heat = race where two runners finish at the same time.

2. *verb*

٢ ـ يُسَخِّن ـ يُحَمِّي

to make hot; heat up the soup while I'm getting the table ready; a heated swimming pool = pool where the water is kept warm.
heats—heating—heated—has heated

heater, *noun*

السخّانة ـ (سخانة الماء سخانة تعمل على الكهرباء)

machine for heating; water heater = machine for heating water in a house; electric heater = heating machine which runs on electricity.

135

heavy

heating, *noun* التدفئة (تدفئة مركزية)
way of warming a house; **the heating has been switched off; central heating** = heating of a whole house from one heater.

heavy ['hevɪ] *adjective*
أ) ثقيل
(a) which weighs a lot; **this box is so heavy I can hardly lift it.**
ب) كثير ـ غزير
(b) strong; in large quantities; **heavy rain fell; don't go to bed after you've had a heavy meal; there has been a heavy fall of snow during the night; there was heavy traffic in the centre of town; he's making heavy weather of it** = he's having difficulty in doing it well.
heavy—heavier—heaviest

heel [hi:l] *noun*
أ) عَقِب القَدَم (أو الجورب)
(a) back part of your foot; part of a sock into which the back part of your foot fits; **you've got a hole in the heel of your stocking.**
ب) عَقِب الحذاء ـ كَعب
(b) block under the back part of a shoe; **she wore shoes with very high heels.**

height [haɪt] *noun*
عُلوّ ـ طول القامة
measurement of how tall/how high something is; **the height of the ceiling is 3 m; what is the height of that mountain?**

held [held] *see* **hold**
ملاحظة : انظر إلى كلمة **hold**

helicopter ['helɪkɒptə] *noun*
طائرة مروحية
type of aircraft which is lifted off the ground by a large propeller on its roof.

hello [hə'ləʊ] *interjection showing a greeting*

help

مرحباً
Hello, James, where have you been? say hello to her from me; he called out hello from the other side of the street.
also spelt **hallo, hullo**

helmet ['helmɪt] *noun*
خَوْذة
hard hat which you wear to protect your head; **if you ride a motorbike you have to wear a helmet.**

help [help] 1. *noun*
١ ـ أ) مُساعدة
(a) something which makes it easier for you to do something; **he cleaned the car with the help of a big brush; do you need any help?**
ب) نجدة
(b) making somone safe; **they went to his help** = to rescue him; **she was calling for help.**
2. *verb*
٢ ـ أ) يساعد
(a) to make it easier for someone to do something; **can you help me with my homework? I got a friend to help put the piano into the bedroom; he helped the old lady across the street.**
ب) لا يستطيع الامتناع عن
(b) (*with* **cannot**) not to be able to stop doing something; **he couldn't help laughing: he can't help it if he's deaf.**
ت) تفضل ـ إخدم نفسك بنفسك
(c) **help yourself** = to serve yourself with food, etc.; **he helped himself to some pudding; if you want anything to eat just help yourself.**
٣ ـ النجدة
3. **help!** *interjection which you shout when you are in difficulties;* **help, help, call a doctor quickly! help, the brakes aren't working.**
helps—helping—helped—has helped

hen

helper, *noun* مُساعد

person who helps

helpful, *adjective* مفيد ـ مساعد

which helps; **he made a helpful suggestion.**

helpless, *adjective* لا عون له ـ بائس ـ عاجز

not able to do anything.

hen [hen] *noun* دجاجة ـ انثى الطير

female bird, especially a chicken which you keep on a farm; **the hen has laid an egg.**

her [hɜː] **1.** *object pronoun referring to a female person, a female animal and sometimes to machines and countries*
١ ـ هي : (ضمير مؤنث ، للأشخاص وبعض الحيوانات وبعض الأشياء)
have you seen her? tell her to go away; that's her in the white dress; there's a letter for her.

2. *adjective referring to a female, a ship or a country*
٢ ـ خاص بالمفردة الغائبة بوصفها مالكة ، فاعلاً أو مفعولاً
she had lost all her money; have you seen her brother? the cat won't eat her food; Germany is helping her industry to sell more goods abroad.

hers, *pronoun* خاصتها : هذا الكتاب خاصتها

belonging to her; **this book is hers, not mine; she introduced me to a friend of hers** = to one of her friends.

herself, *pronoun referring to a female subject*
هي بنفسها ـ هي نفسها ـ هي بالذات
the cat was washing herself; she is all by herself = all alone; **she did it all by herself** = with no one to help her; **she wrote to me herself; the nurse is ill herself; did your mother enjoy herself?**

hide

here ['hɪə] *adverb* هنا ـ في هذا المكان ـ إلى هنا

in this place; to this place; **I put the book down here next to my cup; we have been living here in London for twenty years; can you come here, please? they brought the money here; here's the newspaper; here comes Frank; here you are** = take this.

Note; when **here** *comes at the beginning of a sentence the following subject comes after the verb if the subject is a noun and not a pronoun:*
here comes the bus/here it comes

hesitate ['hezɪteɪt] *verb* يَتَرَدَّد

not to be able to decide; to stop for a moment while you decide what to do; **I'm hesitating about what to do next; he hesitated for a few seconds, then went into the shop.**

hesitates—hesitating—hesitated—has hesitated

hesitation, *noun* تَرَدُّد

act of hesitating; **after a few minutes' hesitation he went into the shop.**

hi [haɪ] *American interjection showing a greeting*
مرحباً (مستعملة في اميركا)
hi John, did you have a good day?

hide [haɪd] *verb*
۱) يُخْبىء ـ يُخْفي عن الأنظار
(*a*) to put something where no one can see or find it; **he hid the gold coins under the bed; someone has hidden the key to the school.**

ب) يحتجب ـ يختبيء
(*b*) to put yourself where no one can see or find you; **he's hiding from the police; they hid behind the door.**

hides—hiding—hid [hɪd]—**has hidden** ['hɪdn]

one hundred and thirty-seven 137

high

high [haɪ] **1.** *adjective*

١ ـ أ) عالٍ ـ شاهق ـ بالغ ارتفاعه

(a) tall; the office building is 60 m high; which is the highest mountain in the world? the living room has a high ceiling.

ب) بالغ ذروته ـ مرتفع ـ غالٍ

(b) (*referring to numbers*) big; the car goes well at high speeds; prices seem to be higher every year; glass will melt at very high temperatures.

Note: **high** *is used with figures;* **the mountain is 700 metres high**

2. *adverb*

٢ ـ في العلاء ـ عالياً

above; up in the air; the balloon flew high up into the sky; aircraft fly high to avoid storms; the bird went up higher and higher.

high—higher—highest

highly, *adverb*

بإعجاب (هو معجبٌ بها)

he thinks highly of her = he admires her very much.

High School, *noun*

المدرسة الثانوية

school in America for older children.

High Street, *noun*

الشارع الرئيسي

main street in a town, where most of the shops are; he has a shop in the High Street; go down the High Street until you come to the traffic lights.

Note: often written **High St.**

hill [hɪl] *noun*

تل ـ هضبة

piece of high land, but lower than a mountain; his house is on top of a hill; if you climb up the hill, you will get a good view.

him [hɪm] *object pronoun referring to a man, boy or some male animals*

ضمير النصب والجرّ للمفرد الغائب المذكر (للأشخاص وبعض الحيوانات فقط)

have you seen him lately? tell him to come in; there is a letter for him; that's him over there.

himself, *pronoun referring to a male subject*

هو بنفسه ـ هو نفسه

he's all by himself = all alone; he did it all by himself = with no one to help him; he wrote to me himself; the doctor is ill himself; did your father enjoy himself?

hire ['haɪə] *verb*

١) يَسْتَأْجِر

(a) to pay to borrow something for a time; he hired a car for his holiday.

ب) يُؤَجِّر

(b) (*also* **to hire out**) to lend something to someone for money; **a car hire firm** = firm which lends cars which you pay to borrow.

hires—hiring—hired—has hired

his [hɪz] **1.** *adjective*

١ ـ ضمير الغائب المتصل

belonging to him; he's lost all his money; have you met his mother? our dog wants his food.

2. *pronoun*

٢ ـ خاصتُهُ : هذا الكتاب هو خاصتُهُ

belonging to him; this book is his, not mine; he introduced me to a friend of his called Anne.

history ['hɪstri] *noun*

علم التاريخ ـ التاريخ (الأحداث الماضية)

study of what happened in the past; he is writing a history of the First World War; she's reading a history book; I got best marks in History.

no plural

hit [hɪt] *verb*

يَصْدُم ـ يَضرُب

to knock; to go against something hard using a lot of force; the car hit the lamppost and knocked it down; she was hit-

hobby

ting her husband with a bottle; he hit the ball so hard, that we can't find it; I hit my head on the door.
hits—hitting—hit—has hit

hobby ['hɒbɪ] *noun* هواية

thing which you do to amuse yourself when you are not working; **his hobby is collecting stamps; do you have any hobbies?**
plural **hobbies**

hold [həʊld] *verb*

أ) يُمْسك ـ يَقْبض

(*a*) to have, especially in your hand; **he was holding a gun in his right hand; she held the knife between her teeth; hold tight—the ship is moving fast.**

ب) يتَّسع ـ يَسَعُ

(*b*) to contain; **this bottle holds two litres; will the car hold six people? the box isn't big enough to hold all the potatoes.**

ت) يعقد (اجتماعاً)

(*c*) to arrange for something to happen; **we held the meeting in the Town Hall; we are holding the flower show next week.**

ث) يدوم

(*d*) to stay; **will the fine weather hold until next week?**
holds—holding—held [held]—has held

holder, *noun*

حاملة (المستندات أو بعض الأشياء)

thing which holds; **he put the pen back into its holder.**

hold on, *verb*

أ) يمسك بشدة ـ يتمسك بـ

(*a*) to hold something tightly; **hold on to the handle; hold on, we're turning.**

ب) ينتظر

(*b*) to wait; **hold on a moment; you want to speak to Mr Smith—hold on, I'll find him for you.**

home

hold up, *verb*

أ) يرفع عن

(*a*) to lift; **he held up his hand; the tent is held up by four posts.**

ب) يعوق ـ يؤخّر

(*b*) to make late; **we were held up in a traffic jam; the train was held up by the snow.**

ت) يقتحم مكاناً ابتغاء السرقة

(*c*) to attack and rob; **three men held up the bank.**
Note: **the accident held the traffic up** or **held up the traffic** *but only* **the accident held us up**

hold-up, *noun*

أ) تأخير

(*a*) delay; **the accident caused a hold-up on the motorway.**

ب) اقتحام ابتغاء السرقة

(*b*) armed attack; **two people were injured in the bank hold-up.**

hole [həʊl] *noun* ثقب ـ حفرة

opening/space in something; **the boys looked through the hole in the fence; I've got a hole in my sock; the rabbit ran down its hole; you must try to pull the piece of wool through the hole in the needle.**

holiday ['hɒlɪdeɪ] *noun* (*American:* vacation) عطلة

time when you do not have to work or be at school; **we always spend our holidays by the sea; how many days' holiday do you have each year? teachers can rest during the school holidays; Mr Brown isn't in the office—he's on holiday; when do you go on holiday?**
Note: usually used without **the**

home [həʊm] 1. *noun*

١ ـ أ) بيت ـ منزل

(*a*) place where you live; house which you live in; **are you going to be at home**

one hundred and thirty-nine 139

honest

tomorrow? **our home is the house at the corner of the street**; **she's staying at home instead of going to work**; **when do you leave home in the morning?** **make yourself at home!** = act as if you were in your own home.

ب) مأوى ـ بيت مختص بعناية المسنّين أو الأطفال .. الخ

(b) house where people are looked after; **an old people's home**; **a children's home** = a house where children with no parents are looked after.

ت) في الوطن ـ في مقرّه

(c) **at home** = on the local sports ground; **our team is playing at home next Saturday**.

2. *adverb*

٢ ـ نحو أو في أو إلى البيت

towards the place where you usually live; **I'm going home**; **I usually get home at 7 o'clock** = reach the house where I live; **I'll take it home with me**; **she can take the bus home** = she can go home by bus.

Note: used without a preposition: **he went home; she's coming home,** *etc.*

homemade, *adjective*

بيتي الصنع

made at home, and not bought; **a pot of homemade jam.**

homesick, *adjective*

مشوّق للعودة إلى الوطن أو الأسرة

feeling sad because you are away from home.

homework, *noun*

الفرض المنزلي : المذاكرة النمطية

work which children take home from school to do in the evening; **have you done your maths homework? I haven't got any homework, so I can watch TV.**

no plural

honest ['ɒnɪst] *adjective*

صادق ـ فاضل ـ مستقيم

who tells the truth; who doesn't cheat.

hope

honey ['hʌnɪ] *noun*

عسل

sweet stuff produced by bees; **put some honey on your bread.**

no plural

hook [hʊk] 1. *noun*

كُلّاب ـ خُطّاف ـ سنّارة صيد

bent piece of metal used for holding or pulling; **hang your coat on the hook behind the door**; **he caught a fish on his hook.**

2. *verb*

٢ ـ يُكَلّب ـ يصيد بسنارة

to attach something with a hook; to catch (a fish) with a hook; **he hooked his umbrella over the back of the chair**; **she hooked a huge fish.**

hooks—hooking—hooked—has hooked

hop [hɒp] 1. *noun*

١ ـ وثبة على قدم واحدة

little jump standing on one foot.

2. *verb*

٢ ـ يثب على قدم واحدة

to jump on one foot or move about in little jumps; **he hopped up and down**; **the birds were hopping about on the grass.**

hops—hopping—hopped—has hopped

hope [həʊp] *verb*

يأمل ـ يرجو

to expect something will happen; to want something to happen; **we hope to be back home at 6 o'clock**; **I had hoped to be there, but in the end I couldn't go**; **I hope our team wins**; **she hoped she would soon be able to drive a car**; **I hope so** = I want it to happen; **I hope not** = I don't want it to happen; **will you come to the party?—yes, I hope so**; **is it going to rain tomorrow?—I hope not!**

hopes—hoping—hoped—has hoped

hopped

hopped [hɒpt], **hopping** [ˈhɒpɪŋ] *see* **hop**

ملاحظة: انظر إلى كلمة hop

horizon [həˈraɪzn] *noun*

أفق

line where the earth seems to meet the sky; **can you see that ship on the horizon?**

horizontal [hɒrɪˈzɒntl] *adjective*

أفقي

which is lying flat; **a horizontal line.**

horn [hɔːn] *noun*

أ) قرن (البقرة أو بعض الحيوانات)

(*a*) hard part growing on the head of an animal (such as cow); **the cow tried to push him with its horns.**

ب) بوق - نفير (للسيارة)

(*b*) musical instrument; part of a car which makes a loud noise to warn people; **he plays the horn in an orchestra; sound your horn when you come to the corner.**

horrible [ˈhɒrəbl] *adjective*

رهيب - كريه إلى أقصى حد

terrible/unpleasant; **I had a horrible dream last night; the meal in the restaurant was horrible; what horrible weather!**

horrid [ˈhɒrɪd] *adjective*

بشع - بغيض

nasty/unpleasant; **she's a horrid old woman; what horrid weather!**

horse [hɔːs] *noun*

فَرَس - حصان

large animal used for riding or pulling; **she goes out on her horse every morning; some farmers still use horses to plough the fields.**

على صهوة الجواد

on horseback = riding on a horse; **there were six policemen on horseback.**

hour

hose [həʊz] *noun*

خرطوم مياه

long rubber or plastic tube; **he was watering his garden with a hose; the firemen used their hoses to put out the fire.**

hospital [ˈhɒspɪtl] *noun*

مستشفى

place where sick or hurt people are looked after; **she's so ill, she has been sent to hospital; he's been in hospital for several days; the children's hospital is at the end of our street.**

hot [hɒt] *adjective*

ساخن - حار

very warm; with a high temperature; **the water in my bath is too hot; what hot weather we're having! it's usually hot in August; if you're hot, take your coat off.**
hot—hotter—hottest

hot dog, *noun*

سندويش من اللقانق

food made of a hot sausage eaten in a roll of bread.

hotel [həʊˈtel] *noun*

فندق

place where you can buy a meal and rent a room for the night; **all the rooms in the hotel are booked; which is the best hotel in the town? we're staying at the Grand Hotel; aren't there any hotels near the sea? ask the hotel manager if he has found your keys.**

hour [ˈaʊə] *noun*

ساعة (زمنية) - مدة تستغرق ٦٠ دقيقة

period of time lasting sixty minutes; **there are 24 hours in the day; he is paid by the hour** = he is paid for each hour he works; **the hours of work are from 9 to 5; when is your lunch hour?** = when do you stop work for lunch? **I'll be ready in a quarter of an hour/in half an hour** = in 15 minutes/in 30 minutes; **the car was travelling at over 100 miles an hour.**

one hundred and forty-one   141

house

hourly, *adjective*

في كل ساعة

happening every hour; **there's an hourly news programme.**

house [haʊs] *noun*

منزل - بيت

building which someone lives in; **he has a flat in town and house in the country; all the houses in our street look the same; his house has six bedrooms.**
Note: **houses** ['haʊzɪz]

household, *noun & adjective*

أسرة - أهل البيت

(referring to) people living together in a house; **household goods department** = part of a big shop which sells things for the house.

housework, *noun*

تنظيف البيت

cleaning of a house or flat; **I have a lot of housework to do.**

how [haʊ] *adverb*

أ) كيف ؟

(a) (*showing or asking the way in which something is done*) **how do you make chocolate biscuits? how can you get to the post office from here? tell me how fish breathe.**

ب) كم ؟ إلى أي مدى ؟

(b) (*showing or asking in what quantity*) **how big is your car? how long is the flight to Copenhagen? how often do you have a holiday? he showed how strong he was.**

ت) كم - ياله من (للتعبير عن الدهشة)

(c) (*showing surprise*) **how hot it is today! how blue the sky is! how she cried when she hit her thumb with the hammer!**
how are you?/how do you do? *showing greeting*

كيف حالك ؟

how do you do, Mrs Jones; hello, Charles, how are you? the headmaster asked me how I was.

142

hundred

however, *adverb*

أ) كيفما - مهما

(a) in whatever quantity; **however hard he tried, he couldn't swim; I must buy that old clock, however expensive it is.**

ب) رغم ذلك - ومع ذلك

(b) in spite of this; **I never go out on Saturdays, however this Saturday I'm going to a wedding.**

hullo [hə'ləʊ] *interjection showing a greeting*

مرحباً

Hullo John, I'm glad to see you; say hullo to your mother from me; he called hullo from the other side of the street
also spelt **hallo, hello**

human ['hju:mən] **1.** *adjective*

١ - بشري - آدمي - إنساني

referring to any man, woman or child; **a human being** = a person.
2. *noun*

٢ - الإنسان (بصورة عامة)

person; **most animals are afraid of humans.**

humour ['hju:mə] *noun* (*American:* humor)

الفكاهة - روح الفكاهة

ability to be funny or to see something as funny; **he's got no sense of humour** = he doesn't think anything is funny.

hundred ['hʌndrəd] *number* 100

مئة - (العدد ١٠٠) جزء من مئة

he's over a hundred (years old); the house was built several hundred years ago; hundreds of people caught the disease = very many people.
Note: in numbers **hundred** *does not change and is followed by* **and** *when reading:* **491** = four hundred and ninety one; **102** = a hundred and two

one hundred and forty-two

hung

Note: **a hundred and one** (101), **three hundred and six** (306), *etc.*, *but* **hundred and first** (101st), **three hundred and sixth** (306th), *etc.*

hundredth, 100th *adjective & noun*

المِئَة

the clock is correct to one hundredth of a second (100th of a second); tomorrow is grandfather's hundredth birthday.

hung [hʌŋ] *see* **hang**

ملاحظة : انظر إلى كلمة hang

hungry ['hʌŋgrɪ] *adjective*

جائِع

wanting to eat; **I'm hungry; are you hungry? you must be hungry after that long walk; I'm not very hungry—I had a big breakfast; hurry up with the dinner—we're getting hungry.**

hungry—hungrier—hungriest

hunt [hʌnt] *verb*

أ) يُطارِد - يُفَتِّش

(*a*) to look for someone or something; **the police are hunting for the people who held up the bank; I've been hunting in all the shops, but I can't find any shoes that fit me.**

ب) يَصيد - يَصطاد

(*b*) to chase wild animals to kill them; **the cat went out hunting mice; the farmer's sons are hunting rats.**

hunts—hunting—hunted—has hunted

hunter, *noun*

صَيّاد

person who hunts.

hurry ['hʌrɪ] **1.** *noun*

١ - عَجَلة - سُرعة

rush; **he's always in a hurry** = always rushing about; **out of the way—we're in**

hut

a hurry! what's the hurry? = why are you going so fast?

no plural

2. *verb*

٢ - يستعجل - يُسرع - ينقل بعجلة

to go or do something fast; to make someone go faster; **she hurried along the passage; you'll have to hurry if you want to catch the train; don't hurry—we've got plenty of time; don't hurry me, I'm going as fast as I can.**

hurries—hurrying—hurried—has hurried

hurry up, *verb*

يجعل احداً يذهب أو يأتي بسرعة - يستعجل

to go or do something faster; to make someone do something faster; **hurry up—we'll be late; can't you make the waiter hurry up? we'll have to hurry them up if we want them to be there in time.**

hurt [hɜːt] *verb*

يَجرَح - يُؤذي - يُؤلِم

to have pain; to give pain; **he's hurt his hand; she fell down and hurt herself; are you hurt? is he badly hurt? my foot hurts; he was slightly hurt in the crash; two players got hurt in the football game.**

hurts—hurting—hurt—has hurt

husband ['hʌzbənd] *noun*

زوج

man to whom a woman is married; **he's my secretary's husband; I know Mrs Jones, but I have never met her husband.**

hut [hʌt] *noun*

كوخ

small house, usually made of wood.

one hundred and forty-three

Ii

I [aɪ] *pronoun used by the speaker when talking about himself or herself.*
أنا (ضمير الفرد المتكلم) ت (ضمير متصل)
he said: 'I can do it', and he did it; he and I are great friends; the manager said I could have a holiday; I told you I was going to be late.

Note: when it is the object, I becomes me: I gave it to him/he gave it to me; I hit him/he hit me; when it follows the verb be, I usually becomes me: who is it?—it's me!

ice [aɪs] *noun*
أ) جليد ـ رقاقة من جليد
(*a*) frozen water; when the lake freezes, ice covers the surface; don't try to walk on the ice, it isn't thick enough yet; do you want some more ice in your drink? my hands are like ice = are very cold.
ب) مثلوجات « بوظة » « جيلاتي «
(*b*) ice cream; I'll have an ice for my pudding; two chocolate ices, please.
no plural for (a): **some ice; a lump of ice; ices** *means* **ice creams**

ice cream, *noun*
مثلوجات » بوظة «
frozen sweet made of cream, water and fruit juice; a chocolate ice cream; what sort of ice cream do you want—lemon or coffee? come and help me—I can't carry six ice creams.

icicle, *noun*
الدلّاة الجليدية (كتلة جليدية مدلّاة ناشئة عن تجمّد الماء أثناء تقطّره)
long piece of ice hanging from a roof, etc., made by water dripping in cold weather.

icy, *adjective*
جليدي ـ مكسو بالجليد
covered with ice; be careful, the pavements are icy.
icy—icier—iciest

idea [aɪ'dɪə] *noun*
فكرة ـ تَصَوُّر ـ ظَنْ
something which you think of/plan which you make in your mind; I've had an idea—let's all go swimming; what a good idea! I have an idea that the buses don't run on Sundays = I think that the buses don't run; where's your brother?—I've no idea = I don't know; I had no idea it was so late = I didn't know it was so late.

ideal [aɪ'dɪəl] *adjective*
مثالي
very suitable/perfect; this is an ideal place for a picnic; a small car is ideal for shopping in town.

i.e. ['aɪ'iː]
يعني ـ هذا يعني
that is; you must obey the rules, i.e. don't walk on the grass.

if [ɪf] *conjunction*
أ) إذا ـ إن
(*a*) (*showing what might happen*) if it rains, you'll get wet; if I'm free, I'll come for a walk; if you'd told me you were ill, I'd have come to see you; if I won £1000, I'd take a long holiday.
ب) إذا
(*b*) (*asking questions*) do you know if the train is going to be late? I wonder if you've ever been to Russia?

ill

(c) when; if she goes out, she always wears a coat; if he was late, he always used to telephone.

ill [ɪl] *adjective*

مريض - عليل

not well/sick; **eating green apples will make you ill; if you feel ill, you ought to see a doctor; he's not as ill as he was last week.**
ill—worse—worst

illness, *noun*

مَرَض

not being well; **his illness makes him very tired; a lot of children stay away from school because of illness.**
plural illnesses

imagine [ɪˈmædʒɪn] *verb*

يتخيّل - يتصوّر - يظنّ - يعتقد

to see or hear something in your mind; **imagine yourself sitting on the beach in the sun; you can't imagine how difficult it is to get a new telephone; I thought I heard someone shout, but I must have imagined it because there is no one there.**
imagines—imagining—
imagined—has imagined

imagination [ɪmædʒɪˈneɪʃn] *noun*

خيال - تَصَوُّر - ظنّ

being able to see things in your mind; **in his imagination he saw himself sitting on a beach in the sun.**

imitate [ˈɪmɪteɪt] *verb*

يُقَلِّد

to do what someone else does; **when he walks he imitates his father; she is very good at imitating the English teacher.**
imitates—imitating—imitated—
has imitated

immediate [ɪˈmiːdjət] *adjective*

عاجل - فوري

which happens now/without waiting:

improve

this letter needs an immediate reply.

immediately, *adverb*

فَوْراً - توّاً

just after; **he became ill immediately after he came back from holiday; she will telephone you immediately (after) she comes home; if the house catches fire, you must call the firemen immediately.**

important [ɪmˈpɔːtnt] *adjective*

هام - ذو أهمية - ذو شأن

which matters a lot; **is it important for you to get to London tomorrow? I must go to London, because I have an important meeting; he has an important job in the government.**

impossible [ɪmˈpɒsɪbl] *adjective*

مستحيل - صعب جداً - متعذّر

which cannot be done; **it's impossible to get tickets for the concert; it was impossible to get the car out of the garage because of the snow; driving to London is impossible because of the traffic.**

impress [ɪmˈpres] *verb*

يؤثّر - يُخلِّف انطباعاً قوياً (في نفس المرء)

to have an effect on someone so that they admire you; **I'm very impressed by your work; she isn't very impressed by the new maths teacher.**
impresses—impressing—
impressed—has impressed

improve [ɪmˈpruːv] *verb*

يُحسّن - يُدْخِل تحسينات على - يَتَحسّن

to get better; to make better; **he has improved the look of his house by painting it white; he was very ill, but he is improving now; I scored two—can you improve on that?** = can you do better than that?
improves—improving—
improved—has improved

improvement, *noun*

getting better; there is no improvement in his work.

تَحَسُّن

in [ɪn] *preposition & adverb*

أ) في (للدلالة على مكان) : في اليابان - في روسيا - في الحمام ...

(a) (*showing place*) they live in Japan; in Russia it can be very cold during the winter; he's in the bathroom; she's in bed; why are you sitting outside in the snow? is your mother in? = is she at home? the train isn't in yet = hasn't arrived yet.

ب) خلال (للدلالة على زمان) : خلال الخريف - في المساء - في سنة ١٩٦٣

(b) (*showing time*) in the autumn the leaves fall off the trees; in the evening we sit and watch TV; he was born in 1963; I will be back home in January; she should be here in half an hour; he finished the crossword in 20 minutes.

ت) (للدلالة على حالة أو مظهر) : كانت ترتدي أبيضاً - خرج وهو في ثياب النوم

(c) (*showing state*) she was dressed in white; he ran outside in his pyjamas; she's in a hurry; the dictionary is in alphabetical order.

in for, *adverb*

متوقع حصول شيء ما - متورّط

I think we're in for some rain = I think we are going to have some rain; he's in for a nasty shock = he's going to have a nasty shock.

in on, *adverb*

بِعِلْم

is he in on the secret? = does he know the secret?

inch [ɪntʃ] *noun*

إنش - بوصة (قياس للمسافة أو الطول) الإنش يبلغ ٢,٥٤ سنتم

measurement of how long something is (= 2.54 cm); the table is 18 inches (18″) across; she is 5 foot 6 inches tall (5′6″) (say 'she's five foot six').

plural **inches**
Note: with numbers **inch** *is often written* ″: **7½″** = seven and a half inches

include [ɪnˈkluːd] *verb*

يتضمّن - يَشْمُل - يشتمل على

to count something/someone with others; did you include your mother in the people you have asked to the party? there were ten of us, if you include the children; I will be on holiday up to and including next Tuesday; every one had a good time, including the grown-ups.
includes—including—included— has included

income [ˈɪŋkʌm] *noun*

دَخْل - إيراد

money which you receive (usually for work); his income isn't enough to pay the rent.

increase [ˈɪnkriːs] **1.** *noun*

١ - إزدياد - إرتفاع (الأسعار) - زيادة (الرواتب)

getting larger or higher; an increase in the price of petrol; he asked for an increase = he asked to have more money.
2. *verb* [ɪnˈkriːs]

٢ - يرتفع - يزداد

to get larger or higher; the price of petrol has increased twice this year; his salary was increased by 10 per cent.
increases—increasing— increased—has increased

indeed [ɪnˈdiːd] *adverb*

أ) بالفعل ، بالواقع

(a) really; thank you very much indeed for your letter; she is very kind indeed to have given you so much money.

ب) بالفعل - حقّاً

(b) in fact; he is poor—indeed he has no money at all.

independent

independent [ɪndɪˈpendənt] *adjective*

مُستقلّ ـ حرّ

free/not controlled by someone else; **she's a very independent girl; the country became independent on January 1st; an independent member of parliament** = one who does not belong to any political party.

indoors [ɪnˈdɔːz] *adverb*

داخل المبنى أو البيت ـ في الداخل ـ إلى الداخل

inside a building; **you ought to stay indoors until your cold is better; they were playing tennis, but when it started to rain they went indoors.**

indoor [ˈɪndɔː] *adjective*

داخلي ـ يستعمل أو يعيش داخل البيت ولا خارجه (النباتات الداخلية، المسبح المسقوف)

which is inside a building; **the room's full of indoor plants; there's an indoor swimming pool in the town, so we can swim even in winter.**

industry [ˈɪndəstrɪ] *noun*

الصناعة. (صناعة السيارات، الصناعة الخفيفة...) النشاط الصناعي

making goods in factories; **the car industry; heavy industry** = factories which make large products (like cars/aircraft, etc.); **light industry** = factories which make small things (like watches/toys, etc.).

plural: **industries**

industrial [ɪnˈdʌstrɪəl] *adjective*

صناعي : (مدينة صناعية)

referring to industry; **an industrial town** = a town where there are many factories.

infectious [ɪnˈfekʃəs] *adjective*

مُعْدٍ (يقال عن مرض أو ميكروب)

which you can catch from someone else (usually referring to a disease); **mumps and measles are common infectious dis-

injure

eases; he is covered with red spots—is it infectious?**

inluence [ˈɪnfluəns] **1.** *noun*

١ ـ تأثير ـ نفوذ

being able to have an effect on someone/something; **the moon has an influence on the tide; the headmaster has no influence over the teachers in the school** = he cannot make them do what he wants.

2. *verb*

٢ ـ يؤثر في

to have an effect on someone/something; **the crops have been influenced by the bad weather; the government has tried to influence the voters; I liked the film—I wasn't influenced by what the papers said about it.**

influences—influencing—influenced—has influenced

inform [ɪnˈfɔːm] *verb*

يُخْبِر بشيء ـ يُبلَّغ عن

to tell someone; **have you informed the police that your car has been stolen? I must inform you that you will be arrested.**

informs—informing—informed—has informed

information [ɪnfəˈmeɪʃn] *noun*

معلومات ـ حقائق

facts about something; **have you any information about holidays in Greece? the police won't give me any information about how the accident happened; could you send me some more information about the job; you haven't given me enough information about your stolen car; that's a very useful piece/bit of information.**

no plural: **some information; a piece of information**

injure [ˈɪndʒə] *verb*

يَجرح ـ يؤذي ـ ينزل بأحد ضرراً

to hurt; **six people were injured in the accident.**

one hundred and forty-seven   **147**

ink

injures—injuring—injured—has injured

ink [ɪŋk] *noun*

حبر

coloured liquid which is used for writing; **he wrote his name in red ink; my pen's dry—have you any blue ink?** she dropped a bottle of ink on the floor.

inquire [ɪŋ'kwaɪə] *verb*

يسأل ـ يستعلم عن

to ask questions; **have you inquired at the police station about your lost cat?** she inquired about the weather in Spain.
inquires—inquiring—inquired—has inquired
Note: can be spelt **enquire**

inquiry, *noun*

تحقيق ـ استعلام ـ سؤال

question; **she is making inquiries about her cat which is missing;** he wrote in answer to my inquiry about holidays in Greece.
plural **inquiries**
Note: can be spelt **enquiry**

insect ['ɪnsekt] *noun*

حشرة

small animal with six legs and a body in three parts; **flies and butterflies are insects but spiders aren't;** lots of insects were flying round the lamp.

inside [ɪn'saɪd] **1.** *adverb*

١ ـ في الداخل

in; indoors; **come inside—it's starting to rain;** the weather was so bad that we just sat inside and watched TV; the house is dark inside.
2. *preposition*

٢ ـ داخل (الشيء)

in; **there is nothing inside the box;** he was sitting inside his car listening to the radio; I know his house from the outside, but I've never been inside it.
3. *noun*

148

instrument

٣ ـ من الداخل

part which is in something; **I know his house from the outside, but what is the inside like?** the inside of this cake is quite hard; he put his pyjamas on inside out = with the inside part facing out; **he knows London inside out** = very well.

instant ['ɪnstənt] **1.** *noun*

١ ـ لحظة ـ آونة

moment; **come here this instant!** = at once; he stopped running for an instant, and then started again.
2. *adjective*

٢ ـ فوري الذوبان

instant coffee = coffee powder to which you add hot water to make coffee quickly.

instantly, *adverb*

على الفور

immediately; **all the passengers were killed instantly in the crash.**

instead (of) [ɪn'stedəv] *adverb*

بَدَلاً من ـ عوضاً عن

in place of; **he'll go instead of me;** instead of talking to the police, he just ran away; instead of playing football, why don't you help me clean the car? would you like an orange instead of that apple? **if she can't go, can I go instead?** = in her place; we haven't any coffee—would you like some tea instead?

instructions [ɪn'strʌkʃnz] *plural noun*

تعليمات

words which explain how something is used/how to do something; **the instructions are written on the bottle of medicine;** I can't use this machine because I have lost the book of instructions; she gave the taxi driver instructions how to get to her house.

instrument ['ɪnstrəmənt] *noun*

١) آلة ـ أداة

(*a*) piece of equipment; tool; **the doctor had a box of instruments;** I can't test

one hundred and forty-eight

insure

your car—I haven't brought the right instruments.

ب) آلة موسيقية

(b) **musical instrument** = thing with which you make music; **wind instruments** = ones which you blow to make a musical note; **string instruments** = ones with strings which make different notes when you pull them.

insure [ɪn'ʃʊə] *verb*

يُؤَمِّن - يضمن - يَصْدُر صك تأمين : (هل سيارتك مؤمنة ؟)

to agree with a company that they will pay you money if something is lost or damaged; **is your car insured? I insured my luggage for £200.**
insures—insuring—insured—has insured

insurance, *noun*

التأمين - ضمان

agreement with a company that they will pay you money if something is lost or damaged; **she has an insurance against fire; life insurance** = insurance against someone dying; **accident insurance** = insurance against an accident.

intelligent [ɪn'telɪdʒənt] *adjective*

ذكيّ - سريعُ الفَهم - بارع

clever/able to learn quickly; **he's the most intelligent boy in the class.**

intend [ɪn'tend] *verb*

يَقْصِدُ - يَنْوي - يعتزم

to plan to do something; **they intend to go to Spain for their holidays; she's intending to study English at university.**
intends—intending—intended—has intended

interest ['ɪntrəst] 1. *noun*

١ - أ) إهتمام

(a) special attention; **he takes a lot of interest in his students; she has no interest in plants; why doesn't he take more interest in what his sister is doing?**

interrupt

ب) هواية - منفعة شخصية

(b) something which attracts you particularly; **her main interest is the cinema; do you have any special interests apart from your work?**

ت) فائدة (مصرفية)

(c) money which is paid to someone who lends money; **if you put your money in the bank you'll get 10% interest on it; this type of bank account pays 10% interest; what's the interest I'll have to pay if I borrow £1000?**
2. *verb*

٢ - يُثير إنتباه - يثير اهتمام (شخص ما)

to attract someone's attention; **he's specially interested in the cinema; nothing seems to interest her very much; the film didn't interest me at all.**
interests—interesting—interested—has interested

interesting, *adjective*

مُمتع - مُشوِّق

which attracts your attention; **there's an interesting article on fishing in the newspaper; I didn't find the TV programme at all interesting; what's so interesting about old churches?—I find them dull.**

interjection [ɪntə'dʒekʃn] *noun*

التعجب : صوت يُعبِّر عن التعجب أو الحماس أو الوجع : مثل آه أو آخ .

word used to show that you are excited, hurt, annoyed, etc.; **'oh!' and 'help!' are interjections.**

international [ɪntə'næʃnl] *adjective*

دُوَلي - عالمي

between different countries; **an international agreement; I have to make an international phone call.**

interrupt [ɪntə'rʌpt] *verb*

يقطع (الكلام) - يقاطع (الحديث)

to do something (such as to start to speak) when someone else is speaking and so stop them continuing; **I was just starting to tell my story, when I was**

one hundred and forty-nine 149

into

interrupted by the telephone; he couldn't finish his speech because he was being interrupted all the time; I'm sorry to interrupt, but your wife wants to speak to you on the phone.
interrupts—interrupting—interrupted—has interrupted
interruption, noun

تقطيع (الحديث أو العمل)

act of interrupting; he couldn't finish his work because of all the interruptions.

into ['ɪntʊ] preposition

أ) داخل : ذهبت داخل البيت

(a) (showing movement towards the inside) he went into the house; she fell into the swimming pool; put the knives back into their box; you can't get 150 people into that bus; when he came into the room we were all talking about him; are you driving into the centre of the town?

ب) في ، اوب : اصطدمت السيارة بشجرة

(b) against; the car ran into a tree.

ت) إلى : تحولت إلى فراشة

(c) (showing a change) it turned into a butterfly; when does water turn into steam? you ought to change into some clean clothes for the party; she burst into tears = suddenly started crying.

ث) إلى (للدلالة على التقسيم) : إقطعي الكعكة إلى ست قطع

(d) (showing you are dividing) cut the cake into six pieces; four into three won't go = you can't divide three by four.

introduce [ɪntrə'djuːs] verb

يُعَرَّف (شخصاً بآخر) : سأعرفك على اختي

to make two people know each other, when they have never met before; I will introduce you to my sister; can I introduce my new assistant?
introduces—introducing—introduced—has introduced

invent [ɪn'vent] verb

أ) يَخْتَرِع ـ يكتشف

(a) to make something which has never

150

Ireland

been made before; he invented a new type of engine; who invented the telephone? he invents new machines.

ب) يُلَقِّق

(b) to make up, using your imagination; he invented the whole story.
invents—inventing—invented—has invented
invention, noun

اكتشاف ـ اختراع

thing which someone has invented; we have seen his latest invention—a machine for putting fruit into jars.

invite [ɪn'vaɪt] verb

يَدْعُو

to ask someone to do something (especially to come to a party, etc.); how many people have you invited to your party? we invited them to come in; don't invite him—he's too rude; he's been invited to speak at the meeting.
invites—inviting—invited—has invited
invitation [ɪnvɪ'teɪʃn] noun

دَعْوة

letter or card sent to someone asking them to do something; I've had an invitation to their party; he's had an invitation to speak at the meeting.

Ireland ['aɪələnd] noun

ايرلندا

island to the west of Great Britain; country which occupies the south part of this island; we're going to Ireland for our holidays; they live in Ireland.
Northern Ireland noun

ايرلندا الشمالية

part of the United Kingdom which occupies the north part of Ireland.
Irish ['aɪrɪʃ] 1. adjective

١ ـ ايرلندي

referring to Ireland; he speaks English with an Irish accent; the Prime Minister of the Irish Republic.

one hundred and fifty

iron

2. *noun*

٢ - الايرلنديّون

the Irish = people who live in or come from Ireland; **the Irish are good at rugby.**

iron [aɪən] **1.** *noun*

١ - أ) حديد - شيء مصنوع من مادة الحديد

(a) common grey metal; **the house has an iron roof; this hammer is made of iron.**

no plural: **some iron; lumps of iron/ pieces of iron**

ب) مِكواة

(b) metal instrument used to make cloth smooth after washing; **she has two irons—but only one of them works; if the iron is too hot it will make a brown mark on my shirt.**

2. *verb*

٢ - يكوي

to make cloth smooth, using an iron; **he was ironing his shirt when the telephone rang; that shirt doesn't look as though it has been ironed.**

irons—ironing—ironed—has ironed

ironing, *noun*

الكوي (كوي الملابس)

clothes which have been washed and are ready to be ironed; **she was doing the ironing.**

is [ɪz] *see* **be**

ملاحظة : انظر إلى كلمة be

island [ˈaɪlənd] *noun*

جزيرة

piece of land with water all round it; **he lives on a little island in the middle of the river Thames; Australia is really a very large island.**

it

isn't [ɪznt] *see* **be**

ملاحظة : انظر إلى كلمة be

it [ɪt] *subject or object pronoun referring to a thing or an animal*

ضمير الغائب المفرد لجماد أو حيوان

أ) (للدلالة على شيء قد سبق ذكره) : هو ، هي ـ ه ـ ها : مثلاً : قطف تفاحة واسقطها

(a) (*used to show something which has just been mentioned*) **he picked up an apple and then dropped it on the ground; I put my hat down somewhere, and now I can't find it; where's my book?—it's on the chair; the dog's hungry—give it something to eat.**

ب) للدلالة على شيء غير معيّن : (هي) تمطر (السماء) ـ (هو) بعيد عن هنا

(b) (*referring to no particular thing*) **it's raining; it's a long way from here to the post office; is it Tuesday today? it's very difficult to get a ticket at this time of year; what time is it?—it's 6 o'clock; it's silly to walk when we've got a car.**

Note: **it's = it is** *or* **it has**

its [ɪts] *adjective*

صيغة الملكية من it : مثلاً لا أستطيع ان اقود دراجتي لأن عجلاتها مفرغة من الهواء

belonging to it; **I can't use my bicycle— one of its tyres is flat; that firm pays its staff very badly.**

Note: written **its** not **it's**

itself [ɪtˈself] *pronoun referring to a thing or an animal*

(ضمير منفصل يتعلق بشيء أو بحيوان) : نفسه ـ نفسها : بمفرده ـ بمفردها : هذا البيت يقع بمفرده ـ يبدو الحصان وكأنه جرح نفسه

the house stands all by itself = all alone; **the horse seems to have hurt itself; the car started to move all by itself; the cat is washing itself; the wires are all right, so there must be something wrong with the TV itself.**

one hundred and fifty-one 151

Jj

jacket [′dʒækɪt] *noun*

سترة ـ مِعْطف قصير

short coat; **he took his jacket off because it was hot; he was wearing grey trousers and a blue jacket.**

jam [dʒæm] *noun*

١) مُرَبّى (مصنوع من الفاكهة)

(*a*) sweet food made by boiling fruit and sugar; **have some jam on your bread; she made jam out of all the fruit in the garden; open another jar of jam—this one is empty.**

ب) ازدحام السير او المرور ـ شلل حركة السير

(*b*) traffic jam = too much traffic on the road, so that vehicles can't move; **the accident caused a big traffic jam; there are jams every Friday evening.**
no plural for (a); **some jam; a pot of jam**

January [′dʒænjʊərɪ] *noun*

كانون الثاني ـ يناير (اول شهر في السنة)

first month of the year; **her birthday is in January; he was born on January 26th; we never go on holiday in January; he went to Canada last January; today is January 6th.**
Note: **January 6th** *say* 'the sixth of January' *or* 'January the sixth'

jar [dʒɑː] *noun*

جَرَّة ـ مرطبان ـ وعاء زجاجي

usually glass pot for keeping food in; **a jar of fruit; put those nuts into that glass jar.**

jaw [dʒɔː] *noun*

فكْ ـ حنك

bones in your face which move up and down and make your mouth open and shut; **your teeth are fixed in your jaw; he fell down and broke his jaw.**

jealous [′dʒeləs] *adjective*

غيور ـ حسود

feeling annoyed because someone has something which you would like to have; **I'm jealous of him because he gets more money than I do; don't be jealous—he works harder than you do; we're all jealous of his long holidays.**

jeans [dʒiːnz] *plural noun*

« جين » : قماش قطني متين ، ازرق اللون إجمالاً
بنطلون من « الجين »

trousers made of a type of strong cloth, usually blue; **she was wearing jeans and a red pullover; I've bought a new pair of jeans/some new jeans.**
Note: say **a pair of jeans** *if you want to show that there is only one*

jewel [′dʒuːəl] *noun*

جوهرة

valuable stone; **she had jewels in her hair.**

jewellery, *noun*

مجوهرات

job

jewels which are worn; **a burglar stole all her jewellery.**
no plural

job [dʒɒb] *noun*

أ) عَمَل

(a) piece of work; **you've made a good job of mending that table** = you've done it well; **I have a couple of jobs for you to do; have you any little jobs you want doing in the house?**

ب) عَمَل ـ شُغل ـ وظيفة

(b) regular work which you get paid for; **he's got a job in a car factory; he's finding it difficult to get a job because he can't drive; she's applied for a job as a teacher; he lost his job when the factory closed.**

ت) مهمة صعبة

(c) difficulty; **I had a job to find your house; what a job!** = how difficult it is!

ث) أمر سار

(d) **good job** = lucky thing; **it's a good job he can drive.**

ج) هذا هو الامر الصحيح

(e) **it's just the job** = it's just the right thing.

join [dʒɔɪn] *verb*

أ) يرتبط ـ يلتقي ـ يربط

(a) to put things together; to come together; **the two roads join about three kilometres further on; you must join the two wires together.**

ب) ينضم ـ يلتحق (بالجيش) ـ يشارك ـ يلحق

(b) to become a member of a group/a club, etc.; to do something with someone; **we are going to the theatre tomorrow—why don't you join us? will you join me for a cup of coffee? his daughter is going to join the police; he's joined the army.**

joins—joining—joined—has joined

jug

joint [dʒɔɪnt] *noun*

أ) ملتقى شيئين

(a) place where two things are joined; **your elbow is a joint in your arm.**

ب) قطعة لحم كبيرة للشي

(b) large piece of meat for cooking; **we have a joint of beef for dinner.**

joke [dʒəʊk] *noun*

نُكْته ـ مزاح ـ هزل ـ اضحوكة

something said to make people laugh; **he was cracking jokes all the time; she made jokes about his hat.**

journey ['dʒɜːnɪ] *noun*

رحلة ـ سفر

travelling a long distance; **he went on a journey across Russia; he has a difficult journey to work every day.**

judge [dʒʌdʒ] **1.** *noun*

١ ـ قاضٍ

person who makes decisions, especially in law; **the judge ordered him to pay a £50 fine; she's the judge in the flower competition; he's one of the judges in the Olympics.**
2. *verb*

٢ ـ أ) يَحْكُم

(a) to decide which is the best; **she's judging the flowers in the flower show.**

ب) يُقَدِّر ـ يحسب

(b) to calculate; **I'm no good at judging distances.**

judges—judging—judged—has judged

jug [dʒʌg] *noun*

إبريق

large pot with a handle, used for keeping liquids in and pouring them; **milk jug; a jug of milk.**

one hundred and fifty-three   153

juice

juice [dʒuːs] *noun* عصير ـ عُصارة

liquid inside fruit/vegetables, etc.; **a glass of orange juice; a tin of tomato juice.**

juicy, *adjective* كثير العُصارة

with a lot of juice in it; **a juicy orange.**
juicy—juicier—juiciest

July [dʒuːˈlai] *noun*
تمّوز ـ يوليو ـ (الشهر السابع من السنة)

seventh month of the year; **he was born in July; she died last July; we are going to Spain next July; today is July 25th.**
Note: **July 25th:** *say* 'the twenty-fifth of July' *or* 'July the twenty-fifth'

jump [dʒʌmp] **1.** *noun*
١ ـ قفزة ـ وثبة

sudden movement off the ground; **long jump/high jump** = sports where you see who can jump furthest or highest.
2. *verb* ٢ ـ يَقفِز ـ يَثِبُ

to go into the air off the ground; **he jumped over the wall; can you jump across this stream? jump on to that bus—it's going to leave; she jumped down from the chair** = she was standing on the chair and then came down to the floor suddenly; **when they fired the gun, it made me jump** = move suddenly because I was surprised or frightened.

ينطلق قبل الأوان المعيّن

to jump the gun = to go first; before you are supposed to; to do something too early.

يتعدى الآخرين في الطابور (أي لا يحترم أولوية الصف في الطابور)

to jump the queue = to go in front of someone who has been waiting for longer than you have.
jumps—jumping—jumped—has jumped

154

just

June [dʒuːn] *noun*
حزيران ـ يونيو (الشهر السادس من السنة)

sixth month of the year; **he was born in June; her birthday is on June 15th; last June we went to the USA; today is June 7th.**
Note: **June 7th:** *say* 'the seventh of June' *or* 'June the seventh'

just [dʒʌst] *adverb*

أ) بصواب ـ تماماً

(*a*) exactly; **it's just by the door; don't come in just yet—we're not ready; just how many of the children can read? she's just sixteen—her birthday was yesterday; what time is it?—it's just six o'clock.**

ب) منذ لحظات ـ منذ وقت وجيز ـ منذ ثوانٍ

(*b*) (*showing something which happened very recently or will happen very soon*) **I had just got into my bath when the phone rang; I'm just going to the shops; I was just going to phone her, when she phoned me; they've just arrived from New York; he's just leaving for the office.**

ت) فقط

(*c*) only; **I've been there just once; wait just a minute!**

تقريباً

just about = nearly; more or less; **I've just about finished my homework.**

على وشك

just about to = will very soon; **he's just about to leave; we are just about to go to bed when the phone rang.**

أ) في نفس اللحظة

just as = (*a*) at the same time; **just as I got into the bath the phone rang.**

ب) تماماً ـ على وجه الضبط

(*b*) in exactly the same way; **this book is just as good as the film; it is just as cold inside the house as it is outside.**

one hundred and fifty-four

keen

أ) في الوقت الحاضر

just now = (a) at the present time; we're very busy just now.

ب) قبل لحظات

(b) a short time ago; **I saw him just now in the bank.**

Kk

keen [kiːn] *adjective*

أ) مُتَحَمِّس ـ مُولع

(a) eager/willing; **he's keen to do well at school; I'm not very keen to go to see that film; she's keen on dancing** = she likes it very much; **he's keen on football.**

ب) حاد ـ قويّ ـ مُمَيِّز

(b) which can notice differences very well; **he has a keen sense of smell.**
keen—keener—keenest

keep [kiːp] *verb*

أ) يحتفظ بـ

(a) to have for a very long time or for ever; **can I keep the book I borrowed from you? I don't want that paper any more—you can keep it; he's kept my watch and won't give it back.**

ب) يستمر ـ يواصل (حركة او عمل او حالة ما)

(b) to continue to do something; **this watch will keep going even under water; he had to keep running so that the police wouldn't catch him; keep quiet or they'll hear you; the weather has kept fine.**

ت) يُبقي

(c) to make someone stay in a state; **what kept you?** = why are you late? **he kept us waiting for twenty minutes; this coat will keep you warm.**

ث) يراقب عن كثب

(d) **to keep an eye on** = to watch carefully; **he's keeping an eye on the shop while I'm away.**
keeps—keeping—kept [kept]—**has kept**

keep off, *verb*

يتجنب ـ يبقى بعيداً عن

to stay away from; **keep off the grass!**

keep on, *verb*

يتابع ـ يستمر ـ لا ينقطع عن

to continue to do something; **my watch keeps on stopping; the traffic kept on moving although the snow was very deep.**

keep up, *verb*

يبقى على نفس المستوى

to keep at the same level; **you're doing very well—keep it up!** = keep doing the same; **he finds it difficult to keep up his French.**

keep up with, *verb*

يُجاري ـ يظلُّ على مستوى واحد (مع الآخرين)

to go at the same speed; **he couldn't keep up with a car on his bicycle; wages can't keep up with the cost of food; she walked so fast that I had difficulty in keeping up with her.**

kettle ['ketl] *noun*

غلّاية

metal container which you use for boiling water; **the kettle's boiling—let's make the tea.**

key

key [ki:] **1.** *noun*

١ - أ) مفتاح (الباب)

(*a*) piece of metal used to open a lock; **I can't get into the house—I've lost the key to the front door; where did you put your car keys?**

ب) مفتاح (في آلة موسيقية او آلة كاتبة..)

(*b*) part of a piano/a typewriter, etc., which you push down with your fingers.

ت) مفتاح الحلّ - مفتاح الرموز

(*c*) answer to a problem/explanation; **is there a key to explain what these signs mean?**
2. *adjective*

٢ - رئيسي - اساسي

most important; **he has the key position in the firm; oil is a key industry.**

kick [kɪk] **1.** *noun*

١ - رفسة

hitting with your foot; **he gave the ball a kick.**
2. *verb*

٢ - يرفس - يضرب برجله

to hit something with your foot; **he kicked the ball into the goal.**
kicks—kicking—kicked—has kicked

kill [kɪl] *verb*

يقتل - يقضي على

to make something die; **the dry weather has killed all my plants; the car hit the dog and killed it; he was killed in a plane crash.**
kills—killing—killed—has killed

kilogram [ˈkɪləɡræm], **kilo** [ˈkiːləʊ] *noun*

كيلوغرام (الف غرام):

measurement of weight; **two kilos of sugar; he weighs 62 kilos (62 kg).**
Note: when used with numbers, **kilos** *is usually written* **kg**

156

kiss

kilometre [kɪˈlɒmɪtə] *noun* (American: **kilometer**)

كيلومتر (الف متر)

measurement of distance; **it is about twenty kilometres (20 km) from here to the railway station; the speed limit is 80 kilometres per hour (80 kmh).**
Note: when used with numbers **kilometres** *is usually written* **km: 26 km;** *note also* **kilometres per hour** *is usually written* **kmh: eighty kilometres per hour = 80 kmh**

kind [kaɪnd] **1.** *noun*

١ - جنس - نوع

sort/type; **a butterfly is a kind of insect; how many kinds of apples do you have in your garden? we were talking about all kinds of things** = about several subjects.
2. *adjective*

٢ - لطيف - مُعين - عطوف - حنون

friendly; helpful; thinking about other people; **it's very kind of you to lend me your car; how kind of him to ask you to the party; you always should be kind to animals; she's the kindest old lady I know.**
kind—kinder—kindest

king [kɪŋ] *noun*

ملك - عاهل

man who rules a country; **King John; the King and Queen came to visit the town.**
Note: **king** *is spelt with a capital when used with a name or when referring to a particular person*

kiss [kɪs] **1.** *noun*

١ - قُبلة

touching someone with your lips to show love; **she gave her mother a kiss.**
plural **kisses**
2. *verb*

٢ - يُقَبّل

to touch someone with your lips to show that you love or like them; **they kissed**

one hundred and fifty-six

kitchen

each other goodbye; he kissed his daughter and went away.
kiss—kissing—kissed—has kissed

kitchen [kɪtʃn] *noun*

مطبخ

room where you cook food/wash dishes, etc.; **don't come into the kitchen with your dirty shoes on; he put the bread down on the kitchen table; the ice cream is in the fridge in the kitchen.**

knee [ni:] *noun*

ركبة

joint in the middle of your leg; **he was on his knees looking for something under the bed; the baby can go quite fast on his hands and knees; the little girl sat on her grandfather's knee.**

kneel [ni:l] *verb*

يَركَعُ

to be or to go on your knees; **he kneeled/knelt down to look under the car; she was kneeling by the bed.**
kneels—kneeling—kneeled/knelt [nelt]**—has kneeled/knelt**

knew [nju:] *see* **know**

ملاحظة : انظر الى كلمة Know

knife [naɪf] *noun*

سكين

tool with a sharp metal blade fixed in a handle; **to lay the table, you put a knife, fork and spoon for each person; cut your meat up with your knife; bread knife** = special large knife for cutting bread.
plural **knives** [naɪvz]

knit [nɪt] *verb*

يُحَيِّك (بصنارة)

to make something out of wool, using two long needles; **she's knitting a pair of socks; he was wearing a red knitted hat; my mother knitted this scarf for me.**
knits—knitting—knitted—has knitted

knot

knock [nɒk] **1.** *noun*

١ ـ أ) طرقة (على الباب)

(*a*) sound made by hitting something; **there was a knock at the door.**

ب) ضربة ـ خبطة

(*b*) the hitting of something; **he had a knock on the head.**
2. *verb*

٢ ـ يضرب ـ يطرق ـ يقرع (الباب)

to hit something; **he knocked on the door before going in; you need a hammer to knock that nail in.**
knocks—knocking—knocked—has knocked

knock down, *verb*

يهدّم ـ يصرع ـ يضرب به على الارض

to make something fall down by hitting it hard; **they are going to knock down the old church to build a new one; he was knocked down by a car.**
Note: **they knocked the church down** *or* **they knocked down the church** *but only* **they knocked it down**

knock off, *verb*

أ) يصطدم بالشيء ويوقعه

(*a*) to make something fall off by hitting it; **the cat knocked the milk jug off the table.**

ب) يكفّ عن العمل

(*b*) to stop work; **the workmen all knocked off at 4.30.**

knock out, *verb*
to hit someone so hard that he is no longer conscious; **he was knocked out by a blow on the head.**

knot [nɒt] *noun*

عُقْدة

place where two pieces of string are tied

Kitchen

المطبخ

1. cooker	١ ـ طباخة
2. cup	٢ ـ فنجان
3. cupboard	٣ ـ دولاب
4. electric light	٤ ـ إضاءة كهرباء
5. electric plug	٥ ـ المأخذ
6. fridge	٦ ـ ثلاجة
7. frying pan	٧ ـ مقلاة
8. glasses	٨ ـ كؤوس
9. handle	٩ ـ مسكة ـ مقبض
10. jug	١٠ ـ ابريق
11. kettle	١١ ـ غلاية
12. kitchen scales	١٢ ـ ميزان
13. lid	١٣ ـ غطاء
14. matchbox	١٤ ـ علبة كبريت
15. oven	١٥ ـ فرن
16. pan (saucepan)	١٦ ـ وعاء ـ طنجرة
17. plate	١٧ ـ صحن
18. saucer	١٨ ـ وعاء للصلصة
19. shelf	١٩ ـ رف
20. sink	٢٠ ـ مجلى
21. steam	٢١ ـ بخار
22. tap	٢٢ ـ حنفية
23. teacloth	٢٣ ـ فوطة
24. teapot	٢٤ ـ ابريق الشاي
25. tin opener	٢٥ ـ فتاحة العلب

one hundred and fifty-eight

know

together; he tied a knot at the end of the piece of string; tie the two ropes together with a knot.

know [nəʊ] *verb*

أ) يعلَمُ (خبراً او حدثاً) ـ يدري بـ ـ يدرك

(*a*) to be informed about something; **do you know how to get to London from here? I didn't know she was married; he knew he would have to spend a lot of money; do you know the German for 'one—two—three'? he doesn't know where she has gone; I didn't know when he was going to come.**

lake

ب) يعرف ـ (شخصاً او مكاناً)

(*b*) to have met someone/to have been to a place often; **I know your brother—we were at school together; I used to know a man called Johnson; I know Scotland very well.**

knows – knowing – knew [njuː] – has known

knowledge [ˈnɒlɪdʒ] *noun*

معرفة ـ دراية ـ علْم

what is known; **he has no knowledge of what is happening; he has a good knowledge of French.**

Ll

lack [læk] **1.** *noun*

١ ـ عدم وجود ـ إفتقار ـ نقص ـ فقدان ـ احتياج

not having something; **the plants are dying through lack of rain; they could not go on holiday for lack of money.**
2. *verb*

٢ ـ ينقصه ـ يفتقر الى ـ يَعْوَز

not to have enough of something; **the plants lack water; he lacks strength** = he isn't strong enough.

lacks – lacking – lacked – has lacked

ladder [ˈlædə] *noun*

سُلَّم

thing made of a row of bars which you use to climb up or down; **he climbed up a ladder to look at the roof; you have to go down a ladder to get into the hole in the ground.**

one hundred and fifty-nine

lady [ˈleɪdɪ] *noun*

السيّدة ـ (إمرأة ذات مقام او مكانة اجتماعية)

(*polite way of referring to a woman*) **there's a lady waiting to see you; a lady doctor.**
plural **ladies**

laid [leɪd] *see* **lay**

ملاحظة : انظر الى كلمة lay

lain [leɪn] *see* **lie**

ملاحظة : انظر الى كلمة lie

lake [leɪk] *noun*

بُحَيرة

large piece of water surrounded by land; **they went out in a boat on the lake; he swam across the lake.**

lamb

lamb [læm] *noun*

أ) حَمَل

(a) baby sheep; **we saw hundreds of lambs in the fields.**

لحم الحَمَل

(b) meat from a young sheep; **we had roast lamb for dinner.**
Note: no plural when it means meat: **some lamb; a slice of lamb**

lamp [læmp] *noun*

مصْباح ـ قنديل ـ مصباح كهربائي

thing which makes light; **an electric lamp; street lamp** = light in a street.

lamppost, *noun*

مصباح لأضاءة الشارع

tall post in a street, holding a lamp; **the car hit a lamppost and stopped.**

---

land [lænd] **1.** *noun*

١ ـ أ) اليابسة

(a) solid soil; **I am glad to be on land again after ten days at sea.**

ب) بلد

(b) country; **people of many lands.**

ت) منطقة ـ قطعة أرض

(c) part of a country; area of ground; **he owns land in Scotland; I have bought a piece of land to build a house on.**

2. *verb*

٢ ـ يَحُطّ ـ يهبط على الأرض ـ يرسو

to come to earth; **the plane landed at the airport; we will be landing at London Airport in 15 minutes.**
lands—landing—landed—has landed

landing, *noun*

أ) هبوط (الطائرة) ـ نزول ـ حطّ

(a) action of coming to earth; **the plane made a good landing.**

ب) منبسط الدرج

(b) flat space at the top of a flight of stairs; **go up the stairs and wait for me on the landing.**

land up, *verb*

ينتهي به الامر الى

to finish up/to end up (in a place); **we set off for London and landed up in Oxford; he tried to steal a car and landed up in prison.**

language ['læŋgwɪdʒ] *noun*

لُغة

way of speaking/writing used by people of a country or area; **Swedish is a very difficult language; English is a language which is used everywhere; I don't enjoy holidays in a country where I don't speak or understand the language; Chinese is the language spoken by most people in the world.**

---

large [lɑːdʒ] *adjective*

كبير ـ ضخم ـ واسع

very big; **he was carrying one large suitcase and two small ones; I want a large cup of coffee, please; how large is your office?**
large—larger—largest

largely, *adverb*

في معظمه ـ إجمالاً ـ الى حدٍ كبير

mainly/mostly; **the country is largely forest.**

---

last [lɑːst] **1.** *adjective*

١ ـ أ) أخير ـ آخر

(a) which comes at the end; **they live in the last house on the right; you must pay me by the last day of the month; December 31st is the last day of the year; last but one** = the one before the last one; **they live in the last house but one.**

ب) السابق ـ الماضي : (الاسبوع الماضي ، العام الماضي ...)

(b) most recent; **last Monday** = the Monday before today; **last week** = the week before this one; **I saw her last**

late

Thursday; where did you go on holiday last year? last month it rained almost every day; she's been ill for the last ten days.

ت) ما قبل الأخير

(c) before last = the one before the most recent; the Monday before last = two Mondays ago; the week before last = two weeks ago.

2. noun

٢ ـ الأخير

thing/person coming at the end; she was the last to arrive; that's the last of the apples = we have finished the apples.

3. adverb

٣ ـ أ) في المؤخرة

(a) at the end; he came last in the race.

ب) آخر مرّة قبل الزمن الحاضر

(b) most recently; when did you see her last? she was looking ill when I saw her last.

4. verb

٤ ـ يَسْتَمِرّ ـ يَطُول

to stay/to go on; the fine weather won't last; our holidays never seem to last very long; the storm lasted all night.

lasts—lasting—lasted—has lasted

اخيراً ـ بعد تأخر طويل

at last/at long last = in the end/ finally/after a long delay; I walked for hours, and got home at last at 6 o'clock; at long last the train arrived.

lastly, adverb

اخيراً

finally; lastly I want to thank my friends for their help.

late [leɪt] 1. adjective

١ ـ أ) مُتَأَخِّر

(a) after the usual time; after the expected time; the train is ten minutes late; it's too late to change your ticket; if you don't hurry you'll be late.

laugh

ب) متأخر

(b) at the end of a period of time; we had tea in the late afternoon; there are always films on the late evening programmes on TV.

ت) في ساعة متأخرة

(c) towards the end of the day; it's late—I'm going to bed.

ث) الاخيرة

(d) latest = most recent; the radio gives the latest news at 10.00; have you read his latest book?

late—later—last/latest

2. adverb

٢ ـ أ) بعد الوقت المألوف او المنتظر

(a) after the usual time; the train arrived late; we went to bed late last night; she got up late this morning.

ب) في ما بعد ـ بعد زمن ما ـ (جاء بعد شهر)

(b) at a time after the present; after a time which has been mentioned; he came a month later; can I see you later this afternoon? see you later! = I hope to see you again later today.

late—later—last

lately, adverb

مؤخراً ـ حديثاً ـ منذ عهد قريب

recently; have you seen her lately? he's been quite busy lately.

laugh [lɑːf] 1. noun

١ ـ ضحك

sound you make when you are amused; she's got a lovely laugh; he said it with a laugh; he did it for a laugh = as a joke.

2. verb

٢ ـ يضحك ـ يسخر من ـ يهزأ بـ

to make a sound to show you are amused; they all laughed at his jokes; when he fell off his bicycle everyone laughed; don't laugh at him because he's so fat; you mustn't laugh at her hat.

laughs—laughing—laughed—has laughed

laundry

laundry ['lɔ:ndrɪ] *noun*

أ) المغسل : حجرة مخصصة لغسل الملابس (في البيت)
المصبغة : مؤسسة لغسل الملابس

(a) place where clothes, etc., are washed; **you had better send your shirts to the laundry.**

ب) ملابس معدة للغسيل
ملابس مغسولة

(b) clothes, etc., which need to be washed or which have been washed; **have you any laundry to be washed?**
plural **laundries**, *but no plural for (b)*

lavatory ['lævətrɪ] *noun*

مغسلة ـ مكان لغسل اليدين

toilet/place or room where you get rid of water or solid waste from your body; **the ladies' lavatory is to the right.**
plural **lavatories**

law [lɔ:] *noun*

قانون ـ نظام

set of rules which govern a country; **you must always obey the law; driving at night without lights is against the law; Parliament has passed a law forbidding the use of dangerous drugs.**

lawyer ['lɔ:jə] *noun*

المحامي

person who knows about laws and can advise you about them; **if you are arrested, you must try to speak to your lawyer.**

lawn [lɔ:n] *noun*

قطعة أرض منبسطة ومزروعة بنوع خاص من العشب الصغير ـ مرج

area in a garden covered with short grass; **let's have tea outside on the lawn; the lawn needs cutting; the town hall has a large lawn in front of it.**

lay [leɪ] *verb*

أ) يطرح على الارض ـ يبيض (الدجاج)

(a) to put something down; **he laid the book down on the table; they are laying a new carpet in the dining room; the hen has laid an egg.**

ب) يرتّب (الطاولة)

(b) **to lay the table** = to put knives/forks/spoons, etc., on the table ready for a meal; **the table is laid for four people.**

ت) ملاحظة : انظر ايضاً الى كلمة lie

(c) *see also* **lie.**
lays—laying—laid—has laid

lay out, *verb*

يكشف ـ يُظهر

to put out; to spread out; **the map was laid out on the table; the presents are laid out under the Christmas tree.**

lazy ['leɪzɪ] *adjective*

كسول

not wanting to do any work; **he's too lazy to earn a lot of money; she's the laziest girl in the school.**
lazy—lazier—laziest

lb, *see* **pound**

ملاحظة : انظر الى كلمة pound

lead¹ [led] *noun*

أ)رصاص

(a) very heavy soft metal; **you should tie a piece of lead to your fishing line to make it sink.**

ب) رصاص القلم

(b) black part in the middle of a pencil; **the lead's broken—I must sharpen the pencil.**
no plural for (a)

lead² [li:d] **1.** *noun*

١ ـ أ) طوق (للكلاب)

(a) string or thin piece of leather to hold a dog; **dogs must be kept on a lead.**

ب) الطليعة (في سباق)

(b) first place (in a race); **he went into the lead; who's in the lead?**

leaf

2. *verb*

٢ - أ) يتقدم (غيره) - يتقدم على (غيره)

(a) to be in first place; our team was leading at half time; he is leading by two metres.

ب) يقود (احداً نحو او الى) يؤدي الى

(b) to go in front to show the way; she led us to the post office; the path leads to the top of the hill.

ت) يقود - يكون على رأس مجموعة ... يتزعّم

(c) to be in charge of/to be the main person; he is leading a group of businessmen on a tour of Italian factories.

ث) يؤدي الى - يكون السبب في - يُسبب

(d) to lead to = to be the cause of; the discussion led to a violent argument.
leads—leading—led [led]—**has led**

leader, *noun*

زعيم - رئيس (وفد) - قائد (حزب)

person who leads; he is the leader of the group.

lead up to, *verb*

يؤدي - يُسبّب - يكون السبب في

to be the cause of; to take place just before; the events leading up to the war; the discussion led up to an agreement.

leaf [li:f] *noun*

ورقة نبات

flat green part of a plant; in the winter the leaves fall off the trees and grow again in the spring; insects have eaten the leaves of the cabbages.
plural **leaves** [li:vz]; *see also* **leave**

lean [li:n]*verb*

يتكىء على - يُسند على - يَستند على - يتكل على - يميل الى - يُحْني رأسه

to keep upright by resting against something; to bend over; lean the ladder against the wall; he leant his elbows on the table; the ladder is leaning up against

leave

the wall; don't lean over the edge of the roof; he was leaning out of the window.
leans—leaning—leaned/leant [lent]—**has leaned/leant**

learn [l3:n] *verb*

يتعلَّم - يَدْرُس

(a) to find out about something/how to do something; she's learning to swim; we learn English at school; have you learnt how to drive yet?

ب) يَعْلَمُ - يَعْرِفُ - يكتشف

(b) to hear (news); I learnt that they were leaving; when did you learn that she was getting married?
learns—learning—learnt/learned—has learnt/learned

learner, *noun*

الطالب - التلميذ - الطالب المبتدأ

person who is learning; a learner driver = someone who is learning to drive.

least [li:st] *adverb, adjective & noun*

الادنى - الاصغر - الاقل

smallest; less than anything; that's the least of my problems; it's the thing I worry about least of all; it doesn't matter in the least =

على الاطلاق

it doesn't matter at all.

ولكن على الاقل

at least = at any rate; even if the job is dull, at least you have enough money to live on.

leather ['leðə] *noun*

جلْد مدبوغ

skin of animals used to make shoes, etc.; a leather belt; her jacket is made of leather.
no plural

leave [li:v] *verb*

ا) يُغادر - ينصرف

(a) to go away; he left the house; the

led ... lemon

train leaves at 10.00; when does the train leave for Edinburgh?

ب) يترك ــ ينسى

(b) to forget (to do something); to let something stay; **she left her toothbrush at home; someone has left the light on; did you leave the door locked?**

ت) يترك ــ يتخلى عن

(c) not to take; **leave a piece of cake for your brother.**

ث) بقايا ــ ما يتبقى (من شيء)

(d) left *or* left over = remaining; **after paying for the meal and the theatre tickets, I've still got £3 left over; if you eat three apples there will be only two left; there is nobody left in the office.**

leaves—leaving—left [left]**—has left**

leave behind, *verb*

ينسى ان يأخذ معه

to forget to take; not to take; **he left his keys behind in the shop; we had to leave the dog behind at home.**

leave off, *verb*

ا) يتخلى عن

(a) to stop; **he suddenly left off smoking; leave off!** = stop doing that!

ب) ينسى ان يضع او يسجّل

(b) to forget to put on; **she left the address off the envelope; the waiter left the drinks off the bill.**

leave out, *verb*

ينسى ان يضيف او يشمل او يضمّن

to forget to put in; not to include; **he left out the most important detail when he reported the accident to the police; we left him out of the team because he's got a cold.**

Note: **don't leave your sister out** *or* **don't leave out your sister** *but only* **don't leave her out**

led [led] *see* **lead²**

ملاحظة : انظر الى كلمة lead

164

left [left] *adverb, adjective & noun*

أيسر ــ يسرى

referring to the side of the body which usually has the weaker hand; **he can't catch with his left hand; in England, cars drive on the left; his house is on the left side of the street; go down the street and turn left at the traffic lights; keep going left if you want to get to the beach;** *see also* **leave**

ملاحظة : انظر ايضاً الى كلمة leave

left-hand, *adjective*

الجهة اليسرى

on the left side; **look in the left-hand drawer; they live on the left-hand side of the street.**

left-handed, *adjective*

أعسر ــ عامل باليد اليسرى

using the left hand more often than the right for writing; **he's left-handed.**

leg [leg] *noun*

ا) رجل ــ ساق

(a) part of the body with which a person or animal walks; one of the parts of a chair, etc., which touch the floor; **he's standing on one leg; the table has got four legs; some dogs can stand on their back legs; she fell off the wall and broke her leg; he's pulling your leg** = he's making you believe something which is untrue/he's joking.

ب) فخذ (بقر او دجاج ..)

(b) leg of an animal used for food; **a leg of lamb; would you like a chicken leg?**

lemon ['lemən] *noun*

ليمون حامض

bitter yellow fruit; **put some lemon juice on your fish; do you want a piece of lemon in your drink?**

lemonade [lemə'neɪd] *noun*

الليموناضة (عصير الليمون المحلّي)

drink made from lemons; **can I have a glass of lemonade?**

one hundred and sixty-four

lend

lend [lend] *verb*

يُعير - يعترض (مالاً) - يساعد

to give something to someone for a certain period of time; **can you lend me your dictionary? can you lend me £5 till Monday? I lent her my bike and now she won't give it back; to lend a hand** = to help; **can you lend a hand with the cooking?**

lends—lending—lent [lent]—has lent
Note: compare **borrow**

length [leŋkθ] *noun*

طول - امتداد - مسافة

measurement of how long something is; **the garden is 25 metres in length; he swam a length of the pool** = he swam from one end to the other.

lent [lent] *see* **lend**

انظر الى كلمة lend

less [les] **1.** *adjective & noun*

١ - أقل - أدنى

smaller (quantity/size, etc.); **you ought to eat less bread; the bill comes to less than £10; he finished his work in less than an hour.**
2. *adverb*

٢ - بمقدارٍ أقل - بدرجةٍ أقل - أقل

not as much; **she's trying to eat less; the second book is less well known than the first; I want a suitcase which is less heavy than this one.**

lesson ['lesn] *noun*

أمثولة - دَرْس

period of time in school, etc., when you are taught something; **he went to sleep during the maths lesson; we have six lessons of English a week; he's taking/having driving lessons; she gives English lessons at home in the evenings.**

let

let [let] *verb*

أ) يدع - يسمح

(*a*) to allow someone to do something; **let me wash the car; will he let us go home early today? can you let me have two kilos of sugar? they let her borrow their car; let them come in—it's raining hard; can you let me know as soon as possible?** = can you tell me.

ب) يُؤجِّر

(*b*) to allow someone to borrow a house for a time and pay for it; **I'm letting my house to an American family for the summer; this flat is to let at £100 a month.**

ت) هيّا بنا (مصحوبة بالفعل اجمالاً) هيّا بنا نذهب الى السينما - (لنذهب الى السينما) ..

(*c*) (*showing a suggestion*) **let's all go to the cinema; don't let's start yet/let's not start yet.**

lets—letting—let—has let

let down, *verb*

أ) يدعه يسقط - يُدْلي

(*a*) to allow something to go down; **they let down the bucket on a rope.**

ب) يفرّغ من الهواء (إطار)

(*b*) to allow the air to go out of a tyre, etc.; **he let down my back tyre.**

ت) يَخْذل شخصاً - لا يتجاوب معه

(*c*) not to help someone who was expecting you to help; **I asked him to speak at the meeting but he let me down.**

let go, *verb*

يُطْلِق - يُفْلِت

to stop holding on to something; **don't let go of the handle; he held on to the branch, and then had to let go of it.**

let in, *verb*

يدعه يدخل - يسمح له بالدخول - يدعه يتسرّب (سائل ، ماء)

to allow to come in; **don't let the dog in if he's wet; these shoes are no good—they let in water/they let the water in.**

one hundred and sixty-five   **165**

letter

let yourself in for, *verb*

يتورط ـ يُورّط نفسه بـ

to allow something to happen to you; **he didn't realise what he letting himself in for when he said he would paint the house** = didn't realise what a big job it was.

let off, *verb*

أ) يطلق (الرصاص ، القوس)

(*a*) to make a gun, etc., fire; **the gun made a loud noise when they let it off.**

ب) يعفو عن ـ يعذر

(*b*) not to punish someone/not to give someone work; **he was arrested for stealing; but the judge let him off with a fine; the teacher has let us off our homework.**

let on, *verb*

يُفشى (سراً او خبراً)

to tell; **don't let on that I was there.**

let out, *verb*

يُخْرج ـ يدعه يخرج او يُفلت

to allow to go out; **they let the sheep out of the field; don't let the dog out when the postman is coming; he let the air out of my back tyre.**

let up, *verb*

يَتوقف ـ يَكُفُّ عن ـ ينقص ـ يخفّ

to stop/to become less; **the rain didn't let up all day; he's working too hard—he ought to let up a bit.**

Note: **don't let the dog in** *or* **don't let in the dog; he let the bucket down** *or* **he let down the bucket,** *etc., but only* **don't let it in, he let it down,** *etc.*

letter ['letə] *noun*

أ) رسالة

(*a*) message in writing sent from one person to another; **the postman has brought two letters for you; I must write a letter to my mother to tell her how we all are; I've had a letter from the bank manager; can you post this letter for me?**

ب) حرف (من حروف الابجدية)

(*b*) sign used in writing; **A is the first letter of the alphabet; can you think of a word with eight letters beginning with A and ending with T?**

letterbox, *noun*

أ) صندوق البريد

(*a*) box in the road where you post letters; **can you post these letters for me?; there's a letterbox at the corner of the street.**

ب) صندوق البريد (الخاص بالمنزل)

(*b*) hole in a front door through which the postman delivers letters; **the newspaper is too thick to go into the letterbox.**

level ['levl] **1.** *adjective*

أ) أفقي ـ منبسط

(*a*) horizontal/not sloping; **this table isn't level, put a piece of wood under the leg.**

ب) متساو مع ـ على نفس المستوى

(*b*) at the same height as something; **can you hang this picture level with the other one? the water is level with the top of the glass.**

2. *noun*

٢ ـ مستوى ـ سطح : تقع المدينة على ارتفاع ٩٠٠ متر فوق سطح البحر

height; **the room is on a level with the garden; the town is 900 metres above sea level; the government wants to reduce the level of public spending.**

3. *verb*

٣ ـ يُسوّي (الارض) ـ يُسَطِّح ـ يجعله منبسطاً

to make something flat; **they are levelling the ground before they start building; the road goes up and down, and then levels out for a few miles.**

levels - levelling - levelled - has levelled

library

library [ˈlaɪbrərɪ] *noun*

مكتبة عامة ـ مجموعة كتب او مستندات

place where books are kept which can then be borrowed; collection of books/records, etc.; **he has a big library of records; don't forget to take your books back to the library; this book isn't mine—it's a library book.**
plural **libraries**

librarian [laɪˈbreərɪən] *noun*

أمين المكتبة ـ الموظف المسؤول على المكتبة

person who works in a library.

lick [lɪk] *verb*

يلعق ـ يلحس

to make your tongue move over something; **she was licking an ice cream; the cat licked up the spilt milk; he forgot to lick the envelope.**
licks—licking—licked—has licked

lid [lɪd] *noun*

غطاء (صندوق او إناء)

top which covers a container; **put the lid back on the jam jar; I've lost the lid of the kettle.**

lie [laɪ] **1.** *noun*

١ ـ أكذوبة ـ كذب

something which is not true; **he's been telling lies about his brother.**
2. *verb*

٢ ـ يكذب

to say something which is not true; **he was lying when he said he hadn't touched the money; he lied to the police about the accident.**
lies—lying—lied—has lied
3. *verb*

٣ ـ يتمدّد ـ ينبسط

to be in a flat position; **the dog was lying in front of the fire; snow lay 6 inches deep on the ground; there were leaves**

lift

lying all over the pavement; we lay in the sun all afternoon.
lies—lying—lay [leɪ]**—has lain**

lie down, *verb*

يستلقي (على الارض) ـ يستريح (في فراشه)

to put yourself in a flat position; **she lay down on the floor; just as I was lying down the telephone rang.**

lie in, *verb*

يبقى في فراشه مدة اطول من العادة

to stay in bed late in the morning.

life [laɪf] *noun*

حياة ـ عمر

time when you are alive; being alive; **he spent his whole life working on the farm; a miner has a hard life; life insurance** = insurance against death; **she saved my life** = saved me from dying; **there's no sign of life in the house** = it looks as though there is no one in it.

lifebelt, *noun*

حزام النجاة

large ring which helps you to float in water.

lifeboat, *noun*

قارب النجاة (من الغرق)

special boat used to rescue people at sea; **the lifeboat rescued the crew of the sinking ship.**

lift [lɪft] **1.** *noun*

١ ـ أ) المصعد

(*a*) (*American:* **elevator**) machine which takes people from one floor to another in a tall building; **take the lift to the sixth floor; push the button to call the lift.**

ب) نقلة الطريق : نقل شخص ما بالسيارة في سبيل المساعدة

(*b*) ride offered to someone; **can I give you a lift to the station in my car?**
2. *verb*

one hundred and sixty-seven 167

light

٢ - يَرْفع

to raise to a higher position; to pick something up; **this case is so heavy, I can't lift it off the floor; he hurt his back lifting a box down from the shelf.**
lifts—lifting—lifted—has lifted

light [laɪt] **1.** *adjective*

أ) خفيف الوزن - رقيق - خفيف المجهود

(*a*) not heavy; **I can carry this case easily—it's quite light; she was only wearing a light coat; he's not fit, and so can only do light work.**

ب) فاتح اللون

(*b*) pale; **a light blue shirt; our house has a light green door; she has light hair.**

ت) منير - مُشرق

(*c*) bright so that you can see well; **the kitchen is lighter than our dining room; at six o'clock in the morning it was just getting light.**

ب) خفيف - (موسيقى خفيفة)

(*d*) **light music** = not serious music.
light—lighter—lightest
2. *noun*

٢ - أ) نور - ضوء

(*a*) thing which shines and helps you to see; **you can't read by the light of the moon; the light of the sun makes plants green; there's not enough light in here to take a photo.**

ب) وسيلة إنارة - مصباح كهربائي

(*b*) object (usually a glass bulb) which gives out light; **switch on the lights—it's getting dark; the car was travelling with no lights; I could see the red lights of the car in front of me; I'm going to put a light on the wall so that I can read in bed.**

ت) هل لديك شعلة - (الرجاء إشعل لي سيجارتي)

(*c*) **can you give me a light?** = have you a match or lighter to light my cigarette?
3. *verb*

٣ - يُشعل (النار)

to make something start to burn; **can you light the gas under the kettle? I can't get the fire to light; light a match—we can't see in the dark.**
lights—lighting—lit—has lit

lighter, *noun*

ولّاعة - قدّاحة (لاشعال السجاير)

small machine for lighting cigarettes; **can I borrow your lighter—mine has run out of gas?**

lighthouse, *noun*

منارة (لهداية الملاحين)

tall building near the sea which shines a bright light at night to warn ships that rocks are near.

lighting, *noun*

الاضاءة - الانارة

way of giving light; **the lighting is very bad in the dining room—we can't see what we are eating.**

lights, *plural noun*

اشارات المرور الضوئية

red, green and orange lights for making traffic stop and start; **turn right at the lights; he went across the crossroads when the lights were red.**

lightning [ˈlaɪtnɪŋ] *noun*

بَرْق

flash of electricity in the sky, followed by the noise of thunder; **during the storm, lightning struck the town hall clock; a flash of lightning lit the sky.**
no plural: **some lightning; a flash of lightning**

like

like [laɪk] **1.** *preposition*

١ - مثل - كـ : (هو مثل ابيه) - مطابق : (صورتها لا تتطابق مع الحقيقة) - مشابه - مماثل - ميّال الى

nearly the same as/similar to; **he's very like his father; the photo doesn't look like her at all; what was the weather like on holiday? he swims like a fish; it tastes like jam; it sounds like Beethoven; it**

limit

feels like rain = as if it is going to rain; **I feel like a cup of tea** = I want a cup of tea.
2. *verb*

٢ ـ أ) يحب ـ يودّ ـ يرغب ـ يشاء

(*a*) to be pleased with; to enjoy; **do you like butter? he doesn't like fish; I like my new teacher; do you like driving? I like to sit and read quietly in the evening.**

ب) يَوَدّ ان

(*b*) to want; **I'd like you to meet my father; we'd like to go to Sweden; take as much sugar as you like.**

likes—liking—liked—has liked

likely, *adjective*

مُحتمل ـ مُرَجَّح ـ منتظَر

which you expect to happen; **it's likely to rain** = it'll probably rain; **he's not likely to win** = he will probably not win.

likely—likelier—likeliest

liking, *noun*

ميل ـ ولوع

being fond of; **he has a liking for sweets; I've taken a liking to her** = I've started to like her.

limit ['lımıt] **1.** *noun*

١ ـ تُخْم ـ حَدّ

furthest point/place past which you cannot go; **there is a speed limit of 30 miles per hour in towns; there is no age limit for joining the club** = people of all ages can join.
2. *verb*

٢ ـ يحدّ ـ يحدّد

to set a limit to something; **the club is limited to 200 members** = only 200 people may belong to it; **parking is limited to 30 minutes** = you can only park for 30 minutes; **limited company** = business where the owners do not have to pay all the company's debts; **John Smith, Limited.**

limits—limiting—limited—has limited

line

Note: in names of companies **limited** *is often written* **Ltd**

line [laın] **1.** *noun*

١ ـ أ) خطّ ـ سطر

(*a*) long thin mark; **he drew a straight line with his pencil; she has lines on her forehead; you must not park on the yellow lines; I want some notepaper without any lines; the football went over the line.**

ب) سلك ـ خيط ـ حبل ـ خطّ هاتفي او تلغرافيّ ..

(*b*) long wire/string; **fishing line; telephone line; speak more clearly—the line's bad; we had a crossed line** = two telephone conversations were mixed together; **he's on the line now** = he is on the phone waiting to speak to you.

ت) صف (من السيارات او الاشخاص او الكلمات)

(*c*) row (of cars/people/words, etc.); **we stood in line for half an hour waiting to get into the exhibition; no buses came for a long time, then three of them came in a line; the line of cars stretched for three miles from the accident; she only typed two lines and made six mistakes; start at the top line on page 6; can you read that line again?**

ث) سكة الحديد

(*d*) **railway line** = metal rails on which trains run; **don't cross the lines when a train is coming.**
2. *verb*

٢ ـ أ) يَصْتَف ـ يقف في خطّ واحد

(*a*) to make a line; **the soldiers lined the streets** = stood in line along the pavements; **lined paper** = paper with lines printed on it.

ب) يُعَرِّف ـ يزيّن بالخطوط الالبسة او قطعة قماش

(*b*) to put a lining inside a piece of clothing; **she was wearing a dress lined with silk; have you any fur-lined boots?**

lines—lining—lined—has lined

one hundred and sixty-nine   **169**

lip

line up, *verb*

يقف في الصف

to stand in a line; **if you want tickets, line up over here.**

lining, *noun*

بطّانة الثوب ـ تبطين

material put on the inside of a piece of clothing; **a dress with a silk lining.**

lip [lıp] *noun*

شفة

one of two parts round the edge of your mouth; **he licked his lips when he thought of dinner; she fell over and cut her top lip.**

lipstick, *noun*

احمر الشفاه

stick of red colour which you put on your lips; **she put her lipstick on.**

liquid ['lıkwıd] *adjective & noun*

سائل ـ مائع

something (like water) which is not solid and is not a gas; **heat the butter until it is quite liquid; he's ill and needs a lot of liquids.**

list [lıst] **1.** *noun*

١ ـ قائمة

number of things written down one after the other; **there is a list of names in alphabetical order; we couldn't remember what to buy because we forgot the shopping list; he's on the danger list** = he is very seriously ill.
2. *verb*

٢ ـ يضع قائمة ـ يسجل ضمن قائمة ـ يُدَوِّن على لائحة

to write in the form of a list; **the streets are listed at the back of the book; all the restaurants are listed in the yellow pages.**
lists—listing—listed—has listed

170

little

listen ['lısn] *verb*

يستمع ـ يُصْغي الى

to pay attention to something which you hear; **be quiet—I'm listening to the news; if you listened to what I tell you, you wouldn't make so many mistakes; will you listen for the telephone while I'm in the garden** = will you wait to see if it rings?
listens—listening—listened—has listened

listener, *noun*

مستمع

person who listens.

lit [lıt] *see* **light**

ملاحظة: انظر الى كلمة light

litre ['li:tə] *noun (American:* **liter**)

لِتْر: وحدة مكاييل تعادل كيلوغرام من الماء

measurement of liquids; **can you buy a litre of milk? this bucket contains two litres.**

little ['lıtl] **1.** *adjective*

١ ـ أ) صغير

(*a*) small/not big; **they have two children—a boy and a little girl** = a young girl; **he has a ring on his little finger; she stood on my little toe.**

ب) قليل

(*b*) not much; **she eats very little bread; the car uses very little petrol.**
little—less—least
2. *noun*

٢ ـ قليل ـ مقدار قليل

a little = a small amount; **give me a little of that soup; would you like some more coffee?—just a little, please.**
3. *adverb*

٣ ـ قليلاً ـ بقليل

not much; **it was little more than fifteen minutes ago; I see her very little these days.**

one hundred and seventy

live

تدريجياً ـ شيئاً فشيئاً

little by little = not all at the same time; little by little, he got better.

live 1. *adjective* [laɪv]

١ ـ أ) حي

(a) living/not dead; **a real live film star** = an actual film star.

ب) على الهواء(برنامج على الهواء اي غير مسجل)

(b) not recorded; **a live TV programme.**

ت) مشحون بالتيار الكهربائي

(c) carrying electricity; **don't walk on the live rail; watch out—that's a live wire.**

2. *verb* [lɪv]

٢ ـ أ) يقيم ـ يسكن

(a) to have your home in a place; **we live in London; they used to live in Germany; do you like living in the town better than in the country? they live in a house by the river; where do your parents live? they live at 15, London Road.**

ب) يعيش ـ يحيا ـ يقضي حياته

(b) to be alive; **Queen Elizabeth lived in the 16th century; he is very ill, and the doctor doesn't expect him to live much longer.**

lives—living—lived—has lived

lively [ˈlaɪvlɪ] *adjective*

مُفْعَم بالحياة ـ نشيط ـ مثير

active; **my grandfather is very lively; we had a very lively party with dozens of guests.**

live on, *verb*

يعيش على (البيض والخبز)

to use something to stay alive; **he lives on eggs and bread; you can't live on £10 a week; he doesn't earn enough to live on.**

living room, *noun*

حجرة الجلوس

room in a house which the family spend most time in; **we sat in the living room and watched TV; the living room door is shut; they were having tea in the living room.**

lock

load [ləʊd] **1.** *noun*

١ ـ حمولة ـ حمل ـ الكثير من

things which are carried in a vehicle; **a lorry with a load of potatoes; the aircraft had a load of supplies; loads of** = a lot of; **he's got loads of money.**

2. *verb*

٢ ـ يحمّل

to put things into a vehicle; **we're loading the lorry with bags of coal; the ship's loading in the harbour; the aircraft was loaded with supplies for the soldiers.**

loads—loading—loaded—has loaded

loaf [ləʊf] *noun*

رغيف

large piece of bread baked separately; **can you buy me one white loaf and a brown one? have you eaten all that loaf of bread? the baker took the loaves out of the oven.**

plural **loaves** [ləʊvz]

local [ˈləʊkl] *adjective*

مَحَلّي : (الحكومة المحلّية) ـ (نبأ محلّي)..

referring to the place/area near where you live; **we do all our shopping in the local shops; local government** = organization of towns and areas of the country.

lock [lɒk] **1.** *noun*

١ ـ قُفْل

thing which closes a door/a box, etc., so that you can only open it with a key; **you left the key in the lock, so anyone could have opened the door; the lock is very stiff—I can't turn the key.**

2. *verb*

٢ ـ يقفل

one hundred and seventy-one 171

Living Room

حجرة الجلوس

1. armchair	١ـ كرسي ذو ذراعين	12. lamp	١٢ـ مصباح كهربائي
2. bookcase	٢ـ خزانة كتب	13. loudspeaker	١٣ـ مكبر الصوت
3. bookshelf	٣ـ رف للكتب	14. picture	١٤ـ صورة
4. carpet	٤ـ سجادة	15. radio	١٥ـ راديو
5. ceiling	٥ـ كرسي	16. record	١٦ـ اسطوانة
6. chair	٦ـ ساعة جدران	17. record player	١٧ـ لاعبة الاسطوانات
7. clock	٧ـ ساعة جدران	18. rocking chair	١٨ـ كرسي هزاز
8. cushion	٨ـ وسادة	19. rug	١٩ـ بساط
9. fire	٩ـ نار	20. sofa	٢٠ـ الأريكة
10. fireplace	١٠ـ مصطلي ـ مستوقد	21. telephone	٢١ـ هاتف
11. floor	١١ـ الأرض	22. television	٢٢ـ تلفيزيون

172 *one hundred and seventy-two*

lonely

to close a door/a box, etc., so that it has to be opened with a key; **the door's locked—can you climb in through a window? did you remember to lock the car? my father locks all the doors each night before he goes to bed.**

locks—locking—locked—has locked

lock in/lock out, *verb*

يحبس شخصاً الخ .. في الداخل ـ يمنع شخصاً من الدخول

to make someone stay inside/outside because a door is locked; **my mother went shopping and locked my father out; he came back late and found he was locked out; I've left the keys inside and locked myself out; I think we've been locked in.**

lock up, *verb*

أ) يقفل ابواب (مبنى او بيت)

(*a*) to close a building by locking the doors; **don't forget to lock up before you go home; he was locking up the shop when a customer called.**

ب) يضع في صندوق او خزنة او مكان مقفل

(*b*) to keep a person/a thing inside by locking a door; **I'll lock up these jewels in the safe/I'll lock these jewels up in the safe; the police locked him up in prison for the night.**

Note: he locked the jewels up or he locked up the jewels but only he locked them up

lonely ['ləʊnlɪ] *adjective*

مُتَوَحِّد ـ شاعر بالوحدة

sad because you are alone; **come and stay with me—it's lonely being in this big house all by myself; she was so lonely on holiday that she came back early.**

lonely—lonelier—loneliest

long [lɒŋ] **1.** *adjective*

١ ـ طويل

not short; which measures a lot; **a long piece of string; what a long film—it** lasted for more than three hours; **we've been waiting for a long time; do you have long holidays in your job? how long is it before the holidays begin? the table is three feet long; is the Amazon the longest river in the world? your hair is getting long—it needs cutting.**

long—longer—longest

Note: used with figures: **the road is six miles long; a piece of string a metre long**

2. *adverb*

٢ ـ منذ وقت طويل ـ طويلاً ـ لمدة طويلة

for a long time; **have you been waiting long? I couldn't wait any longer; she died long ago.**

long—longer—longest

ما دام ـ طالما ـ إذا ـ شريطة ان

as long as/so long as = provided that; **it's nice to go on a picnic as long as it doesn't rain.**

3. *verb*

٣ ـ يتوق الى ـ يتشوَّق الى

to want something very much; **I'm longing for a cup of tea; they long to be back home.**

longs—longing—longed—has longed

look

look [lʊk] **1.** *noun*

١ ـ أ) نظرة

(*a*) seeing something with your eyes; **take a look at this picture; they had a quick look round the town.**

ب) مظهر ـ هيئة ـ طلعة

(*b*) the way someone/something seems to be; **he has a foreign look about him.**

ت) وسامة ـ جمال

(*c*) **good looks** = beautiful appearance.

2. *verb*

٢ ـ أ) ينظر ـ يراقب

(*a*) to turn your eyes towards something; **look at this picture; we spent all evening looking at TV; can you look in the oven and see if the meat is cooked?**

one hundred and seventy-three 173

look after

she looked out of the window and saw the postman; he was looking under the bed.

ب) يبدو

(b) to be seen to be; to seem; he looks ill; she looks at least eighty = she seems to be at least 80 years old; that cake looks good; what does she look like? he looks like his father; it looks as if it may rain/it looks like rain = it seems that it will rain.

looks—looking—looked—has looked

look after, verb

يعتني بـ - يسهر على

to take care of; the nurses looked after their patients; who's looking after your cat when you're away?

look for, verb

يبحث عن

to try to find; he looked everywhere for his missing watch; the police are looking for the prisoner who has escaped.

look forward to, verb

يتشوّق - يتطلّع الى

to think happily about something which is going to happen; I'm looking forward to my holidays; he isn't looking forward to his exams; I'm looking forward to seeing her again.

look in, verb

يزور - يقوم بزيارة قصيرة

to pay a short visit; I'll look in on my way home.

look out, verb

ينتبه - يحذر

to be careful; look out! the pavement is covered with ice.

look out for, verb

أ) يستمر في البحث عن

(a) to keep looking to try to find; he's looking out for new staff to work in the office; I'll look out for you at the party.

loose

ب) يَحْذَر

(b) to be careful about; look out for ice on the road.

look round, verb

أ) يلتفت - ينظر حوله

(a) to turn to see what is behind you; when he heard footsteps in the road he quickly looked round.

ب) يدرس الاحتمالات قبل اتخاذ قرار ما

(b) to go round looking at something; did you look round the museum? do you want to buy something?—no, I'm just looking round.

look up, verb

أ) ينظر الى أعلى

(a) to aim your eyes upwards; he looked up and saw a bird on the roof; if you look up the chimney you can see the sky.

ب) يبحث عن

(b) to try to find some information in a book; I'll look him up in the telephone book to try to find his address; look up the word in the dictionary if you don't know what it means.

Note: **look the words up** *or* **look up the words** *but only* **look them up**

loose [lu:s] adjective

غير مربوط باحكام

not fixed/not attached; not tight; part of the engine is loose; tie the rope with a loose knot; the knot came loose and the boat floated away.

loose—looser—loosest

loosely, adverb

بطريقة غير حازمة ، غير مُحَكَّمة

not tightly; the boat was only loosely tied to the tree.

loosen, verb

يحلّ - يفك

to make loose; loosen the rope; she loosened the knot.

loosens—loosening—loosened—has loosened

lorry

lorry ['lɒrɪ] *noun*

عربة ضخمة ـ شاحنة

large motor vehicle for carrying goods; he was putting the potatoes on to his lorry; the big lorries make a lot of noise as they go past the house; *see also* **truck**.
plural **lorries**

lose [luːz] *verb*

١) يضيع ـ يفقد

(a) to put something somewhere and not to know where it is; **I can't find my watch—I think I lost it on the bus; don't lose your ticket or you'll have to buy another one.**

ب) يتخلّص من (بعض وزنه) ـ يتأخر (عقارب الساعة) ـ يضيع (الوقت) ـ يفقد (أعصابه)

(b) not to have something any longer; **she has lost weight since last summer** = has got thinner; **my watch loses 10 minutes every day** = is 10 minutes slower; **don't lose any time in posting the letter** = post it as soon as you can; **has he lost his way?** = doesn't he know where he is? **he lost his temper** = he became angry.

ت) يخسر (في مباراة)

(c) not to win; **we lost the match 10-0; did you win?—no, we lost!**
loses—losing—lost [lɒst]—**has lost**

get lost, *verb*

يضيع الطريق ـ يضلّ

not to know where you are; **we went for a walk in the woods and got lost; they're very late—do you think they've got lost?**

loss [lɒs] *noun*

١) خسران ـ فقدان ـ ضياع ـ إضاعة

(a) not having something any more; **loss of weight; with no loss of time** = without any delay.

love

ب) خسارة (الفلوس)

(b) amount of money which you don't have any more; **he made a loss of £10; we sold the car at a loss.**

ت) خسارة (المباراة)

(c) not winning; **the loss of a battle; our team had a series of losses this summer.**
plural **losses**

lot [lɒt] *noun*

١) مقدار كبير ـ عدد كبير ـ كثير من

(a) **a lot of/lots of** = a large number of/a large amount of; **we've lots of time; what a lot of apples! I've seen him quite a lot recently; I'm feeling a lot better now; lots of people go to Spain for their holidays; a lot of people were waiting for the bus.**

ب) الكمية بأكملها ـ كل شيء

(b) **the lot** = everything; **that's the lot; we sold the lot for £10; we bought 3 pounds of potatoes and ate the lot for dinner.**

loud [laʊd] *adjective & adverb*

عالٍ ـ مرتفع (صوت ـ ضجة)

making a sound which you can hear easily; **don't talk too loud—your father is asleep; a loud noise made him jump.**
loud—louder—loudest

loudspeaker, *noun*

مكبّر الصوت

instrument from which sounds come, especially part of a radio/a record player, etc.

love [lʌv] **1.** *noun*

١ ـ حبّ ـ عشق ـ غرام

great liking for someone/something; **give my love to your parents; her great love is music; to fall in love with someone** = to start to like them very much.
2. *verb*

٢ ـ يحبّ ـ يودّ ـ يعشق ـ يولع بـ

to like something/someone a great deal;

one hundred and seventy-five 175

low

to be very fond of; **he loves his children; the children love their teacher; we love going to the sea; he loves cream cakes; I'd love to come with you, but I've got too much work to do.**
loves—loving—loved—has loved

lovely, *adjective*

جميل ـ فاتن ـ رائع

very pleasant; delightful; **a lovely warm day; she was wearing a lovely blue hat.**
lovely—lovelier—loveliest

low [ləʊ] *adjective & adverb*

منخفض ـ واطىء

near the bottom/towards the bottom; not high; **he hit his head on the low ceiling; this shop has the lowest prices in town; the town is surrounded by low hills; the engine works best at low speeds; that aircraft is flying too low—it'll hit the trees; the temperature is too low for oranges to grow here.**
low—lower—lowest

lower [ləʊə] *verb*

يخفّض ـ يُدَلّي

to make something go down; to reduce; **we lowered a bucket into the water; the shops are lowering their prices to attract customers.**
lowers—lowering—lowered—has lowered

Ltd *see* limit

ملاحظة : انظر الى كلمة limit

luck [lʌk] *noun*

حُسْن الحظ ـ توفيق

something, usually good, which happens to you by chance; **good luck with your exams!** = I hope you do well in your exams; **bad luck! hard luck!** = I am sorry you didn't do well; **I wear this ring for luck** = because I hope it will bring me luck; **just my (bad) luck to have homework to do when everyone else is swimming.**

lunch

lucky, *adjective*

محظوظ ـ حَسَن الحظ

having good things which happen; which brings luck; **he is lucky not to have been sent to prison; 13 is my lucky number.**
lucky—luckier—luckiest

luckily, *adverb*

لحسن الحظ ـ لحسن الطالع

by luck; **it started to rain, but luckily I had taken my umbrella.**

luggage ['lʌgɪdʒ] *noun*

حقائب السفر ـ أمتعة

cases/bags, etc., which you take with you when you travel, containing your clothes, etc.; **put all the luggage into the back of the car; we have too much luggage—we will have to pay extra; I can't carry all that luggage—can someone help me?**
no plural: **some luggage; a piece of luggage**

lump [lʌmp] *noun*

قطعة ـ كتلة

mass of something which often has no particular shape; **he made a bowl out of a lump of wood; how many lumps of sugar do you take in your tea?**

lunch [lʌntʃ] *noun*

وجبة الغذاء

meal eaten in the middle of the day; **hurry up—lunch is ready; will it soon be time for lunch? we always have lunch at one o'clock; we are having fish and chips for lunch; I'm not hungry so I don't want a big lunch.**
plural **lunches;** *see also* **dinner**

lunchtime, *noun*

وقت تناول الغذاء

time when you usually have lunch; **it's half past twelve—almost lunchtime.**

176 *one hundred and seventy-six*

lung

lung [lʌŋ] *noun*

رِئَة

one of two parts of the body which suck air in when you breathe; **the doctor listened to his chest to see if his lungs were all right.**

lying [laɪɪŋ] *see* **lie**

ملاحظة : انظر الى كلمة lie

main

Mm

machine [məˈʃiːn] *noun*

آلة

thing which works with a motor; **washing machine; sewing machine; the factory has put in a new machine for making electric light bulbs.**

machinery, *noun*

معدّات ـ آلات

machines; **the factory has put in a lot of new machinery.**
no plural: **some machinery; a piece of machinery**

mad [mæd] *adjective*

أ) أحمق

(*a*) very silly; **you're mad to go out in the snow without a coat; he had a mad idea to walk across America.**

ب) ساخط ـ مغتاظ ـ غاضب

(*b*) very angry; **this noise is driving me mad; I'll go mad if you don't stop that singing.**

ت) مولع

(*c*) very keen; **she's mad about film stars; he's mad on old cars.**
mad—madder—maddest

madam [ˈmædəm] *noun*

سيدتي

(*polite way of referring to a lady whom you are talking to*) **after you, madam;** (*at the beginning of a letter to a lady whom you do not know*) **Dear Madam.**

made [meɪd] *see* **make**

ملاحظة : انظر الى كلمة make

magazine [mægəˈziːn] *noun*

مجلّة

paper which comes out regularly, (every week or month) usually with many pictures in it; **the gardening magazine comes out on Tuesdays; have you got this week's TV magazine?**

mail [meɪl] *noun*

أ) البريد

(*a*) service of sending letters, etc., from one place to another; **you should send the letter by air mail; if the present is valuable, send it by registered mail.**

ب) الرسائل المرسلة بواسطة البريد

(*b*) letters which have been delivered to you; **has the mail come yet? he opened his mail before he had his breakfast.**

main [meɪn] **1.** *adjective*

١ ـ رئيسي ـ اساسي

most important; **the main thing is to work well; our main office is in London; there is always a lot of traffic on main roads; August is the main month for holidays.**
2. *noun*

٢ ـ أ) الخط الرئيسي (من الانابيب)

(*a*) large pipe for delivering water/gas,

177

make

etc.; **a water main burst in the High Street.**

ب) الخط الكهربائي الرئيسي

(b) **the mains** = electric power brought into a house by a wire; **that machine is connected to the mains; does it use a battery or the mains?**

mainly, *adverb*

في الدرجة الاولى ـ خصوصاً ـ الى حدٍ بعيد

largely/mostly; **we have mainly women working in our office; people mainly go on holiday in August.**

make [meɪk] **1.** *noun*

١ ـ صُنْع (من صنع ايطاليا) ـ إنتاج

showing where or by which firm something is made; **an Italian make of car; what make is your new record-player? 2.** *verb*

٢ ـ أ) يَصْنَعُ ـ يُنْتِج

(a) to produce/to build; **he made a table out of pieces of wood; this cup is made of plastic; he is making a cake.**

ب) يهيىء ـ يُعِد

(b) to get ready; **do you want me to make the breakfast? have you made your bed?** = made it tidy after having slept in it.

ت) يساوي (٢ و ٣ تساوي ٥)

(c) to add up to; **two and three make five.**

ث) يكسب (مالاً)

(d) to earn (money); **he made £10 from selling old newspapers.**

ج) يجعل ـ يدفع على ـ يجعله يشعر بـ

(e) to cause someone to feel something; **the smell of cooking makes me hungry; the movement of the boat made him sick; will the present make him happier? he made himself comfortable in the armchair.**

ح) يُجبِر على ـ يساعد على ـ يُرغِم على

(f) to force someone/something to do something; **I made him clean his shoes; the teacher made him stay in after school; the rain will make the grass grow; can't you make the car go any faster?**

makes—making—made [meɪd]**— has made**

make do with, *verb*

يستعمل كبديل مؤقت

to use something, because there is nothing better; **I lost my toothpaste, so I had to make do with soap; the baker had run out of brown bread, so we had to make do with white; all the plates were dirty, so we made do with paper ones.**

make for, *verb*

يتوجه نحو ـ يذهب الى

to go towards; **he is making for London; when he saw her he made straight for the door.**

make of, *verb*

يُكَوِّن فكرةً عن

to think about; **what do you make of the news? I don't know what to make of it.**

make off with, *verb*

يغادر بسرعة ـ ينسَلُّ هارباً

to go away with something/to steal something; **the burglar made off with the jewellery.**

make out, *verb*

أ) يفهم بوضوح

(a) to see clearly; to understand; **I can't make out the details in the photo because the light is bad; she couldn't make out why he didn't want to come.**

ب) يَدَّعي

(b) to say something which is probably not true; **is English weather really as bad as it is made out to be? stop trying to make out that you're the best singer in the world.**

ت) يَعُدّ ـ يُدَوِّن (اسم على شيك)

(c) to write (a name on a cheque); **he made out the cheque to Mr Smith.**

Note: **can you make the writing out?** *or* **can you make out the writing?** *but only* **can you make it out?**

make up, *verb*

أ) يؤلف (قصة كاذبة)

178 *one hundred and seventy-eight*

male

(a) to invent (a story); **he told the police he had seen a man steal a car but in fact he made the whole story up.**

ب) يأخذ قراراً - يُقَرِّر

(b) **to make up your mind** = to decide; **I can't make up my mind what to do; his mind is made up** = he has decided what to do.

Note: **he made the story up** *or* **he made up the story** *but only* **he made it up**

make-up, *noun*

مستحضرات التجميل

things like face powder, lipstick, etc., which you put on your face to make it more beautiful.

male [meɪl] *adjective & noun*

الذَكَر - مُذَكَر

of the same sex as a man; **a male spider; the male is stronger than the female.**

man [mæn] *noun*

ا) رَجُل

(a) male human being; **my father is a very tall man; ask that old man if he wants some tea.**

ب) الانسان - البشر

(b) human being; **men have only existed on earth for a short time compared to fish.**

ت) شخص - المرء

(c) person; **the man in the street** = average, ordinary person; **the man in the street isn't interested in politics.**

plural **men** [men]

manage ['mænɪdʒ] *verb*

ا) يُدير - يُدَبِّر

(a) to control; to be in charge of; **she manages our London office; we want to appoint someone to manage our sales department.**

ب) ينجح في تحقيق

(b) to be able to do something/to succeed in doing something; **did you manage to phone your mother? he managed to get the lid off; can she manage all by herself? how are we going to manage without her?**

manages—managing—managed—has managed

manager, *noun*

مُدير - مُنَسِّق

person in charge of a department in a shop/in a business; **the sales manager; the manager of the sports department.**

manner ['mænə] *noun*

ا) طريقة

(a) way of doing something; **he was behaving in a strange manner.**

ب) أدب - تصرفات حسنة

(b) **manners** = polite way of behaving; **he has very good table manners** = he behaves well when he's eating; **it's bad manners to put your knife in your mouth.**

many ['menɪ] *adjective & pronoun*

عدد كبير - كثير

a large number (of); **many old people live by the seaside; many of us knew him when he was at school; so many people wanted tickets that they sold out quickly; how many apples have you got? he ate twice as many slices of bread as you did; a good many** = a large number; **a good many people thought the film was no good.**

many—more [mɔː]**—most** [məʊst]
Note: **many** *is used with nouns which you can count:* **not many apples** *but* **not much bread**

map [mæp] *noun*

خريطة جغرافية

drawing which shows a town/a country as if seen from the air; **here's a big map of Germany; have you got a street map of London? can you show me the mountains on the map? we soon got lost because we'd forgotten to take a map.**

March

March [mɑːtʃ] *noun*

مارس ـ شهر اذار

third month of the year; **his birthday is in March; today is March 6th; last March we went to Germany.**
Note: **March 6th:** *say* 'the sixth of March' *or* 'March the sixth'

march [mɑːtʃ] *verb*

يسير على طريقة الجنود

to walk in step; **the soldiers marched up the street; quick march!** = order given to soldiers to walk quickly.
marches—marching—marched—has marched

margarine [mɑːgəˈriːn] *noun*

سمن نباتي

vegetable fat which looks like butter and is used instead of butter; **spread some margarine on your bread; she fried the fish in margarine.**

mark [mɑːk] **1.** *noun*

١ ـ أ) علامة ـ لطخة

(*a*) spot/small area of a different colour; **he has ink marks on his shirt; your cup has made a mark on the table; there's a red mark where you hit your head; on your marks!** = get ready at your places (*order given to runners at the beginning of a race*).

ب) نقطة ـ علامة ـ وسام (حصل على أعلى علامة في درس اللغة الفرنسية)

(*b*) number of points given to a student; **he got top marks in French** = he was best in his class; **did you get a good mark for your maths homework? the teacher took marks off for spelling mistakes; is 8 out of 10 a good mark?**
2. *verb*

٢ ـ أ) يُلطّخ ـ يُدوِّن

(*a*) to make a mark; **the table is marked by coffee cups; the tin is marked 'dangerous'** = it has the word 'dangerous' written on it.

mass

ب) يصحح ويمنح علامات (على عمل او مذاكرة او درس)

(*b*) to correct and give points to work; **the teacher is marking our homework; has the maths exam been marked yet?**
marks—marking—marked—has marked

market [ˈmɑːkɪt] *noun*

سوق ـ مجموعة متاجر

place where fruit and vegetables, etc., are sold from small tables, often in the open air; **we bought some vegetables and fish at the market; market day is Saturday.**

marmalade [ˈmɑːməleɪd] *noun*

مُربّى (مصنوع من الفاكهة)

jam made from oranges, lemons or grapefruit; **do you want toast and marmalade for your breakfast? open another pot of marmalade—this one is empty.**
no plural

marry [ˈmærɪ] *verb*

يَتَزوَّج من ـ يُزَوِّج

to make two people husband and wife; to become the husband or wife of someone; **he married the girl next door; they were married in church; how long have you been married? she's married to a soldier; they got married last Saturday.**
marries—marrying—married—has married

mass [mæs] *noun*

كتلة كبيرة ـ مجموعة كبيرة

large number; **there's a mass of dead leaves on the lawn; masses of people went to the exhibition; have some more meat—there's masses left; a mass meeting** = meeting where a large number of people come together.
plural **masses**

master

master ['mɑːstə] *noun*

المعلّم ــ استاذ في التعليم ــ مُدَرِّس

man who teaches in a school; **Mr Jones is the English master.**

mat [mæt] *noun*

أ) حصير ــ ممسحة

(*a*) small carpet; **wipe your shoes on the mat; bath mat** = small carpet which you stand on when you get out of the bath; **door mat** = thick stiff carpet to wipe your shoes on in front of a door.

ب) قطعة قماش أو خشب توضع تحت طبق مائدة .

(*b*) small piece of cloth/wood, etc., which you put under a plate on a table; **put table mats out for everyone.**

match [mætʃ] *noun*

أ) مباراة

(*a*) game between two teams, etc.; **are you going to watch the football match? I won the last two tennis matches I played.**

ب) عُودْ ثقاب ــ عود كبريت

(*b*) small piece of wood or cardboard with a tip which catches fire when you rub it against a rough surface; **a box of matches; he struck a match and lit the fire; the matches are wet—they won't light.**

plural **matches**

matchbox, *noun*

علبة كبريت

small box containing matches.

plural **matchboxes**

material [mə'tɪərɪəl] *noun*

أ) مادة

(*a*) something which can be used to make something; **building materials** = bricks, wood, etc.; **raw materials** = materials like iron or oil which have not been made into anything.

ب) قماش ــ نسيج

(*b*) cloth; **I bought some cotton material to make a skirt.**

May

mathematics [mæθə'mætɪks], **maths** [mæθs] *noun*

الرياضيات ــ علم الرياضيات

study of numbers and measurements; **the maths teacher; I found the maths exam very difficult; my sister is no good at maths; maths is my best subject.**

Note: the verb is in the singular: maths is an important subject

matter ['mætə] **1.** *noun*

١ ــ مسألة ــ شأن ــ أمر

problem; **what's the matter? there's something the matter with the engine** =

مشكلة ــ قضية

there is something which does not work properly; **it's a matter for the police** = something which the police should know about; **as a matter of fact** = really; **as a matter of course** =

في الحقيقة ــ عادةً

in the usual way.
2. *verb*

٢ ــ يَهُمُّ : لا يهمني إذا كنت متأخراً

to be important; **it doesn't matter if you're late; it matters a lot to him; does it matter where we sit?**

matters—mattering—mattered—has mattered

mattress ['mætrəs] *noun*

فِراش ــ فرشة

thick soft part of a bed which you lie on; **this mattress has lumps in it.**

plural **mattresses**

May [meɪ] *noun*

أيّار ــ شهر مايو

fifth month of the year; **she was born in May; today is May 15th; last May we moved to London; are you going away next May?**

Note: **May 15th:** *say* 'the fifteenth of May' *or* 'May the fifteenth'

one hundred and eighty-one 181

may

may [meɪ] *verb used with other verbs*

أ) مُمْكِن ان ـ من الممكن ـ جائز ـ ربّما ـ قد ـ لعلّ

(*a*) *to mean* it is possible; if he doesn't hurry he may miss the train; take your umbrella, it may rain; he may be waiting outside; you may have left your gloves on the train; it may not rain after all; she may not have heard.

ب) يمكنه ان ـ من المسموح ان

(*b*) *to mean* it is allowed; mother says we may come in; you may sit down if you want to; may I ask you a question? may we have tea early today?

I may, you may, he may, we may, they may
Past: [(*a*) only] **might, might not**, usually **mightn't**
Note: **may** and **might** do not have **to** and are always used with other verbs

maybe, *adverb*

ربّما

perhaps; maybe it will be fine tomorrow.

me [miː] *object pronoun used by the person who is speaking, to talk about himself*

ضمير المتكلم في حالتي النصب والخفض

give it to me; can you hear me? he is taller than me; who is it?—it's me!

meal [miːl] *noun*

وجبة ـ وقعة طعام

eating food at table at a particular time; we have three meals a day—breakfast, lunch and dinner; you should only have a light meal in the evening; when they had eaten their evening meal they went for a walk.

mean [miːn] **1.** *adjective*

١ ـ أ) خسيس ـ دنيء

(*a*) nasty/not kind; he played a mean trick on his sister; that was a mean thing to say.

182

mean

ب) بخيل

(*b*) not wanting to give; don't be mean—lend me your football; he's very mean with his money.

mean—meaner—meanest
2. *verb*

٢ ـ أ) يقصد ـ يعني

(*a*) to refer to/to talk about; did he mean Uncle Richard when he was talking about fat men? what do you mean?

ب) يعني ـ تفيد (الاشارة)

(*b*) to show; a red light means that you have to stop; 'Tisch' in German means 'table'; what does that sign mean?—I know what it means, it means that you can't park here on Saturdays.

ت) من المفروض ان ـ يجب ان

(*c*) to be meant to = ought to; we're meant to be there by nine o'clock; this medicine is meant to be used only for coughs; a train is meant to leave every half hour.

means—meaning—meant [ment]—has meant

meaning, *noun*

معنى

what a word means; if you want to find the meaning of this word, look it up in the dictionary.

means, *noun*

أ) وسيلة

(*a*) way of doing something; is there any means of getting to London tonight? a motorbike is a cheap means of travelling.

مهما كلّف الأمر ـ بأي ثمن

by all means = of course; by all means telephone the office if you want to.

بأية حال ـ على الاطلاق

by no means = not at all; he's by no means rich.

ب) الامكانيات المادية

(*b*) money; it is beyond my means = it is too dear for me to buy it.

meanwhile, *adverb*

one hundred and eighty-two

measles

في غضون ذلك

during this time; **he hid in an empty house—meanwhile, the police were coming nearer.**

measles ['mi:zlz] *plural noun*

الحصبة (مرض)

children's disease which makes your skin go red; **she's in bed with measles; have you had measles? he's got measles; they caught measles from their friends at school.**

measure ['meʒə] **1.** *noun*

١ ـ مقياس ـ مكيال ـ معيار

thing used to calculate the size of something; **a metre is a measure of length; tape measure** = long tape with centimetres/inches, etc., marked on it.
2. *verb*

٢ ـ يقيس ـ يبلغ قياسه ...

to find out the size of something; to be a certain size; **the room measures 3 metres by 2 metres; a thermometer measures temperature; how much do you measure round the waist? she measured the room before buying the carpet.**
measures—measuring—measured—has measured

measurement, *noun*

القياس : أخذ قياس الشيء . قياس (مثل الطول والحجم ... الخ)

size/length, etc., of something which you have measured; **what are the measurements of the tent? do you know your waist measurement? he had to take the measurements of the room to calculate how much paint he needed.**

meat [mi:t] *noun*

لحم ـ لحمة

part of an animal which you eat; **can I have some more meat? would you like another slice of meat? this meat is very well cooked.**
no plural: **some meat; a piece of meat/a slice of meat**

melt

medicine ['medsın] *noun*

أ) دواء ـ علاج

(*a*) something which you eat or drink to make you well; **take some cough medicine if your cough is bad; you should take the medicine three times a day.**

ب) الطبّ ـ علم الطب

(*b*) study of diseases and how to cure them; **he is studying medicine because he wants to be a doctor.**
no plural for (b)

medical ['medikl] *adjective*

طبّي

referring to the study of diseases; **a medical student; medical help was provided by the Red Cross.**

meet [mi:t] *verb*

أ) يلتقي بـ ـ يقابل ـ يجتمع إلى

(*a*) to come together (with someone); **I'll meet you at the bus stop; they met at the railway station; let's arrange to meet somewhere before we go to the theatre; I'm meeting her at the post office at six o'clock.**

ب) يتعرف على : لقد سبق وتعرفت عليه

(*b*) to get to know someone; **I think I have met him before; I have never met your mother—come and meet her, then.**
meets—meeting—met—has met

meeting, *noun*

إجتماع ـ مقابلة

coming together of a group of people; **there will be a meeting of the stamp club next Thursday; there were only six people at the meeting.**

melt [melt] *verb*

يذُوب

to change from solid to liquid because of heating; **the butter has melted in the sun; you must melt the chocolate in a pan and pour it over the ice cream.**
melts—melting—melted—has melted

one hundred and eighty-three 183

member

member ['membə] *noun*

عَضْوٌ (في نادي أو المجلس)

person who belongs (to a club, etc.); **he is a member of the golf club; the club is limited to 250 members; Member of Parliament** = person who is elected to Parliament.

memory ['meməri] *noun*

أ) ذاكرة

(a) ability to remember; **he has a very good memory for dates; I have no memory for names; he said the whole poem from memory.**

ب) ذكرى

(b) thing which you remember; **I have wonderful memories of our last holiday.**
plural **memories**

men [men] *see* **man**

ملاحظة : انظر إلى كلمة Man

mend [mend] *verb*

يُصلح (عطب أو خلل) - يرمّم - يصحح - يرتق

to repair/to make something perfect which had a fault; **can you mend my watch? he's trying to mend his car; my trousers are torn—can they be mended?**
mends—mending—mended—has mended

mention ['menʃn] *verb*

يذكر - يشير إلى

to refer to something in a few words; **he mentioned that he was going away for a few days; did she mention the results of the exam? they don't know about the party—shall I mention it to them?**
mentions—mentioning—mentioned—has mentioned

menu ['menju:] *noun*

لائحة الطعام

list of food in a restaurant; **have you any fish on the menu? the waiter brought us the menu; she always chooses the most expensive dish on the menu.**

metre

merry ['meri] *adjective*

سعيد - مبتهج

happy; **Merry Christmas; he wished us a Merry Christmas.**
merry—merrier—merriest

mess [mes] *noun*

فوضى - مجموعة أشياء مختلطة بغير نظام - لا ترتيب

dirt; something which isn't tidy; **the builders made a mess all over the floor; the room is in a mess—you'll have to tidy it up; he made a mess of mending his car** = he did it badly.
plural **messes**

message ['mesɪdʒ] *noun*

رسالة

news/instructions which are sent to someone; **he got a message telling him to go to the police station; your boss has left a message for you; here's a phone message for you.**

messenger ['mesɪndʒə] *noun*

الرسول - الساعي

person who brings a message.

met [met] *see* **meet**

ملاحظة : انظر إلى كلمة meet

metal ['metl] *noun*

معدن

solid material which can carry heat and electricity and is used for making things; **a metal teapot; the spoons are plastic but the knives are metal; this table is made of metal.**

method ['meθəd] *noun*

طريقة - منهج - نظام

way of doing something; **she showed me a new method of making bread.**

metre ['mi:tə] *noun* (*American:* **meter**)

متر (أي ١٠٠ سنتم)

measurement of length; **the room is four metres by three; one square metre =**

184   *one hundred and eighty-four*

لائحة الطعام

MENU

الغذاء	**LUNCH**
حساء الخضار	vegetable soup
حساء الطماطم	tomato soup
عصير الفاكهة ـ عصير الطماطم	fruit juices, tomato juice
دجاج ، أرز	chicken, rice
خروف محمّر	roast lamb
فطيرة باللحمة	meat pie
لحم مملح بارد (عادةً خنزير) وسلطة	ham & salad
خضراوات : بطاطة مسلوقة ، بطاطة مقلية وبازيلا ـ فاصوليا ، جزر وملفوف	vegetables: boiled potatoes, chips, peas, beans, carrots, cabbage
جبنة وبسكوت	cheese & biscuits
سلطة فاكهة طازجة	fresh fruit salad
فطيرة تفاح مع قشطة	apple pie & cream
بوظة ـ جيلاتي	ice cream
فطائر محلّاة	pancakes (two)
حلويات	pastries
قهوة ـ شاي	coffee, tea
حليب بالفاكهة	milk shakes
بيرة	beer
نبيذ ـ خمر	wine
وجبات سريعة	**SNACKS**
(سندويتش) شطائر	sandwiches
نقانق ساخنة	hot dogs
رقائق من النقانق	sausage rolls
الخدمة غير متضمنة في السعر	Service not included

one hundred and eighty-five

mice

area which is one metre by one metre; **the area of the stage is ten square metres.**
Note: with figures **metre** *is usually written* **m** *and* **square metre** *is written* **m²** *(four metres = 34 m; six square metres = 6m²)*

mice [maɪs] *see* **mouse**
ملاحظة : انظر إلى كلمة mouse

mid- [mɪd] *prefix*

منتصف ـ نصف

meaning middle; **the two aircraft hit each other in mid-air; we will be going on holiday in mid-August.**

midday [mɪd'deɪ] *noun*

منتصف النهار ـ الظهر

12 o'clock in the middle of the day; **he caught the midday train to Scotland; she won't be back to her office before midday.**

middle ['mɪdl] *noun*

أ) وسط ـ منتصف

(a) centre; **he was standing in the middle of the room; Zaire is a country in the middle of Africa; I woke up in the middle of the night; she was in the middle of making the dinner when we called; the telephone rang in the middle of the meeting.**

ب) خَصْر

(b) waist; **the water came up to my middle; how much do you measure round the middle?**

middle-aged, *adjective*

الكهولة . خريف العمر (بين ٤٠ و ٦٠ عاماً)

not very young, and not very old; **he's middle-aged; three middle-aged women got on to the bus.**

midnight ['mɪdnaɪt] *noun*

منتصف الليل

12 o'clock at night; **you must go to bed before midnight; I heard the clock strike midnight and then went to sleep.**

186

mile

might [maɪt] *verb used with other verbs*

أ) جائز ـ ممكن

(a) *to mean* it is possible; **it might rain; he might be waiting outside; you might have left your gloves on the train.**

ب) يتوجب ـ يجب ان ـ من الواجب ان

(b) *to mean* something should have been done; **he might have done something to help** = it would have been better if he had done something; **you might have told me** = I wish you had told me.
I might, you might, he might, we might, they might
Negative: **might not,** *usually* **mightn't**
Note: **might** *does not have to and is always used with other verbs.* **Might** *is the past of* **may,** *but can be used as a more polite form of the present when asking for permission*

mild [maɪld] *adjective*

لطيف ـ معتدل ـ خفيف النكهة ـ غير حاد

soft; not hard or cold; not serious; **we had a very mild winter; she's had a mild attack of measles; I like strong mustard—this sort is too mild** = it hasn't a strong taste.
mild—milder—mildest

mile [maɪl] *noun*

أ) ميل (وحدة طول او مسافة تساوي ١٦٠٩,٣٥ متراً)

(a) measurement of length (= 1609 metres); **we walked for miles before we found the post office; the car was travelling at 60 miles per hour; it's 24 miles from here to the sea; it's a three mile walk from here.**

ب) كثير ـ للغاية

(b) **miles** = a lot; **it's miles too big** = far too big; **the string is miles too long** = far too long.
with figures **miles per hour** *is usually written* **mph: 60 miles per hour = 60 mph**

one hundred and eighty-six

military

military ['mɪlɪtrɪ] *adjective*

عسكري - خاص بالجيش

belonging to the army; **he was wearing military uniform; a military hospital** = a hospital for soldiers.

milk [mɪlk] **1.** *noun*

١ - حليب - لبن

white liquid produced by female animals to feed their young, especially that produced by cows; **have you drunk your milk? can I have a glass of milk, please? I must buy some milk; have you enough milk? we've got no milk left.**
no plural: **some milk: a glass of milk/ a bottle of milk**

2. *verb*

٢ - يحلب

to take the milk from an animal; **the farmer was milking the cow; the cows haven't been milked yet.**
milks—milking—milked—has milked

milkman, *noun*

الحلّاب - بائع الحليب أو اللبن

man who delivers bottles of milk to each house in the morning; **tell the milkman to leave six bottles of milk today.**
plural **milkmen**

milk shake, *noun*

شراب من اللبن المخفوق مع بعض الحلويات أو الفاكهة

drink made by mixing milk with sweet stuff; **he drank two chocolate milk shakes.**

millimetre ['mɪlɪmiːtə] *noun* (*American:* **millimeter**)

ميليمتر: وحدة طول تساوي واحداً بالألف من المتر

very small measurement of length; **the wood is only 10 millimetres thick; there are ten millimetres in a centimetre, and a thousand in a metre.**
with figures **millimetre** *is usually written* **mm: 26 mm = 26 millimetres**

mind

million ['mɪljən] number 1,000,000

مليون: عدد ١٠٠٠٠٠٠

the population of the country is 60 million; millions of trees were burnt in the forest fire; the country spends millions of dollars on oil; millions of people spend their holidays in Spain.
Note: no plural with figures: **sixty million**; *with figures* **million** *can be written* **m: £2m = two million pounds**

millionth, *adjective & noun*

جزء من مليون

referring to a million; **a millionth of a second; congratulations—you're our millionth customer!**

mind [maɪnd] **1.** *noun*

عقل - ذهن

place from which thoughts come; **what do you have in mind?** = what are you thinking of? **he's got something on his mind** = he's worrying about something; **let's try to take her mind off her exams** = to stop her worrying about them.

حالة نفسية

state of mind = general feeling; **he's in a very miserable state of mind.**

يقرّر - تتخذ قراراً

to make up your mind = to decide; **I can't make up my mind whether to go on holiday or stay here and work; she couldn't make up her mind what hat to wear.**

يغيّر رأيه

to change your mind = to decide to do something different; **I have decided to go on holiday, and nothing will make me change my mind; he took out his bike, but then changed his mind and went by bus.**

2. *verb*

٢ - أ) ينتبه

(*a*) to be careful about; **mind the step! mind you ride carefully on your bike; mind you get back in time for tea; mind the oven—it's hot!**

mine

ب) يقلق ـ (لا تقلق)
(b) to worry about; **never mind** = don't worry; **you must learn to mind your own business** = not to deal with other people's problems.

ت) ينزعج ـ لديه مانع ان
(c) to be annoyed by; **do you mind if I close the window? they won't mind if you're late; I wouldn't mind a cup of tea** = I'd rather like a cup of tea; **do you mind if we sit down? I don't mind standing up.**
minds—minding—minded—has minded

mine [maın] 1. *pronoun*
١ ـ ملكي ـ خاصتي ـ لي
thing/person belonging to me; **that bike is mine; can I borrow your pen, I've lost mine? Paul is a friend of mine.**
2. *noun*
٢ ـ أ) منجم
(a) deep hole in the ground where coal, etc., is taken out; **a coal mine; a gold mine.**

ب) لُغم
(b) type of bomb which is hidden under the ground or under water; **the lorry went over a mine and was blown up.**
3. *verb*
٣ ـ يحفر منجماً ـ يُعَدِّن ـ يبحث عن معدن تحت الأرض
to dig (coal, etc.) out of the ground; **they are mining gold here.**
mines—mining—mined—has mined

miner, *noun*
عامل المناجم
person who works in a coal mine.

mineral ['mınrəl] *noun*
معدن ـ معدني (مياه معدنية) ـ صنف من المرطبات
stone/coal, etc., which is taken out of the earth; **they mine coal and other minerals in the north of the country; mineral water** = (a) water taken out of the ground and sold in bottles; (b) sweet drink sold in a bottle.

miserable

minister ['mınıstə] *noun*
وزير
member of the government in charge of a department; **the Foreign Minister** = the minister who deals with relations with other countries; *see also* **Prime Minister.**

minute[1] ['mınıt] *noun*
أ) دقيقة (٦٠ ثانية)
(a) a sixtieth part of an hour; **there are sixty minutes in an hour; 12 minutes to four** = 3.48; **12 minutes past three** = 3.12; **I'll meet you in fifteen minutes; the house is about five minutes' walk from the station/is a five minute walk from the station; minute hand** = long hand on a watch or clock which shows the minutes.

ب) لحظة ـ فترة وجيزة
(b) very short space of time; moment; **why don't you sit down for a minute? I won't be a minute** = I'll be very quick; **can you wait a minute?**

minute[2] [maı'nju:t] *adjective*
صغير جداً
very small; **a minute piece of dust got in my eye.**

mirror ['mırə] *noun*
مرآة
piece of glass with a dark back, so that when you look at it you can see yourself; **he looked at his face in the bathroom mirror; driving mirror** = mirror in a car so that the driver can see if any vehicle is behind without turning round.

miserable ['mızrəbl] *adjective*
تعيس ـ حزين ـ بائس ـ سيّىء (الطقس)
very sad/not happy; **she was miserable when he didn't write to her; the weather**

Miss

on holiday was really miserable = very bad.

Miss [mɪs] *noun*

آنسة

name given to young girl or unmarried woman; **Miss Jones; Miss Anne Jones; please, Miss, can I have the bill?**
Note: with a name, Miss can be followed by the surname or the Christian name and surname; without a name, Miss is used to call a waitress or a school teacher

miss [mɪs] **1.** *noun*

١ - عدم الاصابة - اخفاق

not hitting; **he scored a goal and then had two misses; let's give it a miss** = let's not go to see it.
plural **misses**
2. *verb*

٢ - أ) يخطىء المرمى

(a) not to hit; **he missed the goal; they tried to shoot the rabbit but missed.**

ب) يغفل - يفوته شيء ما - يقصّر عن - ينجو من

(b) not to see/to catch, etc.; **we missed the house in the dark; they missed the bus and had to walk home; I missed the article about farming in yesterday's paper; you didn't miss much** = there wasn't much to see/the film, etc., wasn't very good; **he just missed being knocked down** = he was almost knocked down.

ت) يفتقد - يستفقد لـ

(c) to be sad because something is not there; **do you miss your dog? I miss those long walks we used to take; they'll miss you if you go to work in another office.**
misses—missing—missed—has missed

missing, *adjective*

مفقود - ضائع

which is not there/which has been lost; **we're looking for my missing keys; there is a lot of money missing; the police searched for the missing children.**

miss out, *verb*

mix

يفوته شيء ما : (لقد فاتك القسم الأهم من الرسالة)

to leave out/to forget to put in; **you missed out the most important part of the letter.**
Note: **he missed the best part out** *or* **he missed out the best part** *only* **he missed it out**

mistake [mɪ'steɪk] **1.** *noun*

١ - خطأ - غلط

action or thought which is wrong; **I made a mistake; I got on the wrong bus by mistake; by mistake he tried to eat his soup with his fork; there are several mistakes in her work.**
2. *verb*

٢ - يخطىء - يسيء فهم شيء ما

to think wrongly; **I mistook him for his brother** = I thought he was his brother; **he is mistaken in thinking I am your brother; if I'm not mistaken, Dr Smith is your brother.**
mistakes—mistaking—mistook [mɪ'stʊk]**—has mistaken**

mix [mɪks] *verb*

يخلط - يمزج

to put things together; **mix the flour and milk in a bowl; if you mix blue and yellow you will get green.**
mixes—mixing—mixed—has mixed

mixture ['mɪkstʃə] *noun*

خليط

things mixed together; **the walls are painted in a mixture of red and blue; the doctor gave me an unpleasant mixture to drink; cough mixture** = medicine taken to stop you coughing.

mix up, *verb*

يشوش - يتشوش

to mistake; to put out of the right order; **I'm always mixing him up with his brother; all the books got mixed up in the box.**

one hundred and eighty-nine 189

model

model ['mɒdl] *noun*

أ) نسخة

(a) small copy of something larger; **he is making a model plane; have you seen his model trains?**

ب) عارض للأزياء

(b) person who wears new clothes to show them to customers.

ت) موديل سيارة ـ طراز

(c) style of car, etc., produced at a particular time; **this is the latest model; he has a 1979 model Ford.**

modern ['mɒdn] *adjective*

حديث ـ عصري

of the present time; **their house is very modern** = does not look old; **modern languages** = languages which are spoken today; **he's studying French and Spanish in the modern language department.**

moment ['məumənt] *noun*

لحظة ـ فترة وجيزة

very short time; **please wait a moment; I only saw him for a moment; we expect him to arrive at any moment** = very soon; **we only heard of it a moment ago** = just recently.

في الوقت الحاضر

at the moment = now; **I'm rather busy at the moment.**

في هذا الوقت بالذات

for the moment = just now; for a little while; **we won't disturb you for the moment.**

Monday ['mʌndɪ] *noun*

الاثنين (يوم الاثنين)

first day of the week, the day between Sunday and Tuesday; **the shops are shut on Mondays; I saw her last Monday; we're going on holiday next Monday; will you be in the office on Monday afternoon? we go to the cinema every Monday.**

more

money ['mʌnɪ] *noun*

مال ـ عملة ـ نقد

coins or notes which are used for buying things; **how much money have you got? I haven't any money with me; we ran out of money** = we spent all our money; **you spent too much money last week; I want to change my pounds into Spanish money.**

no plural

month [mʌnθ] *noun*

شهر

one of twelve parts of a year; **January is the first month of the year; February is the shortest month; what day of the month is it today? I'm going on holiday next month; it rained a lot last month, in fact it rained all month; a month from today I'll be sitting on the beach** = in a month's time; **we haven't had any homework for months** = for a long time; **he's taken a month's holiday.**

moon [mu:n] *noun*

القمر

star in the sky which goes round the earth and which shines at night; **it is difficult to think that men have walked on the moon; the moon is very bright tonight; there was no moon because there were too many clouds; it only happens once in a blue moon** = very rarely; **new moon** = time when the moon is only a thin curve; **full moon** = time when the moon is a full circle.

more [mɔ:] **1.** *adjective*

١ ـ أكثر ـ مزيد من

extra/which is added; **do you want some more coffee? we need two more men to make a football team; there are many more trains on weekdays than on Sundays; £10—that's more than I can pay.**
2. *noun*

٢ ـ أكثر ـ شيء إضافي

extra thing; **is there any more of this jam?**

morning

3. *adverb used with adjectives to make the comparative*

أكثر ـ بمقدار أكبر

he was more surprised than I was; she is more intelligent than her brother; it was even more unpleasant than I had thought it would be.

تقريباً

more or less = roughly/not quite completely; I've more or less finished my homework.

ابداً ـ على الاطلاق

not ... any more = no longer; he doesn't write to me any more; we don't go abroad on holiday any more.

Note: **more** *is used to make the comparative of long adjectives which do not take -er*

morning ['mɔːnɪŋ] *noun*

الصباح ـ الضحى

first part of the day before 12 o'clock; I go to the office every morning; tomorrow morning he's going to talk on the radio; we'll meet on Tuesday morning; I woke up at four in the morning = at 04.00; have you read the morning paper? we must get the morning plane to Stockholm.

most [məʊst] **1.** *adjective*

معظم

very large number of; most people have breakfast at about 8 o'clock; most children like watching TV; most apples are sweet.

2. *noun*

٢ ـ معظم أغلبية ـ الأكثرية

very large number/amount; most of the work has been done; he sits and writes most of the time; it rained for most of the day; most of the children are over 11.

3. *adverb*

٣ ـ أ) الأكثر

(*a*) *making the superlative* he's the most intelligent child in his class; the most important thing is to be able to speak Russian.

motor

ب) إلى أقصى حد ـ أغلب : (في أغلب الظن سيمتنع عن المجيء بسبب الضباب)

(*b*) very; I find it most annoying that the post doesn't come until 10 o'clock; most probably he will be held up by the fog; you are most kind.

Note: **most** *is used to form the superlative of long adjectives which do not take -est*

mostly, *adverb*

في الأغلب ـ في المقام الأول

most often; sometimes we go abroad for our holidays, but mostly we stay in Britain.

mother ['mʌðə] *noun*

أم ـ والدة ـ ماما

female parent; he lives with his mother; my mother's a doctor; Mother! there's someone asking for you on the telephone

Note: **Mother** *is sometimes used as a name for a mother, but* **Mum** *or* **Mummy** *are more usual*

motor ['məʊtə] *noun*

مُحرّك (السيارة)

engine/part of a machine which makes it work; switch on the motor; the model boat has an electric motor.

motorbike, motorcylce, *noun*

دراجة نارية

two-wheeled cycle driven by a motor; he fell off his motorbike; I'm learning to ride a motorcycle.

motorboat, *noun*

زورق مزوّد بمحرك

boat driven by a motor.

motorcyclist, *noun*

سائق الدراجة النارية

person who rides a motorcycle.

motorist, *noun*

سائق السيارة أو راكبها

person who drives a car.

motorway, *noun*

خط سريع ـ طريق رئيسي

road with very few roads joining it, on

mountain

which traffic can travel fast; **we drove north along the new motorway; if we take the motorway we will get there more quickly; there is a lot of traffic on the motorway.**

mountain ['maʊntn] *noun*

جبل

very high piece of land, much higher than the land which surrounds it; **Everest is the highest mountain in the world; we go climbing in the mountains every weekend; are we nearly at the top of the mountain yet? mountain railway** = special railway which climbs steep mountains.

mouse [maʊs] *noun*

فأر - فأرة

little animal with a long tail, often living in houses; **a mouse ran under the bed; my sister is afraid of mice; John brought a white mouse to school.**
plural **mice** [maɪs]

moustache [məˈstɑːʃ] *noun*

الشارب أو الشاربين

hair which grows above a man's mouth; **the policeman had a big black moustache.**

mouth [maʊθ] *noun*

فَمْ

opening below your nose through which you take in food and drink, and through which you speak; **don't talk with your mouth full; she was sleeping with her mouth open; the cat was carrying a bird in her mouth.**
plural **mouths** [maʊðz]

mouthful, *noun*

مِلء الفم

amount which you can hold in your mouth; **he had a mouthful of bread.**

move [muːv] **1.** *noun*

١ - نقل (شيء ما من مكان إلى آخر)

changing the place of something; **we must make a move** = we must go; **get a**

move

move on! = hurry up; **what's the next move?** = what do we have to do next?
2. *verb*

٢ - أ) ينقل - ينتقل - يتحرّك

(*a*) to change the place of something; to change your own place; **move the chairs away from the table; an animal was moving in the bushes; only the end of the cat's tail was moving; who's moved my book?—I left it on the table; he moved his head; don't move!** = stand still.

ب) ينتقل من منزل إلى منزل آخر

(*b*) to leave one place to go to live in another; **they moved from Edinburgh to London; my husband has got a job in Oxford, but I don't want to move; we are moving back to London.**
moves—moving—moved—has moved

move about, *verb*

يَحْرُك - يتحرك كثيراً

to change the place of something often; to change place often; **he moved the boxed about; crowds of people were moving about in the street.**

move away, *verb*

يبتعد

to change the place of something or your own place, to a place further away; **the ship moved away from the harbour; we're moving away from London** = we are going to live in another town away from London.

move in, *verb*

ينقل اثاثه ومفروشاته إلى مكان
أو منزل جديد

to put your furniture into a new house and start to live there.

movement, *noun*

حركة - تحرّك

changing of the place of something; not being still; **there was a movement in the trees; all you could see was a slight movement of the cat's tail.**

move off, *verb*

Mr.

ينطلق بحركة ما ـ يبدأ بالتحرك

to start moving; **the car moved off; he tried to get on to the train as it was moving off.**

Mr ['mɪstə] *noun*

سيّد : (عادةً تتقدم هذه الكلمة على اسم الشّخص المذكر : السيد د . جونس)

name given to a man; **Mr Jones; Mr John Jones; Dear Mr Smith** (*at beginning of a letter*); **Mr and Mrs Smith.**

Mr is used with a surname, sometimes with the Christian name and surname

Mrs ['mɪsɪz] *noun*

سيّدة : (عادةً تتقدم هذه الكلمة على اسم إمرأة ، مثلاً : السيّدة جونس)

name given to a married woman; **Mrs Jones; Mrs Anne Jones; Dear Mrs Jones** (*at beginning of a letter*); **Mr and Mrs Smith.**

Mrs is used with a surname, sometimes with the Christian name and surname

Ms [mɪz] *noun*

سيّدة

name given to any woman; **Ms Jones; Dear Ms Jones** (*at beginning of a letter*)

Ms is used with a surname

much [mʌtʃ] **1.** *adjective*

١ ـ كثير ـ كم ؟

a lot of; **with much love; how much bread do you want? I never carry much money with me; he eats too much meat; how much does it cost?** = how much money? **how much is that book?**

قدر ما ـ بقدر ما ـ بمقدار ما

as much as = the same quantity; **you haven't eaten as much as she has; he spends as much money as me.**

Note: **much** *is used with nouns which you cannot count;* **not much money** *but* **not many boys**

multiply

2. *adverb*

٢ ـ بكثير ـ إلى حدّ بعيد

very; a lot; **she's feeling much better today; it's much less cold in the south of the country; does it matter very much? that book is much too expensive.**

much—more [mɔː]**—most** [məʊst]

3. *noun*

٣ ـ كثيراً ـ قدر كبير

a lot; **much of the work has been done; you didn't write much in your exam; do you see much of him?** = do you see him often?

mud [mʌd] *noun*

وحل ـ طين

earth and water mixed; **we were up to our ankles in mud; the tractor got stuck in the mud.**

no plural

muddy, *adjective*

موحل ـ عَكِر

full of mud; covered with mud; **don't walk across the kitchen in your muddy boots; he dropped his hat into a pool of muddy water.**

muddy—muddier—muddiest

mudguard, *noun*

وقاء الطين ـ رفرف العجلة

piece of metal over the wheel of a bicycle which stops mud or water being splashed.

multiply ['mʌltɪplaɪ] *verb*

يضرب (عدداً بآخر)

to work out the sum of several numbers repeated several times; **if you multiply 240 by 2 the answer is 480.**

multiplies—multiplying—multiplied—has multiplied

multiplication [mʌltɪplɪ'keɪʃn] *noun*

الضرب (ضرب الأعداد)

sum when one number is multiplied by another; **I can do division but I'm no good at multiplication.**

one hundred and ninety-three

mum [mʌm], **mummy** ['mʌmɪ] *noun*

ماما – أمي

child's name for mother; **go and tell your mum I want to see her; is your mummy at home? my mummy's gone shopping; Mummy! can I have a biscuit?** *spelt* **Mum** *or* **Mummy** *when used to speak to your mother, but* **mum** *or* **mummy** *when used to talk about a mother*

mumps [mʌmps] *plural noun*

النكاف : التهاب الغدّة النكفية

disease which makes the sides of your face become fat; **he caught mumps from the children next door; she's in bed with mumps; he can't go to school—he's got mumps.**

murder ['mɜːdə] **1.** *noun*

١ ـ القتل العَمْد

killing of someone; **he was arrested for murder; the police are looking for the knife used in the murder.**
2. *verb*

٢ ـ يقتل عمداً ـ يقضي على

to kill someone; **he was charged with murdering the old man; she was murdered while she was sleeping.**
murders—murdering—murdered—has murdered

murderer, *noun*

قاتل

person who kills someone.

muscle ['mʌsl] *noun*

عضلة

meat part of the body, which makes the legs and arms, etc., move; **if you do a lot of exercises you develop strong muscles.**

museum [mjuːˈzɪəm] *noun*

مُتْحَف

building in which a collection of interesting things are put on show; **a railway museum** = place where old railway engines, carriages, etc., are put on show; **war museum** = place where old guns, uniforms, etc., are put on show; **a museum of country life; a museum of modern art; the British Museum.**

music ['mjuːzɪk] *noun*

أ) موسيقى

(a) sound made when you sing or play an instrument; **do you like modern music? he's taking music lessons; her music teacher says she plays the piano very well.**

ب) اللحن الموسيقي مُدَوَّن على ورق

(b) written signs which you read to play an instrument; **here's some piano music—try and play it; he can play the piano without any music.**
no plural: **some music; a piece of music**

musical, *adjective*

موسيقي

referring to music; **he doesn't play any musical instrument.**

must [mʌst] *verb used with other verbs*

أ) يجب ان

(a) to mean it is necessary; **you must do your homework or the teacher will be angry; we mustn't be late or we'll miss the TV programme; you must hurry up if you want to catch the bus; must you go so soon?**
Negative: **mustn't, needn't**
Note: **mustn't** = not allowed, **needn't** = not necessary; **we mustn't be late; you needn't hurry**

ب) جائز ان : (جائز ان اكون قد نسيت مظلتي في القطار)

(b) to mean it is likely; **I must have left my umbrella on the train; there's a knock at the door—it must be the doctor; they must be wet after walking in the rain.**
Negative: **can't: it can't be the doctor.**
I must, you must, he must, we must, they must
Past: **had to: I must go to the den-**

mustard

tist's/I had to go to the dentist's yesterday
Negative: **didn't have to**
Perfect: **must have: I must have left it on the train**
Negative: **can't have: I can't have left it on the train**
Note: **must** *does not have* **to** *and is always used with other verbs*

mustard ['mʌstəd] *noun*

الخردل

hot-tasting yellow powder or paste; **do you want some mustard with your beef? have you put any mustard on the ham sandwiches?**
no plural

mutton ['mʌtn] *noun*

لحم الضأن أو الغنم

meat from a sheep; **we're having a leg of mutton for lunch on Sunday.**
Note: **mutton** *is not used as often as* **lamb**

name

my [maɪ] *adjective*

ضمير المتكلم المضاف إليه

belonging to me; **that's my pen you're using! have you seen my new car? I broke my leg when I was playing football.**

myself, *pronoun referring to me*

انا - نفسي - بنفسي

I've hurt myself; I saw it myself; I enjoyed myself very much; I did it all by myself = with no one helping me; **I don't like being all by myself in the big house** = all alone.

mystery ['mɪstrɪ] *noun*

سرّ - لغز - غموض

thing which cannot be explained; **it is a mystery how the burglar got into the house; the police are trying to clear up the mystery of the missing jewels.**
plural **mysteries**

Nn

nail [neɪl] 1. *noun*

١ - (أ) ظفر

(a) hard part at the end of your fingers and toes; **she painted her nails red; nail scissors** = special curved scissors for cutting your nails; *see also* **fingernail, toenail**

ب) مسمار

(b) small piece of pointed metal with a flat end, which you knock into wood, etc., with a hammer; **hang that picture on the nail; put in another nail—the piece of wood is loose.**
2. *verb*

٢ - يُسَمِّر

to attach with nails; **she nailed the pieces of wood together; they were nailing the carpet to the floor; they nailed down the lid of the box.**
nails—nailing—nailed—has nailed

name [neɪm] 1. *noun*

١ - اسم - لقب أو نعت

special word which you use to call someone or something; **his name's John; I've forgotten the name of the shoe shop; Christian name/first name** = particular name given to someone; **her Christian name/her first name is Anne, but I don't know her surname; I know him by name** = I have never met him, but I know who

one hundred and ninety-five 195

narrow

he is; **don't call the teacher names** = don't be rude to the teacher; *see also* **surname**

2. *verb*

٢ ـ يُسَمِّي ـ يدعو ـ يطلق اسماً على ـ يشير إليه باسمه

to call someone or something by a name; **he's named John after his grandfather** = his grandfather was called John too; **can you name the largest town in the USA?**

names—naming—named—has named

narrow ['nærəʊ] *adjective*

ضَيِّق ـ بمشقة (نجاة بمشقة)

not wide; **the road is too narrow for two cars to pass; we had a narrow escape** = we almost didn't escape.

narrow—narrower—narrowest

narrowly, *adverb*

بشق النفس

only just; **we narrowly missed hitting the lamppost.**

nasty ['nɑːstɪ] *adjective*

كريه ـ بغيض ـ شنيع

unpleasant; **this medicine has a nasty taste; he's a nasty man—I don't like him; there's a nasty smell coming from the kitchen.**

nasty—nastier—nastiest

nation ['neɪʃn] *noun*

أمة ـ شعب ـ قوم

country; **all the nations of the world.**

national ['næʃnl] *adjective*

وطني ـ قومي

referring to a particular country; **she's wearing national costume; they're singing a national song.**

nationality [næʃə'nælɪtɪ] *noun*

جنسيّة

the state of belonging to a particular country; **he's of French nationality; what nationality is she?**

near

nature ['neɪtʃə] *noun*

الطبيعة

plants and animals; **nature study** = learning about plants and animals at school.

natural ['nætʃrəl] *adjective*

أ) طبيعي

(*a*) normal/not surprising; **his behaviour was quite natural; it's quite natural for old people to go deaf.**

ب) طبيعي (غير إصطناعي)

(*b*) not made by men; (thing) which comes from nature; **do you think the colour of her hair is natural? natural gas** = gas which is found in the earth and is not made in a factory; **natural history** = study of nature.

naturally, *adverb*

أ) بالتأكيد ـ طبعاً

(*a*) of course; **naturally the little boy was beaten by the big one; do you want to watch the game?—naturally!**

ب) طبيعياً ـ بطريقة طبيعية

(*b*) because of nature, not made; **she has naturally curly hair.**

naughty ['nɔːtɪ] *adjective*

سيىء السلوك ـ مؤذي ـ غير مطيع

badly behaved; **if you're naughty you won't have any ice cream; you naughty boy, stop pulling the cat's tail.**

naughty—naughtier—naughtiest
Note: **naughty** *is usually used of children or small animals*

navy ['neɪvɪ] *noun*

البحريّة : الأسطول البحري

all the warships of a country and the sailors who sail in them; **he's in the navy; we want to join the navy; navy blue** = very dark blue.

plural **navies**

near [nɪə] *adverb, preposition & adjective*

أ) بالقرب من ـ قريب من ـ مجاور لـ

(*a*) close to/not far away from; **the shops**

neat

are near the post office; bring your chair nearer to the fire; the bus stop is nearer to our house than the pub; which is the nearest police station? we had a near miss = we were nearly hit; (*of a car*) the **near side** = the side closer to the side of the road.

ب) قريب ـ في وقت قريب

(*b*) soon/not far in time; **my birthday is on December 21st—it's quite near to Christmas; phone me again nearer the day when you want to see me.**

near—nearer—nearest

nearby [nɪəˈbaɪ] *adverb & adjective*

بمقربة من

not far away; **they live just nearby; we met in a nearby pub.**

nearly, *adverb*

تقريباً

almost; **he's nearly 20 years old; the war lasted nearly ten years; this film isn't nearly as good as the one we saw last week; hurry up, it's nearly time for the bus to come.**

neat [niːt] *adjective*

نظيف ـ مُرَتَّب

tidy/clean; **her room is always neat and tidy; why is his homework never neat?**

neat—neater—neatest

necessary [ˈnesəsəri] *adjective*

ضروري

which has to be done; **it's necessary to pay your tax at the correct date; if you are going abroad it's necessary to have a passport; is all this equipment really necessary?**

neck [nek] *noun*

١) رَقَبَة ـ عنق

(*a*) part of the body which joins your head to your body; **I've got a stiff neck; she wears a gold chain round her neck; he's breathing down my neck all the time** = he's always watching how I'm working; **they're neck and neck** = exactly equal in the race.

needle

ب) عنق المعطف أو القميص ...

(*b*) part of a piece of clothing which goes round your neck; **a pullover with a V neck; what size neck shirts do you wear?**

ت) عنق الزجاجة ـ مضيق ـ بوغاز

(*c*) narrow part; **the neck of a bottle; a neck of land** = narrow piece of land between two pieces of water.

necklace [ˈnekləs] *noun*

عقد ـ قلادة

string of jewels, etc., which is worn round your neck.

need [niːd] **1.** *noun*

١ ـ حاجة ـ ضرورة

what is necessary or wanted; **there's no need for us to wait; to be in need of** = to want something/to be without something; **they're in need of food; are you in need of help?**
2. *verb*

٢ ـ يحتاج إلى

to be necessary for something; to want; **we shall need foreign money for our holiday; painting needs a lot of skill; do you need help? the house needs painting; I'm afraid the TV needs mending again; do you really need all this equipment? the police need to know who saw the accident; you don't need to come if you have a cold; will you be needing me any more or can I go home? I need you to help me with the cleaning; you can take the book—I don't need it any more.**

needs—needing—needed—has needed

needn't *verb used with other verbs*

لا حاجة لـ

to mean it isn't necessary; **you needn't come if you have a cold; he needn't have phoned; he needn't make so much noise in the bath.**

needn't *is not used with* **to** *and is only used with other verbs*

needle [ˈniːdl] *noun*

إبرة ـ صنّارة

thin metal tool with a sharp point used

negative

for sewing or knitting; **she's lost her knitting needles; don't sit down, I've left a needle on that chair.**

negative ['negətɪv] *adjective & noun*

سلبي - رافض

showing 'no'; **'didn't' is the negative of 'did'; the answer's in the negative** = the answer is 'no'.

neighbour ['neɪbə] *noun (American:* neighbor)

جار

person who lives near you; **our next door neighbours** = the people who live in the house next to ours; **the Swedes and Danes are neighbours** = their countries are close together.

neighbourhood, *noun (American:* neighborhood)

الجوار - منطقة مجاورة

area and the people who live in it; **this is a quiet neighbourhood; the postman knows everyone in the neighbourhood.**

neighbouring, *adjective (American:* neighboring)

مجاور

which is close to you; **we go to the neighbouring town to see the doctor as there isn't one in our town; Sweden and Denmark are neighbouring countries.**

neither ['naɪðə] 1. *adjective & pronoun*

١ - ولا واحد من - لا هذا ولا ذاك - لا...ولا

not either of two (people, etc.); **neither of them guessed the right answer; neither brother is fair/neither of the brothers is fair.**

2. *adverb & conjunction*

٢ - ولا

not either; **he doesn't like fish and neither do I** = I don't like fish either; **it's neither too hot nor too cold—it's just right; he isn't tall—but neither is he really very short** = he isn't really very short either.

Note: verb comes before subject after **neither**

never

nephew ['nefjuː] *noun*

ابن الأخ - ابن الأخت

son of your brother or sister; **my sister has two sons, so I have two nephews; an uncle and his nephews.**

nerve [nɜːv] *noun*

عَصَب - هستيريا - انزعاج - وقاحة

one of the many threads in a body which take messages to and from the brain; **she's in a state of nerves** = she's very worried; **he gets on my nerves** = he annoys me; **he had the nerve to tell me to be quick when he's so slow himself** = he was rude enough to tell me to be quick.

nervous, *adjective*

عصبي - قلق

very easily worried; **she's nervous about her exams; don't be nervous—the driving test is quite easy.**

nest [nest] *noun*

عش

place built by birds to lay their eggs; **the birds have built a nest in the apple tree.**

net [net] 1. *noun*

١ - شبكة

material made of string or thread with very large holes; **a fishing net; a tennis net; he hit the ball into the net.**
2. *adjective*

٢ - صافي (الوزن الصافي، الربح الصافي ... الخ)

(*price/weight, etc.*) after taking away anything extra; **net weight** = weight without the container; **net profit** = profit left after all the costs have been paid.

never ['nevə] *adverb*

ابداً - قط - مطلقاً - على الاطلاق

not at any time; not ever; **I'll never forget our holiday in Sweden; I've never been into that shop although I've often walked past it; she never eats meat; never mind!** = don't worry/don't bother about it.

new

new [njuː] *adjective*

أ) جديد - عصري
(a) quite recently made/not used; **take a new piece of paper; this is a new model of car; this bike is new—I didn't buy it secondhand.**

ب) جديد
(b) recently arrived/fresh; **here are the new boys in the school; we bought some new potatoes** = the first potatoes of this year's crop.

ت) حديث - جديد
(c) which has just been got/just been bought; **have you seen his new car? she introduced me to her new teacher.**

new—newer—newest

New Year, *noun*

رأس السنة - العام الجديد
first few days of the year; **I start my new job in the New Year; Happy New Year** = good wishes for the New Year; **New Year's Day** = January 1st.

news, *singular noun*

خبر - نبأ - أخبار - أنباء
spoken or written information about what has happened; **he was watching the 9 o'clock news on TV; did you hear the news on the radio? he told me the news about the fire; have you heard the news?** = have you heard what has happened? **have you had any news about your new job? we always like to hear good news.**

Note: **news** *is singular, not plural*

newsagent, *noun*

صاحب محل لبيع الصحف
person who sells newspapers/magazines in a shop; **go to the newsagent's and get me today's newspaper and the TV magazine.**

newspaper, *noun*

صحيفة - جريدة
sheets of paper (which usually come out each day) with news of what has happened; **a daily newspaper/a weekly newspaper; has today's newspaper been delivered? have you finished the crossword in today's newspaper? yesterday's** newspaper was full of news of the election.

Note: **a newspaper** *is often called* **a paper**

niece

next [nekst] *adjective & adverb*

أ) تالٍ - بعد - في المرة التالية - القادم
(a) coming after in time; **on Wednesday we arrived in London and the next day we left for Scotland; what shall we do next? first the teacher came into the classroom, and next came a policeman; come to see me when you're next in London; next Monday I start my holidays; the next time you go to the post office, can you buy me some of the new stamps? come to see me the week after next; next please!** = asking the next person in the queue to come in/to say what he wants in a shop.

ب) مجاور - الأقرب - بالقرب من - تقريباً (لا شيء تقريباً)
(b) nearest (in place); **the walls are thin—we can hear everything that is said in the next room; he sat down next to me; it costs next to nothing** = very little.

next door, *adjective & adverb*

البيت التالي أو المجاور
in the house next to this one; **she lives next door to my aunt; our next door neighbours are Germans; they have a lot of flowers next door.**

nice [naɪs] *adjective*

ممتع (وقت) - لطيف - طقس - جيّد - مليح
pleasant/fine; **what a nice time we had at the party! come and see us if the weather's nice; it wasn't fine today, so we hope it'll be nicer tomorrow; he had a nice sleep after lunch; we went for a nice ride in his new car; that wasn't a very nice thing to say** = that wasn't very pleasant.

nice—nicer—nicest

niece [niːs] *noun*

بنت الأخ أو الأخت
daughter of your brother or sister; **I've**

night

got three nieces—they're my brother's children; the niece looks like her aunt.

night [naɪt] *noun*

ليل ـ ليلة

part of the day when it is dark; **I don't like going out alone late at night;** it rained a lot during the night; we stayed at home last night, but tomorrow night we're going to a party; if you travel by night you pay less.

nine [naɪn] *number 9*

تسعة (العدد ٩)

he's nine (years old); come to see me tomorrow morning at nine o'clock; you've eaten nine cakes! nine times out of ten = very often.

nineteen, *number 19*

تسعة عشر ـ تسع عشرة

she's nineteen (years old); **the nineteen fifteen train** = the train leaving at 19.15; **in the 1950s** = during the years 1950-1959.

Note: **1950s:** *say* 'the nineteen fifties'

nineteenth, 19th, *adjective & noun*

التاسع عشر

referring to nineteen; he came nineteenth in the race; it's her nineteenth birthday tomorrow; **the nineteenth century** = the period from 1800 to 1899; **the nineteenth of June/ June the nineteenth (June 19th).**

ninety, *number 90*

تسعون

she is ninety (years old); her husband is ninety-two; they are both in their nineties.

Note: **ninety-one** (91), **ninety-two** (92), *etc* **ninety-first** (91st), **ninety-second** (92nd), *etc.*

ninetieth, 90th, *adjective & noun*

التسعون

referring to ninety; **a ninetieth of a second;** she was ninetieth in the competition; it will be grandmother's ninetieth birthday next month.

200

nod

ninth, 9th, *adjective & noun*

التاسع ـ تاسع

referring to nine; **at least a ninth of the children are ill;** she was ninth in her exam; today is the ninth of September/ September the ninth (September 9th); tomorrow is his ninth birthday.

no [nəʊ] *adjective & adverb*

ا) لا ـ كلاّ

(*a*) (*showing the opposite of* **yes**) we asked him if he wanted to come, and he said 'no'; do you want some more coffee?—no, thank you.

ب) لا ـ ليس

(*b*) not any; there's no butter left; there are no shops for miles around; I've had no reply to my letter; **no parking/no smoking/no exit** = do not park/smoke/ go out.

ت) اطلاقاً

(*c*) not at all; **this book is no better than the last one I read;** he's no longer here; he's no good at his job.

nobody ['nəʊbədɪ] *pronoun*

لا أحد

no one/no person; there's nobody in the bathroom; I saw nobody I knew; nobody likes sour milk; nobody else wears long socks like you.

nod [nɒd] **1.** *noun*

١ ـ ايماءة

moving your head forward to show you agree/ to greet someone; he gave me a nod; when we asked if he wanted an ice cream, he gave a nod.

2. *verb*

٢ ـ يميء برأسه (علامة الموافقة أو التحية)

to move your head forward to show you agree/to greet someone; **he nodded to me in the street;** when she asked if anyone wanted an ice cream all the children nodded.

nods—nodding—nodded—has nodded

two hundred

noise

nod off, *verb*

يحني الرأس نعاساً

to begin to go to sleep; **he nodded off in his chair; give me a pinch if I nod off; she's nodding off over her book.**

noise [nɔɪz] *noun*

ضجة - ضجيج - ضوضاء

sound which is often loud or unpleasant; **don't make so much noise—I'm trying to work; the car's making strange noises—perhaps something's wrong with the engine; I thought I heard a noise in the kitchen; he's making such a lot of noise that he can't hear the telephone; we were woken up by noises in the night.**

noisy, *adjective*

ضاجّ

which makes a lot of noise; **a noisy car; a crowd of noisy children.**

noisy—noisier—noisiest

none [nʌn] *pronoun*

أ) لا شيء

(*a*) not any; **a little money is better than none at all; none of the houses has a red door; he was none the worse for his accident** = not at all hurt; **her health is none too good** = not very good.

ب) لا أحد

(*b*) not one; **none of the teachers has a beard; none of the guests left the party early.**

nonsense [ˈnɒnsəns] *noun*

هُراء - توافه - تصرف غير مرضي

something which does not make sense; silly behaviour; **you're talking nonsense; it's nonsense to say that money doesn't matter; take an umbrella!—nonsense, it won't rain; stop that nonsense at once!**

no one [ˈnəʊwʌn] *pronoun*

لا أحد

nobody/no person; **there's no one in the room; I saw no one I knew; no one here likes sour milk; no one else wears long socks like you.**

north

nor [nɔː] *conjunction*

لا ... ولا

neither ... nor = nor one ... and not the other; **she's neither English nor German; neither you nor she looks very well.**

normal [ˈnɔːml] *adjective*

طبيعي - عادي

usual; ordinary; **wet weather is quite normal at this time of year; after the Christmas holidays the trains went back to their normal service.**

normally, *adverb*

عادةً

usually; **I normally have a cup of chocolate before going to bed; we normally go on holiday in August.**

north [nɔːθ] **1.** *noun*

١ - الشمال (عكس الجنوب)

direction when you are facing away from the sun at midday; **snow fell in the north of the country; the wind is blowing from the north.**
2. *adjective*

٢ - الشمالي

referring to the north: **the north coast of Scotland; the north side of the house never gets any sun.**
3. *adverb*

٣ - شمالاً - نحو الشمال

towards the north; **we were travelling north; the house faces north.**

North America, *noun*

اميركا الشمالية

part of America containing the USA and Canada.

northern, [ˈnɔːðn] *adjective*

شمالي

of the north; **they live in the northern part of the country.**

North Pole, *noun*

nose

القطب الشمالي
furthest point at the north of the earth.
North Sea, *noun* بحر الشمال
sea between England and Denmark, Germany, Holland, etc.

nose ['nəuz] *noun* أنف
part of your face which you breathe through and smell with; **he has a red nose; dogs have wet noses; she must have a cold—her nose is running** = liquid is dripping from her nose; **don't wipe your nose on your sleeve—use a handkerchief; he blew his nose several times** = blew through his nose into a handkerchief to get rid of liquid in his nose; **to speak through your nose** = as if your nose is blocked, so that you say 'b' instead of 'm' and 'd' instead of 'n'; **to look down your nose at something** = to look as if you don't think it is very good; **to turn up your nose at something** = to refuse something because you don't feel it is good enough.

not [nɒt] *adverb* أ) لا ـ لم ـ لن
(a) (*used with verbs to show that the action is the opposite—short form is* **n't**) he won't come; she isn't there; he didn't eat his meat; they couldn't go home because of the snow; the service charge is not included.

ب) ليس ـ غير
(b) (*used to make sentences and words have the opposite meaning*) **it is not at all funny; is he coming?—I hope not; I don't want to go—why not? all the family was there—not forgetting old Aunt Jane** = even including; **not a few** = many; **not very well** = rather ill; **I'm not sorry to leave** = I'm glad to leave.

ولا ... أيضاً
not...either = and not...also; **I don't like meat and I don't like fish**

nothing

either; it wasn't fine but it wasn't raining either.

ليس ... فحسب ... بل لم ... فحسب ... بل
not only...but also = not just this ... but this as well; **he isn't only blind, but he's also deaf; the book is not only very long but it's also very bad.**

note [nəut] **1.** *noun*
١ ـ أ) مُذكرة ـ ملاحظة ـ مفكرة
(a) very short letter; a few words written down; **I sent him a note to say I was ill; he made some notes before giving his speech; we must make a note of what we need before we go on holiday.**

ب) ورقة نقدية
(b) (*American:* **bill**) piece of paper money; **he only had a five pound note to pay for the newspaper.**

ت) نغمة موسيقية
(c) musical sound; written sign meaning a musical sound; key on a piano; **he can't sing the high notes; he only played the black notes on the piano.**

2. *verb*
٢ ـ أ) يُدَوِّن
(a) to write down briefly; **the policeman noted down the details of the accident.**

ب) يلاحظ ـ يَنْتبه
(b) to take notice of; **please note that the film starts at 7 o'clock.**

notes—noting—noted—has noted

notebook, *noun* مفكرة ـ مذكرة
small book for making notes

notepaper, *noun* ورق الرسائل
paper for writing letters.
no plural: **some notepaper; a piece of notepaper**

nothing ['nʌθɪŋ] *noun* لا شيء ـ عَدَم
not anything; **there's nothing in the box; when asked about the accident he said**

202

notice

nothing; he said nothing about the accident; he thinks nothing of cycling ten miles to work = he does it easily; **it's nothing to do with you** = it is not your problem; **nothing much happened** = not very much; **there was nothing interesting on the news; there's nothing more to be done; he has nothing left in the bank** = no money left.

notice ['nəʊtɪs] **1.** *noun*

١ ـ أ) إشعار ـ بلاغ

(*a*) piece of writing giving information, usually put in a place where everyone can see it; **he pinned up a notice about the meeting.**

ب) إنذار

(*b*) warning; **they had to leave with ten minutes' notice; it had to be done at short notice** = with very little warning time; **if you want to leave your job, you have to give a month's notice.**

ت) إنتباه ـ ملاحظة

(*c*) attention; **take no notice of what he says** = pay no attention to it/don't worry about it.

2. *verb*

٢ ـ يُلاحظ ـ ينتبه

to see; to take note of; **nobody noticed that I was wearing one blue and one white sock; did you notice what the time was when I started boiling the egg?**
notices—noticing—noticed—has noticed

noticeboard, *noun*

لوحة الاعلانات

flat piece of wood, etc., on a wall, on which notices can be pinned.

nought [nɔːt] number 0

صفر ـ لا شيء

a million is written as a one and six noughts.

noun [naʊn] *noun*

اسم (في علم النحو)

word used to show a person or thing or

nowhere

idea; **'man', 'stone' and 'colour' are all nouns.**

November [nə'vembə] *noun*

تشرين الثاني (شهر نوفمبر)

eleventh month of the year; **today is November 5th; he was born in November; we didn't go away last November.**
Note: **November 5th:** say 'the fifth of November' *or* 'November the fifth'

now [naʊ] **1.** *adverb*

١ ـ الآن ـ حالياً ـ في الوقت الحاضر

at this moment; **I can hear the car coming now; can we go to the beach now? he ought to be in Germany by now; now's the best time for picking apples; a week from now we'll be on holiday; until now she has never had to see a doctor.**
2. *conjunction*

٢ ـ والآن (تستعمل كصيغة لاستهلال الكلام أو السؤال) اما وقد

at this moment; **now (that) I know how to drive I can go on holiday by myself; now that you've reminded me, I do remember seeing him last week.**
3. *interjection*

٣ ـ أ) والآن

(*a*) (*showing warning*) **now then, let's get ready; come on now, pull hard!**

ب) أما الآن

(*b*) (*attracting someone's attention*) **now, let's begin.**

nowadays, *adverb*

في هذه الأيام ـ في الوقت الراهن

at the present time; **everything is very different nowadays from what it was fifty years ago; nowadays most people have cars and fridges.**

nowhere ['nəʊweə] *adverb*

أ) لا مكان ـ ليس في أي مكان ـ إلى لا مكان

(*a*) not in any place/not to any place/not anywhere; **the cat was nowhere to be found; where are you going?—nowhere!**

two hundred and three 203

nuisance

there is nowhere else to put the type-writer.

(ب) على الاطلاق

(b) **nowhere near** = not at all; **the house is nowhere near finished; he has nowhere near done his homework.**

nuisance ['nju:sns] *noun*

إزعاج - أذى

something/someone who is annoying; **what a nuisance—I've lost my front door key! that little boy is a real nuisance.**

number ['nʌmbə] *noun*

أ) عدد - رقم

(a) name of a figure; **13 is my lucky number; they live in flat number 48b; what is your telephone number? I can't remember the number of our car.**

ب) عدد - مجموعة كبيرة - عدة

(b) quantity of people/things; **a large number/large numbers of people are waiting to take their driving tests; a large number of houses were damaged in the fire; only a small number of people were there; I've seen that film a number of times** = several times; **I've been to London any number of times** = so many times I cannot count them; **you could take your driving test any number of times but you still wouldn't pass it.**

obey

Note: when **number** *refers to a plural noun it is followed by a plural verb:* **a number of houses were damaged**

nurse [nɜ:s] **1.** *noun*

١ - مُمَرِّضة

person (usually a woman) who looks after sick people; **she works as a nurse in the local hospital; she's training to be a nurse; male nurse** = man who looks after sick people.
2. *verb*

٢ - يقوم بعمل المُمَرِّض - يرعى المرضى - يقوم بعناية المرضى

to look after sick people; **when he was ill, his sister nursed him until he was better.**
nurses—nursing—nursed—has nursed

nursery school, *noun*

بيت الحضانة

school for little children; **now she is three, we may send her to nursery school in the mornings.**

nut [nʌt] *noun*

جوزة - بندقة

fruit of a tree, with a hard shell and a softer centre which you can eat; **he was eating a bar of milk chocolate with nuts.**

Oo

oar [ɔ:] *noun*

مِجْذاف

long wooden pole with a wide flat end, used for rowing a boat.

obedient [ə'bi:diənt] *adjective*

مطيع - ممتثل

doing what you are told to do; **our dog isn't very obedient—he won't sit down when we tell him to.**

obey [ə'beɪ] *verb*

يطيع - يمتثل

to do what someone or a rule tells you to do; **you ought to obey your father; you must obey the rules.**
obeys—obeying—obeyed—has obeyed

204   *two hundred and four*

object

object ['ɒbdʒɪkt] **1.** *noun*

١ ـ أ) شيء : (شيء أسود كبير سقط في وسط الحقل)

(a) thing; **a big black object fell into the middle of the field.**

ب) هَدَف ـ قَصْد

(b) something which you try to do; **what's the object of your plan?**

ت) مفعول به ـ مجرور

(c) noun or pronoun which follows immediately after a verb or a preposition; **in the sentence 'the dog chased the cat', the word 'cat' is the object of the verb 'chased'.**

2. *verb* [əb'dʒekt]

٢ ـ يعترض على ـ يعارض في ـ يرفض الموافقة على

to refuse to agree to something/not to approve of something; **I object to having to attend long meetings; he objected to my going on holiday; does anyone object if I smoke my pipe?**

objects—objecting—objected—has objected

observe [əb'zɜːv] *verb*

يراقب

to notice/to see something and understand it; **a policeman observed them putting the boxes into a van.**

observes—observing—observed—has observed

obvious ['ɒbviəs] *adjective*

واضح ـ جليّ

which can easily be seen/be noticed; **it's obvious that the car is no good; he made a very obvious mistake.**

obviously, *adverb*

بوضوح ـ بجلاء

naturally; **obviously he was very pleased when he passed his exam.**

occupy ['ɒkjupaɪ] *verb*

يشغل ـ يَحْتَل (مكاناً) ـ يستغرق (زماناً)

to fill up/to take up space or time; **the table occupies the whole corner of the room; how do you occupy your time when you are on holiday? the soldiers occupied the town; is this seat occupied? I'm afraid the manager is occupied at the moment** = busy.

occupies—occupying—occupied—has occupied

occupation [ɒkju'peɪʃn] *noun*

شغل ـ عمل ـ مهنة ـ صنعة

job; **what is his occupation?**

ocean ['əʊʃn] *noun*

محيط (المحيط الهادي ، الأطلسي)

very large sea surrounding the main areas of land on the earth; **the Pacific Ocean; the Atlantic Ocean.**

o'clock [ə'klɒk] *adverb phrase*

وفقاً للساعة ـ حسب الساعة . تماماً : (تمام الساعة)

ملاحظة : تستعمل هذه الكلمة للاشارة على الوقت الكامل ولا تستعمل في الاشارة على الوقت المجزأ : الخامسة تماماً

(*used with numbers to mean the exact hour*) **it's 6 o'clock; I never get up before 8 o'clock; by 10 o'clock everyone was asleep.**

Note: **o'clock** *is only used for the exact hour, not for times which include minutes. It can also be left out:* **we got home at eleven = we got home at eleven o'clock**

October [ɒk'təʊbə] *noun*

تشرين الأول (شهر اكتوبر)

tenth month of the year; **were you born in October? today is October 21st; last October we went to Germany.**

Note: **October 21st:** *say* 'the twenty-first of October' *or* 'October the twenty-first'

odd [ɒd] *adjective*

أ) غريب ـ شاذّ

(a) strange; **I find it odd that he hasn't written to us; how odd that the door**

of — office

wasn't locked; isn't it odd that he is afraid of the telephone?

ب) وتريّ ـ عدد غير شفعي

(b) (number) which cannot be divided by 2; **3, 5, 7 are all odd numbers**; **the houses with odd numbers are on this side of the street.**

ت) مفرد ، ينقصه الجزء المتمم له

(c) not one of a group; **I have two odd socks** = two socks which are not the same; **there was an odd glove left on the table.**

ث) غير اعتيادي ـ غير نظامي

(d) not regular; **he does odd jobs in the house**; **she writes the odd article for the newspaper.**

odd—odder—oddest

---

of [ɒv] *preposition*

أ) أداة إضافة: هو ابن الرجل الذي أصلح السيّارة

(a) (showing connection) **he's the son of the man who mended my car**; **she's a friend of mine**; **where's the lid of the black saucepan?** **what are the dates of Henry VIII?**

ب) من: كم تريد من هذا الصنف

(b) (showing a part/a quantity) **how much of it do you want?** **today is the first of June**; **there are six of them**; **half of the team were ill with flu**; **a pint of milk**; **two kilos of potatoes.**

ت) من أصل: ولد من أصل عشرة أولاد

(c) of = who/which is; **a child of ten** = a child who is ten years old; **the town of Bath is an important town in the west.**

ث) للدلالة على موقع ، مادة ، أو سبب: هو يسكن في المنطقة الجنوبية من المدينة.

(d) (showing position/material/cause) **he lives south of the town**; **the pullover is made of wool**; **he died of his wounds.**

Note: of is often used after verbs or adjectives: to think of; to be fond of; to be tired of; to smell of; to be afraid of, etc.

---

off [ɒf] *adverb & preposition*

(ينصرف) نحو ـ (يقع) بجانب (ينزل) من (ينزع حذاءه) (يقع) من على (ظهر الفرس) من أيام العطلة ...

(a) (showing movement away from a place) **I'm off to France tomorrow**; **the post office is just off the High Street**; **she got off the bus**; **take your shoes off if they are wet**; **take the cloth off the table**; **he fell off his horse**; **he's taking a day off** = a day away from work; (of a car) **the off side** = the side near the middle of the road.

ب) غير دائر . غير شغال ـ مقطوع التيار الكهربائي عنه

(b) not switched on; **switch all the lights off**; **is the TV off?**

Note: off is often used after verbs: to keep off; to take off; to fall off; to break off, etc.

---

offer [ˈɒfə] **1.** *noun*

١ ـ عرض ـ تقدمه

showing that you are ready to give something; **£10 is the best offer I can make** = I'm not ready to pay more; **we had offers of help from everyone in the village**; **special offer** = goods which are on sale at reduced price.

2. *verb*

٢ ـ يَعرْض على ـ يقدّم

to say that you are ready to do or give something; **did he offer to help?** **they didn't even offer me a cup of tea**; **I offered to go with her to the bus stop.**

offers—offering—offered—has offered

---

office [ˈɒfɪs] *noun*

مكتب (الشركة) ـ غرفة (الموظف)

room/building where a business is carried on or where something is organised; **he works in an office in London**; **I'll be staying late at the office this evening**; **she's the manager of our London office**; **Miss Jones's office is next door to mine**; *see also* **post office**

Office

المكتب

1. book	١ - كتاب
2. calculator	٢ - آلة حاسبة
3. card	٣ - بطاقة
4. cassette	٤ - شريط تسجيل
5. cheque	٥ - شيك
6. drawing pin	٦ - دبوس
7. envelope	٧ - غلاف
8. ink	٨ - حبر
9. letter	٩ - رسالة
10. magazine	١٠ - مجلّة
11. notebook	١١ - مفكرة
12. notice	١٢ - ملاحظة
13. noticeboard	١٣ - لوحة الاعلانات
14. page	١٤ - صفحة
15. parcel	١٥ - طرد
16. pen	١٦ - ريشة
17. pencil	١٧ - قلم
18. ruler	١٨ - مسطرة
19. safe	١٩ - خزنة
20. telephone	٢٠ - تلفون - جهاز الهاتف
21. telephone book	٢١ - دفتر التلفون
22. typewriter	٢٢ - آلة كاتبة

two hundred and seven   **207**

officer

officer [ˈɒfɪsə] *noun*

ظابط (في الجيش أو الأسطول)

person in command in the army, navy, air force, etc.; **he's an army officer; a police officer came to look at the damage.**

official [əˈfɪʃl] **1.** *adjective*

١ ـ رسمي ـ نابع عن السلطة ـ قانوني ـ مرخص به

as used by government or people in charge; **an official report; his official title is Manager of the Sales Department.**
2. *noun*

٢ ـ موظف حكومي

person in an important government job; **an official from the Tax Office came to look at our accounts; she's an official in the Department of Education.**

often [ˈɒfn] *adverb*

كثيراً ما ـ غالباً

many times/frequently; **I often go to Paris on business; do you often have chicken for dinner? how often do the trains go to London? I go to the cinema every so often** = not very frequently.

oh [əʊ] *interjection*

آهِ : صوت يعبر عن الدهشة أو الألم أو الرغبة .

(*showing surprise/interest/excitement*) **Oh look, there's the train! Oh, Mr Jones, can you come here, please? you must come to the police station—Oh no I won't!**

oil [ɔɪl] **1.** *noun*

زيت ـ نفط ـ بترول

any of various sorts of thick liquid used in cooking/engineering/painting etc.; **cooking oil; vegetable oil; he fond of painting in oils; an oil painting; an oil well; an oil field** = large area where oil is found underground.
2. *verb*

on

يُزَيِّت

to put oil on a machine, etc.; **you should oil the car door because it makes a noise.**
oils—oiling—oiled—has oiled

OK [əʊˈkeɪ] *noun & interjection*

حسناً ـ أنا (أو نحن) موافق ـ حسن

all right; **shall we start now?—OK, let's go; I was ill yesterday, but I'm OK now; he gave our plan the OK** = he approved our plan.

old [əʊld] *adjective*

ا) عجوز ـ متقدم في السن ـ قديم

(*a*) having lived/existed for a long time; not young; **my grandfather is an old man—he's eighty; my mother's getting old; an old church; I don't like this old music—play something modern.**

ب) بالٍ ـ عتيق

(*b*) having been used for a long time/not new; **I'll have to wear my old clothes to paint the house; she sold her old car and bought a new one.**

ت) بالغ سنّاً معيناً . (هي بلغت اليوم العاشرةَ من عمرها . وأنت ما هو عمرك ؟)

(*c*) having a certain age; **she's ten years old today; how old are you?** = what is your age?

ث) تستعمل كتعبير مودة عن شخص ما: (يا صديقي العزيز)

(*d*) (*used as a pleasant way of talking about someone*) **hello, old boy! the old man** = your father/the boss/the headmaster, etc.
old—older—oldest

on [ɒn] **1.** *preposition*

١ ـ ا) على : (ضع الكتاب على الطاولة)

(*a*) touching or lying on the top or outside of something; **put the book on the table; flies can walk on the ceiling.**

ب) بواسطة ، بـ : عَلّق الصورة بالكُلّاب

(*b*) hanging from; **hang the picture on the hook.**

once

ت) إلى : (وصل إلى القطار) في : (في الصفحة الرابعة)
(c) (showing movement or position) he got on the train; it's on page 4; the house is on the right side of the road.

ث) من : (هي من موظفي المدرسة)
(d) belonging to; she's on the staff of the school; he's on the committee.

ج) بُغية ، في سبيل : سافر في سبيل العمل
(e) busy doing something; he's gone to Germany on business; they're on holiday.

ح) تستعمل للدلالة على الوقت أو اليوم أو التاريخ : (في أيام الأحد)
(f) (showing time/day/date) on Sundays; on Monday we went to the zoo; on December 25th; on my arrival = when I arrived.

خ) على : (سيراً على الأقدام)
(g) (showing means of travel) he went away on foot; she's going on her bike.

د) (عن موضوع ما) : كتاب عن الحيوانات
(h) about; he wrote a book on African animals.

ذ) دائر ـ شغّال ـ جار ـ بواسطة
(i) (showing an instrument/machine which is used) he played a piece of music on the piano; she was on the telephone for half an hour; the play was on the radio yesterday; I watched the football game on TV.

2. adverb

٢ ـ أ) على رأسه ـ على جسمه ـ على النار ـ على التيار الكهربائي
(a) in position; being worn; put the kettle on; have you put your boots on? because it was cold he kept his coat on in the house.

ب) شغّال : الغاز شغّال ـ النور شغّال ـ التلفزيون دائر
(b) working; the gas is on; you've left the light on; turn the engine on; switch the TV on; what's on at the cinema?

ت) باستمرار ـ بدون توقف
(c) continuing/not stopping; he worked

one

on until the evening; she went on talking; go on—don't stop.

ث) بعد ـ في ما بعد ـ من الآن فصاعداً
(d) (showing that time has passed) later on; from that time on.

Note: on is often used after verbs: to sit on; to jump on; to put on; to lie on, etc.

once [wʌns] 1. *adverb*

أ) مرةً واحدة
(a) one time; take the medicine once a day; the magazine comes out once a month; how many times did you see the dentist?—only once.

ب) ذات مرةٍ ـ يوماً ...
(b) at a time in the past; I knew him once; once, when I was going home, I fell off my bike.

2. *conjunction*

٢ ـ حالما
as soon as; once you start you can't stop; once I'm on holiday, I'll swim every day.

at once, *adverb*

أ) على الفور ـ فوراً
(a) immediately; do it at once! the doctor came at once.

ب) في نفس الوقت
(b) at the same time; don't all speak at once.

one [wʌn] 1.

١ ـ أ) العدد واحد
(a) number 1; our little boy is one year old; hs grandfather is a hundred and one.

ب) واحد ـ واحدة ـ أوحد ـ وحيد
(b) single thing; there's only one left; this is the last page but one = the page before the last.

2. *adjective & pronoun*

٢ ـ أ) واحد ـ أي واحد ـ أحد
(a) single (thing); there's only one cake left; which one do you want—the green one or the black one? one of the boys will help you; I've lost my pen—have you got one?

onion

ب) المرء (عامةً) ـ الانسان
(b) you; one just can't do that sort of thing, can one? one can't afford to drive a large car these days.

ت) بعضكم بعضاً
(c) **one another** = each other; **you should write to one another more often.**
Note: **one** (1) *but* **first** (1st)

one-way street, *noun*
شارع وحيد الاتجاه
street where the traffic only goes in one direction; **you can't turn left—it's a one-way street.**

onion ['ʌnjən] *noun*
بصل ـ بصلة
vegetable with a round white root which makes you cry when you cut it; **we had onion soup for dinner.**

only ['əʊnlɪ] **1.** *adjective*
الوحيد ـ الوحيدة : (هـذه هي ساعتي الوحيدة ـ هي بنتي الوحيدة)
one single (thing or person); **it's the only watch I've got; she's an only child** = there are no other children in her family.
2. *adverb*

٢ ـ أ) فحسب ـ فقط
(a) and no one/nothing else; **I've only got three pounds; only you can help us; staff only can use this lift; only children are allowed in free.**

ب) إلاّ : لم تصلني بطاقتها إلاّ البارحة
(b) as recently as; **only yesterday I got a postcard from her.**

ليت ـ يا ليت
if only (*phrase showing a strong wish*) = **if only I had known; if only she had phoned the police.**

بالكاد
only just = almost not; **he only just caught the bus** = he almost missed the bus.

210

open

في منتهى ... للغاية
only too = extremely; **I'm only too happy to help.**

open ['əʊpn] **1.** *adjective*

١ ـ أ) مفتوح
(a) not shut; **that box is open; leave the door open—it's hot in here; why is the oven door open?**

ب) فاتح أبوابه ـ متاح الدخول إليه : (هل المتاجر تفتح أبوابها أيام الأحد ؟)
(b) which you can go into; **are the shops open on Sundays? the exhibition is open from 10 a.m. to 5 p.m.**

ت) غير مطوق بحواجز ـ طلق (الهواء الطلق)
(c) without any walls/any protection; **the field is open on three sides; I like being out in the open air; the competition is open to everyone** = anyone can enter it.
2. *verb*

٢ ـ أ) يفتح
to make open; **open the door—the cat wants to go out; can you open that box?**

ب) يفتتح ـ ينشىء ـ يؤسس يفتح أبوابه (متجر)
(b) to start up; **a new shop is going to open next door to us; the shops open early in the morning.**
opens—opening—opened—has opened

opener, *noun*
فتّاحة العلب أو الزجاجات
tool for opening; **a tin opener; a bottle opener.**

opening, *noun*

أ) إفتتاح ـ فتح
(a) the action of opening; **opening time for the exhibition is 10.00 a.m.**

ب) فتحة ـ ثغرة
(b) place where something opens; **the sheep got out through an opening in the hedge.**

two hundred and ten

opeation

open on to, *verb*

يطلّ على : (النوافذ تطل على الشارع)

to lead out on to/to look out on to; **the door opens directly on to the garden; the windows open on to the street.**

operation [ɒpəˈreɪʃn] *noun*

عمليّة جراحية

act of cutting open someone's body to cure something; **she's had an operation on her foot; the operation was successful.**

opinion [əˈpɪnjən] *noun*

رأي - اعتقاد

what people think about something; **what's your opinion of the situation? ask the bank manager for his opinion about what we should do; he has a very high/a very low opinion of his assistant** = he thinks he is very good/very bad.

opportunity [ɒpəˈtjuːnɪti] *noun*

فرصة - مناسبة

situation which allows you to do something; **if you start work early, that will give you the opportunity to finish before dinner; I'd like to learn to fly a plane, but I've never had the opportunity to do so.**
plural **opportunuties**

oppose [əˈpoʊz] *verb*

يعارض - يقاوم - يتصدى لـ - يواجه

to work to stop something/to try to stop something happening; **he opposed his boss at the meeting; she is opposed to taking a long holiday this year.**
opposes - opposing - opposed - has opposed

opposite [ˈɒpəzɪt] *1. adjective & preposition*

١ - مقابل - مواجه - معاكس - مضاد

facing/on the other side; **their house is just opposite the post office; it's not on this side of the street—it's on the oppo-**

orchestra

site side; his car hit a lorry going in the opposite direction; will you sit opposite my mother?
2. noun

الضدّ - النقيض - العكس - مختلف كليّا

something which is completely different; **'big' is the opposite of 'small'; what's the opposite of 'black'? he's just the opposite of his brother; he said one thing, and then did the opposite.**

or [ɔː] *conjunction*

أ) أو - أم - (شاي أو قهوة)

(a) (*showing something else which is possible*) **you can come with us or you can stay at home; I don't mind if I have tea or coffee; did she die in an accident or was she murdered?**

ب) أو

(b) (*showing a rough figure*) **six or seven people came; it costs £4 or so** = roughly £4.

وإلاّ : البس معطفك وإلاّ ستشعر بالبرد

or else = if not; **you must wear a coat or else you'll catch cold; he has to get up early or else he'll miss his train.**

orange [ˈɒrɪndʒ] *1. noun*

١ - برتقال - ليمون البرتقال

sweet tropical fruit, coloured between yellow and red; **I have an orange for breakfast; I like orange ice cream; can I have a glass of orange juice?**
2. adjective & noun

٢ - برتقالي - اللون البرتقالي

the colour of an orange/ a colour between yellow and red; **does he always wear an orange tie? they painted the kitchen ceiling orange; I'd like to paint the front door a dark orange.**

orchestra [ˈɔːkɪstrə] *noun*

جوقة موسيقية

large group of people who play music together; **the school orchestra played music by Beethoven.**

two hundred and eleven 211

order

order [ˈɔːdə] **1.** *noun*

١ - أ) أمر

(a) saying that something has to be done; **he gave an order to the soldiers; if you can't obey orders, you shouldn't be a policeman.**

ب) طلب تجاري - طلبية

(b) asking for something to be served/to be sent; **we've had a large order for machinery from Japan; he gave the waiter his order; the waiter brought him the wrong order.**

ث) ترتيب (ترتيب الأسماء بالأحرف الأبجدية)

(c) arrangement of things in a special way; **the names on the list are in alphabetical order; the books in the library are all in the wrong order/ all out of order** = not in the right places.

ث) حالة - وضع

(d) correct running of a machine, etc.; **the lift is out of order** = it is not working; **are your papers in order?** = are they correct?

بغيّة ان - لكي

in order that = so that; **people on bikes should wear orange coats in order that drivers can see them in the dark.**

لأجل - لكي

in order to = to/so as to; **he ran fast in order to catch the bus; she bent down in order to pick up her book.**
2. *verb*

٢ - أ) يأمر

(a) to say that something has to be done; to tell someone to do something; **he ordered the gate of the castle to be shut; the doctor ordered three weeks' rest; I don't like being ordered about** = I don't like people always telling me what to do.

ب) يطلب

(b) to ask for something to be served/to be sent; **he ordered chicken and chips and a glass of beer; we've ordered a new electric typewriter.**

212

other

orders—ordering—ordered—has ordered

ordinary [ˈɔːdnrɪ] *adjective*

عادي - اعتيادي - مألوف

normal/not special; **I'll wear my ordinary suit to the office; he leads a very ordinary life; the film is quite out of the ordinary** = quite different from other films.

organize [ˈɔːɡənaɪz] *verb*

يُنَظِّم - يُرتّب

to arrange things/to put things into a special order; **you must organize your work properly; she organized a meeting to complain about the noise.**

organizes—organizing—organized—has organized

organization, *noun*

ا) تنظيم

(a) way or organizing; **you have to have good organization if you want the factory to work well.**

ب) مُنَظَّمَة : (منظمة الشباب)

(b) group which is organized; **a youth organization; an organization which sends food to poor people; she belongs to an organization which looks after old people.**

other [ˈʌðə] *adjective & pronoun*

ا) آخر - أخرى - آخرون - غير

(a) not the same/different (person or thing); **the two boys went swimming while the other members of the family sat on the beach; I don't like these cakes—can I have one of the other ones/ one of the others? which others do you want? any other sort would do; can't we go to some other place on holiday next year?**

ب) الآخر - الأخرى - الآخرون

(b) second one of two; **one pencil is red, and the other (one) is blue; one girl is tall, but the other (one) is short.**

two hundred and twelve

ought

ت) آخر (في قرية أو في أخرى) سابق ، في وقت مضى : منذ بضعة أيام

(c) (showing an idea which is not clear) he went to stay in some village or other by the sea; she met some boy or other at the party; **the other day/the other week** = a day or two ago/a week or two ago.

واحد تلوَ الآخر

one after the other = following in line; they fell down one after the other; they all got colds one after the other.

كل اثنين : (كل سيارتين ، كل يومين)

every other = every second; the police stopped every other car = the first, third, fifth cars, etc.; he wrote a letter every other day = on Tuesday, Thursday, Saturday, etc.

ought [ɔːt] *verb used with other verbs*

١) يجب ـ يُستحسن ـ يتعين

(a) *to mean* it would be a good idea to; you ought to go to the cinema; he ought to see a doctor if his cough is no better; you oughtn't to eat so many cakes; she ought to have told you before she went away.

ب) يُتَوقع ان

(b) *to mean* it is probable that; he ought to pass his exams easily; she ought to get home by 6 o'clock; they ought to have arrived by now.

I ought, you ought, he ought, we ought, they ought
Past: ought to have
Negative: ought not, ought not to have, usually oughtn't, oughtn't to have
Note: ought is followed by to, ought and ought to have do not follow to and are only used with other verbs

our ['auə] *adjective*

» ـ نا « ـ ملكنا ـ خاصتنا (بيتنا ـ كلبنا)

belonging to us; our house is near the post office; we have lost our dog; one of our children has got measles.

out

ours, *pronoun*

ملكنا ـ خاصتنا

thing/person belonging to us; that house is ours; is that their son?—no, he's ours; some friends of ours told us to go; can we borrow your car, ours won't start?

ourselves, *pronoun*

أنفسنا ـ نحن

referring to us we organized ourselves into two groups; we were enjoying ourselves; we did it all by ourselves = with no one to help us; we don't like being all by ourselves = all alone.

out [aʊt] *adverb*

١) خارج البيت

(a) not in; away from; no one answered the phone—they must all be out; the rabbit got out of its cage; he pulled out a gun; take the camera out of its box; the water came out of the hole in the pipe.

ب) بعيد عن

(b) away; the tide is out; the ship is out at sea.

مخطىء (في الحساب أو في العد)

(c) wrong (when you are calculating); I am £10 out = I have £10 too much or too little; she was out in her answer to the sum.

ت) من بين ـ من أصل : (لديه ١٠ من أصل ١٢)

(d) among (in a total); he got 10 out of 12 for his exam; nine times out of ten she's wrong = nearly all the time.

Note: out is often used with verbs: to jump out; to get out; to come out, etc.
Note: out is often followed by of

outdoor, *adjective*

في الهواء الطلق

in the open air; an outdoor swimming pool.

outdoors, *adverb*

في الهواء الطلق

in the open air; you should sit outdoors instead of sitting in the house.

two hundred and thirteen 213

oven

outing, *noun*

رحلة صغيرة ـ نزهة

short trip; **we're going on an outing to the seaside.**

output, *noun*

نتاج ـ محصول ـ مردود

amount which a firm/a person/a machine produces; **output is falling; the factory has an output of 200 tons per day.**

outside 1. *noun*

١ ـ الخارج ـ خارج الشيء : (خارج البيت مدهون بالأبيض)

surface of something/part which is not inside; **the outside of the house is painted white; the apple looked nice on the outside, but the inside was rotten.**

2. *adjective*

٢ ـ خارجي

which is on the outside; **the outside walls of the house.**

3. *adverb & preposition*

٣ ـ في الخارج ـ في خارج شيء : (تركت دراجتي خارج الباب)

not inside/beyond the walls of something; **I left my bike outside the front door; come and sit outside in the garden; his coat's all wet—it must be raining outside.**

oven ['ʌvn] *noun*

فرن

inside part of a cooker which is heated and which you cook food in; **I've put a cake in the oven; your dinner's in the oven.**

over ['əʊvə] **1.** *preposition*

١ ـ أ) فوق ـ على

(a) on top of; higher than; **she spread a cloth over the table; the plane flew over our house; the water was soon over her ankles.**

214

over

ب) على الجانب الآخر

(b) on the other side; to the other side; **he lives over the road from the post office; she threw the bottle over the wall; they jumped over the railway lines.**

ت) من أعلى ـ من فوق

(c) from the top of; **he fell over the edge; she looked over the edge.**

ث) على مدى ـ طوال

(d) during; **over the last few months he's grown quite tall; we talked about it over dinner.**

ج) أكثر من ـ وما فوق

(e) more than; **children over 5 years old; it costs over £50; we've been waiting for over two hours.**

2. *adverb*

٢ ـ أ) بالكامل

(a) everywhere; **he's dirty all over.**

ب) عدة مرات ـ تكراراً

(b) several times; **he played the record over and over again; they did it ten times over.**

ت) سقط : (سقطت الزجاجة)

(c) down from being upright; **the bottle fell over; he knocked the bottle over; she leaned over and picked up the cushion.**

ث) مُنْتَه : (ان اللعبة قد انتهت)

(d) finished; **is the game over yet? when the war was over we had more food to eat.**

ج) وما فوق

(e) more than; **children of 14 and over pay full price; there are reduced prices for groups of 30 and over.**

ح) زيادة

(f) not used/left behind; **you can keep what's left over; I have two cards over.**

Note: **over** *is used after many verbs:* **to run over; to fall over; to come over; to look over,** *etc.*

overalls, *plural noun*

ثوب فضفاض يرتدى فوق الثياب العادية لحمايتها من الأوساخ

one-piece suit worn over other clothes to keep them clean when working; **he was wearing a pair of blue overalls.**

two hundred and fourteen

overcoat

overcoat, *noun*

معطف

thick coat which you wear over other clothes outside; **put on your overcoat—it's snowing.**

overcrowded, *adjective*

مزدحم ـ مكتظ بالسكان

with too many people inside; **the building is overcrowded; the overcrowded boat sank.**

overnight, *adverb & adjective*

طوال الليل ـ بين عشية وضحاها

lasting all night; for the night; **we stayed overnight in France; will the food stay fresh overnight? they took the overnight train to Scotland.**

overtake, *verb*

يتجاوز

to go past someone travelling in front of you; **he overtook three lorries on the motorway; we were overtaken by a bus.**

overtakes—overtaking—overtook—has overtaken

owe [əʊ] *verb*

أ) يكون مدينًا لـ : هو مدين لي بخمسة جنيهات استرليني

(*a*) to have money which you should pay someone; **he owes me £5; how much do I owe you for the petrol?**

ب) يدين بكذا : أدينه بحياتي

(*b*) to have something because of what someone has done; **I owe him my life** = I am alive because he saved my life; **he owes a lot to his father** = his father has helped him a lot.

own

بفضل ـ بسبب ـ بداعي

owing to = because of; due to; **the train is late owing to fog.**

owes—owing—owed—has owed

own [əʊn] **1.** *adjective*

١ ـ يملك

belonging to you alone; **I have my own car; he has his own shop.**

2. *noun*

٢ ـ أ) ملكي ـ ملكه ـ ملكها ملكهم ... الخ

(*a*) **my own/his own,** etc. = mine/his; **he has a car of his own; she has a house of her own; they have a garden of their own.**

ب) بمفردي ـ بمفرده ـ بمفردهـا ـ بمفردهم ... الخ

(*b*) **on my own/on his own,** etc. = alone; **I'm on my own today; he did it on his own.**

3. *verb*

to have/to possess; **I don't own a car; who owns this land?**

owns—owning—owned—has owned

owner, *noun*

المالك (مالك السيارة أو بيت ...)

person who owns; **the police are looking for the owner of the car; who's the owner of this house?**

own up (to), *verb*

يعترف بـ ـ يقرّ بـ

to say that you have done something wrong; **she owned up to having stolen the jewels; he owned up to his mistake; the teacher asked who had written rude words on the board, but no one would own up.**

two hundred and fifteen 215

Pp

p [piː] *letter*

مختصر لفظة Pence وهي الجزء المئوي من الجنيه الاسترليني

used to show a price in pence; **this book costs 60p; you should get a ticket from the 20p machine** = the machine which gives tickets worth 20p; *see also* **penny**

pack [pæk] **1.** *noun*

١ ـ رُزمة ـ علبة ـ حزمة

group of things put together (in a box); **a pack of cards.**
2. *verb*

٢ ـ أ) يرزم ـ يُوضب ـ يُعلّب

(a) to put things into a suitcase/to put things in boxes ready for sending; **she's packed her suitcase; have you finished packing yet, it's time to start? I packed my toothbrush at the bottom of the bag; the glasses are packed in boxes to stop them being broken.**

ب) يحشر ـ يحشد

(b) to squeeze a lot of people or things into something; **how can you pack ten people into that little car? the trains are packed with people going on holiday; the shelves were packed with books.**

packs—packing—packed—has packed

package ['pækɪdʒ] *noun*

طرد بريدي

parcel/something wrapped up for posting; **the postman brought this package for you; tie the package carefully before taking it to the post office; package tour** = tour where everything (hotel, food, travel, etc.) is arranged and paid for before you leave.

packet, *noun*

علبة . رزمة صغيرة : (كم علبة سجاير تدخن يومياً)

small parcel/box; **a packet of cigarettes; how many packets do you smoke a day?** = how many packets of cigarettes.

pack up, *verb*

أ) يوضب ـ يرزم امتعته ـ يحزم

(a) to put things away (before leaving); **they packed up the picnic things when the rain started.**

ب) يكف عن العمل

(b) to stop working/to break down; **the engine packed up when we were on the motorway.**

page [peɪdʒ] *noun*

صفحة

one of the sides of the sheets of paper used in books, newspapers, etc.; **the paper has 32 pages; turn over the page; look at the next page; the answer to the crossword is on page 23; open the book at page 24.**

Note: with numbers, the word 'the' is left out: **on the next page; on page 50**

paid [peɪd] *see* **pay**

ملاحظة : انظر إلى كلمة pay

pain [peɪn] *noun*

أ) وجع ـ ألم

(a) feeling when you are hurt; **I have pains in my legs after playing tennis; she says she has a pain in her back.**

ب) يبذل جهداً كبيراً

(b) **to take pains** = to be very careful when you are doing something; **he took**

216   two hundred and sixteen

paint

a lot of pains with his homework; they took great pains to be at the meeting on time.

painful, *adjective*

مؤلم ـ موجع

which hurts; his foot is so painful he can hardly walk; your eye looks very red—is it painful?

paint [peɪnt] **1.** *noun*

١ ـ دهان ـ صبغة

coloured liquid which you use to give something a colour/to make a picture; we gave the front door two coats of paint; she got a box of paints for her birthday; I need a 2½ litre tin of blue paint; the paint's coming off the ceiling. **2.** *verb*

٢ ـ أ) يدهن ـ يطلي

(a) to cover something with paint; he's painting the outside of the house; we painted the front door red.

ب) يصور ـ يرسم بالاصباغ

(b) to make a picture of something using paint; he painted a picture of his mother; she's painting the old church; the sea is very difficult to paint.

paints—painting—painted—has painted

painter, *noun*

الدهان ـ الرسام

person who paints; the painter's coming today to paint the bathroom; Rembrandt was a famous painter.

painting, *noun*

صورة ـ رسمة

picture; do you like this painting of my mother?

pair [peə] *noun*

أ) زوج ـ اثنين

(a) two things taken together; she's bought a new pair of shoes; these socks are a pair = they go together.

ب) شيء مؤلف من قطعتين متقابلتين

(b) two things joined together to make

pan

one; I'm looking for a clean pair of pyjamas; where's my pair of brown trousers? this pair of scissors isn't very sharp.

pajamas [pə'dʒɑːməz] *plural noun American* = **pyjamas**

ملابس النوم ـ قميص النوم

palace ['pæləs] *noun*

بلاط ـ قصر ـ مبنى ضخم

large house where a king or president lives; the soldiers stood in front of the president's palace; the Queen lives in Buckingham Palace.

pale [peɪl] *adjective*

شاحب ـ باهت

light coloured; she turned pale at the sight of blood = she went white; he was wearing pale grey trousers; this blue is too dark—have you something paler?

pale—paler—palest

palm [pɑːm] *noun*

أ) راحة اليد

(a) soft inside part of your hand; he held the egg in the palm of his hand; if you look at the lines on your palm you can see what will happen to you in the future.

ب) نخلة ـ نخيل

(b) type of tall tropical tree with a bare trunk and long leaves at the top; he climbed up a palm tree.

pan [pæn] *noun*

مقلاة ـ وعاء

metal container which you heat on a stove and use for cooking; put the potatoes into a pan of boiling water; use a larger pan if you're boiling lots of eggs; the handle of the frying pan is hot; *see also* **frying pan, saucepan**

pancake, *noun*

فطيرة محلاة

thin soft cake made in a frying pan, using a mixture of eggs, flour, milk,

two hundred and seventeen 217

paper

etc.; we eat pancakes with jam; who wants another pancake?
Note: pancakes are always eaten in the UK on a Tuesday in February (Shrove Tuesday or Pancake Day)

paper ['peɪpə] *noun*

١) ورق - ورقة

(a) thin sheet of material which you write on, and which is used to make books/newspapers, etc.; she uses pink paper when she writes to her friend; the parcel was wrapped up in brown paper; can you give me another piece of paper/ another sheet of paper? this paper's too thin to write on; I bought a box of paper handkerchiefs; he floated a paper boat on the lake.

ب) صحيفة - جريدة

(b) newspaper; I read the paper in the train on my way to work; did you see the picture of our school in yesterday's paper? the local paper comes out on Fridays; has the evening paper been delivered yet? Sunday papers are so big that it takes me all day to read them.

ت) امتحان خطي

(c) exam; the French paper was very hard; she wrote a good maths paper.
Note: no plural for (a); some paper; a sheet of paper/a piece of paper

paper boy, *noun*

موزع الصحف : الذي يوزع الصحف على البيوت

boy whose job is to deliver newspapers to houses.

paragraph ['pærəgrɑːf] *noun*

مقطع (من نص) - فقرة

group of several sentences in a book/letter/newspaper, etc., which starts with a small space at the beginning of the first line; look at the second paragraph on page 2; start a new paragraph.

parallel ['pærəlel] *adjective*

متواز - مواز

(lines) which are side by side and the same distance apart, but which never join; railway lines are parallel; the lines of writing should be parallel to the top of the page.

parcel ['pɑːsl] *noun*

طرد

something wrapped and tied, ready for sending; the postman brought this parcel for you; look at all the parcels round the Christmas tree! tie that parcel up well before you take it to the post office.

pardon ['pɑːdn] **1.** *noun*

١ - تسامح - غفران - مسامحة : عدم المؤاخذة

action of forgiving; I beg your pardon = please excuse me; pardon? = what did you say?
2. *verb*

٢ - يسامح - يصفح عن

to forgive.
pardons—pardoning—pardoned—has pardoned

parents ['peərənts] *plural noun*

أهل - الأبوين - الأب والأم

father and mother; my parents live in London; she went to live with her parents; did your parents tell you they had sold their house?
Note: parent is not often used in the singular

park [pɑːk] **1.** *noun*

١ - أ) حديقة عامة

(a) open public place with grass and trees; Hyde Park is in the middle of London; you can ride across the park on a horse, but cars are not allowed in.

ب) موقف سيارات

(b) car park = special place where you can leave a car while you are not using it; leave your car in the hotel car park; the car park's full.
2. *verb*

٢ - يوقف سيارته في مكان ما

to leave your car in a place while you are

parliament

not using it; **you can park your car at the back of the hotel; don't park on the grass; the bus ran into a parked car; no parking** = sign showing that you must not park your car.

parks — parking — parked — has parked

parliament ['pɑ:ləmənt] *noun*

البرلمان : مجلس النواب

group of people who are elected to govern the country; **he was elected to Parliament in 1970; Parliament will meet again next week; the Houses of Parliament** = big building in London where the British Parliament meets; **Member of Parliament** = person who has been elected to Parliament.

Note: **Parliament** *is usually used without* **the**

part [pɑ:t] *noun*

أ) جزء ـ قسم ـ عضو ـ قطعة (من جهاز)

(*a*) piece; **parts of the book are good; we live in the south part of London; part of the year he works in France; spare parts** = pieces used to put in place of broken parts of a car, etc.

ب) دور (في مسرحية أو معركة أو حدث ما)

(*b*) **to play a part** = to do something (in an action); **he played an important part in putting out the fire; to take part** = to be active; to join in; **he took part in the battle; did she take part in the fight?**

partly, *adverb*

جزئياً

not completely; **the house is partly finished; I'm only partly happy with the result.**

particular [pə'tɪkjʊlə] *adjective*

خصوصي ـ بالذات

special and different from all others; **I don't like that particular restaurant.**

بالأخص ـ خاصةً ـ خصوصاً

in particular = especially; **he's good at languages, in particular Italian and**

two hundred and nineteen

pass

Greek; **she likes Shakespeare's plays, 'Hamlet' in particular.**

particularly, *adverb*

خاصةً ـ خصوصاً

especially; **he is particularly fond of cakes.**

party ['pɑ:tɪ] *noun*

أ) حفلة

(*a*) meeting of several people on a special occasion; **we're having a party on Saturday night; can you come to our party next Saturday? she had fifteen people to her birthday party.**

ب) مجموعة

(*b*) group of people; **there were parties of tourists visiting all the churches.**

ت) حزب سياسي

(*c*) group of people who believe in a certain type of politics; **he joined a political party; which party does the Prime Minister belong to?**

plural **parties**

pass [pɑ:s] *verb*

أ) يجتاز ـ يمرّ ـ يَعْبُرُ

(*a*) to go past; **on the way to the bank you pass the church on your left; I passed him on the stairs; when you're passing the post office, can you put this letter in the letter box?**

ب) يعطي باليد إلى ، يناول (ناولني السكر من فضلك)

(*b*) to move something towards someone; **can you pass me the sugar? he passed the ball to the goalkeeper; they passed the dirty plates to the person at the end of the table.**

ت) يجتاز بنجاح ـ ينجح (في الامتحان)

(*c*) to be successful in an examination; **he passed in maths, but failed in English; she passed her driving test.**

ث) يصدر حكماً أو قانوناً

(*d*) to make a law; **Parliament has passed a law against drugs.**

passes — passing — passed — has passed

219

passage

pass out, *verb*

يُغمى عليه ـ يصاب باغماء

to faint; **when we told her her father was ill, she passed out.**

passage ['pæsɪdʒ] *noun*

مَمَرّ ـ طريق ضيّق

corridor/long narrow way between rooms; **I passed her in the passage; he rushed down the passage and into the street; go to the end of this passage and turn left.**

passenger ['pæsɪndʒə] *noun*

الراكب ـ المسافر

person who is travelling in a car/bus/plane, etc., but who is not the driver or member of the crew; **the car can take three passengers on the back seat; the plane is carrying 125 passengers and a crew of 6.**

passive ['pæsɪv] *noun*

مبني للمجهول ـ مشتق من الفعل المجهول

form of a verb which shows that something has happened to the subject, such as **he was bitten by a dog.**

passport ['pɑːspɔːt] *noun*

جواز سفر

official book which shows who you are and allows you to go from one country to another.

past [pɑːst] **1.** *preposition*

١ ـ أ) بعد (نصف الساعة بعد العاشرة) ـ في وقت منصرم

(*a*) after; **it's past ten o'clock; it was past dinner time; the train leaves at twenty past two; it's already half past three; it's five past nine—we've missed the news on TV.**

ب) مروراً بـ ـ إلى ما أبعد من

(*b*) from one side to the other in front of something; **go past the post office and turn left; he walked past me without** saying hello; **the car drove past at 50 miles an hour.**

2. *adjective*

٢ ـ ماضٍ ـ منصرم

(time) which has passed; **she has spent the past hour talking about her holidays.**

3. *noun*

٣ ـ أ) الماضي ـ الوقت الماضي

(*a*) time before the present; **in the past we always went to Scotland for our holidays.**

ب) صيغة الماضي

(*b*) (*also* **past tense**) form of a verb which shows something which happened before now; **'he went' is the past of the verb 'to go'.**

Note: **past** *is used for times between* **o'clock** *and* **half past**: *4.05 = five past four; 4.15 = a quarter past four; 4.25 = twenty five past four; 4.30 = half past four. For times after half past, see* **to**

past *is also used with many verbs:* **to go past; to drive past; to fly past,** *etc.*

paste [peɪst] **1.** *noun*

١ ـ أ) عجينة إلصاق

(*a*) thin glue for sticking paper; **put some paste on the back of the picture before you stick it in the book.**

ب) عجينة

(*b*) soft material, esp. food; **he spread fish paste on his bread; do you like meat paste sandwiches?** *see also* **toothpaste**

2. *verb*

٢ ـ يلصق

to glue; **he pasted the pictures into his book; they pasted the picture on to the wall.**

pastes—pasting—pasted—has pasted

pastry ['peɪstrɪ] *noun*

معجنات

mixture of flour, water and fat, used to make pies; this mixture when it is cooked; **she was rolling the pastry on the**

path

kitchen table; these pies are made of very hard pastry.
no plural: **some pastry;** *the plural* **pastries** *means cakes made out of pastry*

path [pɑːθ] *noun*

أ) سبيل ـ طريق ضيّق
(*a*) narrow way for walking; **the path goes across the field; follow the path until it comes to the river.**

ب) درب
(*b*) direction in which something moves; **the house stood in the path of the motorway** = where the motorway was going to be built.

patience ['peɪʃns] *noun*

أ) صبر
(*a*) being able to wait for a long time without getting annoyed; **if you want to catch a fish, you must have patience; he lost patience waiting for the bus** = began to get annoyed because he had to wait so long.

ب) ضربٌ من لعب الورق يلعبه شخص واحد عادةً
(*b*) type of card game for one person; **she was playing patience.**
no plural

patient 1. *adjective*

١ ـ صبور
(person) who can wait a long time without getting annoyed; **you have to be patient if you are at the end of a long queue.**
2. *noun*

٢ ـ المريض
person who is in hospital, or who is being looked after by a doctor; **the patients are all asleep in their beds; the doctor is taking the patient's temperature.**

patiently, *adverb*

بصبر
without getting annoyed; **they waited patiently for two hours.**

pay

pattern ['pætən] *noun*

أ) نموذج
(*a*) something which you copy to make something; **to knit this pullover, you have to follow the pattern.**

ب) رسم ـ طرز ـ نقش
(*b*) lines/flowers, etc., repeated again and again on cloth, etc.; **her dress has a pattern of white and red spots; I don't like the pattern on this carpet.**

pause [pɔːz] **1.** *noun*

١ ـ استراحة قصيرة . توقف مؤقت
short break; **there was a pause in the conversation.**
2. *verb*

٢ ـ يتوقف لمدة قصيرة ـ يتردّد
to stop doing something for a short time; **he paused for a moment and then went on speaking.**
pauses — pausing — paused — has paused

pavement ['peɪvmənt] *noun* (*American:* **sidewalk**)

رصيف
hard path at the side of a street; **the restaurant has put some tables out on the pavement; you can park your car on the pavement for a few minutes; it's dangerous to cycle on the pavement; the pavements are slippery after yesterday's snow.**

pay [peɪ] *verb*

أ) يدفع
(*a*) to give money for something; **I paid £100 for my watch; did he pay for the coffee? how much do you pay for petrol? I'll pay for both of us** = I will pay for the tickets, etc., for both.

ب) يستخدم مقابل مبلغ من المال
(*b*) to give money to someone for doing something; to give money to someone who sells you something; **please pay the waiter for your meal; I paid him 50p for washing the car; I'll pay you 50p to wash**

two hundred and twenty-one **221**

pea

the car; **they paid him £10 for his old bike.**

ت) يقوم بزيارة

(c) **to pay a visit** = to visit; **we'll pay my mother a visit when we are in town.**

pays—paying—paid [peid]—**has paid**

Note: you **pay him to wash the car** before he washes it, but you **pay him for washing the car** after he has washed it

pay back, *verb*

يردّ الدين

to give someone money which you owe them; **I paid for your meal—when will you pay me back?**

pay up, *verb*

يدفع بالكامل ـ يردّ الدين بالكامل

to pay all the money which you owe; **he paid up quickly when they started to take out their guns.**

pea [pi:] *noun*

بسلّة ـ بازيلاً (نوع من الخضار)

green vegetable with little round green seeds which you eat; **with the meat we'll have potatoes and peas; don't eat your peas with your knife!**

peace [pi:s] *noun*

أ) سلْم ـ حالة سلْم ـ سلام

(a) not being at war; **after the long war, there were thirty years of peace.**

ب) هدوء ـ طمأنينة ـ جوّ آمن

(b) being quiet; **I like the peace of the country better than the noise of the town.**

no plural

peaceful, *adjective*

هادىء ـ آمن

quiet; **the village is so peaceful.**

peanut [′pi:nʌt] *noun*

فول سوداني

type of small nut which you often eat with salt; **he bought a bag of peanuts to eat in the cinema; peanut butter** = paste made from crushed peanuts which you can spread on bread.

pence

pedal [′pedl] *noun*

دوّاسة ـ دعسة

thing which you push with your foot and which makes a piece of machinery work; **bicycle pedal; he took his feet off the pedals as he was riding down the hill; brake pedal** = pedal which works a brake.

pedestrian [pɪ′destrɪən] *noun*

المارّ ـ راجل ـ ماشٍ

person who goes about on foot; **you have to watch out for pedestrians when you're driving in a busy town; always cross the road at a pedestrian crossing** = place marked with white lines where you can walk across a street.

peel [pi:l] **1.** *noun*

١ ـ قشرة (الثمرة أو الخضار)

skin on a fruit or vegetable; **put the apple peel into the dustbin; you can boil potatoes with their peel on.**

no plural

2. *verb*

٢ ـ يَقْشِر ـ يُقَشِّر

to take the peel or skin off a fruit or vegetable; **he was peeling an orange; peel the potatoes before you cook them.**

peels—peeling—peeled—has peeled

pen [pen] *noun*

ريشة الكتابة ـ قلم حبر

thing for writing with which uses ink; **I've lost my pen—can I borrow yours? if you haven't got a pen you can write in pencil.**

pence [pens] *see* **penny**

ملاحظة : انظر إلى كلمة penny

222   *two hundred and twenty-two*

pencil

pencil ['pensl] *noun*

قلم رصاص - ريشة الرسام

thing for writing with, made of wood with a lead in the centre; **can I borrow your knife?—I want to sharpen my pencil; you must not write your examination answers in pencil.**

penknife ['pennaɪf] *noun*

سكين الجيب

small pocket knife which folds up; **he cut his name on the table with his penknife.**

plural **penknives** ['pennaɪvz]

penny ['penɪ] *noun*

بنس : جزء مئوي من الجنيه الاسترليني

small British coin, which is one hundredth of a pound; **this book only costs 60 pence; the meat came to £3.25, and you gave me £4, so I must give you seventy five pence change.**

Note: plural **pennies** *is used to refer to the coin, but* **pence** *refers to the price. In prices,* **pence** *is always written* **p** *and often said as* [piː]; **this book costs 60p** (*say* **sixty p** *or* **sixty pence**)

people ['piːpl] *plural noun*

الناس - عامة الشعب - شعب

men, women or children; **how many people are there in the room? there were thirty people waiting to see the doctor; so many people tried to see the film that they had to go on showing it for several months; several people in our office went to Spain on holiday; here's a photograph of the people we met on holiday.**

pepper ['pepə] *noun*

فلفل

a powder used in cooking, made from black or white seeds; **pepper makes me sneeze; don't put so much pepper in your soup.**

no plural

perfect

per [pɜː] *preposition*

ا) بـ - من : (عشرة بالألف أو من الألف)

(*a*) out of; **ten per thousand** = ten out of every thousand; **there are about six bad eggs per hundred.**

ب) في : لا تتجاوز السيارة سرعة ٦٠ كيلومتراً في الساعة

(*b*) in each/for each; **the car can't go faster than sixty miles per hour; we eat about 10 loaves of bread per week; tomatoes cost 10p per kilo; we paid her £3 per hour.**

per cent, *adverb & noun*

بالمئة (٥٠ بالمئة - ٧٥ بالمئة)

out of each hundred; **fifty per cent of the people 50%) voted in the election** = half of them; **seventy five per cent 75%) of the cars are less than two years old** = three quarters of them.

ملاحظة : تختصر هذه اللفظة في الكتابة بالاشارة/%.

Note: **per cent** *is written* **%** *when used with figures*

perfect ['pɜːfɪkt] *adjective*

١ - كامل - خال من الاغلاط - خال من العيوب - مثالي - خالص - صرف .

without any mistakes; exactly right; **he speaks perfect English; she drew a perfect circle; it's a perfect day for a picnic.**
2. *noun* (*also* **perfect tense**)

٢ - صيغة الفعل التام

form of a verb which shows something which happened before now; **'he has gone' is the perfect of 'to go'.**

perfectly, *adverb*

تماماً - على نحو كامل

without any mistakes; completely; **she can speak English perfectly; it was a perfectly beautiful holiday.**

perform [pə'fɔːm] *verb*

ا) يقوم بعمل فنّي كالرقص أو الغناء أو التمثيل

(*a*) to sing/dance/act in front of people who are watching; **the school performed Shakespeare's 'Hamlet'.**

two hundred and twenty-three   **223**

perhaps

ب) ينجز بطريقة ناجحة ـ يؤدي نتيجة مرضية

(b) to work well; to get good results; **our Rugby team performed very well; the car hasn't been performing very well.**
performs—performing—performed—has performed

performance, noun

تأدية ـ مسرحية ـ حفلة موسيقية ... الخ

showing of a film/a play; **did you enjoy the performance of 'Hamlet'?**

perhaps [pəˈhæps] adverb

ربما ـ لعلّ

possibly; it may be; **perhaps he'll come; they're late—perhaps the snow's very thick; do you think it's going to rain?—perhaps not, I can see some blue sky.**

period [ˈpɪərɪəd] noun

أ) مدّة

(a) length of time; **I can swim under the water for short periods; this happened at a period when food was scarce.**

ب) وقت محدد ـ فترة الدراسة

(b) time for a lesson in school; **we have three periods of maths a week; I had to miss the English period because I was seeing the headmaster.**

permission [pəˈmɪʃn] noun

الإجازة أو الترخيص بالشيء

allowing someone to do something; **you have my permission to use the telephone; he left the school without permission.**

permit [ˈpɜːmɪt] 1. noun

رخصة ـ إجازة

written paper which allows you to do something; **he has a permit to use the library; you must have a permit to park in the college car park; the shop has a permit to sell alcohol.**
2. verb [pəˈmɪt]

٢ ـ يسمح بـ

to allow someone to do something; **smoking is not permitted in the theatre;**

petrol

this ticket permits you to park at any time.
permits—permitting—permitted—has permitted

person [ˈpɜːsn] noun

شخص

man/woman; **this ticket admits three persons; she's a very interesting person; he was there in person** = he was there himself.

personal, adjective

شخصي ـ خصوصي

referring to a person/belonging to a person; **he lost all his personal property in the fire.**

persuade [pəˈsweɪd] verb

يُقْنِع

to speak to someone to get him to do what you want; **he persuaded me to sing a song; the policeman persuaded her not to shoot.**
persuades—persuading—persuaded—has persuaded

pet [pet] noun

حيوان داجن (مثل الهرّ أو الكلب ...)

animal which you keep in your home; **we keep a lot of pets—a cat, two dogs and a white mouse.**

petrol [ˈpetrəl] noun (American: gas)

نفط ـ بترول ـ بنزين

liquid used to drive a car engine, etc.; **my car doesn't use very much petrol; I ran out of petrol on the motorway; petrol prices seem to be going up all the time.**
no plural: some petrol; a gallon of petrol

petrol station, noun

محطة بنزين

place where you can buy petrol for your car; **stop at the next petrol station—we've got hardly any petrol left.**

224 *two hundred and twenty-four*

phone

phone [fəun] **1.** *noun*

هاتف ــ تلفون ــ جهاز هاتفي

telephone/machine which you use to speak to someone a long distance away; the phone's ringing; can you answer the phone for me—I'm in the bath; he lifted the phone and called the police.

أ) على الخط

on the phone = (*a*) speaking by telephone; don't make a noise—Daddy's on the phone; there's someone on the phone who wants to speak to you.

ب) مزوّد بالخط الهاتفي

(*b*) with a telephone in the house; are you on the phone? they're not on the phone = they haven't got a telephone. **2.** *verb*

٢ ــ يخاطب بالتلفون

to call someone by telephone; your sister phoned yesterday; phone the doctor—the baby's ill; can you phone me tomorrow morning? I want to phone New York.

phones—phoning—phoned—has phoned

phone back, *verb*

يردّ على المكالمة الهاتفية

to reply by telephone; Mr Smith is out—can you phone back in an hour? she phoned back very late at night.

phone book, *noun*

دليل الهاتف

book which gives the names of people and shops in a town in alphabetical order, with their addresses and phone numbers; this restaurant isn't in the phone book.

phone box, *noun*

كشك الهاتف

tall square box with windows, with a public telephone inside; you can call from the phone box at the corner of the street; I wanted to use the phone box, but I didn't have any 10p coins.

phone number, *noun*

pick

رقم الهاتف

number which refers to a particular phone; what's your phone number? if I tell you my phone number you'll keep on phoning me; my phone number's 405 9935.

photo [ˈfəutəu] *noun*

صورة فوتوغرافية

photograph/picture taken with a camera; here's a photo of our house; let me show you our holiday photos.

photograph [ˈfəutəgrɑːf] **1.** *noun*

١ ــ صورة فوتوغرافية ــ صورة ضوئية

picture taken with a camera; a black and white photograph of the church; she's taking a photograph of the dogs; he pinned her photograph on the wall; have you got a photograph of your children? **2.** *verb*

٢ ــ يلتقط صورة

to take a picture with a camera; he was photographing the birds on the lake.

photographs—photographing—photographed—has photographed

photographer [fəˈtɒgrəfə] *noun*

المصوّر الفوتوغرافي ــ المصوّر الضوئي

person who takes photographs.

phrase [freiz] *noun*

تعبير ــ عبارة

group of words, not usually containing a verb; 'the big green door' and 'along the road' are phrases.

piano [ˈpjænəu] *noun*

بيانو (آلة موسيقية)

musical instrument with black and white keys which you press to make music; he's learning to play the piano; she plays the piano all day long; she played the song on the piano.

pick [pɪk] **1.** *noun*

١ ــ إنتقاء ــ اختيار

what you choose; take your pick = choose which one you want.

two hundred and twenty-five 225

picnic

2. *verb*

٢ - أ) يختار - ينتقي

(a) to choose; **the captain picked his team; he was picked to play goalkeeper.**

ب) يقطف (الفاكهة ، الأزهار)

(b) to take fruit or flowers from plants; **we've picked all the apples; she was picking roses in the garden.**

ت) ينشل - ينتشل - ينزع بإصبعه أو بواسطة عود

(c) to take away small pieces of something with your fingers/with a tool; **he picked the bits of grass off his coat; she was picking her teeth with a pin** = taking away little bits of food which were stuck between her teeth.

ث) يسرق (من جيوب المارة)

(d) **to pick someone's pocket** = to steal something from someone's pocket; **my pocket's been picked!**

picks—picking—picked—has picked

pick on, *verb*

يضايق - يزعج

to choose someone in order to attack them; **why do you always pick on children who are smaller than you? stop picking on me all the time.**

pick out, *verb*

يختار - يميّز

to choose; **he picked out all the good apples in the box.**

pick up, *verb*

أ) يلتقط عن الأرض

(a) to lift something up which is lying on the ground; **she picked up the books which had fallen on the floor; he dropped his money and bent down to pick it up.**

ب) يتعلّم بسرعة - يلتقط بعض الكلام

(b) to learn something easily without being taught; **I was never taught to type—I just picked it up; she picked up some Chinese when she was living in China.**

226

picture

ت) يأخذ ركاب بسيارته

(c) to give someone a lift in a car; **I'll pick you up at your office; can you come to pick me up at 6 o'clock?**

ث) يتعرف على

(d) to meet and make friends with someone by chance; **he picked up a girl in a snack bar.**

ج) يقبض على

(e) to catch; **the police picked him up at the airport.**

ح) ينتعش - ينشط - يجدد قواه

(f) to get stronger/better; to increase; **he was ill for months, but he's picking up now; the car began to pick up speed; business is picking up.**

Note: **pick your money up** *or* **pick up your money** *but only* **pick it up**

picnic ['pɪknɪk] 1. *noun*

١ - نزهة يتناول فيها الطعام المجهز في البيت

trip with a meal eaten in the open air; **let's go on a picnic on Saturday; we went on a picnic last week and it rained; they stopped the car and had a picnic in the wood.**

2. *verb*

٢ - يقوم بنزهة ويجهز الأكل في الهواء الطلق

to eat a picnic; **we were picnicking by the side of the road.**

picnics—picnicking—picnicked—has picnicked

picture ['pɪktʃə] *noun*

أ) صورة - لوحة زيتية - صورة ضوئية

(a) drawing/painting/photograph, etc., of something; **he's painting a picture of the church; have you seen the picture she drew of the house? the book has several pictures of wild flowers; he cut out the picture of the Prime Minister from the newspaper; let me put you in the picture** = let me give you all the information about the problem.

two hundred and twenty-six

pie

(ب) السينما
(b) **pictures** = cinema; **we go to the pictures every Friday evening.**

pie [paɪ] *noun*

فطيرة

cooked food, usually made of pastry with meat or fruit inside; **we had apple pie and ice cream; let's buy a pork pie to eat on the picnic; cottage pie** = meat cooked in a dish with potatoes on top.

piece [piːs] *noun*

قطعة - جزء

(small) bit of something; **can I have another piece of cake? I want two pieces of paper; the watch came to pieces in my hand** = broke into several bits; **he dropped the plate and it smashed to pieces; to mend the clock, he had to take it to pieces** = to put it into pieces to see what was wrong with it.

ملاحظة: تستعمل أيضاً كلمة piece للتعبير عن القليل من الشيء أو فكرة مبهمة: (بعض النصائح)
Note: **piece** *is often used to show one bit of something which has no plural;* **furniture: a piece of furniture; wood: a piece of wood; toast: a piece of toast; news: a piece of news; advice: a piece of advice**

pig [pɪg] *noun*

خنزير

fat farm animal which gives meat; **the pigs were lying in the mud.**
Note: the meat from a **pig** *is called* **pork, bacon** *or* **ham**

pile [paɪl] **1.** *noun*

١ - ركام - كومة - تكديس

heap/lots of things put on top of each other; **there were piles of old books on the floor; throw those bricks on to the pile.**

piles of = a lot of; **we've got piles of work to do.**

pin

2. *verb* (*also* **to pile up**)

٢ - يركّم - يكوّم - يكدّس

to put things on top of each other; **he piled (up) the bricks by the side of the house; the books were piled (up) on the table; she was piling boxes on top of each other.**
piles—piling—piled—has piled

pillar box [ˈpɪləbɒks] *noun*

صندوق بريد عمودي

round red box in the street which you put letters into so that they can be sent by post; **can you post this letter in the pillar box at the end of the road?**
plural **pillar boxes**

pillow [ˈpɪləʊ] *noun*

وسادة - مخدّة

soft cushion on a bed which you put your head on when you lie down.

pilot [ˈpaɪlət] *noun*

أ) ربّان الطائرة
(a) person who flies a plane; **don't talk to the pilot when the plane is landing.**
ب) قبطان السفينة
(b) person who guides boats into or out of a harbour.

pin [pɪn] **1.** *noun*

١ - دبّوس - مسمار صغير

small sharp piece of metal for attaching papers, etc., together; **he kept his trousers up with a pin; fasten the papers together with a pin; drawing pin** = pin with a large flat head, used for pinning papers; **he pinned the notice up with a drawing pin.**

2. *verb*

يُدبّس - يثبت بالدبابيس

to attach with a pin; **the papers were pinned together; the notices are pinned to the wall of the office.**
pins—pinning—pinned—has pinned

pin up, *verb*

two hundred and twenty-seven 227

pinch

يُعلّق بالدبابيس

to attach something to a wall with a pin; the notice is pinned up outside the entrance; he was pinning the sign up on a tree.

Note: **pin the notice up** *or* **pin up the notice** *but only* **pin it up**

pinch [pɪntʃ] **1.** *noun*

١ ـ قرصة ـ قبصة

squeezing your thumb and first finger together; amount of something which you hold between your thumb and first finger; **he gave me a pinch; put a pinch of salt into the water; you can take what he says with a pinch of salt** = you should not believe everything he says.
plural **pinches**

2. *verb*

٢ ـ ١) يقرص

(a) to squeeze something tightly between your thumb and first finger; **she pinched my arm.**

ب) يسرق

(b) to steal; **they pinched some sweets from the shop; someone has pinched my bike.**

pinches—pinching—pinched—has pinched

pink [pɪŋk] *noun & adjective*

زهر (اللون الزهر)

of a colour like very pale red; **these pink roses smell nice; her hat was a dark pink.**

pint [paɪnt] *noun*

مقياس للسوائل يعادل ٠,٥٦ من اللتر

measure of liquids (= about .56 of a litre); **ask the milkman to leave two pints of milk; a pint of beer, please; he drank half a pint of coffee.**

pipe [paɪp] *noun*

أ) أنبوب

(a) long round hollow tube for water, gas, etc.; **the water pipes are under the street; he made a hole in the gas pipe and the gas started to come out.**

ب) غليون للتدخين

(b) thing with a small bowl and a tube which you put in your mouth, used for smoking tobacco; **he was smoking a pipe; can I have another match—my pipe has gone out; it's difficult to light a pipe when it is windy.**

pity ['pɪtɪ] **1.** *noun*

١ ـ أ) شفقة ـ رحمة

(a) a feeling for someone who has had bad luck/who is not well/who has done badly, etc.; **I felt pity for the runner who came last in the race.**

ب) داع للأسف : انه أمر يدعو للأسف ان المطر تسّاقط لما ذهبنا بنزهة

(b) (*showing that you are sorry*) **it's a pity that . . .** = it is sad that . . .; **it's a pity that it rained when we went on the picnic; what a pity that she was ill and couldn't run in the race.**

no plural

2. *verb*

٢ ـ يشفق على ـ يشعر بالشفقة على

to feel sorry for someone who has had bad luck/who is not well/who has done badly, etc.; **I pity you having to stay in and look after the baby when we all go to the cinema.**

pities—pitying—pitied—has pitied

place [pleɪs] **1.** *noun*

أ) مكان

(a) spot; where something is; where something happens or happened; **this is the place where we had the accident; put the books back in the right place; there were papers lying all over the place** = everywhere.

ب) بيت ـ مسكن ـ مأوى

(b) home; **why don't we all go back to my place for a cup of coffee?**

plain

(c) seat; ت) مكان مخصص لشخص ما ـ مقعد
this is Mr Smith's place; is this anybody's place? yes, I'm afraid this place is taken; I changed places with Jane = we each took the other's seat.

ث) مرتبة (في سباق أو مباراة)
(d) position (in a race); the German runners were in the first three places = they were first, second and third in the race; he's in first place = he is winning.

ج) الصفحة حيث توقف القارىء عن القراءة
(e) page where you have stopped reading a book; I put a piece of paper to mark my place; I've lost my place and can't remember where I've got to.

يحدث ـ يحصل : ان الاقتتال حدث في المطعم
to take place = to happen; the argument took place in the restaurant; the action of the film takes place in Russia.
2. verb

٢ ـ يضع
to put; he placed his hat carefully on the table; can you place the books in the right order?

places—placing—placed—has placed

plain [pleɪn] 1. adjective

١ ـ أ) واضح ـ سهل الفهم ـ مفهوم
(a) easy to see/easy to understand; it's plain that he didn't hear the motorcycle; I want to make it plain that we will not pay you any more money.

ب) بسيط ـ عادي
(b) simple/ordinary; I like plain country cooking best; plain chocolate = dark brown bitter chocolate.

plain—plainer—plainest

2. noun

٢ ـ سهل ـ أرض منبسطة
large flat area of land; the wind whistled across the plain.

plainly, adverb

plant

بوضوح ـ بصراحة
clearly; he was plainly worried by his exams.

plan [plæn] 1. noun

١ ـ أ) خطّة
(a) way of doing things which you arrange in advance; we've prepared a plan for saving money each week; the burglars made a plan to get into the house by the kitchen window.

ب) خريطة ـ تصميم
(b) drawing of the way something is built/is arranged; here are the plans for the new school; this is the plan of the office; I can't find our street on the town plan = on the map of the town.
2. verb

٢ ـ يخطط ـ يصمم
to arrange how you are going to build something/to do something; to intend to do something; she planned her kitchen herself; they've planned a whole new town; we are planning to go on holiday in August; I wasn't planning to stay up late = I thought I would go to bed early.

plans—planning—planned—has planned

plane [pleɪn] noun

أ) طائرة
(a) aircraft/machine which flies; when does this plane leave for Copenhagen? the plane to Glasgow is full—you will have to wait for the next one; there are six planes a day to New York.

ب) المسحاج ـ فارة النجار
(b) tool for making wood smooth.

plant [plɑːnt] 1. noun

١ ـ نبتة ـ نبات ـ شتلة ـ غرسة
living thing which grows in the ground and has leaves and flowers; a tomato plant; these plants are growing very tall; house plants/pot plants = plants which you grow in pots in the house; plant pot = special pot for growing plants in.
2. verb

two hundred and twenty-nine 229

plaster

٢ - يغرس - يزرع
to put a plant in the ground; **I've planted an apple tree in the garden.**
plants—planting—planted—has planted

plaster ['plɑ:stə] *noun*
أ) جص . مسحوق أبيض يستعمل لتلميس الجدران
(a) white powder which is mixed with water and used to make inside walls/to cover broken legs, etc.; **the ceiling is made of plaster; after his accident he had his leg in plaster for two months.**
ب) اللصوق : شريط لاصق لكساء الجرح
(b) **sticking plaster** = sticky tape used to cover a small wound; **put a piece of sticking plaster on your cut.**
no plural: **some plaster; some sticking plaster; a piece of sticking plaster**

plastic ['plæstɪk] *adjective & noun*
بلاستيك (مادة مستخرجة من النفط ومستعملة في تصنيع الكثير من الأشياء)
hard material made from oil, and used to make many objects; **take the plastic plates on the picnic; I want a plastic bag to put my sandwiches in; don't put that plate in the oven—it's made of plastic; these seats in the car are made of plastic and get very hot in the summer.**
no plural: **it's made of plastic**

plate [pleɪt] *noun*
أ) صحن - طبق
(a) flat round thing for putting your food on; **put the sausages on a plate; pass your dirty plates to the person at the end of the table.**
ب) ملء الصحن
(b) food which is on a plate; **she held out a plate of cakes; he ate two plates of meat.**
ت) شريحة معدنية أو زجاجية
(c) flat sheet of metal/glass, etc.; **a plate glass window** = a very large window,

play

such as in a shop; **number plate** = plate on the front and back of a car which shows its number.

platform ['plætfɔ:m] *noun*
أ) رصيف في محطة للسكة الحديدية
(a) high pavement by the side of the railway lines at a station, so that passengers can get on or off the trains easily; **there were crowds waiting on the platform; the train to Edinburgh will leave from platform 6; the Birmingham train is leaving from the next platform; I was in such a hurry that I left my suitcase on the platform.**
ب) مِنْبَر
(b) high place in a hall for speakers to stand on; **the speaker went up on to the platform; someone in the crowd threw a tomato at the speaker on the platform.**

play [pleɪ] **1.** *noun*
١ - أ) مسرحية
(a) something written, which is acted in a theatre/on TV; **did you watch the play last night? we're going to see a new play at the National Theatre; we have to read two of Shakespeare's plays for our English exam.**
ب) لَعِب - لهو
(b) way of amusing yourself; taking part in a game; **play will start at 3 o'clock** = the game/match will start; **the ball went out of play** = went off the field; **it's child's play** = it is very easy.
2. *verb*
٢ - أ) يلعب - يلهو
(a) to amuse yourself; **he was playing with his sister; the children were playing in the garden; let's play at doctors and nurses** = let's pretend to be doctors and nurses.
ب) يشترك في لعبة أو مباراة
(b) to take part in a game; **he plays football for the school team; can you play cricket? I don't play tennis in the winter.**

pleasant

ت) يعزف (لحن أو قطعة موسيقية)
(c) to make music on a musical instrument or to put on a record; don't talk while he's playing the violin; I can't play the piano very well; let me play you my new record.

ث) يلعب (دوراً) في مسرحية
(d) to act as a person in a film/play; he played Harry Lime in 'The Third Man'.

plays—playing—played—has played

player, noun

اللاعب

person who plays; you need eleven players for a football team; tennis players have to be fit; three of our players are ill.

playground, noun

ملعب (خاصةً ملعب للأطفال)

place (usually round a school) where children can play; if it's raining you can't go into the playground during break; they were playing quietly in the playground.

playing cards, noun

لعب الورق - (الكوتشينة)

set of pieces of stiff paper with pictures or patterns on them, used for playing various games; see also **card**.

playing field, noun

ملعب رياضي

large field where sports can be played; two football matches are being played on our playing field.

pleasant ['pleznt] adjective

سار - مُرْضٍ

which makes you happy/which you like; what a pleasant picnic; the weather is very pleasant.

pleasant—pleasanter—pleasantest

pleasantly, adverb

بطريقة مُسرّة ، لطيفة

in a pleasant way; he answered me pleasantly.

plug

please [pli:z] interjection

يسرّ - يرضي - يحبّ

used to make an order polite; shut the door, please; please come in; can I have another cup of coffee, please? do you want some more cake?—yes, please; who wants some more coffee?—me, please!

pleased, adjective

مسرور

happy; I'm pleased with my new car; she isn't pleased with her exam results; he wasn't pleased when we broke his bedroom window; I'd be very pleased to help you if I can; was she pleased to get your letter?

pleasure ['pleʒə] noun

مشيئة - رغبة - سرور

pleasant feeling; sitting in the garden is my greatest pleasure; I'll do the job with pleasure = I will be very glad to do it; it gives me great pleasure to be here today.

plenty ['plentı] noun

وافر - كثير - كثيراً - جداً - بوفرة

large amount/lots; you've got plenty of time; we've plenty of food left after the party; plenty of people were waiting for the bus; have you enough milk?—yes, we've got plenty.

no plural

plough [plau] 1. noun

١ - محراث

farm machine for turning over the soil.
2. verb

٢ - يحرث الأرض

to turn over the soil with a plough; the farmer was ploughing the field.

ploughs—ploughing—ploughed—has ploughed

plug [plʌg] 1. noun

١ - أ) مأخذ كهربائي - قابس
(a) electric object on the end of a wire, with pins which go into holes to allow the electricity to go into a machine; the

plural

refrigerator has stopped working—I think that a wire has broken in the plug.

ب ـ سدادة ـ سطام

(b) rubber object used to stop water running out of a bath, etc.

2. *verb* (*usually* **to plug in**)

٢ ـ يوصل بالقابس الكهربائي

to attach an electric machine to the mains with a plug; **have you plugged the radio in? the light won't work—it isn't plugged in!**

plugs—plugging—plugged—has plugged

plural [ˈpluərəl] *adjective & noun*

جمع ـ صيغة الجمع

form of a word showing there is more than one; **'children' is the plural of 'child'; 'is' is the third person singular of the verb 'to be' and 'are' is the plural; 'they' is a plural pronoun.**

p.m. [ˈpiːˈem] *adverb*

بعد الظهر

after 12 o'clock midday; **I have to meet someone at 2 p.m.; she's catching the 7 p.m. train to Edinburgh.**

Note: **p.m.** *is used to show the exact hour and the word* **o'clock** *is left out*

pocket [ˈpɒkɪt] *noun*

جيب

small bag attached to the inside of a coat, etc., which you can keep your handkerchief/your keys, etc., in; **I've looked in my coat pockets but I can't find my keys; there's a hole in my pocket, and all my money fell out; he was walking along with his hands in his pockets; put your hands in your pockets if you want to keep them warm.**

آلة حاسبة صغيرة (للجيب)

pocket calculator = small calculator which you can put in your pocket.

قاموس صغير (للجيب)

pocket dictionary = small dictionary which you can put in your pocket.

232

point

مقدار قليل من المال مخصص للنفقات الصغيرة

pocket money = money given by parents to children each week to spend; **how much pocket money do you get? I can't buy any more sweets, I spent all my pocket money on a new penknife.**

poem [ˈpəʊɪm] *noun*

قصيدة

piece of writing, especially with lines of the same length which rhyme; **do you like this poem about the autumn? he spends all his time writing poems.**

poet, *noun*

شاعر

person who writes poems; **Byron and Keats are famous English poets.**

poetry, *noun*

شِعْر ـ كتابة شعرية

type of writing done by a poet; **we have to study English poetry of the nineteenth century; he was reading a poetry book.**

no plural

point [pɔɪnt] **1.** *noun*

١ ـ أ) سن ـ رأس ـ طرف

(a) sharp end; **he's broken the point of his pencil; this needle hasn't got a very sharp point.**

ب) نقطة (تستعمل للدلالة على انتهاء الجملة)

(b) dot used to show the division between whole numbers and parts of numbers; **3.256** *say* **'three point two five six'.**

ت) مرحلة ـ موقع

(c) particular time/place; **we walked for miles and came back to the point where we'd started from; the lights went off at that point** = at that moment; **I was on the point of phoning you** = I was just going to phone you.

ث) غرض ـ غاية ـ قصد

(d) meaning/reason; **there's no point in trying to phone him—he's gone away; the point of the meeting is to discuss how**

two hundred and thirty-two

poison

we can save money; **I see your point** = I see what you mean.

ج) رقم (الرقم الذي يحصل عليه أحد اللاعبين في لعبة أو مباراة)

(e) score in a game; **he scored three points; that shot gives you ten points.**

ح) درجة

(f) mark in a series of numbers; **what's the freezing point of water?**

2. *verb*

٢ ـ يشير بإصبعه إلى ـ يوجه (مسدسه) نحو

to aim (a gun/your finger) at; to show with your finger; **the policeman is pointing at you; he pointed his gun at the door; don't point at people—it's rude.**
points—pointing—pointed—has pointed

pointed, *adjective*

حادّ ـ مروس

with a sharp point; **a pointed stick.**

point out, *verb*

يشير إلى ـ يلفت نظر المرء إلى

to show; **he pointed out all the mistakes in my homework.**
Note: **he pointed the mistakes out** *or* **he pointed out the mistakes** *but only* **he pointed them out**

poison ['pɔɪzn] *noun*

سُمّ

something which can kill you if you eat or drink it; **I think someone has put poison in my soup; try putting some poison on the floor if you want to kill the mice.**

poisonous, *adjective*

سام ـ خطر ـ مؤذٍ

full of poison; **don't eat those seeds—they're poisonous; I wish I knew which leaves are good to eat and which are poisonous.**

pole [pəʊl] *noun*

١) عمود ـ سارية

(a) long wooden or metal stick; **the flag is attached to a tall pole; the tent is held up by two poles; the car ran into a telephone pole.**

ب) قطب (أحد قطبي الأرض الشمالي والجنوبي)

(b) one of the two points at the ends of the earth; **who was the first man to get to the North Pole?**

polar, *adjective*

قطبي

referring to the North or South Pole; **a polar bear.**

police [pə'liːs] *noun* (*usually plural*)

الشرطة

group of people (in uniform) who control traffic, who try to stop crimes and who try to catch criminals; **the police are looking for three armed men; if someone steals your car, you must tell the police; the phone number of the police is 999; call the police—someone's taken all my money! he was knocked down by a police car.**

policeman, policewoman, *noun*

شرطي ـ شرطية

member of the police; **three policemen were hiding behind the wall; if you don't know how to find the post office—ask a policeman.**
plural **policemen, policewomen**

police station, *noun*

مخفر الشرطة

building in a town with the offices of the police in it; **they arrested two men and took them to the police station.**

polish ['pɒlɪʃ] **1.** *noun*

١ ـ أ) مادة صاقلة أو ملمعة

(a) something used to make things shiny; **put some polish on the table; we haven't any black shoe polish left.**

ب) صقل ـ تلميع

(b) making something shiny; **give the car a good polish; I'll give the table a polish.**

2. *verb*

٢ ـ يلمّع ـ يجلو ـ يصقل

to rub something until it is shiny; **you**

two hundred and thirty-three 233

polite

should polish your shoes before you go to the party; has he polished the car?
polishes—polishing—polished—has polished

polite [pə'laɪt] *adjective*

مهذّب ـ مؤدّب

not rude; behaving in a pleasant way; with good manners; **you should always be polite to your teacher; it wasn't very polite to go away without saying thank you; it is polite to say 'please' when you are asking for something; he's a very polite little boy.**

politely, *adverb*

بتهذيب ـ بأدب

in a polite way; **if you ask her politely she will give you some cake.**

political [pə'lɪtɪkl] *adjective*

سياسي ـ (يقال عن حزب أو تجمع)

referring to a certain way of running a country; **political party** = group of people who believe the country should be run in one particular way.

politician [pɒlɪ'tɪʃn] *noun*

سياسي (رجل يتعاطى السياسة)

person who is an active member of a political party, especially a Member of Parliament.

politics, *noun*

السياسة ـ علم السياسة

study of how a country should be governed; **he is going into politics** = he is going to be an active member of a political party.

pool [puːl] *noun*

أ) بركة

(a) small amount of liquid not contained in anything; **there was a pool of blood on the floor.**

ب) مسبح

(b) **(swimming) pool** = special tank of water for swimming in; **the competition will be held in the open air pool; our school has an indoor pool; come out—**

pork

you've been in the pool long enough; we have a heated swimming pool in our garden.

poor [pɔː] *adjective*

أ) فقير

(a) (person) who has little or no money; **they are very poor, now that their father has no work; poor people can get extra money from the government; it is one of the poorest countries in the world.**

ب) رديء ـ غير خصب ـ قليل البراعة

(b) not very good; **this soil's poor—it's not good for growing fruit trees; their football team is very poor this year—they haven't won a single match; these bananas are very poor quality; he's in poor health.**

ث) مسكين ـ مثير للشفقة

(c) (*showing you are sorry*) **poor John—he's got to stay in bed while we're going for a picnic; my poor feet—I've been walking all day!**
poor—poorer—poorest

popular ['pɒpjʊlə] *adjective*

رائج ـ شائع بين عامة الناس ـ متمتع بشعبية كبيرة ـ محبوب من الجماهير

which is liked by a lot of people; **Spain is a popular place for summer holidays; this film has been very popular; cold milk is a popular drink with children; the maths teacher isn't very popular with our class—he gives us too much homework.**

population [pɒpjʊ'leɪʃn] *noun*

السكان ـ عدد السكان

number of people who live in one place; **the population is increasing by 2% each year; what is the population of Denmark?**

pork [pɔːk] *noun*

لحم خنزير

meat from a pig; **we're having roast pork for lunch; would you like some**

two hundred and thirty-four

porridge

more pork? can I have another slice of pork, please? pork sausages = sausages made from pork.
no plural: some pork; a piece of pork/a slice of pork

porridge ['pɒrɪdʒ] *noun*
عصيدة : نوع من القمح المغلي
hot food which you eat at breakfast, made of a sort of cereal cooked in water; you eat porridge with milk and sugar; do you want any more porridge?
no plural: some porridge; a bowl of porridge

port [pɔːt] *noun*
مرفأ ـ ميناء
town which has a harbour; **Dover is an important port for ferries to France; Grimsby is a big fishing port.**

porter ['pɔːtə] *noun*
البواب ـ الحمال ـ العتال
person who carries luggage for you at a railway station or airport.

position [pə'zɪʃn] *noun*
موضع ملائم ـ وضع ـ ترتيب ـ حالة ـ مركز اجتماعي ـ موقف من قضية ـ حالة ـ مرتبة ـ الوضع الصحيح
place (where something is); the way something is held/the way something stands/lies, etc.; **it was a difficult job putting the piano into position; she found herself in a very difficult position; he was in third position in the race; you need to have the brush in the right position to paint properly.**

possess [pə'zes] *verb*
يملك
to own; **he possessed two large houses; how many cars does she possess?**
possesses—possessing—possessed—has possessed

post

possession, *noun*
إمتلاك ـ مُلك ـ ممتلكات
thing which you own; **he lost all his possessions in the fire.**

possible ['pɒsɪbl] *adjective*
مؤهل بأن يكون ـ ممكن ـ جائز حدوثه ـ محتمل
which can happen/which is likely to happen; **that field is a possible place for a house; it's possible that the train will be late because of the fog.**

بقدر المستطاع ـ بقدر الامكان
as possible (*used to make a superlative*) **go as far away as possible; I would like it done as quickly as possible; give me as much time as possible; this is the cheapest possible way of going to France.**

possibility [pɒsɪ'bɪlɪti] *noun*
امكانية
chance/being likely to happen; **is there any possibility that the plane will be late?**

possibly, *adverb*
ا) من الممكن ان ـ ربما
(*a*) perhaps; **the train will possibly be late; it is possibly the worst weather we have ever had.**

ب) بأية حال ـ مهما حدث
(*b*) (*used to make a word stronger*) **you can't possibly eat all those sausages!**

post [pəʊst] **1.** *noun*
١ ـ ا) عمود خشبي
(*a*) large wooden pole put in the ground; **the gate is attached to a gate post; he kicked the ball but it bounced off the post.**

ب) وظيفة ـ عمل
(*b*) job; **she has applied for a post in the library.**

ت) البريد
(*c*) letters, etc., sent by mail; **has the post come yet? there was nothing for you in the post this morning; send the parcel**

235

pot

by post; can you put this letter in the post for me?
2. *verb*

٢ ـ يرسل بالبريد

to send a letter, etc., by mail; he went to post his Christmas cards; the letter was posted ten days ago; if you're going to the post office, can you post this parcel for me?

posts—posting—posted—has posted

postage, *noun*

أجرة بريدية

money which you pay to send something by post; what is the postage for a letter to Australia?

no plural

postcard, *noun*

بطاقة بريدية

piece of card (often with a picture on one side), which you send to someone with a message on it; send me a postcard when you get to Italy; she sent me a postcard of the hotel where she was staying.

postman, *noun*

ساعي البريد

person who delivers letters to houses; has the postman been yet? give this letter back to the postman—it's not for us.

plural postmen

post office, *noun*

مكتب البريد

building where you can buy stamps/ send letters and parcels/where letters and parcels are collected, etc.; can you take this parcel to the post office for me? the post office is shut on Saturday afternoons.

pot [pɒt] *noun*

قِدْر (معدنية أو فخارية)

container made of china/glass, etc.; plant the flowers in a bigger pot; we made ten pots of jam.

236

pour

potato [pəˈteɪtəʊ] *noun*

بطاطس ـ بطاطا

common vegetable which grows under the ground; boiled potatoes; do you want any more potatoes? potatoes in their jackets = potatoes cooked with their skins on.

plural potatoes

pound [paʊnd] *noun*

أ) الباوند : (رطل انكليزي)

(a) measure of weight (about 450 grams); I want a pound of onions and three pounds of potatoes; the baby only weighed four pounds when he was born; how much is sugar?—it's 20p a pound. *Note: with numbers* pound *is usually written* lb; it weighs 26lb; take 6lb of sugar.

ب) عملة مستعملة في بريطانيا وبعض الدول الأخرى : جنيه استرليني

(b) money used in Britain and several other countries; the meal cost several pounds; he gets more than a pound in pocket money; the price is over fifty pounds (£50); he gave me a five pound note.

Note: with numbers pound *is usually written* £: £20; £6,000, *etc.*
Note: with the word note, pound *is singular;* five pounds *but* a five pound note

pour [pɔː] *verb*

أ) يصب ـ يسكب

(a) to make liquid go from a container; she poured the tea into my cup; pour the dirty water down the sink; he poured out two glasses of water; can you pour me another cup of tea?

ب) ينصب بغزارة ـ ينهمر ـ يتدفق

(b) (*of liquid, etc.*) to come out fast/to come on to something fast; smoke poured out of the window; people poured on to the platform; oil was pouring out of the hole in the pipe; it was pouring with rain = it was raining hard.

pours—pouring—poured—has poured

two hundred and thirty-six

powder / prefer

pour down, *verb*

يتساقط المطر بغزارة

to rain hard; **we couldn't go for a walk because it was pouring; the rain poured down for days.**

powder ['paʊdə] *noun*

مسحوق ‐ مسحوق التجميل ‐ مسحوق الوجه

fine dry dust, made from crushing something hard; **face powder** = powder which has a pleasant smell, and which you put on your face.

power ['paʊə] *noun*

أ) قوة ‐ طاقة

(a) force which drives something; **the engine runs on electric power; the wheel is turned by water power; power cut** = break in the supply of electricity.

ب) سلطة ‐ نفوذ

(b) control; **the party has a lot of power in the town council; the general came to power in 1962** = became the president.

powerful, *adjective*

قوي ‐ جبّار ‐ فعّال

very strong; **the motor isn't powerful enough to drive the car up hills.**

practical ['præktɪkl] *adjective*

عمليّ

which works in practice; **she gave me some practical advice; he's a practical man** = he's good at mending or building things in the house.

practically, *adverb*

تقريباً ‐ بالفعل

almost; **I've practically finished my homework.**

practice ['præktɪs] *noun*

أ) تطبيق

(a) actual working; **it's a good idea, but will it work in practice?**

ب) ممارسة ‐ مزاولة

(b) exercises; **he does his piano practice every day; with practice, you should be able to play tennis quite well.**

practise ['præktɪs] *verb*

يمارس ‐ يزاول ‐ يُطبّق عمليا

to do exercises; to do something over and over again to become good at it; **he practises the piano every day; she's practising her Spanish songs; if you don't practise you'll never play tennis well.**

practises—practising—practised—has practised

praise [preɪz] **1.** *noun*

١ ‐ مدحة ‐ تسبيح ‐ تمجيد

words which show that you admire someone/something; **he wrote a poem in praise of the new church; she was full of praise for your work.**

2. *verb*

٢ ‐ يُطري ‐ يثني علي ‐ يمجّد ‐ يسبّح

to show that you admire/approve of someone or something; **he praised the policeman who had saved the little boy from drowning; the judges praised the winners in the competition.**

praises—praising—praised—has praised

pray [preɪ] *verb*

يصلّي

to speak to God/to ask God for something; to hope very much that something will happen; **they are praying for fine weather; we prayed for his sister** = we asked God to save her.

prays—praying—prayed—has prayed

prayer [preə] *noun*

صلاة

words spoken to God; **he said his prayers before he went to bed.**

prefer [prɪ'fɜː] *verb*

يُفَضِّل

to like something/to like to do something better than something else; **I don't**

two hundred and thirty-seven 237

prefix

want to sit in the garden—I prefer watching TV inside; which do you prefer—chocolate or orange ice cream? I prefer English cars to foreign ones; we prefer to go on holiday in June because the weather is better; I don't want to go to the cinema—I'd prefer to stay at home.
prefers—preferring—preferred—has preferred

prefix ['pri:fɪks] *noun*
البادئة : أداة توضع في بدء الكلمة لتغير معناها أو لتكوين كلمة جديدة
word which goes in front of another word and is joined to it; **in the word 'impossible', 'im-' is a prefix which means 'not'.**

prepare [prɪ'peə] *verb*
يُهَيِّء - يتهيأ - يجهّز - يستعد - يعدّ
to get ready; to get something ready; **they are preparing to go on holiday next week; she was preparing the dinner when the milkman called.**
prepares—preparing—prepared—has prepared

prepared, *adjective*
مُجَهَّز - مُسْتَعَد - مُحَضَّر
ready; **are you prepared to leave immediately? they weren't prepared for the letter from the bank manager** = they were surprised to get it.

preposition [prepə'zɪʃn] *noun*
حرف جر
word which is used with a noun or pronoun to show how it is connected to another word; **prepositions are words such as 'near', 'next to', 'through', in the sentences 'his house is near the Post Office', 'she sat down next to me', 'he drove through the town'.**

present ['preznt] **1.** *noun*
١ - أ) هدية
(*a*) thing which you give to someone; **he gave me a watch as a present; do you give

press

your children big presents at Christmas? how many birthday presents did you get? all the Christmas presents are piled under the tree.**
ب) الزمن الحاضر
(*b*) the time we are in now; **at present** = now.
ت) فعل المضارع (الدال على الحاضر)
(*c*) form of a verb which shows the time we are in now; **the present of 'to give' is 'he gives' or 'he is giving'.**
2. *adjective* ['preznt]
٢ - أ) حاضر : (ما هو عنوانه الحاضر)
(*a*) being at the time we are in now; **what is your present address? the present situation; present tense** = form of a verb which shows the time we are in now; **the present tense of 'to sit' is 'he sits' or 'he is sitting'.**
ب) موجود - حاضر : هل كنت حاضراً عندما مات العجوز
(*b*) being there when something happened; **were you present when the old man died?**
3. *verb* [prɪ'zent]
٣ - أ) يهب - يمنح - يهدي
(*a*) to give; **when he retired, the firm presented him with a watch.**
ب) يقدّم (برنامج)
(*b*) to introduce a show (on TV, etc.); **he's presenting a programme on wild animals.**
presents—presenting—presented—has presented

president ['prezɪdnt] *noun*
رئيس (جمهورية أو نادي ..)
head of a republic/a club, etc.; **the President of the USA; we've elected him president for the next year.**
Note: can be used with names: **President Kennedy,** *etc.*

press [pres] **1.** *noun*
١ - الصحافة
newspapers and magazines; **the British press reported a plane crash in Africa;**

pretend

the press has not mentioned the problem; I read about it in the press.
no plural
2. *verb*

٢ - أ) يعصر - يضغط

(*a*) to push/to squeeze; **press the button if you want a cup of coffee; they all pressed round him.**

ب) يكوي

(*b*) to iron; **your trousers need pressing.**
presses—pressing—pressed—has pressed

pressure ['preʃə] *noun*

ضغط

action of squeezing/of forcing; force of something which is pushing down, etc.; **there is not enough air pressure in your tyres; to put pressure on someone to do something** = to try to force someone to do something; **he did it under pressure** = because he was forced to do it; **blood pressure** = force of the blood as it is being pumped round the body.

pretend [prɪ'tend] *verb*

يزعم - يدّعي - يتظاهر بـ

to imitate something (especially to try to trick someone); to act as if something is true when you know it isn't; **he got into the house by pretending to be a policeman; she pretended she was Australian; the children were pretending to be doctors and nurses; he hasn't got a headache—he's pretending to have one so that he can go home.**
pretends—pretending—pretended—has pretended

pretty ['prɪtɪ] *adjective*

جميل - ظريف - وسيم

pleasant to look at; **he has two pretty daughters; she is prettier than her sister; what a pretty little village!**
pretty—prettier—prettiest
Note: used of things or girls, but never of men

primary

prevent [prɪ'vent] *verb*

يحول دون - يمنع - يعوق

to stop something happening; **the fog prevented the planes (from) taking off; something must have prevented her (from) coming; we must try to prevent anyone (from) knowing about this; cars have red lights to try to prevent accidents.**
prevents—preventing—prevented—has prevented

price [praɪs] 1. *noun*

١ - سعر - ثمن - قيمة

amount of money which you have to pay to buy something; **the price of meat is going up; we can't pay such a high price; don't go to that greengrocer's—his prices are too high; that TV is very cheap—at that price you could buy two.**
2. *verb*

يُسَعِّر

to give something a price; **the table is priced at £25; it won't sell—it is too highly priced.**
prices—pricing—priced—has priced

pride [praɪd] *noun*

مفخرة - كبرياء - غرور

pleasure which you take in what you do or have done/in something which belongs to you; **he takes pride in always being on time; she takes a lot of pride in her garden.**

primary ['praɪmərɪ] *adjective*

أ) أساسي - رئيسي

(*a*) basic; most important; **the primary colours** = simple colours like red, blue and yellow which can be mixed to make all the other colours.

ب) ابتدائي - بدائي

(*b*) referring to the first years of school; **primary education** = education for small children; **primary school** = school for small children (up to the age of eleven).

two hundred and thirty-nine 239

Prime Minister

Prime Minister [praɪm'mɪnɪstə] *noun*

رئيس الحكومة

head of a government (in Britain and many other countries); **the French Prime Minister; the Prime Minister of Australia.**

Note: is sometimes used with a name: **Prime Minister Wilson,** *etc.*

print [prɪnt] **1.** *noun*

١ ـ أ) طباعة ـ طبعة

(a) letters marked on a page; **the print in that book is so small that I can't read it.**

ب) صورة مطبوعة

(b) photograph; **can you develop this film and make black and white prints of it?**

2. *verb*

٢ ـ أ) يطبع

(a) to mark letters on paper with a machine; **the book is printed in the USA; this newspaper is printed on pink paper.**

ب) يكتب بأحرف كبيرة ومتفرقة

(b) to write using only capital letters; **please print your name and address.**

prints—printing—printed—has printed

prison [prɪzn] *noun*

سجن ـ حبس

place where people are kept when they have been found guilty of a crime; **he was sent to prison for four years; his mother's in prison; they escaped from prison.**

Note: often used without **the**

prisoner, *noun*

سجين ـ أسير

person who is in prison; **the prisoners tried to escape by climbing over the wall.**

private ['praɪvɪt] *adjective*

شخصي ـ خصوصي

personal/belonging to one person, not to the public; **this is a private house; he won't talk about his private life** = about what he does at home, away from the office, etc.; **we were having a private conversation** = we were talking together without anyone else listening.

produce

prize [praɪz] *noun*

جائزة

something given to someone who wins; **the person with the highest marks has a prize of £10; there are several good prizes in the competition; a prize pig** = pig which has won prizes in shows.

probable ['prɒbəbl] *adjective*

جائز ـ محتمل

likely; **it's probable that the ship sank in a storm; this horse is a probable winner.**

probably, *adverb*

من المحتمل ـ ربما ـ على الأرجح

likely to happen; **they're probably going to be late because of the fog; he's probably forgotten about the meeting; we'll probably see you next week.**

problem ['prɒbləm] *noun*

مشكلة ـ مسألة مستعصية

something which is difficult to find an answer to; **I couldn't do the problems in the maths exam; the government is trying to deal with the problem of crime/ with the crime problem.**

produce [prə'djuːs] *verb*

يُنتج ـ يَصْنَعْ ـ يُصَنَّع ـ يولد (طاقة) ـ يُحدث

to make; **the company is producing a new sort of toothpaste; he hit the piano hard, but only produced a little noise; if you bring the two electric wires together you'll produce a flash; the country doesn't produce enough oil; we produce so many vegetables that we sell them to our neighbours.**

produces—producing—produced—has produced

product ['prɒdʌkt] *noun*

إنتاج ـ محصول ـ غلة ـ مُنتج

thing which is produced; **we sell electri-**

profession

cal products; coal is an important product in the north of the country.

production [prəˈdʌkʃn] *noun*

إنتاج

making of something; **production of cars was held up by the strike; we are trying to increase production.**

no plural

profession [prəˈfeʃn] *noun*

مهنة ـ صنعة

type of job for which you need special training; **the teaching profession; he's a doctor by profession** = his job is being a doctor.

professional, *adjective & noun*

مهني ـ حِرَفي

(person) who is paid to play a sport; **a professional footballer; she has become a professional.**

profit [ˈprɒfɪt] *noun*

ربْح ـ كَسْب ـ نَفْع

money which you make in business; **we sold the car and made a profit of £200** = we got £200 more than we paid for it; **he sold his car at a profit** = he made money by selling it.

programme [ˈprəʊɡræm] *noun* (American: **program**)

أ) برنامج

(a) show on TV or radio; **we watched a programme on wild animals of the desert; did you see that funny programme last night? there's a sports programme after the news.**

ب) منهاج ـ بيان

(b) paper in a theatre or at a football match, etc., which gives information about the play or match and the names of the people acting or playing in it; **can I look at your programme? the programme costs 25p.**

two hundred and forty-one

proof

promise [ˈprɒmɪs] **1.** *noun*

١ ـ وعد ـ تَعَهُّد ـ عهد

saying that you will certainly do something; **he gave his promise that he would work harder; she broke her promise that she would pay us the money** = she did not pay although she said she would. **2.** *verb*

٢ ـ يَتَعهّد ـ يَعِدُ

to say that you will certainly do something; **he promised to send us a postcard when he arrived; promise me you'll go to bed early; she promised she would pay back the money.**

promises—promising—promised—has promised

promising, *adjective*

ينتظر ان يكون ناجحاً

(person) who seems likely to be successful; **he's a promising student.**

pronoun [ˈprəʊnaʊn] *noun*

ضمير

word used instead of a noun; **'I', 'you', 'they', etc., are pronouns; 'he', 'it' and 'me' are pronouns in the sentence 'he gave it to me'.**

pronounce [prəˈnaʊns] *verb*

يلقي كلمة ـ يَلْفُظْ ـ ينطق

to say a word; **he didn't pronounce the name very clearly; how do you pronounce the word 'laugh'?**

pronounces—pronouncing—pronounced—has pronounced

pronunciation [prənʌnsɪˈeɪʃn] *noun*

طريقة اللفظ ـ لهجة كلامية

way of speaking (a word); **the pronunciation is given for the words in this dictionary; what's the correct pronunciation of 'through'?**

proof [pruːf] *noun*

برهان ـ دليل

something which shows that something is true; **the police have proof that he was**

241

propellor

not at home when the old woman was murdered; you say he stole your bicycle—but do you have any proof of it?

propellor [prə'pelə] *noun*

الدافع ـ المدسرة ـ المروحة

thing made of several blades, which turns round very fast and is used to drive a boat or an aircraft; **a helicopter has a large propeller on its roof.**

proper ['prɒpə] *adjective*

مناسب ـ ملائم ـ مميّز ـ صحيح

right/correct; **he didn't put the book back into its proper place; what is the proper way to hold a screwdriver? the envelope did not have the proper address.**

properly, *adverb*

كما ينبغي ـ حسب الأصول

rightly/correctly; **they didn't put the wheel on the car properly; the envelope wasn't properly addressed.**

property ['prɒpətɪ] *noun*

أ) ملك ـ ملكيّة ـ خصوصيّة

(*a*) thing which belongs to someone; **that piano is my property; lost property office** = office (in a station, etc.) where you can look for bags, etc., which you have lost.

ب) ممتلكات

(*b*) buildings and land; **he has a lot of property in north London; not much private property was destroyed in the war.**

protect [prə'tekt] *verb*

يَحْمي ـ يحفظ ـ يقي ـ يصون

to stop something which might harm; **the house is protected from the wind by a row of tall trees; they were protected from the cold by their thick coats; the harbour is protected by a high wall; the white coat will protect your clothes in the** factory; the police were protecting the Prime Minister against attack.
protects—protecting—protected—has protected

protection, *noun*

حماية ـ وقاية

thing which protects; **that thin coat is no protection against the rain; the President has police protection** = is protected by the police.

proud [praʊd] *adjective*

فخور ـ مفتخر ـ مغرور

feeling pleased because of something you have done/because of something which belongs to you; **she was proud of her exam results; hitting an old lady is nothing to be proud of; he's very proud of his cooking; she's proud of her children; I'm proud to be here today.**
proud—prouder—proudest

proudly, *adverb*

بفخر ـ بكل اعتزاز

in a proud way; **he proudly showed us his new car.**

prove [pruːv] *verb*

أ) يبرهن ـ يُثْبِت

(*a*) to show that something is true/correct; **the police think he's a burglar, but they can't prove it; can you prove that you were at home on the day the old woman was murdered?**

ب) يتكشّف عن صفة ما

(*b*) to happen; **the weather proved to be even worse than they expected; the film proved to be very bad.**
proves—proving—proved—has proved

provide [prə'vaɪd] *verb*

يزوّد ـ يُجَهّز

to supply; **the hotel will provide us with sandwiches; they'll bring the food, but we'll have to provide the drink.**
provides—providing—provided—has provided

242   *two hundred and forty-two*

pub

provided that, *conjunction*

بشرط ان - شريطة ان

on condition that; I will come provided that the weather is fine; he said he would make a speech provided that someone told him what to say.

pub [pʌb] *noun*

حانة - خمّارة

short for public house; let's stop at the next pub and get some sandwiches; there's a pub in the village where children can sit in the garden.

public ['pʌblɪk] *adjective*

عمومي - شعبي - حكومي

used by people in general; not private; go to the public library to see if there is a book on sailing; the last Monday in August is a public holiday.

public house, *noun*

حانة - خمّارة

place where you can buy and drink alcohol, and often get food as well; there are three public houses in the village, but no shops; children are not allowed in public houses.

Note: a public house *is usually called* a pub

pudding ['pʊdɪŋ] *noun*

١) البودينغ : حلوى مطبوخة

(a) usually sweet food which has been cooked; **Christmas pudding** = special pudding (like hot cake) eaten at Christmas; **rice pudding** = rice, milk and sugar cooked together.

ب) حلوى يتناولها البريطانيون في آخر الطعام

(b) sweet dish at the end of a meal; what's for pudding? I've eaten so much, I don't want any pudding; we're having ice cream for pudding.

pull [pʌl] *verb*

يسحب لجانبه - يجذب إليه

to move something towards you; to

pull

move something which is coming behind you; you have to pull that door to open it, not push; the plough is pulled by a tractor; he pulled a piece of paper out of his pocket; I don't like people who pull my hair.

يخدع - يضحك على

to pull someone's leg = to make them believe something which is wrong as a joke; don't believe what he says—he's pulling your leg.

pulls—pulling—pulled—has pulled

pull down, *verb*

يُدمّر - يهُدّم

to knock down (a building); they pulled down an old house to build a row of shops.

pull in(to), *verb*

يتوقف على جانب الطريق

to drive close to the side of the road and stop; he pulled into the side of the road when he saw the ambulance coming.

pull off, *verb*

يُنْجز بنجاح رغم المصاعب

to make a success of something; the burglars pulled off a big crime.

pull out, *verb*

يرحل ، ينسحب (بسيارته)

to drive a car away from the side of the road.

pullover, *noun*

كنزة صوفية تلبس من خلال الرأس

knitted piece of clothing which you pull over your head to put it on; I like your new pullover; my mother's knitting me a pullover.

pull together, *verb*

يملك أعصابه - يُهدّىء أعصابه

to pull yourself together = to become calmer; although he was very angry he soon pulled himself together.

pull up, *verb*

١) يسحب إليه ، إلى جانبه

(a) to bring something closer; pull your chair up to the table.

two hundred and forty-three 243

pump

ب) يتوقف

(b) to stop (in a car, etc.); **a car pulled up and the driver asked us the way; he didn't pull up in time and hit the back of the car in front.**

pump [pʌmp] **1.** *noun*

١ ـ مضخّة ـ منفخ

machine which forces liquids or air into or out of something; **bicycle pump** = pump which you use to blow up the tyres on a bicycle; **petrol pump** = machine (at a garage) which provides petrol.
2. *verb*

يَضخّ ـ ينفخ الهواء في

to force liquid or air with a pump; **he was pumping up his tyres; I can't pump any more air into this balloon; they tried to pump the water out of the boat.**
~~pumps—pumping—pumped—has pumped~~

punish [ˈpʌnɪʃ] *verb*

يعاقب ـ يقاصص

to make someone suffer because he has done something wrong; **you will be punished for talking in class; I'll punish him by taking away his chocolate.**
~~punishes—punishing—punished—has punished~~

punishment, *noun*

عقاب ـ قصاص

action of punishing; **as a punishment, you mustn't watch TV for three days.**

pupil [ˈpjuːpl] *noun*

تلميذ

child at school; **how many pupils are there in your school?**

pure [ˈpjʊə] *adjective*

نقي ـ صافٍ

very clean; not mixed with other things; **this gold is 100% pure; this pullover is made of pure wool; is the water pure?**
~~pure—purer—purest~~

push

purely, *adverb*

فقط

only; **he says he likes you purely because you've got money.**

purpose [ˈpɜːpəs] *noun*

غاية ـ غرض ـ عزم

aim/plan; **what's the purpose of going by plane when it's much cheaper by car? I think he set fire to the house on purpose** = because he planned to do it.

purposely, *adverb*

قصداً ـ عمداً

on purpose; **she purposely stayed at home instead of coming to work.**

purse [pɜːs] *noun*

كسيس أو جزدان لوضع الأموال والدراهم

small bag for carrying money; **she dropped her purse on the floor of the bus; I put my ticket in my purse so that I wouldn't forget it.**

push [pʊʃ] *verb*

أ) يدفع إلى الأمام

(a) to make something move away from you; to make something which is in front of you move; **they had to push their car to get it to start; we can't lift the piano, we'll have to push it into the corner; I had to push my bike home because I had a flat tyre; did he fall into the river, or was he pushed?**

ب) يضغط (بيده أو اصبعه)

(b) to press with your finger; **push button A to make the machine start; (in a lift) which floor number do you want me to push?** = which button.
~~pushes—pushing—pushed—has pushed~~

push off, *verb*

ينطلق ـ يرحل

to start (on a journey); **it's time for us to push off now; push off!** = go away!

put

put [put] *verb*

أ) يضع

(*a*) to place; **put your books down on the table; he put the milk in the fridge; do you want me to put another record on? can you help me put up the curtains?**

ب) يقول

(*b*) to say (in words); **if you put it like that, it sounds quite pleasant; I want to put a question to the speaker.**

puts – putting – put – has put

put away, *verb*

يضع جانباً - يضع في مكانه المألوف

to clear things away; **put your toys away before you go to bed.**

put back, *verb*

يُعيد - يضع الشيء في مكانه ثانيةً

to put something where it was before; **put that book back on the shelf; shall I put the milk back in the fridge? to put the clocks back** = to turn the clocks back one hour (at the beginning of the summer).

put off, *verb*

ا) يُرجيء - يُؤَجّل

(*a*) to arrange for something to take place later; **the meeting has been put off until next week.**

Note: **we put the meeting off** *or* **we put off the meeting** *but only* **we put it off**

ب) يزعج - يضايق - يغيظ

(*b*) to upset someone so that he can't work well; to say something which makes someone decide not to do something; **don't sing while I'm writing, you're putting me off; he told a story about the hospital which put me off my food; I was going to see that film, but my brother put me off.**

put on, *verb*

ا) يرتدي - يَلْبس

(*a*) to dress yourself with a piece of clothing; **put your coat on; put on your coat if you're going out.**

ب) يضع قيد الاستعمال

(*b*) to switch on; **put the light on, it's getting dark.**

Note: **put your own coat on** *or* **put on your coat** *but only* **put it on**

put out, *verb*

يطفيء (النور) - يوقف تشغيل (آلة)

to switch off; **don't forget to put out the light when you go to bed.**

Note: **put the light out** *or* **put out the light** *but only* **put it out**

put up, *verb*

يستضيف

to give someone a place to sleep in your house; **can you put me up for the night?**

put up with, *verb*

يتحمّل - يَتَقبّل الإزعاج

to accept someone/something even though he or it is unpleasant; **if you live near an airport you have to put up with a lot of noise; how can you put up with all those children?**

puzzle ['pʌzl] *noun*

حيرة - ارتباك - لعبة محيرة

problem; game where you have to find the answer to a problem; **it's a puzzle to me why he doesn't sell his house; she's finished the crossword puzzle.**

pyjamas

pyjamas [pə'dʒɑːməz] *plural noun* (*American:* **pajamas**)

ملابس النوم

light shirt and trousers which you wear in bed; **I must buy another pair of pyjamas; he ran into the street in his pyjamas.**

Note: **a pair of pyjamas** *means one shirt and one pair of trousers*

Qq

quality ['kwɒlɪtɪ] *noun*

أ) جودة

(*a*) how good something is; **the cloth is of very high quality; those tomatoes are of poor quality.**

ب) صفة حميدة ــ صفة حسنة

(*b*) good points about a person; **he has many qualities.**
plural **qualities**

quantity ['kwɒntɪtɪ] *noun*

كميّة ــ مقدار

how much there is of something; **a large quantity of rubbish; there was only a small quantity of milk left; we have a quantity of waste paper** = quite a lot of waste paper.
plural **quantities**

quarrel ['kwɒrəl] **1.** *noun*

١ ــ نزاع ــ خلاف

argument; **they had a quarrel over who should pay for the meal; we had a quarrel about the colour of the carpet.**
2. *verb*

٢ ــ يتنازع ــ يتشاجر

to argue; **they quarrelled about the colour of the carpet; he quarrelled with the grocer over the price of sugar.**
quarrels—quarrelling—quarrelled—has quarrelled

quarter ['kwɔːtə] *noun*

أ) رُبع

(*a*) one of four parts which make a whole/a fourth; **cut the apple into quarters; the bottle is only a quarter full; a quarter of our staff are ill; I want a quarter of a pound of coffee.**

ب) رُبع ساعة

(*b*) **a quarter of an hour** = 15 minutes; **it's (a) quarter to four** = it's 3.45; **at (a) quarter past seven** = at 7.15.
Note: **a quarter and three quarters are often written ¼ and ¾**

queen [kwiːn] *noun*

مَلكة

wife of a king; woman who rules a country; **the Queen lives in Buckingham Palace; Queen Victoria was queen for many years.**
Note: **queen** *is spelt with a capital when used with a name or when referring to a particular person*

question ['kwestʃn] *noun*

أ) سؤال

(*a*) sentence which needs an answer; **he asked the teacher a question; the teacher couldn't answer all our questions; I didn't answer two of the questions in the exam.**

ب) مشكلة ــ مسألة ــ قضية

(*b*) problem or matter; **the question is—do we want to spend a lot of money on a new car? it is out of the question** = it is quite impossible.

question mark, *noun*

علامة استفهام

sign (?) used in writing to show that a question is being asked.

queue [kjuː] **1.** *noun*

١ ــ طابور ــ صف (من الناس)

line (of people, etc.) waiting for something; **they stood in a queue for tickets to the theatre; there were queues of cars**

quick

waiting for the ferry; **he jumped the queue** = he went in front of people who had been waiting for longer than he had.
2. *verb* (*also* **to queue up**)

٢ ـ ينتظر في الطابور ـ يقف بالصفّ

to wait in a line for something; **we had to queue (up) to get some petrol; they queued (up) for hours to get into the theatre; I don't like queuing.**

queues—queuing—queued—has queued

quick [kwɪk] *adjective*

سريع
زكي ـ لامع ـ رشيق

fast; **which is the quickest way to get to the post office? I had a quick lunch and then got back to work; she is much quicker at sums than her sister; if you went by air it would be quicker than taking the train.**

quick—quicker—quickest

quickly, *adverb*

بسرعة

without taking much time; **he finished his meal very quickly because he wanted to watch a TV programme; the firemen quickly put the fire out.**

quiet [ˈkwaɪət] *adjective*

هادىء ـ ساكن

with no noise/no excitement; **the chil-dren are very quiet—they must be doing something naughty; please keep quiet—I'm trying to work; we had a quiet weekend working in the garden; it's a quiet little town.**

quiet—quieter—quietest

quietly, *adverb*

بهدوء ـ بسكون ـ بلا ضجّة

without making any noise; **the burglar went quietly upstairs; he shut the door quietly.**

race

quite [kwaɪt] *adverb*

أ) إلى حدّ ما ـ نوعاً ما

(*a*) more or less; **it's quite a good film; she's quite a fast typist; the book is quite interesting, but I liked the TV programme best.**

ب) تماماً ـ فعلاً

(*b*) completely; **he's quite mad; you're quite right; I quite understand why you want to go to bed; have you finished?—not quite.**

بضعة ـ كثير ـ عدد كبير ـ وافر

quite a few/quite a lot = several/many; **quite a few people were sick; quite a lot of the cars were new; she spent quite a lot of the time lying in bed.**

Note the order of words: **he's quite a good student** *but* **he's a fairly good student**

Rr

rabbit [ˈræbɪt] *noun*

أرنب

common wild animal with grey fur, long ears and a short white tail, also kept as a pet; **the rabbit went down its hole.**

race [reɪs] **1.** *noun*

١ ـ أ) سباق ـ مسابقة

(*a*) competition to see which person/horse/car, etc., is the fastest; **he won the 100 metres race; we watched a bicycle**

radio

race; **I like watching horse races on TV.**

ب) جنس - عِرق - سُلالة

(b) group of people with similar bodies; **the white races.**

2. *verb*

٢ - يسابق - يدخل في سباق

to run/ride, etc., to see who is the fastest; **let's race to see who gets to school first; I'll race you to the sweet shop.**

races—racing—raced—has raced

radio ['reɪdɪəʊ] *noun*

راديو - الاذاعة

way of sending out and receiving messages using waves that travel through the air; machine which does this; **he got the message by radio; did you hear the programme on the radio about Germany? switch on the radio—it's time for the news; I was listening to the news on the car radio.**

rail [reɪl] *noun*

أ) سكة حديدية

(a) metal bar, especially one which trains run along; **don't step on that rail—it's electric; the little boy ran across the rails in front of the train.**

ب) مواصلات بواسطة القطار

(b) trains used as a means of transport; **I go to work by rail; British Rail =** the British railway system.

railings, *plural noun*

سياج

fence made of metal bars; **he looked through the railings at the animals in the zoo.**

railway, *noun* (*American:* **railroad**)

سكة حديدية

organization which uses trains to carry passengers and goods; **a railway station; the French railway system.**

rain [reɪn] **1.** *noun*

١ - مطر

drops of water which fall from the clouds; **the ground is very dry—we've had no rain for weeks; yesterday London had 3 cm of rain; don't go out in the rain without an umbrella; the rain will help the plants grow.**

no plural: some rain; a drop of rain

2. *verb*

٢ - تمتطر (السماء) - ينهمر المطر - تتساقط الأمطار

to fall as drops of water from the clouds; **it started to rain as soon as we sat on the grass; you can't go for a picnic when it's raining; it rained all day yesterday.**

rains—raining—rained—has rained

Note: **to rain** *is only used with* **it**

rainbow, *noun*

قوس قزح

coloured half circle which shines in the sky when it is sunny and raining at the same time.

raincoat, *noun*

معطف واق للمطر

coat which keeps off water, which you wear when it is raining; **put on your raincoat if it's raining; he took off his raincoat and hung it in the hall.**

rainstorm, *noun*

عاصفة مطريّة

storm with a lot of rain; **the streets were flooded in the rainstorm last night.**

rainy, *adjective*

مُمطر

when it rains; **the rainy weather spoilt our holiday.**

rainy—rainier—rainiest

raise [reɪz] *verb*

أ) يرفع (ذراعه)

(a) to lift; **he raised his arm; don't raise your voice.**

ب) يزيد (أسعار المواصلات)

(b) to increase; **they've raised the bus fares again.**

raises—raising—raised—has raised

ran

ran [ræn] *see* **run**

ملاحظة : انظر إلى كلمة **run**

rang [ræŋ] *see* **ring**

ملاحظة : انظر إلى كلمة **ring**

rapid ['ræpɪd] *adjective*

سريع ـ متلاحق

fast; we heard rapid footsteps on the stairs; the enemy made a rapid attack.

rapidly, *adverb*

بسرعة

quickly; he read the names out rapidly.

rare [reə] *adjective*

نادر ـ غير مألوف ـ فريد

not common; (something) of which there are very few; this is one of the rarest stamps; these animals are getting rarer every year.

rare—rarer—rarest

rarely, *adverb*

نادراً ـ قلّما

not often; seldom; he rarely comes to London now.

rat [ræt] *noun*

جرذ ـ فأر

common small grey animal with a long tail, which lives under houses and eats rubbish.

rate [reɪt] *noun*

سعر ـ قيمة ـ نسبة

amount of something compared to something else; a high rate of interest; birth rate = number of children born per 1,000 of population.

مهما تكن الظروف ـ بأية حال

at any rate = whatever may happen; are you going to the party?—we're going, at any rate.

rather ['rɑːðə] *adverb*

أ) إلى حدّ ما ـ نوعاً ما

(a) quite; it's rather cold outside; her hat is rather a pretty shade of green.

reach

ب) مفضلاً ذلك على

(b) used with would to mean prefer; I'd rather stay at home than go to the party; are you going to pay for everybody?—I'd rather not; she'd rather we stayed with her; they'd rather we went with them.

ت) الافضل هو ان

(c) (showing that something is preferred) rather than wait for a bus, we decided to walk home; rather than have to pay, he said he had no money.

بالاحرى ـ بالاصح

or rather = or to be more correct; his father is English, or rather Scottish.

raw [rɔː] *adjective*

نَيِّء ـ فَجّ

not cooked; he eats his meat raw; too much raw fruit can make you ill.

razor ['reɪzə] *noun*

موسى للحلاقة ـ المحلاق

sharp knife or small machine for cutting off the hair on your face; he was shaving with his electric razor; she used a razor blade to sharpen her pencil.

Rd *see* **road**

ملاحظة : انظر إلى كلمة **road**

reach [riːtʃ] **1.** *noun*

١ ـ متناول ـ حوزة ـ متناول (اليد) ـ وصول

distance which you can stretch out your hand to; distance which you can travel easily; you should keep medicines out of the reach of the children; the house is within easy reach of the station.

2. *verb*

٢ ـ أ) يمدّ يده للحصول على ـ يحصّل

(a) to stretch out your hand to; he reached across the table and put a potato on my plate; the little boy is tall enough to reach the cupboard; can you reach me down the box from the top shelf = stretch out your hand and bring down the box.

two hundred and forty-nine 249

read

(b) يَصِلُ إلى - يَبْلُغ

(b) to arrive at; **we only reached the hotel at midnight; what time are we supposed to reach London? the letter never reached him** = he never received it; **the amount in my bank account has now reached £1000.**

reaches—reaching—reached—has reached

read [ri:d] verb

يقرأ

to look at and understand written words; **I can read Russian but I can't speak it; he was reading the newspaper; I can't read the instructions on the medicine bottle—the letters are too small; he plays the piano by ear, but he can't read music; I'm reading about the American election; the teacher read out all our marks** = read them in a loud voice.

reads—reading—read [red]—has read [red]

ready ['redɪ] adjective

جاهز - مُهَيَّأ

prepared to do something; fit to be used or eaten; **we can't eat yet—the dinner isn't ready; wait for me, I'll be ready in two minutes; are you ready to go to school? the children are ready for bed** = have their pyjamas on, etc.; **he's ready for anything** = prepared to do anything.

real [rɪəl] adjective

ا) أصلي - غير زائف

(a) which does not imitate; **is your watch real gold? this plastic fruit looks very real/looks like the real thing.**

ب) حقيقي

(b) which exists; **have you ever seen a real live elephant?**

really, adverb

ا) بالفعل - حقاً - صحيحاً

(a) in fact; **is he really American? did she really mean what she said? he really believes that the earth is flat; did the house really belong to your father?**

receive

ب) (للدلالة على العجب) : صحيح !

(b) (used to show surprise) **you really ought to have your hair cut; he doesn't like chocolate—really, how odd!**

realize ['rɪəlaɪz] verb

يُدرك - يَفْهَم

to understand; **he realized that he was becoming deaf; did she realize that the car was going too fast? I realize that the holiday will be expensive.**

realizes—realizing—realized—has realized

reason ['ri:zn] noun

سبب - داعٍ - مُبَرِّر

thing which explains why something happens; **what was the reason for the train being late? they said the train would be late, but didn't give any reason; the reason he's gone to live in Greece is that it's warmer there than here.**

reasonable, adjective

معقول - عاقل - سليم التفكير - معتدل

sensible/acting in a normal way; **the manager was very reasonable when I said I had left all my money at home.**

receipt [rɪ'si:t] noun

وصل - ايصال

piece of paper showing that you have paid for something; **keep your receipt—you'll have to show it if you want to change your pullover for another one.**

receive [rɪ'si:v] verb

يَسْتلم - يَتَسلَّم

to get something which has been sent or given to you; **he received a lot of cards on his birthday; did you ever receive the cheque I sent you? he received a gold watch when he retired.**

receives—receiving—received—has received

250   *two hundred and fifty*

recent

recent ['ri:snt] *adjective*

حديث ـ جديد

which happened not very long ago; **his recent film about the war; the Prime Minister's recent speech.**

recently, *adverb*

مؤخراً ـ في الآونة الأخيرة ـ حديثاً ـ منذ عهدٍ حديث

not long ago; lately; **have you ever been to Sweden?—I was there quite recently; he's recently joined the tennis club.**

recognize ['rekəgnaɪz] *verb*

يُمَيِّز ـ يتعرّف ـ يعرف

to know something/someone because you have seen it/him before; **the police recognized the writing on the letter; I recognized her by the hat she was wearing; you've had your hair cut—I didn't recognize you!**

recognizes—recognizing—recognized—has recognized

recommend [rekə'mend] *verb*

١) ينصح ـ يوصي بـ

(*a*) to suggest that it would be a good thing if someone did something; **the doctor recommended that he should stay in bed; I wouldn't recommend you to go there; I don't recommend going on a long car ride if you don't like travelling.**

ب) يقترح

(*b*) to say something is good; **this restaurant is recommended in the guide book; I would certainly recommend that dictionary.**

record ['rekɔ:d] **1.** *noun*

١ ـ أ) إسطوانة

(*a*) flat, round piece of black plastic which has sound printed on it, and which you play on a special machine; **I bought her an Elvis Presley record for her birthday; I don't like his new record—do you? some records are expensive, so I borrow them from the re-**

reduce

cord library; put another Beethoven record on.

ب) رقم قياسي (في الرياضة)

(*b*) success in sport which is better than any other; **he holds the world record for the 1000 metres; she broke the world record/she set up a new world record in the last Olympics** = she did better than the last record; **they're trying to set a new record for eating sausages.**

2. *verb* [rɪ'kɔ:d]

٢ ـ يسجل على أسطوانة أو على شريط ـ تسجيلي

to fix a sound on a flat round piece of plastic or on a plastic tape; **he recorded the conversation on his pocket tape-recorder; this music has been badly recorded.**

records—recording—recorded—has recorded

recorder, *see* **tape recorder**

tape recorder ملاحظة : انظر إلى كلمة

record-player, *noun*

آلة استنطاق الأسطوانات

machine for playing records; **shall I put my new record on the record-player? switch the record-player off—I want to watch TV.**

red [red] *adjective & noun*

أحمر ـ حمراء

of a colour like the colour of blood; **he has red hair; they live in the house with a red door; I'm painting the chair red; he turned red when we asked him what he had done with the money; have you any paint of a darker red than this one? you have to stop when the traffic lights are red.**

red—redder—reddest

Red Cross, *noun*

الصليب الأحمر

international organization which provides medical help.

reduce [rɪ'dju:s] *verb*

يُخفِّض ـ يخفف

to make something smaller or lower;

two hundred and fifty-one 251

refer to

you must reduce speed when you come to the traffic lights; we've reduced the temperature in the office.
reduces—reducing—reduced—has reduced

refer to [rɪˈfɜːtʊ] *verb*

يرجع إلى ـ يحيل إلى

to talk about or write about something/someone; **are you referring to me? he referred to the letter he had just received.**
refers—referring—referred—has referred

referee [refəˈriː] *noun*

حَكَم (في قضية أو مباراة)

person who sees that a game is played according to the rules; **the referee blew his whistle; our best player was told off by the referee.**

referigerator [rɪˈfrɪdʒəreɪtə] *noun*

ثلاجة

machine in the kitchen for keeping food cold; **put the milk in the refrigerator; a refrigerator is very useful in hot weather; shut the refrigerator door.**
Note: often called a **fridge** [frɪdʒ]

refuse [rɪˈfjuːz] *verb*

يرفض

to say that you will not do something; not to accept; **he came to the party but he refused to talk to anyone; they refused my offer of a lift home; we asked them to come to dinner, but they refused.**
refuses—refusing—refused—has refused

register [ˈredʒɪstə] *verb*

يُسجّل

to write a name on a list, especially to write your name and address when you arrive at a hotel; **they registered at the hotel at 6 p.m. and then went out for dinner.**
registers—registering—registered—has registered

registered letter, *noun*

رسالة مسجلة

important letter which has been noted at a post office and which will be delivered carefully.

registered mail, *noun*

بريد مسجل

system in the post office for taking special care of important letters.

regret [rɪˈgret] *verb*

ا) يأسف ـ يندم على

(*a*) to be sorry that something has happened; **he regretted doing it, but he had been told to.**

ب) يأسف ـ يعتذر

(*b*) to be sorry that something has happened or will happen; **I regret to have to tell you that your father is ill.**
regrets—regretting—regretted—has regretted

regular [ˈregjʊlə] *adjective*

مُنتظم ـ مطّرد

which takes place again and again after the same period of time; which happens at the same time each day; **11 o'clock is my regular time for going to bed; if you don't have regular meals you will be ill; regular visits to the dentist are important; is this your regular train?** = the train you catch each day.

regularly, *adverb*

بطريقة منتظمة ـ بانتظام

happening often after the same period of time; **he is regularly late for work; she regularly goes to bed after midnight; you should go to the dentist regularly.**

related [rɪˈleɪtɪd] *adjective*

نسيب ـ قريب

belonging to the same family; **they are related—his mother is her aunt; she is**

252   two hundred and fifty-two

relation

related to the family who run the butcher's shop in the village.

relation [rɪ'leɪʃn], **relative** ['relətɪv] *noun*

القريب ـ النسيب

member of a family; **all our relations came for grandmother's birthday party; she doesn't speak to any of her relatives; we have relatives in Australia but I've never met them.**

relatively, *adverb*

نسبياً

quite/more or less; **this train is relatively fast; the tickets were relatively cheap.**

religion [rɪ'lɪdʒn] *noun*

دين ـ عقيدة

believing in gods or in one god; **he's a follower of the Christian religion.**

religious, *adjective*

ديني ـ متدين

referring to religion; **they held a religious ceremony to mark the beginning of the school term.**

rely on [rɪ'laɪ ɒn]

يعتمد على ـ يتكل على ـ يضع ثقته بـ

to depend on/to be sure that someone will do something; **we're relying on you to pay for the tickets; don't rely on the weather being good for your picnic.**
relies—relying—relied—has relied

remain [rɪ'meɪn] *verb*

١) يبقى ـ يظلّ

(*a*) to stay; **several people remained behind when the speaker left; the weather will remain cold for several days.**

ب) يتبقى

(*b*) to be left; **two problems remain to be dealt with.**
remains—remaining—remained—has remained

remains, *plural noun*

remove

بقايا ـ آثار ـ خراب ـ فضلات (الأكل أو الطعام)

things left behind; **after the fire the remains of the house had to be pulled down; we'll have the remains of the pie for our supper.**

remark [rɪ'mɑːk] *noun*

تعليق ـ ملاحظة (شفهية أو خطية)

thing said; **he made some rude remarks about the teachers; she passed some remarks about his dirty shoes** = she said she did not like his dirty shoes.

remember [rɪ'membə] *verb*

يَتَذَكّر ـ يَذْكُر

to bring back into your mind something which you have seen or heard before; **do you remember the football game where we lost 20-0? my grandfather can remember seeing the first planes flying; I can't remember where I put my book; I don't remember having been to this restaurant before; I remember her very well; it's odd that she can never remember how to get to their house; remember me to your father** = pass my good wishes to your father.
remembers—remembering—remembered—has remembered

remind [rɪ'maɪnd] *verb*

يُذَكِّر

to make someone remember something; **remind me to write to my aunt; he reminds me of someone I used to know in Africa** = he looks like someone I knew in Africa.
reminds—reminding—reminded—has reminded

remove [rɪ'muːv] *verb*

ينزع ـ يزيل ـ ينقل

to take away; **they removed the TV set when we couldn't pay the bill; the police came to remove my car because it was parked in a no parking area.**
removes—removing—removed—has removed

two hundred and fifty-three 253

rent

rent [rent] 1. *noun*

١ ـ إيجار

money which you pay to live in or use a house/a flat which belongs to someone else; **they had to get out of their flat when they couldn't pay the rent.**
2. *verb*

٢ ـ أ) يستأجر

(*a*) to pay money to live in or use a house/flat, etc.; **we rent this office from the government; when I go on holiday I'll rent a car.**

ب) يُؤَجِر

(*b*) to let a house/flat, etc., to someone; **when we went to the USA, we rented our house to a Swedish family.**

rents—renting—rented—has rented

repair [rɪˈpeə] *verb*

يُصْلِح ـ يُرَمِّم

to mend; to make something good again; **my shoes need repairing; the workmen have repaired the broken gas pipe.**

repairs—repairing—repaired—has repaired

repairs, *plural noun*

تصليحات ـ إصلاح ـ ترميم

mending of something; **they have done some repairs to the roof.**

repeat [rɪˈpiːt] *verb*

يقول ثانيةً ـ يردّد ـ يكرّر

to say something again; **could you repeat the address so that I can write it down?; he kept repeating that he wanted a drink; she keeps repeating herself =**

يعيد الكلام

she keeps saying the same thing again and again.

repeats—repeating—repeated—has repeated

reply [rɪˈplaɪ] 1. *noun*

١ ـ جواب (على طلب أو رسالة)

answer; **we've had no reply to our letter;**

rescue

I've had so many replies that I can't answer them all.

plural **replies**

2. *verb*

٢ ـ يجيب

to answer; **when I asked him how to get to the post office, he replied that he didn't know; she wrote to the company three weeks ago, but they still haven't replied.**

replies—replying—replied—has replied

report [rɪˈpɔːt] 1. *noun*

١ ـ أ) تقرير

(*a*) statement by a teacher about a pupil's work; **she had a very good report—all the teachers said she did well.**

ب) بيان ـ تقرير

(*b*) statement by a government committee; **they wrote a report on the problem of crime in large towns.**
2. *verb*

٢ ـ ينقل (خبراً أو قولاً) يبلّغ عن ـ ينقل نبأ لـ

to tell the police about someone or something; **we had better report this accident to the police; you'll get reported if you go on singing like that—it's after midnight.**

reports—reporting—reported—has reported

reporter, *noun*

المراسل الصحفي ـ المذيع

person who writes about news in a newspaper; **a crime reporter/a sports reporter.**

republic [rɪˈpʌblɪk] *noun*

جمهورية

country which is governed by an elected president and not by a king; **the German republic.**

rescue [ˈreskjuː] 1. *noun*

١ ـ إسعاف ـ اغاثة ـ إنقاذ

saving (of someone from danger); **the**

254 *two hundred and fifty-four*

reserve

rescue of the school children lost on the mountain; six policemen took part in the rescue.
2. *verb*

٢ - يُسْعِف - يُنْقِذ

to save (from danger); **the firemen rescued ten people from the burning house; he tried to rescue his cat which was up a tree.**
rescues—rescuing—rescued—has rescued

reserve [rɪ'zɜːv] 1. *noun*

١ - احتياط

something kept in case it will be needed later; **our reserves of oil are low; we're keeping these sandwiches in reserve in case more people come to the party.**
2. *verb*

٢ - أ) يحجز (مقاعد)

(*a*) to keep something for someone; **I'm reserving the seat next to me for my sister.**

ب) يحجز - يحفظ

(*b*) to book a seat/a table; **I've reserved a table for six people; can I reserve some seats by telephone?**
reserves—reserving—reserved—has reserved

resign [rɪ'zaɪn] *verb*

يستقيل (من عمله)

to give up a job; **he has resigned and gone to work for another company; if you don't pay me more I'll resign.**
resigns—resigning—resigned—has resigned

rest [rest] 1. *noun*

١ - أ) راحة - استراحة

(*a*) lying down/being calm; **what you need is a good night's rest; I had a few minutes' rest and then I started work again.**

ب) توقف - تجميد

(*b*) not moving; **the car came to rest at the bottom of the hill.**

result

ت) الباقي - ما تبقى من - بقايا (الطعام)

(*c*) what is left; **here are John and Jim, but where are the rest of the children? the cat drank the rest of the milk; he put the rest of his dinner in the dustbin; she gave away three apples and ate the rest herself.**

Note: **rest** *takes a singular verb when it refers to a singular;* **here's the rest of the milk; where's the rest of the string? the rest of the money has been stolen;** *it takes the plural when it refers to a plural:* **here are the rest of the children; where are the rest of the bricks? the rest of the books have been stolen**

2. *verb*

٢ - أ) يرتاح - يهدأ - يستريح

(*a*) to lie down/to be calm; **don't disturb your mother—she's resting; they walked for ten miles, then rested for ten minutes, then walked again.**

ب) يركّز على - يرتكز على

(*b*) to lean something against something; **he rested his bike against the wall.**
rests—resting—rested—has rested

restaurant ['restrɒnt] *noun*

مطعم

place where you can buy a meal; **let's not stay at home tonight—let's go to the restaurant in the High Street; he's waiting for me at the restaurant.**

result [rɪ'zʌlt] 1. *noun*

١ - أ) نتيجة (امتحانات)

(*a*) score (in a game)/marks (in an exam); **the result of the game was a draw; I've been told my maths results—I passed.**

ب) فائدة - جدوى - نتيجة

(*b*) something which happens because of something; **he had a cold, with the result that he had to stay in bed; I complained that the price was too high, but with no result; as a result of the accident, six people had to go to hospital; the re-**

Restaurant

المطعم

1. bill	12. pepper	١٢ ـ بهار
2. bottle	13. plate	١٣ ـ صحن
3. candle	14. salt	١٤ ـ ملح
4. chair	15. saucer	١٥ ـ صحن الفنجان
5. cup	16. spoon	١٦ ـ ملعقة
6. fork	17. table	١٧ ـ طاولة
7. glass	18. tablecloth	١٨ ـ غطاء الطاولة
8. knife	19. teapot	١٩ ـ إبريق الشاي
9. menu	20. waiter	٢٠ ـ النادل
10. milk jug	21. waitress	٢١ ـ النادلة
11. mustard	22. wine	٢٢ ـ نبيذ ـ خمر

١ ـ الحساب — 1. bill
٢ ـ زجاجة — 2. bottle
٣ ـ شمعة — 3. candle
٤ ـ كرسي — 4. chair
٥ ـ فنجان — 5. cup
٦ ـ شوكة — 6. fork
٧ ـ كباية ـ كأس — 7. glass
٨ ـ سكين — 8. knife
٩ ـ لائحة الطعام — 9. menu
١٠ ـ ابريق الحليب — 10. milk jug
١١ ـ خردل — 11. mustard

256 *two hundred and fifty-six*

retire

sult of all our discussions was that nothing was decided.
2. *verb*

٢ ـ يتسبّب ـ يُؤَدّي إلى ـ ينشأ أو ينتج عن

to happen because of something; **the accident resulted in a traffic jam; his illness resulted in his being away from work for several weeks.**

results—resulting—resulted—has resulted

retire [rɪ'taɪə] *verb*

يتقاعد ـ يحيل إلى التقاعد

to stop work at a certain age; **most men retire at 65, but women only go on working until they are 60; he retired after twenty years in the factory; both my parents are retired.**

retires—retiring—retired—has retired

return [rɪ'tɜːn] 1. *noun*

١ ـ أ) عودة

(a) coming back/going back; **on his return to work he was given a present; can you send me your reply by return of post?** = by the next post back; **many Happy Returns of the Day!** = best wishes for a happy birthday.

ب) بطاقة ذهاب وإياب

(b) ticket to go somewhere and come back; **I want two returns to London; buy a return ticket—it's cheaper than two singles; day return** = ticket where you go somewhere and come back in the same day.

2. *verb*

٢ ـ أ) يعود إلى

(a) to come back/to go back; **they returned from holiday last week; he hasn't returned to work since he was ill.**

ب) يعيد ـ يرجع ـ يردّ (الأشياء المقروضة له)

(b) to give back; **I must return my books to the library; she borrowed my knife and never returned it.**

returns—returning—returned—has returned

two hundred and fifty-seven

rid

rhyme [raɪm] 1. *noun*

١ ـ سجع ـ قافية ـ ايقاع

same sound in two words used in poetry; **don't be silly—'blow' isn't a rhyme for 'cow'; I can't finish my poem because I can't think of a rhyme for 'scissors'.**

2. *verb*

٢ ـ يتساجع ـ يتقافى مع

to have the same sound (in poetry); **don't be silly—'blow' doesn't rhyme with 'cow'/'blow' and 'cow' don't rhyme.**

rhymes—rhyming—rhymed—has rhymed

rice [raɪs] *noun*

الاُرزّ ـ الرُّزّ

common food plant, grown in hot countries, of which you eat the seeds; **he was eating a bowl of rice;** *see also* **pudding.** *no plural:* **some rice; a bowl of rice/a spoonful of rice.**

rich [rɪtʃ] *adjective*

أ) ثريّ ـ غنيّ

(a) having a lot of money; **he's so rich that he doesn't know what to do with his money; if I were a rich man, I'd go to warm places in the winter; she doesn't spend any money and so gets richer and richer.**

ب) قويّ (لون)

(b) dark (colour); **he painted the ceiling a rich chocolate colour.**

ت) غنيّ بالموارد الطبيعية أو بالتراث ...

(c) with many minerals/treasures, etc.; **the country is rich in coal; the town is rich in old churches; the museum has a rich collection of Italian paintings.**

ث) شديد الحلاوة (طعام)

(d) very sweet (food); **this cake's too rich for me.**

rich—richer—richest

rid [rɪd] *verb*

يتخلص من

to get/to get rid of something = to throw

257

ride

something away/to make something go away; **to be rid of something** = not to have something unpleasant any more; I'm trying to get rid of my old car; he can't get rid of his cold—he's had it for weeks; I'm very glad to be rid of my cold.

ride [raɪd] **1.** *noun*

١ ـ ركوب على الخيل ـ رحلة (في سيارة أو حافلة ...)

trip on a horse/on a bike/in a car, etc.; I'm going for a ride on my bike; do you want to come for a bike ride? can I have a ride on the black horse? we all went for a ride in his new car; the shops are only a short bus ride from our house.

2. *verb*

٢ ـ يذهب على متن دراجة أو فرس أو حيوان

to go for a trip on a horse/on a bike, etc.; I was riding my bike when it started to rain; have you ever ridden (on) an elephant? she's learning to ride a bicycle.

rides—riding—rode [rəʊd]—has ridden [ˈrɪdn]

riding school, *noun*

مدرسة تدريب على ركوب الفرس

school where you learn to ride horses.

right [raɪt] **1.** *adjective*

١ ـ أ) صحيح

(*a*) correct/not wrong; you're right—they didn't win; he's always right; he gave the right answer every time; I think the answer's 240—quite right! is your watch right? is that the right time? this isn't the right train for London; put the books back in the right place; if you don't put the bottle the right way up, all the milk will run out of it; is this right way to get to the post office? see also **all right**.

ب) أيْمن ـ يُمْني

(*b*) not left/referring to the hand which most people use to write with; in England, you mustn't drive on the right side

of the road; she was holding her bag in her right hand; my right arm is stronger than my left.

2. *noun*

٢ ـ أ) اليمين ـ اليد اليمنى ـ الجانب الأيمن

(*a*) the side opposite the left/the side of the hand which most people write with; in England you mustn't drive on the right; in Germany you must keep to the right; when you get to the traffic lights, turn to the right; who was that girl sitting on your right? = at the right side of you; take the second street on the right.

ب) إنصاف ـ حق ـ عدل

(*b*) what you should be allowed to do or to have; you've got no right to read my letters; everyone has the right to say what they like about the government.

3. *adverb*

٣ ـ أ) مباشرةً ـ على نحو مستقيم

(*a*) straight; keep right on to the end of the road; instead of turning he went right on into a tree.

ب) فوراً

(*b*) (*also* **right away**) immediately; he phoned the police right after the accident; the doctor came right away.

ت) تماماً ـ بالضبط

(*c*) exactly/completely; his house is right at the end of the road; the TV went wrong right in the middle of the programme; go right along to the end of the corridor; don't stand right in front of the TV—no one can see the picture.

ث) على نحو منطبق على الحقيقة

(*d*) correctly; he guessed right; nothing seems to be going right.

ج) على جهة اليمين ـ على اليمين

(*e*) to the right-hand side; turn right at the traffic lights; look right and left before you cross the road.

right-hand, *adjective*

على اليمين

on the right side; look in the right-hand drawer; he lives on the right-hand side of the street.

ring

right-handed, *adjective*

يميني : منجز باليد اليمنى

using the right hand more often than the left; **he's right-handed.**

ring [rɪŋ] **1.** *noun*

١ – أ) حلقة – خاتم

(*a*) circle of metal, etc.; **she has a gold ring on her finger.**

ب) مستديرة – دائرة

(*b*) circle of people or things; **we all sat in a ring.**

ت) رنين (الجرس) – قرع الجرس

(*c*) noise of an electric bell; **there was a ring at the door.**

ث) مكالمة هاتفية

(*d*) call on the phone; **I'll give you a ring tomorrow.**

2. *verb*

٢ – أ) يرنّ (الجرس) – يقرع

(*a*) to make a sound with a bell; **he rang at the door; the bells were ringing; ring your bicycle bell and people will get out of the way; is that your phone ringing? that rings a bell** = it reminds me of something.

ب) يتلفن – يجري مكالمة هاتفية مع

(*b*) to telephone; **he rang me when I was in bed; don't ring tomorrow—I'll be out.**

rings—ringing—rang [ræŋ]—**has rung** [rʌŋ]

ring back, *verb*

يتصل بغية الجواب على مكالمة سابقة

to telephone in reply; **he said he would ring me back in an hour, but he hasn't.**

ring off, *verb*

ينهي مكالمة هاتفية – يقفل الخط

to stop a telephone call; to put down the phone; **when I started to talk he just rang off.**

ring up, *verb*

يتصل هاتفياً

to make a telephone call; **someone rang you up while you were out; she rang up** the police to say that her dog was missing.

Note: **I rang my father up** *or* **I rang up my father** *but only* **I rang him up.**

ripe [raɪp] *adjective*

يانع – ناضج

(fruit) which is ready to eat; **that apple isn't ripe—it will make you ill; are oranges ripe in the winter?**

ripe—riper—ripest

rise [raɪz] *verb*

يشرق (الشمس) – يصعد – يرتفع (السعر)

to go up; **the sun rises in the east; the road rises steeply; prices have risen this year.**

rises—rising—rose [rəʊz]—**has risen** ['rɪzn]

risk [rɪsk] **1.** *noun*

١ – مجازفة – مخاطرة – خطر

possible harm or bad result; **is there any risk of being caught by the police? they ran the risk of being caught** = they did it, even though they might have been caught; **there's not much risk of rain** = it is not likely to rain.

2. *verb*

٢ – يخاطر – يجازف

to do something which may possibly harm or have bad results; **I'll risk going out without a coat; he risked his life to save the little girl.**

risks—risking—risked—has risked

river ['rɪvə] *noun*

نهر

wide stream of water which goes across land and into the sea or a lake; **he's trying to swim across the river; don't fall into the river—it's very deep; London is on the River Thames.**

Note: with names it is usually **the River: the River Thames; the River Amazon; the River Nile**

two hundred and fifty-nine   **259**

road

road [rəʊd] *noun*

طريق

hard way used by cars/lorries, etc., to travel along; **in England, you drive on the left side of the road; be careful—the road's covered with ice; look both ways when you cross the road; where do you live?—15, London Road.**
Note: often used in names: **London Road, York Road,** *etc., and often written* **Rd: London Rd,** *etc.*

roast [rəʊst] *verb*

يَشْوي - يُحَمِّص

to cook meat in an oven; **the pork is roasting in the oven; I like roast chicken.**
roasts—roasting—roasted—has roasted
Note: as an adjective, use **roast**: **roast beef/roast pork,** *etc.*

rob [rɒb] *verb*

يسرق - يسلب

to steal from someone or a place; **he was robbed of all his money; three men robbed the bank.**
robs—robbing—robbed—has robbed

robber, *noun*

السارق - لصّ

person who steals from someone; **they were attacked by robbers.**

rock [rɒk] **1.** *noun*

١ - أ) صخر

(*a*) stone as part of the earth; **the house is built on hard rock; the road is cut out of the rock.**

ب) صخرة

(*b*) large piece of stone; **rocks fell down the mountain; the ship hit some rocks and sank.**
2. *verb*

٢ - يهزّ - يُهزْهِزُ

to move from side to side instead of standing still; **the waves are rocking the boat; he rocked backwards and forwards on his chair.**
rocks—rocking—rocked—has rocked

rocking chair, *noun*

الكرسي الهزّاز

chair fixed on curved pieces, so that it can rock backwards and forwards.

rode [rəʊd] *see* **ride**

ملاحظة : انظر إلى كلمة ride

roll [rəʊl] **1.** *noun*

١ - أ) لَفَّة

(*a*) something which has been turned over and over on itself; **a roll of paper; toilet roll** = roll of toilet paper; **sausage roll** = small pastry with sausage meat inside.

ب) أصابع في المعجنات المحشية بالجبن أو اللحم ... الخ)

(*b*) very small loaf of bread for one person, sometimes cut in half and used to make a sandwich; **cheese roll/ham roll** = roll with cheese or ham in it.
2. *verb*

٢ - يدحرج - يتدحرج

to make something go forward by turning it over and over; to go forward by turning over and over; **he rolled the ball across the table; the football rolled down the stairs; the penny rolled under the piano.**
rolls—rolling—rolled—has rolled

roll up, *verb*

يَلفّ

to turn something flat over and over until it is a tube; **he rolled up the carpet; she rolled the newspaper up.**
Note: **she rolled up the carpet** *or* **she rolled the carpet up** *but only* **she rolled it up**

roof

roof [ruːf] *noun*

سقف ـ سطح بيت أو سيارة

part of a building/a car, etc., which covers it and protects it; **the cat walked**

room

across the roof of the house; the roof needs mending—the rain's coming in; put your suitcases on the roof of the car.

room [ru:m] *noun*

أ) غرفة ـ حجرة (في بيت)

(*a*) part of a house, divided with walls; here's the dining room; our flat has five rooms, and a kitchen and bathroom.

ب) غرفة (في فندق)

(*b*) room in a hotel or bedroom; I want to book a room for two nights; here's your room—it's just opposite mine.

ت) مجال

(*c*) space for something; this table takes up a lot of room; there isn't enough room for three people; we can't have a piano in our house—there just isn't any room.
no plural (c): **some room; no room; too much room**

root [ru:t] *noun*

جذر

part of a plant which goes down into the ground; **root crops** = vegetables like carrots where you eat the roots but not the leaves.

rope [rəup] *noun*

حَبْل

very thick string made of several thin pieces twisted together; they pulled the car out of the river with a rope; he climbed down from the window on a rope.

rose [rəuz] **1.** *noun*

١ ـ وردة

common garden flower which grows on a bush; she was picking a bunch of roses; this red rose has a beautiful smell.
2. *verb see* **rise**

٢ ـ ملاحظة : انظر إلى كلمة rise

rotten ['rɒtn] *adjective*

نَتِن ـ فاسد

(food) which has become bad; all these apples are rotten; don't eat that

round

potato—it's rotten; a bag of rotten oranges.

rough [rʌf] *adjective*

أ) خشن

(*a*) not smooth; a rough road led to the farm; the sea was rough—we were all sick.

ب) استقرابي ـ غير نهائي

(*b*) not finished/not very correct; he made a rough drawing of the scene of the accident; I can only make a rough guess at what happened.

ت) شاق ـ عنيف ـ قاس

(*c*) violent; we had a rough game of football.
rough—rougher—roughest

roughly, *adverb*

أ) بقسوة ـ بشدة ـ بعنف

(*a*) in a violent way; they played roughly.

ب) تقريباً

(*b*) more or less; the cost will be roughly £25; I can't say exactly, but I can tell you roughly how big it is.

round [raund] **1.** *adjective*

١ ـ مستدير

shaped like a circle; a round carpet; we sat at a round table.
2. *adverb & preposition*

٢ ـ أ) بشكل مستدير

(*a*) in a circle; the wheels went round and round; we ran round the house; the wall goes right round the house.

ب) إلى الوراء (انظر إلى الوراء)

(*b*) backwards; he turned round; don't look round when you're driving.

ت) من يد إلى يد ـ من شخص إلى شخص ... الخ

(*c*) from one person to another; they passed round the plate of cakes; there aren't enough cakes to go round = not enough for one for each person.

ث) في عدة اتجاهات

(*d*) here and there/in various places; we walked round the shops.

two hundred and sixty-one

row

3. *noun*

٣ - أ) جولة

(a) regular trip; **the postman's round** = the streets he goes down every day; **a newspaper round** = the houses which one boy delivers newspapers to.

ب) دورة

(b) **round of drinks** = drinks bought for several people by one person; **I'll buy the next round; a round of toast** = piece or pieces of toast from one slice of bread.

ت) جولة (في مباراة)

(c) part of a competition; **if you answer all the questions, you will go on to the next round.**

roundabout, *noun*

أ) مستديرة (طريق مستديرة)

(a) place where several roads meet, and traffic has to move in a circle to avoid accidents; **turn right at the next roundabout.**

ب) دوارة الخيل

(b) heavy wheel which turns, and which children ride on; **I want a ride on the roundabout.**

row¹ [rəu] **1.** *noun*

١ - صفّ (من الأشياء أو الناس)

line of things/people, etc.; **there were rows of empty seats in the cinema; try and find a seat in the front row; stand in a row facing the camera.**

2. *verb*

٢ - يجذف

to make a boat go forward by using oars; **he's learning to row/he takes rowing lessons; we rowed the boat across the river.**

rows—rowing—rowed—has rowed

rowing boat, *noun*

مركب تجذيف

small boat for rowing; **let's hire a rowing boat and go on the river.**

262

rubber

row² [rau] *noun*

خلاف عنيف

loud noise/big argument; **I had a row with my boss; the engine is making an awful row; stop that row!—I'm trying to work.**

royal ['rɔɪəl] *adjective*

مَلَكي

referring to a king or queen; **when we were in Copenhagen we visited the royal gardens; the Royal Family** = the family of a king or queen.

rub [rʌb] *verb*

أ) يَحْتك - يَحفّ

(a) to move something backwards and forwards across the surface of something; **he rubbed the table with a cloth.**

ب) يفرك

(b) to move your hands backwards and forwards across something; **she rubbed her knee after she knocked it against the corner of the table; have you hurt your elbow?—come here, and let me rub it for you; he was rubbing his hands with excitement** = was rubbing them together.

rubs—rubbing—rubbed—has rubbed

rub out, *verb*

يمحو - يزيل

to take away marks made by a pencil; **he rubbed out his mistakes; this pencil won't rub out.**

Note: **he rubbed the word out** or **he rubbed out the word** but only **he rubbed it out**

rubber ['rʌbə] *noun*

أ) مطاط

(a) material which we can stretch, made from liquid which comes from a tropical tree; **cars have rubber tyres; they were blowing up a rubber boat; some boots are made of rubber.**

ب) ممحاة

(b) piece of soft material used to take

two hundred and sixty-two

rubbish

away pencil marks; **can you lend me your rubber, I've made a mistake.**
no plural for (a)

rubber band, *noun*

شريط لاصق

thin circle of rubber used to attach things together; **the cards were held together with a rubber band.**

rubbish ['rʌbɪʃ] *noun*

نفاية ـ نفايات (١

(a) things which are not needed and are thrown away; **put all that rubbish in the dustbin; there is so much rubbish that we will have to burn it.**

ب) كلام فارغ

(b) nonsense; **he's talking rubbish; I've never heard such rubbish; it's getting cold!—rubbish! it's hotter than yesterday.**
no plural

rude [ru:d] *adjective*

غليظ ـ غير مهذّب

not polite; **he was rude to his customers; you mustn't be rude to your teachers; she was very rude about my painting = she said she thought it was bad; he's the rudest man I know.**
rude—ruder—rudest

rug [rʌg] *noun*

بساط ـ سجادة

small carpet, often one on top of a large carpet; **he sat on the rug in front of the fire.**

rugby ['rʌgbɪ] *noun*

الركبي : نوع من لعبة كرة القدم

type of football played with a long ball which can be thrown as well as kicked; **he's in our rugby team; they both got hurt playing rugby; we've lost our last two rugby matches; we had a good game of rugby on Saturday; did you watch the rugby game on TV?**
no plural

run

ruin ['ru:ɪn] *verb*

يُخَرِّب ـ يُحْبط

to spoil something completely; **our holiday was ruined by the bad weather; he is ruining his chances of getting more money by being rude to the boss.**
ruins—ruining—ruined—has ruined

ruins, *plural noun*

خراب ـ دمار ـ بقايا ـ آثار

remains of buildings which have been damaged; **firemen searched the ruins to see if anyone was still alive; have you visited the castle ruins/the ruins of the castle?**

rule [ru:l] **1.** *noun*

١ ـ قاعدة ـ قانون

general way of behaving; statement of what you should or should not do in a game, etc.; **I make it a rule not to smoke before breakfast; you have to play the game according to the rules; the referee's job is to make sure that the players don't break the rules.**

عادةً

as a rule = in a general way/usually; **as a rule he gets to the office before 9 a.m.**
2. *verb*

٢ ـ يحكم (بلداً)

to control a country; **a republic is ruled by a president.**
rules—ruling—rules—has ruled

ruler ['ru:lə] *noun*

مسطرة

flat piece of wood/plastic/metal, etc., which you use to draw straight lines; **this line isn't straight—use a ruler next time.**

run [rʌn] **1.** *noun*

١ ـ أ) ركض

(a) going quickly on foot; **he went for a run before breakfast; I was tired out after that long run.**

ب) رحلة قصيرة بالسيارة

(b) short trip by car; **let's go for a run in your new car.**

two hundred and sixty-three   263

rung

2. *verb*

٢ - أ) يركض

(*a*) to go quickly on foot; he ran upstairs; don't run across the road; he's running in the 100 metres race.

ب) يستمرّ في العمل

(*b*) (*of buses/trains, etc.*) to be working; the trains aren't running today because of the fog; the bus is running late because of the traffic; this bus doesn't run on Sundays.

ت) يستمرّ في تشغيل (المحرك أو الآلة ...).

(*c*) (*of machines*) to work; he left his car engine running.

ث) يمتدّ (تمتدّ الطريق شمالاً وجنوباً .)

(*d*) to go; the main street runs north and south; the film runs for two hours.

ج) يدير - يقوم بادارة (متجر أو شركة)

(*e*) to direct a business; to use a car regularly; to organize a club, etc.; he runs a shoe shop; I want someone to run the sales department for me; he can't afford to run two cars; she runs the youth club; the army is running the country.

ح) يوصل بسيارة : (سأوصلك بسيارتي إلى المحطة)

(*f*) to drive; I'll run you to the station = I will take you there in my car.

runs—running—ran [ræn]—has run

run away, *verb*

يفرّ - يهرب

to go away fast; to escape; he's running away from the police; she threw a stone through the window and ran away; he ran away from school when he was 14.

run in, *verb*

يترفق بمحرك السيارة الجديدة

to make a new engine work gently until it is working well; I'm running in my new car.

run into, *verb*

يصطدم بـ

to go fast and hit something (usually in a vehicle); he ran into a tree; the bus ran into the lamppost.

runner, *noun*

راكض - مشترك بسباق الركض

person who runs; there are ten runners in the race.

run out of, *verb*

ينفذ - ينتهي

to have none left of something; we've run out of petrol; I must go to the shops—we're running out of jam.

run over, *verb*

يصدم - يَدْهَس

to knock someone down by hitting them with a vehicle; he was run over by a bus; he drove without looking and ran over a dog.

Note: he ran over a dog *or* he ran a dog over *but only* he ran it over

runway, *noun*

مدرجة (لهبوط الطيارة واقلاعها)

track on which planes land and take off at an airport.

rung [rʌŋ] *see* **ring**

ملاحظة : انظر إلى كلمة ring

rush [rʌʃ] **1.** *noun*

١ - إندفاع - عجلة بالغة

going fast; there was a rush for the door = everyone ran towards the door.

2. *verb*

٢ - يندفع - يدفع بعجلة أو بعنف

to go fast; he rushed into the room; she was rushed to hospital; why was everyone rushing to the door?

rushes—rushing—rushed—has rushed

rush hour, *noun*

فترة الضغط أو الازدحام

فترة يشتد فيها ازدحام الناس في الشوارع وسبل المواصلات

time of day when everyone is trying to travel to work or back home from work; you can't drive fast in the rush hour traffic; if we leave the office early we'll avoid the rush hour.

Ss

sack [sæk] **1.** *noun*

١ - أ) كيس

(*a*) large bag made of strong rough cloth; **we bought a sack of potatoes; I've ordered three sacks of coal.**

ب) الاستغناء عن الخدمة ـ الطرد من العمل

(*b*) being told to leave your job; **he got the sack/he was given the sack because he was always late for work.**
2. *verb*

٢ ـ يصرف من الخدمة

to tell someone to leave his job; **she was sacked because she was always late.**
sacks—sacking—sacked—has sacked

sad [sæd] *adjective*

حزين ـ كئيب ـ مُحْزِن

miserable/not happy; **she's sad because her little cat has died; it was such a sad film that we cried; reading poetry makes me sad.**
sad—sadder—saddest

safe [seɪf] **1.** *adjective*

١ ـ آمن ـ مأمون ـ مضمون ـ غير مؤذٍ ـ باعث على الشعور بالأمن

not in danger; not likely to hurt you or cause damage; **the town is safe from attack; you should keep medicines high up so that they are safe from children; I keep my money in a safe place; even if the school is on fire, all the children are safe; is this snake safe to touch? it isn't safe to touch the bomb; is it safe to go into the house now? don't play with the gas cooker—it isn't safe.**
safe—safer—safest

2. *noun*

٢ ـ خزنة ـ خزينة

strong box for keeping money/jewels, etc., in; **he puts his gold coins in the safe every night.**

safely, *adverb*

بأمان ـ بدون أذى ـ بسلامة

without danger; without being hurt; **although the plane was on fire, all the passengers got out safely; he stopped the car safely although the brakes weren't working.**

safety, *noun*

أمان ـ سلامة : (تدابير وقائية للسلامة على الطريق ـ حزام الأمان ـ دبّوس أفرنجي)

being safe; **road safety** = care taken by people on the roads to avoid accidents; **safety belt** = belt which you wear in a car or a plane to stop you being hurt if there is an accident; **safety pin** = pin whose point fits into a little cover when it is fastened, and so can't hurt you.
no plural

said [sed] *see* **say**

ملاحظة : انظر إلى كلمة say

sail [seɪl] **1.** *noun*

١ ـ أ) شراع السفينة

(*a*) large piece of cloth which makes a boat go forward when it is blown by the wind; **the wind blew so hard it tore our sails; look at those little boats with their blue sails.**

ب) رحلة في مركب شراعي

(*b*) short trip on a boat; **let's go for a sail across the harbour.**
2. *verb*

٢ ـ يسافر بمركب شراعي

to travel on water; to control a sailing

two hundred and sixty-five 265

sake

boat; hurry up—the ferry sails at 11.30; she was the first woman to sail alone around the world; the children were sailing their little boats in the park; we go sailing every weekend.

sails—sailing—sailed—has sailed

sailing boat, noun

مركب شراعي

boat which uses sails rather than a motor.

sailor, noun

بَحَّار ـ ملّاح

person who sails; the sailors and the passengers stood on the deck; he wants to be a sailor, so he's going to join the navy; I'm a bad sailor = I feel sick when I travel on a boat.

sake [seɪk] noun

أ) من أجل

(a) **for the sake of** = to help; so as to get; for the sake of his health he stopped smoking cigarettes; is it worth working so hard just for the sake of £10 a week?

ب) تكريماً لـ ـ لكي تكون في حسن ظنّ (أحدِ ما)

(b) **for someone's sake** = to please someone; write her a letter for my sake; you ought to be nicer to your sister for your mother's sake.

salad ['sæləd] noun

سلطة

dish of cold vegetables, often raw; cold meat or fish served with cold vegetables; I'll have a chicken salad; we had ham and tomato salad; **fruit salad** = various fresh fruit cut up and mixed together.

no plural

salary ['sælərɪ] noun

راتب ـ مرتَّب

money given to a worker every month; he has a very good salary; he has applied for a job with a salary of £10,000 a year.

plural **salaries**

same

sale [seɪl] noun

أ) بيع

(a) giving something to someone for money; this house is for sale; some of these towels are on sale in the market.

ب) بيع بأسعار مخفّضة

(b) selling things at cheap prices; our store is having a sale of china this week; I bought this hat for 50p in a sale.

ت) مبيعات

(c) **sales** = money which a business receives; our sales have gone up this year.

salesman, noun

البائع

person who sells; ask the salesman to show you the new car.

plural **salesmen**

salt [sɒlt] noun

مَلْح

white powder used to make food, especially meat, fish and vegetables, taste better; did you put any salt in this soup? put some more salt on your fish; fish which live in the sea can only live in salt water.

no plural: some salt; a spoonful of salt

salty, adjective

مالح

tasting of salt; sea water is very salty; this soup is very salty—I think you've put too much salt in it.

salty—saltier—saltiest

same [seɪm] adjective & pronoun

نفسه ـ عينه : (ألم تسأم بالقيام بنفس العمل يوماً بعد يوم ؟)

looking/tasting/sounding, etc., exactly alike; showing that two things are of one kind; you get very bored having to do the same work day after day; she was wearing the same dress as she wore last year; they all live in the same street; everyone else was looking tired—but he stayed the same; these two drinks taste the same;

sand

coffee looks the same as tea, but has quite a different taste.

all the same, *adverb*

بالرغم من ذلك ـ ومع ذلك

in spite of this; **I don't like parties, but I shall come to yours all the same.**

sand [sænd] *noun*

رَمْل ـ تربة رمليّة

very small pieces of stone which you find on a beach or in the desert; **the children were playing in the sand; they raced across the sand on their motor-bikes.**

no plural

sandy, *adjective*

رملي : (شاطىء رملي)

covered with sand; **a sandy beach.**

sandal ['sændl] *noun*

صَنْدَلَ ـ خُفّ ـ حذاء خفيف

light shoe with holes in the top, which you wear in the summer; **he's bought a new pair of sandals for his holiday; she was wearing blue sandals.**

sandwich ['sændwɪtʃ] *noun*

سندويتش ـ شطيرة

two slices of bread with meat, etc., in between; **a ham sandwich; two cheese sandwiches; what sort of sandwiches do you want me to make for the picnic? we had a sandwich and some beer in the pub.**

plural **sandwiches**

sang [sæŋ] *see* **sing**

ملاحظة : انظر إلى كلمة sing

sank [sæŋk] *see* **sink**

ملاحظة : انظر إلى كلمة sink

sat [sæt] *see* **sit**

ملاحظة : انظر إلى كلمة sit

saucer

satisfy ['sætɪsfaɪ] *verb*

يرضي ـ يقنع ـ يشبع

to make someone pleased; **is he satisfied with his new car? they weren't satisfied with the service in the restaurant.**

satisfies—satisfying—satisfied—has satisfied

satisfaction [sætɪs'fækʃn] *noun*

ارضاء ـ ارتياح ـ إشباع

being pleased; **to his great satisfaction, his daughter married a very rich man.**

satisfactory, *adjective*

مرض

quite good; good enough; **his marks in maths are satisfactory, but in English they are bad.**

Saturday ['sætədɪ] *noun*

السبت ـ يوم السبت

sixth day of the week/day between Friday and Sunday; **we go shopping on Saturdays; I saw him at a party last Saturday; today is Saturday, September 20th; we'll go to the cinema next Saturday.**

sauce [sɔːs] *noun*

صلصة ـ مرق التوابل

liquid which you eat with food or pour over it; **we eat apple sauce with pork; do you want any chocolate sauce on your ice cream? he poured a whole bottle of tomato sauce on his chips.**

saucepan, *noun*

الكَفْت ـ قِدْر صغير ذات مقبض

metal pan with high sides and a long handle in which you cook things on a stove; **put the potatoes in the saucepan; the soup has stuck to the bottom of the saucepan.**

saucer ['sɔːsə] *noun*

صحن الفنجان (الصُحَيْفَة)

small plate which you stand a cup on; **he poured so much tea into his cup that it all ran into the saucer; get out another cup and saucer—your uncle is coming to tea.**

two hundred and sixty-seven 267

sausage

sausage ['sɒsɪdʒ] *noun*

سجق ــ نقانق

food made of chopped meat in a long tube which you eat; **we had sausages and fried eggs for breakfast; when you go to the butcher's, can you buy me a pound of pork sausages?**

save [seɪv] *verb*

ا) يُنْقِذ (أحداً) من

(*a*) to stop someone from being hurt or killed; to stop something from being damaged; **the policeman saved the little boy from being burnt in the fire; how many people were saved when the ship sank? he saved my life** = he stopped me being killed.

ب) يَقْتصد (المال)

(*b*) to keep (money, etc.) so that you can use it later; **I'm saving to buy a car; they save all the old pieces of bread to give to the birds; if you save £1 each week, you'll have £52 in a year's time.**

ت) يُوَفِّر (المال) : (إذا ذهبت إلى العمل سيراً على الأقدام ، تكون قد وفرت ٣ جنيهات بالأسبوع)

(*c*) not to waste (time, money, etc.); **if you walk to work you will save £3 a week on bus fares; he delivered the letter himself so as to save buying a stamp; if you travel by air you'll save a lot of time; if you have your car mended now it will save you a lot of trouble later.**

saves—saving—saved—has saved

save up, *verb*

يقتصد ــ يضع الأموال جانباً تحسباً للمستقبل

to keep money so that you can use it later; **I'm saving up to buy a new car.**

savings, *plural noun*

المال المُوَفَّر

money which you have saved; **he put all his savings in the bank; she spent all her savings on a holiday in Australia.**

Note: **I've saved my money up** *or* **I've saved up my money** *but only* **I've saved it up**

scales

saw¹ [sɔː] **1.** *noun*

۱ ــ منشار

tool with a long metal blade with teeth along its edge, used for cutting wood, etc.; **he cut his hand on the saw; this saw doesn't cut well—it needs to be sharpened; chain saw** = saw made of a chain with teeth in it, which turns very fast when driven by a motor.

2. *verb*

۲ ــ ينشر ــ يقص بالمنشار

to cut with a saw; **he was sawing wood; they sawed the tree into small pieces; he said he was going to saw the piece of wood in half.**

saws—sawing—sawed—has sawn [sɔːn]

saw² *see* **see**

ملاحظة : انظر إلى كلمة see

say [seɪ] *verb*

ا) يقول

(*a*) to speak words; **he said he wanted to come with us; don't forget to say 'thank you'; I was just saying that we never hear from Uncle John, when he phoned; can you translate what he said? the TV says it will be fine tomorrow.**

ب) تتضمن كلاماً ــ يشير إلى

(*b*) to put in writing; **their letter says that they will arrive on Monday; the timetable says that there are no trains on Sundays.**

يقترح ــ مثلاً ــ في سبيل المثل

(*c*) to suggest; **choose a number—let's say sixteen; let's meet next week—shall we say Thursday?**

says [sez]—saying—said [sed]—has said

scales [skeɪlz] *plural noun*

ميزان

machine for weighing; **he weighed the sugar on the kitchen scales; the bathroom scales must be wrong—I'm heavier than I was yesterday.**

scarce

scarce [skeəs] *adjective*

نادر ـ قليل

not common; of which there is not very much; **fresh vegetables are getting scarce; when meat is scarce, you should try to eat fish; to make yourself scarce** = to run away and hide; **when father is annoyed, we all make ourselves scarce.**

scarce—scarcer—scarcest

scarcely, *adverb*

نادراً ـ بصعوبة ـ بشق النفس

hardly/almost not; **I scarcely know her; she could scarcely speak.**

scarf [skɑːf] *noun*

منديل ـ وشاح ـ لفاع

long piece of cloth which you wear round your neck to keep yourself warm; square piece of cloth which a woman can wear over her hair; **the boys were wearing their school scarves; put a scarf over your hair—it's starting to rain.**

plural **scarves** [skɑːvz]

scene [siːn] *noun*

مسرح الأحداث ـ المكان الذي حصل فيه حدث ما

place where something happens; **five minutes after the accident, an ambulance arrived on the scene; the police were at the scene of the crime.**

scent [sent] *noun*

أ) عطر ـ عبير ـ رائحة زكية

(a) pleasant smell; **the scent of roses; these flowers have no scent.**

ب) عطر ـ طيب

(b) liquid with a pleasant smell which you put on your body; **she was wearing a new scent; he gave her a bottle of scent.**

school [skuːl] *noun*

مدرسة

place where people (usually children) are taught; **he's four, so he'll be going to school this year; do you like school? what did you do at school today? she ran**

score

away from school; he left school and joined the navy; which school do you go to? there are two schools near our house.

المدرسة الابتدائية

primary school = school for small children.

المدرسة الثانويّة

secondary school = school for children after the age of eleven or twelve.

schoolboy, schoolgirl, schoolchildren, *nouns*

تلميذ مدرسة ـ تلميذة مدرسة ـ تلاميذ مدرسة

boy or girl or children who go to school.

science ['saɪəns] *noun*

علم ـ معرفة

study which is based on looking at and noting facts, especially facts which are arranged into a system; **he's no good at languages, but very good at science.**

scientific [saɪən'tɪfɪk] *adjective*

علمي

referring to science; **he carried out scientific experiments.**

scientist ['saɪəntɪst] *noun*

العالِم

person who studies science.

scissors ['sɪzəz] *plural noun*

مقص

thing for cutting, made of two blades and two handles; **the hairdresser was cutting my hair with his scissors; I must buy another pair of scissors; someone has borrowed my scissors and hasn't given them back.**

Note: you can say **a pair of scissors** *if you want to show that there is only one tool*

score [skɔː] **1.** *noun*

١ ـ أ) علامة (عدد النقاط التي يحوز عليها أحد الفرقاء)

(a) number of points made in a game; **the football match ended with a score of 2-0; what's the score in the match so far?**

two hundred and sixty-nine   **269**

Scotland

ب) عدد كبير من
(b) scores of = many; scores of people caught flu; I've seen that film scores of times.
2. verb

٢ ـ يسجل نقاط في مباراة
to make a point in a game; he scored three goals; she scored twenty five!
scores—scoring—scored—has scored

Scotland ['skɒtlənd] *noun*
اسكتلندا (منطقة من المملكة المتحدة)
country which is part of Great Britain, and is north of England; he went to live in Scotland; are you going to Scotland for your holiday?

Scot, *noun*
اسكتلندي (شخص)
person who lives in or comes from Scotland; he's a Scot; the Scots work hard.

Scotch, *adjective*
اسكتلندي (شيء) : البيض الاسكتلندي
referring to Scotland; Scotch eggs = boiled eggs covered with meat and fried.

Scottish, *adjective*
اسكتلندي (شيء) : الجبال الاسكتلندية
referring to Scotland; the Scottish mountains.

Note: in Scotland, Scottish is preferred instead of Scotch, and Scotch is never used to refer to people

scrape [skreɪp] *verb*
يَكْشِط ـ يَحُكّ
to move something sharp across an area taking off the surface; to remove the surface of something; he was scraping the paint off the door with a knife; she fell off her bike and scraped her knee.
scrapes—scraping—scraped—has scraped

scratch [skrætʃ] *verb*
يحكّ بظفره ـ يحفر ـ يخدش
to move a sharp point across a surface; they scratched the top of the table as they were carrying it upstairs; be careful not to scratch yourself on that rose tree; he scratched his name on the wall of the school.

ابتداءاً من لا شيء
from scratch = from the beginning; we'll have to start again from scratch.
scratches—scratching—scratched—has scratched

scream [skri:m] **1.** *noun*
١ ـ صرخة ـ صياح
loud sharp cry; you could hear the screams of the people in the burning building.
2. verb

٢ ـ يصرخ ـ يصيح
to make a loud sharp cry; she screamed when a man suddenly opened the door; all the children screamed with laughter.
screams—screaming—screamed—has screamed

screw [skru:] **1.** *noun*
١ ـ لَوْلَب
metal nail with a twisting line round it, so that when you push and turn it, it goes into something solid; he took out the screws and the car door fell off; the parts of the chair are held together with two screws.
2. verb

١ ـ ا) يُثَبَّت باللولب
(a) to attach with a screw; the table is screwed down to the deck of the ship; he screwed the lid on to the box.
ب) يثبت (شيئاً) لولبياً ـ يغلف (علبة) بالبرم
(b) to attach something by twisting it; don't forget to screw the lid back on to the pot of jam.
screws—screwing—screwed—has screwed

screwdriver, *noun*
مفك ـ مفك البراغي
tool with a long handle and a small blade, used for putting screws in.

sea

sea [siː] *noun*

بَحْر

salt water which covers a large part of the earth; I like swimming in the sea better than in a river; the sea's rough—I hope I won't be sick; to get to Germany you have to cross the North Sea; send your furniture to Australia by sea—it would be much more expensive by air.
Note: in names Sea is written with a capital letter. Sea is usually used with the: the sea's too cold; the North Sea, etc.

seaman, *noun*

بحار ـ ملّاح

man who works on a ship.
plural **seamen**

seasick, *adjective*

مصاب بدوار البحر

ill because of the movement of a ship; she didn't enjoy the trip because she was seasick all the time; I'll stay on deck because I'm feeling seasick.

seaside, *noun*

شاطىء البحر

land on the edge of the sea; we go to the seaside for our holidays; I like a seaside holiday; this seaside town is empty in the winter.

seaweed, *noun*

العشب البحري

plant which grows in the sea; the beach is covered with seaweed.
no plural: some seaweed; a piece of seaweed

search [sɜːtʃ] 1. *noun*

١ ـ يستكشف ـ يفحص ـ يفتش

trying to find something; we went to every shop in search of a German book, but couldn't find it; the police sent out search parties to look for people lost in the snow; we all joined in the search for his wallet = we all tried to find it.
2. *verb*

٢ ـ يبحث ـ يفتش

to look for something; we've searched everywhere but can't find mother's watch; they're searching the mountains for people lost in the snow; the customs man searched my suitcase.
searches—searching—searched—has searched

second

season [ˈsiːzən] *noun*

أ) فصل (الربيع ـ الصيف ـ الخريف أو الشتاء)

(*a*) one of four parts of a year; spring, summer, autumn and winter are the four seasons.

ب) موسم ـ أوان

(*b*) any part of the year when something usually happens; the cricket season lasts from April to September; the town is very crowded during the holiday season; when are pears in season? apples are out of season just now.

season ticket, *noun*

بطاقة موسمية (تسمح لحاملها التنقل بالقطار أو الحافلة خلال بضعة أشهر أو سنة كاملة

railway or bus ticket which you can use for a whole year or several months.

seat [siːt] *noun*

مقعد

something which you sit on; sit in the front seat of the car; I want two seats in the front row; I couldn't find a seat on the bus, so I had to stand; this chair isn't very comfortable—it has a wooden seat; why is your bicycle seat so narrow? take a seat, please, the doctor will see you in a few minutes.

seat belt, *noun*

حزام المقعد ـ حزام التثبيت (في سيارة أو طائرة)

belt which you wear in a car or plane to stop you being hurt if there is an accident.

second [ˈsekənd] 1. *noun*

١ ـ أ) ثانية : (٦٠/١ من الدقيقة)

(*a*) one of the sixty parts of a minute; the bomb will go off in ten seconds.

two hundred and seventy-one **271**

secret

(b) very short time; **I saw him a second ago; wait for me—I'll only take a second to get ready.**

ب) لحظة

ت) ثان - ثانية - (المرتبة الثانية)

(c) something/someone that comes after the first thing or person; **the German runner was first, the British runner was second; today is the second of January/January the second (January 2nd); Charles the Second (Charles II) was king at the time of the fire of London.**

Note: in dates **second** *is usually written* **2nd: April 2nd, 1973; November 2nd, 1980;** *with names of kings and queens* **second** *is usually written* **II: Queen Elizabeth II**

2. 2nd *adjective*

ثان - ثانية : (فبراير هو الشهر الثاني من السنة)

coming after the first; **February is the second month in the year; it's Mary's second birthday next week; B is the second letter in the alphabet; men's clothes are on the second floor; this is the second tallest building in the world** = there is one building which is taller; **she's the second most intelligent girl in the school; that's the second time the telephone has rung while I'm in the bath.**

secondary, *adjective*

ثانوي - (المدرسة الثانوية)

which is not the most important; which comes second; **secondary school** = school for children after the age of eleven or twelve.

second class, *noun*

الدرجة الثانية (في قطار أو طائرة)

ordinary seats in a train; **a second class ticket to Edinburgh; she travels second class because it is cheaper.**

second hand, *noun*

عقرب الثواني في الساعة

long hand on a watch which turns round fast and shows the seconds.

see

secondhand, *adjective & adverb*

مستعمل (سيارة مستعملة)

not new/which someone else has owned before; **he's just bought a secondhand car; I bought this car secondhand.**

secret ['siːkrət] *noun & adjective*

سِرّ

something which is hidden/which is not known; **I won't tell you what your birthday present will be—it's a secret; he hid his money in a secret place; can you keep a secret?** = can you not tell anyone if I tell you a secret?

secretary ['sekrətərɪ] *noun*

سكرتير (أمين السر)

person who writes letters/answers the telephone, etc., for someone else; **my secretary will tell you when you can come to see me.**
plural **secretaries**

see [siː] *verb*

ا) يرى - يبصر

(a) to use your eyes to notice things; **can you see that house over there? cats can see in the dark; I can see the bus coming; we saw the car hit the tree.**

ب) يشاهد (فيلماً او مباراة) يتابع (برنامجاً)

(b) to watch a film, etc.; **have you seen the film at the cinema? I saw the football match on TV.**

ت) يقابل

(c) to go with someone; **the policeman saw the old lady across the road; my secretary will see you to the door; let me see you home; they saw me off at the airport** = they went with me to say goodbye.

ث) يفهم - يدرك

(d) to understand; **I don't see why you need so much money; don't you see that we have to be at the station by ten o'clock? I see—you want to borrow a lot of money.**

seed

ج) يتأكد بنفسه من

(e) to make sure that something happens; to check; **can you see that the children are in bed by nine o'clock?** would you see if the post has arrived?

ح) يلتقي - يزور

(f) to meet/to visit; **I see him often, because he lives quite close to me; see you on Thursday! see you again soon! I saw him last Christmas; you should see a doctor about your cough.**

sees—seeing—saw [sɔː]**—has seen**

see through, *verb*

يدرك تماماً حقيقة امرءٍ

to understand everything about someone/something; **I saw through his plan.**

see to, *verb*

يتحقق - يقوم بعمل حسب اللزوم

to arrange to deal with/to make sure that something happens; **can you see to it that the children are in bed by nine o'clock? will you see to the Christmas cards?** = will you deal with them?

seed [siːd] *noun*

بزرة - حبَّة

part of a plant which you put in the ground so that it will grow into a new plant; **I'll sow some carrot seeds; these seeds are so small that you can hardly see them.**

seem [siːm] *verb*

يبدو

to appear/to look as if; **he seems to like his new job; they seem to be having a good time; I seem to have lost my wallet; it seems that they got lost in the snow; they seem very pleasant; it seems strange that no one answered your letter; it seems to me that we ought to buy a new car** = I think that we ought to buy one.

seems—seeming—seemed—has seemed

seldom ['seldəm] *adverb*

نادراً

not often; rarely; **I seldom go to the**

send

cinema; we very seldom go out on Saturdays; he's seldom at home when you phone him.

*Note: **seldom** is usually placed in front of the verb*

self- [self] *prefix referring to yourself*

نفسي - نفسه - نفسها

self-defence, *noun*

الدفاع عن النفس

defending yourself.

selfish, *adjective*

أناني - محبٌّ لنفسه

doing things only for yourself; keeping things for yourself; **don't be selfish—let me have one of your chocolates.**

self-service, *noun & adjective*

الخدمة النفسيّة : (خدمة المرء نفسه بنفسه في المطعم اي أنه يختار ما يشاء من الطعام ويضعها في طبقه او على طاولته)

shop, etc., where you take things yourself and pay for them as you go out; **self-service restaurant** = restaurant where you take the food to the table yourself; **self-service petrol station** = one where you put the petrol into the car yourself.

sell [sel] *verb*

يبيع

to give something to someone for money; **I sold my bike to my brother; we sold our car for £500; they sold him their house; they sell vegetables in that shop, but you can't buy meat there.**

sells—selling—sold [səʊld]**—has sold**

sell out, *verb*

بيع كامل المخزون (من سلعة ما)

to sell all of something; **we've sold out of potatoes** = we have no potatoes left.

send [send] *verb*

يُرسل

to make something/someone go from one place to another; **he sent me to the**

sensation

butcher's to buy some meat; we send 100 cards to our friends every Christmas; I'll send you a card when I get home.
sends—sending—sent—has sent

send away for, *verb* (*also* **send off for**)

يرسل بالبريد طالباً شيئاً ما

to write to ask someone to send you something, usually when you have seen an advertisement; **I sent away for a watch which I saw advertised in the paper.**

send back, *verb*

يعيد شيئاً بالبريد

to return something; **if you don't like your present, send it back and I'll buy you something different.**

Note: **send the present back** *or* **send back the present** *but only* **send it back**

send for, *verb*

يستدعي

to ask someone to come; **we had to send for the doctor; send for the police!**

send off, *verb*

يرسل بالبريد

to post; **I sent the letter off without a stamp.**

Note: **send the letter off** *or* **send off the letter** *but only* **send it off**

send off for *see* **send away for**

send up, *verb*

يطلق في الهواء

to make something go up; **they sent up a balloon; the cold weather sent up the price of vegetables.**

sensation [sen'seɪʃn] *noun*

أ) شعور - إحساس

(*a*) feeling; **I had an odd sensation as if I was floating in the air.**

ب) حدث مثير - إهتياج

(*b*) great excitement; **the new film made a sensation.**

separate

sense [sens] *noun*

أ) حاسة (من الحواس الخمس)

(*a*) one of the five ways in which you notice something (seeing, hearing, touching, smelling and tasting); **he lost his sense of smell.**

ب) الحس (روح النكته)

(*b*) way of feeling; **he has no sense of humour** = he doesn't often think things are funny.

ت) معنى

(*c*) meaning; **this letter doesn't make sense** = it doesn't mean anything.

ث) شيء معقول - فهم

(*d*) reasonable behaviour; **it makes sense to save money** = it's sensible.

sensible ['sensɪbl] *adjective*

مُدرِك - واعٍ - عاقل

reasonable/not stupid or mad; **he made a very sensible suggestion.**

sensitive ['sensɪtɪv] *adjective*

أ) حساس الشعور

(*a*) (person) who is easily annoyed; **don't mention her hair—she's very sensitive about it.**

ب) مصاب بحساسية

(*b*) which hurts easily; **his arm is still sensitive where he hurt it.**

sent [sent] *see* **send**

ملاحظة : انظر الى كلمة send

sentence ['sentəns] *noun*

حُكم قضائي (بعقوبة)

words put together to make a complete statement, usually ending in a full stop; **the second sentence in his letter doesn't mean anything.**

separate ['seprət] **1.** *adjective*

١ - منفصل - مفترق - مختلف

not together; **keep the water and the oil separate; I am sending you the book in a separate parcel; can we have two separate bills, please?**

274 *two hundred and seventy-four*

September

2. *verb* ['sepəreɪt]

٢ - يَفْصِل - يُفَرِّق - يفرز

to make things or people be separate; you must separate the big stones from the sand; the family got separated in the crowd; let's separate, and meet again in thirty minutes.

separates—separating— separated—has separated

separately, *adverb*

كلٌ على حدى

not together; we want to pay for the two meals separately.

September [sep'tembə] *noun*

أيلول (شهر سبتمبر)

ninth month of the year; **my birthday is in September; today is September 21st; we're going on holiday next September.**
Note: **September 21st:** *say* 'the twenty-first of September' *or* 'September the twenty-first'

series ['sɪəriːz] *noun*

سلسلة

group of things which come one after the other; **there has been a series of accidents at this corner; she wrote a series of letters to the police.**

serious ['sɪəriəs] *adjective*

ا) وقور - رزين - جدي

(*a*) not funny; **I'm being serious** = I am not joking.

ب) خطير - سيىء

(*b*) very important/very bad; **he's had a serious illness; there was a serious accident on the motorway.**

seriously, *adverb*

جدياً - بطريقة خطيرة

in a serious way; **he is seriously thinking of going to work in Canada; she is seriously ill.**

serve [sɜːv] *verb*

ا) يخدم على المائدة

(*a*) to give people food at table; **let me**

serve

serve the potatoes; have you served the children? serve yourself if you want some more meat.

ب) يقضي وقتاً في خدمة ...

(*b*) to work for; **he served in the Police Force for twenty years.**

ت) يوفّر الخدمات لـ

(*c*) to help a customer in a shop, etc.; to provide a service; **are you being served? the bus serves the villages in the hills.**

ث) يستهل ضرب الكرة (في لعبة التنس)

(*d*) (*in games like tennis*) to start the game by hitting the ball.

serves—serving—served—has served

servant, *noun*

خادم

person who is paid to work for a family.

service, *noun*

ا) خدمة

(*a*) working for someone/helping someone in a shop or restaurant; **did he enjoy his service in the Police Force? service charge** = money which you pay for service in a restaurant; **the service is not included in the bill** = the bill does not include any money for service; **the car has just had its 10,000 kilometre service** = it has been checked by the garage after 10,000 kilometres.

ب) مصلحة (الصحة) - دائرة رسميّة - القوات المسلحة

(*b*) group of people working together; **the health service** = doctors, nurses, hospitals, etc., all taken together; **the services** = the army, the navy and the air force.

ت) خدمات - شبكة خدمات

(*c*) providing things which people need; **the bus service is very bad; the main services** = water, gas and electricity.

ث) القدّاس - صلاة عامة

(*d*) regular religious ceremony; **I'm going to the nine o'clock service on Sunday.**

set

set [set] 1. *noun*

أ) «طقم» ـ (مجموعة من اواني للشاي او القهوة) ـ مجموعة من الادوات المختلفة والمتكاملة

(a) group of things which are used together; **a set of tools; a tea set** = cups, saucers, plates, etc.

ب) آلة ـ جهاز (تلفزيون او راديو)

(b) machine; **a TV set**.

2. *verb*

٢ ـ أ) يُرتّب (المائدة)

(a) to put in a special place; **he set the table** = he put the knives and forks, plates, cups, etc., on the table.

ب) يضبط (الساعة)

(b) to arrange; **I've set my watch to the correct time; the bomb was set to go off at ten o'clock.**

ت) يحدّد ـ يقرّر

(c) to give work to someone; **the teacher set us our maths homework; this book has been set for the exam** = we have to study it for the exam.

ث) يُضْرِم (النار) في

(d) to make something happen; **the house was set on fire; the prisoner was set free.**

ج) يغرب (تغرب الشمس)

(e) to go down; **the sun sets in the west.**

ح) يُلَحِّن

(f) to write music to go with words; **the poem was set to music.**

sets—setting—set—has set

set about, *verb*

يبدأ ـ يباشر بـ

to start to do something; **he set about building a boat; I haven't started yet because I don't know how to set about it.**

set back, *verb*

أ) يعوق ـ يؤخّر

(a) to make late; **the bad weather has set the crops back by three weeks.**

ب) يقع وراء ـ يكون منصوباً وراء

(b) to place back; **the house is set back from the road** = is not built near the road.

276

seven

set down, *verb*

يُنزل (الركاب) من

to let passengers get off; **the bus set down several passengers at the post office.**

set off, *verb*

يبدأ بالرحيل ـ ينطلق

to begin a trip; **we're setting off for Italy tomorrow; he set off on a long walk over the mountains.**

set out, *verb*

يبدأ رحلة

to begin a trip; **they set out into the snow; we're setting out early tomorrow.**

set to, *verb*

يبدأ بالعمل بنشاط

to start to work hard; **he set to, and soon built a boat.**

seven ['sevn] number 7

سبعة (الرقم ٧)

there are seven bottles of milk in the fridge; she's seven (years old); the train leaves at seven (o'clock).

seventeen, number 17

سبعة عشر ـ سبع عشرة (الرقم ١٧)

she's seventeen (years old); the train leaves at seventeen sixteen (17.16).

seventeenth 17th, *adjective & noun*

السابع عشر

today is the seventeenth of September/ September the seventeenth (September 17th); the seventeenth letter of the alphabet; it's my seventeenth birthday next week.

seventh, 7th, *adjective & noun*

السابع ـ سابع

the seventh of June/June the seventh (June 7th); a seventh of the bottle; Charles the Seventh (Charles VII); it's his seventh birthday on Wednesday.

Note: in dates **seventh** *is usually written* **7th: August 7th, 1980; May 7th, 1965;** *with names of kings and queens* **seventh** *is usually written* **VII; King Henry VII**

two hundred and seventy-six

several

seventieth, 70th, *adjective & noun*

السبعين

the seventieth film which I have seen this year; tomorrow is grandfather's seventieth birthday.

seventy, number 70

سبعين (الرقم ٧٠)

he's seventy (years old); she's in her seventies = she is between 70 and 79 years old.

Note: **seventy-one (71), seventy-two (72),** etc., but **seventy-first (71st), seventy-second (72nd),** etc.

several ['sevrəl] *adjective & pronoun*

بضعة ـ عدة ـ مختلف

more than a few, but not very many; I've met him several times; several of us are going to the film; several houses were damaged in the storm.

sew [səʊ] *verb*

يخيّط ـ يمارس الخياطة

to attach or make using a needle and a thread; can you sew this button on my coat? she's sewing some curtains.
sews—sewing—sewed—has sewn

sewing machine, *noun*

آلة خياطة ـ ماكينة خياطة

small machine which is used in the house to sew clothes, etc.

sex [seks] *noun*

الجنس (ذكر او انثى)

one of two groups (male and female) into which animals and plants can be divided; please write on the form your name, age, and sex.
plural **sexes**

shade [ʃeɪd] *noun*

١) ظلّ ـ ظلّة ـ فَيء ـ عتمة ـ ظلام

(a) dark place which is not in the light of the sun; we'll sit in the shade of the apple tree; the sun's too hot—let's sit in the shade.

shall

ب) فارق دقيق (في اللون)

(b) type of colour; another shade of blue; a darker shade of red.

shadow ['ʃædəʊ] *noun*

ظلّ ـ خيال

shade made by something which is in the light; I can see the shadow of a man on the pavement; what a strange shadow the tree makes!

shake [ʃeɪk] **1.** *noun*

١ ـ أ) اهتزاز ـ ارتعاش ـ مصافحة

(a) action of moving quickly up and down or from side to side; give your watch a good shake to start it.

ب) مشروب مؤلف من الحليب المخفوق والممزوج ببعض الفاكهة او الحلوى : (المخفوق اللبني)

(b) drink made by mixing milk and sweet stuff; a milk shake; can I have a chocolate milk shake?
2. *verb*

٢ ـ يهزّ ـ يهتزّ ـ يخض ـ يخفق ـ يرتعش ـ يصافح

to move quickly from side to side or up and down; he shook his watch to see if it would go; the buildings shook in the storm; don't shake the box—you'll break the glasses; she shook her head = she moved her head from side to side to mean 'no'; he shook hands with me = he greeted me by shaking my right hand with his.
shakes—shaking—shook [ʃʊk]—has shaken

shall [ʃæl] *verb used with other verbs*

أ) صيغة المستقبل

(a) to make the future; we shall leave for Italy on Saturday; I shan't say anything; we shan't be home until after 9 o'clock.

ب) تستعمل كمقدمة لسؤال

(b) to show a suggestion; shall I shut the door? shall we wait? shall we go to the cinema tonight?

two hundred and seventy-seven

shallow

Negative: **shan't** [ʃɑːnt]
Past: **should, should not,** *usually* **shouldn't**
Note: **shall** *is mainly used with* **I** *and* **we**

shallow [ˈʃæləʊ] *adjective*

ضحل ـ قليل العمق

not deep; the water was so shallow that the boat touched the bottom; if you can't swim, stay in the shallow end of the swimming pool.

shallow—shallower—shallowest

shame [ʃeɪm] *noun*

١) خجل ـ خزي ـ عار

(a) feeling very sorry about something you have done; he was full of shame for what he had done.

ب) اسف : (ياللاسف انك لم تأت الى الحفلة)

(b) (*showing that you are sorry that something has happened*) what a shame you can't come to the party! = what a pity! it's a shame that it rained when we went on the picnic = it's a pity.

shan't [ʃɑːnt] *see* **shall**

ملاحظة : انظر الى كلمة shall.

shape [ʃeɪp] *noun*

شكل ـ هيئة ـ مظهر

form/how something looks; she's got a ring in the shape of a letter A; my pullover's beginning to lose its shape = beginning to stretch.

shaped, *adjective*

ذو شكل محدّد

with a particular shape; her hat is shaped like a beehive.

shapeless, *adjective*

عديم الشكل ـ مشوه

with no particular shape; she was wearing a shapeless dress.

sharp

share [ʃeə] 1. *noun*

١ ـ ١) حصّة ـ نصيب

(a) part of a whole which belongs to someone; don't eat my share of the cake; has he done his share of the work?

ب) سهم مالي

(b) small part of a company; he bought 300 shares in Marks and Spencers.
2. *verb*

٢ ـ ١) يوزّع الحصص على

(a) to divide something between several people; we have to share the cake between seven people; he doesn't want to share his sweets.

ب) يشارك ـ يشترك في ـ يشاطر ـ يتقاسم

(b) to use something which someone else also uses; we share a bathroom with the flat next door; he doesn't want to share his toys with the other children; we only have one room empty in the hotel—do you mind sharing it?

shares—sharing—shared—has shared

sharp [ʃɑːp] *adjective*

١) حاد ـ قاطع ـ لاذع

(a) which cuts easily; be careful with that knife—it's very sharp; I cut my foot on the sharp stones.

ب) حاد

(b) which bends suddenly; a sharp corner; the car made a sharp turn across the road.

ت) ثاقب

(c) with a high sound; he gave a sharp cry.

sharp—sharper—sharpest

sharpen, *verb*

يجعله حاداً ـ يبري (القلم) ـ يشحذ (السكين)

to make sharp; he sharpened his pencil with a knife; this knife doesn't cut well—it needs sharpening.

sharpens—sharpening—sharpened—has sharpened

shave

shave [ʃeɪv] **1.** *noun*

١ ـ حلاقة (الشعر او الذقن)

cutting off the hair on your face with a razor; **he hasn't had a shave for two days; I need a shave; where's the plug for the razor?—I want a shave.**
2. *verb*

٢ ـ يَحْلُقُ (بالموسى)

to cut off the hair on your face with a razor; **he cut himself while shaving; he hasn't shaved for two days.**
shaves—shaving—shaved—has shaved

she [ʃiː] *pronoun referring to a female person, a female animal and sometimes to machines and countries.*

هي، (ضمير منفصل مؤنث)

she's my aunt; she and I are going on holiday together; I'm angry with Anne—she's taken my bike; she's a nice little cat; get off the ship—she's sinking.
Note: when it is the object, **she** *becomes* **her: she hit the ball/the ball hit her;** *when it follows the verb* **be, she** *usually becomes* **her: who's that?—it's her, the girl we met yesterday.**

sheep [ʃiːp] *noun*

خروف ـ نعجة

farm animal, kept to give wool and also used as meat; **he's looking after his sheep; the sheep are in the field.**
no plural: **one sheep; ten sheep**
Note: the meat from a **sheep** *is called* **lamb,** *or sometimes* **mutton**

sheet [ʃiːt] *noun*

١) الملاءة ـ الشرشف

(*a*) large piece of cloth which you put on a bed; **she pulled the sheet over her head and went to sleep.**

ب) لوح ـ شريحة ـ صفحة من الورق

(*b*) large flat piece; **a sheet of glass; give me two sheets of paper.**

shine

shelf [ʃelf] *noun*

رفّ

flat piece of wood attached to a wall or inside a cupboard which things can be put on; **put the books back on the shelves; the jam's on the top shelf.**
plural **shelves** [ʃelvz]

shell [ʃel] **1.** *noun*

١ ـ أ) قشرة (البيض او الثمرة)

(*a*) hard outside of an egg, a nut or of some animals; **to eat a boiled egg you have to take off the shell.**

ب) قذيفة مدفعية

(*b*) type of bomb fired from a gun; **the shells were falling near the castle.**
2. *verb*

٢ ـ يضرب بالقنابل ـ يقصف بالمدافع

to hit something with a shell from a gun; **the guns shelled the town.**
shells—shelling—shelled—has shelled

shelter [ˈʃeltə] **1.** *noun*

١ ـ ملجأ ـ حماية

place where people or things can be protected (usually from bad weather); **he took shelter from the rain; you should keep your new bike under shelter; bus shelter** = small building with a roof where you can wait for a bus; **the people stood in the bus shelter out of the rain.**
2. *verb*

٢ ـ يلجأ ـ يحتمي

to stand in a shelter; **he sheltered from the rain under a big tree; the sheep were sheltering from the snow behind a wall.**
shelters—sheltering—sheltered—has sheltered

shine [ʃaɪn] *verb*

يضيء ـ يلمع ـ يلمّع ـ يشعّ

to be bright with light; **the sun's shining so I think it'll be hot today; he polished his shoes until they shone; the glasses shone in the sunshine; why do cats' eyes shine in the dark?**
shines—shining—shone [ʃɒn]**—has shone**

two hundred and seventy-nine 279

ship

shiny, *adjective*

لَمّاع ـ مشرق ـ صافٍ

which shines; **the table has a shiny surface.**

shiny—shinier—shiniest

ship [ʃɪp] *noun*

سفينة ـ مركب ـ زورق

large machine which floats on water and carries cargo and passengers; **we went across to the United States by ship; she'a fine passenger ship; the navy has many ships.**

Note: a ship is often referred to as she/her

shirt [ʃɜːt] *noun*

قميص

light piece of clothing which you wear on the top part of your body under a pullover, jacket or coat; **he wore a dark suit and a white shirt; when he came home his suitcase was full of dirty shirts; it's so hot that I'm going to take my shirt off.**

shock [ʃɒk] **1.** *noun*

١ ـ أ) صدمة ـ مفاجأة بشعة

(a) unpleasant surprise; **he had a shock when the waiter gave him the bill; it was a shock to see how ill she was.**

ب) صدمة كهربائية

(b) electric shock = sudden pain when you touch an electric wire; **when she touched the cooker she got a shock; don't touch that wire—it'll give you a shock.**

2. *verb*

٢ ـ يَصْدُم

to give someone an unpleasant surprise; **I was shocked to hear he was dead.**

shocks—shocking—shocked—has shocked

shoe [ʃuː] *noun*

حذاء

piece of clothing made of leather or hard material which you wear on your foot; **he's bought a new pair of shoes; she put her shoes on and went out; I must take my shoes off—my feet hurt.**

shone [ʃɒn] *see* **shine**

ملاحظة: انظر الى كلمة shine

shook [ʃʊk] *see* **shake**

ملاحظة: انظر الى كلمة shake

shoot [ʃuːt] *verb*

أ) يطلق النار او الرصاص على

(a) to fire a gun; to hit someone by firing a gun; **the soldiers were shooting into the houses; he was shot by a policeman as he tried to run away; he shot two rabbits.**

ب) ينطلق ـ يندفع بقوة

(b) to go very fast; **he shot into the room; she shot up the stairs; the car shot out of the garage.**

shoots—shooting—shot [ʃɒt]—has shot

shoot down, *verb*

يصيب ـ يطلق القنابل ويصيب

to make an aircraft crash by hitting it with a shell; **we shot down three aircraft.**

shop [ʃɒp] **1.** *noun*

١ ـ مَتْجَر ـ حانوت

place where you can buy things; **the furniture shop is opposite the post office; all the shops are shut on Sundays; don't go to that shop—it's much too dear; I buy my food at the shop on the corner.**

2. *verb*

٢ ـ يَتَسَوَّق ـ يتبضّع ـ يتحوّج

to buy things in a shop; **we've been shopping; he's out shopping.**

shops—shopping—shopped—has shopped

shop around, *verb*

يذهب في رحلة تسويقية ـ يتفقد الاسواق

to go to various shops to find which one is the cheapest before you buy what you

shore

want; **if you want a cheap radio, you ought to shop around.**

shopkeeper, noun

صاحب المتجر

person who owns a shop.

shopper, noun

الزبون ـ الشاري ـ المتسوِّق

person who buys things in a shop.

shopping, noun

أ) تسويق ـ شراء بضائع او حاجيات من المتجر

(a) buying things in a shop; **I do all my shopping on Saturday mornings; she's doing her shopping; have you done any shopping?**

ب) المشتريات

(b) things which you have bought in a shop; **put all your shopping on the table; he slipped and dropped all his shopping.**
no plural: **some shopping; a lot of shopping**

shore [ʃɔː] noun

شاطىء

land at the edge of the sea or lake; **we walked along the shore; these plants grow on the shores of the lake.**

short [ʃɔːt] adjective

أ) قصير : (حبل قصير)

(a) not long in space; **I need a short piece of string—about 25 centimetres; the shortest way to the station is to go along the High Street.**

ب) وجيز : (فترة وجيزة)

(b) not long in time; **he was here a short time ago; they had a short holiday in Greece; I had a short sleep on the train.**

ت) قصير القامة

(c) not tall; **John is shorter than his brother.**

ث) مفتقر لـ ـ بحالة نقص

(d) short of = with not enough of; **we're short of sugar; I can't pay as I'm rather short of money.**

should

ج) مُخْتَصَر

(e) (word) which is written or spoken with fewer letters than usual; **Co. is short for Company; his name is Robert, but we call him Bob for short.**
short—shorter—shortest

shortly, adverb

بعد وقت وجيز ـ قريباً

soon; **he left the house shortly after breakfast.**

shorts, plural noun

الشورت (بنطلون قصير)

short trousers which end above your knees; **he was wearing a pair of football shorts; you can't go into the church in shorts.**

shot [ʃɒt] noun

إطلاق النار ـ طلقة ناريّة

action of shooting; **the police fired a shot at the car;** *see also* **shoot**

should [ʃʊd] verb used with other verbs

أ) تستعمل للوجوب : يجب عليك الاّ تأكل هذا المقدار من الشكولاتا
من المفروض ان ـ عليه ، عليها ، عليهم ان

(a) to mean ought to *when you think something is correct or when you expect something to happen;* **you shouldn't eat so many chocolates; he should go to see the doctor if his cold gets worse; we shouldn't have come to this party—it's terrible; they should have arrived by now.**

ب) تستعمل للتعبير عن الاستحالة او الشرط : (لكان بودي ان اسافر لو كان لديّ المال الكافي)

(b) to mean would; **I should like to go to Greece if I had enough money.**
Negative: **should not,** *usually* **shouldn't**
Note: **should** *is the past of* **shall: shall we go to the cinema?—I suggested we should go to the cinema**

two hundred and eighty-one 281

shoulder

shoulder ['ʃəʊldə] *noun*

أ) كَتف ـ مَنْكِب

(a) top part of the body between the top of the arm and the neck; **he carried his gun over his shoulder; the policeman touched him on the shoulder; his shoulders are very wide because he spends a lot of time rowing; she looked over her shoulder to see who was following her.**

ب) كَتفيّة

(b) part of a piece of clothing which covers the shoulder; **the shoulders of this shirt are too narrow.**

shout [ʃaʊt] **1.** *noun*

١ ـ صيحة ـ صرخة

loud cry from someone; **I heard a shout for help; there were shouts of surprise when the result was announced.**

2. *verb*

٢ ـ يصرخ ـ يصيح

to say something very loudly; **they shouted for help; shout when you're ready.**

shouts—shouting—shouted—has shouted

show [ʃəʊ] **1.** *noun*

١ ـ أ) معرض ـ استعراض

(a) things which are put out for people to look at; **we are going to the flower show; a show house** = new house which is filled with furniture by the builders so that people can look inside it and decide to buy houses like it.

ب) حفلة مسرحية ـ تمثيلية

(b) something which is on at a theatre; **'My Fair Lady' is a wonderful show; we're going to a show tonight.**

2. *verb*

٢ ـ يعرض ـ يُظْهِر ـ يُري ـ يشير ـ يبدو

to let someone see something/to point out something to someone; **can I show you my stamp collection? he showed her his new car; show me where you fell down; ask the policeman to show you the way to the post office; can you show me** how to get to the post office? he showed me how the camera worked; my watch shows the date as well as the time.

shows—showing—showed—has shown

show in, *verb*

يؤشر بالدخول

to bring a guest/visitor into a room, etc.; **is that Mr Smith?—please show him in.**

show off, *verb*

يسعى لالفات الانظار ـ يتباهى

to show how much better you are than others; **don't look at her—she's showing off; he's showing off his new car.**

show out, *verb*

يرافق حتى الباب

to lead someone to the door; **I'll show you out.**

show over, show round, *verb*

يُري شخصاً على مكان ما

to lead a visitor round a place; **the guide showed us over the castle/showed us round the castle.**

show up, *verb*

أ) يحضر ـ يأتي ـ يصل

(a) to arrive; **we invited twenty people to the party, but no one showed up.**

ب) يفضح

(b) to do something which shows someone to be worse than you; **she's so clever that she shows us all up.**

ت) يبدو بوضوح

(c) to be seen clearly; **this orange jacket shows up in the dark when I ride my bike.**

shower ['ʃaʊə] *noun*

أ) وابل من المطر او الثلج

(a) small amount of rain or snow which falls for a short time; **we often have showers in April; the TV says that there will be snow showers tonight.**

ب) مضخة ماء للاستحمام

(b) arrangement in a bathroom for washing your body under drops of water; **we've fixed a shower over the bath;**

Shrove

each room in the hotel has a toilet and a shower; **shower curtain** = curtain to pull when you are having a shower.

ت) حمام بواسطة المضخة (الدوش)

(c) washing your body under a shower of water; **she has a shower every morning before breakfast; I don't like cold showers!**

Shrove [ʃrəʊv] *see* **pancake**

ملاحظة : انظر الى pancake

shut [ʃʌt] **1.** *adjective*

١ ـ مُغْلَق

closed/not open; **all the shops are shut on Sundays; we tried to go in, but the door was shut.**
2. *verb*

٢ ـ يُغْلِق (الباب) ـ يَقْفُل

to close something which is open; **please shut the window—it's getting cold; I've brought you a present—shut your eyes and guess what it is; pubs shut at 3 o'clock.**

shuts – shutting – shut – has shut

shut down, *verb*

يغلق (المصنع) ـ يبطل عن العمل

to close completely; **the factory shut down for the Christmas holiday.**

shut in, *verb*

يحجز في الداخل

to lock inside; **the door closed and we were shut in.**

shut off, *verb*

يوقف ـ يفصل التيار الكهربائي

to switch something off; **can you shut off the electricity?**

Note: he shut the electricity off *or* he shut off the electricity *but only* he shut it off

shut out, *verb*

يمنعه من الدخول

to lock outside; **I'm shut out of the car—I left my keys inside.**

shut up, *verb*

side

أ) يحتجز داخل مكان مغلوق ـ يحبس

(a) to close something inside; **shut the dog up in the kitchen.**

ب) يسكت ـ يصمت

(b) to stop making a noise/to stop speaking; **shut up! I'm trying to listen to the news.**

sick [sɪk] *adjective*

أ) مريض ـ عليل

(a) ill/not well; **she's sick in bed.**

ب) مصاب بالغثيان

(b) having an illness where you bring up food from your stomach to your mouth; **when I got up this morning I felt sick; he ate too many cakes and was sick all over the floor.**

ت) متخم حتى السأم

(c) **to be sick of** = to have had too much of; **I'm sick of hearing all that noise; I'm sick and tired of looking after all these children.**

ث) يضايق ـ يغضب

(d) **to make someone sick** = to make someone annoyed; **the way he spends money makes me sick.**

sickness, *noun*

مرض

not being well; **there is a lot of sickness in the winter.**

side [saɪd] **1.** *noun*

جانب

(a) one of the parts which (with the top and bottom) make a box or (with the front and back) make a house; **turn the box on to its side; the garden is by the side of the house.**

ب) صفحة ـ وجه

(b) flat surface; **write on one side of the piece of paper.**

ت) ناحية

(c) one of two parts/two edges of something; one of two parts separated by something; **he lives on the other side of the street; she jumped over the wall to get to the other side; in England cars**

two hundred and eighty-three 283

sight

drive on the left-hand side of the road; we live on the south side of London; their house is on the sunny side of the street.

ث) فريق ـ طرف

(d) sports team; **our side was beaten 3-0; which side does he play for?**

ج) جنب

(e) part of the body between the top of the legs and the shoulder; **lie down on your side; she stood by my side; all the soldiers stood side by side** = one next to the other.

ح) يشاركه في رأيه ـ يقف بجانبه

(f) **to be on someone's side** = to have the same point of view; **I'm on your side; whose side are you on?**

2. *adjective*

٢ ـ ثانوي ـ جانبي

at the side; if your shoes are dirty, use the side door, not the front door.

sidewalk, *noun*

pavement ملاحظة : انظر الى كلمة

American = **pavement**

sideways *adverb*

من الجنب ـ على الجانب

to the side/from the side; they all walked sideways; if you look at him sideways you'll see how big his nose is.

sight [saɪt] *noun*

أ) بصر ـ حاسة البصر

(a) one of the five senses/being able to see; **he lost his sight in the war** = he became blind.

ب) رؤية : (لا تستطيع رؤية الدّم)

(b) seeing; **she can't stand the sight of blood; I caught sight of the mountain in the distance** = I saw it for a moment; **the mountain came into sight** = it appeared; **they waved until the ship was out of sight** = until they couldn't see it any more.

ت) مشهد ـ شيء جدير بالمشاهدة

(c) something which you see (especially something famous or odd); **the guide took us to see the sights of the town; she looks a sight in that red hat.**

284

silence

ث) المُصَوِّبة : جهاز التسديد في البندقية

(d) **sights** = part of a gun which you look through to aim.

sign [saɪn] **1.** *noun*

أ) إشارة ـ لافتة اعلانية

(a) movement/drawing, etc., which means something; **he made a sign with his hand and the cars began to go forward; go straight on until you come to a sign marked 'town centre'; the shop has a big sign outside it saying 'for sale'.**

ب) أثر ـ دليل ـ علامة

(b) mark/something which shows; **is there any sign of the snow stopping? there's no sign of how the burglar got into the house.**

2. *verb*

٢ ـ يوقع ـ يضع توقيعه على

to write your name on a form/cheque, etc., or at the end of a letter; **he's forgotten to sign the cheque; the manager signed the letter; sign here, please.**

signs—signing—signed—has signed

signal [ˈsɪɡnəl] *noun*

إشارة ـ علامة

movement/flag/light, etc., which shows that you should do something; **he waved a flag which was the signal for the race to start; the traffic signals aren't working.**

signature [ˈsɪɡnətʃə] *noun*

توقيع

name which someone writes when he signs; **I can't read his signature; her signature is easy to recognize.**

silence [ˈsaɪləns] *noun*

صمت ـ سكوت ـ سكون ـ انعدام الصوت

lack of noise/not talking; **the crowd waited in silence; the teacher asked for silence.**

6silent, *adjective*

صامت ـ ساكت ـ ساكن

not making any noise; not talking; **they kept silent for the whole meeting.**

two hundred and eighty-four

silk

silently, *adverb*

بدون ضجة - بكل سكون

without any noise; **they walked silently into the church.**

silk [sɪlk] *noun*

حرير

soft, expensive material made from a thread produced by an insect; **she was wearing a silk shirt; this tie is made of silk.**

no plural: **some silk; a piece of silk**

silly ['sɪlɪ] *adjective*

سخيف - ساذج - احمق

stupid; **don't be silly—you can't eat raw potatoes; what a silly question!**

silly—sillier—silliest

silver ['sɪlvə] *noun*

فِضّة (معدن الفِضّة)

(*a*) valuable white metal; **a silver teapot; this ring is silver; the handle of the knife is made of silver.**

ب) شيء مصنوع من الفِضّة (الفِضّيّة)

(*b*) things made of silver; **don't forget to polish the silver.**

no plural

silver wedding, *noun*

ذكرى الزواج الخامسة والعشرون

day when you have been married for twenty-five years.

similar ['sɪmɪlə] *adjective*

شبيه - مماثل - متشابه

which looks/tastes, etc., the same; **the two houses are quite similar; his job is similar to mine; have you something similar but not as expensive?**

similarly, *adverb*

بصورة مماثلة او متشابهة

in the same way; **he is very fond of sport; similarly his sister plays tennis every day.**

two hundred and eighty-five

sing

simple ['sɪmpl] *adjective*

ا) بسيط - سهل

(*a*) easy; **the answer is quite simple; I didn't think the exam was very simple.**

ب) عادي - بسيط

(*b*) ordinary/not very special; **we had a simple meal of bread and soup; it's a very simple plan.**

simple—simpler—simplest

simply, *adverb*

ا) ببساطة - بكل بساطة

(*a*) in a simple way; **he described what happened very simply.**

ب) فقط

(*b*) only; **he did it simply to see what you would say.**

since [sɪns] **1.** *adverb & preposition*

١ - منذ - منذ ذلك الحين

from that time on; **he was rude to the teacher and has had bad marks ever since; we've been working since 2 o'clock; since we got home, it has rained every day.**

2. *conjunction*

٢ - لأن - نظراً لـ - بما أن

because; **he can't come with us since he's ill; since it's such a fine day, let's go for a picnic.**

sincere [sɪn'sɪə] *adjective*

صادق - وفي - مخلص

very honest; **was he sincere when he promised he would work better?**

sincerely, *adverb*

بصدق - باخلاص

in a sincere way; **Yours sincerely** = words which you put at the end of a letter before your signature.

sing [sɪŋ] *verb*

يُغَنّي - يُنْشد

to make music with your voice; **he was singing as he worked; can you sing that**

285

single

song again? she was singing a song about roses.

sings—singing—sang [sæŋ]—has sung [sʌŋ]

singer, *noun*

مغنٍّ ـ مغنّية

person who sings.

single ['sɪŋgl] **1.** *adjective*

١ ـ أ) واحد ـ واحد فقط ـ لشخص واحد

(*a*) one/for one person; I haven't seen a single newspaper; I want a single room for one night; do you want a double bed or two single beds?

ب) عازب ـ غير متزوّج

(*b*) not married; he's still single.

ت) بطاقة (قطار او طائرة) للذهاب دون العودة

(*c*) **single ticket** = ticket for a trip in one direction only/not a return ticket.

2. *noun*

٢ ـ أ) بطاقة للسفر في اتجاه واحد

(*a*) ticket for one trip; I want two singles to London.

ب) مباراة ثنائية (بين خصمين)

(*b*) **singles** = tennis game played between two people; the men's singles.

singular ['sɪŋgjʊlə] *adjective & noun*

مفرد

form of a word showing that there is only one; 'mouse' is the singular, and 'mice' is the plural; 'is' is the singular of the verb 'to be' and 'are' is the plural; 'he' is a singular pronoun.

sink [sɪŋk] **1.** *noun*

١ ـ بالوعة ـ مغسلة

place in a kitchen where you wash the dishes; put the dirty plates in the sink.

2. *verb*

٢ ـ أ) يغرق ـ يغوص ـ يهبط الى قعر الماء

(*a*) to go to the bottom of water/not to float; get off the ship—she's sinking; the boat sank because there were too many people in it; they sank the ship with a bomb.

sit

ب) يغطس ـ يغرق (في فراشه) ـ يهبط (القلب) يغرب (الشمس)

(*b*) to go down; he sank into an armchair; the sun's sinking in the west; my heart sank = I felt very sad/disappointed.

sinks—sinking—sank [sʌŋk]—has sunk [sʌŋk]

sir [sɜː] *noun*

أ) سيدي ـ (يستعمل كطريقة مهذبة لمخاطبة رجل ما)

(*a*) (*usually used by someone serving in a shop or restaurant*) polite way of referring to a man who you are talking to; would you like to order your lunch, sir? please sit here, sir.

ب) سيدي العزيز: طريقة مهذبة لاستهلال رسالة عمل

(*b*) polite way of writing to a man who you do not know; **Dear Sir.**

sister ['sɪstə] *noun*

اخت ـ شقيقة

female who has the same father and mother as another child; she's my sister; he has three sisters; his sister works in a bank.

sit [sɪt] *verb*

أ) يجلس ـ يقعد

(*a*) to be resting with your behind on something; he was sitting on the floor; you can sit on the table if you like; sit next to me; she was sitting in bed eating her breakfast.

ب) يقدم (امتحاناً)

(*b*) to take an examination; she failed and had to sit the examination again.

sits—sitting—sat [sɒt]—has sat

sit down, *verb*

يجلس (على كرسي)

to take a seat; everyone sat down and the film began; don't sit down—that chair's just been painted.

286 *two hundred and eighty-six*

situation

sitting-room, *noun*

غرفة الجلوس

room where you can sit in comfortable chairs; let's watch TV in the sitting-room; shut the sitting-room door, please.

sit up, *verb*

أ) يجلس منتصباً (في فراشه)

(*a*) to sit with your back straight; to move from a lying to a sitting position; he sat up in bed; sit up straight!

ب) يطيل السهر

(*b*) to stay up without going to bed; we sat up until 2 a.m.

situation [sɪtjʊˈeɪʃn] *noun*

حال ـ حالة ـ وضع ـ منصب ـ موقع

how things are; position; we're in a difficult situation; this has made the situation very difficult for us.

six [sɪks] number 6

ستة (العدد ستة)

she's six (years old); come and have a cup of coffee at six (o'clock); there are six chocolates left.

sixteen, number 16

ستة عشر (العدد ١٦)

he's sixteen (years old).

sixteenth, **16th**, *adjective & noun*

سادس عشر

he was sixteenth in the race; the sixteenth of August/August the sixteenth (August 16th); his sixteenth birthday is next week.

sixth, **6th**, *adjective & noun*

السادس (المرتبة السادسة)

they live on the sixth floor; F is the sixth letter of the alphabet; he spent a sixth of the money; ten minutes is a sixth of an hour; the sixth of February/February the sixth (February 6th); Henry the Sixth (Henry VI); tomorrow is my son's sixth birthday.

Note: in dates sixth is usually written 6th: April 6th, 1980; December 6th,

skeleton

1976; with names of kings and queens sixth is usually written VI: King Henry VI

sixty, number 60

ستون (العدد ٦٠)

he's sixty (years old); I bought sixty books yesterday; she's in her sixties = she is between 60 and 69 years old.

Note: sixty-one (61), sixty-two (62) etc., but sixty-first (61st), sixty-second (62nd), etc.

sixtieth, **60th**, *adjective & noun*

الستون (المرتبة الستون)

he was sixtieth out of 120; a minute is a sixtieth of an hour; it's father's sixtieth birthday tomorrow.

size [saɪz] *noun*

حجم ـ قياس ـ مقاس ـ كبر ـ ضخامة ـ مقدار

how big something is; that onion's the size of a tennis ball; he has a garage about the same size as our house; what's the size of a normal swimming pool? she takes size 7 in shoes; what size shirts do you wear?

skate [skeɪt] 1. *noun*

١ ـ المُزلِج : قطعة معدنية حادة تشد على الحذاء للتزلج

sharp blade worn under a boot to slide on ice; she was putting on her skates.
2. *verb*

٢ ـ يتزلّج

to slide on ice wearing skates; we went skating on the ice; there is a big skating competition next week; she skates very well.

skates—skating—skated—has skated

skeleton [ˈskelɪtən] *noun*

الهيكل العظمي

all the bones which make your body or an animal's body.

ski

ski [skiː] 1. *noun*

١ ـ الزحلوقة : احدى آدتين يتزحلق بهما

long piece of wood which you attach to a boot, to allow you to slide on snow.
2. *verb*

٢ ـ يتزحلق على الثلج

to slide on snow wearing skis; **he skied down the mountain; we go skiing every weekend.**
skis—skiing—skied [skiːd]—**has skied**

skill [skɪl] *noun*

مهارة ـ رشاقة ـ براعة

being able to do something which is difficult; something which you get by training; **you need special skills to become a doctor.**

skilled, *adjective*

بارع ـ ماهر

having a particular skill by training; **he's a skilled workman.**

skin [skɪn] *noun*

جلد ـ بشرة

outside surface of a human's or an animal's body or of a fruit; **his skin turned brown in the sun; the skin of a cow can be used to make leather; a banana skin.**

skirt [skɜːt] *noun*

تنّورة

piece of clothing worn by women covering the lower part of the body from the waist to the knees or ankles; **I like wearing jeans better than wearing a skirt; her skirt's so long it touches the ground.**

sky [skaɪ] *noun*

السماء

space above the earth which is blue (or grey) during the day and black at night; **look at all the clouds in the sky; when the sky's grey it means it'll be wet; the birds are flying high in the sky.**
plural **skies**

slice

sleep [sliːp] 1. *noun*

١ ـ نَوْم ـ رقاد

resting (usually at night) when your eyes are closed and you do not know what is happening; **she needs eight hours' sleep a night; get a good night's sleep—we have a lot of work to do tomorrow; she had a short sleep in the middle of the afternoon; to go to sleep** = to start sleeping; **I'm trying to go to sleep; he went to sleep in front of the TV set.**
2. *verb*

٢ ـ ينام ـ يرقد ـ يغرق في النوم

to be asleep/to rest with your eyes closed and not knowing what is happening; **he always sleeps for eight hours each night; she slept for the whole of the TV programme; don't disturb him—he's trying to sleep.**
sleeps—sleeping—slept [slept]—**has slept**

sleep in, *verb*

يطول به النوم ـ ينام اكثر من المعتاد

to sleep later than usual in the morning.

sleepy, *adjective*

نعسان ـ ناعس

feeling ready to go to sleep; **I'm feeling sleepier and sleepier; the children are very sleepy by ten o'clock.**
sleepy—sleepier—sleepiest

sleeve [sliːv] *noun*

كُمّ ـ رُدْن

part of a piece of clothing which you put your arm into; **one sleeve of this coat is longer than the other; I often wear shirts with short sleeves in the summer.**

slept [slept] *see* **sleep**

ملاحظة : انظر الى كلمة sleep

slice [slaɪs] *noun*

شريحة ـ حصة

thin flat piece of food which has been cut off something larger; **cut me another slice of bread; he ate six slices of ham.**

slide

slide [slaɪd] 1. *noun*

١ ـ سلايد : صورة ملونة مظهرة على مادة بلاستيكيّة وشفافة

coloured photo on plastic which you can see through; **turn out the lights—I'll show you my holiday slides.**

2. *verb*

٢ ـ ينزلق

to move smoothly across a slippery surface; **the door slid open; the van has sliding doors; let's go sliding on the ice.**

slides—sliding—slid [slɪd]—has slid

slight [slaɪt] *adjective*

خفيف ـ طفيف ـ ضعيف ـ قليل ـ نحيل

not very large/not very serious; **there's been a slight frost; he has a slight temperature; she's had slight accident.**

slight—slighter—slightest

slightly, *adverb*

قليلاً ـ بشكل طفيف

not very much; **the new box is slightly larger than the old one; I only know him slightly.**

slip [slɪp] *verb*

أ) ينزلق

(*a*) to slide by mistake; **he slipped on the ice and fell down.**

ب) يجري بخفّة ـ ينطلق بسرعة

(*b*) to go quickly; **she slipped upstairs when no one was watching; I'll just slip out to the shops for a moment.**

slips—slipping—slipped—has slipped

slipper, *noun*

خفّ ـ شبشب

comfortable light shoe which is worn indoors; **he took off his shoes and put on his slippers.**

slippery, *adjective*

زَلِق : (انتبه ، ان الصقيع يجعل الارض زلقة)

so smooth that you may easily slip; **watch out—the ice is slippery!**

small

slope [sləʊp] 1. *noun*

١ ـ مُنْحَدَر ـ انحدار

surface which is neither flat nor upright; **a steep slope; the house is built on the slope of the mountain.**

2. *verb*

٢ ـ ينحدر : (ينحدر الطريق نحو النهر)

to be neither flat nor upright; **the path slopes upwards; the road sloped down to the river.**

slopes—sloping—sloped—has sloped

slow [sləʊ] *adjective*

أ) بطيء ـ متمهّل

(*a*) not fast; taking a long time to do something; **the car was going at a slow speed; the train was very slow; he's very slow at answering my letters.**

ب) متأخر : ساعتك متأخرة بثلاث دقائق

(*b*) showing a time which is earlier than the right time; **my watch is three minutes slow.**

slow—slower—slowest

slow down, *verb*

يخفف سيره ـ يخفض سرعته

to go more slowly; to make something go more slowly; **the snow slowed down the cars; the bus slowed down as it came to the traffic lights.**

slowly, *adverb*

ببطء ـ بتمهّل

in a slow way/not fast; **the car was going very slowly when it hit the wall; we walked slowly round the museum; the teacher must speak slowly so that the children can understand.**

small [smɔːl] *adjective*

صغير

little/not big; **small cars use less petrol than big ones; I'm selling my house and buying a smaller one; he only paid a small sum of money; she's smaller than her brother, but her mother's the smallest person in the family; this book isn't small enough to put in your pocket; my**

two hundred and eighty-nine   289

smell

son's too small to ride a bike = he is too young.

smalI—smaller—smallest

smell [smel] 1. *noun*

١ ـ الشمّ ـ حاسة الشم ـ رائحة

one of the five senses/something which you can feel through your nose; **dogs have a good sense of smell; the smell of roses makes me sneeze; what a lovely smell of roast meat! do you like the smell of onions? what a nasty smell! there's a smell of burning/there's a burning smell; there's a funny smell in the kitchen.**

usually used in the singular

2. *verb*

٢ ـ أ) يشمّ

(*a*) to notice the smell of something; **I can smell smoke; dogs can smell strangers; can you smell cooking? I can't smell anything when I've got a cold; smell these flowers!**

ب) تفوح منه رائحة

(*b*) to produce a smell; **this cheese smells very strong; the dinner smells good; the air smells fresh; there's something which smells funny in the kitchen; it smells of gas in here.**

smells—smelling—smelled/ smelt [smelt] —has smelled/has smelt

smelly, *adjective*

ذو رائحة كريهة

which has a nasty smell; **a smelly river; a smelly old dog.**

smelly—smellier—smelliest

smile [smaıl] 1. *noun*

١ ـ إبتسامة ـ ابتسام

way of showing that you are pleased/ happy by turning your mouth up at the corners; **she gave me a friendly smile; he gave a big smile when he read his exam results.**

2. *verb*

٢ ـ يبتسم

to show that you are pleased by turning your mouth up at the corners; **she smiled at me; stop smiling—it's very serious; smile please—I'm taking a photo.**

smiles—smiling—smiled—has smiled

smoke [sməuk] 1. *noun*

١ ـ دخان

white, grey or black gas which is given off by something burning; **the room was full of cigarette smoke; can you smell smoke? I like the smell of cigar smoke; clouds of smoke poured out of the burning ship.**

2. *verb*

٢ ـ أ) يتصاعد منه الدخان

(*a*) to give off smoke; **the ruins of the house are still smoking.**

ب) يُدَخِّن (سيجارة او غليون)

(*b*) to suck in smoke from a cigarette/ cigar/pipe, etc.; **she was smoking a cigarette; he only smokes a pipe; she doesn't smoke; we always sit in the 'no smoking' area; smoking can make you ill; if you want to play tennis, you shouldn't smoke.**

smokes—smoking—smoked—has smoked

smoker, *noun*

المُدَخِّن

person who often smokes cigarettes.

smoky, *adjective*

داخن ـ مفعم بالدخان

full of smoke; **a smoky room.**

smooth [smu:ð] 1. *adjective*

١ ـ املس ـ ناعم

flat/not rough; **the table is quite smooth; we had a very smooth ride in our new car.**

smooth—smoother—smoothest

2. *verb*

٢ ـ يُمهَد ـ يُمْلِس ـ يهدّىء (الامور)

to make something smooth; **she smoothed down the sheets on the bed; he**

snack

tried to smooth over the problem = to make things easier.

smooths—smoothing—smoothed—has smoothed

smoothly, adverb

بهدوء

in a smooth way; **the car came to a stop very smoothly.**

snack [snæk] noun

وجبة خفيفة

very small meal; **let's have a snack at the station; I always have a snack at 11 o'clock in the morning.**

snack bar, noun

مطعم يقدّم وجبات خفيفة

small shop where you can buy snacks.

snake [sneɪk] noun

أفعى

long smooth animal with no legs which moves by sliding; **she's afraid of snakes; some snakes can kill you.**

sneeze [sniːz] 1. noun

أ) عَطْسة - عُطاس

sudden blowing out of air through your nose and mouth when you have a cold, etc.; **she gave a loud sneeze; his sneezes woke me up!**
2. verb

ب) يعطس

to blow air suddenly out of your nose and mouth because you have a cold, etc.; **she sneezed three times; the smell of flowers make me sneeze.**

sneezes—sneezing—sneezed—has sneezed

snore [snɔː] verb

يَشخِر

to make a loud noise in your nose and throat when you are asleep; **he snored so much that none of us could get to sleep; can't you stop him snoring?**

snores—snoring—snored—has snored

two hundred and ninety-one

snow

snow [snəʊ] 1. noun

١ - ثلج - تساقط الثلج

light white pieces of frozen water which fall from the sky when it is cold; **look at all the snow which has fallen during the night; the mountains are covered with snow; the trains will be late because the lines are covered with snow; ten centimetres of snow had fallen during the night.**

no plural: **some snow; a lot of snow**

2. verb

٢ - يتساقط الثلج - تثلج (السماء)

to fall as snow; **it's snowing! it snowed all night; do you think it's going to snow? it never snows here.**

snows—snowing—snowed—has snowed

Note: **to snow** *is always used with* **it**

snowball, noun

كرة ثلج

ball made with snow; **they threw snowballs at the teacher; he broke a window with a snowball.**

snowed up, adjective

مكسيّ بالثلج

surrounded by snow, so that you cannot travel; **we were snowed up for six days.**

snowman, noun

الانسان الثلجي (شكل انسان مصنوع من الثلج)

shape of a man made of snow; **they made a snowman in the school playground; if the sun comes out, your snowmen will melt.**

plural **snowmen**

snowstorm, noun

عاصفة ثلجية

storm when the wind blows and snow falls.

snowy, adjective

مُثلِج

covered with snow; (weather) when it is snowing; **snowy weather; if it's snowy, you should stay indoors; this is the snow-**

291

so

iest winter I can remember; they walked through the snowy streets to the shops.
snowy—snowier—snowiest

so ([səu] **1.** *adverb*

أ) كثيراً ـ لدرجة أن

(*a*) (*showing how much*) it's so cold that the river has frozen; we enjoyed ourselves so much that we're going to the same place for our holiday next year; the pudding was so sweet that it made me feel ill; she's not so intelligent as her sister.

ب) وهكذا ـ ايضاً

(*b*) also; he was late and so was I; we all caught flu, and so did the teacher; I like fish—so do I; he can cook well—so can his wife.

ت) كذلك : (وهو كذلك ـ وانا اظنّ كذلك)

(*c*) (*showing that the answer is 'yes'*) is this the train for London?—I think so; did the burglars steal all your records?—I'm afraid so; are you coming to the party?—I hope so; will you be at the meeting?—I suppose so.

2. *conjunction*

٢ ـ أ) لهذا السبب ـ كذلك

(*a*) for this reason; it was raining, so we didn't go for a walk; she caught a cold, so she couldn't come to the party.

ب) لكي ـ بُغْيَة

(*b*) so that = in order that; so as to = in order to; people on bicycles should wear orange coats so that drivers can see them in the dark; we ran to the station so as not to miss the train.

so far, *adverb*

حتى الآن

until now; he said he would phone me, but so far he hasn't done so; how do you like your new job so far?

soap [səup] *noun*

صابون

stuff which you use to wash with, made from oils and usually with a pleasant smell; I must buy some more soap; they went away on holiday and forgot to take any soap with them; I've put a new bar of soap in the bathroom; this soap has a strong smell—it makes me sneeze.
no plural: some soap; a bar of soap/a cake of soap/a piece of soap

society [sə'saɪətɪ] *noun*

أ) المجتمع ـ مجتمع ـ جمعية

(*a*) people in general and the way in which they live together; money is too important in our society; society has to be protected from dangerous criminals. (*b*) group of people who are interested in the same thing; a local history society; a society for the protection of birds.
plural societies

sock [sɒk] *noun*

جورب قصير

piece of clothing which you wear on your foot inside your shoe; he's wearing blue socks and a blue tie; I'm almost ready—I only have to put my socks and shoes on; tennis socks/football socks = special socks for playing tennis or football; knee socks = long socks which go up to your knee; you'll have to pull your socks up = you will have to try to do better.

sofa ['səufə] *noun*

الاريكة ـ كَنَبْ

long soft seat for several people; we sat on the sofa and watched TV.

soft [sɒft] *adjective*

أ) ناعم

(*a*) not hard; the seats in this car are too soft; he was sitting in a big soft armchair; do you like soft ice cream.

ب) خفيف (صوت)

(*b*) not loud; she talked in such a soft voice that we could hardly hear her.

ت) خفيف ـ ضعيف (ضوء)

(*c*) not bright; the soft lighting made the room look warm.
soft—softer—softest

soil

softly, *adverb*

بنعومة ـ بلطف

in a gentle way; quietly/not loudly; not brightly; **I touched her hair softly; she speaks very softly; they crept softly up the stairs; the lights were shining softly.**

soil [sɔıl] *noun*

تُربة

earth in which plants grow; **put some soil in a pot and plant your seeds in it.**
no plural **some soil; a bag of soil**

sold [səuld] *see* **sell**

ملاحظة : انظر الى كلمة sell

soldier [ˈsəuldʒə] *noun*

جندي

man who is in the army; **the soldiers attacked the railway station; soldiers wear brown uniforms.**

solid [ˈsɒlɪd] *adjective*

ا) صلب ـ متين

(a) hard/not liquid; **water turns solid when it freezes.**

ب) صاف (معدن ، ذهب)

(b) made all of one material; **the table is made of solid metal; a solid gold plate.**

some [sʌm] *adjective & pronoun*

ا) بعض (الاشخاص)

(a) certain; **some people drive much too fast; some days it was so hot that we had to stay indoors.**

ب) بعض (قليل من)

(b) several/not many; **can you cut some slices of bread? some of these apples are green; there are some people waiting in the queue; I've bought some oranges.**

ت) بعض (كمية قليلة من)

(c) a certain quantity; **can you buy some petrol when you go to town? do you want any sugar?—no, I've already taken some.**

some is used with plural nouns and with nouns which have no plural:

song

some people; some apples; some bread, etc.

somebody [ˈsʌmbədɪ], **someone** [ˈsʌmwʌn] *pronoun*

أحدٌ ـ شخص ما

a certain person; **somebody/someone has stolen my car; there's somebody/someone in the telephone box; if somebody/someone phones, say I will be back at 4 o'clock; I know somebody/someone who's a policeman.**

somehow, *adverb*

بطريقة ما ـ بطريقة او بأخرى

in one way or another; **we must get to London by 4 o'clock somehow.**

something, *pronoun*

شيء ما

a certain thing; **there's something at the bottom of the bag; something's wrong with the engine; can I have something to eat?**

sometimes, *adverb*

في بعض الاحيان ـ احياناً

at certain various times; at a particular time; **sometimes it is cold in the summer; sometimes the car goes well, and sometimes it doesn't go at all; I sometimes go to London on business.**

somewhere, *adverb*

في مكان ما

in/at a certain place; **I left my keys somewhere in the office; this restaurant is full—let's go somewhere else; he lives somewhere in Scotland.**

son [sʌn] *noun*

إبن

male child of a parent; **they have two sons and one daughter; her son's gone to work in France; my son Simon likes rowing.**

song [sɒŋ] *noun*

أغنية

words and music which are sung; **she was singing a song in the bath; have you a record of his latest song?**

soon

soon [suːn] *adverb*

أ) قريباً ـ عاجلاً ـ باكراً (عاجلاً او آجلاً)
(*a*) in a short time from now; **we'll soon be home; it will soon be dinnertime; I want to see you as soon as possible; I'll see you next week—can't you come any sooner? when did the fire start?—soon after 9 o'clock; sooner or later** = at some time in the future; **he drives so badly that sooner or later the police will catch him.**

ب) يُفَضِّل
(*b*) **would sooner** = would rather/prefer; **I'd sooner stay at home than go to the party;** *see also* **rather**.

فوراً عندما
as soon as = immediately; **as soon as he sat down the telephone rang.**
soon—sooner—soonest

sorry ['sɒrɪ] **1.** *adjective*

١ ـ آسف ـ متأسف ـ حزين
showing that you regret; **I'm sorry it rained when you went on holiday; she trod on my toe and didn't say she was sorry; we were all sorry to hear you been ill; to feel sorry for someone** = to pity someone; **I feel sorry for her—her husband is so unpleasant.**
2. *interjection*

٢ ـ عدم المؤاخذة
used to excuse yourself; **sorry! I didn't see that you were in the bathroom; sorry! I've got the wrong number; can you give me a cigarette?—sorry! I haven't any left.**

sort [sɔːt] *noun*

نوع
type/kind/group of things which are alike; **all sorts of people came to the party; what sort of day did you have at the office? there are three sorts of ice cream to choose from—which sort do you like best? I don't like this sort of coffee.**

نوعاً ما
sort of = rather/more or less; **I'm feeling sort of tired.**

sound [saʊnd] **1.** *noun*

١ ـ صوت ـ ضجّة ـ ضجيج
something which you can hear; **the sound of music came through the open window; can you hear the sound of a train? I don't like the sound of that** = I am not very keen on that/I don't think that is a good idea.
2. *verb*

٢ ـ يُصَوِّت ـ يبدو ـ يشبه
to make a sound; **he sounded his horn when he came to the corner; that sounds strange** = what I hears seems strange; **it sounds like a car** = I think I can hear a car; **that sounds like my father** = (i) it is similar to the way my father talks, (ii) I think I can hear my father coming.
sounds—sounding—sounded—has sounded

soup [suːp] *noun*

حساء
liquid which you eat hot in a bowl or plate at the beginning of a meal; **I don't like onion soup; do you want some soup? we had vegetable soup for dinner; open a tin of soup—I'm hungry; soup bowl/ soup plate/soup spoon** = special bowl/ plate/spoon for eating soup.
no plural: **some soup; a bowl of soup**

sour [saʊə] *adjective*

أ) حامض
(*a*) not sweet; **these oranges are as sour as lemons.**

ب) رائب
(*b*) **sour milk** = milk which has gone bad; **you can put sour cream in your soup.**
sour—sourer—sourest

294 *two hundred and ninety-four*

south

south [sauθ] 1. *noun*

١ - جنوب

direction of where the sun is at midday; **the town is to the south of the mountains; the wind is blowing from the south.**
2. *adjective*

٢ - جنوبيّ

referring to the south; **the south coast of England; the south side of the river.**
3. *adverb*

٣ - نحو الجنوب - في اتجاه الجنوب

towards the south; **birds fly south in the winter; go due south for ten kilometres.**

South America, *noun*

ب) بعض (قليل من)

part of America containing Brazil, Argentina, Chile and several other countries.

southern ['sʌðən] *adjective*

جنوبيّ

of the south; **they live in the southern part of the country.**

South Pole, *noun*

القطب الجنوبي

furthest point at the south of the earth.

souvenir [suːvəˈnɪə] *noun*

تذكار

something which reminds you of a place; **this is a souvenir of our holiday in Sweden.**

sow [səu] *verb*

يَبذُر

to put seeds into earth so that they will grow; **sow your seeds in spring; he's sown his beans.**

sows—sowing—sowed—has sown

space [speɪs] *noun*

مدى - مساحة - فراغ - مكان - حيّز

place/empty area between things; **park your car in that space over there; write your name and address in the space at the top of the paper; this table takes up a lot of space.**

two hundred and ninety-five

special

spade [speɪd] *noun*

ا) رَفْش - مجراف

(*a*) tool used for digging; **he dug a hole in the ground with his spade.**

ب) البستوني (في ورق اللعب)

(*b*) one of the suits in a game of cards shaped like a black heart; **the ten of spades.**

spare [speə] 1. *adjective*

١ - احتياطي - إضافي - فائض

extra/which is not used; **you need a spare wheel in case one of your tyres is flat; can I spend the night in your spare bedroom? what do you do in your spare time?** = when you are not working.
2. *verb*

٢ - يستحيط - يستبقي - يضع جانباً كاحتياط - يوفّر - يوفّر على - يستغني عن

to be able to give or spend; **can you spare the time to go on holiday? can you spare me a cigarette? I want to buy that car, but I can't spare the money.**

spares—sparing—spared—has spared

speak [spiːk] *verb*

يَتَكَلَّم - يخاطب - ينطق

to say words; to talk; **he walked past me without speaking; she was speaking to the milkman; can he speak English? I must speak to him about his son.**

speaks—speaking—spoke [spəuk]—has spoken

speaker, *noun*

مُذيع

person who speaks; **he is a funny speaker** = he makes funny speeches; *see also* **loudspeaker.**

speak up, *verb*

يتكلم بصوت عال

to speak louder; **speak up—I can't hear you!**

special [ˈspeʃl] *adjective*

استثنائي - غير اعتيادي - خاص

which refers to one particular thing; not

295

spectacles

ordinary; **this is a very special day—it's my birthday; he has a special pair of scissors for cutting his hair; there is nothing very special about his new car** = it is quite ordinary.

specially, adverb

خاصةً ـ بالاخص ـ خصوصاً

particularly; **the weather has been specially good; she is specially good at making cakes;** *see also* **especially**.

spectacles ['spektəklz] *plural noun*

نظارات

glasses which you wear in front of your eyes to help you see better; **he has broken his spectacles; she was wearing a pair of spectacles with gold frames.**

sped [sped] *see* **speed**

ملاحظة : انظر الى كلمة **speed**

speech [spiːtʃ] *noun*

أ) خطاب ـ خطبة ـ حديث

(*a*) talk given in public; **she made a funny speech at the dinner; all the speeches were much too long.**

ب) لغة ـ لهجة

(*b*) language; **the parts of speech** = different types of words which are used in different ways (like nouns/verbs, etc.).

plural **speeches,** *but no plural for (b)*

speed [spiːd] **1.** *noun*

١ ـ سرعة

how fast you move; **the car was travelling at high speed; if you go at a speed of 30 miles per hour you'll use less petrol; the ship was going at full speed.**
2. *verb*

٢ ـ يُسرع ـ يُعَجّل ـ يُسَرِّع

to go fast; **the car sped across the road; he was arrested for speeding** = for going too fast.

speeds—speeding—sped [sped]—**has sped**

spend

speed limit, *noun*

السرعة القصوى

highest speed at which you are allowed to drive; **the speed limit in towns is 30 miles per hour.**

speed up, *verb*

يُسرع ـ يزيد من سرعته

to go faster; to make something go faster; to do something faster; **can't you speed up your work?**

spell [spel] **1.** *noun*

١ ـ فترة

short period; **we had a spell of cold weather; the cold spell lasted a week.**
2. *verb*

٢ ـ يَتَهجَّى (لفظةٍ)

to write or say correctly the letters which make a word; **how do you spell your name? you've spelt his name wrong; L-A-U-G-H spells 'laugh'; his name is Steven, but I don't know if it's spelt PH or V** = if it is Stephen or Steven.

spells—spelling—spelled/spelt—has spelled/has spelt

spelling, *noun*

تهجئة

way in which words are spelt; **he writes very well, but his spelling is bad.**

spend [spend] *verb*

أ) ينفق (اموالاً)

(*a*) to pay money in a shop, restaurant, etc.; **I spent £6 on a new tie; I don't like spending too much money on food; he has saved up all his pocket money and is going to spend it on Christmas presents.**

ب) يُمْضي (الوقت)

(*b*) to pass time; **we spent our holidays in France last year; he spent two hours mending the car; why don't you come to spend the weekend with us? don't spend hours doing your homework.**

spends—spending—spent—has spent

spider

spider ['spaɪdə] *noun*

عنكبوت

small animal with eight legs, which makes a web to catch flies; **she's afraid of spiders; help! there's a spider in the bath.**

spill [spɪl] *verb*

يَدْلُق ـ يندلق ـ يتناثر

to let liquid fall by mistake; **I spilled my soup down my shirt; the cat knocked over the bottle and the milk spilled all over the table.**

spills—spilling—spilled/spilt [spɪlt] —has spilled/has spilt

spite [spaɪt] *noun*

بالرغم من ـ على الرغم من

in spite of = although (something has happened); **we went for a walk in spite of the snow; he went to the party in spite of the fact that he had a cold.**

splash [splæʃ] **1.** *noun*

١ ـ غوصة في الماء ـ إرتشاش

noise made by liquid being thrown; **he fell into the swimming pool with a big splash; you could hear the splash of the waves on the rocks.**

plural **splashes**

2. *verb*

٢ ـ يتساقط على شكل قطرات

to make a noise of liquid being thrown; to cover with drops of liquid; **the waves splashed against the rocks; the children were splashing about in the pool; the bus splashed me with dirty water; when you're painting the ceiling, be careful not to splash paint on to the carpet.**

splashes—splashing—splashed— has splashed

splendid ['splendɪd] *adjective*

رائع ـ ممتاز ـ عظيم

wonderful/very very good/excellent; **we had a splendid holiday in Sweden; what**

spoon

splendid weather for a picnic! you've passed your exams?—splendid!

split [splɪt] **1.** *noun*

١ ـ شَقّ ـ شقاق

thin crack in something solid; **there is a split in this piece of wood; do you know that you've got a split in the back of your trousers? banana split** = dessert made with bananas, cream, ice cream and nuts.

2. *verb*

٢ ـ يَشقُّ ـ يقسم ـ يَشطُر ـ يَفْلُق

to divide something into parts; to make something crack or tear; **if you get any fatter, you'll split your trousers; my trousers split when I bent down; the committee has split into three groups; let's split the money between us.**

splits—splitting—split—has split

split up, *verb*

يَفْلُق ـ يقسم الى جزئين ـ يشطر

to divide into parts; to separate; **the tourists split up into two groups; let's split up and meet at the post office in half an hour.**

spoil [spɔɪl] *verb*

يُتْلِف ـ يَعْطُب ـ يفسد

to ruin/to make bad/to damage; **the bad weather spoilt our holidays; the film was spoilt by the bad sound; don't spoil my dinner by talking about hospitals.**

spoils—spoiling—spoiled/spoilt— has spoiled/spoilt

spoke [spəʊk], **spoken** ['spəʊkn] *see* **speak**

ملاحظة : انظر الى كلمة speak

spoon [spuːn] **1.** *noun*

١ ـ ملعقة

long tool with a handle at one end and a small bowl at the other, used for eating; **eat your pudding with your spoon, not with your knife; have you got a big spoon**

two hundred and ninety-seven 297

sport

to serve the peas? **soup spoon** = special spoon for eating soup.
2. *verb*

٢ ـ يتناول بالملعقة ـ يسكب بالملعقة ـ يستخرج بالملعقة

to move something with a spoon; **he spooned the sugar into his tea; she was spooning out jam on to all the plates.**

spoons—spooning—spooned— has spooned

spoonful, *noun*

ملء ملعقة

quantity which a spoon can hold; **he put two spoonfuls of sugar into his tea.**

sport [spɔːt] *noun*

رياضة

game which you play; all games; **I like watching sport on TV; do you like the sports programmes on TV? the only sport I play is football; he doesn't play any sport at all.**

sports car, *noun*

سيارة رياضية

fast open car.

sports day, *noun*

يوم المباراة الرياضية

day at a school where teams play various sports for prizes.

sportsfield/sportsground, *noun*

ملعب

big field where sports are played.

sportsman, *noun*

الرياضي

person who plays a sport; **he's an Olympic sportsman.**

plural **sportsmen**

spot [spɒt] **1.** *noun*

١ ـ أ) مكان

(*a*) place; **this is a good spot for a picnic; this is the spot where the accident took place; he was killed on the spot** = immediately.

298

spring

ب) نقطة مستديرة

(*b*) small round mark; **he has a blue tie with red spots; you've got spots of mud on your coat; he must be ill—his face is covered with red spots.**

ت) بقعة ـ مقدار قليل ـ قطرة

(*c*) small drop; small amount; **spots of rain were falling; would you like a spot of food? we're having a spot of trouble with the car.**

2. *verb*

٢ ـ يكتشف ـ يلاحظ

to notice; **he spotted a mistake in my homework; did you spot the number of the car?**

spots—spotting—spotted—has spotted

sprang [spræŋ] *see* **sprung**

ملاحظة : انظر الى كلمة **spring**

spread [spred] *verb*

أ) ينشر ـ يذيع (خبراً) ـ ينتشر

(*a*) to send out/to go out over a wide area; **don't spread the news—it's supposed to be a secret; the soliders spread out across the fields; the fire spread to the house next door.**

ب) يبسط ـ يكسو

(*b*) to cover with; **she spread a cloth over the table; he was spreading jam on his bread; don't spread too much glue on the paper.**

spreads—spreading—spread— has spread

spring [sprɪŋ] **1.** *noun*

١ ـ أ) الربيع : (فصل من فصول السنة)

(*a*) season of the year between winter and summer; **in spring, the trees grow new leaves; we always go on holiday in the spring; they started work last spring/ in the spring of last year; what beautiful spring flowers!**

ب) نابض ـ زُنْبَرَك

(*b*) wire which is twisted round and round and which goes back to its first

two hundred and ninety-eight

square

shape after you have pulled it; strong pieces of metal which allow a car to go easily over bumps; **there are no springs in this bed; there's a spring to keep the door shut; my car needs new springs.**
2. *verb*

٢ - يهبُّ (من فراشه)

to jump; **he sprang out of bed; the door sprang open.**
springs—springing—sprang [spræŋ]**—has sprung** [sprʌŋ]

square [skweə] *noun & adjective*

أ) مربَّع

(a) shape with four equal sides and four corners of 90°; **the floor is covered with black and white squares; it's difficult to fit six people round a small square table; this piece of paper isn't square; ten square metres** = area of 10 metres × 10 metres.

ب) ساحة - ميدان

(b) open area in a town, surrounded by big buildings; **the tourists were visiting Trafalgar Square; Red Square is in the middle of Moscow.**
Note: **ten square metres** *is usually written* **10m²**

squash [skwɒʃ] 1. *noun*

١ - عصير

fruit drink to which you add water; **a glass of orange squash.**
2. *verb*

٢ - يسحق - يهرس - ينسحق - ينهرس

to make something flat; to press together; **he sat on my hat and squashed it; don't put the cakes at the bottom of the bag—they'll get squashed; we all squashed into his little car.**
squashes—squashing—squashed—has squashed

squeeze [skwi:z] *verb*

يعصر - يضغط على - يكبس - ينحشر

to crush/to press hard; to press together; **he squeezed the juice out of the lemon; they all squeezed into the little car.**
squeezes—squeezing—squeezed—has squeezed

staff [stɑ:f] *noun*

مجموعة الموظفين او الاساتذة (في مؤسسة او في مدرسة)

people who work in a school/business, etc.; **we have 25 teaching staff; the firm has a staff of 100; the staff don't like the new offices.**
Note: when used as a subject, **staff** *takes a plural verb;* **a staff of 25** *but* **the staff work very hard**

stage [steɪdʒ] *noun*

خشبة المسرح

part of a theatre where the actors act; **he came on to the stage and started to sing.**

stairs [steəz] *plural noun*

سُلَّم - درجة (في سلَّم)

steps which go up or down from one floor of a building to the next; **he ran up the stairs to his bedroom; she fell down the stairs and broke her leg;** *see also* **downstairs, upstairs.**
Note: **stair** *is sometimes used in the singular for one step:* **she was sitting on the bottom stair**

staircase, *noun*

بيت السلَّم - درج

several stairs which go from one floor in a building to another; **he fell down the staircase; this staircase goes down to the ground floor.**

stamp [stæmp] 1. *noun*

١ - أ) طابع (بريدي او اميري)

(a) small piece of paper with a price printed on it which you stick on a letter to show that you have paid for it to be sent by mail; **you need a 14p stamp for that letter; did you remember to put a stamp on my letter before you posted it? he collects stamps and old coins.**

two hundred and ninety-nine 299

stand

ب) خَتْم ـ دَمْغَة ـ آلة دامغة
(b) machine for making a mark on something; mark made on something; he has a stamp for marking the date on letters; the customs put their stamp on the parcel.
2. *verb*

٢ ـ يلصق طابعاً بريدياً ـ يدمغ (جواز السفر)
(a) to stick a stamp on something; to mark something with a stamp; **did they stamp your passport when you entered the country? send a stamped addressed envelope for a reply** = an envelope with your address and a stamp on it.

ب) يضرب شيئاً بأخمص قدمه
(b) to bang your foot on the ground; **they stamped on the floor and shouted; he stamped out of the room; the soldiers stamped across the square.**

stamps—stamping—stamped—has stamped

stand [stænd] 1. *noun*

١ ـ أ) مسند ـ قاعدة ـ منصب
(a) something which holds something up; **put the pot back on the stand.**

ب) مُدَرَّج
(b) seats where you watch a football match, etc.; **the stands were crowded.**
2. *verb*

٢ ـ أ) ينتصب
(a) to be upright; to put upright; **stand the ladder against the wall; the box was standing in the middle of the room; she stood the clock on the table.**

ب) يقف (على رجليه)
(b) to be on your feet/not to be sitting or lying; **I'm so tired I can hardly keep standing; there are no seats left, so we'll have to stand; don't just stand there—come and help; stand on a chair if you want to reach the top of the cupboard.**

ت) يتحمّل ـ يطيق
(c) not to be annoyed by; **I can't stand all this noise; what a dirty office—I don't** know how you can stand it; **she stopped going to her German class because she couldn't stand the teacher.**

stands—standing—stood [stud]**—has stood**

stand around, *verb*

يقف موقف المتفرج
to stand not doing anything; **they just stood around and watched.**

stand back, *verb*

يرجع الى الوراء
to take a step or two backwards; **the police told the crowd to stand back as the cyclists were passing.**

stand for, *verb*

يعني
to mean; **what do the letters GPO stand for?**

stand in for, *verb*

يَحُلُّ محلَّ
to take the place of someone; **I'm standing in for Mr Smith because he's ill.**

stand out, *verb*

يبرز
to be very clear against a background; **the blue picture stands out very well against the white wall.**

stand up, *verb*

أ) يقف على رجليه
(a) to get up from being on a seat; **when the teacher came into the room all the children stood up; please don't stand up!**

ب) ينتصب ـ يقف منتصباً
(b) to hold yourself upright; **stand up straight.**

ت) يُوَقَّف ـ يَنصُبُ
(c) to put something upright; **stand all those books up; he stood his umbrella up in the corner of the room.**

stand up for, *verb*

يُؤَيِّد ـ يناصر
to try to defend someone/something in an argument; **you must stand up for your rights.**

300   **three hundred**

star

star [stɑː] *noun*

أ) نجم ـ نجمة

(a) small bright light which you see in the sky at night; **look at all those stars—the weather will be fine tomorrow.**

ب) نجم سينمائي ـ ممثل مشهور ـ ممثلة مشهورة

(b) famous person who acts in a play or film; **she's the star of the new film; a film star.**

stare [steə] *verb*

يُحَدِّق

to look straight at someone/something for a long time; **he stared at his plate; it's rude to stare at people; she kept staring at me.**

stares—staring—stared—has stared

start [stɑːt] **1.** *noun*

١ ـ إبتداء ـ بداية ـ استهلال ـ مطلع

beginning; **it took 3 hours from start to finish; we must make an early start** = we must leave early.
2. *verb*

٢ ـ أ) يبدأ ـ يبتدىء ـ يستهلّ ـ يباشر

(a) to begin; **he started eating his sandwiches; it's staring to rain; have you started your new job yet? we'll start by learning the alphabet; we must start to get ready or we'll miss the train; when does the film start?**

ب) ينصرف

(b) to leave; **let's start at 8 o'clock.**

ت) يسيّر ـ يشغّل

(c) to begin to work; to make something begin to work; **I can't start the car/the car won't start.**

starts—starting—started—has started

start off, *verb*

يبدأ ـ يباشر

to begin; **you start off and I'll follow; we'll start off with soup and then have some fish.**

station

start out, *verb*

يخرج ـ ينصرف

to leave; **he started out two hours ago.**

start up, *verb*

يبدأ عملاً ـ يباشر عملاً

to make a business begin to work; **he's starting up a restaurant.**

state [steɪt] **1.** *noun*

١ ـ أ) حالة ـ حالة سيئة

(a) way in which something is; **the house isn't in a very good state; his state of health is getting worse.**

ب) ولاية ـ بلد ـ دولة

(b) independent country or part of a country with its own government; **the African states; the United States of America; the State of California; the electricity industry is owned by the State; state schools** = schools which are organized by the government.
2. *verb*

٢ ـ يُصرِّح ـ يعلن عن

to say clearly; **the stated that she had never been to Paris; the form states the details of the job.**

states—stating—stated—has stated

statement, *noun*

تصريح ـ بيان

clear description of something; **he made a statement to the police; the government made a statement about prices; bank statement** = paper showing how much money you have in your bank account.

States, *plural noun*

الولايات المتحدة الاميركية

the USA; **we're going to the States for Christmas; I was in the States last year.**

station [ˈsteɪʃn] *noun*

أ) محطة (للسكك الحديدية)

(a) place where trains stop for passengers to get on or off; **can you tell me the way to the station? the train doesn't stop at the next station; there's an under-**

three hundred and one　　　　**301**

stay

ground station at the corner of the street; I'll try and have something to eat at the station bar.

ب) موقف الباصات
(b) **bus station/coach station** = place where coaches or buses begin and end their journeys; **we had to wait at the coach station for an hour.**

ت) مركز (الشرطة - الاطفاء ...) محطة ارسال (تلفيزيونية او اذاعية)
(c) large building for some service; **fire station/police station**; **power station** = factory which makes electricity; **service station** = garage which sells petrol and repairs cars; **TV station/radio station** = main building where TV or radio programmes are produced.

stay [steɪ] 1. *noun*

١ - إقامة - فترة الاقامة
time which you spend in a place; **I'm only here for a short stay.**
2. *verb*

٢ - يقيم - يبقى - يظلُّ - ينزل - يمكث - يلازم (الفراش)
to stop in a place for some time; **I'll stay at home tomorrow; we'll stay in Edinburgh on our way to the north of Scotland; how long will you be staying in New York? she's ill and has to stay in bed; they came for tea and stayed until ten o'clock.**
stays—staying—stayed—has stayed

stay away, *verb*

يبقى جانباً - يقف بعيداً عن
not to come or go to something; **he doesn't like big parties, so he stayed away.**

stay in, *verb*

يلازم البيت
to stay at home; **I won't come to the party—I'm staying in tonight.**

stay out, *verb*

يغيب عن البيت
not to come home; **don't stay out after ten o'clock.**

302

steer

stay up, *verb*

يبقى صاحياً - لا ينام
not to go to bed; **we stayed up very late last night; little children shouldn't stay up watching TV; I'm staying up to watch the late football match on TV.**

steal [stiːl] *verb*

يسلب - ينهب
to take something which does not belong to you; **the burglar stole all the jewellery; someone has stolen my car.**
steals—stealing—stole [stəʊl]—has stolen

steam [stiːm] *noun*

بخار
hot gas which comes off boiling water; **steam was coming out of the kettle; the train was pulled by an old steam engine.**

steel [stiːl] *noun*

فولاذ
strong metal used for making knives/cars, etc.; **he has glasses with steel frames; you need a pair of steel scissors—those plastic ones won't cut paper!**
no plural

steep [stiːp] *adjective*

شديد الانحدار - شاهق - عال - باهظ
which slopes up or down a lot; **the car had difficulty in going up the steep hill; there's been a steep increase in prices.**
steep—steeper—steepest

steer [stɪə] *verb*

يوجّه (السيارة او المركب)
to make a car/a boat go in a certain direction; **he steered the boat into the harbour; steer towards that rock.**
steers—steering—steered—has steered

steering wheel, *noun*

عجلة القيادة (في السيارة)
wheel in a car which you hold, and turn to make the car turn.

three hundred and two

step

step [step] **1.** *noun*

١ - أ) خطوة

(a) movement of your foot when walking; he took two steps forward; she took a big step sideways; **step by step** = little by little.

ب) مشية - وقع الاقدام

(b) regular movement of feet; **out of step/in step** = moving at a different rate/at the same rate as everyone/everthing else; **try to keep in step;** wages are out of step with the rise in prices.

ت) درجة (من درجات السلّم)

(c) place where you walk going up or down; there is a step down into the kitchen; be careful, there are two steps up into the bathroom; to go from the house into the garden you have to go down several stone steps.

ث) إجراء - (يتخذ اجراءات)

(d) action; we must take steps to make sure that we do not lose money; the first step is to find out how much money we spend = the first thing to do.

2. *verb*

٢ - يمشي - يتقدم - يتخطى - ينزل من - يقفز - يخرج

to move forward on foot; he stepped out into the street; she stepped off the bus; step over that heap of rubbish.
steps—stepping—stepped—has stepped

step in, *verb*

يتدخّل في شأن

to act where you were not concerned before; everything was working very well until the government stepped in.

step up, *verb*

يزيد - يضاعف

to increase; we are trying to step up production.

stick [stɪk] **1.** *noun*

١ - أ) عود - قضيب - عصا

(a) piece of wood; **collect some dry sticks to light a fire.**

stick

ب) عصا للمشي

(b) **walking stick** = long piece of wood which you use to help you to walk; **the blind man had a white stick; he has to walk with two sticks.**

2. *verb*

٢ - أ) يَغْرُزُ - يشك - يطعن

(a) to push something sharp into something; he stuck a pin into me; the nurse stuck a needle into my arm.

ب) يُلْصِق

(b) to attach (with glue); he stuck the stamp on the envelope; she tried to stick the handle on to the cup with glue.

ت) يمكث - يبقى في مكان معين

(c) to stay and not to move; stick close to me and you won't get lost; the car got stuck in the mud; the door's stuck and we can't open it.

ث) يضع في مكان معيّن

(d) to push/to put; he stuck the letter in his pocket; stick all those books in the back of the car.

ج) يطبق - يتحمّل

(e) not to be annoyed by; I can't stick people who make a lot of noise; *see also* **stand**
sticks—sticking—stuck [stʌk]—**has stuck**

sticking plaster, *noun*

اللاصوق : لزقة للجراح السطحية

sticky tape used to cover a small wound; **put a piece of sticking plaster on your cut.**

no plural: **some sticking plaster; a piece of sticking plaster**

stick out, *verb*

يبرز - يُخرج - يَبْرُز

to push out; to be further out; **the doctor asked him to stick out his tongue/to stick his tongue out; his wallet was sticking out of his pocket.**

Note: **he stuck his tongue out** *or* **he stuck out his tongue** *but only* **he stuck it out**

stick up, *verb*

still

أ) يعلّق (على الجدران)
(a) to attach to a wall; **he stuck up a notice on the wall.**

ب) يَبْرُز ـ يَنْتَأ الى أعلى
(b) to push up; to be further up; **the guns were sticking up out of a box.**

stick up for, verb

يدافع عن ـ يؤيّد
to try to defend someone/something in an argument; **he stuck up for her when the head teacher wanted to sack her;** see also **stand up for.**

sticky, adjective

لزج ـ دَبق
which is covered with glue; **there's something sticky on the table; don't sit on that chair—the paint's still sticky.**
sticky—stickier—stickiest

stiff [stɪf] adjective

أ) صلب ـ جاسيء
(a) which cannot be bent or moved easily; **my knee is stiff after playing football; can you open this pot of jam?—the lid's very stiff; brush your coat with a stiff brush; he's frozen stiff** = very cold.

ب) صعب ـ شاق
(b) difficult; **you have to take a stiff driving test.**
stiff—stiffer—stiffest

still [stɪl] **1.** adjective

١ ـ ساكن ـ غير متحرك ـ هادئ
not moving; **stand still while I take your photograph; the surface of the water was completely still.**
2. adverb

٢ ـ أ) حتى الآن ـ لا يزال
(a) until now/until then/continuing; **they came for tea and they were still here at ten o'clock; I've still got some money left; they're still talking about the election.**

ب) ومع ذلك
(b) even; **there were fifty people in the room and still more tried to get in; it has been cold all day, and it will be still colder tonight.**

ت) بالرغم من ذلك
(c) however; in spite of that; **it wasn't very fine—still, it didn't rain; he still went on holiday although he had no money.**

stir [stɜː] verb

يُحَرِّك ـ يمزج بالتحرك
to mix a liquid; **he stirred his cup of tea; she was stirring the soup.**
stirs—stirring—stirred—has stirred

stir up, verb

يعكر صفوه : (هي دائماً تعكر صفو الجوّ في المكتب)
to make (trouble); **she's always stirring up trouble in the office.**

stocking ['stɒkɪŋ] noun

جورب
long light piece of clothing worn by women which covers all your leg and your foot; **she was wearing blue stockings and white shoes.**

stole [stəʊl], **stolen** ['stəʊln] see **steal**

ملاحظة : انظر الى كلمة steal

stomach ['stʌmək] noun

مَعِدة ـ بطن
part of the front of the body lower than the chest; **he hit him in the stomach; he crept across the room on his stomach; stomach ache** = pain in the stomach caused by eating too much food, etc.

stone [stəʊn] noun

أ) حَجَر
(a) hard material, found in the ground, and used for building; **a big stone bridge; the houses in the town are all built of stone; these stone floors are very cold.**

304 *three hundred and four*

stood　　　　　　　　　　　　　　　　　　　　　　　**store**

ب) حجرة - حجارة
(b) small piece of stone; **don't throw stones at the cars; she's got a stone in her shoe; the beach is covered with sharp stones.**

ت) الحجر : وحدة وزن بريطانية تعادل ١٤ باوناً او ٦,٣٥ كيلوغراماً
(c) measure of weight (= 14 pounds or 6.35 kilograms); **he tried to lose weight and lost three stone; she weighs eight stone.**
Note: no plural for (a): some stone; a piece of stone; a block of stone
No plural for (c): she weighs ten stone

stony, *adjective*

حجري - صخري
covered with stones; **a stony beach.**
stony—stonier—stoniest

stood [stʊd] *see* **stand**
ملاحظة : انظر الى كلمة **stand**

stop [stɒp] **1.** *noun*

١ - ١) تَوَقُّف - نهاية
(a) end of something, especially of a movement; **the car came to a stop at the bottom of the hill; we must put a stop to crime; all work came to a stop when the firm couldn't pay any wages.**

ب) نقطة توقف - محطة
(b) place where a bus lets passengers get on or off; **we waited for twenty minutes at the bus stop; the bus stop is just in front of the post office; I must get off at the next stop.**

ت) علامة وقف (في الكتابة)
(c) **full stop** = dot (.) at the end of a written sentence.
2. *verb*

٢ - ١) يُوْقِف
(a) not to move any more; to make something not move any more; **the policeman stopped the traffic to let the children cross the road; the car didn't stop at the red lights; fast trains don't stop at this station; the bus just went past**

without stopping; **stop him! he's stolen my watch!**

ب) يكفُّ عن - ينقطع عن
(b) not to do something any more; **can't you stop that noise? the clock has stopped at 3.30; it's stopped raining; last week it rained for three days without stopping; he stopped work and went home.**

ت) يتوقف - ينزل (في مكان)
(c) to stay in a place for a time; **we stopped for a few days in Stockholm; we'll be stopping in Rome for the weekend; can you stop at the butcher's on your way home and buy some meat for dinner?**

ث) يمنع - يضع حداً لـ - يصدُّ
(d) **to stop someone/something (from) doing something** = to prevent someone/something from doing something; **the weather stopped us from playing cricket; can the police stop the children from stealing sweets? can't you stop your watch making such a loud noise?**
stops—stopping—stopped—has stopped

stop over, *verb*

يتوقف (خلال رحلة)
to spend a night in a place on a long journey; **we'll stop over in Amsterdam on the way to Moscow.**

stop up, *verb*

أ) يبقى مستيقظاً
(a) not to go to bed; **are you going to stop up to watch the late football match?**

ب) يسدُّ
(b) to block; **you can stop up the hole with a piece of wood.**
Note: **stop the hole up** *or* **stop up the hole** *but only* **stop it up**

store [stɔː] **1.** *noun*

١ - ١) محل تجاري كبير
(a) shop (usually a big shop); **you can buy shoes in the big stores in town; does this store have a restaurant?**

three hundred and five　　　　　　　**305**

storm

ب) مخزون ـ مقدار وافر

(b) food, etc., kept to use later; **we have a big store of wood for the winter; we have bought stores for the long journey.**
2. *verb*

٢ ـ يُخَزِّن

to keep food, etc., to use later; **we'll store all our apples in that cupboard.**
stores—storing—stored—has stored

storm [stɔ:m] *noun*

عاصفة

very bad weather with a high wind; **two ships sank in the storm; the storm blew down two trees; we often have storms in March.**

stormy, *adjective*

عاصف

with storms; **a period of stormy weather.**
stormy—stormier—stormiest

story ['stɔ:rɪ] *noun*

أ) خبر ـ قصة ـ حكاية

(a) telling of what happened; **tell the policeman your story; it's a long story** = it is difficult to explain what happened; **the film is the story of two children and a little white dog; he writes stories about the war.**

ب) اكذوبة ـ خرافة

(b) lie/something which is not true; **don't tell stories.**
plural **stories**

stove [stəʊv] *noun*

موقد : جهاز للطبخ

machine for cooking; **we have a gas stove in the kitchen.**

straight [streɪt] 1. *adjective*

١ ـ أ) مستقيم ـ غير جعد

(a) not curved; **a straight road; draw a straight line; he has long straight hair.**

ب) مرتّب ـ حسن الترتيب

(b) tidy/in its proper place; **your tie isn't straight; we'll try to put the room straight after the party; let's get it straight** = let us understand clearly what happened/understand the situation.
straight—straighter—straightest
2. *adverb*

٢ ـ أ) دغري ـ بخط مستقيم

(a) in a straight line/not curving; **keep straight on until you come to the traffic lights; the road goes straight for three miles.**

ب) مباشرةً ـ فوراً

(b) immediately; **I'll come straight back; he went straight to the police.**

ت) بلا تردّد

(c) without stopping or changing direction; **he drank the milk straight out of the bottle; he ran straight across the road without looking; she looked him straight in the face.**

straight away, *adverb*

حالاً ـ توّاً

immediately/at once; **I need the money straight away.**

strange [streɪndʒ] *adjective*

أ) غريب ـ غير مألوف

(a) odd/not usual; **the car engine is making a strange sound; he said some very strange things about his boss.**

ب) غير مألوف

(b) which you have never seen before/where you have never been before; **it's difficult to get to sleep in a strange room; we went to Hong Kong and had lots of strange food to eat.**
strange—stranger—strangest

stranger, *noun*

الأجنبي ـ الغريب

person whom you have never met; person in a place where he has never been before; **he's a complete stranger; don't accept presents from strangers; I'm a stranger here—I'm afraid I don't know where the post office is.**

stream

stream [stri:m] *noun*

أ) نهر - نهير - سيل

(a) small river; **he jumped over the mountain stream.**

ب) موكب متصل (موكب السيارات)

(b) mass of cars/people, etc., all going in the same direction; **streams of cars were going towards the coast; you can't cross the stream of traffic.**

street [stri:t] *noun*

شارع

road in a town, with houses or shops on each side; **the main street is very busy on Saturday mornings; go down the street to the traffic lights; the post office is on the opposite side of the street; where do you live?—16 Oxford Street; High Street** = the main shopping street in a town; **his shop in in the High Street.**
Note: often used in names: **Oxford Street, High Street,** *etc., and usually written* **St: Oxford St**

strength [streŋθ] *noun*

قوة - مقدرة

being strong; **he kicked the ball with all his strength; he doesn't know his own strength** = he doesn't know how strong he really is.
no plural

stretch [stretʃ] *verb*

أ) يمدّ - يمدّد - يبسط - يمط

(a) to pull out; to make longer; **the wire was stretched between two poles; you've stretched your pullover by pulling it over your head** = made it become too big.

ب) يتمدد - يتمطى

(b) to put out your arms and legs as far as they will go; **he stretched out his hand and took a book frm the shelf; the cat got up from the chair and stretched; she lay stretched out on the floor.**

ت) يمتدّ

(c) to go on for a great distance; **the sea**

three hundred and seven

strong

stretched all round us; the road stretches for miles.
stretches—stretching—stretched—has stretched

strike [straɪk] **1.** *noun*

١ - إضراب عن العمل

stopping of work by workers; **the office staff are on strike; the strike by the bus drivers lasted two weeks.**
2. *verb*

٢ - أ) يوجّه ضربةً

(a) to hit; **he struck a policeman with a bottle; the car went down the hill and struck a tree.**

ب) يؤثر في النفس

(b) to surprise; to make someone think; **I was struck by what she said; it strikes me that she was telling a lie** = it seems to me.

ت) يضرب عن العمل

(c) to stop work; **the staff are striking for more money.**

ث) يعلن عن طريق ضربات : ساعة بيج بن تعلن العاشرة

(d) (of a clock) to ring a bell to show the hour; **Big Ben struck ten.**

ج) يولع (عوداً)

(e) to light (a match).
strikes—striking—struck [strʌk]—has struck

string [strɪŋ] *noun*

أ) حبل - سلك - خيط

(a) thin threads twisted together; **tie the parcel up with a piece of string; I bought a ball of string; this string isn't strong enough; have you any more string?**

ب) وتر (لآلة موسيقية)

(b) long thread on a musical instrument which makes a note when you hit it; **a guitar has six strings.**
no plural for (a): **some string; a piece of string**

strong [strɒŋ] *adjective*

أ) قويّ - جبار

(a) who/which has a lot of force/a lot of

307

Streets

الشوارع

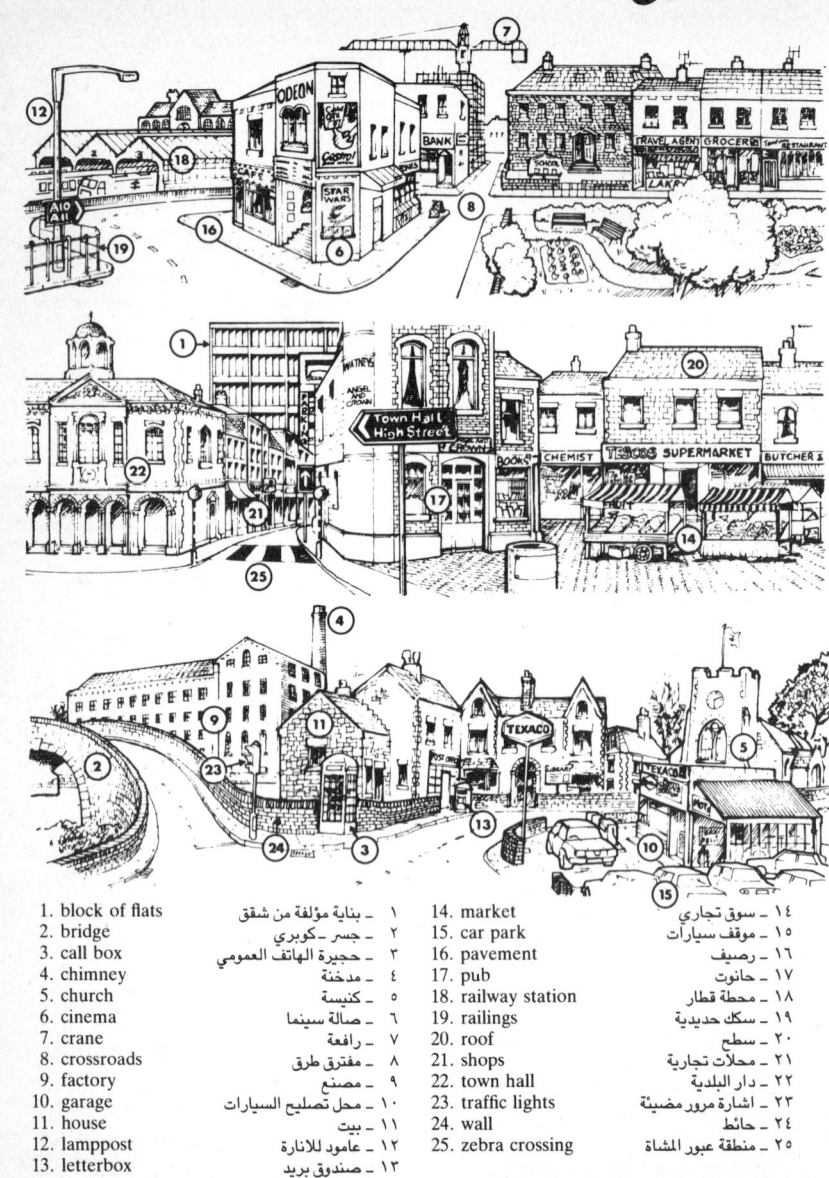

1. block of flats	بناية مؤلفة من شقق	١
2. bridge	جسر – كوبري	٢
3. call box	حجيرة الهاتف العمومي	٣
4. chimney	مدخنة	٤
5. church	كنيسة	٥
6. cinema	صالة سينما	٦
7. crane	رافعة	٧
8. crossroads	مفترق طرق	٨
9. factory	مصنع	٩
10. garage	محل تصليح السيارات	١٠
11. house	بيت	١١
12. lamppost	عامود للانارة	١٢
13. letterbox	صندوق بريد	١٣
14. market	سوق تجاري	١٤
15. car park	موقف سيارات	١٥
16. pavement	رصيف	١٦
17. pub	حانوت	١٧
18. railway station	محطة قطار	١٨
19. railings	سكك حديدية	١٩
20. roof	سطح	٢٠
21. shops	محلات تجارية	٢١
22. town hall	دار البلدية	٢٢
23. traffic lights	اشارة مرور مضيئة	٢٣
24. wall	حائط	٢٤
25. zebra crossing	منطقة عبور المشاة	٢٥

308   *three hundred and eight*

struck

strength; **is he strong enough to pick up that box? the rope's broken—we need something stronger; the strong wind blew all the leaves off the trees.**

ب) حادّ الرائحة او المذاق او المفعول او الكحول

(b) with a powerful smell/taste, etc.; **this cheese is too strong; this tea is too strong—put some water in it; what I want is a cup of strong black coffee; there was a strong smell of onions; strong drink is bad for you** = alcohol is bad for you.

strong—stronger—strongest

struck [strʌk] *see* **strike**

ملاحظة : انظر الى كلمة strike

stuck [stʌk] *see* **stick**

ملاحظة : انظر الى كلمة stick

student ['stju:dnt] *noun*

طالب

person who is studying at a college or university; **all the science students are working for their exams.**

study ['stʌdı] 1. *noun*

١ ـ دراسة ـ درس ـ بحث

learning about something; **she's finished her studies** = has finished her course at university, etc.; **he's making a study of diseases of fish.**

plural studies

2. *verb*

٢ ـ يدرس ـ يقوم بأبحاث

to learn about something; **he's studying maths; don't make any noise—we're all studying for our exams.**

studies—studying—studied—has studied

stuff [stʌf] 1. *noun*

امتعة ـ اشياء ـ مواد ـ ممتلكات شخصية ـ نسيج ـ طعام ـ البسة

material/things (especially when you don't know what it is); **put some dry**

three hundred and nine

subtract

stuff in the bottom of the box; there's some green stuff on the table—I don't know what it is; there's still some stuff left in the car.

2. *verb*

٢ ـ يحشو ـ يتخم

to push hard into; **he stuffed the papers into his pocket; she was stuffing her clothes into a suitcase.**

stuffs—stuffing—stuffed—has stuffed

stupid ['stju:pɪd] *adjective*

أحمق ـ أبله ـ غبيّ

silly/not very clever; **don't be stupid—you can't drive a car if you haven't passed your test; he's a stupid boy—he spends all his time watching TV instead of doing his homework.**

subject ['sʌbdʒekt] *noun*

أ) الفاعل : (في الجملة : وقع الكلب في الماء ، ان كلمة كلب هي فاعل لفعل وقع)

(a) word which shows the person or thing doing an action; **in the sentence 'the dog fell into the water' the word 'dog' is the subject.**

ب) موضوع : (لديّ ثلاث مواضيع تحت الدراسة)

(b) thing which is being talked about, written about or studied; **I have to study three subjects—English, maths and science; what subject does Mr Smith teach?—he teaches English; the subject of his book is English history; she's talking on the subject 'the place of women in Parliament'; let's change the subject** = let's talk about something else.

subtract [sʌb'trækt] *verb*

يطرح (عدداً من عدد آخر)

to take one number away from another; **subtract 24 from 86 and the answer is 62.**

subtracts—subtracting—subtracted—has subtracted

subtraction [sʌb'trækʃn] *noun*

الطرح (عملية الطرح)

taking one number from another; **I'm**

309

succeed

good at subtraction, but I can't do division.

succeed [sək'si:d] *verb*

يَنْجَحُ - يُفْلِح

to do well; to do what you have been trying to do; **he tried to climb up the tree but didn't succeed; she succeeded in opening the box; this book tells you how to succeed in business.**

succeeds—succeeding—succeeded—has succeeded

success [sək'ses] *noun*

١) نجاح - فَلاَحْ

(a) doing something well; doing what you have been trying to do; **I've been trying to get a job, but with no success.**

ب) عمل ناجح - حدث ناجح

(b) somebody/something which does well; **the party was not a success; this new film is a great success.**

plural **successes**

successful, *adjective*

ناجح

which does well; **a successful party; he's a successful businessman.**

successfully, *adverb*

بنجاح

well; **he successfully finished his studies.**

such [sʌtʃ] *adjective*

١) مثل - كَـ

(a) like; of this sort; **people such as doctors need to study for many years; there is no such thing as a plastic frying pan; the customs are looking for such things as drugs or alcohol; there is no such day as February 30th; he was asking for Miss Jones, but there is no such person working here.**

ب) كبير - هائل - للغاية

(b) so large/so great; **there was such a crowd of people that there were not enough chairs; he's such a slow worker; people can't afford to drive such large cars.**

310

sugar

suck [sʌk] *verb*

يمصّ - يمتصّ - يرضع

to pull liquid or air into your mouth; to have something in your mouth which you like with your tongue; **he sucked all the juice out of the orange; she was sucking a big sweet; the baby's sucking its thumb.**

sucks—sucking—sucked—has sucked

sudden ['sʌdn] *adjective*

مفاجىء - فجائي - سريع

which happens quickly; which surprises; **there was a sudden bang and smoke poured out of the engine; don't drive too fast—there's a sudden bend in the road.**

فجأةً

all of a sudden = happening quickly and making you surprised; **all of a sudden the lights went out.**

suddenly, *adverb*

فجأةً

happening quickly and making you surprised; **the car stopped suddenly; he suddenly sneezed**

suffer ['sʌfə] *verb*

يتألّم - يتوجع - يعاني

to feel pain; to have an illness; to be in a bad situation; **she suffers from headaches; he suffers from not being able to hear well; if you watch too much TV, your homework will suffer** = will be badly done.

suffers—suffering—suffered—has suffered

sugar ['ʃʊgə] *noun*

سُكَّر

white or brown sweet stuff which you use to make food sweet; **do you take sugar in your coffee? there's too much sugar in this pudding; can you buy a bag of sugar—we have none left.**

no plural: **some sugar; a bag of sugar; a lump of sugar**

three hundred and ten

suggest

suggest [sə'dʒest] *verb*

يقترح - يعرض فكرة او اقتراحاً - يوحي to mention an idea; **I suggest we stop for a cup of coffee; she suggested that we should ask John to the party; we've suggested to the headmaster that he should talk to the parents.**

suggests—suggesting—suggested—has suggested

suggestion, *noun*

اقتراح - ايحاء

idea which has been mentioned; **I don't agree with your suggestion that we should stop for coffee; can I make a suggestion? it was my suggestion that we should all go for a walk.**

suit [suːt] **1.** *noun*

١ - (أ) بذلة - طاقم - طقم

(a) various pieces of clothing (jacket and trousers or skirt) made of the same cloth and worn at the same time; **he had a dark grey suit on; she was wearing a blue suit.**

ب) جميع اوراق اللعب ذات النقش الواحد : (السباتي او البستوني ... الخ)

(b) one of the four groups of cards with the same pattern in a pack of cards; **hearts and diamonds are the two red suits; to follow suit** = to do what everyone else does; **he jumped on to the bus and we all followed suit.**

2. *verb*

٢ - (أ) يلائم - يتلائم - يتمشى مع

(a) to fit your appearance; **green suits you; that hat suits her.**

ب) يناسب - يرضي

(b) to be convenient; **I'll do it when it suits me** = when it is convenient for me; **that suits me fine** = that is very convenient.

suits—suiting—suited—has suited

suitable, *adjective*

ملائم - مناسب

which fits/which is convenient; **the most suitable date for the meeting would be October 18th.**

three hundred and eleven

sun

suitcase, *noun*

حقيبة سفر

box with a handle which you carry your clothes in when you are travelling; **she was putting her clothes into a suitcase; your suitcase is very heavy.**

sum [sʌm] *noun*

١) الجمع (عملية الجمع في الرياضيات) - مجموع

(a) problem in maths; **he's no good at sums; I can't do this sum; she tried to do the sum in her head** = without writing it down.

ب) مبلغ

(b) total amount (of money); **she received the sum of £25.**

summer ['sʌmə] *noun*

صيف - فصل الصيف

hottest season of the year, the season between spring and autumn; **most people go on holiday in the summer; last summer we went to Greece; summer is the hottest part of the year; I haven't any summer clothes—it is never very warm here.**

sun [sʌn] *noun*

الشمس

very hot star round which the earth travels and which gives light and heat; **we can go for a walk now that the sun's shining again; the sun's so hot that we'll have to sit in the shade; you can't spend all day just sitting in the sun** = sitting in the sunshine; **the sun rises in the east.**

sunglasses, *plural noun*

نظارات واقية من الشمس - نظارات شمس

dark glasses which you wear to protect your eyes from the sun; **he kept bumping into the chairs because he wore his sunglasses in the house.**

sunny, *adjective*

مشمس

with the sun shining; **a sunny day; the sunny side of the street.**

sunny—sunnier—sunniest

311

Sunday

sunrise, *noun*
الشروق : شروق الشمس
time when the sun comes up in the morning.

sunset, *noun*
الغروب : غروب الشمس
time when the sun goes down in the evening.

sunshine, *noun*
أشعة الشمس
light from the sun; **the sunshine hurts my eyes.**

Sunday ['sʌndɪ] *noun*
الاحد : (يوم الاحد)
day between Saturday and Monday; **last Sunday we went on a picnic; the shops are closed on Sundays; shall we meet next Sunday? today is Sunday, October 18th.**

sung [sʌŋ] *see* **sing**
ملاحظة : انظر الى كلمة sing

sunk [sʌŋk] *see* **sink**
ملاحظة : انظر الى كلمة sink

superlative [suːˈpɜːlətɪv] *noun*
دال على صيغة التفضيل
form of an adjective or adverb which shows the highest level; **'fattest'** is the superlative of **'fat'; 'fastest'** is the superlative of **'fast'.**

supermarket [ˈsuːpəmɑːkɪt] *noun*
السوق المركزية : متجر كبير للبيع عن طريق الخدمة الذاتية
large shop which sells mainly food, where you take things from the shelves and pay for them as you leave; **go to the supermarket and get me some coffee; the supermarket stays open late on Friday evenings.**

supper [ˈsʌpə] *noun*
عشاء ـ طعام العشاء
meal which you eat in the evening; **what did you eat for supper? we have supper at about seven o'clock; come and have supper with us tomorrow.**
see note at **dinner**

supply [səˈplaɪ] **1.** *noun*
١ ـ أ) تـزويـد ـ مـواد استهـلاكيـة ـ امدادات ـ ذخيرة
(*a*) something which is provided; **the electricity supply has broken down; the army dropped supplies to the farms which were cut off by the snow.**
ب) مؤونة ـ مخزون
(*b*) something which is kept for later use; **we have a good supply of wood for the winter; eggs are in short supply at the moment** = there are not many eggs in the shops.
plural **supplies**

2. *verb*
٢ ـ يزوّد ـ يمدّ بـ ـ يجهّز ـ يسدّ حاجةً
to provide/to give something which is needed; **the army is supplying the farms with food; bread is supplied by the local baker; the town is supplied with water from the river; can you supply me with information about the accident? he couldn't supply any information about holidays in Russia.**
supplies—supplying—supplied—has supplied

suppose [səˈpəʊz] *verb*
أ) يفترض ـ يتصوّر ـ يعتقد ـ يظنّ
(*a*) to think; to imagine; **I suppose she will be late as usual; I supposed everyone knew about the party; are you going to the party tonight?—I suppose so; I don't suppose anyone will come; he's supposed to be a good doctor** = people say he is a good doctor.
ب) من المفروض ان : (من المفروض ان تلازم فراشك)
(*b*) **to be supposed to** = ought to; **you're supposed to be in bed.**
ت) على إفتراض ان ـ إفرض أن
(*c*) **suppose/supposing** = if we imagine/ what happens if; **suppose/supposing it**

sure

rains tomorrow, shall we still go on the picnic? suppose/supposing he's had an accident?
supposes—supposing—supposed—has supposed

sure [ʃʊə] *adjective*

أكيد ـ متأكد ـ يقين

certain; **I'm sure he'll come to the party; are you sure she'll lend you her car? are you sure you haven't lost the key? it's sure to be cold in Canada in January; make sure/be sure you lock all the doors.**

surely, *adverb*

طبعاً ـ بكل تأكيد

of course (*used mostly in questions where a particular answer is expected*) **surely you don't expect him to go out in the rain? surely his name is John not James?**

surface ['sɜːfɪs] *noun*

سطح ـ (سطح الماء)

top part of something which the air touches; **the fish came to the surface of the water to breathe; the table has a shiny surface.**

surname ['sɜːneɪm] *noun*

لقب ـ إسم الاسرة

family name; **I know he's called John, but what's his surname? write your first name and surname on the form.**

surprise [səˈpraɪz] 1. *noun*

١ ـ مفاجأة

feeling caused by something which you did not expect to happen; **let's hide behind the door and give him a surprise; they made her a big birthday cake as a surprise; what a surprise to meet him in the supermarket.**
2. *verb*

٢ ـ يفاجىء

to give someone a surprise; **I'm sur-**

sweep

prised to hear that he is in prison; I shouldn't be surprised if it snows.
surprises—surprising—surprised—has surprised

surround [səˈraʊnd] *verb*

يحيط بـ ـ يحاوط

to be all around something; **an island is a piece of land surrounded by water; the garden is surrounded by a high wall; she's always surrounded by young men.**
surrounds—surrounding—surrounded—has surrounded

suspect [səˈspekt] *verb*

يَتَّهم

to think that someone may have done something wrong; **the police suspect that he was lying; she is suspected of having killed her brother.**
suspects—suspecting—suspected—has suspected

suspicious [səˈspɪʃəs] *adjective*

مشبوه ـ مريب ـ مثير للشك

thinking that someone may have done something wrong; **don't mention money—we don't want to make him suspicious; I'm suspicious about why she had to go to Germany quickly.**

swallow ['swɒləʊ] *verb*

يبتلع ـ يلتهم

to make food go down from your mouth to your stomach; **chew your food well or you won't be able to swallow it; give him a glass of water—he's swallowed a fly; he swallowed his dinner and went out = he ate his dinner quickly.**
swallows—swallowing—swallowed—has swallowed

swam [swæm] *see* **swim**

ملاحظة : انظر الى كلمة swim

sweep [swiːp] *verb*

أ) يكنس

(*a*) to clean with a brush; **he swept the**

three hundred and thirteen 313

sweet

dead leaves into a pile; don't forget to sweep the kitchen floor.

ب) يمرّ بسرعة

(b) to go fast; **the traffic swept past our house; the crowd swept into the street.**

sweeps—sweeping—swept—has swept

sweet [swi:t] 1. *adjective*

١ - حلو

tasting like sugar; not sour/bitter; **my tea's too sweet—I put sugar in it twice; do you like sweet food? oranges are sweeter than lemons; he's got a sweet tooth** = he likes sweet things.

sweet—sweeter—sweetest

2. *noun*

٢ - ١) حلوى - قطعة صغيرة من الحلوى

(a) (*American*: **candy**) small piece of sweet food, made with sugar; **be brought a bag of sweets to suck in the car; eating sweets is bad for your teeth.**

ب) حلاوة

(b) sweet food eaten at the end of a meal; pudding; **what's for sweet? I want ice cream for sweet; I haven't eaten my sweet yet.**

swept [swept] *see* **sweep**

ملاحظة : انظر الى كلمة sweep

swim [swɪm] 1. *noun*

١ - سباحة

moving in the water, using your arms and legs to push you along; **we went for a swim before breakfast; it's too cold to have a swim; I went for three swims yesterday.**

2. *verb*

٢ - يسبح

to move in water using your arms and legs to push you along; **he can't swim; she's learning to swim; I swam across the river twice; can you swim under the water? let's go swimming this afternoon.**

swims—swimming—swam [swæm]—has swum [swʌm]

314

swum

swimmer, *noun*

السابح - السبّاح

person who is swimming.

swimming pool, *noun*

مسبح

large bath of water for swimming in; **our school has an indoor swimming pool; we have a little swimming pool in the garden; he swam two lengths of the swimming pool.**

swing [swɪŋ] *verb*

ا) يتأرجح - يتمايل

(a) to move from side to side or forwards and backwards; **he was swinging on a rope; the door swung open.**

ب) يدور - يلتفت - يتقلّب

(b) to turn suddenly; **he swung round and shouted something; the car swung across the road and hit a tree.**

swings—swinging—swung [swʌŋ]—has swung

switch [swɪtʃ] 1. *noun*

١ - مفتاح كهربائي

button which you push to stop or start something electric; **push the red switch to start the engine; the light switch is behind the door.**

plural **switches**

2. *verb*

٢ - يشغّل التيار او يقطع التيار الكهربائي :

to switch on/off = to make an electric machine start/stop; **can you switch the TV off when you go to bed? he forgot to switch off his car lights/to switch his car lights off; switch on the radio/switch the radio on—it's time for the news.**

switches—switching—switched—has switched

Note: **he switched the radio off** *or* **he switched off the radio** *but only* **he switched it off**

swum [swʌm] *see* **swim**

ملاحظة : انظر الى كلمة swim

three hundred and fourteen

swung

swung [swʌŋ] *see* **swing**
ملاحظة : انظر الى كلمة **swing**

system [ˈsɪstəm] *noun*
شبكة (السكك الحديدية) - نظام (تعليمي) - جهاز (هاتفي)

arrangement of things so that they work together; **the country's railway system; I don't understand the education system; he has a funny system of bells to wake himself up in the morning.**

Tt

table [teɪbl] *noun*
طاولة - مائدة

piece of furniture with a flat top and legs, which is used to eat at/to work at, etc.; **a dining room table; a kitchen table; can you set the table please?** = put the knives/forks/spoons/plates, etc., on a table ready for a meal; **let me help you clear the table** = take away the dirty knives/forks/spoons/plates, etc., after a meal.

tablecloth, *noun*
٢ - السمّاط : غطاء المائدة

cloth which you put on a table for a meal.

tail [teɪl] *noun*
أ) ذنب - ذيل

(a) back part of an animal at the end of the body just above the legs, usually sticking out; **the cat was moving its tail from side to side; some birds have very long tails; a fish swims with its tail.**

ب) قفا الدرهم - قفا قطعة النقد المعدنيّة
(b) side of a coin opposite the head; **let's play heads or tails** = lets throw the coin in the air to see which side comes down on top.

take [teɪk] *verb*
أ) يأخذ من

(a) to pick something up; **he took the book from the shelf; she took the newspaper off the table.**

ب) يأخذ معه
(b) to go with something to another place; **can you take this letter to the post office? she was taking her children to school; he's taken the car to the garage.**

ت) يأخذ - يسلب - يستولي على
(c) to steal; **who's taken my pen? someone has taken my car.**

ث) يحجز (مقعداً) - يجلس على مقعد
(d) to occupy; **this seat is taken; please take a seat.**

ج) يجري (فحصاً ، امتحاناً)
(e) to do an examination or test; **he's taking his exams tomorrow so he has to go to bed early; she took her driving test three times before she passed.**

ح) يتناول (الدواء)
(f) to eat/to drink (often); **do you take sugar in your coffee? he has to take the medicine three times a day.**

خ) يقبل - يتقبّل
(g) to accept; **if he offers you the job, take it.**

د) يذهب في عطلة - يستحمّ - يلتقط (صورة) - يرتاح
(h) to do certain actions; **I'm going to take a holiday; has he taken his bath yet? he took a picture of the Houses of Parliament; hurry up and take the photo, it's starting to rain; you should go and take a rest.**

three hundred and fifteen 315

talk

ذ) يحتاج الى ـ يتوجب ـ يستغرق (من الوقت)

(i) to need; **it took three men to lift the car; we took three days/it took us three days to walk to Edinburgh; how long does it take to get to school by bus? he must have been hungry—it didn't take him long to eat all his dinner.**

ر) يستوعب ـ يستطيع احتواء

(j) to accept/to hold; **this machine only takes 10p coins; his car can take four passengers.**

takes—taking—took [tuk]—has taken

take after, verb

يحذو حذو ـ يُشْبه

to be like (a parent); **he takes after his father.**

take away, verb

ا) ينقل ـ يُبْعد عن

(a) to remove something/someone; **take that knife away from him; the police came and took him away.**

ب) يطرح من (عدد)

(b) to subtract one number from another; **if you take six away from ten, you have four.**

Note: **take away** *is usually shown by the sign* −; **10−4=6** (ten take away four equals six)

take back, verb

ا) يَرُدّ

(a) to go back with something; **this shirt is too small—I'll take it back to the shop.**

ب) يسترد

(b) to accept something which someone has returned; **I went to the shop with the shirt which I had just bought, but they wouldn't take it back.**

take in, verb

ا) يفهم ـ يدرك ـ يستوعب

(a) to understand; **he didn't take in what I said.**

ب) يخدع

(b) to trick; **don't be taken in by what he says.**

316

talk

take off, verb

ا) يخلع (ملابسه) ـ ينزع

(a) to remove (especially clothes); **he took off all his clothes/he took all his clothes off; take your shoes off before you come into the house.**

ب) يقلع (قلعت الطائرة في الساعة الرابعة والنصف)

(b) to fly into the air; **the plane took off at 4.30.**

take on, verb

يستخدم (عمالاً او موظفين)

to agree to do a job/to agree to have someone as a worker; **he's taken on two more jobs; the company has taken on three secretaries.**

take over, verb

ا) يشتري (شركة)

(a) to buy (a business); **the firm was taken over last year.**

ب) يتولى السلطة او المسؤولية

(b) to start to be in charge of something in place of someone else; **I'll take over from you now; when the maths teacher was ill, the history teacher had to take over his class.**

take up, verb

ا) يحْتَلّ ـ يملأ (فراغاً)

(a) to occupy; **this table takes up a lot of room; playing football takes up too much time.**

ب) يستأنف ـ يبدأ بـ

(b) to start to do (a sport, etc.); **he's taken up tennis.**

Note: **he took his shoes off** *or* **he took off his shoes; she took the shirt back** *or* **took back the shirt** *but only* **took them off, took it back,** *etc.*

talk [tɔːk] *verb*

يتكلم
يقول ـ يتحدث

to speak; **the tourists were talking German; I don't understand what they're talking about; I must talk to the man at the garage about the car engine;**

three hundred and sixteen

tall

he's talking of going to the USA on holiday.

talks—talking—talked—has talked

talk over, *verb*

يناقش - يجادل

to discuss; go and talk things over with the bank manager.

talk round, *verb*

يقنع (احداً) بتغير رأيه

to persuade someone to change his mind; I talked him round.

tall [tɔ:l] *adjective*

متطاول - عالٍ - طويل القامة

high (usually higher than others); a tall building; can you see that tall tree over there? he's the tallest in his class—he's taller than all the others; how tall are you? I'm 5 foot 7 (5'7") tall.

tall—taller—tallest

Note: **tall** *is used with numbers:* **the tree is 10 metres tall; he's 6 foot tall**

tap [tæp] *noun (American:* faucet)

حنفيّة - سدادة

pipe with a handle which you turn to make a liquid or gas come out; turn the cold water tap off—my bath's too cold; have you turned the gas taps off?

tape [teɪp] *noun*

ا) شريط

(a) long thin flat piece of plastic/of cloth; **tape measure/measuring tape** = tape with marks on it showing centimetres or inches.

ب) شريط تسجيلي

(b) long thin piece of plastic on which sound is recorded; have you heard his latest tape? let me play you the tape I bought today.

tape recorder, *noun*

مُسجّلة الصوت

machine which records sound on tape; he recorded the conversation on his tape recorder.

three hundred and seventeen

tea

taste [teɪst] **1.** *noun*

١ - حاسة الذّوق - طعم - مذاق

one of the five senses, which you notice through your tongue; I don't like the taste of onions; this ice cream has no taste at all.

2. *verb*

٢ - يتذوّق - يذوق - يكون ذا طعم معيّن

to notice the taste of something with your tongue; to have a taste; can you taste the salt in this soup? this cake tastes of salt; I have a cold so I can't taste anything; what is it?—it tastes like jam.

tastes—tasting—tasted—has tasted

taught [tɔ:t] *see* **teach**

ملاحظة : انظر الى كلمة teach

tax [tæks] *noun*

ضريبة - رسم

money which is paid to the government; there's a 10% tax on petrol; you always have to pay tax on the money you earn; no one likes paying tax.

plural **taxes**

taxi ['tæksɪ] *noun*

سيارة أجرة للركاب - التاكسي

car (with a driver) which you can hire; I must call a taxi; why are there no taxis at the station today? there are no buses after 10 o'clock, so we had to take a taxi to the airport.

taxi driver, *noun*

سائق التاكسي

person who drives a taxi.

tea [ti:] *noun*

ا) الشاي

(a) drink made from water which has been poured on to the dried leaves of a plant which grows in hot countries; the dried leaves of this plant; we've got no tea left—can you buy some at the supermarket? put some tea into the pot and add boiling water; would you like

317

teach

another cup of tea/some more tea? I don't like tea—can I have coffee instead?

ب) فنجان من الشاي

(b) a cup of tea; **two teas, please, and two pieces of cake.**

ت) حفلة شاي يُتناول فيها الشاي مع الكعك والخبز والزبدة والحليب

(c) afternoon meal, at which you drink tea and eat bread, cake, etc.; **come and have tea with us tomorrow; have you had your tea yet? they've asked us to tea; we always have tea at four o'clock.**

no plural for (a); **teas** *means* **cups of tea**

tea-bag, *noun*

كيس شاي (مصنوع من الورق عادة)

small paper bag with tea in it which you put into the pot with hot water.

teacloth, *noun*

فوطة لتنشيف الاواني

cloth which you use for drying dishes.

teacup, *noun*

فنجان شاي

large cup for drinking tea.

teapot, *noun*

إبريق الشاي

special pot which is used for making tea; **put some tea into the teapot and add boiling water.**

teaspoon, *noun*

ملعقة شاي

small spoon for stirring tea.

teatime, *noun*

ساعة الشاي (عادةً عند الغروب)

time when you usually have tea; **come on, it's teatime! there is an interesting TV programme which is on at teatime.**

teach [tiːtʃ] *verb*

يُعَلِّم ـ يُدَرِّس

to give lessons; to show someone how to do something; **he taught me how to drive; she teaches French in our school; she taught herself typing; who taught you to swim?**

318

tear

teaches—teaching—taught [tɔːt] **—has taught**

teacher, *noun*

مُعَلِّم ـ مُدَرِّس

person who teaches; **Mr Smith is our English teacher; the music teacher is ill today.**

team [tiːm] *noun*

فريق

group of people who play a game together/who work together; **there are eleven people in a cricket team; she plays for the school team; which football team is your favourite? our team played badly last Saturday.**

tear[1] [tɪə] *noun*

دمعة

drop of water which comes in your eye when you cry; **tears ran down her face; he burst into tears** = he suddenly started to cry; **she ran out of the room in tears** = she was crying.

tear[2] [teə] *verb*

ا) يُمَزِّق

(a) to make a hole in something by pulling; **he tore a hole in his trousers/he tore his trousers.**

ب) يمزّق

(b) to pull something (especially paper or cloth) to pieces; **I tore the letter into little bits.**

ت) يتنقّل بسرعة ـ يشق طريقه

(c) to go fast; **he tore across the room; the cars were tearing past.**

tears—tearing—tore [tɔː] **—has torn** [tɔːn]

tear off, *verb*

ينزع بقوة ـ يمزّق

to pull off by tearing; **he tore off the next page in his notebook.**

tear out, *verb*

ينزع بقوة ـ يقتلع

to pull something out by tearing; **he tore a page out of his notebook.**

three hundred and eighteen

teeth

tear up, *verb*

يمزق قطعاً قطعاً

to pull something to pieces; **she tore up the letter; they tore up the old newspapers; they used torn up newspapers to pack the cups into the box.**

teeth [ti:θ] *see* **tooth**

ملاحظة : انظر الى كلمة tooth

telegram ['telɪgræm] *noun*

برقية

message sent by the post office along wires; **we've had a telegram to say he's coming; send a telegram to your mother.**

telephone ['telɪfəʊn] **1.** *noun*

١ - هاتف - جهاز الهاتف

machine which you can use to speak to someone a long distance away; **the telephone's ringing; can you answer the telephone for me—I'm in the bath; he lifted the telephone and called the police.**

أ) على الخط

on the telephone = (*a*) speaking by telephone; **don't make a noise—Daddy's on the telephone; there's someone on the telephone who wants to speak to you.**

ب) مزوّد بالخط الهاتفي

(*b*) with a telephone in the house; **are you on the telephone? they're not on the telephone.**

2. *verb*

٢ - يتصل هاتفياً بـ

to call someone by telephone; **your sister telephoned yesterday; telephone the doctor—the baby's ill; can you telephone New York from here?**
telephones—telephoning—telephoned—has telephoned
Note: **phone** *is nearly always used instead of* **telephone**

telephone book, *noun*

دليل الهاتف

book which gives the names of people in a town in alphabetical order with their addresses and phone numbers; **this restaurant isn't in the telephone book.**

telephone box, *noun*

حجيرة الهاتف العمومي

tall square box with windows, with a public telephone inside; **I'm phoning from the telephone box outside the post office.**
plural **telephone boxes**

telephone number, *noun*

رقم الهاتف

number which refers to a particular phone; **what's your telephone number? his telephone number's 405 9935.**

television [telɪ'vɪʒn] *noun*

أ) تلفزيون

(*a*) pictures which are sent through the air and appear on a special machine; **we watch television every night; is there any sport on television tonight? television programmes are never interesting on Saturdays.**

ب) جهاز تلفزيون

(*b*) machine which shows television pictures; **I've bought a colour television; the television has broken down; turn off the television—that programme's awful! when he comes home in the evening he just turns on the television and goes to sleep.**
Note: **television** *is often written or spoken as* **TV** ['ti:'vi:]

television set, *noun*

جهاز تلفزيون

machine which shows television pictures; **we've bought a new television set.**

tell [tel] *verb*

أ) يروي - يقول - يُخبر

(*a*) to say something to someone; **he told me a long story; she told the police she had seen the accident; do you think he is telling the truth? don't tell your mother you've been to the pub!**

ب) يعلم - يعطي تعليمات

(*b*) to give information/instructions; **can**

three hundred and nineteen 319

temper

you tell me how to get to the post office? the teacher told the children to sit down; tell me when to start; nobody told me about the picnic.

(ت) يميّز

(c) to notice the difference between two things; can you tell the difference between butter and margarine? you can tell he's annoyed by the way his ears go red.

tells—telling—told [təuld]—has told

tell off, verb

يوبّخ

to tell someone that he has done something wrong; he was told off for being late; the teacher will tell us off if we don't do our homework.

Note: she told the boys off *or* she told off the boys *but only* told them off

temper ['tempə] noun

مزاج سيّء ـ حالة إنفعال

(usually bad) state of mind; he's in a (bad) temper = he is annoyed; he lost his temper = he became very angry; see also **bad-tempered**.

temperature ['temprətʃə] noun

أ) درجة الحرارة

(a) heat measured in degrees; what's the temperature of boiling water? the temperature in the desert is very hot; the car won't start when the temperature's very low; put the thermometer in your mouth—I want to take your temperature.

ب) حمّى ـ ازدياد في درجة حرارة الجسم

(b) illness when your body is hotter than normal; he's in bed with a temperature; the doctor says she's got a temperature.

ten [ten] number 10

عشرة (العدد ١٠)

he bought ten oranges for £1; he's ten (years old); the train leaves at ten (o'clock).

320

term

tenth [tenθ] **10th** adjective & noun

العاشر ـ العاشرة

the tenth of June/June the tenth (June 10th); that's the tenth letter I've written today; he spends a tenth of his money on food; her tenth birthday is on Wednesday.

tennis ['tenɪs] noun

كرة المضرب ـ التنس

game for two or four people, where a ball is hit backwards and forwards over a net; would you like a game of tennis? I'm no good at tennis; he's having tennis lessons; let's play with this tennis ball.

no plural

tense [tens] noun

صيغة الفعل (ماضي او مضارع)

form of a verb which shows when an action takes place; the past tense of 'go' is 'went'.

tent [tent] noun

خيمة

small shelter made of cloth, held up by poles and attached to the ground with ropes; when we go camping we take our tent in the back of our car; his tent was blown down by the wind.

term [tɜːm] noun

أ) مدى زماني ـ أمد ـ أجل ـ مدّة

(a) length of time; during his term as President; he was sent to prison for a term of five years.

ب) فصل دراسي ـ دورة دراسية

(b) part of a school year when lessons are taught; there are three terms in the school year; we play cricket during the summer term and football in the autumn and spring terms; term ends on July 27th; next term, I'm starting to learn German; half term = short holiday in the middle of a term.

(ت) شروط

(c) something which has to be agreed

three hundred and twenty

terrible

before something else is done; **what are the terms of the agreement?**

ث) علاقة شخصية

(d) way of getting on with someone; **we're on good terms with the people next door; he's on bad terms with everyone.**

terrible ['terɪbl] *adjective*

رهيب ـ كريه ـ بغيض

very bad; **he had a terrible accident; the last meal I had in that restaurant was terrible.**

terribly, *adverb*

للغاية ـ الى اقصى حد

very; **he's terribly kind; these chocolates are terribly expensive.**

test [test] **1.** *noun*

١ ـ إختبار ـ إمتحان ـ فحص طبّي

short examination to see if something works well/to see if you can do something, etc.; **we've had a maths test this morning; he's passed his driving test; the doctor's going to do a blood test.**
2. *verb*

٢ ـ يختبر ـ يمتحن

to examine to see if something is working well/if you can do something, etc.; **I must have my eyes tested; the teacher tested his French; have you tested your new car in the snow?**
tests—testing—tested—has tested

textbook ['teksbʊk] *noun*

الكتاب المدرسي

book which is used by children at school/by students at university.

than [ðæn *or* ðən] *conjunction*

من : (بيتي اكبر من بيتك)

used to show a second thing which is being compared; **my house is bigger than yours; it's colder today than it was yesterday; I know London better than Edinburgh; more than thirty people were waiting for the bus.**

that

thank [θæŋk] *verb*

يشكر

to show that you are grateful to someone for doing something; **he thanked me for having helped him; she thanked them for coming to see her; I must thank him for his present.**
thanks—thanking—thanked—has thanked

thanks, *plural noun & interjection*

شكراً

words which show you are grateful; **please give him my thanks for his present; we got no thanks for all our help; do you want some more coffee?—no thanks, I've had plenty; do you want a lift to the station?—thanks, it's a long way to walk.**

thanks to, *adverb*

بفضل ـ بسبب ـ نتيجةً لـ

because of/as a result of; **thanks to your father's map, we found our way to the post office; thanks to the rain, we couldn't have the picnic.**

thank you, *interjection*

شكراً ـ أشكرك

(*showing that you are grateful*) **thank you for the present; did you say thank you to your mother for the book? do you want some more coffee?—no thank you, I've had plenty; do you want a lift to the station?—thank you, it's a long way to walk.**

that [ðæt *or* ðət] **1.** *adjective & pronoun*

١ ـ أ) ذلك ـ تلك ـ ذاك

(a) (*used to show something which is further away—the opposite of* **this**) **that book is the one I was talking about, not this one; can you see that tall man standing by the door? what's the name of that restaurant where we had dinner yesterday? who's that sitting at the next table?**
plural **those**

ب) الذي ـ التي

(b) (*used to join a subject or object to a verb*) **where is the letter that he sent you?**

three hundred and twenty-one 321

the

they live in a house that has red windows; here's the box that you left in the bedroom.
Note: with an object **that** *can be left out:* **where's the letter he sent you? here's the box you left in the bedroom**
With a subject **that** *can be changed to* **which** *(for things and animals) or* **who** *(for people);* **a house that has red windows/a house which has red windows; the man that stole the car/the man who stole the car**

2. *conjunction*

١ - أ) أنّ : (قال لي أن ..)
(a) *(after verbs like* **hope, know, tell, say** *and adjectives like* **glad, sorry, happy***)* he told me that she was out; she said that she was tired; he didn't know that we were coming; I'm glad that you were able to come.

ب) الى حدّ انه : (الطقس حارّ الى حدٍ اني أشعر بالعطش باستمرار)
(b) *(after* **so/such** *+ adjective or noun)* it's so hot here that it makes me thirsty; the meat was so good that I ate all of it; it was raining so hard that we couldn't have our picnic; we had such bad weather that our holiday was spoilt; there was such a crowd that we couldn't get into the cinema.
Note: **that** *is often left out:* **he didn't know we were coming; it's so hot here it makes me thirsty**

the [ðə; ðɪ *before a vowel*] *article*

ا) لام التعريف ـ « الـ » التعريف
(a) *(meaning something in particular)* where's the parcel which came today? there's the dog from next door.

ب) تستعمل للاشياء الفريدة من نوعها : « الـ » شمس ـ « الـ » قمر
(b) *(used with something of which only one exists)* the sun was shining; men have walked on the moon.

ت) تستعمل للتعبير عن شيء بالاجمال : « الـ » هاتف
(c) *(meaning something in general)* do you like listening to the radio? I never use the telephone; the streets are crowded at Christmas.

ث) تستعمل للتعبير عن شيء غير اعتيادي : هذا هو « الـ » مكان
(d) [ðiː] *(meaning something very special)* that's the shop for men's clothes = the best shop; he's the doctor for children; that's not the Charlie Chaplin is it? = not the real Charlie Chaplin?

ج) تستعمل في المقارنة
(e) *(used to compare)* the less you work the fatter you get; the sooner you do it the better; that's the best way to do it; he's the tallest boy in our school.

theatre [ˈθɪətə] *noun* (*American:* **theater**)

مسرح
building in which plays are shown; we're going to the theatre tonight; is there a good play at the theatre this week?

their [ðeə] *adjective*

« هم » ـ « هنّ » : (بيتهم ـ منزلهنّ)
belonging to them; here's their house; they were eating their dinner.

theirs, *pronoun*

خاصتهم ـ خاصتهن ـ ملكهم ـ ملكهن
belonging to them; which house is theirs? he's a friend of theirs; they want to borrow my car—theirs won't start.

them [ðem] *object pronoun*

هم ـ هنّ ـ هي : (لا اجد « هم » قل لـ « هم » ـ إضرب « هن »
(referring to a plural) do you like chocolates?—no, I don't like them very much; the children are waiting outside—tell them to come in; if you are going to visit your parents can you take them this present?

themselves, *plural pronoun*

انفسهم ـ انفسهنّ
(referring to a plural subject) cats clean themselves very carefully; the old ladies

then

were all by themselves in the house = all alone; they did it all by themselves = with no one to help them; the doctors were all ill themselves.

then [ðen] 1. *adverb*

١ - أ) آنذاك - آنئذٍ

(a) at that time; the police said he killed his sister in London on April 23rd, but he was in Scotland then; can you come to a party next week?—no, I shall be on holiday then.

ب) بعدئذ

(b) after that; he sat down and then they brought cups of coffee; we had a busy holiday—we went to France, and then to Italy and then to Germany.

2. *conjunction*

٢ - إذن - اذا

and so/therefore; if you don't like fish then you'll have to eat meat; then you already knew that he had died?

there [ðeə] 1. *adverb*

١ - هناك - في ذلك المكان - ثمة

in that place/to that place; we'll go there at 10 o'clock; is the car still there? where's the tea?—there, on the top shelf; have you ever been to Canada?— yes, I went there three years ago.

2. *interjection*

٢ - أ) اداة تدل على الشفقة : (لا - لا - لا تبكِ)

(a) (showing pity) there, there, don't cry; there, if you sit down, you'll soon feel better.

ب) اداة تدل على ان المتكلم هو على حق : (هكذا اذاً - هل رأيت ؟)

(b) (showing you were right) there, what did I tell you, we've missed the train.

ت) اداة تدل على حزم او اتخاذ قرار

(c) (making a decision) I'll go to the party all by myself, so there!

ث) اداة تدل اعطاء شيء لشخص ما : ها هو ما تريد !

(d) (used when giving something to someone) there you are!

they

3. *pronoun*

موجود - يوجد : (يوجد كلب كبير في الحديقة)

(used as the subject of verbs (usually with the verb to be) when the real subject follows the verb) there's a big dog in the garden; there's a page missing in this book; were there many people at the meeting? is there anything to drink? there seems to have been an accident; there isn't any sugar left.

therefore ['ðeəfɔː] *adverb*

لهذا السبب

for this reason; there's a lot of snow, therefore the trains will be late; the children are growing up and therefore can look after themselves.

thermometer [θə'mɔmitə] *noun*

المكشاف الحراري

instrument for measuring temperature; the thermometer showed only 2°—it was very cold.

these [ðiːz] *see* **this**

ملاحظة : انظر الى كلمة this

they [ðeɪ] *plural pronoun*

أ) ضمير منفصل بمعنى هم - هن - هي (في الجمع)

(a) (referring to people or things) where are the cups and saucers?—they're in the cupboard; who are those people in uniform?—they're army officers; the children went out in the snow with no coats on, so they all caught colds.

ب) ضمير منفصل للجمع بمعنى هم ، هن ، للتعبير عن عامة الناس بدون تحديد

(b) (referring to people in general) they say it's going to be hot; they tell me that you've got married.

Note: when it is the object, they becomes them: we gave it to them; he hit them with a stick; when it follows the verb be, they usually becomes them: who's that?—it's them!

three hundred and twenty-three   **323**

thick

thick [θɪk] *adjective*

أ) سميك ـ ثخين
(a) not thin/with a lot of space between the two surfaces; **a thick slice of cake; the walls are two metres thick; this orange has a very thick skin; a thick piece of string; he was carrying a thick pile of papers.**

ب) كثيف
(b) close together; **a thick forest of trees; the lawn was covered with thick grass.**

ت) غليظ القوام
(c) (liquid) which does not flow easily; **this paint is too thick—add some water to it; a bowl of good thick soup.**

ث) كثير الضباب او الغشاوة
(d) which you can't see through easily; **the plane couldn't land because of thick fog.**

thick—thicker—thickest

thief [θiːf] *noun*

لصّ
person who steals; **thieves broke into the shop and stole 100 watches.**

plural **thieves** [θiːvz]

thin [θɪn] *adjective*

أ) نحيل ـ نحيف
(a) not fat; **his legs are very thin; she's getting too thin—she should eat more.**

ب) رقيق ـ (ورقة رقيقة) ـ رفيع
(b) not thick; **a thin slice of bread; a thin sheet of paper; a thin piece of string.**

ت) متفرق
(c) not close together; **the ground was covered with thin grass.**

ث) رقيق القوام (حليب او زيت ..)
(d) (liquid) which flows easily; **thin soup; add water until the paint is thin.**

ج) شفاف ـ رقيق (ستائر رقيقة)
(e) which you can see through; **thin curtains.**

thin—thinner—thinnest

think

thing [θɪŋ] *noun*

أ) شيء (كل شيء غير انسان او حيوان او نبات)
(a) something which is not living/not a plant or animal; **what's that black thing in the garden? what's that green thing for?**

ب) طريقة وديّة للتعبير عن شخص
(b) usually kind way of talking to a person or animal; **his mother's such a nice old thing; you silly thing!—why did you do that?**

ب) أمتعة ـ حاجيات ـ أجهزة ـ أشياء معينة
(c) **things** = clothes/equipment; **have you brought your football things? I left my painting things in the car.**

ت) حالة ـ الاحوال : (كيف الاحوال) ـ حدث ـ أمر ـ مسألة
(d) something which is referred to in general; **how are things going? don't take things so seriously; it was a good thing the train was late** = it was lucky for us that the train was late; **she just sat there and didn't say a thing; the first thing to do is phone the police; what a silly thing to do!**

think [θɪŋk] *verb*

أ) يفكّر
(a) to use your mind; **think before you say anything; he never thinks about what people might say.**

ب) يعتقد ـ يظنّ
(b) to believe/to have an opinion; **I think she is prettier than her sister; what do you think we ought to do now? everyone thought he was mad; what do you think of the film? he's thought to be in Canada** = people believe he is in Canada; **he's in Canada, isn't he?—I don't think so.**

ت) يتوقع
(c) to expect; **I think it's going to rain; I didn't think the train would be late.**

ث) ينوي
(d) to plan; **he's thinking of going to**

third

work in Canada; have you thought about going to work in Canada?
thinks — thinking — thought [θɔːt] — has thought

think over, verb

ينظر جدياً في مسألة

to think about a plan or suggestion very carefully; **think it over, and give me your answer tomorrow.**

think up, verb

يَعُدُّ خطأ

to invent; **he thought up a plan for making money.**

third [θɜːd] **3rd,** noun & adjective

ثالث ـ الثالث

referring to three; **my birthday is on the third of September/September the third (September 3rd); he was third in the race; they live in the third house on the left; King James the Third (James III); it's his third birthday on Friday.**
Note: with dates **third** *is usually written* **3rd: September 3rd, 1974; March 3rd, 1981;** *with names of kings and queens* **third** *is usually written* **III: King Charles III**

thirst [θɜːst] noun

عطش ـ ظَمَأ

feeling that you want to drink.

thirsty, adjective

ظامىء ـ متعطش

wanting to drink; **I'm thirsty, give me a drink of water; if you're thirsty, have some orange juice.**
thirsty — thirstier — thirstiest

thirteen [θɜːˈtiːn] number 13

ثلاثة عشر ـ ثلاث عشرة (العدد ١٣)

she's thirteen (years old).

thirteenth, 13th, adjective & noun

الثالث عشر ـ جزء من ١٣

she came thirteenth in the race; the thirteenth of August/August the thirteenth (August 13th); it's his thirteenth birthday on Monday.

thought

thirty [ˈθɜːtɪ] number 30

ثلاثون (العدد ٣٠)

he's thirty (years old); she has thirty pairs of shoes; he's in his thirties = he is between 30 and 39 years old.
Note: **thirty-one (31), thirty-two (32), etc., but thirty-first (31st), thirty-second (32nd), etc.**

thirtieth, 30th, adjective & noun

الثلاثون

he was thirtieth in the race; the thirtieth of June/June the thirtieth (June 30th); it was her thirtieth birthday last week.

this [ðɪs] adjective & pronoun

أ) هذا ـ هذه

(a) (used to show something which is nearer—the opposite of **that**) **this is the book I was talking about; this little girl is my sister's daughter; I think I have been to this restaurant before; this is Mr Martin; these apples are bad.**

ب) هذا ـ هذه

(b) (used to refer to a part of today, the recent past or a period of time which will soon arrive) **I saw him this morning; they are coming to have tea with us this afternoon; I'll be seeing him this week; she's retiring this year; we're going to Greece this summer.**
plural **these**

those [ðəʊz] see **that**

ملاحظة : انظر إلى كلمة that

though [ðəʊ] conjunction

برغم ذلك ـ ومع ذلك

in spite of the fact that; **though he's small, he can hit very hard; though it was snowing, it wasn't very cold outside;** see also **although**

وكأنّ ـ كأنّ

as though = as if; **it looks as though it will rain.**

thought [θɔːt] see **think**

ملاحظة : انظر الى كلمة think

three hundred and twenty-five **325**

thousand

thousand ['θaʊznd] number 1000

الف ـ (العدد ١٠٠٠)

I paid two thousand pounds for it (£2,000); thousands of people escaped from the fire = very many people.

Note: after numbers thousands does not have an -s: two thousand; ten thousand

thread [θred] 1. *noun*

١ ـ خيط

thin piece of cotton, etc.; I need some strong thread to sew on my button.
2. *verb*

٢ ـ يُسْلِك (الخيط) في سم الابرة

to put a thread/string, etc., through a hole; can you thread this needle for me?

threads—threading—threaded—has threaded

threaten ['θretn] *verb*

يهدّد ـ يحذر

to warn that something unpleasant will happen; he threatened to call the police; the burglar threatened her with a gun.

threatens—threatening—threatened—has threatened

three [θriː] number 3

ثلاثة ـ ثلاث (العدد ٣)

she's three (years old); can you see me at three (o'clock)? three men stole my car.

Note: three (3) but third (3rd)

threw [θruː] *see* **throw**

ملاحظة : انظر الى كلمة throw

throat [θrəʊt] *noun*

حنجرة ـ حلق ـ حلقوم

front part of your neck below the chin, tube which goes down from your mouth inside your neck; he held her by the throat; a piece of meat got stuck in his throat; he cleared his throat = gave a little cough.

through [θruː] *adverb & preposition*

١) خلال ـ من خلال

(a) crossing the inside of something/going in at one side and coming out of the other side; he went through the door; she looked through the window; the water runs through the pipe; the air comes in through the hole in the wall; the road goes straight through the centre of the town; she pushed the needle through the ball of wool.

ب) عبر ـ طوال

(b) during a period of time; she went on talking all through the film.

ت) بواسطة

(c) by; I sent the letter through the post; we heard of it through my sister.

ث) عبر ـ بواسطة

(d) speaking by telephone; I'm trying to get through to Germany; can you put me through to the manager?

Note: through is often used after verbs: to go through; to fall through; to see through, etc.

throughout, *preposition & adverb*

في كل مكان من (البلاد ، البيت) طوال (الليل ، الموسم ...)

everywhere; all through; roads are blocked by snow throughout the country; heavy rain fell throughout the night.

throw [θrəʊ] *verb*

يرمي ـ يقذف ـ يلقي

to send something through the air; how far can you throw this ball? she threw the stone through the window; he threw the letter into the dustbin; he threw the cushion at his sister.

throws—throwing—threw [θruː]—has thrown

throw away, *verb*

يطرح ـ يرمي في النفايات

to get rid of something which you don't need; don't throw away that old bike—we can mend it; she threw away all her old clothes.

Note: throw that paper away or throw away that paper but only throw it away

throw off, *verb*

thumb

يتخلص من

to get rid of; **I've had a cold for weeks, and I can't throw it off.**

throw out, verb

أ) يرمي خارجاً ـ يطرد

(a) to put outside using force; **when he couldn't pay the bill, he was thrown out of the restaurant.**

ب) يتخلص

(b) to get rid of something which you don't need; **we're throwing out this old carpet.**

throw up, verb

أ) يتقيّأ

(a) to be sick; **the dog has thrown up all over the kitchen floor.**

ب) يتخلّى عن

(b) to give up something; **she threw up her job and went to live in the country.**

thumb [θʌm] noun

إبهام اليد

short thick finger which is separated from the other four fingers on your hand; **he hit his thumb with the hammer; the baby was sucking its thumb.**

thunder ['θʌndə] noun

رعد ـ (الرعد)

loud noise in the air caused by lightning; **listen to the thunder! when there's thunder, the cat hides under the bed.**

thunderstorm, noun

عاصفة رعديّة

storm with rain and thunder and lightning; **we were caught on the mountain by a thunderstorm.**

Thursday ['θɜːzdɪ] noun

الخميس (يوم الخميس)

day between Wednesday and Friday, the fourth day of the week; **she was ill last Thursday; I go to my evening class on Thursdays; shall we meet next Thursday? today is Thursday, October 27th.**

ticket

tick [tɪk] **1.** noun

١ ـ أ) علامة صغيرة تكتب على الورق للفت النظر على كلمة أو جملة او مقطع ... الخ

(a) mark on paper to show that something is right; **he put a tick next to each name on the list; put a tick if you want breakfast in your room.**

ب) تكّة الساعة

(b) small sound made by a clock; **the room was very quiet—I could only hear the tick of the clock.**

2. verb

٢ ـ أ) يضع علامة على الورق ـ يؤشر بعلامة صغيرة

(a) to mark with a tick; **he ticked the names of the children who were present; please tick if you want breakfast in your room.**

ب) يتكّ (تتك الساعة)

(b) to make a small sound; **the room was so quiet—all we could hear was the clock ticking; run away—the bomb's ticking!**
ticks—ticking—ticked—has ticked

tick off, verb

يوبّخ

to tell someone that what they have done is wrong; **he was ticked off by the police for parking on the yellow line.**

ticket ['tɪkɪt] noun

أ) بطاقة سفر ـ تذكرة سفر

(a) piece of paper/card which allows you to travel; **you can't get on the train without a ticket; I've lost my plane tickets—how can I get to New York?**

ب) بطاقة دخول ـ تذكرة دخول

(b) piece of paper which allows you to go into a cinema/an exhibition, etc.; **two tickets for the 6.30 show please; I went to several theatres but there were no tickets left anywhere.**

ت) بطاقة غرامة

(c) paper which you get when you leave a car parked wrongly, telling you that you will have to pay a fine; **don't leave**

three hundred and twenty-seven

tide

your car on the yellow line—you'll get a ticket!

tide [taɪd] *noun*

المدّ والجزر

movement of the sea which comes up and goes down each day; **high tide is at four o'clock; at low tide/when the tide is out you can walk for miles on the sand.**

tidy ['taɪdɪ] **1.** *adjective*

١ - مُرَتَّب - حَسَن - نظيف - محب للترتيب

neat/in good order; **you must keep your room tidy.**

tidy—tidier—tidiest

2. *verb*

٢ - يرتّب

to make something tidy; **she was tidying her room.**

tidies—tidying—tidied—has tidied

tidy away, *verb*

يرتب - يضع جانباً كل الاشياء غير اللازمة

to put something away so that everything is neat; **he tidied away all the books on the desk.**

tidy up, *verb*

يرتّب تماماً - يضع كل شيء في مكانه

to make something completely tidy; **can't you tidy up all those papers? you must tidy up your room before your parents come back.**

tie [taɪ] **1.** *noun*

١ - رباط العنق - (كرافات)

long piece of cloth which men wear in a knot round their necks under the collar of their shirts; **he wore a blue tie with white spots; you can't come into the restaurant if you haven't got a tie on.**

2. *verb*

٢ - يربط

to attach with a knot; **the parcel is tied with string; he was tying his horse to the fence; the burglars tied her hands behind her back.**

ties—tying—tied—has tied

time

tie up, *verb*

أ) يربط بإحكام

(*a*) to attach tightly; **the parcel is tied up with string; that dog ought to be tied up or it will bite someone.**

ب) يكون مشغولاً إلى اقصى حد - يكون منهمكاً في شغله

(*b*) to be tied up = to be busy; **I'm rather tied up at the moment—can I phone you tomorrow?**

tight [taɪt] **1.** *adjective*

١ - مُغْلَق بإحكام - مشدود

which fits firmly; not loose; **the lid is so tight I can't open it; my trousers are so tight I can't fasten the top button; her dress is so tight that she can't bend down.**

2. *adverb*

٢ - بإحكام

firmly; **shut the door tight; hold (on) tight!**

tight—tighter—tightest

tighten, *verb*

يشدّ - يربط بإحكام - يُضَيِّق - يجعله مغلقاً تماماً

to make tight; **can you tighten this screw? the lid needs tightening.**

tightens—tightening—tightened—has tightened

tightly, *adverb*

بإحكام

in a tight way; **he put the lid on tightly; hold on to the handle tightly.**

till [tɪl] *preposition*

حتى - إلى - إلى ان

until/up to the time when; **I won't be home till nine o'clock; he worked from morning till night.**

time [taɪm] **1.** *noun*

١ - أ) وقت : (لديك الوقت الكافي)

(*a*) quantity of hours/days/weeks, etc.; **you don't need to hurry—you've plenty of time; have you got time for a cup of**

three hundred and twenty-eight

tin

tea? he spends all his time reading the newspaper; don't waste time putting your shoes on—jump out of the window now.

ب) زمن (لم اره منذ زمن طويل) ـ مدّة

(b) certain period; I haven't seen him for a long time; it didn't take him much time to get here; it took her a long time to get better; we had a letter from her a short time ago; we're going on holiday in three weeks' time = three weeks from now.

ت) الساعة : (الساعة الآن تماما السادسة والدقيقة ٣٥)

(c) particular point in the day shown in hours and minutes; what time is it?/what's the time? the time is exactly 6.35; can you tell me the time please? he's only four—he can't tell the time yet = he can't read the time on a clock.

ث) حين : (لم اسمع الانفجار لاني كنت نائماً في ذلك الحين)

(d) particular point when something happens; I didn't hear the bang as I was asleep at the time; by the time the police arrived the burglars had run away; you can't sing and drink at the same time.

ج) ساعة الافتتاح او الاغلاق في متجر او مصنع ... الخ ـ الوقت المخصص لشيء معين ـ وقت النوم ـ وقت الصلاة ...

(e) hour at which something usually happens; closing time is 10.30; it's dinner time—I'm hungry; is it time to go to bed? see also **bedtime, dinnertime, lunchtime, teatime.**

ح) اوقات ـ ايام : (امضينا اوقات جميلة)

(f) period when things are pleasant or bad; we had a good time at the party.

خ) مرّة : رأيت هذا الفلم ٣ مرات

(g) one of several moments/periods when something happens; I've seen that film three times; that's the last time I'll ask you to sing a song; next time you come, bring your football.

د ـ أضعاف ـ (في الرياضيات) : ضرب : ستة ضرب اربعة تساوي ٢٤

(h) times = multiplied by; six times four is twenty four; this box is ten times as heavy as that one; she's a hundred times prettier than her sister.

ضمن الوقت المناسب او المحدّد

in time = not late; we ran fast and got to the station in time to catch the train; hurry if you want to be in time for the train; we were just in time to see the soldiers march past.

في الوقت المناسب او المحدّد

on time = happening at the right time; the train arrived on time; he's never on time.

2. *verb*

٢ ـ يُوَقِّت ـ يَعُدُّ الوقت

to count how many hours and minutes; if you run round the football pitch, I'll time you; can you time these eggs?—they have to cook for three minutes; the police timed the car—it was going at 70 miles an hour.

times—timing—timed—has timed

timetable, *noun*

جدول مواعيد

list which shows the times of classes in school/of trains leaving, etc.; look up the trains to London in the timetable; we have three English lessons on the timetable today.

tin [tɪn] *noun*

أ) علبة من القصدير

(a) round metal box in which food can be kept for a long time; let's open a tin of soup; I bought three tins of food for the cat.

ب) علبة معدنية

(b) any metal box; put the cakes into that tin; I gave her a tin of biscuits for her birthday.

tinned, *adjective*

معلّب : (فاكهة مُعَلَّبة)

in a tin; do you like tinned fruit better than fresh fruit?

tin opener, *noun*

three hundred and twenty-nine 329

tiny

tool for opening tins; **we took a tin of fruit for the picnic, but we forgot the tin opener!**

tiny ['taını] *adjective*

صغير جداً ـ بالغ الصغر

very small; **a tiny baby; this plant has tiny blue flowers.**

tiny—tinier—tiniest

tip [tɪp] **1.** *noun*

١) الاسلّة : طرف الشيء المستدق ـ رأس ـ قمة

(*a*) end of something long; **she touched it with the tips of her fingers; he has a stick with a metal tip.**

ب) النفحة (بقشيش)

(*b*) money given to someone who has provided a service; **I gave the taxi driver a £1 tip; should I give the waiter a tip? is a tip included in the bill?**

2. *verb*

٢ ـ أ) يقلب ـ ينقلب ـ يفرّغ

(*a*) to make something empty/to pour something out; **he picked up the bucket and tipped the apples on to the floor; she tipped the money out of her bag.**

ب) يمنح بقشيشاً ـ يَنْفَح

(*b*) to give money to someone who has helped you; **I tipped the waiter £1; shall I tip the driver?**

tips—tipping—tipped—has tipped

tip over/tip up, *verb*

يقلب ـ يميل

to lean and fall over; to make something lean so that it falls over; **he tipped over the bottle; the lorry tipped over; my cup tipped over and all my tea spilled on to the table.**

tire ['taɪə] *noun*

ملاحظة : انظر الى كلمة **type**

American = **tyre**

to

tired ['taɪəd] *adjective*

أ) مُتْعَب

(*a*) feeling sleepy; feeling that you need rest; **I'm tired—I'll go to bed; if you feel tired, lie down on my bed; I'm tired after that long walk.**

ب) يسأم من . يكون سئماً من

(*b*) **to be tired of something** = to be bored with something, to have had enough of something; **I'm tired of hearing the baby cry; she's tired of having to do all the work; can't we play another game—I'm tired of this one.**

tired out, *adjective*

مُنْهَك

feeling very sleepy/feeling that you must have rest; **I'm tired out after that long walk; let her sit down—she's tired out.**

title ['taɪtl] *noun*

عنوان (كتاب او مسرحية او فيلم ...)

name of a book/play/film, etc.; **the title of his next film was 'The Third Man'; what's the title of that book you're reading?**

to [tu: *or* tə] **1.** *preposition*

١ ـ أ) الى (للتعبير على الوجهة او المكان) : ذهب الى المحطة

(*a*) (*showing direction/place*) **he went to the station; I'm going to the butcher's; is this the way to the post office? the church is to the east of the town; take one step to the left.**

ب) الى (للتعبير عن الوقت) : (من الاثنين الى السبت) قبل : (١٥ دقيقة قبل السادسة)

(*b*) (*showing time*) **from Monday to Saturday; he slept from ten to eight o'clock; it's ten to six; the time is a quarter to seven.**

ت) لـ : (إعط الكتاب « لـ » المعلم) تجاه : (كن لطيفاً تجاه المسنين)

(*c*) (*showing person/aniaml who gets something*) **give the book to the teacher, pass the sugar to your father; you must be kind to old people.**

330   *three hundred and thirty*

toast

ث) مقابل : (للمقارنة في نتيجة مباراة) : خسر الفريق بستة اهداف مقابل اربعة
(d) (showing connection) they lost by six goals to four; there are two dollars to the pound; there are three keys to the front door; in this class there are 35 children to one teacher.

ج) على : (للتفضيل) : أُفضّل الزبدة على السمنة
(e) (showing that you are comparing) I prefer butter to margarine; you can't compare tinned fruit to fresh fruit.

2. used before a verb

٢ ـ أ) اداة تستعمل قبل الافعال
(a) (following verbs) he remembered to switch off the light; they tried to run away; she agreed to come with us; we decided to leave the office early.

ب) اداة للتعبير عن نيّة او هدف مترقب
(b) (showing purpose) they came to help us; the doctor left to go to the hospital.

ت) اداة تستعمل بعد الصفة
(c) (used after adjectives) she was too tired to walk; are these apples good to eat? I'm sorry to be late.

Note: to is used for times between half past and o'clock: 4.35 = twenty-five to five; 4.45 = a quarter to five; 4.50 = ten to five

toast [təʊst] *noun*

شريحة خبز محمص

slices of bread which have been cooked until they are brown; do you want toast and honey for your breakfast? I want some more toast; can you make another piece of toast?

no plural: some toast; a piece of toast

tobacco [tə'bækəʊ] *noun*

تبغ (للتدخين)

dried leaves of a plant which are used to make cigarettes and cigars, and which you can smoke in a pipe; these cigarettes are made of American tobacco; I must buy a packet of tobacco.

no plural: some tobacco

three hundred and thirty-one

toilet

today [tə'deɪ] *adverb & noun*

اليوم ـ هذا اليوم

this day; he said he was coming to see me today, but he hasn't come yet; today's my birthday; what's the date today? have you ready today's newspaper?

no plural

Note: to refer to the morning/afternoon, etc. of today, say this morning/this afternoon, etc.

toe [təʊ] *noun*

إصبع القدم

part of the body—one of the five parts at the end of your foot; he trod on my toe; big toe/little toe = biggest/smallest of the five toes.

toenail, *noun*

ظفر اصبع القدم

thin hard part covering the end of a toe.

together [tə'geðə] *adverb*

ا) سويةً ـ معاً

(a) in a group; we must stay together or we'll get lost; let's go to the cinema together.

ب) مع بعضهم البعض ـ مع بعضها البعض ـ مع بعضهن البعض

(b) one thing with another; tie the two chairs together; can you stick the pieces of the cup together again? add all these numbers together; we've had three lunches and three beers—how much is it all together?

toilet ['tɔɪlət] *noun*

حمّام ـ مرحاض

lavatory/place or room where you get rid of water or solid waste from your body; where's the men's toilet? I want to got to the toilet.

toilet paper, *noun*

ورق المرحاض

special paper for wiping yourself when you go to the toilet.

331

told

toilet roll, noun

ورق المرحاض

roll of toilet paper.

told [təʊld] see **tell**

ملاحظة : انظر الى كلمة **tell**

tomato [tə'mɑːtəʊ] noun

طماطم ـ بندورة

red fruit which is used in salads and cooking; **have another tomato; a bowl of tomato salad; tomato sauce** = red sauce made with tomatoes; **put some tomato sauce on your chips.**
plural **tomatoes**

tomorrow [tə'mɒrəʊ] adverb & noun

غداً

the day after today; **today's Tuesday, so tomorrow must be Wednesday; can you meet me tomorrow morning? tomorrow is my birthday; we are going to the cinema tomorrow evening.**

ton [tʌn] noun

الطُنّ : وحدة وزن تساوي ١٠٠٠ كيلوغرام
very large measure of weight; **that piece of metal weighs three tons.**

tongue [tʌŋ] noun

ا) لسان

(a) part of the body—the long piece inside your mouth which can move and is used for tasting and speaking; **don't stick your tongue out at the teacher; he said it with his tongue in his cheek** = he was not really serious.

ب) لغة

(b) language; **his mother tongue is English** = his first language/the language which he spoke when he was a child.

tonight [tə'naɪt] adverb & noun

في هذه الليلة ـ هذه الليلة

the night/evening of today; **we're having a party tonight; can you phone me at 11.30 tonight? is there anything interesting on TV tonight? tonight's programmes are very boring.**

tooth

too [tuː] adverb

ا) اكثر مما ينبغي

(a) more than necessary; **he has too much money; it's too cold for you to play outside; these shoes are too small.**

ب) ايضاً ، كذلك

(b) also; **he had some cake and I had some too; she, too, has a cold/she has a cold too.**

took [tʊk] see **take**

ملاحظة : انظر الى كلمة **take**

tool [tuːl] noun

اداة ـ وسيلة

thing which you use with your hands for doing work; **I keep my hammer in the tool box; have you got a tool for taking the wheels off a car?**

tooth [tuːθ] noun

ا) سِنّ ، ضرس : (لا تنس ان تنظف اسنانك بعد تناول الفطار)

(a) one of a set of bones in the mouth, which you use to chew food with; **don't forget to clean your teeth after breakfast; I must see the dentist—one of my teeth hurts; he had to have a tooth out** = had to have a bad tooth taken out by the dentist; **he has a sweet tooth** = he likes eating sweet things.

ب) سِنّ من اسنان المنشار

(b) one of the row of pointed pieces on a saw.
plural **teeth** [tiːθ]

toothache, noun

وجع الاضراس او الاسنان

pain in your teeth; **I must see the dentist—I've got toothache.**
no plural

toothbrush, noun

top

فرشاة الاسنان

small brush which you use to clean your teeth.
plural **toothbrushes**

toothpaste, *noun*

معجون الاسنان

soft material which you spread on a toothbrush and then use to clean your teeth; **I must buy some toothpaste; here's a tube of toothpaste.**
no plural: **some toothpaste; a tube of toothpaste**

top [tɒp] **1.** *noun*

١ - ا) قمة - رأس

(*a*) highest point; **he climbed to the top of the mountain; the bird is sitting on the top of the tree.**

ب) سطح

(*b*) flat upper surface; **he sat on the top of his car; take the top off the box; the table has a black top; the cake has sugar and fruit on top; on top of** = on; **put the book on top of the others.**

ت) ذروة - المرتبة العليا

(*c*) most important place; highest place; **look at the top of the next page; our team is at the top in the competition.**
2. *adjective*

٢ - الاعلى - العليا - الاحسن

in the highest place; **my office is on the top floor of the building; the jam is on the top shelf; he's the top boy in the class** = he has the best marks; **he's one of the top players in the world** = he's one of the best players.

torch [tɔːtʃ] *noun*

مشعل كهربائي

electric light which you can carry in your hand; **the policeman shone his torch into the room; I can't see anything in the dark—have you got a torch?**
plural **torches**

tore [tɔː] **torn** [tɔːn] *see* **tear**

ملاحظة: انظر الى كلمة **tear**

three hundred and thirty-three

touch

total [təʊtl] *adjective & noun*

مجموع

complete/whole (amount); **what's the total cost? the total which you have to pay is at the bottom of the bill.**

totally, *adverb*

تماماً - بالكلية

completely; **the house was totally destroyed.**

touch [tʌtʃ] **1.** *noun*

١ - ا) إتصال : (ساكون على إتصال معك في الاسبوع المقبل)

(*a*) passing of news and information; **I'll be in touch with you next week** = I'll phone/write, etc., to you; **we've lost touch with him now that he's gone to live in the States.**

ب) لمس

(*b*) feeling gently; **I felt a touch on my arm.**

ت) مقدار طفيف

(*c*) very small amount; **add a few touches of green to the picture; there's a touch of frost in the air.**
plural **touches,** *but no plural for (a)*
2. *verb*

٢ - ا) يَلْمُس - يَمَسّ

(*a*) to feel with your fingers; to be so close to something that you press against it; **the policeman touched me on the shoulder; don't touch that door—the paint isn't dry yet; he's so small that his feet don't touch the floor when he sits on a chair; there is a mark on the wall where the chair has touched it.**

ب) يتناول - ياكل او يشرب - يتعاطى

(*b*) **I never touch coffee** = I never drink it.
touches—touching—touched—has touched

touch down, *verb*

يحطّ - (حطت الطائرة على الارض) يهبط على الارض

to land; **the plane touched down at 3.15.**

touch up, *verb*

333

tour

« يُرَوْتِش » يزيل اثار خمش او عطب
to add a small amount of paint; **I must touch up the car where it has been scratched.**

tour [tuə] *noun*

جولة ـ زيارة (الى متحف او مدينة ..)
journey which takes you round various places and brings you back to where you started from; **we're going on a coach tour to Germany; he took us on a tour of the old castle.**

tourist ['tuərɪst] *noun*

سائح
person who goes on holiday to visit places; **the town is full of tourists in the summer; tourist office** = office which gives information to tourists on what to see and do.

towards [tə'wɔːdz] *preposition*

ا) نحو ـ باتجاه
(a) in the direction of; **he ran towards the policeman; the car was going towards London; the ship is sailing towards the rocks.**

ب) حوالي ـ قرب ـ عند : (عند اواخر الأسبوع)
(b) near (in time); **can we meet towards the end of next week; we went on holiday towards the middle of August.**

ت) كجزء من المال المخصص لغرض ما ـ من أصل
(c) as part of the money to pay for something; **they gave me £5 a week towards the cost of food.**

ث) من : كان تصرفه مني لطيفاً
(d) to; **he behaved very kindly towards me.**

towel ['tauəl] *noun*

فوطة ـ منشفة
piece of soft cloth which is used for drying; **she rubbed her hair with a towel; I can't dry myself; my towel fell into the water.**

trace

tower ['tauə] *noun*

بُرج ـ قلعة
very tall building; **let's climb to the top of the church tower; control tower** = tall building at an airport which contains the radio station.

town [taun] *noun*

مدينة ـ بلدة
place where people live and work, with houses, shops, offices, factories, etc.; **we go to do our shopping in the next town; which is the nearest town to your farm? this town is important for its car factories; let's go to town for an evening meal; his office is in town.**

Note: **to town** and **in town** *do not need* **the**

town council, *noun*

المجلس البلدي
elected committee which runs a town.

town hall, *noun*

دار البلدية
main building in a town, where the town council meets, and where many of the council departments are.

toy [tɔɪ] *noun*

لعبة ـ دُمْيَة
thing for children to play with; **he's playing with his toy soldiers; put all your toys away before you go to bed; our children love going to the toy shop.**

trace [treɪs] **1.** *noun*

ا ـ أ) أثر ـ آثار ـ مقدار طفيف
(a) very small amount; small mark; **there's a trace of onion in the soup; the police found traces of blood in the shop.**

ب) لا يوجد أثر من ...
(b) **there's no trace of** = there are no signs of; **there's no trace of a car having been past here; there's no trace of your letter—it must have been lost by the Post Office.**

2. *verb*

334 *three hundred and thirty-four*

track

٢ - يقتفي الأثر - يكتشف مكان وجود شخص أو شيء

to follow tracks to try to find where someone has gone; **the police have traced her to New York; I can't trace your letter.**

traces—tracing—traced—has traced

track [træk] *noun*

أ) أثر اقدام او إطار او عجلة ...

(*a*) mark left by an animal/a car, etc., which has gone past; **look—there's a track of a bicycle in the sand; I'm trying to keep track of the money we're spending** = trying to count how much money; **I've lost track of how many times I've seen that film** = I can't count how many times.

ب) درب - طريق

(*b*) path, especially for racing; **he's running round the track.**

ت) خط السكة الحديدية

(*c*) line of rails; **the engine went off the track.**

track suit, *noun*

ملابس الرياضة

warm suit made of trousers and a jacket, worn when practising sports.

tractor [ˈtræktə] *noun*

جرّارة

farm vehicle with large wheels, used for pulling a plough or other machines; **he drove his tractor across the field.**

traffic [ˈtræfɪk] *noun*

المرور - حركة المرور - حركة سير السيارات

cars/lorries/buses, etc., travelling on a road; **there's a lot of traffic on Friday nights; the lights turned red, and the traffic stopped; there's so much traffic that it's quicker to take the underground.**

no plural: some traffic; a lot of traffic
traffic jam, *noun*

translate

ازدحام السيارات - عرقلة مجرى المرور

too much traffic on the road, which means that it cannot move; **the accident caused a big traffic jam; there are traffic jams every Friday evening.**

traffic lights, *plural noun*

إشارات المرور الضوئية

red, green and orange lights for making traffic stop and start; **turn right at the next traffic lights; he went across the crossroads when the traffic lights were red.**

train [treɪn] **1.** *noun*

١ - قطار

set of coaches pulled by an engine on the railway; **the train to Edinburgh leaves from platform 3; I go to work every day by train; hurry up if you want to catch the next train; we missed the last train and had to take a taxi.**

2. *verb*

٢ - أ) يُدَرِّب

(*a*) to teach someone or an animal how to do something; **he's trained his dog to carry the newspaper from the shop; he's training to be a pilot.**

ب) يتدرب - يتمرّن - يقوم بتمارين رياضية

(*b*) to practise for a sport; **she's training for the 100 metres race.**

trains—training—trained—has trained

translate [trænsˈleɪt] *verb*

يُتَرجم

to put something which is said or written into another language; **he asked me to translate the letter into German; this book is translated from the Chinese.**

translates—translating—translated—has translated

translation, *noun*

ترجمة

something which has been translated; **here's the translation of the letter from your Japanese friend.**

three hundred and thirty-five   **335**

transport

transport ['trænspɔːt] *noun*

نَقْل (البضائع او الركاب)

moving goods or people; **the car is the commonest means of transport; does the city have an underground transport system?**

trap [træp] **1.** *noun*

١ ـ فَخّ ـ مصيدة ـ شَرَك

something which catches an animal or person; **we caught the wild cat in a trap; the burglars were caught in a police trap.**

2. *verb*

٢ ـ يحبس ـ يوقع في شَرَك ـ ينصب فخاً

to catch someone/an animal, so that they can't move; **we were trapped in the lift for two hours; the police trapped the burglars inside the bank.**

traps—trapping—trapped—has trapped

trap door, *noun*

باب افقي في سقف او ارضية

small door in a ceiling or floor.

travel ['trævl] *verb*

يسافر ـ ينتقل من مكان إلى آخر

to move from one country to another/from one place to another; **he travels to work by car; they're travelling to India by bus; they travelled across the States by bicycle.**

travels—travelling—travelled—has travelled

travel agent, *noun*

وكيل سفريات

person who sells tickets/organizes tours, etc.; **I bought my plane tickets at the travel agent's.**

traveller, *noun (American:* **traveler***)*

المسافر

person who travels.

traveller's cheque, *noun (American:* **traveler's check***)*

شيك سياحي

cheque which you buy at a bank before you travel and which you can then use in a foreign country.

treasure ['treʒə] *noun*

كنز ـ ثروة

store of money/jewels/gold, etc.; **they found some treasure when they were digging a hole in the garden; the burglars hid the treasure in a garage.**

no plural: **some treasure; a piece of treasure; treasures** *means* **valuable things**

treat [triːt] *verb*

أ) يُعَامل

(*a*) to deal with; **he was badly treated by the police; she treats her dogs very kindly.**

ب) يعالج ـ (مريض)

(*b*) to look after a sick or hurt person; **after the accident the passengers were treated in hospital for cuts; he's being treated by his doctor for heart disease.**

ت) يستضيف ـ يُكرم

(*c*) to give someone a special present; **I'll treat you all to an ice cream; he treated himself to a long holiday in Africa.**

treats—treating—treated—has treated

treatment, *noun*

أ) معاملة

(*a*) way of dealing with someone; **the treatment of prisoners by the police.**

ب) معالجة (مريض)

(*b*) way of looking after a sick or hurt person; **this is a new treatment for heart disease; she's in hospital for treatment to her back.**

tree [triː] *noun*

شجرة

very large plant, with a trunk and branches; **he climbed up a tree; birds make their nests in trees; we have six apple trees in the garden; let's have our picnic under this tree.**

Travel and Transport

السفر والنقل

1. airport	١ ـ مطار	14. headlight	١٤ ـ الاضواء الامامية
2. bicycle	٢ ـ درّاجة	15. helicopter	١٥ ـ طائرة مروحيّة
3. bus	٣ ـ حافلة	16. lorry	١٦ ـ شاحنة
4. car	٤ ـ سيارة	17. motorbike	١٧ ـ درّاجة نارية
5. carriage	٥ ـ عربة	18. mudguard	١٨ ـ عازلة الوحول
6. coach	٦ ـ ناقلة ركاب	19. passenger	١٩ ـ راكب
7. control tower	٧ ـ برج المراقبة	20. plane	٢٠ ـ طائرة
8. cyclist	٨ ـ راكب الدراجة	21. roof	٢١ ـ سطح السيارة
9. door	٩ ـ باب	22. seat	٢٢ ـ مقعد
10. driver	١٠ ـ سائق	23. tyre	٢٣ ـ إطار
11. engine (of a train)	١١ ـ محرك القطار	24. van	٢٤ ـ شاحنة صغيرة
12. engine (of a car)	١٢ ـ محرك السيارة	25. wheel	٢٥ ـ عجلة
13. handlebars	١٣ ـ مقود الدراجة	26. window	٢٦ ـ نافذة

three hundred and thirty-seven

trick

trick [trɪk] **1.** *noun*

١ ـ حيلة ـ خدعة ـ مزاح

clever action which can confuse someone; he did some card tricks; she did a trick and made a handkerchief come out of his ear; they played a trick on the teacher.

2. *verb*

٢ ـ يحتال على ـ يخدع

to confuse somone; he was tricked into signing the paper; she was tricked out of her money = she was made to lose her money.

tricks—tricking—tricked—has tricked

tried [traɪd], **tries** [traɪz] *see* **try**

ملاحظة : انظر الى كلمة try

trip [trɪp] **1.** *noun*

١ ـ سفر ـ رحلة

journey; we went on a boat trip down the Thames; he's on a business trip to Canada; a day trip to Stratford costs £25 = a trip lasting one day.

2. *verb*

٢ ـ تزلُّ به القدم

to knock your foot on something, so that you fall down; he tripped over the piece of wood; she tripped and sat down in the mud.

trips—tripping—tripped—has tripped

trip up, *verb*

يقع على الارض ـ يوقع ـ يخلّ بتوازنه

to fall down; to make someone fall down; they put a piece of string across the path and tripped up the postman/ tripped the postman up; he tripped up and fell on his face.

tropics ['trɒpɪks] *plural noun*

المدارين (اي مدار السرطان والجدي) المناطق القريبة من خط الاستواء

hot parts of the world; he lives in the tropics; this fruit comes from the tropics.

trunk

tropical, *adjective*

مداري . استوائي

coming from the tropics; **a tropical plant;** do you like tropical fruit such as bananas?

trouble ['trʌbl] *noun*

أ) مشكلة ـ ازعاج ـ حالة اضطراب

(*a*) problem/difficult situation; the trouble is that this old car won't start; it's no trouble—I can do it easily; the children are no trouble at all; he has money troubles; they got into trouble with the police; it's asking for trouble = it is likely to cause problems; **he got his friend into trouble** = he made his friend do something wrong.

ب) عناء

(*b*) thinking carefully about something; he took the trouble to write.

trousers ['traʊzəz] *plural noun*

بنطلون ـ سروال

clothes which cover your legs and the bottom part of your body; he tore his trousers; he was wearing a blue jacket and brown trousers; I've bought two pairs of trousers.

Note: to show one piece of clothing, say **a pair of trousers**

truck [trʌk] *noun*

شاحنة كبيرة

large lorry.

true [truː] *adjective*

صحيح ـ صادق

correct/right; what he says is true; it's true that she is married; is it true that you went to Scotland on holiday?

trunk [trʌŋk] *noun*

أ) جزع (الشجرة)

(*a*) main part of a tree; the tree trunk is 3 metres round; can you jump over that tree trunk?

338   *three hundred and thirty-eight*

try

(ب) خرطوم (الفيل)
(b) long nose of an elephant; **the elephant picked up the banana with its trunk.**

(ت) صندوق الثياب
(c) large box for sending clothes, books, etc.; **I have two suitcases and a trunk.**

try [traɪ] **1.** *noun*

١ - أ) محاولة
(a) making an effort to do something; **she's going to have a try at flying a plane; he had two tries before he passed his driving test.**

ب) هدف (في لعبة كرة القدم)
(b) goal scored in rugby; **they scored two tries.**

plural **tries**

2. *verb*

٢ - أ) يحاول
(a) to make an effort to do something; **he tried to climb up the tree; don't try to drive if you've never driven before; let me try to start the car.**

ب) يجرّب - يختبر
(b) to test/to see if something is good; **try one of my cakes; have you tried this new toothpaste; have you tried eating fish with jam?**

tries [traɪz]—**trying**—**tried** [traɪd]—**has tried**

try on, *verb*

يقيس (ثوباً او حذاءً)
to put on a piece of clothing to see if it fits; **try the shoes on before you buy them; did you try on the shirt?**

try out, *verb*

يختبر
to test/to see if something is good; **try out the car before you buy it.**

Note: **try this hat on** *or* **try on this hat; try out the car** *or* **try the car out,** *but only* **try it on, try it out**

tube [tjuːb] *noun*

أ) أنبوب
(a) long pipe; **a plastic tube takes the petrol from the tank to the engine.**

turn

ب) أنبوب (من معجون الأسنان)
(b) soft pipe with a lid, which is filled with some sort of liquid; **a tube of toothpaste; a tube of glue.**

ت) السكة الحديدية التحت أرضية لمدينة لندن
(c) the London underground railway; **I go to work by tube; I met her on the tube yesterday morning; take the tube to the Tower of London.**

Tuesday [ˈtjuːzdɪ] *noun*

الثلاثاء (يوم الثلاثاء)
day between Monday and Wednesday, the second day of the week; **he came to see me last Tuesday; I go to the library on Tuesdays; shall we meet next Tuesday? today is Tuesday, October 28th.**

tune [tjuːn] *noun*

لحن - مقطوعة موسيقية
piece of music which you can whistle or sing; **he was whistling a tune which he'd heard on TV; play a tune on the piano.**

turn [tɜːn] **1.** *noun*

١ - أ) دورة
(a) movement in a circle; **he gave the screw two turns.**

ب) منعطف - انعطاف
(b) change of direction; **the car made a sudden turn to the right; take the next turn to the left** = the next road on the left; **the car did a U-turn** = turned round and went back in the opposite direction.

ت) دور : (إنتظر دورك)
(c) chance to do something in order; **wait for your turn to see the doctor; it's your turn to play now; let me go first—it's my turn, not yours; don't go out of turn** = when it is not your turn; **they took it in turns to carry the box/they took turns to carry the box** = each of them carried it for a while and then passed it to the next person.

2. *verb*

three hundred and thirty-nine 339

turn

أ) يرفض
(a) to refuse; **he was offered a job, but he turned it down; she turned down a job/ turned a job down in the library.**

ب) يُخَفِّض ـ يخفف (الصوت أو النار)
(b) to make less strong; **turn down the radio—it's too loud; turn down the gas/ turn the gas down—it's too hot.**

turn in, *verb*

يذهب للنوم
(a) to go to bed; **it's time to turn in.**

turning, *noun*

منعطف
(a) road which goes away from another road; **take the next turning to the left.**

turn off, *verb*

أ) يقطع التيار الكهربائي ـ يطفىء النور أو التلفزيون ... الخ
(a) to switch off; **don't forget to turn the TV off; turn off the lights/turn the lights off—I'm going to show my film.**

ب) ينحرف عن الطريق
(b) to leave a road you are travelling on; **he turned off the High Street into a car park; turn off the main road at the next crossroads.**

turn on, *verb*

يشعل (النور أو التلفزيون)
to switch on; **turn the lights on/turn on the lights—it's getting dark; can you turn on the TV/turn the TV on—it's time for the news.**

turn out, *verb*

أ) يطرد
(a) to make someone go out; **they were turned out of their house.**

ب) ينتج
(b) to produce; **the factory turns out 2,000 cars a week.**

ت) يطفىء (النور)
(c) to switch off; **turn out the lights/turn the lights out—I'm going to show a film.**

ث) يَحْصُل ـ يَجْري ـ يَحْدُث
(d) to happen; **it turned out that he knew my sister; everything turned out all right.**

٢ ـ أ) يدور ـ يدير ـ ينقلب على عقبيه
(a) to go round in a circle; to make something go round in a circle; **the wheels are turning slowly; turn the key to the left to open the door; the hands of the clock turned slowly to ten o'clock; the boat turned upside down.**

ب) ينعطف ـ يدور حول منعطف ـ يغيّر اتجاهه
(c) to change direction; **turn right at the next traffic lights; he turned the corner; the road turns to the left; the tide has turned = has started to go up or down.**

ت) يلتفت
(c) to move your head or body so that you face in another direction; **he turned to look at the camera.**

ث) يغيّر لونه ـ يَتغيّر إلى ـ يحوّل إلى ـ يتحوّل إلى
(d) to change into something different; **the leaves turn brown in the autumn; his hair's turned grey; we are turning this field into a football ground.**

ج) يتجاوز (الوقت المحدد أو العمر): قد تجاوز الخمسين عاماً
(e) to go past a time; **it's turned eight, and he still hasn't come home; he's turned fifty = he is is more than 50 years old.**

turns—turning—turned—has turned

turn away, *verb*

١) يصرف ـ يطرد
(a) to send people away; **the cinema is full, so we have to turn people away.**

ب) ينصرف ـ يرحل
(b) to move away; **she turned away because she didn't want to be photographed.**

turn back, *verb*

يعود ـ يرجع
to go back in the opposite direction; **the weather was so bad that we had to turn back and go home.**

turn down, *verb*

340   *three hundred and forty*

TV

ج) يخرج - يُغادر المنزل
(e) to come out; the whole school turned out to see the race.

turn over, verb

أ) يقلب - ينقلب
(a) to roll over; the lorry turned over; the boat turned over.

ب) يتصفح (كتاباً)
(b) to turn the page of a book; turn over the page/turn the page over; you turned over two pages together.

turn round, verb

يلتفت

to move your head or body so that you face in another direction; he turned round to look at the camera; she turned round to see who was following her.

turn up, verb

أ) يجيء - يظهر - يثبت انه
(a) to arrive; to be found; half the people didn't turn up until nine o'clock; the little boy finally turned up in Edinburgh = he was finally found in Edinburgh; my pen turned up in my coat pocket.

ب) يرفع (صوت الراديو أو النور)
(b) to make stronger; can you turn up the radio/turn the radio up—I can't hear it; turn up the gas/turn the gas up, the kettle hasn't boiled yet.

Note: **turn the radio down** or **turn down the radio; turn the light off** or **turn off the light,** etc., *but only* **turn it down, turn it off,** etc.

TV ['tiː'viː] noun, short for **television**
تلفزيون
do you watch TV every night? is there any sport on TV tonight? he's bought a colour TV; our TV set has broken down; some TV programmes make me go to sleep.

twelve [twelv] number 12

إثنا عشر - اثنتا عشرة (العدد ١٢)
he's twelve (years old); come for a cup of coffee at twelve o'clock; there are twelve months in a year.

three hundred and forty-one

twist

Note: **twelve o'clock** *is also called* **midday; twelve o'clock at night** *is* **midnight**

twelfth [twelfθ] 12th, adjective & noun

الثاني عشر - ثاني عشر
he came twelfth in the race; today is the twelfth of November/November the twelfth (November 12th); it's her twelfth birthday next week.

twenty ['twentɪ] number 20

عشرون (العدد ٢٠)
she's twenty (years old); he's in his twenties = he is between 20 and 29 years old.

Note: **twenty-one** (21), **twenty-two** (22), *etc.,* **but twenty-first** (21st), **twenty-second** (22nd), *etc.*

twentieth, 20th, adjective & noun
العشرون
she was twentieth in her class; today is the twentieth of December/December the twentieth (December 20th); it's her twentieth birthday on Tuesday.

twice [twaɪs] adverb

مرتين - ضِعْف
two times; I've already seen that film twice; twice two is four; he's twice as old as I am; she earns twice as much money as her sister; this book is twice as big as that one/is twice the size of that one.

twist [twɪst] verb

أ) يَفْتُل - يَجْدُل
(a) to turn round and round; to bend; the road twisted round the mountain; he twisted the metal bar into the shape of an S; threads are twisted together to make string.

ب) يلوي (الحديد أو الذراع)
(b) to bend something in a wrong way; the fire twisted the metal roof; he twisted his ankle = hurt it by bending it in an odd direction.

twists—twisting—twisted—has twisted

341

two

two [tu:] *number* 2

إثنين - إثنتين (العدد ٢)

there are only two chocolates left in the box; his son's two (years old); they didn't come home until two (o'clock).

واحد أو اثنين

one or two = some/a few; there were only one or two people in the shop.

Note: **two** (2), *but* **second** (2nd)

tying [taɪŋ] *see* **tie**

ملاحظة: انظر إلى كلمة **tie**

type [taɪp] **1.** *noun*

١ - نوع - طراز

sort/kind; you can have two types of cloth for your chairs; this is a new type of apple.
2. *verb*

under

٢ - يضرب على الآلة الكاتبة

to write with a typewriter; he's learning to type; I can only type with two fingers; she's typing all day long.

types—typing—typed—has typed

typewriter, *noun*

آلة كاتبة

machine which prints letters on to a piece of paper when you press the keys; she has a new electric typewriter; a typewriter's no use to me—I can't type.

typist, *noun*

الطابع (أو الضارب) على الآلة الكاتبة

person who types.

tyre [ˈtaɪə] *noun* (*American:* **tire**)

إطار العجلة المطاطي للسيارة

rubber cover which goes round a wheel and which is filled with air; my bike's got a flat tyre.

Uu

ugly [ˈʌgli] *adjective*

شنيع - قبيح - بشع - مروّع

not beautiful/not pleasant to look at; she was wearing an ugly hat; they live in an ugly little house.

ugly—uglier—ugliest

UK [juːˈkeɪ] *see* **unite**

ملاحظة: انظر إلى كلمة **unite**

umbrella [ʌmˈbrelə] *noun*

مظلّة

round cover of folded cloth which you open up and hold over your head to keep the rain off; can I come under your umbrella? he has an umbrella with red, white and blue stripes; the wind tore my umbrella.

unable [ʌnˈeɪbl] *adjective*

عاجز - غير قادر

not able; he was unable to come to the meeting; after her accident, she was unable to walk.

uncle [ˈʌŋkl] *noun*

العمّ أو الخال أو زوج العمّة أو الخالة

brother of your father or mother; husband of your aunt; look, here's Uncle John.

under [ˈʌndə] *preposition*

أ) تحت

(*a*) in or to a place where something else is on top or above; he hid under the table; my pencil's rolled under the piano; can you swim under water? = below the surface of the water.

understand

ب) دون ـ ما يقلُّ عن : (عمرها دون الثلاثين عاماً)

less than; she's under thirty = she is less than 30 years old; the car was sold for under £100; he ran the race in under six minutes.

Note: under is often used with verbs: to look under; to go under, etc.

underground 1. adverb & adjective

١ ـ تحت الأرضي ـ تحارضي

under the ground; the railway line goes underground for a short distance; he took an underground corridor to the next building.
2. noun

٢ ـ شبكة السكك الحديدية التحارضية

railway in a town, which runs under the ground; he goes to work by underground; she took the underground to go to the centre of the town.

underneath, preposition & adverb

تحت (شيء ما) مباشرة

under; he wore a long green pullover underneath his coat; look and see if my pencil is underneath the piano.

understand [ʌndəˈstænd] verb

أ) يدرك ـ يفهم

(a) to know; to see what something means; do you understand how this machine works? he doesn't understand English, so don't try to talk to him; I hardly speak any Chinese, but I made myself understood.

ب) يستنتج

(b) to have information; I understood you were going to be late? we understand he's getting married next week.

understands—understanding— understood—has understood

undress [ʌnˈdres] verb

ينزع ثيابه ـ يخلع ملابسه ـ يتعرّى

to take your clothes off; he undressed and got into bed; before you get undres-

sed, can you see if the garage door is shut?

undresses—undressing— undressed—has undressed

unhappy [ʌnˈhæpɪ] adjective

تعيس ـ شقي ـ حزين

sad/not happy; she's unhappy because her cat's ill; he looked very unhappy when he came out of the headmaster's room.

unhappy—unhappier— unhappiest

unhappily, adverb

بتعاسة ـ بحزن ـ بشقاء

sadly; she stared unhappily out of the window.

uniform [ˈjuːnɪfɔːm] noun

بزّة ـ بذلة خاصة أو نظامية

special clothes worn by everyone in a group, especially soldiers, policemen, etc.; the policemen were in uniform; was he wearing uniform? the children all have to wear school uniform.

unite [juːˈnaɪt] verb

يوحّد ـ يَلُمُّ ـ يتحد : (الولايات المتحدة الأميركية ، المملكة المتحدة ... الخ)

to bring together/to join together; the United States (of America) = very large country south of Canada in North America; the United Kingdom = country formed of England, Scotland, Wales and Northern Ireland.

unites—uniting—united—has united

Note: the United States of America is usually called the US or the USA; the United Kingdom is usually called the UK

university [juːnɪˈvɜːsɪtɪ] noun

جامعة

place where you study after leaving school; the university is on the south side of the town; he's studying history at uni-

unless

versity; are you going to university when you leave school?
plural **universities**
Note: use **the** *only when you refer to a particular university*

unless [ʌn'les] *conjunction*

إلاّ إذا ـ ما لم

if not; **unless you start at once, you'll be late** = if you do not start at once; **don't telephone unless the message is important** = if the message isn't important; **we'll have our picnic in the field, unless it rains** = if it doesn't rain; **don't come unless you want to** = if you don't want to.

unload [ʌn'ləʊd] *verb*

يُفرغ حمولة أو يتخلص من عبء

to take things off a vehicle, etc.; **the ship is unloading her cargo in the dock; can you help me unload the bricks from the lorry?**
unloads—unloading—unloaded—has unloaded

unlucky [ʌn'lʌkɪ] *adjective*

مشؤوم ـ منحوس ـ قليل الحظ

not lucky; **it's unlucky to walk under a ladder; Friday 13th is my unlucky day.**
unlucky—unluckier—unluckiest

unpleasant [ʌn'plezənt] *adjective*

كريه ـ بغيض

not nice/not pleasant; **what an unpleasant smell! our teacher was unpleasant when I told him I couldn't go to school.**

untidy [ʌn'taɪdɪ] *adjective*

مهمل ـ غير مرتب

not tidy; **your room is so untidy that you can't find anything in it.**

until [ʌn'tɪl] *preposition*

حتى ذلك الحين ـ حتى

till/up to the time when; **I won't be home until after eleven o'clock; until yesterday, I was very well.**

344

upper

up [ʌp] *adverb & preposition*

أ) فوق ـ إلى فوق

(*a*) in or to a high place; **he climbed up the stairs; she was going up a ladder; lift your hands up; why is the cat up there on the cupboard?**

ب) بارتفاع ـ على ارتفاع

(*b*) to a higher level; **the temperature has gone up; prices seem to go up every day.**

ت) على طول ـ إلى آخر (الطريق)

(*c*) along; **go up the street to the traffic lights and then turn left.**

ث) مستيقظ ـ غير نائم

(*d*) not in bed; **he's still up—he should be in bed; she stayed up all night.**

ج) شمالا ـ نحو الشمال

(*e*) towards the north; **I'll be going up to Scotland next week (from London).**

ح) ماذا يجري ـ ما هي المشكلة ؟

(*f*) **what's up?** = what is the matter? **what's up with the car?—it's making a strange noise.**

خ) انتهى الوقت المحدّد

(*g*) **your time's up** = you have had all the time allowed.
Note: **up** *is often used after verbs:* **to keep up; to look up; to turn up,** *etc.*

up to, *preposition*

أ) حتى أو إلى كذا

(*a*) as many as; **the bus will hold up to sixty passengers.**

ب) ماذا تفعل ؟

(*b*) **what are you up to?** = what are you doing?

up to date, *adjective & adverb*

عصري ـ حديث ـ ملائم للذوق العصري

very modern/using very recent information; **is this railway timetable up to date? I keep myself up to date by reading the newspaper every day.**

upper ['ʌpə] *adjective*

الأعلى ـ العليا (الطبقة العليا من البيت)

at the top/higher; **the upper part of the house was destroyed by fire; the upper**

three hundred and forty-four

upright

forms in the school are taking their exams this year.

upright ['ʌpraɪt] *adjective & adverb*
عمودي ـ بشكل عمودي ـ منتصب
standing straight up; hold the stick upright; he kept himself upright by holding on to the wall.

upside down ['ʌpsaɪd'daʊn] *adverb*
مقلوب رأس على عقب
with the top turned to the bottom; don't hold the box upside down—everything will fall out; the car ran off the road and ended up upside down in a field; the boys were hanging upside down from a tree; he's not reading that book—he's holding it upside down.

upstairs [ʌp'steəz] *adverb & noun*
فوق ـ في الدور الأعلى ـ العلوي
on or to the top floor of a house; my father's upstairs—I'll ask him to come down; can you go upstairs and get my coat from the bedroom? the upstairs of the house is smaller than the downstairs.

upwards, *adverb*
صاعد ـ متجه إلى أعلى ـ إلى أعلى
towards the top; the path slopes upwards.

urgent ['ɜːdʒənt] *adjective*
مُلح ـ متطلب عملاً عاجلاً
which has to be done quickly; he had an urgent message to go to the hospital.

us [ʌs] *object pronoun used by the person who is speaking to talk about himself and other people with him*
نحن ـ « نا » (ضمير متصل) أعطانا « نا »
he gave us £1 to buy ourselves some ice cream; who is it?—it's us! our class is very happy—the teacher has given us a holiday.

US [juː'es], **USA** [juːes'eɪ] *see* **unite**
ملاحظة : انظر إلى كلمة unite

used to

use¹ [juːs] *noun*
أ) طريقة استعمال ـ استعمال ـ امكانية استعمال
(a) way in which something can be used; being used; can you find a use for this piece of wood? the cooker has been in daily use for ten years; our flat has no kitchen, but we have the use of the kitchen in the flat downstairs; to make use of something = to use; you should make more use of your dictionary = you should use it more.

ب) فائدة ـ غرض ـ معنى ـ هدف ـ منفعة ـ حاجة ضرورة
(b) value/being useful; what's the use of telling her what to do, when she never does what you want? it's no use sitting here and saying the car needs washing, let's go out and wash it.

use² [juːz] *verb*
أ) يستعمل ـ يستخدم
(a) to take a tool, etc., and do something with it; someone's used my knife to open a tin of fruit; he used the money to buy a car; did you use a sewing machine to make your dress? can I use these scissors for cutting flowers? he was using the electric saw when it slipped.

ب) يستهلك ـ يحرق
(b) to take something and burn it, etc., to make an engine work or to produce heat, light, etc.; this car uses a lot of petrol; we're using too much gas and electricity.

uses—using—used [juːzd]—has used

used [juːzd] *adjective*
مستعمل ـ مستخدم ـ عتيق
which is not new; a used car; this typewriter's worth a lot of money—it's hardly used.

used to ['juːsttʊ]
أ) يكون متعوّداً على
(a) to be used to something/to doing something = not to object to something, because you do it often; he's used to

three hundred and forty-five 345

vacation

getting up early; she's used to hard work; we're not used to eating so much.

ب) يعتاد على

(b) **to get used to something/to doing something** = to do something often or for a period of time, so that it becomes a habit; **you'll soon get used to your new job; he never got used to getting up early.**

ت) عبارة للتعبير عن شيء كان يحصل أو كان موجوداً في الماضي بطريقة دائمة أو عادية (كان يوجد فرن في هذه القرية ـ لما كنت صبياً، كنّا نذهب إلى شاطىء البحر...)

(c) (*showing that something happened often or regularly in the past*) **there used to be a baker's shop in the village; when I was a boy, we used to go to the seaside every year for our holidays; she used to teach history at our school; didn't he use to go to work on his bike?**

Note the forms used in the negative and questions: **he used to go by bike; he didn't use to go by bike/he used not to go by bike; didn't he use to go by bike?**

useful, *adjective*

مفيد ـ نافع

who/which can help you to do something; **I find this knife very useful in the garden; he's a very useful man in the office.**

useless, *adjective*

عقيم ـ عديم الجدوى

which does not help; **this knife is useless—it isn't sharp; she's useless at numbers** = she is no good with numbers.

use up, *verb*

يستهلك ـ يستنفد

to finish something; **we've used up all our sugar; he's used up all my cigarettes.**
Note: **we've used all the sugar up** *or* **we've used up all the sugar** *but only* **we've used it up**

usual ['ju:ʒʊəl] *adjective*

معتاد ـ مألوف ـ اعتيادي

which happens often/which you do often; **I'll take my usual train this morning; the postman was late, as usual; let's meet at the usual time; as usual, it rained on my birthday.**

usually, *adverb*

عادة

very often/mostly; **he usually gets to work at 9 o'clock; she usually has an apple for lunch.**

U-turn, *see* **turn**

Vv

vacation [vəˈkeɪʃn] *noun*

عطلة

American = **holiday**

vain [veɪn] *adjective*

بدون جدوى ـ عبثاً

in vain = without any success; **we waited in vain for a bus; they tried in vain to start the car.**

valley [ˈvælɪ] *noun*

وادي

low land between hills, with a river running through it: **the valley of the Thames/the Thames valley; the town is in the bottom of the valley.**

value [ˈvæljuː] *noun*

قيمة ـ قدر

346 three hundred and forty-six

van

what something is worth; **what's the value of this house? this is very good value** = it is well worth its price.

valuable, *adjective*

قيّم - ثمين - نفيس

worth a lot of money; **the burglar stole some valuable books.**

van [væn] *noun*

شاحنة صغيرة (لنقل السلع)

small vehicle for carrying goods by road or rail; **here comes the bread van; the furniture shop delivered the chairs by van; guard's van** = wagon on a train in which the guard rides.

various ['veəriəs] *adjective*

مختلف - عدّة

several/of different sorts; **we've met on various occasions; there are various ways of getting to London from here; he has written various books on birds.**

vegetable ['vedʒtəbl] *noun*

نبات من الخُضَر (مثل البطاطة والخس والطماطم)

plant grown for food, not usually sweet; **we have potatoes, cabbages and other sorts of vegetables in the garden; what vegetables do you want with your meat?—peas and carrots, please; I'll have a bowl of vegetable soup.**

vehicle ['vɪəkl] *noun*

مركبة - عربة - اداة نقل برّي من سلع أو ركاب

machine on wheels which travels on land, carrying people or goods; **motor vehicles are not allowed on this path; goods vehicles can park here for 30 minutes.**

verb [vɜːb] *noun*

فعل

word showing action/being/feeling, etc.; **in the sentence 'he kicked the ball', the word 'kicked' is a verb.**

view

vertical ['vɜːtɪkl] *adjective*

عمودي - منتصب

which is standing upright; **a vertical line**

very ['veri] **1.** *adverb*

١ - جداً - إلى حدّ بعيد

(*used to make an adjective stronger*) **it's very hot in here—let's open the window; she's very tall; this meat isn't very good.**
2. *adjective*

٢ - بالذات - مطلق - تماماً - عين - نفس

exactly the right one/exactly the same; **he's the very man you want; it happens at the very beginning of the film** = right at the beginning.

very many, *adjective*

كثير - مقدار كبير - عديد

a lot of; **there weren't very many people at the party; we went swimming very many times.**
Note: **very many** *is used with things you can count:* **very many cars**

very much 1. *adverb*

كثيراً - جزيلاً (شكراً جزيلاً) - بكثير

greatly; **I like ice cream very much; thank you very much for your present; it's very much colder today; she's very much better.**
2. *adjective*

٢ - كثيراً - مقدار كبير

a lot of; **he doesn't do very much work; she hasn't got very much money.**
Note: **very much** *is used with things which you cannot count:* **very much money**

victory ['vɪktrɪ] *noun*

انتصار - نصر - ظَفَر

win (in a game or battle); **the victory of the Scottish team over the English.**
plural **victories**

view [vjuː] *noun*

١) مَنْظَر - مَشْهد

(*a*) what you can see from a certain place; **from my window there's a wonderful view over London; you get a**

347

village

good view of the sea from the top of the hill; this photograph is a side view of our house.

ب) وجهة نظر ـ فكرة ـ رأي ـ ظنّ ـ اعتقاد

(b) way of thinking about something; **in my view, the government ought to do something to help poor people; I try to see the headmaster's point of view** = I try to understand the way he thinks.

ت) نظراً لـ ـ بسبب

(c) **in view of** = because of; **in view of the weather, we had the party indoors.**

village ['vɪlɪdʒ] noun

قرية ـ بلدة

small group of houses in the country, with a church, pub and usually some shops; **we live in a little mountain village; go to the village baker's to get some bread; there aren't many children in the village school.**

violence ['vaɪələns] noun

عنف

rough action; use of force; **the game was spoilt by violence.**

violent, adjective

عنيف ـ شديد ـ قاسٍ

using a lot of force; very rough; **there was a violent storm during the night; the game of football was very violent—several players were hurt.**

visit ['vɪzɪt] 1. noun

١ ـ زيارة

short stay with someone/short stay in a town or country; **he's on a visit to China; let's pay a visit to your mother; they had a visit from the doctor.**

2. verb

٢ ـ يزور ـ يقوم بزيارة ـ يعود (مريضاً)

to stay a short time with someone/to stay a short time in a town or country; **I must visit my brother in hospital; we are going to visit the factory; he's visiting friends in France.**

visits—visiting—visited—has visited

voyage

visitor, noun

الزائر ـ القائم بزيارة

person who visits; **how many visitors are staying in the hotel this weekend? we had a visitor last night—old Uncle Charles.**

voice [vɔɪs] noun

صوت

sound made when you speak or sing; **I didn't recognize your voice over the phone; he's got a cold and has lost his voice** = he can't speak; **she spoke for a few minutes in a low voice** = very quietly.

vote [vəʊt] 1. noun

١ ـ صوت (في الانتخابات) ـ تصويت ـ ورقة اقتراع ـ اقتراع

making a mark on a piece of paper/lifting your hand, etc. to elect someone or to make a decision; **there were 10 votes for Mr Smith and only 2 for Mr Jones, so Mr Smith was elected; my vote goes to Mr Smith's plan; if we can't agree, let's have/take a vote.**

2. verb

٢ ـ يصوّت ـ يقترع ـ ينتخب

to make a mark on a piece of paper to elect someone/to lift your hand to make a decision, etc.; **we all voted for Mr Smith; only people over 18 can vote in the election; I vote that we have the picnic in the woods** = I suggest that we have a picnic.

votes—voting—voted—has voted

voter, noun

المقترع ـ الناخب

person who votes.

voyage ['vɔɪɪdʒ] noun

رحلة طويلة

long journey, especially by boat; **he went on a voyage round the world.**

W w

wage [weɪdʒ] *noun*

راتب أسبوعي أو شهري

money which you get each week for work which you have done; **he gets a good wage at the factory; wages have gone up a lot this year; I'm going to collect my wages.**

Note: usually used in the plural

wagon ['wægn] *noun*

عربة (من عربات القطار)

vehicle used on the railway; **a goods wagon; a coal wagon.**

waist [weɪst] *noun*

خَصْر - وسط (الجسم)

narrow part of your body below your chest and above your behind; **he measures 85 centimetres round the waist.**

wait [weɪt] *verb*

ينتظر

to stay somewhere until something happens or someone arrives; **wait here while I fetch a policeman; he waited for the bus for half an hour; he gets annoyed if you keep him waiting; wait a minute, I've got a stone in my shoe; sorry to have kept you waiting!**

waits—waiting—waited—has waited

waiter, *noun*

النادل : القائم على خدمة الزبائن في مطعم

man who brings food to people in a restaurant; **the waiter brought us the soup; how much shall we give the waiter as a tip?** *see also* **waitress.**

waiting room, *noun*

غرفة الانتظار

room where you wait at a doctor's, dentist's or at a railway station; **go into the waiting room—the doctor will see you in ten minutes.**

waitress, *noun*

النادلة : القائمة على خدمة الزبائن في مطعم

woman who brings food to people in a restaurant; **the waitress brought us the soup; shall we give the waitress a tip?** *see also* **waiter.**

plural **waitresses**

wake [weɪk] **1.** *noun*

١ ـ الاثر الذي تخلفه السفينة الجارية في المياه

waves made by a ship as it goes past; **the little boat rocked in the wake of the ferry.**

2. *verb*

٢ ـ يوقظ ـ يستيقظ

to interrupt someone's sleep; to stop sleeping; **the telephone woke me/I was woken by the telephone; can't you wake her?—no, she's fast asleep.**

wakes—waking—woke [wəʊk]*—has woken*

wake up, *verb*

يوقظ ـ يستيقظ

to interrupt someone's sleep; to stop sleeping; **he woke up in the middle of the night; he was woken up by the sound of the telephone; wake up! it's past nine o'clock.**

Note: **I woke my mother up** *or* **I woke up my mother** *but only* **I woke her up**

three hundred and forty-nine

Wales

Wales [weɪlz] *noun*

مقاطعة ويلز البريطانية

country which is part of Great Britain, and is to the west of England; **we're going to Wales for our holiday; he's gone to live in Wales.**

Welsh [welʃ] **1.** *adjective*

١ ـ من مقاطعة ويلز

referring to Wales; **the Welsh mountains are very beautiful.**

2. *noun*

٢ ـ ١) من سكان ويلز

(a) **the Welsh** = the people who live in or come from Wales; **the Welsh are very good singers.**

ب) لغة ويلز: اللغة التي يتكلمها سكان ويلز

(b) language spoken in Wales; **he speaks Welsh; Welsh words are very difficult to pronounce.**

walk [wɔːk] **1.** *noun*

١ ـ مسيرة ـ نزهة ـ مشي

journey on foot; **we all went for a walk in the park; the post office is only five minutes' walk from here** = you can go there on foot in five minutes; **he's taking the dog for a walk; does anyone want to come for a walk?**

2. *verb*

٢ ـ يمشي ـ يسير على القدمين ـ يقوم بنزهة صغيرة على القدمين

to go on foot; **I'll walk to the bus stop with you; she walked across the room; he was walking along the street; can you walk to school, or do you have to take the bus? they all walked up the hill.**

walks—walking—walked—has walked

walk about, *verb*

يمشي في مختلف الاتجاهات

to walk in various directions; **they spent hours walking about the town, looking for a restaurant.**

walk off with, *verb*

يختلس ـ يأخذ ما ليس له

to go away with; to steal; **the burglar walked off with all our jewellery; she walked off with the prize** = she won the prize easily.

wall [wɔːl] *noun*

سور ـ حائط ـ جدار

bricks/stones, etc., piled up to make one of the sides of a building/of a room or to surround a space; **he's building a wall all round his garden; we have a lot of photographs on the walls of the dining room; there's a clock on the wall over his desk; the car went into the wall; can you climb over the garden wall?**

wallet ['wɒlɪt] *noun*

محفظة جيب

small leather case for holding paper money/tickets, etc., and which you keep in your pocket; **someone's stolen my wallet from my back pocket.**

want [wɒnt] *verb*

١) يريد ـ يرغب

(a) to hope that you will do something/that something will happen/that you will have something; **he wants a bicycle for his birthday; they want to go to Africa on holiday; she wants to be an air hostess; he wants me to go to see him.**

ب) يحتاج

(b) to need; **we haven't enough space for all the furniture—we want a bigger house; your hair wants cutting; the house wants painting.**

ت) يطارد ـ يلاحق

(c) to look for someone; **he's wanted by the police.**

wants—wanting—wanted—has wanted

war [wɔː] *noun*

حرب ـ حالة حرب

fighting between countries; **in 1814 Britain was at war with France/Britain and France were at war; millions of people were killed in the Second World War.**

wardrobe

warship, *noun*

سفينة حربية

ship with guns, which is used for fighting, not for carrying goods.

wardrobe ['wɔ:drəub] *noun*

خزانة الثياب

large cupboard where you can hang clothes up; **put your coat in the wardrobe; the wardrobe's full of her old dresses.**

warm [wɔ:m] **1.** *adjective*

١ - دافِئ - حار

quite hot/pleasantly hot; **it's cold outside in the snow, but it's nice and warm in the house; they tried to keep warm by jumping up and down; are you warm enough, or do you want another blanket?**

warms—warmer—warmest

2. *verb*

٢ - يُدْفِئ - يُسَخِّن

to make hotter; **warm yourself by the fire; he was warming his hands over the fire; sit down while I warm some soup.**

warms—warming—warmed—has warmed

warm up, *verb*

يسخّن - يدفّئ - يعيد التسخين

to make hotter; **this soup will warm you up; I'll warm up some milk to make cocoa.**

warn [wɔ:n] *verb*

يُحذِّر - ينذر - ينبّه إلى

to tell that a danger is possible; **the children were warned not to go too near the fire; I warned you about that electric wire; the police warned us against playing near the railway line.**

warns—warning—warned—has warned

warning, *noun*

تحذير - انذار - تنبيه - إشعار

telling about a danger; **the police gave a warning about a dangerous criminal;** did you read the warning notice? there's a warning of the bottle on medicine; every packet of cigarettes has a health warning printed on it.

without warning = very suddenly; **without warning the car ran off the road into a wall.**

فجأةً - بدون تحذير

was [wɒz] *see* **be**

انظر إلى كلمة be

wash

wash [wɒʃ] **1.** *noun*

١ - غسيل - غسل

action of cleaning using water; **he went to the bathroom to have a wash; I need a wash—where's the bathroom?**

2. *verb*

٢ - يغسل

to clean using water; **wash your hands before dinner! we must wash the car before we go on holiday; they were washing the windows when it started to rain; your hair needs washing; can you wash this raincoat?—no, you have to take it to the cleaner's.**

washes—washing—washed—has washed

wash down, *verb*

يغسل تماماً مستعملاً كثيراً من الماء

to clean with a lot of water; **let's wash down the van; the sailors were washing down the deck of the ship.**

washing, *noun*

الغسيل

clothes which have been washed, or which are ready to be washed; **look at that pile of washing; put the washing in the washing machine; the washing's drying in the wind.**

no plural

washing machine, *noun*

غسّالة

machine for washing clothes.

washing up, *noun*

three hundred and fifty-one

351

wasn't

غسيل الأواني والصحون ـ جلي الصحون

cleaning of cups/plates/knives/forks, etc. with water; **can you help me do the washing up? there was so much washing up after the party, that it took us hours to do it.**

wash off, verb

ينزع الأوساخ ـ يغسل

to take off by washing; **I'll wash the mud off my boots.**

wash up, verb

يغسل ـ يجلي الصحون

to clean cups/plates/knives/forks, etc., with water; **let's wash up these plates; Daddy's washing up, while I'm watching the TV.**

Note: **wash the plates up** *or* **wash up the plates** *but only* **wash them up**

wasn't ['wɒznt] *see* **be**

ملاحظة : انظر إلى كلمة be

waste [weɪst] **1.** *noun*

أ) نفاية ـ فضلة

(a) rubbish; **put all the waste in the dustbin.**

ب) إضاعة ـ ضياع ـ تبديد

(b) not being any use; **it's a waste of time trying to telephone—she's not in; that car's a waste of money—it keeps going wrong.**

2. *adjective*

٢ ـ عديم النفع ـ غير صالح للاستعمال

useless/which is no use; **throw all your waste paper into the dustbin.**

3. *verb*

٣ ـ أ) يضيع ـ يتبدد ـ ينفق ـ يروح هدراً

(a) to use more than you need; **I've wasted three sheets of paper; they waste a lot of food.**

ب) يضيع (الوقت أو المال)

(b) not to use something in a useful way; **she wasted several hours waiting for him to come to fetch her; he wastes his pocket money on sweets.**

wastes—wasting—wasted—has wasted

352

water

wasteful, *adjective*

مسرف في الانفاق ـ مبذر

which wastes; **it's wasteful of electricity to leave the lights on all day.**

watch [wɒtʃ] **1.** *noun*

١ ـ أ) ساعة يد

(a) small clock which you wear on your wrist or which you carry in your pocket; **he looked at his watch; what time is it by your watch?**

ب) مراقبة ـ حراسة

(b) looking at something; **the police are on the watch for burglars; she was keeping a watch on the saucepan of milk to make sure it didn't boil over.**

plural **watches;** no plural for (b)

2. *verb*

٢ ـ أ) يشاهد (برنامج أو مباراة)

(a) to look at; **did you watch TV last night? I watched a programme on sport; we'll watch him play football; she was watching the children playing.**

ب) يراقب ـ ينتبه ـ يحرس

(b) to look at something carefully to make sure that nothing happens; **watch the saucepan—I don't want the milk to boil over; will you watch the baby while I go shopping?**

watches—watching—watched—has watched

watch out, *verb*

ينتبه إلى ـ يَحْذَر

to be careful; **watch out! the paint is still wet; you have to watch out for ice on the roads in winter.**

water ['wɔːtə] **1.** *noun*

١ ـ ماء

common liquid which makes rain, rivers, the sea, etc., and which you drink and use in cooking; **can I have a glass of water, please? the hotel has hot and cold water in each bedroom; he dived and swam across the pool under**

three hundred and fifty-two

wave

water; boil the potatoes in a pan of water.

no plural: **some water; a drop of water**

2. *verb*

٢ - يروي بالماء - يسقي - يزوّد بالماء

to pour water on a plant to make it grow; the weather's very dry—we'll have to water the garden; he was watering the flowers.

waters—watering—watered—has watered

waterfall, *noun*

شلّال

place where a stream falls down rocks; let's have our picnic by the waterfall; which is the biggest waterfall in the world—is it Niagara?

waterproof, *adjective*

صامد للماء - ضدّ الماء

which will not let water through; is your raincoat really waterproof? if your watch is waterproof you can wear it when you go swimming.

wave [weɪv] 1. *noun*

١ - موج - موجة

high mass of water on the sea, which moves forward; can you hear the noise of the waves on the beach? the ship was sunk by the waves.

2. *verb*

٢ - يُلَوِّح

to move up and down and from side to side, especially to move your hand in this way; the children were waving flags; she waved her handkerchief as the train left; wave to your mother—she's on the other side of the street; I waved to the waiter and asked him to bring the bill; the flags were waving in the wind.

waves—waving—waved—has waved

way [weɪ] *noun*

١) طريق - سبيل

(a) road/path which goes somewhere; my friend lives across the way.

way

ب) إتجاه

(b) right road/path to somewhere; can you tell me the way to the post office? the policeman showed us the way to the station; he made his way through the crowd; we lost our way and had to ask someone; I'm just on my way to school.

ت) وجهة

(c) particular direction; this is a one-way street; which way is the wind blowing? = is it blowing north, south, etc.? come this way, please.

ث) طريقة مميزة

(d) means of doing something; grandmother showed me the way to make bread; she spoke in a friendly way; is there another way of doing it? he always does it that way; I wish I knew a way of making money quickly.

ج) مسافة - وقت

(e) distance/time; the post office is a long way from here; we've a long way to go before we've finished our work; I'll walk part of the way home with you.

ح) مجال : افسح المجال

(f) space in which someone wants to be/which someone wants to use; get out of the way—there's a car coming; keep out of father's way—he thinks you broke the window; he's always in the way.

وبالمناسبة - وعلى فكرة

by the way (*used to introduce something which is not very important or to change the subject which is being talked about*) by the way, did you see the TV programme on cars yesterday?

way in, *noun*

المدخل

entrance; is this the way in? the way in is through the big blue door.

way out, *noun*

المخرج

exit; is this the way out? we couldn't find the way out in the dark.

way up, *noun*

الطرف الأعلى

way in which something stands; keep the

three hundred and fifty-three 353

we

box the right way up = with the top on top; you're holding the book the wrong way up = holding it upside down.

we [wiː] *pronoun*

نحن ـ « نا » (ضمير متصل أو منفصل)

(*used by speakers when referring to themselves*) the policeman said we could go across the road; we came to London by train; our class went to the cinema—we all enjoyed ourselves very much.
Note: when it is the object we becomes us: we gave it to him/he gave it to us, when it follows the verb be, we usually becomes us: who is it?—it's us!

weak [wiːk] *adjective*

١) ضعيف ـ واهن

(*a*) not strong; after his illness he was very weak; this tea is very weak—you've put too much water in it.

ب) ركيك

(*b*) not good at; he's very weak at maths; maths is his weakest subject.
weak—weaker—weakest

wealth [welθ] *noun*

غنىً ـ وفرة ـ ثروة

being rich; a lot of money; he's famous for his wealth.

wealthy, *adjective*

ثري ـ غنيّ

having a lot of money; he's a very wealthy man.
wealthy—wealthier—wealthiest

weapon ['wepn] *noun*

سلاح

thing which you use to fight with; the soldiers were carrying guns and other weapons; he used a broken bottle as a weapon.

wear [weə] *verb*

١) يرتدي ـ يلبس

(*a*) to carry on your body (especially a piece of clothing); I'll wear my brown coat today; the police are looking for a man wearing a blue raincoat; everyone was wearing uniform; she's wearing my watch.

ب) يبلى ـ يرهق ـ ينهك

(*b*) to become damaged through being used a lot; the car tyres are worn; I've worn a hole in my trousers.
wears—wearing—wore [wɔː]—has worn

wear off, *verb*

يزيل ـ يزول

to disappear gradually; the writing on the wall has worn off; the effect of the cough medicine has worn off.

wear out, *verb*

١) يبلي

(*a*) to use something so much that it is broken/useless; he wore out three pairs of shoes; the engine has worn out = has been working so much that it is useless.

ب) يرهق ـ ينهك

(*b*) worn out = very tired; after that game of football I am quite worn out; she came home worn out after a day at the office.

weather ['weðə] *noun*

الطقس ـ حالة الطقس

conditions outside—that is, if it is raining/hot/cold/windy/sunny, etc.; what's the weather like today? the TV said the weather was going to be bad; the weather's always cold in the mountains; look at the rain—is this your normal summer weather? if the weather's fine, perhaps we'll have a picnic.
no plural

web [web] *noun*

نسيج العنكبوت

kind of net made by a spider.

wedding ['wedɪŋ] *noun*

عرس ـ زفاف ـ زواج

ceremony when two people are mar-

Wednesday

ried; **I'm going to my brother's wedding; the wedding's next week; was it fine for the wedding?**

Wednesday ['wenzdɪ] *noun*

الأربعاء ـ نهار الأربعاء

day between Tuesday and Thursday, the third day of the week; **I saw her last Wednesday; we've got a day off next Wednesday; all the shops are shut on Wednesdays; can you come to tea on Wednesday afternoon?**

week [wiːk] *noun*

أسبوع

period of seven days; **there are 52 weeks in the year; we have two weeks' holiday at Christmas; my aunt's coming to stay with us next week; what day of the week is it today?** = is it Monday, Tuesday, etc.? **we go to the cinema once a week; a week from now I'll be on holiday.**

weekday, *noun*

يوم عادي : كل يوم من أيام الأسبوع ما عدا السبت أو الأحد

normal working day (not Saturday or Sunday); **the office is open on weekdays.**

weekend, *noun*

نهاية الأسبوع : السبت والأحد

Saturday and Sunday; period from Friday evening to Sunday evening; **what are you doing at the weekend? we're going away for the weekend; come to spend the weekend with me; I went to London last weekend; we usually go to the country at weekends.**

weekly, *adjective & adverb*

كل أسبوع ـ أسبوعياً

which happens/appears once a week; **we have a weekly paper which tells us all the local information; we pay the milkman weekly.**

weigh [weɪ] *verb*

يَزِن (شيئاً) ـ يبلغ وزنه : (هل تزن هذه البطاطة ـ هذه السمكة تزن نصف كيلو)

to measure how heavy something is; to

well

be heavy/to have a certain weight; **can you weigh these potatoes for me? this piece of fish weighs 500 grams; how much do you weigh? I weigh 120 pounds/I weigh 54 kilos.**

weighs—weighing—weighed—has weighed

weight [weɪt] *noun*

أ) وزن

(*a*) how heavy something is; **what's the weight of this bag of potatoes? what's your weight? I'm trying to lose weight** = to get thinner; **he's put on a lot of weight** = he is a lot fatter.

ب) ثقل ـ أثقال : (إذا رفعت الأثقال فسيؤلمك ظهرك)

(*b*) something which is heavy; **if you lift heavy weights, you may hurt your back; put a weight on the pile of papers to stop them blowing away.**

welcome ['welkəm] **1.** *noun*

١ ـ ترحيب ـ أهلاً وسهلاً .

action of greeting someone; **they gave us a warm welcome** = a friendly welcome.

2. *verb*

٢ ـ يرحب

(*a*) to greet someone; **they welcomed us to the office; we were welcomed by the dogs when we got home.**

٣ ـ يتقبّل بسرور

(*b*) to be glad to hear news; to accept; **I welcome the news that he has passed his exams; I would welcome any advice on how to make bread, because I've never made it before.**

welcomes—welcoming—welcomed—has welcomed

well [wel] **1.** *noun*

١ ـ بئر

very deep hole in the ground with water or oil at the bottom; **they pulled the water up from a well; there are many oil wells in the North Sea.**

2. *adverb*

three hundred and fifty-five

Welsh

٢ - ا) جيداً
(a) in a good way; **he can speak Russian quite well; she did her homework very well; the shop's small, but it's doing well; does the manager work well?**

ب) بكثير
(b) a lot; **it's well after 9 o'clock; it's well worth trying to get a ticket; he's well over sixty** = more than sixty years old.

أيضاً
as well = also; **I'm bringing my cat, but can I bring the dogs as well?; you can't have a piece of cake and ice cream as well.**

ليس فحسب ... بل
as well as = not only, but also; **he's deaf as well as blind; the shop sells sweets as well as newspapers.**
3. *adjective*

٣ - بصحة جيدة
healthy; **you're looking well! he's quite well after his flu; he's not very well, and has had to stay in bed.**
4. *interjection*

٤ - حسناً
(*which starts a sentence, and often has no meaning*) **well, as I was saying; well, the washing up's finished, so what shall we do now?** (*showing surprise*) **well, well! here's old Mr Smith!**

Welsh [welʃ] *see* **Wales**
ملاحظة : انظر إلى كلمة Wales

went [went] *see* **go**
ملاحظة : انظر إلى كلمة go

were [wɜː], **weren't** [wɜːnt] *see* **be**
ملاحظة : انظر إلى كلمة be

west [west] 1. *noun*

١ - غرب - الغرب
direction of where the sun sets; **the sun rises in the east and sets in the west; the town is to the west of the river.**
2. *adjective*

what

٢ - الغربيّ
referring to the west; **the west coast of the United States; he lives in the west end of the town.**
3. *adverb*

٣ - نحو الغرب - غرباً
towards the west; **the ship's sailing west; if you go west for ten kilometres, you'll come to a little village.**

western ['westən] 1. *adjective*

١ - غربيّ
of the west; **Great Britain is in Western Europe; they live in the western part of Canada.**
2. *noun*

٢ - فيلم اميركي عن رعاة البقر
film about cowboys; **I like watching old westerns on TV.**

wet [wet] *adjective*

ا) رطب - مبتل
(a) covered with water; **I didn't have an umbrella, so I got wet waiting for the bus in the rain; I'm wet through** = very wet; **the carpet's all wet where you spilt your tea.**

ب) رطب - ممطر (طقس ممطر)
(b) rainy; **February is the wettest month of the year.**

ت) غير جاف
(c) not yet dry; **don't sit there—the paint on the chair is still wet.**

wet—wetter—wettest

what [wɒt] *adjective & pronoun*

ا) ما - الذي
(a) the thing which; **I saw what was in the box; did you see what he gave me for my birthday? what he likes most is just sitting the sun.**

ب) ما (للاستفهام) - ماذا :
(ما هو اسمك ؟)
(b) (*asking a question*) **what time is it? what's the time? what's his name? what did you say? what's the German for 'table'? what's the matter with Mrs Smith? what happened to you? what kind of car do you drive?**

356 *three hundred and fifty-six*

wheel

ت) ما هذا ... كله ؟ (للعجب) يا دِ : (يا للرجل البغيض !) (ياله من بيت جميل)

(c) (*showing surprise*) what a lot of potatoes you've eaten! what a nasty man! what a beautiful house! what lovely weather!

Note: after **what** *used to ask a question, the verb is put before the subject:* **what's the time?** *but* **they don't know what the time is**

what about (*showing a suggestion*)

ما رأيك في (كسؤال أو اقتراح) : (ما رأيك إذا توقفنا هنا ؟)

what about stopping here for a picnic? what about something to drink? we've sent cards to everyone we know—what about old Mrs Smith?

whatever, *adjective & pronoun*

ا) كل ما ـ أي شيء مهما : (سأشتريه مهما كان السعر)

(a) (*strong form of* **what**) anything; it doesn't matter what; you can eat whatever you like; he does whatever he feels like doing; I'll buy it whatever the price is = however much it costs.

ب) ما

(b) (*strong form of* **what** *in questions*) whatever made you do that?

what for

ا) لماذا ؟ لأي غرض ؟

(a) why; what are you painting the door for? what's he sitting on the floor for? we're going out—what for? he's phoning the police—what for?

ب) ما هو غرض ذا أو ذاك

(b) what's that handle for? = what does that handle do? what's this little button for?

wheel [wi:l] . *noun*

ا) عجلة (السيارة أو الدراجة)

(a) round part on which a bicycle/a car, etc., runs; a bicycle has two wheels—a front wheel and a back wheel; I had to change a wheel because I had a flat tyre.

when

ب) عجلة ـ دولاب

(b) similar round thing; in English cars, the steering wheel is on the right hand side.

2. *verb*

٢ ـ يندفع في دراجة أو عربة

to push along something which has wheels; he wheeled his bike into the house; she was wheeling her motorbike down the steps.

wheels—wheeling—wheeled— has wheeled

wheeled, *adjective*

مُزوّد بعجلات

with wheels; a three-wheeled vehicle.

when [wen] **1.** *adverb*

ا ـ متى ؟

(*asking a question*) at what time; when does the last train leave? when did you see the film? when are we going to have our dinner? since when has he been in your class?

Note: after **when** *used to ask a question, the verb is put before the subject:* **when does the film start?** *but* **he doesn't know when the film starts; when is he coming?** *but* **they can't tell me when he is coming.**

2. *conjunction*

٢ ـ ا) لما ـ عندما ـ متى

(a) at the time that; when I was young, we were living in London; when you leave the house, don't forget to lock the door; do you remember when we all went to the seaside in your old car? tell me when you're feeling hungry; we were all singing when he came in.

ب) بعد ان

(b) after; when we had finished, we sat down; switch off the TV when the news has finished; when you've had your breakfast, please do the washing up.

whenever, *adverb*

كلّما ـ في أي وقت كان

at any time that; come whenever you like; I go to see her whenever I can.

---

three hundred and fifty-seven   **357**

where

where [weə] *adverb*

أ) أين ؟

(a) (*asking a question*) in what place/to what place; **where are my glasses? where's the restaurant? where did you put the book? where are you going for your holiday? do you know where the manager is?**

ب) حيث - في المكان الذي

(b) (*showing place*) **stay where you are; he still lives in the town where he was born; here's where he hides his money.**
Note: after **where** *used to ask a question, the verb is put before the subject;* **where is the bottle?** *but* **he doesn't know where the bottle is**

wherever, *adverb*

أينما - في أي مكان

to/in any place; **wherever I go, I meet interesting people; I'd like to find her, wherever she may be.**

whether [ˈweðə] *conjunction*

ما إذا - سواء - أ ... أم

if; **I don't know whether it's true; we hope to go on a picnic, but it depends on whether the weather's fine; do you know whether the manager is in or not? whether you're tall or short—it doesn't matter.**

which [wɪtʃ] *adjective & pronoun*

أ) أي ؟ أي من ...

(a) (*asking a question*) what person/thing; **which hat shall I wear? in which hand do you hold a pen? which boy is the one you saw? which of you girls wants to help with the washing up?**

ب) الذي - التي :
(تستعمل للأشياء فقط ولا تستعمل للأشخاص)

(b) (*only used with things, not people*) the thing that; **the house which is opposite the post office; here's the bread which we bought this morning.**
Note: with an object **which** *can be left out:* **here's the bread we bought this morning.**

whistle

while [waɪl] **1.** *noun*

١ - أ) فترة زمانية

(a) length of time; **we had to wait a little while for the bus; he went away a little while ago; it's nice to go to the cinema once in a while** = from time to time.

ب) جدير بأن ينفق المرء أمواله أو جهده أو وقته

(b) **to be worth while** = to be worth doing; **it's worth while having two keys to the door, in case you lose one.**
2. *conjunction*

٢ - أ) في حين - بينما

(a) during the period that; at the same time that; **while I was making the breakfast, everyone else was in bed; you can't do your homework while you're watching TV; while he was on holiday he caught flu; I'll lay the table while you have a bath.**

ب) في حين

(b) (*showing difference*) **he earns £120 a week while I only earn £90.**

whisper [ˈwɪspə] **1.** *noun*

١ - همس

very quiet words; **he spoke in a whisper.**
2. *verb*

ب - يهمس

to speak in a very quiet voice; **he was whispering to his wife during the whole film; she whispered to me that she felt ill.**
whispers—whispering—whispered—has whispered

whistle [ˈwɪsl] **1.** *noun*

١ - أ) صفارة

(a) small instrument which makes a loud high sound when you blow it; **the whistle blew—it was the end of the game; the policeman blew his whistle.**

ب) صَفير

(b) loud high sound which you make by almost closing your mouth and blowing through the hole; **he gave a loud whistle.**
2. *verb*

٢ - يُصَفِّر

to make a loud high sound by blowing

358   *three hundred and fifty-eight*

white

air through your lips; **he whistled and his dog came running up; she was whistling a tune.**
whistles—whistling—whistled—has whistled

white [waɪt] *adjective & noun*

أبيض

of a colour like snow or milk; **he was wearing a white shirt; a white car always looks dirty; the snow was so white that it made my eyes hurt; do you like your coffee black or white?** = without milk or with milk.
white—whiter—whitest

who [huː] *pronoun*

أ) من ؟

(*a*) (*asking a question*) which person/which people; **who's knocking at the door? who are all those people in uniform? who threw the stone through the window? who are you going home with? who was she talking to? who did you see at the party?**

ب) الذي ـ التي ـ الذين ـ اللواتي ـ اللذان

(*b*) the person that/the people that; **the friend who came to see us yesterday works for the post office; people who didn't get tickets early can't get into the cinema; there's the man who I saw at the pub; do you remember the man who helped to push the car?**
Note: with an object **who** *can be left out;* **there's the man I saw at the pub**
Note: when **who** *is used as an object, it sometimes is written* **whom** [huːm]: **whom was she talking to? there's the man whom I saw in the pub**

whoever, *pronoun*

أيًّا كان ـ كلُّ مَنْ

anyone who; **whoever finds the money can keep it.**

whole [həʊl] **1.** *adjective*

١ ـ كامل ـ تام

complete/all (of something); **he's eaten

wide

the whole cake; she stayed in bed a whole week; the whole country was covered with snow; the whole school caught flu** = all the children.
2. *noun*

٢ ـ كل ـ جميع

all/everything; **he stayed in bed the whole of the morning; did you see the whole of the film?—no I only saw the first half of it.**

whom [huːm] *see* **who**

ملاحظة : انظر إلى كلمة who

whose [huːz] *pronoun*

أ) لمن ؟ : (لمن هذه السيارة ؟)

(*a*) (*asking a question*) belonging to which person; **whose car is that? whose are these books?**

ب) الــذي ـ التي ـ الــذين ... الــخ : (الأشخاص الذين سرقت سيارتهم) .

(*b*) referring to who; **the people whose car was stolen; the man whose hat you sat on.**

why [waɪ] *adverb*

لماذا ؟

(*asking a question*) for what reason; **why did you phone me in the middle of the night? why isn't he at work today? why is the sky blue? she told me why she didn't go to the party; I asked him why the train was late; why go by train when the bus is cheaper? why not take the car?**
Note: after **why** *used to ask a question, the verb is put before the subject:* **why isn't he at work today?** *but* **they don't know why he wasn't at work**

wide [waɪd] *adjective*

واسع ـ عريض ـ رَحْب

having a certain width; which measures a lot from one side to the other; not narrow; **how wide is the River Thames? the cupboard's 3 metres wide; the main road is wider than our street.**
wide—wider—widest

wife

width [wɪdθ] *noun*

عَرْض

measurement from side to side; **what's the width of the river? the carpet is 3 metres in width.**

wife [waɪf] *noun*

زوجة ـ عقيلة

woman who is married to a man; **she's the manager's wife; I know Mr Jones but I've never met his wife.**
plural **wives** [waɪvz]

wild [waɪld] *adjective*

ا) بَرِّيّ ـ وحشي

living freely in nature; **he was attacked by a wild animal; you can find all sorts of wild flowers in the mountains.**

(ب) غاضب ـ متهوّر

(b) very angry; **he was wild when he saw that someone had painted white spots on his car; the teacher was wild with me when I threw a book at him.**

(ت) مولع ـ متحمس

(c) **wild about** = liking very much; **she's wild about horses** = she likes horses very much.

wild—wilder—wildest

will [wɪl] *verb, used with other verbs*

ا) (فعل مساعد يفيد معنى التسويف المستقبل): سوف ...

(a) (to form the future) **they will be here soon; will you be staying long in Italy? I won't be able to come to tea; if you ask him to sing, he'll say 'no'.**

ب) (للتعبير عن حتميّة أمر سيحدث) : سوف بالتأكيد ـ حتماً سوف

(b) to be certain to happen; **the cat will keep eating the dog's food.**

ت) (للطلب بطريقة مهذبة)

(c) (to make a polite form of asking someone to do something) **will you all please sit down? will someone turn the light off?**

ث) للتعبير عن الرغبة : يريد ـ يرغب

(d) (showing that you are eager to do something) **leave the washing up—I'll do it; the car won't start.**
Negative: **will not** *usually* **won't** [wəʊnt]
Past: **would, would not** *usually* **wouldn't**
Note: **will** *is often shortened to* **'ll: he'll = he will**

willing, *adjective*

راغب ـ مستعد

eager to help; **is anyone willing to wash the car? I need two willing boys to move the piano.**

win [wɪn] 1. *noun*

ا ـ فوز

beating someone in a game; **our team has only had two wins this year.**
2. *verb*

٢ ـ ا) يفوز ـ يتغلّب على

(a) to beat someone in a game; to be first in a race, etc.; **our team won their match yesterday; he won the race easily; which team's winning?**

ب) يكسب ـ يربح ـ ينال

(b) to get (a prize, etc.); **he won first prize in the music competition; I won a holiday in Greece in a competition in the paper.**

wins—winning—won [wʌn]**— has won**

winner, *noun*

الفائز ـ الرابح

person who wins; **the winner of the 100 metres race; the winner of the music competition.**

wind[1] [wɪnd] *noun*

ريح

air which moves outdoors; **the wind blew the leaves off the trees; don't try to put your umbrella up in this wind; there's no wind at all—the smoke from the fire is going straight up; the flags were blowing in the wind; wind instruments** = musical instruments which you have to blow to make a note.

wind²   wide

windy, *adjective*

عاصف ـ مزروعٌ بالرياح

with a lot of wind; **a windy day; what windy weather!**
windy—windier—windiest

wind² [waɪnd] *verb*

أ) يُدَوِّر (الساعة)

(*a*) to turn (a key, etc. to make a machine work); **do you need to wind your watch? my watch needs winding every day.**

ب) يلفّ

(*b*) to twist round and round; **he wound the string into a ball; she wound the towel round her head.**
winds—winding—wound [waʊnd]—has wound

wind up, *verb*

أ) يلف ـ يتعوّج

(*a*) to twist round and round; **he was winding the string up into a ball; the road winds up the mountain.**

ب) يُدَوِّر

(*b*) to turn (a key to make a machine work); **have you wound up the clock/ wound the clock up?**

ت) ينهي

(*c*) to finish; **he wound up his speech with a story about his father.**
Note: **wind the clock up** *or* **wind up the clock** *but only* **wind it up**

window ['wɪndəʊ] *noun*

نافذة

opening in a wall/door, etc., which is filled with glass; **look out of the window—you can see the garden; it's dangerous to lean out of the train window; he threw a stone through the car window; the burglar climbed in through the window; I saw a camera in the shop window.**

wine [waɪn] *noun*

نبيذ ـ خمرة

alcoholic drink made from the juice of grapes; **let's have a bottle of red wine; pour the wine into the glasses; three glasses of red wine, please.**
Note: usually singular: **some wine; a glass of wine;** *plural* **wines** *means different sorts of wine*

wing [wɪŋ] *noun*

جناح (الطير أو الطائرة)

one of two parts of a bird, butterfly or aircraft which it uses to fly with; **the butterfly has white spots on its wings; the plane has V-shaped wings.**

winner ['wɪnə] *see* **win**

ملاحظة : انظر إلى كلمة win

winter ['wɪntə] *noun*

شتاء ـ فصل الشتاء

coldest season of the year, the season between autumn and spring; **we can't play outside in the winter because it's too cold; last winter there wasn't any snow; if we go on holiday in winter we try to go to a hot country.**

wipe [waɪp] *verb*

تمسح ـ ينظف بالمسح

to clean/to dry something with a cloth; **I've washed the plates—can someone wipe them? you need a handkerchief to wipe your nose; please wipe the mud off your shoes before you come into the kitchen.**
wipes—wiping—wiped—has wiped

wipe out, *verb*

يقضي على ـ يمحو

to kill; **the whole army was wiped out in the war.**

wire ['waɪə] *noun*

سلك ـ سلك معدني أو كهربائي أو هاتفي

thin metal thread; **tie the basket to your bike with a piece of wire; electric wire** = wire along which electricity goes; **you have to be careful with this iron—the wire's loose.**

three hundred and sixty-one   361

wise

wise [waɪz] *adjective*

ذكيّ ـ واعٍ ـ عاقل ـ مُتَعقِّل

very intelligent and careful; **it was wise of him to take his umbrella because it soon started to rain.**

wisely, *adverb*

بحكمة ـ بتعقّل

in a wise way; **he wisely took his umbrella with him.**

wish [wɪʃ] **1.** *noun*

١ ـ أمنية ـ رغبة

what you want to happen; **best wishes for a Happy New Year; please give my best wishes to your mother; he has no wish to go to prison** = he does not want to go.

plural **wishes**

2. *verb*

٢ ـ أ) يرغب ـ يبتغي

(*a*) to want something to happen; **I wish it didn't always rain on my birthday; I wish I could live on an island; I wish you spent more time on your homework; I wish you wouldn't talk so loudly; I wish I hadn't eaten so much; the headmaster wishes to see you.**

ب) يتمنّى

(*b*) to show that you hope something good will happen; **he wished me good luck; he wished me a happy Christmas.**

wishes—wishing—wished—has wished

with [wɪθ] *preposition*

١) مع

(*a*) (*showing things/people that are together*) **he came here with his sister; they're staying with us for the weekend; I like ice cream with my apple pie.**

ب) و ... (جاء وقبعته على رأسه)

(*b*) (*showing something which you have*) **he came in with his hat on; she's the girl with blue eyes; the house with the red door.**

ت) بـ ـ بواسطة

(*c*) (*showing something which is used*) **he cut the bread with a knife; he has to walk with a stick; she was eating her pudding with a spoon; they were attacking the enemy with bombs; it's pouring with rain.**

ث) بسبب

(*d*) because of; **my hands were blue with cold; he was sick with flu.**

Note: **with** *is used with many adjectives and verbs:* **to agree with; to be pleased with,** *etc.*

without [wɪ'ðaʊt] *preposition*

أ) من غير

(*a*) not having; not with; **I'll come without my sister; they lived for days without any food; he was stuck in Italy without any money; how can you do your shopping without a car? he was arrested for travelling without a ticket.**

ب) بدون

(*b*) not doing something; **she sang for two hours without stopping; they lived in the mountains for months without seeing anybody.**

wives [waɪvz] *see* **wife**

ملاحظة : انظر إلى كلمة wife

woke [wəʊk], **woken** [wəʊkn] *see* **wake**

ملاحظة : انظر إلى كلمة wake

woman ['wʊmən] *noun*

إمرأة

female adult person; **there were three women at the next table; an old woman asked me the way to the post office; a woman doctor came to see me; are there any women train drivers?**

plural **women** ['wɪmɪn]

won [wʌn] *see* **win**

ملاحظة : انظر إلى كلمة win

wonder ['wʌndə] *verb*

يتساءل ـ يتمنى لو يعرف

to want to know something; to think

won't

about something; **I wonder why he always wears a green tie? I wonder where the teacher's gone? he's wondering what to do next; we're wondering who'll be the next president.**

wonders—wondering—wondered—has wondered

wonderful, *adjective*

رائع ـ مدهش

very good/splendid; **we had a wonderful holiday in Sweden; the weather was wonderful; you've passed your driving test?—wonderful!**

won't [wəʊnt] *see* **will not**

ملاحظة : انظر إلى كلمة will not

wood [wʊd] *noun*

أ) غابة

(a) many trees together; **the road goes straight through the wood; let's look for flowers in that wood.**

ب) خشب ـ حطب

(b) material that a tree is made of; **the chairs are made of wood; he hit him on the head with a piece of wood; he put some more wood on the fire.**

no plural for (b): **some wood; a piece of wood**

wooden, *adjective*

خشبيّ

made of wood; **a wooden chair; she stirred the soup with a wooden spoon.**

wool [wʊl] *noun*

أ) صوف

(a) hair from a sheep; **in the summer the wool is sent to the market.**

ب) نسيج صوفي

(b) long threads of hair from a sheep, twisted together; **she's used three balls of wool to make my pullover; are these socks made of wool?**

ت) مادة بشكل صوف

(c) material which looks like sheep's wool; **put some cotton wool on the cut on your finger; steel wool** = thin threads of steel put together in a ball, used to clean pans.

no plural: **some wool; a piece of wool**

woollen, *adjective* (*American:* woolen)

صوفي ـ مصنوع من الصوف

made of wool; **a woollen pullover; a woollen carpet.**

woolly, *adjective*

مكسوّ بالصوف ـ يشبه الصوف

covered with wool; looking like wool; **a woolly sheep; soft woolly clouds in the sky.**

word [wɜːd] *noun*

كلمة ـ لفظة

separate piece of language, in writing and speech not joined to other separate pieces; **there are seven words in this sentence; he saw me but didn't say a word; you spelt the word 'through' with two 'g's—that's a mistake; to have a word with the teacher; in other words** = to explain something in a different way; **the manager's ill, in other words I have to do twice as much work.**

wore [wɔː] *see* **wear**

ملاحظة : انظر إلى كلمة wear

work [wɜːk] **1.** *noun*

١ ـ أ) عمل

(a) something which you do using your strength or your brain; **digging holes in the ground is hard work; don't ask me to go out—I've got too much to do; he doesn't do much work—he just sits and watches TV; when you've finished that piece of work, I've got something more for you to do.**

ب) مهمّة ـ شغل

(b) job/something which you do regularly to earn money; **I go to work by train every day; we start work at 9 o'clock in the morning; he doesn't come back from work until 7 o'clock at night; he's out of work** = he has no job.

world

ت) قطعة ـ انجاز ـ جزء من مؤلفات
(c) something which has been made/painted/written, etc., by someone; **a work of art; here are the complete works of Shakespeare** = everything which Shakespeare wrote.

ث) معمل ـ مصنع
(d) **works** = factory; **a car works**.
no plural for (a) and (b): **some work; a piece of work**

2. *verb*

٢ ـ ١ ـ أ) يعمل ـ يقوم بعمل ما
(a) to use your strength or brain to do something; **if you work hard you'll pass your exams; he doesn't work very hard so he doesn't earn much money.**

ب) يُدير ـ يشغل (آلة)
(b) (*of a machine*) to run; to make a machine run; **the clock isn't working; the bell works by electricity; the car didn't work well; he works the biggest machine in the factory.**

ت) يَعْمَل (في شركة أو مصنع ...)
(c) to have a job; **he works in a car factory; she used to work in a butcher's shop; he had to stop working because he was so ill; I don't like working in London.**

ث) ينجح ـ يتم بنجاح
(d) to succeed; **do you think your plan will work? if it doesn't work, try again.**
works—working—worked—has worked

worker, *noun*

أ) شخص مجتهد ـ شخص بطيء في عمله
(a) person who works; **he's a good worker; she's a slow worker.**

ب) عامل ـ شغيل
(b) person who works with his hands; **the workers left the factory.**

workman, *noun*

عامل ـ شغيل
man who works with his hands; **three workmen came to mend the pipe.**
plural **workmen**

work out, *verb*

أ) يحسب
(a) to calculate; **I'm trying to work out how much petrol the car uses; she can't work this sum out.**

ب) ينجح
(b) to succeed; **everything worked out all right in the end.**

workshop, *noun*

مشغل ـ ورشة
very small factory; place where things are made; **he's making a table in the workshop behind the house.**

world [wɜːld] *noun*

عالم ـ العالم
the earth on which we live; **you can fly right round the world; he travels all over the world on business.**

worn [wɔːn] *see* **wear**
ملاحظة : انظر إلى كلمة wear

worn out [ˈwɔːnˈaʊt] *see* **wear out**
ملاحظة : انظر إلى كلمة wear out

worry [ˈwʌrɪ] *verb*

يَقْلَق ـ يُقلِق
to be afraid and not sure because of something; **she's worrying about her exams; I worry when my daughter stays out late; are you worried by the cost of food? they're worried that they won't have enough petrol.**
worries—worrying—worried—has worried

worse [wɜːs] **1.** *adjective*

١ ـ أ) أسوأ ـ أردأ
(a) less good (as compared to something else); **the weather is even worse than last week; this TV film is worse than the one I watched last night; I'm worse at English than at geography; that boy is very naughty—but his sister is worse.**

ب) أسوأ
(b) more ill (than someone else/than at another time); **he was feeling quite well**

worst

yesterday, but is much worse today; she's got worse since she started taking the medicine.
2. *adverb*

٢ ـ على درجة أسوأ ـ على نحو أسوأ

less well (as compared to something else); **he drives worse than his sister.**

worse *is the comparative of* **bad**, **badly** *and* **ill**

worst [wɜːst] 1. *adjective*

١ ـ الأسوأ ـ الأردأ

worse than anything else; **this is the worst film I've seen this year; she has the worst marks for English; he's the worst swimmer in our team.**
2. *adverb*

٢ ـ الأسوأ ـ على أسوأ طريقة

less well than anything/anyone else; less well than at any other time; **which team played worst? he works worst when he's tired.**

worst *is the superlative of* **bad** *and* **badly**

worth [wɜːθ] 1. *adjective*

١ ـ أ) ذو قيمة عالية أو مادية

(*a*) with a certain value; **this house is worth £20,000; that car isn't worth £6,000! what's your car worth?**

ب) جدير بـ

(*b*) useful to do; **that film is worth seeing; it's worth knowing something about car engines.**
2. *noun*

٢ ـ يساوي كذا ـ تساوي قيمته كذا

value; **I want £5 worth of petrol; he bought several pounds' worth of fruit.**

would [wʊd] *verb used with other verbs*

أ) (للطلب بطريقة مهذبة)

(*a*) (*to make the polite form of asking someone to do something*) **would someone please turn off the light? would you please sit down? I asked him if he would help us.**

wound

ب) (للتعبير عن الرغبة في شيء ما)

(*b*) (*past of* **will**, *showing that you are eager to do something*) **he wouldn't come with us, even though we asked him twice; of course the car wouldn't go when we wanted it to; he forgot my birthday again this year—he would!** = it is something which he always does.

ت) (للتعبير عن العادة أو عمل مألوف في الماضي)

(*c*) (*showing something which often used to happen in the past*) **she would get up at eight o'clock every morning; he would always be standing outside the station selling newspapers, until one day he died; my uncle would often bring me chocolates.**

ث) (للتعبير عن النية في الماضي)

(*d*) (*used as a past of* **will**) **they said they would be here by nine o'clock; she hoped she would be able to come.**

ج) (تابعة لشرط)

(*e*) (*following a condition*) **if he could come he would; if she were still alive, she would/she'd be a hundred years old today; if you invited him, he would/he'd come; if it rained we would/we'd stay at home.**

Negative: **would not** *usually* **wouldn't**
Note: **would** *is the past of* **will**; **would** *is often shortened to* **'d**: **she'd be a hundred; he'd stay at home; would** *does not have* **to** *and is only used with other verbs*

would rather, *verb*

يُفَضِّل

to prefer; **I'd rather stay at home than go to the party; are you going to pay for everybody?—I'd rather not; they'd rather we went with them.**

wound¹ [waʊnd] *see* **wind²**

ملاحظة : انظر إلى كلمة wind

wound² [wuːnd] 1. *noun*

١ ـ جرح

bad cut made on the body, usually in

wrap

fighting; **the nurses were bandaging the soldiers' wounds.**
2. *verb*

٢ - يجرح

to hurt someone badly in a fight; **he was wounded in the war; the police wounded the burglar as he was trying to escape.**
wounds—wounding—wounded—has wounded

wrap [ræp] *verb* (*usually* **wrap up**)

يغطّي - يغلّف

to cover something all round with paper/cloth, etc.; **he's wrapping up the Christmas presents; look at this parcel wrapped up in blue paper; wrap yourself up in your blanket if you're cold.**
wraps—wrapping—wrapped—has wrapped

wrist [rɪst] *noun*

المعصم

joint where your hand is connected to your arm; **wrist watch** = watch which you wear attached to your wrist.

write [raɪt] *verb*

١) يكتب

(*a*) to put words or numbers on paper, etc.; **she wrote a few words on the back of an envelope; who wrote 'Teacher go home' on the blackboard? I'll write my name and address for you on a piece of paper; can you write your telephone number on the top of the letter? he's written a book about the police.**

ب) يراسل - يبعث برسالة إلى

(*b*) to write a letter and send it to someone; **have you written to your mother yet? she writes to me every week; don't forget to write as soon as you get to Hong Kong.**
writes—writing—wrote [rəʊt]**—has written**

write back, *verb*

يرد على الرسالة

to answer by letter; **he got my letter, and wrote back immediately.**

wrong

write down, *verb*

يكتب - يدوّن - يسجل

to write on paper, etc.; **he wrote down the number of the car; she wrote down all the information on the back of an envelope.**

write out, *verb*

يدوّن - يكتب

to write something long; **I'll write out a list of the things I need.**
Note: **write the list out** *or* **write out the list** *but only* **write it out**

writer, *noun*

كاتب - مؤلف

person who writes; **do you know who is the writer of this letter? he's the writer of six books.**

writing, *noun*

كتابة

something which is written; **don't phone, please answer in writing; I have his answer here in writing; can't you type your letters?—your writing's so bad I can't read it;** *see also* **handwriting.**

writing paper, *noun*

ورق للرسائل

good paper used for writing letters.

wrong [rɒŋ] 1. *adjective*

١ - خاطىء - مغلوط - غير صحيح - مخطىء

not correct; **what's the time?—I don't know, my watch is wrong; I'm sorry, I was wrong—he does live opposite the post office; there's no one called Smith living here—you've come to the wrong house; I think we're on the wrong road—we should be going to London, not away from it; can I speak to Mr Smith please—sorry, you've got the wrong number; what's wrong with the soup?—there's nothing wrong with it, I'm just not hungry.**
2. *adverb*

خطأ - بطريقة خاطئة

badly; **everything has gone wrong today;**

yard

you've spelt my name wrong; I think you've added up the bill wrong.

wrongly, adverb

على نحو خاطىء

not correctly; the waiter added up the bill wrongly; she spelt my name wrongly.

wrote [rəʊt] see **write**

ملاحظة : انظر إلى كلمة **write**

yesterday

Yy

yard [jɑːd] noun

١) ياردة (وحدة لقياس الطول تعادل ٩١ سنتمترا)

(a) measurement of length (= 0.91 metres); the post office is only a hundred yards away; the piece of string is ten yards long; can you move the chairs a couple of yards to the left?

ب) سطيحة

(b) area at the back of a house (usually with a hard surface), but not a garden.

ت) بالاميركية : حديقة

(c) American = **garden**.

year [jɜː] noun

١) سنة ـ عام

(a) period of time, lasting twelve months, from January 1st to December 31st; in the year 1492 Columbus discovered America; last year we went to France on holiday; next year I'm going to work in Africa; the weather has been very bad this year; the New Year = the first few days of the year; I start my new job in the New Year; New Year's Day = January 1st.

ب) سنة كاملة

(b) any period of twelve months; he was born two hundred years ago; she's ten years old tomorrow; the school year starts in September; how many years have you been living in this village?

yearly, adjective & adverb

سنوياً

every year.

yellow [ˈjeləʊ] adjective & noun

أصفر ـ اللون الأصفر

of a colour like that of the sun or of gold; he's painted his car bright yellow; she's wearing a yellow hat; look at the field of yellow flowers; do you have any paint of a lighter yellow than this?

yellow—yellower—yellowest

yellow pages, noun

دليل الهاتف

telephone book which lists shops and businesses; look up 'Restaurants' in the yellow pages.

yes [jes] adverb

نَعَم ـ أجل

(showing the opposite of **no**) we asked him if he wanted to come and he said 'yes'; do you want any more coffee?—yes, please; does she like horses?—yes, she does; didn't he go to school in Scotland?—yes, he did.

yesterday [ˈjestədɪ] adverb & noun

البارحة

the day before today; yesterday was November 13th, so today must be the 14th; we went to London yesterday morning; he came for tea yesterday afternoon; the day before yesterday.

three hundred and sixty-seven 367

yet

yet [jet] **1.** *adverb*

١ - حتى الآن - بعد

until now; **has the postman come yet?** I haven't seen him yet; he hasn't read the newspaper yet; have you done your homework yet?

2. *conjunction*

٢ - مع ذلك - على الرغم من ذلك

but/still; she's fat and yet she can run very fast; it was pouring with rain and yet the children went out for their picnic.

you [ju:] *pronoun*

أ) ضمير المخاطب : أنتَ - أنتِ - انتما - انتم - انتن - لكَ - لكِ - كما - كم - كنّ

(*a*) (*referring to someone we are speaking to*) you're taller than me/than I am; I'll give you my phone number and you'll give me yours; you go first; Hello, how are you? are you both well?

ب) المرء (إجمالاً) : لا أحد يعلم ...

(*b*) (*referring to anybody*) you never know what will happen; you need to be very clever to go to university.

Note: **you** *is both singular and plural*

young [jʌŋ] *adjective*

صغير السن - شاب - خاص بالشباب

not old; he's a young man—he's only twenty-one; my sister's younger than me/than I am; he's the youngest boy in the class; this is a TV programme for young children.

young—younger—youngest

your [jɔ:] *adjective*

خاصتكَ - ملكك (صيغة الملكية)

belonging to you; **have you brought your toothbrush with you?** this is a present for your sister; your trousers are dirty.

youth

yours, *pronoun*

لكَ - لكِ - لكما - لكم - لكنّ : (هذا الكتاب لك وليس لي)

belonging to you; **this book is yours, not mine;** you said he was a friend of yours = one of your friends.

yourself, *pronoun*

انت بنفسك - أنت بنفسك - انتما ، انتم - انتن ... الخ

(*referring to* **you** *as a subject*) you were washing the car yourself; did you cut yourself on the knife? are you all by yourself? = all alone; did you build the house all by yourself? = with no one to help you; did you both hurt yourselves? look at yourselves in the mirror? I hope you all enjoy yourselves.

plural **yourselves** *refers to* **you** *as a plural subject*

youth [ju:θ] *noun*

أ) شاب

(*a*) young man; **two youths came towards me;** he was attacked by six youths in a pub.

ب) الشباب - أيام الصبا

(*b*) time when you are young; **I did a lot of sport in my youth.**

plural **youths** [ju:ðz] *for (a); no plural for (b)*

youth club, *noun*

نادي الشباب

club for young people; **we're joining the youth club;** the youth club's going on a picnic next Saturday.

youth hostel, *noun*

بيت الشباب

building where young people can stay cheaply when they are walking on holiday in the countryside.

Zz

zebra ['zebrə] *noun*

حمار وحشي : العتابي

animal like a horse with black and white lines on it; **zebra crossing** = place where you can cross the road safely on a path painted black and white.

zero ['zɪərəʊ] number 0

صِفر

the answer is zero; the temperature fell to zero (0°); it's very cold—it's below zero.

zip [zɪp] 1. *noun*

زمَام منزلق

thing for fastening clothes, made of two lines of small teeth which join together; her dress is fastened with a zip at the back; can you do up this zip for me/do this zip up for me?
2. *verb*

٢ ـ يفتح أو يغلق بزمام منزلق

to zip up = to do up a zip; to be fastened with a zip; this dress zips up at the back; can you zip up this dress for me/zip this dress up for me?

zips—zipping—zipped—has zipped
Note: **zip the dress up** *or* **zip up the dress** *but only* **zip it up**

zoo [zu:] *noun*

حديقة الحيوانات

place where wild animals are kept, and which people can go to visit; we went to the zoo on Sunday afternoon; I had a ride on an elephant at the zoo.

three hundred and sixty-nine

مقدمـة

يتضمن هذا القاموس ٢٠٠٠ كلمة الاكثر استعمالا في اللغة الانجليزية . والى جانب هذه الكلمات الاساسية ستجدون العديد من الكلمات المشتقة منها والعبارات المركبة ، وهذا ما يجعل من قاموس الالفي كلمة هذا مرجعا اوسع بكثير مما يوحي به عنوانه .

وان كنتم طلّابا في درس اللغة الانجليزية ، فلا شك ان هذا القاموس سيساعدكم في عدة مجالات . اولا ، ان جميع الكلمات في القاموس واردة ومستعملة في جميع مناهج تعليم اللغة الانجليزية للصفوف الابتدائية . ومن جهة اخرى ان كل كلمة اساسية مترجمة وطريقة لفظها بالانجليزية مدونة . وستجدون ايضا بعض الامثلة عن الطريقة التي تستعمل بها الكلمة في بعض الجمل والتعابير الانجليزية .

وفي حال بعض الكلمات الغامضة او غير المفهومة تلقائيا فقد حرصنا على ترجمة الجملة او العبارة التي تتضمن هذه الكلمة بالكامل . ومما يجدر بالاشارة هو العديد من الملاحظات والتفسيرات الصرفية او المتعلقة بقواعد اللغة الانجليزية والتي هي مدونة ضمن الاشرطة الرمادية في آخر المقاطع .

هاراب

المعجم المدرسي
انجليزي - عربي

HARRAP'S ENGLISH-ARABIC BASIC LEARNER'S DICTIONARY

P. H. Collin

Edited by Nagi Abboud

قاموس مختصر
انجليزي عربي
للمبتدىء في
درس الانجليزية

خطوط الغلاف : حسَن المسعود

AL-MOUHIT

HARRAP